MySQL®

Administrator's Guide

MySQL®

Administrator's Guide

MySQL AB

800 East 96th Street, Indianapolis, Indiana 46240 USA

MySQL Administrator's Guide

International Standard Book Number: 0-672-32634-5

Library of Congress Catalog Card Number: 2003110974

Printed in the United States of America

First Printing: July 2004

06   05   04   4   3   2   1

Trademarks

Warning and Disclaimer

Bulk Sales

Pearson offers excellent discounts on this book when ordered in quantity for bulk purchases or special sales. For more information, please contact

U.S. Corporate and Government Sales
1-800-382-3419
corpsales@pearsontechgroup.com

For sales outside of the U.S., please contact

International Sales
1-317-428-3341
international@pearsontechgroup.com

ASSOCIATE PUBLISHER Mark Taber	**MANAGING EDITOR** Charlotte Clapp	**INDEXER** Mandie Frank	**BOOK DESIGNER** Gary Adair
ACQUISITIONS EDITOR Shelley Johnston	**PROJECT EDITOR** Andy Beaster	**PROOFREADER** Jennifer Timpe	
DEVELOPMENT EDITOR Damon Jordan	**COPY EDITOR** Mike Henry	**PUBLISHING COORDINATOR** Vanessa Evans	

MySQL® Press is the exclusive publisher of technology books and materials that have been authorized by MySQL AB. MySQL Press books are written and reviewed by the world's leading authorities on MySQL technologies, and are edited, produced, and distributed by the Que/Sams Publishing group of Pearson Education, the worldwide leader in integrated education and computer technology publishing. For more information on MySQL Press and MySQL Press books, please go to **www.mysqlpress.com**.

MYSQL HQ
MySQL AB
Bangårdsgatan 8
S-753 20 Uppsala
Sweden

UNITED STATES
MySQL Inc.
2510 Fairview Avenue East
Seattle, WA 98102
USA

GERMANY, AUSTRIA AND SWITZERLAND
MySQL GmbH
Schlosserstraße 4
D-72622 Nürtingen
Germany

FINLAND
MySQL Finland Oy
Tekniikantie 21
FIN-02150 Espoo
Finland

FRANCE
MySQL AB (France)
123, rue du Faubourg St. Antoine
75011, Paris
France

MySQL® AB develops, markets, and supports a family of high-performance, affordable database servers and tools. MySQL AB is the sole owner of the MySQL server source code, the MySQL trademark, and the mysql.com domain. For more information on MySQL AB and MySQL AB products, please go to **www.mysql.com** or the following areas of the MySQL Web site:

- Training information: **www.mysql.com/training**
- Support services: **www.mysql.com/support**
- Consulting services: **www.mysql.com/consulting**

About this Book

The *MySQL Administrator's Guide* is made up of those sections in the *MySQL Reference Manual* (available online in several formats and languages at http://www.mysql.com) that focus on the SQL language used to perform database queries in MySQL. It covers language structure, functions and operators, column types, and SQL statement syntax.

The original *MySQL Reference Manual* was written by Michael "Monty" Widenius and David Axmark, and it is currently maintained by the documentation team in the MySQL development department.

These members of the documentation team helped produce this book: Paul DuBois, Stefan Hinz, and Arjen Lentz.

We Want to Hear from You!

As the reader of this book, *you* are our most important critic and commentator. We value your opinion and want to know what we're doing right, what we could do better, what areas you'd like to see us publish in, and any other words of wisdom you're willing to pass our way.

You can email or write me directly to let me know what you did or didn't like about this book—as well as what we can do to make our books stronger.

Please note that I cannot help you with technical problems related to the topic of this book, and that due to the high volume of mail I receive, I might not be able to reply to every message.

When you write, please be sure to include this book's title and author as well as your name and phone or email address. I will carefully review your comments and share them with the author and editors who worked on the book.

Email: mysqlpress@pearsoned.com

Mail: Mark Taber
                Associate Publisher
                Pearson Education/MySQL Press
                800 East 96th Street
                Indianapolis, IN 46240 USA

Contents at a Glance

1	General Information	1
2	Installing MySQL	63
3	Using MySQL Programs	197
4	Database Administration	207
5	Replication in MySQL	369
6	MySQL Optimization	405
7	MySQL Client and Utility Programs	467
8	MySQL Storage Engines and Table Types	515
9	The InnoDB Storage Engine	539
10	Introduction to MaxDB	599
A	Troubleshooting Problems with MySQL Programs	607
B	Environment Variables	631
	Index	633

Table of Contents

1 General Information   1

1.1 About This Manual..1

    1.1.1 Conventions Used in This Manual 2

1.2 Overview of the MySQL Database Management System 4

    1.2.1 History of MySQL...5

    1.2.2 The Main Features of MySQL...........................6

    1.2.3 MySQL Stability...8

    1.2.4 How Big MySQL Tables Can Be........................9

    1.2.5 Year 2000 Compliance 11

1.3 Overview of MySQL AB 12

    1.3.1 The Business Model and Services of MySQL AB 13

    1.3.2 Contact Information 16

1.4 MySQL Support and Licensing 17

    1.4.1 Support Offered by MySQL AB 17

    1.4.2 Copyrights and Licenses Used by MySQL 18

    1.4.3 MySQL Licenses 18

    1.4.4 MySQL AB Logos and Trademarks......................21

1.5 MySQL Development Roadmap 22

    1.5.1 MySQL 4.0 in a Nutshell..............................23

    1.5.2 MySQL 4.1 in a Nutshell..............................25

    1.5.3 MySQL 5.0: The Next Development Release..............27

1.6 MySQL and the Future (the TODO) 27

    1.6.1 New Features Planned for 4.1...........................27

    1.6.2 New Features Planned for 5.0...........................28

    1.6.3 New Features Planned for 5.1...........................29

    1.6.4 New Features Planned for the Near Future 29

    1.6.5 New Features Planned for the Mid-Term Future 32

    1.6.6 New Features We Don't Plan to Implement 33

1.7 MySQL Information Sources 33

    1.7.1 MySQL Mailing Lists....................................33

    1.7.2 MySQL Community Support on IRC (Internet Relay Chat)..........42

1.8 MySQL Standards Compliance 42

    1.8.1 What Standards MySQL Follows.......................43

    1.8.2 Selecting SQL Modes....................................43

    1.8.3 Running MySQL in ANSI Mode 44

1.8.4 MySQL Extensions to Standard SQL 44

1.8.5 MySQL Differences from Standard SQL 47

1.8.6 How MySQL Deals with Constraints 54

1.8.7 Known Errors and Design Deficiencies in MySQL 56

2 Installing MySQL   63

2.1 General Installation Issues 64

2.1.1 Operating Systems Supported by MySQL 64

2.1.2 Choosing Which MySQL Distribution to Install 66

2.1.3 How to Get MySQL 78

2.1.4 Verifying Package Integrity Using MD5 Checksums or
GnuPG 78

2.1.5 Installation Layouts 82

2.2 Standard MySQL Installation Using a Binary Distribution 83

2.2.1 Installing MySQL on Windows 84

2.2.2 Installing MySQL on Linux 96

2.2.3 Installing MySQL on Mac OS X 99

2.2.4 Installing MySQL on NetWare 102

2.2.5 Installing MySQL on Other Unix-Like Systems 104

2.3 MySQL Installation Using a Source Distribution 107

2.3.1 Source Installation Overview 108

2.3.2 Typical configure Options 111

2.3.3 Installing from the Development Source Tree 114

2.3.4 Dealing with Problems Compiling MySQL 117

2.3.5 MIT-pthreads Notes 121

2.3.6 Installing MySQL from Source on Windows 122

2.3.7 Compiling MySQL Clients on Windows 127

2.4 Post-Installation Setup and Testing 127

2.4.1 Windows Post-Installation Procedures 127

2.4.2 Unix Post-Installation Procedures 128

2.4.3 Starting and Stopping MySQL Automatically 135

2.4.4 Starting and Troubleshooting the MySQL Server 138

2.4.5 Securing the Initial MySQL Accounts 141

2.5 Upgrading/Downgrading MySQL 144

2.5.1 Upgrading from Version 4.1 to 5.0 146

2.5.2 Upgrading from Version 4.0 to 4.1 146

2.5.3 Upgrading from Version 3.23 to 4.0 151

2.5.4 Upgrading from Version 3.22 to 3.23 155

2.5.5 Upgrading from Version 3.21 to 3.22 157

2.5.6 Upgrading from Version 3.20 to 3.21 158

2.5.7 Upgrading MySQL Under Windows 159

2.5.8 Upgrading the Grant Tables 160

2.5.9 Copying MySQL Databases to Another Machine 160

2.6 Operating System–Specific Notes 162

2.6.1 Linux Notes 162

2.6.2 Mac OS X Notes 171

2.6.3 Solaris Notes 171

2.6.4 BSD Notes 176

2.6.5 Other Unix Notes 179

2.6.6 OS/2 Notes 190

2.6.7 BeOS Notes 191

2.7 Perl Installation Notes 191

2.7.1 Installing Perl on Unix 191

2.7.2 Installing ActiveState Perl on Windows 192

2.7.3 Problems Using the Perl DBI/DBD Interface 193

3 Using MySQL Programs   197

3.1 Overview of MySQL Programs 197

3.2 Invoking MySQL Programs 198

3.3 Specifying Program Options 199

3.3.1 Using Options on the Command Line 199

3.3.2 Using Option Files 201

3.3.3 Using Environment Variables to Specify Options 205

3.3.4 Using Options to Set Program Variables 206

4 Database Administration   207

4.1 The MySQL Server and Server Startup Scripts 207

4.1.1 Overview of the Server-Side Scripts and Utilities 207

4.1.2 The mysqld-max Extended MySQL Server 208

4.1.3 The mysqld_safe Server Startup Script 211

4.1.4 The mysql.server Server Startup Script 214

4.1.5 The mysqld_multi Program for Managing
Multiple MySQL Servers 215

4.2 Configuring the MySQL Server 219

4.2.1 mysqld Command-Line Options 219

4.2.2 The Server SQL Mode 229

4.2.3 Server System Variables 231
4.2.4 Server Status Variables 260
4.3 General Security Issues 267
   4.3.1 General Security Guidelines 267
   4.3.2 Making MySQL Secure Against Attackers 270
   4.3.3 Startup Options for `mysqld` Concerning Security 272
   4.3.4 Security Issues with `LOAD DATA LOCAL` 273
4.4 The MySQL Access Privilege System 274
   4.4.1 What the Privilege System Does 274
   4.4.2 How the Privilege System Works 274
   4.4.3 Privileges Provided by MySQL 278
   4.4.4 Connecting to the MySQL Server 282
   4.4.5 Access Control, Stage 1: Connection Verification 283
   4.4.6 Access Control, Stage 2: Request Verification 287
   4.4.7 When Privilege Changes Take Effect 290
   4.4.8 Causes of `Access denied` Errors 290
   4.4.9 Password Hashing in MySQL 4.1 296
4.5 MySQL User Account Management 302
   4.5.1 MySQL Usernames and Passwords 302
   4.5.2 Adding New User Accounts to MySQL 303
   4.5.3 Removing User Accounts from MySQL 307
   4.5.4 Limiting Account Resources 308
   4.5.5 Assigning Account Passwords 309
   4.5.6 Keeping Your Password Secure 311
   4.5.7 Using Secure Connections 312
4.6 Disaster Prevention and Recovery 320
   4.6.1 Database Backups 320
   4.6.2 Table Maintenance and Crash Recovery 321
   4.6.3 Setting Up a Table Maintenance Schedule 335
   4.6.4 Getting Information About a Table 336
4.7 MySQL Localization and International Usage 342
   4.7.1 The Character Set Used for Data and Sorting 342
   4.7.2 Setting the Error Message Language 344
   4.7.3 Adding a New Character Set 344
   4.7.4 The Character Definition Arrays 346
   4.7.5 String Collating Support 347

4.7.6 Multi-Byte Character Support 347
4.7.7 Problems with Character Sets 347
4.8 The MySQL Log Files 348
4.8.1 The Error Log 348
4.8.2 The General Query Log 349
4.8.3 The Update Log 350
4.8.4 The Binary Log 350
4.8.5 The Slow Query Log 353
4.8.6 Log File Maintenance 354
4.9 Running Multiple MySQL Servers on the Same Machine . . 355
4.9.1 Running Multiple Servers on Windows 357
4.9.2 Running Multiple Servers on Unix 360
4.9.3 Using Client Programs in a Multiple-Server
Environment 362
4.10 The MySQL Query Cache 363
4.10.1 How the Query Cache Operates 363
4.10.2 Query Cache SELECT Options 365
4.10.3 Query Cache Configuration 365
4.10.4 Query Cache Status and Maintenance 367

5 Replication in MySQL   369
5.1 Introduction to Replication 369
5.2 Replication Implementation Overview 370
5.3 Replication Implementation Details 371
5.3.1 Replication Master Thread States 373
5.3.2 Replication Slave I/O Thread States 373
5.3.3 Replication Slave SQL Thread States 374
5.3.4 Replication Relay and Status Files 375
5.4 How to Set Up Replication 377
5.5 Replication Compatibility Between MySQL Versions 381
5.6 Upgrading a Replication Setup 382
5.6.1 Upgrading Replication to 4.0 or 4.1 382
5.6.2 Upgrading Replication to 5.0 383
5.7 Replication Features and Known Problems 384
5.8 Replication Startup Options 387
5.9 Replication FAQ 396
5.10 Troubleshooting Replication 403
5.11 Reporting Replication Bugs 404

6 MySQL Optimization   **405**

6.1 Optimization Overview 405

    6.1.1 MySQL Design Limitations and Tradeoffs 406

    6.1.2 Designing Applications for Portability 406

    6.1.3 What We Have Used MySQL For 407

    6.1.4 The MySQL Benchmark Suite 408

    6.1.5 Using Your Own Benchmarks 409

6.2 Optimizing SELECT Statements and Other Queries 410

    6.2.1 EXPLAIN Syntax (Get Information About a SELECT) 411

    6.2.2 Estimating Query Performance 420

    6.2.3 Speed of SELECT Queries 420

    6.2.4 How MySQL Optimizes WHERE Clauses 421

    6.2.5 How MySQL Optimizes OR Clauses 423

    6.2.6 How MySQL Optimizes IS NULL 423

    6.2.7 How MySQL Optimizes DISTINCT 425

    6.2.8 How MySQL Optimizes LEFT JOIN and RIGHT
JOIN 425

    6.2.9 How MySQL Optimizes ORDER BY 426

    6.2.10 How MySQL Optimizes LIMIT 428

    6.2.11 How to Avoid Table Scans 429

    6.2.12 Speed of INSERT Queries 430

    6.2.13 Speed of UPDATE Queries 432

    6.2.14 Speed of DELETE Queries 432

    6.2.15 Other Optimization Tips 432

6.3 Locking Issues 435

    6.3.1 Locking Methods 435

    6.3.2 Table Locking Issues 438

6.4 Optimizing Database Structure 440

    6.4.1 Design Choices 440

    6.4.2 Make Your Data as Small as Possible 440

    6.4.3 Column Indexes 441

    6.4.4 Multiple-Column Indexes 442

    6.4.5 How MySQL Uses Indexes 443

    6.4.6 The MyISAM Key Cache 446

    6.4.7 How MySQL Counts Open Tables 451

    6.4.8 How MySQL Opens and Closes Tables 452

    6.4.9 Drawbacks to Creating Many Tables in the Same
Database 453

6.5 Optimizing the MySQL Server 454

    6.5.1 System Factors and Startup Parameter Tuning............ 454

    6.5.2 Tuning Server Parameters 454

    6.5.3 How Compiling and Linking Affects the Speed of
    MySQL 457

    6.5.4 How MySQL Uses Memory.................................. 459

    6.5.5 How MySQL Uses DNS 461

6.6 Disk Issues 461

    6.6.1 Using Symbolic Links 462

7 MySQL Client and Utility Programs   **467**

7.1 Overview of the Client-Side Scripts and Utilities 467

7.2 `myisampack`, the MySQL Compressed Read-Only Table
Generator 469

7.3 `mysql`, the Command-Line Tool 476

    7.3.1 `mysql` Commands 481

    7.3.2 Executing SQL Statements from a Text File............ 485

    7.3.3 `mysql` Tips 485

7.4 `mysqladmin`, Administering a MySQL Server 487

7.5 The `mysqlbinlog` Binary Log Utility 492

7.6 `mysqlcc`, the MySQL Control Center 495

7.7 The `mysqlcheck` Table Maintenance and Repair Program 497

7.8 The `mysqldump` Database Backup Program 500

7.9 The `mysqlhotcopy` Database Backup Program 506

7.10 The `mysqlimport` Data Import Program...................... 508

7.11 `mysqlshow`, Showing Databases, Tables, and Columns 511

7.12 `perror`, Explaining Error Codes 512

7.13 The `replace` String-Replacement Utility 513

8 MySQL Storage Engines and Table Types   **515**

8.1 The `MyISAM` Storage Engine 517

    8.1.1 `MyISAM` Startup Options 519

    8.1.2 Space Needed for Keys 520

    8.1.3 `MyISAM` Table Storage Formats 521

    8.1.4 `MyISAM` Table Problems................................... 523

8.2 The `MERGE` Storage Engine 525

    8.2.1 `MERGE` Table Problems 528

8.3 The `MEMORY` (`HEAP`) Storage Engine 529

8.4 The BDB (BerkeleyDB) Storage Engine 531

    8.4.1 Operating Systems Supported by BDB 531

    8.4.2 Installing BDB 532

    8.4.3 BDB Startup Options 532

    8.4.4 Characteristics of BDB Tables 534

    8.4.5 Things We Need to Fix for BDB 536

    8.4.6 Restrictions on BDB Tables 536

    8.4.7 Errors That May Occur When Using BDB Tables 536

8.5 The ISAM Storage Engine 537

9 The InnoDB Storage Engine   **539**

9.1 InnoDB Overview 539

9.2 InnoDB Contact Information 540

9.3 InnoDB in MySQL 3.23 540

9.4 InnoDB Configuration 541

9.5 InnoDB Startup Options 546

9.6 Creating the InnoDB Tablespace 550

    9.6.1 Dealing with InnoDB Initialization Problems 551

9.7 Creating InnoDB Tables 551

    9.7.1 How to Use Transactions in InnoDB with
    Different APIs 552

    9.7.2 Converting MyISAM Tables to InnoDB 553

    9.7.3 How an AUTO_INCREMENT Column Works in
    InnoDB 554

    9.7.4 FOREIGN KEY Constraints 554

    9.7.5 InnoDB and MySQL Replication 558

    9.7.6 Using Per-Table Tablespaces 559

9.8 Adding and Removing InnoDB Data and Log Files 561

9.9 Backing Up and Recovering an InnoDB Database 563

    9.9.1 Forcing Recovery 564

    9.9.2 Checkpoints 565

9.10 Moving an InnoDB Database to Another Machine 566

9.11 InnoDB Transaction Model and Locking 567

    9.11.1 InnoDB and AUTOCOMMIT 567

    9.11.2 InnoDB and TRANSACTION ISOLATION
    LEVEL 567

    9.11.3 Consistent Non-Locking Read 569

    9.11.4 Locking Reads SELECT ... FOR UPDATE and
    SELECT ... LOCK IN SHARE MODE 569

9.11.5 Next-Key Locking: Avoiding the Phantom Problem 571

9.11.6 An Example of How the Consistent Read Works in
InnoDB 571

9.11.7 Locks Set by Different SQL Statements in InnoDB 572

9.11.8 When Does MySQL Implicitly Commit or Roll
Back a Transaction? 574

9.11.9 Deadlock Detection and Rollback 574

9.11.10 How to Cope with Deadlocks 575

9.12 InnoDB Performance Tuning Tips 576

9.12.1 SHOW INNODB STATUS and the InnoDB Monitors 578

9.13 Implementation of Multi-Versioning 583

9.14 Table and Index Structures 584

9.14.1 Physical Structure of an Index 585

9.14.2 Insert Buffering 585

9.14.3 Adaptive Hash Indexes 585

9.14.4 Physical Record Structure 586

9.15 File Space Management and Disk I/O 586

9.15.1 Disk I/O 586

9.15.2 Using Raw Devices for the Tablespace 587

9.15.3 File Space Management 588

9.15.4 Defragmenting a Table 588

9.16 Error Handling 589

9.16.1 InnoDB Error Codes 589

9.16.2 Operating System Error Codes 590

9.17 Restrictions on InnoDB Tables 594

9.18 InnoDB Troubleshooting 596

9.18.1 Troubleshooting InnoDB Data Dictionary
Operations 597

10 Introduction to MaxDB   599

10.1 History of MaxDB 599

10.2 Licensing and Support 599

10.3 MaxDB-Related Links 600

10.4 Basic Concepts of MaxDB 600

10.5 Feature Differences Between MaxDB and MySQL 600

10.6 Interoperability Features Between MaxDB and MySQL 601

10.7 Reserved Words in MaxDB 601

A Troubleshooting Problems with MySQL Programs   607

A.1 How to Determine What Is Causing a Problem 607
A.2 Common Errors When Using MySQL Programs 608
   A.2.1 Access denied 609
   A.2.2 Can't connect to [local] MySQL server 609
   A.2.3 Client does not support authentication protocol 611
   A.2.4 Password Fails When Entered Interactively 612
   A.2.5 Host 'host_name' is blocked 612
   A.2.6 Too many connections 613
   A.2.7 Out of memory 613
   A.2.8 MySQL server has gone away 613
   A.2.9 Packet too large 615
   A.2.10 Communication Errors and Aborted Connections 616
   A.2.11 The table is full 617
   A.2.12 Can't create/write to file 618
   A.2.13 Commands out of sync 618
   A.2.14 Ignoring user 618
   A.2.15 Table 'tbl_name' doesn't exist 619
   A.2.16 Can't initialize character set 619
   A.2.17 File Not Found 620
A.3 Installation-Related Issues 621
   A.3.1 Problems Linking to the MySQL Client Library 621
   A.3.2 How to Run MySQL as a Normal User 622
   A.3.3 Problems with File Permissions 623
A.4 Administration-Related Issues 623
   A.4.1 How to Reset the Root Password 623
   A.4.2 What to Do If MySQL Keeps Crashing 625
   A.4.3 How MySQL Handles a Full Disk 628
   A.4.4 Where MySQL Stores Temporary Files 628
   A.4.5 How to Protect or Change the MySQL Socket File
   /tmp/mysql.sock 629
   A.4.6 Time Zone Problems 630

B Environment Variables   631

Index   633

General Information

The MySQL® software delivers a very fast, multi-threaded, multi-user, and robust SQL (Structured Query Language) database server. MySQL Server is intended for mission-critical, heavy-load production systems as well as for embedding into mass-deployed software. MySQL is a registered trademark of MySQL AB.

The MySQL software is Dual Licensed. Users can choose to use the MySQL software as an Open Source/Free Software product under the terms of the GNU General Public License or can purchase a standard commercial license from MySQL AB. See Section 1.4, "MySQL Support and Licensing."

The MySQL Web site (`http://www.mysql.com/`) provides the latest information about the MySQL software.

1.1 About This Guide

This guide is made up of those chapters from the *MySQL Reference Manual* that focus on database administration topics. It covers software installation, server configuration and day-to-day operation, table maintenance, and replication. A companion guide, the *MySQL Language Reference*, serves as a reference to the SQL language used to perform database queries in MySQL. It covers language structure, functions and operators, column types, and SQL statement syntax.

This guide is current up to MySQL 5.0.1, but is also applicable for older versions of the MySQL software (such as 3.23 or 4.0-production) because functional changes are indicated with reference to a version number.

Because this guide serves as a reference, it does not provide general instruction on SQL or relational database concepts. It also will not teach you how to use your operating system or command line interpreter.

The MySQL Database Software is under constant development, and the Reference Manual is updated frequently as well. The most recent version of the manual is available online in searchable form at `http://dev.mysql.com/doc/`. Other formats also are available, including HTML, PDF, and Windows CHM versions.

If you have any suggestions concerning additions or corrections to this manual, please send them to the documentation team at docs@mysql.com.

This manual was initially written by David Axmark and Michael "Monty" Widenius. It is now maintained by the MySQL Documentation Team, consisting of Arjen Lentz, Paul DuBois, and Stefan Hinz.

The copyright (2004) to this manual is owned by the Swedish company MySQL AB. See Section 1.4.2, "Copyrights and Licenses Used by MySQL."

1.1.1 Conventions Used in This Manual

This manual uses certain typographical conventions:

- `constant`

  Constant-width font is used for command names and options; SQL statements; database, table, and column names; C and Perl code; filenames; URLs; and environment variables. Example: "To see how `mysqladmin` works, invoke it with the `--help` option."

- **`constant bold`**

  Bold constant-width font is used to indicate input that you type in examples.

- *`constant italic`*

  Italic constant-width font is used to indicate variable input for which you should substitute a value of your own choosing.

- '`c`'

  Constant-width font with surrounding quotes is used to indicate character sequences. Example: "To specify a wildcard, use the '%' character."

- *italic*

  Italic font is used for emphasis, *like this*.

- **boldface**

  Boldface font is used in table headings and to convey **especially strong emphasis**.

When commands are shown that are meant to be executed from within a particular program, the program is indicated by a prompt shown before the command. For example, `shell>` indicates a command that you execute from your login shell, and `mysql>` indicates a statement that you execute from the `mysql` client program.

```
shell> type a shell command here
mysql> type a mysql statement here
```

The "shell" is your command interpreter. On Unix, this is typically a program such as `sh` or `csh`. On Windows, the equivalent program is `command.com` or `cmd.exe`, typically run in a console window.

When you enter a command or statement shown in an example, do not type the prompt shown in the example.

In example commands, input that you type is indicated in bold type. Variable input for which you should substitute a value that you choose is indicated in italic type. Database, table, and column names must often be substituted into statements. To indicate that such substitution is necessary, this manual uses *db_name*, *tbl_name*, and *col_name*. For example, you might see a statement like this:

```
mysql> SELECT col_name FROM db_name.tbl_name;
```

This means that if you were to enter a similar statement, you would supply your own database, table, and column names, perhaps like this:

```
mysql> SELECT author_name FROM biblio_db.author_list;
```

SQL keywords are not case sensitive and may be written in uppercase or lowercase. This manual uses uppercase.

In syntax descriptions, square brackets ('[' and ']') are used to indicate optional words or clauses. For example, in the following statement, IF EXISTS is optional:

```
DROP TABLE [IF EXISTS] tbl_name
```

When a syntax element consists of a number of alternatives, the alternatives are separated by vertical bars ('|'). When one member from a set of choices *may* be chosen, the alternatives are listed within square brackets ('[' and ']'):

```
TRIM([[BOTH | LEADING | TRAILING] [remstr] FROM] str)
```

When one member from a set of choices *must* be chosen, the alternatives are listed within braces ('{' and '}'):

```
{DESCRIBE | DESC} tbl_name [col_name | wild]
```

An ellipsis (...) indicates the omission of a section of a statement, typically to provide a shorter version of more complex syntax. For example, INSERT ... SELECT is shorthand for the form of INSERT statement that is followed by a SELECT statement.

An ellipsis can also indicate that the preceding syntax element of a statement may be repeated. In the following example, multiple *reset_option* values may be given, with each of those after the first preceded by commas:

```
RESET reset_option [,reset_option] ...
```

Commands for setting shell variables are shown using Bourne shell syntax. For example, the sequence to set an environment variable and run a command looks like this in Bourne shell syntax:

```
shell> VARNAME=value some_command
```

If you are using `csh` or `tcsh`, you must issue commands somewhat differently. You would execute the sequence just shown like this:

```
shell> setenv VARNAME value
shell> some_command
```

1.2 Overview of the MySQL Database Management System

MySQL, the most popular Open Source SQL database management system, is developed, distributed, and supported by MySQL AB. MySQL AB is a commercial company, founded by the MySQL developers, that builds its business by providing services around the MySQL database management system. See Section 1.3, "Overview of MySQL AB."

The MySQL Web site (`http://www.mysql.com/`) provides the latest information about MySQL software and MySQL AB.

- MySQL is a database management system.

  A database is a structured collection of data. It may be anything from a simple shopping list to a picture gallery or the vast amounts of information in a corporate network. To add, access, and process data stored in a computer database, you need a database management system such as MySQL Server. Since computers are very good at handling large amounts of data, database management systems play a central role in computing, as standalone utilities, or as parts of other applications.

- MySQL is a relational database management system.

  A relational database stores data in separate tables rather than putting all the data in one big storeroom. This adds speed and flexibility. The SQL part of "MySQL" stands for "Structured Query Language." SQL is the most common standardized language used to access databases and is defined by the ANSI/ISO SQL Standard. The SQL standard has been evolving since 1986 and several versions exist. In this manual, "SQL-92" refers to the standard released in 1992, "SQL:1999" refers to the standard released in 1999, and "SQL:2003" refers to the current version of the standard. We use the phrase "the SQL standard" to mean the current version of the SQL Standard at any time.

- MySQL software is Open Source.

  Open Source means that it is possible for anyone to use and modify the software. Anybody can download the MySQL software from the Internet and use it without paying anything. If you wish, you may study the source code and change it to suit your needs. The MySQL software uses the GPL (GNU General Public License) to define what you may and may not do with the software in different situations. If you feel uncomfortable with the GPL or need to embed MySQL code into a commercial application, you can buy a commercially licensed version from us. See Section 1.4.3, "MySQL Licenses."

- The MySQL Database Server is very fast, reliable, and easy to use.

  If that is what you are looking for, you should give it a try. MySQL Server also has a practical set of features developed in close cooperation with our users. You can find a performance comparison of MySQL Server with other database managers at `http://dev.mysql.com/tech-resources/crash-me.php`.

  MySQL Server was originally developed to handle large databases much faster than existing solutions and has been successfully used in highly demanding production environments for several years. Although under constant development, MySQL Server today offers a rich and useful set of functions. Its connectivity, speed, and security make MySQL Server highly suited for accessing databases on the Internet.

- MySQL Server works in client/server or embedded systems.

  The MySQL Database Software is a client/server system that consists of a multi-threaded SQL server that supports different backends, several different client programs and libraries, administrative tools, and a wide range of application programming interfaces (APIs).

  We also provide MySQL Server as an embedded multi-threaded library that you can link into your application to get a smaller, faster, easier-to-manage product.

- A large amount of contributed MySQL software is available.

  It is very likely that you will find that your favorite application or language already supports the MySQL Database Server.

The official way to pronounce "MySQL" is "My Ess Que Ell" (not "my sequel"), but we don't mind if you pronounce it as "my sequel" or in some other localized way.

1.2.1 History of MySQL

We started out with the intention of using mSQL to connect to our tables using our own fast low-level (ISAM) routines. However, after some testing, we came to the conclusion that mSQL was not fast enough or flexible enough for our needs. This resulted in a new SQL interface to our database but with almost the same API interface as mSQL. This API was designed to allow third-party code that was written for use with mSQL to be ported easily for use with MySQL.

The derivation of the name MySQL is not clear. Our base directory and a large number of our libraries and tools have had the prefix "my" for well over 10 years. However, co-founder Monty Widenius's daughter is also named My. Which of the two gave its name to MySQL is still a mystery, even for us.

The name of the MySQL Dolphin (our logo) is "Sakila," which was chosen by the founders of MySQL AB from a huge list of names suggested by users in our "Name the Dolphin" contest. The winning name was submitted by Ambrose Twebaze, an Open Source software developer from Swaziland, Africa. According to Ambrose, the name Sakila has its roots in SiSwati, the local language of Swaziland. Sakila is also the name of a town in Arusha, Tanzania, near Ambrose's country of origin, Uganda.

1.2.2 The Main Features of MySQL

The following list describes some of the important characteristics of the MySQL Database Software. See also Section 1.5, "MySQL Development Roadmap," for more information about current and upcoming features.

- Internals and Portability
    - Written in C and C++.
    - Tested with a broad range of different compilers.
    - Works on many different platforms.
    - Uses GNU Automake, Autoconf, and Libtool for portability.
    - APIs for C, C++, Eiffel, Java, Perl, PHP, Python, Ruby, and Tcl are available.
    - Fully multi-threaded using kernel threads. It can easily use multiple CPUs if they are available.
    - Provides transactional and non-transactional storage engines.
    - Uses very fast B-tree disk tables (MyISAM) with index compression.
    - Relatively easy to add another storage engine. This is useful if you want to add an SQL interface to an in-house database.
    - A very fast thread-based memory allocation system.
    - Very fast joins using an optimized one-sweep multi-join.
    - In-memory hash tables, which are used as temporary tables.
    - SQL functions are implemented using a highly optimized class library and should be as fast as possible. Usually there is no memory allocation at all after query initialization.
    - The MySQL code is tested both with commercial and Open Source memory leakage detectors.
    - The server is available as a separate program for use in a client/server networked environment. It is also available as a library that can be embedded (linked) into standalone applications. Such applications can be used in isolation or in environments where no network is available.
- Column Types
    - Many column types: signed/unsigned integers 1, 2, 3, 4, and 8 bytes long, FLOAT, DOUBLE, CHAR, VARCHAR, TEXT, BLOB, DATE, TIME, DATETIME, TIMESTAMP, YEAR, SET, ENUM, and OpenGIS spatial types.
    - Fixed-length and variable-length records.

- Statements and Functions
  - Full operator and function support in the SELECT and WHERE clauses of queries. For example:

    ```
    mysql> SELECT CONCAT(first_name, ' ', last_name)
        -> FROM citizen
        -> WHERE income/dependents > 10000 AND age > 30;
    ```

  - Full support for SQL GROUP BY and ORDER BY clauses. Support for group functions (COUNT(), COUNT(DISTINCT ...), AVG(), STD(), SUM(), MAX(), MIN(), and GROUP_CONCAT()).
  - Support for LEFT OUTER JOIN and RIGHT OUTER JOIN with both standard SQL and ODBC syntax.
  - Support for aliases on tables and columns as required by standard SQL.
  - DELETE, INSERT, REPLACE, and UPDATE return the number of rows that were changed (affected). It is possible to return the number of rows matched instead by setting a flag when connecting to the server.
  - The MySQL-specific SHOW command can be used to retrieve information about databases, tables, and indexes. The EXPLAIN command can be used to determine how the optimizer resolves a query.
  - Function names do not clash with table or column names. For example, ABS is a valid column name. The only restriction is that for a function call, no spaces are allowed between the function name and the '(' that follows it.
  - You can mix tables from different databases in the same query (as of MySQL 3.22).
- Security
  - A privilege and password system that is very flexible and secure, and that allows host-based verification. Passwords are secure because all password traffic is encrypted when you connect to a server.
- Scalability and Limits
  - Handles large databases. We use MySQL Server with databases that contain 50 million records. We also know of users who use MySQL Server with 60,000 tables and about 5,000,000,000 rows.
  - Up to 64 indexes per table are allowed (32 before MySQL 4.1.2). Each index may consist of 1 to 16 columns or parts of columns. The maximum index width is 1000 bytes (500 before MySQL 4.1.2). An index may use a prefix of a column for CHAR, VARCHAR, BLOB, or TEXT column types.
- Connectivity
  - Clients can connect to the MySQL server using TCP/IP sockets on any platform. On Windows systems in the NT family (NT, 2000, or XP), clients can connect using named pipes. On Unix systems, clients can connect using Unix domain socket files.

- The Connector/ODBC interface provides MySQL support for client programs that use ODBC (Open Database Connectivity) connections. For example, you can use MS Access to connect to your MySQL server. Clients can be run on Windows or Unix. Connector/ODBC source is available. All ODBC 2.5 functions are supported, as are many others.

- The Connector/JDBC interface provides MySQL support for Java client programs that use JDBC connections. Clients can be run on Windows or Unix. Connector/JDBC source is available.

- Localization

  - The server can provide error messages to clients in many languages.

  - Full support for several different character sets, including `latin1` (ISO-8859-1), `german`, `big5`, `ujis`, and more. For example, the Scandinavian characters 'â', 'ä' and 'ö' are allowed in table and column names. Unicode support is available as of MySQL 4.1.

  - All data is saved in the chosen character set. All comparisons for normal string columns are case-insensitive.

  - Sorting is done according to the chosen character set (using Swedish collation by default). It is possible to change this when the MySQL server is started. To see an example of very advanced sorting, look at the Czech sorting code. MySQL Server supports many different character sets that can be specified at compile time and runtime.

- Clients and Tools

  - The MySQL server has built-in support for SQL statements to check, optimize, and repair tables. These statements are available from the command line through the `mysqlcheck` client. MySQL also includes `myisamchk`, a very fast command-line utility for performing these operations on `MyISAM` tables.

  - All MySQL programs can be invoked with the `--help` or `-?` options to obtain online assistance.

1.2.3 MySQL Stability

This section addresses the questions, *"How stable is MySQL Server?"* and, *"Can I depend on MySQL Server in this project?"* We will try to clarify these issues and answer some important questions that concern many potential users. The information in this section is based on data gathered from the mailing lists, which are very active in identifying problems as well as reporting types of use.

The original code stems back to the early 1980s. It provides a stable code base, and the `ISAM` table format used by the original storage engine remains backward-compatible. At TcX, the predecessor of MySQL AB, MySQL code has worked in projects since mid-1996, without any problems. When the MySQL Database Software initially was released to a wider public, our new users quickly found some pieces of untested code. Each new release since then has had fewer portability problems, even though each new release has also had many new features.

Each release of the MySQL Server has been usable. Problems have occurred only when users try code from the "gray zones." Naturally, new users don't know what the gray zones are; this section therefore attempts to document those areas that are currently known. The descriptions mostly deal with Version 3.23 and 4.0 of MySQL Server. All known and reported bugs are fixed in the latest version, with the exception of those listed in the bugs section, which are design-related. See Section 1.8.7, "Known Errors and Design Deficiencies in MySQL."

The MySQL Server design is multi-layered with independent modules. Some of the newer modules are listed here with an indication of how well-tested each of them is:

- Replication (Gamma)

  Large groups of servers using replication are in production use, with good results. Work on enhanced replication features is continuing in MySQL 5.x.

- InnoDB tables (Stable)

  The InnoDB transactional storage engine has been declared stable in the MySQL 3.23 tree, starting from version 3.23.49. InnoDB is being used in large, heavy-load production systems.

- BDB tables (Gamma)

  The Berkeley DB code is very stable, but we are still improving the BDB transactional storage engine interface in MySQL Server, so it will take some time before this is as well tested as the other table types.

- Full-text searches (Beta)

  Full-text searching works but is not yet widely used. Important enhancements have been implemented in MySQL 4.0.

- Connector/ODBC 3.51 (Stable)

  Connector/ODBC 3.51 uses ODBC SDK 3.51 and is in wide production use. Some issues brought up appear to be application-related and independent of the ODBC driver or underlying database server.

- Automatic recovery of MyISAM tables (Gamma)

  This status applies only to the new code in the MyISAM storage engine that checks when opening a table whether it was closed properly and executes an automatic check or repair of the table if it wasn't.

1.2.4 How Big MySQL Tables Can Be

MySQL 3.22 had a 4GB (4 gigabyte) limit on table size. With the MyISAM storage engine in MySQL 3.23, the maximum table size was increased to 8 million terabytes (2^{63} bytes). With this larger allowed table size, the maximum effective table size for MySQL databases now usually is determined by operating system constraints on file sizes, not by MySQL internal limits.

The InnoDB storage engine maintains InnoDB tables within a tablespace that can be created from several files. This allows a table to exceed the maximum individual file size. The tablespace can include raw disk partitions, which allows extremely large tables. The maximum tablespace size is 64TB.

The following table lists some examples of operating system file-size limits:

Operating System	File Size Limit
Linux-Intel 32-bit	2GB, much more when using LFS
Linux-Alpha	8TB (?)
Solaris 2.5.1	2GB (4GB possible with patch)
Solaris 2.6	4GB (can be changed with flag)
Solaris 2.7 Intel	4GB
Solaris 2.7 UltraSPARC	512GB
NetWare w/NSS filesystem	8TB

On Linux 2.2, you can get MyISAM tables larger than 2GB in size by using the Large File Support (LFS) patch for the ext2 filesystem. On Linux 2.4, patches also exist for ReiserFS to get support for big files. Most current Linux distributions are based on kernel 2.4 and already include all the required LFS patches. However, the maximum available file size still depends on several factors, one of them being the filesystem used to store MySQL tables.

For a detailed overview about LFS in Linux, have a look at Andreas Jaeger's "Large File Support in Linux" page at http://www.suse.de/~aj/linux_lfs.html.

By default, MySQL creates MyISAM tables with an internal structure that allows a maximum size of about 4GB. You can check the maximum table size for a table with the SHOW TABLE STATUS statement or with myisamchk -dv tbl_name.

If you need a MyISAM table that will be larger than 4GB in size (and your operating system supports large files), the CREATE TABLE statement allows AVG_ROW_LENGTH and MAX_ROWS options. You can also change these options with ALTER TABLE after the table has been created, to increase the table's maximum allowable size.

Other ways to work around file-size limits for MyISAM tables are as follows:

- If your large table is read-only, you can use myisampack to compress it. myisampack usually compresses a table by at least 50%, so you can have, in effect, much bigger tables. myisampack also can merge multiple tables into a single table.

- Another way to get around the operating system file limit for MyISAM data files is by using the RAID options.

- MySQL includes a MERGE library that allows you to handle a collection of MyISAM tables that have identical structure as a single MERGE table.

1.2.5 Year 2000 Compliance

The MySQL Server itself has no problems with Year 2000 (Y2K) compliance:

- MySQL Server uses Unix time functions that handle dates into the year 2037 for TIMESTAMP values. For DATE and DATETIME values, dates through the year 9999 are accepted.

- All MySQL date functions are implemented in one source file, sql/time.cc, and are coded very carefully to be year 2000-safe.

- In MySQL 3.22 and later, the YEAR column type can store years 0 and 1901 to 2155 in one byte and display them using two or four digits. All two-digit years are considered to be in the range 1970 to 2069, which means that if you store 01 in a YEAR column, MySQL Server treats it as 2001.

The following simple demonstration illustrates that MySQL Server has no problems with DATE or DATETIME values through the year 9999, and no problems with TIMESTAMP values until after the year 2030:

```
mysql> DROP TABLE IF EXISTS y2k;
Query OK, 0 rows affected (0.01 sec)

mysql> CREATE TABLE y2k (date DATE,
    ->                    date_time DATETIME,
    ->                    time_stamp TIMESTAMP);
Query OK, 0 rows affected (0.01 sec)

mysql> INSERT INTO y2k VALUES
    -> ('1998-12-31','1998-12-31 23:59:59',19981231235959),
    -> ('1999-01-01','1999-01-01 00:00:00',19990101000000),
    -> ('1999-09-09','1999-09-09 23:59:59',19990909235959),
    -> ('2000-01-01','2000-01-01 00:00:00',20000101000000),
    -> ('2000-02-28','2000-02-28 00:00:00',20000228000000),
    -> ('2000-02-29','2000-02-29 00:00:00',20000229000000),
    -> ('2000-03-01','2000-03-01 00:00:00',20000301000000),
    -> ('2000-12-31','2000-12-31 23:59:59',20001231235959) ,
    -> ('2001-01-01','2001-01-01 00:00:00',20010101000000),
    -> ('2004-12-31','2004-12-31 23:59:59',20041231235959),
    -> ('2005-01-01','2005-01-01 00:00:00',20050101000000),
    -> ('2030-01-01','2030-01-01 00:00:00',20300101000000),
    -> ('2040-01-01','2040-01-01 00:00:00',20400101000000),
    -> ('9999-12-31','9999-12-31 23:59:59',99991231235959);
Query OK, 14 rows affected (0.01 sec)
Records: 14  Duplicates: 0  Warnings: 2
```

```
mysql> SELECT * FROM y2k;
+------------+---------------------+----------------+
| date       | date_time           | time_stamp     |
+------------+---------------------+----------------+
| 1998-12-31 | 1998-12-31 23:59:59 | 19981231235959 |
| 1999-01-01 | 1999-01-01 00:00:00 | 19990101000000 |
| 1999-09-09 | 1999-09-09 23:59:59 | 19990909235959 |
| 2000-01-01 | 2000-01-01 00:00:00 | 20000101000000 |
| 2000-02-28 | 2000-02-28 00:00:00 | 20000228000000 |
| 2000-02-29 | 2000-02-29 00:00:00 | 20000229000000 |
| 2000-03-01 | 2000-03-01 00:00:00 | 20000301000000 |
| 2000-12-31 | 2000-12-31 23:59:59 | 20001231235959 |
| 2001-01-01 | 2001-01-01 00:00:00 | 20010101000000 |
| 2004-12-31 | 2004-12-31 23:59:59 | 20041231235959 |
| 2005-01-01 | 2005-01-01 00:00:00 | 20050101000000 |
| 2030-01-01 | 2030-01-01 00:00:00 | 20300101000000 |
| 2040-01-01 | 2040-01-01 00:00:00 | 00000000000000 |
| 9999-12-31 | 9999-12-31 23:59:59 | 00000000000000 |
+------------+---------------------+----------------+
14 rows in set (0.00 sec)
```

The final two TIMESTAMP column values are zero because the final year values (2040, 9999) exceed the TIMESTAMP maximum. The TIMESTAMP data type, which is used to store the current time, supports values that range from 19700101000000 to 20300101000000 on 32-bit machines (signed value). On 64-bit machines, TIMESTAMP handles values up to 2106 (unsigned value).

Although MySQL Server itself is Y2K-safe, you may run into problems if you use it with applications that are not Y2K-safe. For example, many old applications store or manipulate years using two-digit values (which are ambiguous) rather than four-digit values. This problem may be compounded by applications that use values such as 00 or 99 as "missing" value indicators. Unfortunately, these problems may be difficult to fix because different applications may be written by different programmers, each of whom may use a different set of conventions and date-handling functions.

Thus, even though MySQL Server has no Y2K problems, it is the application's responsibility to provide unambiguous input.

1.3 Overview of MySQL AB

MySQL AB is the company of the MySQL founders and main developers. MySQL AB was originally established in Sweden by David Axmark, Allan Larsson, and Michael "Monty" Widenius.

The developers of the MySQL server are all employed by the company. We are a virtual organization with people in a dozen countries around the world. We communicate extensively over the Internet every day with one another and with our users, supporters, and partners.

We are dedicated to developing the MySQL database software and promoting it to new users. MySQL AB owns the copyright to the MySQL source code, the MySQL logo and trademark, and this manual. See Section 1.2, "Overview of the MySQL Database Management System."

The MySQL core values show our dedication to MySQL and Open Source.

These core values direct how MySQL AB works with the MySQL server software:

- To be the best and the most widely used database in the world
- To be available and affordable by all
- To be easy to use
- To be continuously improved while remaining fast and safe
- To be fun to use and improve
- To be free from bugs

These are the core values of the company MySQL AB and its employees:

- We subscribe to the Open Source philosophy and support the Open Source community
- We aim to be good citizens
- We prefer partners that share our values and mindset
- We answer email and provide support
- We are a virtual company, networking with others
- We work against software patents

The MySQL Web site (http://www.mysql.com/) provides the latest information about MySQL and MySQL AB.

By the way, the "AB" part of the company name is the acronym for the Swedish "aktiebolag," or "stock company." It translates to "MySQL, Inc." In fact, MySQL, Inc. and MySQL GmbH are examples of MySQL AB subsidiaries. They are located in the United States and Germany, respectively.

1.3.1 The Business Model and Services of MySQL AB

One of the most common questions we encounter is, "*How can you make a living from something you give away for free?*" This is how:

- MySQL AB makes money on support, services, commercial licenses, and royalties.
- We use these revenues to fund product development and to expand the MySQL business.

The company has been profitable since its inception. In October 2001, we accepted venture financing from leading Scandinavian investors and a handful of business angels. This investment is used to solidify our business model and build a basis for sustainable growth.

1.3.1.1 Support

MySQL AB is run and owned by the founders and main developers of the MySQL database. The developers are committed to providing support to customers and other users in order to stay in touch with their needs and problems. All our support is provided by qualified developers. Really tricky questions are answered by Michael "Monty" Widenius, principal author of the MySQL Server.

Paying customers receive high-quality support directly from MySQL AB. MySQL AB also provides the MySQL mailing lists as a community resource where anyone may ask questions.

For more information and ordering support at various levels, see Section 1.4, "MySQL Support and Licensing."

1.3.1.2 Training and Certification

MySQL AB delivers MySQL and related training worldwide. We offer both open courses and in-house courses tailored to the specific needs of your company. MySQL Training is also available through our partners, the Authorized MySQL Training Centers.

Our training material uses the same sample databases used in our documentation and our sample applications, and is always updated to reflect the latest MySQL version. Our trainers are backed by the development team to guarantee the quality of the training and the continuous development of the course material. This also ensures that no questions raised during the courses remain unanswered.

Attending our training courses will enable you to achieve your MySQL application goals. You will also:

- Save time
- Improve the performance of your applications
- Reduce or eliminate the need for additional hardware, decreasing cost
- Enhance security
- Increase customer and co-worker satisfaction
- Prepare yourself for MySQL Certification

If you are interested in our training as a potential participant or as a training partner, please visit the training section at `http://www.mysql.com/training/`, or send email to `training@mysql.com`.

For details about the MySQL Certification Program, please see `http://www.mysql.com/certification/`.

1.3.1.3 Consulting

MySQL AB and its Authorized Partners offer consulting services to users of MySQL Server and to those who embed MySQL Server in their own software, all over the world.

Our consultants can help you design and tune your databases, construct efficient queries, tune your platform for optimal performance, resolve migration issues, set up replication, build robust transactional applications, and more. We also help customers embed MySQL Server in their products and applications for large-scale deployment.

Our consultants work in close collaboration with our development team, which ensures the technical quality of our professional services. Consulting assignments range from two-day power-start sessions to projects that span weeks and months. Our expertise covers not only MySQL Server, it also extends into programming and scripting languages such as PHP, Perl, and more.

If you are interested in our consulting services or want to become a consulting partner, please visit the consulting section of our Web site at `http://www.mysql.com/consulting/` or contact our consulting staff at `consulting@mysql.com`.

1.3.1.4 Commercial Licenses

The MySQL database is released under the GNU General Public License (GPL). This means that the MySQL software can be used free of charge under the GPL. If you do not want to be bound by the GPL terms (such as the requirement that your application must also be GPL), you may purchase a commercial license for the same product from MySQL AB; see `https://order.mysql.com/`. Since MySQL AB owns the copyright to the MySQL source code, we are able to employ Dual Licensing, which means that the same product is available under GPL and under a commercial license. This does not in any way affect the Open Source commitment of MySQL AB. For details about when a commercial license is required, please see Section 1.4.3, "MySQL Licenses."

We also sell commercial licenses of third-party Open Source GPL software that adds value to MySQL Server. A good example is the `InnoDB` transactional storage engine that offers `ACID` support, row-level locking, crash recovery, multi-versioning, foreign key support, and more.

1.3.1.5 Partnering

MySQL AB has a worldwide partner program that covers training courses, consulting and support, publications, plus reselling and distributing MySQL and related products. MySQL AB Partners get visibility on the `http://www.mysql.com/` Web site and the right to use special versions of the MySQL trademarks to identify their products and promote their business.

If you are interested in becoming a MySQL AB Partner, please email `partner@mysql.com`.

The word MySQL and the MySQL dolphin logo are trademarks of MySQL AB. See Section 1.4.4, "MySQL AB Logos and Trademarks." These trademarks represent a significant value that the MySQL founders have built over the years.

The MySQL Web site (`http://www.mysql.com/`) is popular among developers and users. In December 2003, we served 16 million page views. Our visitors represent a group that makes purchase decisions and recommendations for both software and hardware. Twelve percent of our visitors authorize purchase decisions, and only nine percent have no involvement at all in purchase decisions. More than 65% have made one or more online business purchases within the last half-year, and 70% plan to make one in the next few months.

1.3.2 Contact Information

The MySQL Web site (http://www.mysql.com/) provides the latest information about MySQL and MySQL AB.

For press services and inquiries not covered in our news releases (http://www.mysql.com/news-and-events/), please send email to press@mysql.com.

If you have a support contract with MySQL AB, you will get timely, precise answers to your technical questions about the MySQL software. For more information, see Section 1.4.1, "Support Offered by MySQL AB." On our Web site, see http://www.mysql.com/support/, or send email to sales@mysql.com.

For information about MySQL training, please visit the training section at http://www.mysql.com/training/, or send email to training@mysql.com. See Section 1.3.1.2, "Training and Certification."

For information on the MySQL Certification Program, please see http://www.mysql.com/certification/. See Section 1.3.1.2, "Training and Certification."

If you're interested in consulting, please visit the consulting section of our Web site at http://www.mysql.com/consulting/, or send email to consulting@mysql.com. See Section 1.3.1.3, "Consulting."

Commercial licenses may be purchased online at https://order.mysql.com/. There you will also find information on how to fax your purchase order to MySQL AB. More information about licensing can be found at http://www.mysql.com/products/pricing.html. If you have questions regarding licensing or you want a quote for high-volume licensing, please fill in the contact form on our Web site (http://www.mysql.com/), or send email to licensing@mysql.com (for licensing questions) or to sales@mysql.com (for sales inquiries). See Section 1.4.3, "MySQL Licenses."

If you represent a business that is interested in partnering with MySQL AB, please send email to partner@mysql.com. See Section 1.3.1.5, "Partnering."

For more information on the MySQL trademark policy, refer to http://www.mysql.com/company/trademark.html, or send email to trademark@mysql.com. See Section 1.4.4, "MySQL AB Logos and Trademarks."

If you are interested in any of the MySQL AB jobs listed in our jobs section (http://www.mysql.com/company/jobs/), please send email to jobs@mysql.com. Please do not send your CV as an attachment, but rather as plain text at the end of your email message.

For general discussion among our many users, please direct your attention to the appropriate mailing list. See Section 1.7.1, "MySQL Mailing Lists."

Reports of errors (often called "bugs"), as well as questions and comments, should be sent to the general MySQL mailing list. See Section 1.7.1.1, "The MySQL Mailing Lists." If you have found a sensitive security bug in MySQL Server, please let us know immediately by sending email to security@mysql.com. See Section 1.7.1.3, "How to Report Bugs or Problems."

If you have benchmark results that we can publish, please contact us via email at benchmarks@mysql.com.

If you have suggestions concerning additions or corrections to this manual, please send them to the documentation team via email at docs@mysql.com.

For questions or comments about the workings or content of the MySQL Web site (http://www.mysql.com/), please send email to webmaster@mysql.com.

MySQL AB has a privacy policy, which can be read at http://www.mysql.com/company/privacy.html. For any queries regarding this policy, please send email to privacy@mysql.com.

For all other inquiries, please send email to info@mysql.com.

1.4 MySQL Support and Licensing

This section describes MySQL support and licensing arrangements.

1.4.1 Support Offered by MySQL AB

Technical support from MySQL AB means individualized answers to your unique problems direct from the software engineers who code the MySQL database engine.

We try to take a broad and inclusive view of technical support. Almost any problem involving MySQL software is important to us if it's important to you. Typically customers seek help on how to get different commands and utilities to work, remove performance bottlenecks, restore crashed systems, understand the impact of operating system or networking issues on MySQL, set up best practices for backup and recovery, utilize APIs, and so on. Our support covers only the MySQL server and our own utilities, not third-party products that access the MySQL server, although we try to help with these where we can.

Detailed information about our various support options is given at http://www.mysql.com/support/, where support contracts can also be ordered online. To contact our sales staff, send email to sales@mysql.com.

Technical support is like life insurance. You can live happily without it for years. However, when your hour arrives, it becomes critically important, but it's too late to buy it. If you use MySQL Server for important applications and encounter sudden difficulties, it may be too time-consuming to figure out all the answers yourself. You may need immediate access to the most experienced MySQL troubleshooters available, those employed by MySQL AB.

1.4.2 Copyrights and Licenses Used by MySQL

MySQL AB owns the copyright to the MySQL source code, the MySQL logos and trademarks, and this manual. See Section 1.3, "Overview of MySQL AB." Several different licenses are relevant to the MySQL distribution:

1. All the MySQL-specific source in the server, the `mysqlclient` library and the client, as well as the GNU `readline` library, are covered by the GNU General Public License. See `http://www.fsf.org/licenses/`. The text of this license can be found as the file `COPYING` in MySQL distributions.

2. The GNU `getopt` library is covered by the GNU Lesser General Public License. See `http://www.fsf.org/licenses/`.

3. Some parts of the source (the `regexp` library) are covered by a Berkeley-style copyright.

4. Older versions of MySQL (3.22 and earlier) are subject to a stricter license (`http://www.mysql.com/products/mypl.html`). See the documentation of the specific version for information.

5. The *MySQL Reference Manual* is *not* distributed under a GPL-style license. Use of the manual is subject to the following terms:

   - Conversion to other formats is allowed, but the actual content may not be altered or edited in any way.

   - You may create a printed copy for your own personal use.

   - For all other uses, such as selling printed copies or using (parts of) the manual in another publication, prior written agreement from MySQL AB is required.

   Please send an email message to `docs@mysql.com` for more information or if you are interested in doing a translation.

For information about how the MySQL licenses work in practice, please refer to Section 1.4.3, "MySQL Licenses," and Section 1.4.4, "MySQL AB Logos and Trademarks."

1.4.3 MySQL Licenses

The MySQL software is released under the GNU General Public License (GPL), which is probably the best known Open Source license. The formal terms of the GPL license can be found at `http://www.fsf.org/licenses/`. See also `http://www.fsf.org/licenses/gpl-faq.html` and `http://www.gnu.org/philosophy/enforcing-gpl.html`.

Our GPL licensing is supported by an optional license exception that enables many Free/Libre and Open Source Software ("FLOSS") applications to include the GPL-licensed MySQL client libraries despite the fact that not all FLOSS licenses are compatible with the GPL. For details, see `http://www.mysql.com/products/licensing/foss-exception.html`.

Because the MySQL software is released under the GPL, it may often be used for free, but for certain uses you may want or need to buy commercial licenses from MySQL AB at `https://order.mysql.com/`. See `http://www.mysql.com/products/licensing.html` for more information.

Older versions of MySQL (3.22 and earlier) are subject to a stricter license (`http://www.mysql.com/products/mypl.html`). See the documentation of the specific version for information.

Please note that the use of the MySQL software under commercial license, GPL, or the old MySQL license does not automatically give you the right to use MySQL AB trademarks. See Section 1.4.4, "MySQL AB Logos and Trademarks."

1.4.3.1 Using the MySQL Software Under a Commercial License

The GPL license is contagious in the sense that when a program is linked to a GPL program, all the source code for all the parts of the resulting product must also be released under the GPL. If you do not follow this GPL requirement, you break the license terms and forfeit your right to use the GPL program altogether. You also risk damages.

You need a commercial license under these conditions:

- When you link a program with any GPL code from the MySQL software and don't want the resulting product to be licensed under GPL, perhaps because you want to build a commercial product or keep the added non-GPL code closed source for other reasons. When purchasing commercial licenses, you are not using the MySQL software under GPL even though it's the same code.

- When you distribute a non-GPL application that works *only* with the MySQL software and ship it with the MySQL software. This type of solution is considered to be linking even if it's done over a network.

- When you distribute copies of the MySQL software without providing the source code as required under the GPL license.

- When you want to support the further development of the MySQL database even if you don't formally need a commercial license. Purchasing support directly from MySQL AB is another good way of contributing to the development of the MySQL software, with immediate advantages for you. See Section 1.4.1, "Support Offered by MySQL AB."

Our GPL licensing is supported by an optional license exception that enables many Free/Libre and Open Source Software ("FLOSS") applications to include the GPL-licensed MySQL client libraries despite the fact that not all FLOSS licenses are compatible with the GPL. For details, see `http://www.mysql.com/products/licensing/foss-exception.html`.

If you require a commercial license, you will need one for each installation of the MySQL software. This covers any number of CPUs on a machine, and there is no artificial limit on the number of clients that connect to the server in any way.

For commercial licenses, please visit our Web site at
`http://www.mysql.com/products/licensing.html`. For support contracts, see
`http://www.mysql.com/support/`. If you have special needs, please contact our sales staff via
email at `sales@mysql.com`.

1.4.3.2 Using the MySQL Software for Free Under GPL

You can use the MySQL software for free under the GPL if you adhere to the conditions of
the GPL. For additional details about the GPL, including answers to common questions,
see the generic FAQ from the Free Software Foundation at
`http://www.fsf.org/licenses/gpl-faq.html`.

Our GPL licensing is supported by an optional license exception that enables many
Free/Libre and Open Source Software ("FLOSS") applications to include the GPL-licensed
MySQL client libraries despite the fact that not all FLOSS licenses are compatible with the
GPL. For details, see `http://www.mysql.com/products/licensing/foss-exception.html`.

Common uses of the GPL include:

- When you distribute both your own application and the MySQL source code under the
  GPL with your product.

- When you distribute the MySQL source code bundled with other programs that are
  not linked to or dependent on the MySQL system for their functionality even if you
  sell the distribution commercially. This is called "mere aggregation" in the GPL
  license.

- When you are not distributing *any* part of the MySQL system, you can use it for free.

- When you are an Internet Service Provider (ISP), offering Web hosting with MySQL
  servers for your customers. We encourage people to use ISPs that have MySQL support, because doing so will give them the confidence that their ISP will, in fact, have
  the resources to solve any problems they may experience with the MySQL installation.
  Even if an ISP does not have a commercial license for MySQL Server, their customers
  should at least be given read access to the source of the MySQL installation so that the
  customers can verify that it is correctly patched.

- When you use the MySQL database software in conjunction with a Web server, you do
  not need a commercial license (so long as it is not a product you distribute). This is true
  even if you run a commercial Web server that uses MySQL Server, because you are not
  distributing any part of the MySQL system. However, in this case we would like you to
  purchase MySQL support because the MySQL software is helping your enterprise.

If your use of MySQL database software does not require a commercial license, we encour-
age you to purchase support from MySQL AB anyway. This way you contribute toward
MySQL development and also gain immediate advantages for yourself. See Section 1.4.1,
"Support Offered by MySQL AB."

If you use the MySQL database software in a commercial context such that you profit by its use, we ask that you further the development of the MySQL software by purchasing some level of support. We feel that if the MySQL database helps your business, it is reasonable to ask that you help MySQL AB. (Otherwise, if you ask us support questions, you are not only using for free something into which we've put a lot a work, you're asking us to provide free support, too.)

1.4.4 MySQL AB Logos and Trademarks

Many users of the MySQL database want to display the MySQL AB dolphin logo on their Web sites, books, or boxed products. We welcome and encourage this, although it should be noted that the word MySQL and the MySQL dolphin logo are trademarks of MySQL AB and may only be used as stated in our trademark policy at `http://www.mysql.com/company/trademark.html`.

1.4.4.1 The Original MySQL Logo

The MySQL dolphin logo was designed by the Finnish advertising agency Priority in 2001. The dolphin was chosen as a suitable symbol for the MySQL database management system, which is like a smart, fast, and lean animal, effortlessly navigating oceans of data. We also happen to like dolphins.

The original MySQL logo may only be used by representatives of MySQL AB and by those having a written agreement allowing them to do so.

1.4.4.2 MySQL Logos That May Be Used Without Written Permission

We have designed a set of special *Conditional Use* logos that may be downloaded from our Web site at `http://www.mysql.com/press/logos.html` and used on third-party Web sites without written permission from MySQL AB. The use of these logos is not entirely unrestricted but, as the name implies, subject to our trademark policy that is also available on our Web site. You should read through the trademark policy if you plan to use them. The requirements are basically as follows:

- Use the logo you need as displayed on the `http://www.mysql.com/` site. You may scale it to fit your needs, but may not change colors or design, or alter the graphics in any way.
- Make it evident that you, and not MySQL AB, are the creator and owner of the site that displays the MySQL trademark.
- Don't use the trademark in a way that is detrimental to MySQL AB or to the value of MySQL AB trademarks. We reserve the right to revoke the right to use the MySQL AB trademark.
- If you use the trademark on a Web site, make it clickable, leading directly to `http://www.mysql.com/`.
- If you use the MySQL database under GPL in an application, your application must be Open Source and must be able to connect to a MySQL server.

Contact us via email at trademark@mysql.com to inquire about special arrangements to fit your needs.

1.4.4.3 When You Need Written Permission to Use MySQL Logos

You need written permission from MySQL AB before using MySQL logos in the following cases:

- When displaying any MySQL AB logo anywhere except on your Web site.
- When displaying any MySQL AB logo except the *Conditional Use* logos (mentioned previously) on Web sites or elsewhere.

Due to legal and commercial reasons, we monitor the use of MySQL trademarks on products, books, and other items. We usually require a fee for displaying MySQL AB logos on commercial products, since we think it is reasonable that some of the revenue is returned to fund further development of the MySQL database.

1.4.4.4 MySQL AB Partnership Logos

MySQL partnership logos may be used only by companies and persons having a written partnership agreement with MySQL AB. Partnerships include certification as a MySQL trainer or consultant. For more information, please see Section 1.3.1.5, "Partnering."

1.4.4.5 Using the Word MySQL in Printed Text or Presentations

MySQL AB welcomes references to the MySQL database, but it should be noted that the word MySQL is a trademark of MySQL AB. Because of this, you must append the trademark notice symbol (®) to the first or most prominent use of the word MySQL in a text and, where appropriate, state that MySQL is a trademark of MySQL AB. For more information, please refer to our trademark policy at
http://www.mysql.com/company/trademark.html.

1.4.4.6 Using the Word MySQL in Company and Product Names

Use of the word MySQL in company or product names or in Internet domain names is not allowed without written permission from MySQL AB.

1.5 MySQL Development Roadmap

This section provides a snapshot of the MySQL development roadmap, including major features implemented or planned for MySQL 4.0, 4.1, 5.0, and 5.1. The following sections provide information for each release series.

The production release series is MySQL 4.0, which was declared stable for production use as of Version 4.0.12, released in March 2003. This means that future 4.0 development will be limited only to making bug fixes. For the older MySQL 3.23 series, only critical bug fixes will be made.

Active MySQL development currently is taking place in the MySQL 4.1 and 5.0 release series. This means that new features are being added to MySQL 4.1 and MySQL 5.0. 4.1 is available in beta status, and 5.0 is available in alpha status.

Plans for some of the most requested features are summarized in the following table.

Feature	MySQL Series
Unions	4.0
Subqueries	4.1
R-trees	4.1 (for `MyISAM` tables)
Stored procedures	5.0
Views	5.0
Cursors	5.0
Foreign keys	5.1 (already implemented in 3.23 for `InnoDB`)
Triggers	5.1
Full outer join	5.1
Constraints	5.1

1.5.1 MySQL 4.0 in a Nutshell

Long awaited by our users, MySQL Server 4.0 is now available in production status.

MySQL 4.0 is available for download at `http://dev.mysql.com/` and from our mirrors. MySQL 4.0 has been tested by a large number of users and is in production use at many large sites.

The major new features of MySQL Server 4.0 are geared toward our existing business and community users, enhancing the MySQL database software as the solution for mission-critical, heavy-load database systems. Other new features target the users of embedded databases.

1.5.1.1 Features Available in MySQL 4.0

- Speed enhancements
    - MySQL 4.0 has a query cache that can give a huge speed boost to applications with repetitive queries.
    - Version 4.0 further increases the speed of MySQL Server in a number of areas, such as bulk `INSERT` statements, searching on packed indexes, full-text searching (using `FULLTEXT` indexes), and `COUNT(DISTINCT)`.
- Embedded MySQL Server introduced
    - The new Embedded Server library can easily be used to create standalone and embedded applications. The embedded server provides an alternative to using MySQL in a client/server environment.

- InnoDB storage engine as standard
  - The InnoDB storage engine is now offered as a standard feature of the MySQL server. This means full support for ACID transactions, foreign keys with cascading UPDATE and DELETE, and row-level locking are now standard features.
- New functionality
  - The enhanced FULLTEXT search properties of MySQL Server 4.0 enables FULLTEXT indexing of large text masses with both binary and natural-language searching logic. You can customize minimal word length and define your own stop word lists in any human language, enabling a new set of applications to be built with MySQL Server.
- Standards compliance, portability, and migration
  - Many users will also be happy to learn that MySQL Server now supports the UNION statement, a long-awaited standard SQL feature.
  - MySQL now runs natively on the Novell NetWare platform beginning with NetWare 6.0.
  - Features to simplify migration from other database systems to MySQL Server include TRUNCATE TABLE (as in Oracle).
- Internationalization
  - Our German, Austrian, and Swiss users will note that MySQL 4.0 now supports a new character set, latin1_de, which ensures that the *German sorting order* sorts words with umlauts in the same order as do German telephone books.
- Usability enhancements

  In the process of implementing features for new users, we have not forgotten requests from our loyal community of existing users.
  - Most mysqld parameters (startup options) can now be set without taking down the server. This is a convenient feature for database administrators (DBAs).
  - Multiple-table DELETE and UPDATE statements have been added.
  - On Windows, symbolic link handling at the database level is enabled by default. On Unix, the MyISAM storage engine now supports symbolic linking at the table level (and not just the database level as before).
  - SQL_CALC_FOUND_ROWS and FOUND_ROWS() are new functions that make it possible to find out the number of rows a SELECT query that includes a LIMIT clause would have returned without that clause.

The news section of the online manual includes a more in-depth list of features. See
http://dev.mysql.com/doc/mysql/en/News.html.

1.5.1.2 The Embedded MySQL Server

The `libmysqld` embedded server library makes MySQL Server suitable for a vastly expanded realm of applications. By using this library, developers can embed MySQL Server into various applications and electronics devices, where the end user has no knowledge of there actually being an underlying database. Embedded MySQL Server is ideal for use behind the scenes in Internet appliances, public kiosks, turnkey hardware/software combination units, high performance Internet servers, self-contained databases distributed on CD-ROM, and so on.

Many users of `libmysqld` will benefit from the MySQL Dual Licensing. For those not wishing to be bound by the GPL, the software is also made available under a commercial license. The embedded MySQL library uses the same interface as the normal client library, so it is convenient and easy to use.

1.5.2 MySQL 4.1 in a Nutshell

MySQL Server 4.0 laid the foundation for new features implemented in MySQL 4.1, such as subqueries and Unicode support, and for the work on stored procedures being done in version 5.0. These features come at the top of the wish list of many of our customers.

With these additions, critics of the MySQL Database Server have to be more imaginative than ever in pointing out deficiencies in the MySQL database management system. Already well-known for its stability, speed, and ease of use, MySQL Server is able to fulfill the requirement checklists of very demanding buyers.

1.5.2.1 Features Available in MySQL 4.1

The MySQL 4.1 features listed in this section already are implemented. A few other MySQL 4.1 features are still planned. See Section 1.6.1, "New Features Planned for 4.1."

The set of features being added to version 4.1 is mostly fixed. Most new features being coded are or will be available in MySQL 5.0. See Section 1.6.2, "New Features Planned for 5.0."

MySQL 4.1 is currently in the beta stage, and binaries are available for download at `http://dev.mysql.com/downloads/mysql/4.1.html`. All binary releases pass our extensive test suite without any errors on the platforms on which we test.

For those wishing to use the most recent development source for MySQL 4.1, we make our 4.1 BitKeeper repository publicly available.

MySQL 4.1 is going through the steps of *Alpha* (during which time new features might still be added/changed), *Beta* (when we have feature freeze and only bug corrections will be done), and *Gamma* (indicating that a production release is just weeks ahead). At the end of this process, MySQL 4.1 will become the new production release.

- Support for subqueries and derived tables
    - A "subquery" is a SELECT statement nested within another statement. A "derived table" (an unnamed view) is a subquery in the FROM clause of another statement.
- Speed enhancements
    - Faster binary client/server protocol with support for prepared statements and parameter binding.
    - BTREE indexing is now supported for HEAP tables, significantly improving response time for non-exact searches.
- New functionality
    - CREATE TABLE *tbl_name2* LIKE *tbl_name1* allows you to create, with a single statement, a new table with a structure exactly like that of an existing table.
    - The MyISAM storage engine now supports OpenGIS spatial types for storing geographical data.
    - Replication can be done over SSL connections.
- Standards compliance, portability, and migration
    - The new client/server protocol adds the ability to pass multiple warnings to the client, rather than only a single result. This makes it much easier to track problems that occur in operations such as bulk data loading.
    - SHOW WARNINGS shows warnings for the last command.
- Internationalization
    - To support applications that require the use of local languages, the MySQL software now offers extensive Unicode support through the utf8 and ucs2 character sets.
    - Character sets can now be defined per column, table, and database. This allows for a high degree of flexibility in application design, particularly for multi-language Web sites.
- Usability enhancements
    - In response to popular demand, we have added a server-based HELP command that can be used to get help information for SQL statements. The advantage of having this information on the server side is that the information is always applicable to the particular server version that you actually are using. Because this information is available by issuing an SQL statement, any client can be written to access it. For example, the help command of the mysql command-line client has been modified to have this capability.
    - In the new client/server protocol, multiple statements can be issued with a single call.

- The new client/server protocol also supports returning multiple result sets. This might occur as a result of sending multiple statements, for example.

- A new INSERT ... ON DUPLICATE KEY UPDATE ... syntax has been implemented. This allows you to UPDATE an existing row if the INSERT would have caused a duplicate in a PRIMARY or UNIQUE index.

- A new aggregate function, GROUP_CONCAT(), adds the extremely useful capability of concatenating column values from grouped rows into a single result string.

The news section of the online manual includes a more in-depth list of features. See http://dev.mysql.com/doc/mysql/en/News.html.

1.5.3 MySQL 5.0: The Next Development Release

New development for MySQL is focused on the 5.0 release, featuring stored procedures and other new features. See Section 1.6.2, "New Features Planned for 5.0."

For those wishing to take a look at the bleeding edge of MySQL development, we make our BitKeeper repository for MySQL version 5.0 publicly available. As of December 2003, binary builds of version 5.0 are also available.

1.6 MySQL and the Future (the TODO)

This section summarizes the features that we plan to implement in MySQL Server. The items are ordered by release series. Within a list, items are shown in approximately the order they will be done.

Note: If you are an enterprise-level user with an urgent need for a particular feature, please contact sales@mysql.com to discuss sponsoring options. Targeted financing by sponsor companies allows us to allocate additional resources for specific purposes. One example of a feature sponsored in the past is replication.

1.6.1 New Features Planned for 4.1

The following features are not yet implemented in MySQL 4.1, but are planned for implementation as MySQL 4.1 moves into its beta phase. For a list what is already done in MySQL 4.1, see Section 1.5.2.1, "Features Available in MySQL 4.1."

- Stable OpenSSL support (MySQL 4.0 supports rudimentary, not 100% tested, support for OpenSSL).
- More testing of prepared statements.
- More testing of multiple character sets for one table.

1.6.2 New Features Planned for 5.0

The following features are planned for inclusion into MySQL 5.0. Some of the features such as stored procedures are complete and are included in MySQL 5.0 alpha, which is available now. Others such as cursors are only partially available. Expect these and other features to mature and be fully supported in upcoming releases.

Note that because we have many developers that are working on different projects, there will also be many additional features. There is also a small chance that some of these features will be added to MySQL 4.1. For a list what is already done in MySQL 4.1, see Section 1.5.2.1, "Features Available in MySQL 4.1."

For those wishing to take a look at the bleeding edge of MySQL development, we make our BitKeeper repository for MySQL version 5.0 publicly available. As of December 2003, binary builds of version 5.0 are also available.

- Stored Procedures
  - Stored procedures currently are implemented, based on the SQL:2003 standard.
- New functionality
  - Elementary cursor support.
  - The ability to specify explicitly for MyISAM tables that an index should be created as an RTREE index. (In MySQL 4.1, RTREE indexes are used internally for geometrical data that use GIS data types, but cannot be created on request.)
  - Dynamic length rows for MEMORY tables.
- Standards compliance, portability and migration
  - Add true VARCHAR support (column lengths longer than 255, and no stripping of trailing whitespace). There is already support for this in the MyISAM storage engine, but it is not yet available at the user level.
- Speed enhancements
  - SHOW COLUMNS FROM *tbl_name* (used by the mysql client to allow expansions of column names) should not open the table, only the definition file. This will require less memory and be much faster.
  - Allow DELETE on MyISAM tables to use the record cache. To do this, we need to update the threads record cache when we update the .MYD file.
  - Better support for MEMORY tables:
    - Dynamic length rows.
    - Faster row handling (less copying).
- Usability enhancements
  - Resolving the issue of RENAME TABLE on a table used in an active MERGE table possibly corrupting the table.

The news section of the online manual includes a more in-depth list of features. See `http://dev.mysql.com/doc/mysql/en/News.html`.

1.6.3 New Features Planned for 5.1

- New functionality
  - `FOREIGN KEY` support for all table types, not just `InnoDB`.
  - Column-level constraints.
  - Online backup with very low performance penalty. The online backup will make it easy to add a new replication slave without taking down the master.
- Speed enhancements
  - New text-based table definition file format (`.frm` files) and a table cache for table definitions. This will enable us to do faster queries of table structures and do more efficient foreign key support.
  - Optimize the `BIT` type to take one bit. (`BIT` now takes one byte; it is treated as a synonym for `TINYINT`.)
- Usability enhancements

  - Add options to the client/server protocol to get progress notes for long running commands.
  - Implement `RENAME DATABASE`. To make this safe for all storage engines, it should work as follows:
    1. Create the new database.
    2. For every table, do a rename of the table to another database, as we do with the `RENAME` command.
    3. Drop the old database.
  - New internal file interface change. This will make all file handling much more general and make it easier to add extensions like RAID.

1.6.4 New Features Planned for the Near Future

- New functionality
  - Views, implemented in stepwise fashion up to full functionality.
  - Oracle-like `CONNECT BY PRIOR` to search tree-like (hierarchical) structures.
  - Add all missing standard SQL and ODBC 3.0 types.
  - Add `SUM(DISTINCT)`.
  - `INSERT SQL_CONCURRENT` and `mysqld --concurrent-insert` to do a concurrent insert at the end of a table if the table is read-locked.
  - Allow variables to be updated in `UPDATE` statements. For example: `UPDATE foo SET @a:=a+b,a=@a, b=@a+c`.

- Change when user variables are updated so that you can use them with GROUP BY, as in the following statement: SELECT id, @a:=COUNT(*), SUM(sum_col)/@a FROM tbl_name GROUP BY id.

- Add an IMAGE option to LOAD DATA INFILE to not update TIMESTAMP and AUTO_INCREMENT columns.

- Add LOAD DATA INFILE ... UPDATE syntax that works like this:

    - For tables with primary keys, if an input record contains a primary key value, existing rows matching that primary key value are updated from the remainder of the input columns. However, columns corresponding to columns that are *missing* from the input record are not touched.

    - For tables with primary keys, if an input record does not contain the primary key value or is missing some part of the key, the record is treated as LOAD DATA INFILE ... REPLACE INTO.

- Make LOAD DATA INFILE understand syntax like this:

```
LOAD DATA INFILE 'file_name.txt' INTO TABLE tbl_name
    TEXT_FIELDS (text_col1, text_col2, text_col3)
    SET table_col1=CONCAT(text_col1, text_col2),
        table_col3=23
    IGNORE text_col3
```

    This can be used to skip over extra columns in the text file, or update columns based on expressions of the read data.

- New functions for working with SET type columns:

    - ADD_TO_SET(value,set)

    - REMOVE_FROM_SET(value,set)

- If you abort mysql in the middle of a query, you should open another connection and kill the old running query. Alternatively, an attempt should be made to detect this in the server.

- Add a storage engine interface for table information so that you can use it as a system table. This would be a bit slow if you requested information about all tables, but very flexible. SHOW INFO FROM tbl_name for basic table information should be implemented.

- Allow SELECT a FROM tbl_name1 LEFT JOIN tbl_name2 USING (a); in this case a is assumed to come from tbl_name1.

- DELETE and REPLACE options to the UPDATE statement (this will delete rows when a duplicate-key error occurs while updating).

- Change the format of DATETIME to store fractions of seconds.

- Make it possible to use the new GNU regexp library instead of the current one (the new library should be much faster than the current one).

- Standards compliance, portability and migration
  - Don't add automatic DEFAULT values to columns. Produce an error for any INSERT statement that is missing a value for a column that has no DEFAULT.
  - Add ANY(), EVERY(), and SOME() group functions. In standard SQL, these work only on boolean columns, but we can extend these to work on any columns or expressions by treating a value of zero as FALSE and non-zero values as TRUE.
  - Fix the type of MAX(*column*) to be the same as the column type:

    ```
    mysql> CREATE TABLE t1 (a DATE);
    mysql> INSERT INTO t1 VALUES (NOW());
    mysql> CREATE TABLE t2 SELECT MAX(a) FROM t1;
    mysql> SHOW COLUMNS FROM t2;
    ```

- Speed enhancements
  - Don't allow more than a defined number of threads to run MyISAM recovery at the same time.
  - Change INSERT INTO... SELECT to optionally use concurrent inserts.
  - Add an option to periodically flush key pages for tables with delayed keys if they haven't been used in a while.
  - Allow join on key parts (optimization issue).
  - Add a log file analyzer that can extract information about which tables are hit most often, how often multiple-table joins are executed, and so on. This should help users identify areas of table design that could be optimized to execute much more efficient queries.

- Usability enhancements
  - Return the original column types when doing SELECT MIN(*column*) ... GROUP BY.
  - Make it possible to specify long_query_time with a granularity in microseconds.
  - Link the myisampack code into the server so that it can perform PACK or COMPRESS operations.
  - Add a temporary key buffer cache during INSERT/DELETE/UPDATE so that we can gracefully recover if the index file gets full.
  - If you perform an ALTER TABLE on a table that is symlinked to another disk, create temporary tables on that disk.
  - Implement a DATE/DATETIME type that handles time zone information properly, to make dealing with dates in different time zones easier.
  - Fix configure so that all libraries (like MyISAM) can be compiled without threads.
  - Allow user variables as LIMIT arguments; for example, LIMIT @a,@b.
  - Automatic output from mysql to a Web browser.

- LOCK DATABASES (with various options).

- Many more variables for SHOW STATUS. Record reads and updates. Selects on a single table and selects with joins. Mean number of tables in selects. Number of ORDER BY and GROUP BY queries.

- mysqladmin copy *database new-database*; this requires a COPY operation to be added to mysqld.

- Processlist output should indicate the number of queries/threads.

- SHOW HOSTS for printing information about the hostname cache.

- Change table names from empty strings to NULL for calculated columns.

- Don't use Item_copy_string on numerical values to avoid number-to-string-to-number conversion in case of SELECT COUNT(*)*(id+0) FROM *tbl_name* GROUP BY id.

- Change so that ALTER TABLE doesn't abort clients that execute INSERT DELAYED.

- Fix so that when columns are referenced in an UPDATE clause, they contain the old values from before the update started.

- New operating systems
  - Port the MySQL clients to LynxOS.

1.6.5 New Features Planned for the Mid-Term Future

- Implement function: get_changed_tables(*timeout,table1,table2,...*).

- Change reading through tables to use mmap() when possible. Now only compressed tables use mmap().

- Make the automatic timestamp code nicer. Add timestamps to the update log with SET TIMESTAMP=*val*;.

- Use read/write mutex in some places to get more speed.

- Automatically close some tables if a table, temporary table, or temporary file gets error 23 (too many open files).

- Better constant propagation. When an occurrence of *col_name=n* is found in an expression, for some constant *n*, replace other occurrences of *col_name* within the expression with *n*. Currently, this is done only for some simple cases.

- Change all const expressions with calculated expressions if possible.

- Optimize *key = expr* comparisons. At the moment, only *key = column* or *key = constant* comparisons are optimized.

- Join some of the copy functions for nicer code.

- Change sql_yacc.yy to an inline parser to reduce its size and get better error messages.

- Change the parser to use only one rule per different number of arguments in function.

- Use of full calculation names in the order part (for Access97).
- `MINUS`, `INTERSECT`, and `FULL OUTER JOIN`. (Currently `UNION` and `LEFT|RIGHT OUTER JOIN` are supported.)
- Allow `SQL_OPTION MAX_SELECT_TIME=val`, for placing a time limit on a query.
- Allow updates to be logged to a database.
- Enhance `LIMIT` to allow retrieval of data from the end of a result set.
- Alarm around client connect/read/write functions.
- Please note the changes to `mysqld_safe`: According to FSSTND (which Debian tries to follow), PID files should go into `/var/run/<progname>.pid` and log files into `/var/log`. It would be nice if you could put the "DATADIR" in the first declaration of "pidfile" and "log" so that the placement of these files can be changed with a single statement.
- Allow a client to request logging.
- Allow the `LOAD DATA INFILE` statement to read files that have been compressed with `gzip`.
- Fix sorting and grouping of `BLOB` columns (partly solved now).
- Change to use semaphores when counting threads. One should first implement a semaphore library for MIT-pthreads.
- Add full support for `JOIN` with parentheses.
- As an alternative to the one-thread-per-connection model, manage a pool of threads to handle queries.
- Allow `GET_LOCK()` to obtain more than one lock. When doing this, it is also necessary to handle the possible deadlocks this change will introduce.

1.6.6 New Features We Don't Plan to Implement

We aim toward full compliance with ANSI/ISO SQL. There are no features we plan not to implement.

1.7 MySQL Information Sources

1.7.1 MySQL Mailing Lists

This section introduces the MySQL mailing lists and provides guidelines as to how the lists should be used. When you subscribe to a mailing list, you will receive all postings to the list as email messages. You can also send your own questions and answers to the list.

1.7.1.1 The MySQL Mailing Lists

To subscribe to or unsubscribe from any of the mailing lists described in this section, visit `http://lists.mysql.com/`. Please *do not* send messages about subscribing or unsubscribing to any of the mailing lists, because such messages are distributed automatically to thousands of other users.

Your local site may have many subscribers to a MySQL mailing list. If so, the site may have a local mailing list, so that messages sent from `lists.mysql.com` to your site are propagated to the local list. In such cases, please contact your system administrator to be added to or dropped from the local MySQL list.

If you wish to have traffic for a mailing list go to a separate mailbox in your mail program, set up a filter based on the message headers. You can use either the `List-ID:` or `Delivered-To:` headers to identify list messages.

The MySQL mailing lists are as follows:

- `announce`

  This list is for announcements of new versions of MySQL and related programs. This is a low-volume list to which all MySQL users should subscribe.

- `mysql`

  This is the main list for general MySQL discussion. Please note that some topics are better discussed on the more-specialized lists. If you post to the wrong list, you may not get an answer.

- `mysql-digest`

  This is the `mysql` list in digest form. Subscribing to this list means that you will get all list messages, sent as one large mail message once a day.

- `bugs`

  This list will be of interest to you if you want to stay informed about issues reported since the last release of MySQL or if you want to be actively involved in the process of bug hunting and fixing. See Section 1.7.1.3, "How to Report Bugs or Problems."

- `bugs-digest`

  This is the `bugs` list in digest form.

- `internals`

  This list is for people who work on the MySQL code. This is also the forum for discussions on MySQL development and for posting patches.

- `internals-digest`

  This is the `internals` list in digest form.

- `mysqldoc`

  This list is for people who work on the MySQL documentation: people from MySQL AB, translators, and other community members.

- `mysqldoc-digest`

  This is the `mysqldoc` list in digest form.

- benchmarks

  This list is for anyone interested in performance issues. Discussions concentrate on database performance (not limited to MySQL), but also include broader categories such as performance of the kernel, filesystem, disk system, and so on.

- benchmarks-digest

  This is the benchmarks list in digest form.

- packagers

  This list is for discussions on packaging and distributing MySQL. This is the forum used by distribution maintainers to exchange ideas on packaging MySQL and on ensuring that MySQL looks and feels as similar as possible on all supported platforms and operating systems.

- packagers-digest

  This is the packagers list in digest form.

- java

  This list is for discussions about the MySQL server and Java. It is mostly used to discuss JDBC drivers, including MySQL Connector/J.

- java-digest

  This is the java list in digest form.

- win32

  This list is for all topics concerning the MySQL software on Microsoft operating systems, such as Windows 9x, Me, NT, 2000, and XP.

- win32-digest

  This is the win32 list in digest form.

- myodbc

  This list is for all topics concerning connecting to the MySQL server with ODBC.

- myodbc-digest

  This is the myodbc list in digest form.

- gui-tools

  This list is for all topics concerning the MySQL GUI tools, including MySQL Administrator and the MySQL Control Center graphical client.

- gui-tools-digest

  This is the mysqlcc list in digest form.

- plusplus

  This list is for all topics concerning programming with the C++ API for MySQL.

- plusplus-digest

This is the plusplus list in digest form.

- msql-mysql-modules

  This list is for all topics concerning the Perl support for MySQL with msql-mysql-modules, which is now named DBD::mysql.

- msql-mysql-modules-digest

  This is the msql-mysql-modules list in digest form.

If you're unable to get an answer to your questions from a MySQL mailing list, one option is to purchase support from MySQL AB. This will put you in direct contact with MySQL developers. See Section 1.4.1, "Support Offered by MySQL AB."

The following table shows some MySQL mailing lists in languages other than English. These lists are not operated by MySQL AB.

- mysql-france-subscribe@yahoogroups.com

  A French mailing list.

- list@tinc.net

  A Korean mailing list. Email subscribe mysql your@email.address to this list.

- mysql-de-request@lists.4t2.com

  A German mailing list. Email subscribe mysql-de your@email.address to this list. You can find information about this mailing list at http://www.4t2.com/mysql/.

- mysql-br-request@listas.linkway.com.br

  A Portuguese mailing list. Email subscribe mysql-br your@email.address to this list.

- mysql-alta@elistas.net

  A Spanish mailing list. Email subscribe mysql your@email.address to this list.

1.7.1.2 Asking Questions or Reporting Bugs

Before posting a bug report or question, please do the following:

- Start by searching the MySQL online manual at http://dev.mysql.com/doc/. We try to keep the manual up to date by updating it frequently with solutions to newly found problems. The change history (http://dev.mysql.com/doc/mysql/en/News.html) can be particularly useful since it is quite possible that a newer version already contains a solution to your problem.

- Search in the bugs database at http://bugs.mysql.com/ to see whether the bug has already been reported and fixed.

- Search the MySQL mailing list archives at http://lists.mysql.com/.

- You can also use http://www.mysql.com/search/ to search all the Web pages (including the manual) that are located at the MySQL AB Web site.

If you can't find an answer in the manual or the archives, check with your local MySQL expert. If you still can't find an answer to your question, please follow the guidelines on sending mail to a MySQL mailing list, outlined in the next section, before contacting us.

1.7.1.3 How to Report Bugs or Problems

The normal place to report bugs is `http://bugs.mysql.com/`, which is the address for our bugs database. This database is public, and can be browsed and searched by anyone. If you log in to the system, you will also be able to enter new reports.

Writing a good bug report takes patience, but doing it right the first time saves time both for us and for yourself. A good bug report, containing a full test case for the bug, makes it very likely that we will fix the bug in the next release. This section will help you write your report correctly so that you don't waste your time doing things that may not help us much or at all.

We encourage everyone to use the `mysqlbug` script to generate a bug report (or a report about any problem). `mysqlbug` can be found in the `scripts` directory (source distribution) and in the `bin` directory under your MySQL installation directory (binary distribution). If you are unable to use `mysqlbug` (for example, if you are running on Windows), it is still vital that you include all the necessary information noted in this section (most importantly, a description of the operating system and the MySQL version).

The `mysqlbug` script helps you generate a report by determining much of the following information automatically, but if something important is missing, please include it with your message. Please read this section carefully and make sure that all the information described here is included in your report.

Preferably, you should test the problem using the latest production or development version of MySQL Server before posting. Anyone should be able to repeat the bug by just using `mysql test < ` *`script_file`* on the included test case or by running the shell or Perl script that is included in the bug report.

All bugs posted in the bugs database at `http://bugs.mysql.com/` will be corrected or documented in the next MySQL release. If only minor code changes are needed to correct a problem, we may also post a patch that fixes the problem.

If you have found a sensitive security bug in MySQL, you can send email to `security@mysql.com`.

If you have a repeatable bug report, please report it to the bugs database at `http://bugs.mysql.com/`. Note that even in this case it's good to run the `mysqlbug` script first to find information about your system. Any bug that we are able to repeat has a high chance of being fixed in the next MySQL release.

To report other problems, you can use one of the MySQL mailing lists.

Remember that it is possible for us to respond to a message containing too much information, but not to one containing too little. People often omit facts because they think they know the cause of a problem and assume that some details don't matter. A good principle is this: If you are in doubt about stating something, state it. It is faster and less troublesome to write a couple more lines in your report than to wait longer for the answer if we must ask you to provide information that was missing from the initial report.

The most common errors made in bug reports are (a) not including the version number of the MySQL distribution used, and (b) not fully describing the platform on which the MySQL server is installed (including the platform type and version number). This is highly relevant information, and in 99 cases out of 100, the bug report is useless without it. Very often we get questions like, "Why doesn't this work for me?" Then we find that the feature requested wasn't implemented in that MySQL version, or that a bug described in a report has already been fixed in newer MySQL versions. Sometimes the error is platform-dependent; in such cases, it is next to impossible for us to fix anything without knowing the operating system and the version number of the platform.

If you compiled MySQL from source, remember also to provide information about your compiler, if it is related to the problem. Often people find bugs in compilers and think the problem is MySQL-related. Most compilers are under development all the time and become better version by version. To determine whether your problem depends on your compiler, we need to know what compiler you use. Note that every compiling problem should be regarded as a bug and reported accordingly.

It is most helpful when a good description of the problem is included in the bug report. That is, give a good example of everything you did that led to the problem and describe, in exact detail, the problem itself. The best reports are those that include a full example showing how to reproduce the bug or problem.

If a program produces an error message, it is very important to include the message in your report. If we try to search for something from the archives using programs, it is better that the error message reported exactly matches the one that the program produces. (Even the lettercase should be observed.) You should never try to reproduce from memory what the error message was; instead, copy and paste the entire message into your report.

If you have a problem with Connector/ODBC (MyODBC), please try to generate a MyODBC trace file and send it with your report.

Please remember that many of the people who will read your report will do so using an 80-column display. When generating reports or examples using the `mysql` command-line tool, you should therefore use the `--vertical` option (or the `\G` statement terminator) for output that would exceed the available width for such a display (for example, with the EXPLAIN SELECT statement; see the example later in this section).

Please include the following information in your report:

- The version number of the MySQL distribution you are using (for example, MySQL 4.0.12). You can find out which version you are running by executing `mysqladmin version`. The `mysqladmin` program can be found in the `bin` directory under your MySQL installation directory.

- The manufacturer and model of the machine on which you experience the problem.

- The operating system name and version. If you work with Windows, you can usually get the name and version number by double-clicking your My Computer icon and pulling down the Help/About Windows menu. For most Unix-like operating systems, you can get this information by executing the command `uname -a`.

- Sometimes the amount of memory (real and virtual) is relevant. If in doubt, include these values.

- If you are using a source distribution of the MySQL software, the name and version number of the compiler used are needed. If you have a binary distribution, the distribution name is needed.

- If the problem occurs during compilation, include the exact error messages and also a few lines of context around the offending code in the file where the error occurs.

- If `mysqld` died, you should also report the query that crashed `mysqld`. You can usually find this out by running `mysqld` with query logging enabled, and then looking in the log after `mysqld` crashes.

- If a database table is related to the problem, include the output from `mysqldump --no-data` *db_name* *tbl_name*. This is very easy to do and is a powerful way to get information about any table in a database. The information will help us create a situation matching the one you have.

- For speed-related bugs or problems with SELECT statements, you should always include the output of EXPLAIN SELECT ..., and at least the number of rows that the SELECT statement produces. You should also include the output from SHOW CREATE TABLE *tbl_name* for each involved table. The more information you give about your situation, the more likely it is that someone can help you.

  The following is an example of a very good bug report. It should be posted with the `mysqlbug` script. The example uses the `mysql` command-line tool. Note the use of the `\G` statement terminator for statements whose output width would otherwise exceed that of an 80-column display device.

```
mysql> SHOW VARIABLES;
mysql> SHOW COLUMNS FROM ...\G
        <output from SHOW COLUMNS>
mysql> EXPLAIN SELECT ...\G
        <output from EXPLAIN>
mysql> FLUSH STATUS;
mysql> SELECT ...;
        <A short version of the output from SELECT,
        including the time taken to run the query>
mysql> SHOW STATUS;
        <output from SHOW STATUS>
```

- If a bug or problem occurs while running `mysqld`, try to provide an input script that will reproduce the anomaly. This script should include any necessary source files. The more closely the script can reproduce your situation, the better. If you can make a reproducible test case, you should post it on `http://bugs.mysql.com/` for high-priority treatment.

If you can't provide a script, you should at least include the output from `mysqladmin variables extended-status processlist` in your mail to provide some information on how your system is performing.

- If you can't produce a test case with only a few rows, or if the test table is too big to be mailed to the mailing list (more than 10 rows), you should dump your tables using `mysqldump` and create a `README` file that describes your problem.

  Create a compressed archive of your files using `tar` and `gzip` or `zip`, and use FTP to transfer the archive to `ftp://ftp.mysql.com/pub/mysql/upload/`. Then enter the problem into our bugs database at `http://bugs.mysql.com/`.

- If you think that the MySQL server produces a strange result from a query, include not only the result, but also your opinion of what the result should be, and an account describing the basis for your opinion.

- When giving an example of the problem, it's better to use the variable names, table names, and so on that exist in your actual situation than to come up with new names. The problem could be related to the name of a variable or table. These cases are rare, perhaps, but it is better to be safe than sorry. After all, it should be easier for you to provide an example that uses your actual situation, and it is by all means better for us. In case you have data that you don't want to show to others, you can use FTP to transfer it to `ftp://ftp.mysql.com/pub/mysql/upload/`. If the information is really top secret and you don't want to show it even to us, then go ahead and provide an example using other names, but please regard this as the last choice.

- Include all the options given to the relevant programs, if possible. For example, indicate the options that you use when you start the `mysqld` server as well as the options that you use to run any MySQL client programs. The options to programs such as `mysqld` and `mysql`, and to the `configure` script, are often keys to answers and are very relevant. It is never a bad idea to include them. If you use any modules, such as Perl or PHP, please include the version numbers of those as well.

- If your question is related to the privilege system, please include the output of `mysqlaccess`, the output of `mysqladmin reload`, and all the error messages you get when trying to connect. When you test your privileges, you should first run `mysqlaccess`. After this, execute `mysqladmin reload version` and try to connect with the program that gives you trouble. `mysqlaccess` can be found in the `bin` directory under your MySQL installation directory.

- If you have a patch for a bug, do include it. But don't assume that the patch is all we need, or that we will use it, if you don't provide some necessary information such as test cases showing the bug that your patch fixes. We might find problems with your patch or we might not understand it at all; if so, we can't use it.

If we can't verify exactly what the purpose of the patch is, we won't use it. Test cases will help us here. Show that the patch will handle all the situations that may occur. If we find a borderline case (even a rare one) where the patch won't work, it may be useless.

- Guesses about what the bug is, why it occurs, or what it depends on are usually wrong. Even the MySQL team can't guess such things without first using a debugger to determine the real cause of a bug.

- Indicate in your bug report that you have checked the reference manual and mail archive so that others know you have tried to solve the problem yourself.

- If you get a `parse error`, please check your syntax closely. If you can't find something wrong with it, it's extremely likely that your current version of MySQL Server doesn't support the syntax you are using. If you are using the current version and the manual at `http://dev.mysql.com/doc/` doesn't cover the syntax you are using, MySQL Server doesn't support your query. In this case, your only options are to implement the syntax yourself or email `licensing@mysql.com` and ask for an offer to implement it.

  If the manual covers the syntax you are using, but you have an older version of MySQL Server, you should check the MySQL change history to see when the syntax was implemented. In this case, you have the option of upgrading to a newer version of MySQL Server.

- If your problem is that your data appears corrupt or you get errors when you access a particular table, you should first check and then try to repair your tables with `CHECK TABLE` and `REPAIR TABLE` or with `myisamchk`.

  If you are running Windows, please verify that `lower_case_table_names` is 1 or 2 with `SHOW VARIABLES LIKE 'lower_case_table_names'`.

- If you often get corrupted tables, you should try to find out when and why this happens. In this case, the error log in the MySQL data directory may contain some information about what happened. (This is the file with the `.err` suffix in the name.) Please include any relevant information from this file in your bug report. Normally `mysqld` should *never* crash a table if nothing killed it in the middle of an update. If you can find the cause of `mysqld` dying, it's much easier for us to provide you with a fix for the problem.

- If possible, download and install the most recent version of MySQL Server and check whether it solves your problem. All versions of the MySQL software are thoroughly tested and should work without problems. We believe in making everything as backward-compatible as possible, and you should be able to switch MySQL versions without difficulty.

If you are a support customer, please cross-post the bug report to `mysql-support@mysql.com` for higher-priority treatment, as well as to the appropriate mailing list to see whether someone else has experienced (and perhaps solved) the problem.

When answers are sent to you individually and not to the mailing list, it is considered good etiquette to summarize the answers and send the summary to the mailing list so that others may have the benefit of responses you received that helped you solve your problem.

1.7.1.4 Guidelines for Answering Questions on the Mailing List

If you consider your answer to have broad interest, you may want to post it to the mailing list instead of replying directly to the individual who asked. Try to make your answer general enough that people other than the original poster may benefit from it. When you post to the list, please make sure that your answer is not a duplication of a previous answer.

Try to summarize the essential part of the question in your reply; don't feel obliged to quote the entire original message.

Please don't post mail messages from your browser with HTML mode turned on. Many users don't read mail with a browser.

1.7.2 MySQL Community Support on IRC (Internet Relay Chat)

In addition to the various MySQL mailing lists, you can find experienced community people on IRC (Internet Relay Chat). These are the best networks/channels currently known to us:

- **freenode** (see http://www.freenode.net/ for servers)
  - #mysql Primarily MySQL questions, but other database and SQL questions are welcome.
  - #mysqlphp Questions about MySQL+PHP, a popular combination.
  - #mysqlperl Questions about MySQL+Perl, another popular combination.
- **EFnet** (see http://www.efnet.org/ for servers)
  - #mysql MySQL questions.

If you are looking for IRC client software to connect to an IRC network, take a look at X-Chat (http://www.xchat.org/). X-Chat (GPL licensed) is available for Unix as well as for Windows platforms.

1.8 MySQL Standards Compliance

This section describes how MySQL relates to the ANSI/ISO SQL standards. MySQL Server has many extensions to the SQL standard, and here you will find out what they are and how to use them. You will also find information about functionality missing from MySQL Server, and how to work around some differences.

The SQL standard has been evolving since 1986 and several versions exist. In this manual, "SQL-92" refers to the standard released in 1992, "SQL:1999" refers to the standard released in 1999, and "SQL:2003" refers to the current version of the standard. We use the phrase "the SQL standard" to mean the current version of the SQL Standard at any time.

Our goal is to not restrict MySQL Server usability for any usage without a very good reason for doing so. Even if we don't have the resources to perform development for every possible use, we are always willing to help and offer suggestions to people who are trying to use MySQL Server in new territories.

One of our main goals with the product is to continue to work toward compliance with the SQL standard, but without sacrificing speed or reliability. We are not afraid to add extensions to SQL or support for non-SQL features if this greatly increases the usability of MySQL Server for a large segment of our user base. The HANDLER interface in MySQL Server 4.0 is an example of this strategy.

We will continue to support transactional and non-transactional databases to satisfy both mission-critical 24/7 usage and heavy Web or logging usage.

MySQL Server was originally designed to work with medium size databases (10-100 million rows, or about 100MB per table) on small computer systems. Today MySQL Server handles terabyte-size databases, but the code can also be compiled in a reduced version suitable for hand-held and embedded devices. The compact design of the MySQL server makes development in both directions possible without any conflicts in the source tree.

Currently, we are not targeting realtime support, although MySQL replication capabilities already offer significant functionality.

Database cluster support is planned through integration of our acquired NDB Cluster technology into a new storage engine, available in 2004.

We are also looking at providing XML support in the database server.

1.8.1 What Standards MySQL Follows

We are aiming toward supporting the full ANSI/ISO SQL standard, but without making concessions to speed and quality of the code.

ODBC levels 0–3.51.

1.8.2 Selecting SQL Modes

The MySQL server can operate in different SQL modes, and can apply these modes differentially for different clients. This allows applications to tailor server operation to their own requirements.

Modes define what SQL syntax MySQL should support and what kind of validation checks it should perform on the data. This makes it easier to use MySQL in a lot of different environments and to use MySQL together with other database servers.

You can set the default SQL mode by starting `mysqld` with the `--sql-mode="modes"` option. Beginning with MySQL 4.1, you can also change the mode after startup time by setting the `sql_mode` variable with a `SET [SESSION|GLOBAL] sql_mode='modes'` statement.

1.8.3 Running MySQL in ANSI Mode

You can tell `mysqld` to use the ANSI mode with the `--ansi` startup option.

Running the server in ANSI mode is the same as starting it with these options (specify the `--sql_mode` value on a single line):

```
--transaction-isolation=SERIALIZABLE
--sql-mode=REAL_AS_FLOAT,PIPES_AS_CONCAT,ANSI_QUOTES,
IGNORE_SPACE,ONLY_FULL_GROUP_BY
```

In MySQL 4.1, you can achieve the same effect with these two statements (specify the `sql_mode` value on a single line):

```
SET GLOBAL TRANSACTION ISOLATION LEVEL SERIALIZABLE;
SET GLOBAL sql_mode = 'REAL_AS_FLOAT,PIPES_AS_CONCAT,ANSI_QUOTES,
IGNORE_SPACE,ONLY_FULL_GROUP_BY';
```

See Section 1.8.2, "Selecting SQL Modes."

In MySQL 4.1.1, the `sql_mode` options shown can be also be set with this statement:

```
SET GLOBAL sql_mode='ansi';
```

In this case, the value of the `sql_mode` variable will be set to all options that are relevant for ANSI mode. You can check the result like this:

```
mysql> SET GLOBAL sql_mode='ansi';
mysql> SELECT @@global.sql_mode;
        -> 'REAL_AS_FLOAT,PIPES_AS_CONCAT,ANSI_QUOTES,
              IGNORE_SPACE,ONLY_FULL_GROUP_BY,ANSI';
```

1.8.4 MySQL Extensions to Standard SQL

MySQL Server includes some extensions that you probably will not find in other SQL databases. Be warned that if you use them, your code will not be portable to other SQL servers. In some cases, you can write code that includes MySQL extensions, but is still portable, by using comments of the form `/*! ... */`. In this case, MySQL Server will parse and execute the code within the comment as it would any other MySQL statement, but other SQL servers will ignore the extensions. For example:

```
SELECT /*! STRAIGHT_JOIN */ col_name FROM table1,table2 WHERE ...
```

If you add a version number after the '!' character, the syntax within the comment will be executed only if the MySQL version is equal to or newer than the specified version number:

```
CREATE /*!32302 TEMPORARY */ TABLE t (a INT);
```

This means that if you have Version 3.23.02 or newer, MySQL Server will use the TEMPORARY keyword.

The following descriptions list MySQL extensions, organized by category.

- Organization of data on disk

  MySQL Server maps each database to a directory under the MySQL data directory, and tables within a database to filenames in the database directory. This has a few implications:

  - Database names and table names are case sensitive in MySQL Server on operating systems that have case-sensitive filenames (such as most Unix systems).

  - You can use standard system commands to back up, rename, move, delete, and copy tables that are managed by the MyISAM or ISAM storage engines. For example, to rename a MyISAM table, rename the .MYD, .MYI, and .frm files to which the table corresponds.

  Database, table, index, column, or alias names may begin with a digit (but may not consist solely of digits).

- General language syntax

  - Strings may be enclosed by either '"' or ''', not just by '''.

  - Use of '\' as an escape character in strings.

  - In SQL statements, you can access tables from different databases with the db_name.tbl_name syntax. Some SQL servers provide the same functionality but call this User space. MySQL Server doesn't support tablespaces such as used in statements like this: CREATE TABLE ralph.my_table...IN my_tablespace.

- SQL statement syntax

  - The ANALYZE TABLE, CHECK TABLE, OPTIMIZE TABLE, and REPAIR TABLE statements.

  - The CREATE DATABASE and DROP DATABASE statements.

  - The DO statement.

  - EXPLAIN SELECT to get a description of how tables are joined.

  - The FLUSH and RESET statements.

  - The SET statement.

  - The SHOW statement.

  - Use of LOAD DATA INFILE. In many cases, this syntax is compatible with Oracle's LOAD DATA INFILE.

  - Use of RENAME TABLE.

  - Use of REPLACE instead of DELETE + INSERT.

  - Use of CHANGE col_name, DROP col_name, or DROP INDEX, IGNORE or RENAME in an ALTER TABLE statement. Use of multiple ADD, ALTER, DROP, or CHANGE clauses in an ALTER TABLE statement.

- Use of index names, indexes on a prefix of a field, and use of INDEX or KEY in a CREATE TABLE statement.
- Use of TEMPORARY or IF NOT EXISTS with CREATE TABLE.
- Use of IF EXISTS with DROP TABLE.
- You can drop multiple tables with a single DROP TABLE statement.
- The ORDER BY and LIMIT clauses of the UPDATE and DELETE statements.
- INSERT INTO ... SET *col_name* = ... syntax.
- The DELAYED clause of the INSERT and REPLACE statements.
- The LOW_PRIORITY clause of the INSERT, REPLACE, DELETE, and UPDATE statements.
- Use of INTO OUTFILE and STRAIGHT_JOIN in a SELECT statement.
- The SQL_SMALL_RESULT option in a SELECT statement.
- You don't need to name all selected columns in the GROUP BY part. This gives better performance for some very specific, but quite normal queries.
- You can specify ASC and DESC with GROUP BY.
- The ability to set variables in a statement with the := assignment operator:
  ```
  mysql> SELECT @a:=SUM(total),@b=COUNT(*),@a/@b AS avg
      -> FROM test_table;
  mysql> SELECT @t1:=(@t2:=1)+@t3:=4,@t1,@t2,@t3;
  ```

- Column types
  - The column types MEDIUMINT, SET, ENUM, and the different BLOB and TEXT types.
  - The column attributes AUTO_INCREMENT, BINARY, NULL, UNSIGNED, and ZEROFILL.
- Functions and operators
  - To make it easier for users who come from other SQL environments, MySQL Server supports aliases for many functions. For example, all string functions support both standard SQL syntax and ODBC syntax.
  - MySQL Server understands the || and && operators to mean logical OR and AND, as in the C programming language. In MySQL Server, || and OR are synonyms, as are && and AND. Because of this nice syntax, MySQL Server doesn't support the standard SQL || operator for string concatenation; use CONCAT() instead. Because CONCAT() takes any number of arguments, it's easy to convert use of the || operator to MySQL Server.
  - Use of COUNT(DISTINCT *list*) where *list* has more than one element.
  - All string comparisons are case-insensitive by default, with sort ordering determined by the current character set (ISO-8859-1 Latin1 by default). If you don't like this, you should declare your columns with the BINARY attribute or use the BINARY cast, which causes comparisons to be done using the underlying character code values rather then a lexical ordering.

- The % operator is a synonym for MOD(). That is, N % M is equivalent to MOD(N,M). % is supported for C programmers and for compatibility with PostgreSQL.

- The =, <>, <=, <, >=, >, <<, >>, <=>, AND, OR, or LIKE operators may be used in column comparisons to the left of the FROM in SELECT statements. For example:

  ```
  mysql> SELECT col1=1 AND col2=2 FROM tbl_name;
  ```

- The LAST_INSERT_ID() function that returns the most recent AUTO_INCREMENT value.

- LIKE is allowed on numeric columns.

- The REGEXP and NOT REGEXP extended regular expression operators.

- CONCAT() or CHAR() with one argument or more than two arguments. (In MySQL Server, these functions can take any number of arguments.)

- The BIT_COUNT(), CASE, ELT(), FROM_DAYS(), FORMAT(), IF(), PASSWORD(), ENCRYPT(), MD5(), ENCODE(), DECODE(), PERIOD_ADD(), PERIOD_DIFF(), TO_DAYS(), and WEEKDAY() functions.

- Use of TRIM() to trim substrings. Standard SQL supports removal of single characters only.

- The GROUP BY functions STD(), BIT_OR(), BIT_AND(), BIT_XOR(), and GROUP_CONCAT().

For a prioritized list indicating when new extensions will be added to MySQL Server, you should consult the online MySQL TODO list at http://dev.mysql.com/doc/mysql/en/TODO.html. That is the latest version of the TODO list in this manual. See Section 1.6, "MySQL and the Future (the TODO)."

1.8.5 MySQL Differences from Standard SQL

We try to make MySQL Server follow the ANSI SQL standard and the ODBC SQL standard, but MySQL Server performs operations differently in some cases:

- For VARCHAR columns, trailing spaces are removed when the value is stored. See Section 1.8.7, "Known Errors and Design Deficiencies in MySQL."

- In some cases, CHAR columns are silently converted to VARCHAR columns when you define a table or alter its structure.

- Privileges for a table are not automatically revoked when you delete a table. You must explicitly issue a REVOKE statement to revoke privileges for a table.

1.8.5.1 Subqueries

MySQL 4.1 supports subqueries and derived tables. A "subquery" is a SELECT statement nested within another statement. A "derived table" (an unnamed view) is a subquery in the FROM clause of another statement.

For MySQL versions older than 4.1, most subqueries can be rewritten using joins or other methods.

1.8.5.2 SELECT INTO TABLE

MySQL Server doesn't support the Sybase SQL extension: SELECT ... INTO TABLE .... Instead, MySQL Server supports the standard SQL syntax INSERT INTO ... SELECT ..., which is basically the same thing.

```
INSERT INTO tbl_temp2 (fld_id)
    SELECT tbl_temp1.fld_order_id
    FROM tbl_temp1 WHERE tbl_temp1.fld_order_id > 100;
```

Alternatively, you can use SELECT INTO OUTFILE ... or CREATE TABLE ... SELECT.

From version 5.0, MySQL supports SELECT ... INTO with user variables. The same syntax may also be used inside stored procedures using cursors and local variables.

1.8.5.3 Transactions and Atomic Operations

MySQL Server (version 3.23-max and all versions 4.0 and above) supports transactions with the InnoDB and BDB transactional storage engines. InnoDB provides *full* ACID compliance.

The other non-transactional storage engines in MySQL Server (such as MyISAM) follow a different paradigm for data integrity called "atomic operations." In transactional terms, MyISAM tables effectively always operate in AUTOCOMMIT=1 mode. Atomic operations often offer comparable integrity with higher performance.

With MySQL Server supporting both paradigms, you can decide whether your applications are best served by the speed of atomic operations or the use of transactional features. This choice can be made on a per-table basis.

As noted, the trade-off for transactional versus non-transactional table types lies mostly in performance. Transactional tables have significantly higher memory and diskspace requirements, and more CPU overhead. On the other hand, transactional table types such as InnoDB also offer many significant features. MySQL Server's modular design allows the concurrent use of different storage engines to suit different requirements and deliver optimum performance in all situations.

But how do you use the features of MySQL Server to maintain rigorous integrity even with the non-transactional MyISAM tables, and how do these features compare with the transactional table types?

1. If your applications are written in a way that is dependent on being able to call ROLLBACK rather than COMMIT in critical situations, transactions are more convenient. Transactions also ensure that unfinished updates or corrupting activities are not committed to the database; the server is given the opportunity to do an automatic rollback and your database is saved.

If you use non-transactional tables, MySQL Server in almost all cases allows you to resolve potential problems by including simple checks before updates and by running simple scripts that check the databases for inconsistencies and automatically repair or warn if such an inconsistency occurs. Note that just by using the MySQL log or even adding one extra log, you can normally fix tables perfectly with no data integrity loss.

2. More often than not, critical transactional updates can be rewritten to be atomic. Generally speaking, all integrity problems that transactions solve can be done with LOCK TABLES or atomic updates, ensuring that you never will get an automatic abort from the server, which is a common problem with transactional database systems.

3. Even a transactional system can lose data if the server goes down. The difference between different systems lies in just how small the time-lag is where they could lose data. No system is 100% secure, only "secure enough." Even Oracle, reputed to be the safest of transactional database systems, is reported to sometimes lose data in such situations.

   To be safe with MySQL Server, whether or not using transactional tables, you only need to have backups and have binary logging turned on. With this, you can recover from any situation that you could with any other transactional database system. It is always good to have backups, regardless of which database system you use.

The transactional paradigm has its benefits and its drawbacks. Many users and application developers depend on the ease with which they can code around problems where an abort appears to be, or is necessary. However, even if you are new to the atomic operations paradigm, or more familiar with transactions, do consider the speed benefit that non-transactional tables can offer on the order of three to five times the speed of the fastest and most optimally tuned transactional tables.

In situations where integrity is of highest importance, MySQL Server offers transaction-level reliability and integrity even for non-transactional tables. If you lock tables with LOCK TABLES, all updates will stall until any integrity checks are made. If you obtain a READ LOCAL lock (as opposed to a write lock) for a table that allows concurrent inserts at the end of the table, reads are allowed, as are inserts by other clients. The new inserted records will not be seen by the client that has the read lock until it releases the lock. With INSERT DELAYED, you can queue inserts into a local queue, until the locks are released, without having the client wait for the insert to complete.

"Atomic," in the sense that we mean it, is nothing magical. It only means that you can be sure that while each specific update is running, no other user can interfere with it, and there will never be an automatic rollback (which can happen with transactional tables if you are not very careful). MySQL Server also guarantees that there will not be any dirty reads.

Following are some techniques for working with non-transactional tables:

- Loops that need transactions normally can be coded with the help of LOCK TABLES, and you don't need cursors to update records on the fly.

- To avoid using ROLLBACK, you can use the following strategy:

  1. Use LOCK TABLES to lock all the tables you want to access.

  2. Test the conditions that must be true before performing the update.

  3. Update if everything is okay.

  4. Use UNLOCK TABLES to release your locks.

  This is usually a much faster method than using transactions with possible rollbacks, although not always. The only situation this solution doesn't handle is when someone kills the threads in the middle of an update. In this case, all locks will be released but some of the updates may not have been executed.

- You can also use functions to update records in a single operation. You can get a very efficient application by using the following techniques:

  - Modify columns relative to their current value.

  - Update only those columns that actually have changed.

  For example, when we are doing updates to some customer information, we update only the customer data that has changed and test only that none of the changed data, or data that depends on the changed data, has changed compared to the original row. The test for changed data is done with the WHERE clause in the UPDATE statement. If the record wasn't updated, we give the client a message: "Some of the data you have changed has been changed by another user." Then we show the old row versus the new row in a window so that the user can decide which version of the customer record to use.

  This gives us something that is similar to column locking but is actually even better because we only update some of the columns, using values that are relative to their current values. This means that typical UPDATE statements look something like these:

```
UPDATE tablename SET pay_back=pay_back+125;
```

```
UPDATE customer
  SET
    customer_date='current_date',
    address='new address',
    phone='new phone',
    money_owed_to_us=money_owed_to_us-125
  WHERE
    customer_id=id AND address='old address' AND phone='old phone';
```

  This is very efficient and works even if another client has changed the values in the pay_back or money_owed_to_us columns.

- In many cases, users have wanted LOCK TABLES and/or ROLLBACK for the purpose of managing unique identifiers. This can be handled much more efficiently without locking or rolling back by using an AUTO_INCREMENT column and either the LAST_INSERT_ID() SQL function or the mysql_insert_id() C API function.

You can generally code around the need for row-level locking. Some situations really do need it, and InnoDB tables support row-level locking. With MyISAM tables, you can use a flag column in the table and do something like the following:

```
UPDATE tbl_name SET row_flag=1 WHERE id=ID;
```

MySQL returns 1 for the number of affected rows if the row was found and row_flag wasn't already 1 in the original row.

You can think of it as though MySQL Server changed the preceding query to:

```
UPDATE tbl_name SET row_flag=1 WHERE id=ID AND row_flag <> 1;
```

1.8.5.4 Stored Procedures and Triggers

Stored procedures are implemented in MySQL version 5.0.

Triggers are scheduled for implementation in MySQL version 5.1. A "trigger" is effectively a type of stored procedure, one that is invoked when a particular event occurs. For example, you could set up a stored procedure that is triggered each time a record is deleted from a transactional table, and that stored procedure automatically deletes the corresponding customer from a customer table when all their transactions are deleted.

1.8.5.5 Foreign Keys

In MySQL Server 3.23.44 and up, the InnoDB storage engine supports checking of foreign key constraints, including CASCADE, ON DELETE, and ON UPDATE.

For storage engines other than InnoDB, MySQL Server parses the FOREIGN KEY syntax in CREATE TABLE statements, but does not use or store it. In the future, the implementation will be extended to store this information in the table specification file so that it may be retrieved by mysqldump and ODBC. At a later stage, foreign key constraints will be implemented for MyISAM tables as well.

Foreign key enforcement offers several benefits to database developers:

- Assuming proper design of the relationships, foreign key constraints make it more difficult for a programmer to introduce an inconsistency into the database.
- Centralized checking of constraints by the database server makes it unnecessary to perform these checks on the application side. This eliminates the possibility that different applications may not all check the constraints in the same way.
- Using cascading updates and deletes can simplify the application code.
- Properly designed foreign key rules aid in documenting relationships between tables.

Do keep in mind that these benefits come at the cost of additional overhead for the database server to perform the necessary checks. Additional checking by the server affects performance, which for some applications may be sufficiently undesirable as to be avoided if possible. (Some major commercial applications have coded the foreign-key logic at the application level for this reason.)

MySQL gives database developers the choice of which approach to use. If you don't need foreign keys and want to avoid the overhead associated with enforcing referential integrity, you can choose another table type instead, such as MyISAM. For example, the MyISAM storage engine offers very fast performance for applications that perform only INSERT and SELECT operations, because the inserts can be performed concurrently with retrievals.

If you choose not to take advantage of referential integrity checks, keep the following considerations in mind:

- In the absence of server-side foreign key relationship checking, the application itself must handle relationship issues. For example, it must take care to insert rows into tables in the proper order, and to avoid creating orphaned child records. It must also be able to recover from errors that occur in the middle of multiple-record insert operations.

- If ON DELETE is the only referential integrity capability an application needs, note that as of MySQL Server 4.0, you can use multiple-table DELETE statements to delete rows from many tables with a single statement.

- A workaround for the lack of ON DELETE is to add the appropriate DELETE statement to your application when you delete records from a table that has a foreign key. In practice, this is often as quick as using foreign keys, and is more portable.

Be aware that the use of foreign keys can in some instances lead to problems:

- Foreign key support addresses many referential integrity issues, but it is still necessary to design key relationships carefully to avoid circular rules or incorrect combinations of cascading deletes.

- It is not uncommon for a DBA to create a topology of relationships that makes it difficult to restore individual tables from a backup. (MySQL alleviates this difficulty by allowing you to temporarily disable foreign key checks when reloading a table that depends on other tables. As of MySQL 4.1.1, mysqldump generates dump files that take advantage of this capability automatically when reloaded.)

Note that foreign keys in SQL are used to check and enforce referential integrity, not to join tables. If you want to get results from multiple tables from a SELECT statement, you do this by performing a join between them:

```
SELECT * FROM t1, t2 WHERE t1.id = t2.id;
```

The FOREIGN KEY syntax without ON DELETE ... is often used by ODBC applications to produce automatic WHERE clauses.

1.8.5.6 Views

Views currently are being implemented, and will appear in the 5.0 version of MySQL Server. Unnamed views (*derived tables*, a subquery in the FROM clause of a SELECT) are already implemented in version 4.1.

Historically, MySQL Server has been most used in applications and on Web systems where the application writer has full control over database usage. Usage has shifted over time, and so we find that an increasing number of users now regard views as an important feature.

Views are useful for allowing users to access a set of relations (tables) as if it were a single table, and limiting their access to just that. Views can also be used to restrict access to rows (a subset of a particular table). To restrict access to columns, views are not required because MySQL Server has a sophisticated privilege system.

Many DBMS don't allow updates to a view. Instead, you have to perform the updates on the individual tables. In designing an implementation of views, our goal, as much as is possible within the confines of SQL, is full compliance with "Codd's Rule #6" for relational database systems: All views that are theoretically updatable, should in practice also be updatable.

1.8.5.7 '--' as the Start of a Comment

Some other SQL databases use '--' to start comments. MySQL Server uses '#' as the start comment character. You can also use the C comment style /* this is a comment */ with MySQL Server.

MySQL Server 3.23.3 and above support the '--' comment style, provided the comment is followed by a space (or by a control character such as a newline). The requirement for a space is to prevent problems with automatically generated SQL queries that have used something like the following code, where we automatically insert the value of the payment for !payment!:

```
UPDATE account SET credit=credit-!payment!
```

Think about what happens if the value of payment is a negative value such as -1:

```
UPDATE account SET credit=credit--1
```

credit--1 is a legal expression in SQL, but if -- is interpreted as the start of a comment, part of the expression is discarded. The result is a statement that has a completely different meaning than intended:

```
UPDATE account SET credit=credit
```

The statement produces no change in value at all! This illustrates that allowing comments to start with '--' can have serious consequences.

Using our implementation of this method of commenting in MySQL Server 3.23.3 and up, credit--1 is actually safe.

Another safe feature is that the mysql command-line client removes all lines that start with '--'.

The following information is relevant only if you are running a MySQL version earlier than 3.23.3:

If you have an SQL program in a text file that contains '--' comments, you should use the `replace` utility as follows to convert the comments to use '#' characters:

```
shell> replace " --" " #" < text-file-with-funny-comments.sql \
       | mysql db_name
```

instead of the usual:

```
shell> mysql db_name < text-file-with-funny-comments.sql
```

You can also edit the command file "in place" to change the '--' comments to '#' comments:

```
shell> replace " --" " #" -- text-file-with-funny-comments.sql
```

Change them back with this command:

```
shell> replace " #" " --" -- text-file-with-funny-comments.sql
```

1.8.6 How MySQL Deals with Constraints

MySQL allows you to work with both transactional tables that allow rollback and non-transactional tables that do not, so constraint handling is a bit different in MySQL than in other databases.

We have to handle the case when you have updated a lot of rows in a non-transactional table that cannot roll back when an error occurs.

The basic philosophy is to try to give an error for anything that we can detect at compile time but try to recover from any errors we get at runtime. We do this in most cases, but not yet for all. See Section 1.6.4, "New Features Planned for the Near Future."

The options MySQL has when an error occurs are to stop the statement in the middle or to recover as well as possible from the problem and continue.

The following sections describe what happens for the different types of constraints.

1.8.6.1 Constraint PRIMARY KEY / UNIQUE

Normally you will get an error when you try to INSERT or UPDATE a row that causes a primary key, unique key, or foreign key violation. If you are using a transactional storage engine such as InnoDB, MySQL will automatically roll back the transaction. If you are using a non-transactional storage engine, MySQL will stop at the incorrect row and leave any remaining rows unprocessed.

To make life easier, MySQL supports an IGNORE keyword for most commands that can cause a key violation (such as INSERT IGNORE and UPDATE IGNORE). In this case, MySQL will ignore any key violation and continue with processing the next row. You can get information about what MySQL did with the `mysql_info()` C API function. In MySQL 4.1 and up, you also can use the `SHOW WARNINGS` statement.

Note that, for the moment, only `InnoDB` tables support foreign keys. Foreign key support in `MyISAM` tables is scheduled for implementation in MySQL 5.1.

1.8.6.2 Constraint `NOT NULL` and `DEFAULT` Values

To be able to support easy handling of non-transactional tables, all columns in MySQL have default values.

If you insert an "incorrect" value in a column, such as a `NULL` in a `NOT NULL` column or a too-large numerical value in a numerical column, MySQL sets the column to the "best possible value" instead of producing an error:

- If you try to store a value outside the range in a numerical column, MySQL Server instead stores zero, the smallest possible value, or the largest possible value in the column.

- For strings, MySQL Server stores either the empty string or the longest possible string that can be in the column.

- If you try to store a string that doesn't start with a number into a numerical column, MySQL Server stores 0.

- If you try to store `NULL` into a column that doesn't take `NULL` values, MySQL Server stores 0 or `''` (the empty string) instead. This last behavior can, for single-row inserts, be changed when MySQL is built by using the `-DONT_USE_DEFAULT_FIELDS` compile option.) This causes `INSERT` statements to generate an error unless you explicitly specify values for all columns that require a non-`NULL` value.

- MySQL allows you to store some incorrect date values into `DATE` and `DATETIME` columns (like `'2000-02-31'` or `'2000-02-00'`). The idea is that it's not the job of the SQL server to validate dates. If MySQL can store a date value and retrieve exactly the same value, MySQL stores it as given. If the date is totally wrong (outside the server's ability to store it), the special date value `'0000-00-00'` is stored in the column instead.

The reason for the preceding rules is that we can't check these conditions until the query has begun executing. We can't just roll back if we encounter a problem after updating a few rows, because the table type may not support rollback. The option of terminating the statement is not that good; in this case, the update would be "half done," which is probably the worst possible scenario. In this case, it's better to "do the best you can" and then continue as if nothing happened.

This means that you should generally not use MySQL to check column content. Instead, the application should ensure that it passes only legal values to MySQL.

In MySQL 5.0, we plan to improve this by providing warnings when automatic column conversions occur, plus an option to let you roll back statements that attempt to perform a disallowed column value assignment, as long as the statement uses only transactional tables.

1.8.6.3 Constraint ENUM and SET

In MySQL 4.x, ENUM is not a real constraint, but is a more efficient way to define columns that can contain only a given set of values. This is for the same reasons that NOT NULL is not honored.

If you insert an incorrect value into an ENUM column, it is set to the reserved enumeration value of 0, which is displayed as an empty string in string context.

If you insert an incorrect value into a SET column, the incorrect value is ignored. For example, if the column can contain the values 'a', 'b', and 'c', an attempt to assign 'a,x,b,y' results in a value of 'a,b'.

1.8.7 Known Errors and Design Deficiencies in MySQL

1.8.7.1 Errors in 3.23 Fixed in a Later MySQL Version

The following known errors or bugs are not fixed in MySQL 3.23 because fixing them would involve changing a lot of code that could introduce other even worse bugs. The bugs are also classified as "not fatal" or "bearable."

- You can get a deadlock (hung thread) if you use LOCK TABLE to lock multiple tables and then in the same connection use DROP TABLE to drop one of them while another thread is trying to lock it. (To break the deadlock, you can use KILL to terminate any of the threads involved.) This issue is resolved as of MySQL 4.0.12.

- SELECT MAX(key_column) FROM t1,t2,t3... where one of the tables that are empty doesn't return NULL but instead returns the maximum value for the column. This issue is resolved as of MySQL 4.0.11.

- DELETE FROM heap_table without a WHERE clause doesn't work on a locked HEAP table.

1.8.7.2 Errors in 4.0 Fixed in a Later MySQL Version

The following known errors or bugs are not fixed in MySQL 4.0 because fixing them would involve changing a lot of code that could introduce other even worse bugs. The bugs are also classified as "not fatal" or "bearable."

- In a UNION, the first SELECT determines the type, max_length, and NULL properties for the resulting columns. This issue is resolved as of MySQL 4.1.1; the property values are based on the rows from all UNION parts.

- In DELETE with many tables, you can't refer to tables to be deleted through an alias. This is fixed as of MySQL 4.1.

1.8.7.3 Open Bugs and Design Deficiencies in MySQL

The following problems are known and fixing them is a high priority:

- Dropping a FOREIGN KEY constraint doesn't work in replication because the constraint may have another name on the slave.

- REPLACE (and LOAD DATA with the REPLACE option) does not trigger ON DELETE CASCADE.

- You cannot mix UNION ALL and UNION DISTINCT in the same query. If you use ALL for one UNION, it is used for all of them.

- If one user has a long-running transaction and another user drops a table that is updated in the transaction, there is small chance that the binary log may contain the DROP TABLE command before the table is used in the transaction itself. We plan to fix this in 5.0 by having the DROP TABLE wait until the table is not used in any transaction.

- When inserting a big integer value (between 2^{63} and $2^{64}-1$) into a decimal/string column, it is inserted as a negative value because the number is evaluated in a signed integer context. We plan to fix this in MySQL 4.1.

- FLUSH TABLES WITH READ LOCK does not block CREATE TABLE or COMMIT, which may cause a problem with the binary log position when doing a full backup of tables and the binary log.

- ANALYZE TABLE on a BDB table may in some cases make the table unusable until you restart mysqld. If this happens, you will see errors of the following form in the MySQL error file:

```
001207 22:07:56  bdb:  log_flush: LSN past current end-of-log
```

- MySQL accepts parentheses in the FROM clause of a SELECT statement, but silently ignores them. The reason for not giving an error is that many clients that automatically generate queries add parentheses in the FROM clause even where they are not needed.

- Concatenating many RIGHT JOINS or combining LEFT and RIGHT join in the same query may not give a correct answer because MySQL only generates NULL rows for the table preceding a LEFT or before a RIGHT join. This will be fixed in 5.0 at the same time we add support for parentheses in the FROM clause.

- Don't execute ALTER TABLE on a BDB table on which you are running multiple-statement transactions until all those transactions complete. (The transaction will probably be ignored.)

- ANALYZE TABLE, OPTIMIZE TABLE, and REPAIR TABLE may cause problems on tables for which you are using INSERT DELAYED.

- Doing a LOCK TABLE ... and FLUSH TABLES ... doesn't guarantee that there isn't a half-finished transaction in progress on the table.

- BDB tables are a bit slow to open. If you have many BDB tables in a database, it will take a long time to use the mysql client on the database if you are not using the -A option or if you are using rehash. This is especially noticeable when you have a large table cache.

- Replication uses query-level logging: The master writes the executed queries to the binary log. This is a very fast, compact, and efficient logging method that works perfectly in most cases. Although we have never heard of it actually occurring, it is theoretically possible for the data on the master and slave to become different if a query is designed in such a way that the data modification is non-deterministic; that is, left to the will of the query optimizer. (That generally is not a good practice anyway, even outside of replication!) For example:

- CREATE ... SELECT or INSERT ... SELECT statements that insert zero or NULL values into an AUTO_INCREMENT column.
- DELETE if you are deleting rows from a table that has foreign keys with ON DELETE CASCADE properties.
- REPLACE ... SELECT, INSERT IGNORE ... SELECT if you have duplicate key values in the inserted data.

If and only if all these queries have no ORDER BY clause guaranteeing a deterministic order.

For example, for INSERT ... SELECT with no ORDER BY, the SELECT may return rows in a different order (which will result in a row having different ranks, hence getting a different number in the AUTO_INCREMENT column), depending on the choices made by the optimizers on the master and slave. A query will be optimized differently on the master and slave only if:

- The files used by the two queries are not exactly the same; for example, OPTIMIZE TABLE was run on the master tables and not on the slave tables. (To fix this, OPTIMIZE TABLE, ANALYZE TABLE, and REPAIR TABLE are written to the binary log as of MySQL 4.1.1).
- The table is stored using a different storage engine on the master than on the slave. (It is possible to use different storage engines on the master and slave. For example, you can use InnoDB on the master, but MyISAM on the slave if the slave has less available disk space.)
- MySQL buffer sizes (key_buffer_size, and so on) are different on the master and slave.
- The master and slave run different MySQL versions, and the optimizer code differs between these versions.

This problem may also affect database restoration using mysqlbinlog|mysql.

The easiest way to avoid this problem in all cases is to add an ORDER BY clause to such non-deterministic queries to ensure that the rows are always stored or modified in the same order. In future MySQL versions, we will automatically add an ORDER BY clause when needed.

The following problems are known and will be fixed in due time:

- Log file names are based on the server hostname (if you don't specify a filename with the startup option). For now you have to use options like --log-bin=old_host_name-bin if you change your hostname to something else. Another option is to just rename the old files to reflect your hostname change.
- mysqlbinlog will not delete temporary files left after a LOAD DATA INFILE command.
- RENAME doesn't work with TEMPORARY tables or tables used in a MERGE table.

- When using the RPAD() function in a query that has to be resolved by using a temporary table, all resulting strings will have rightmost spaces removed. This is an example of such a query:

```
SELECT RPAD(t1.column1, 50, ' ') AS f2, RPAD(t2.column2, 50, ' ') AS f1
FROM table1 as t1 LEFT JOIN table2 AS t2 ON t1.record=t2.joinID
ORDER BY t2.record;
```

  The final result of this bug is that you will not be able to get spaces on the right side of the resulting values. The problem also occurs for any other string function that adds spaces to the right.

  The reason for this is due to the fact that HEAP tables, which are used first for temporary tables, are not capable of handling VARCHAR columns.

  This behavior exists in all versions of MySQL. It will be fixed in one of the 4.1 series releases.

- Due to the way table definition files are stored, you cannot use character 255 (CHAR(255)) in table names, column names, or enumerations. This is scheduled to be fixed in version 5.1 when we have new table definition format files.

- When using SET CHARACTER SET, you can't use translated characters in database, table, and column names.

- You can't use '_' or '%' with ESCAPE in LIKE ... ESCAPE.

- If you have a DECIMAL column in which the same number is stored in different formats (for example, +01.00, 1.00, 01.00), GROUP BY may regard each value as a different value.

- You cannot build the server in another directory when using MIT-pthreads. Because this requires changes to MIT-pthreads, we are not likely to fix this.

- BLOB values can't "reliably" be used in GROUP BY or ORDER BY or DISTINCT. Only the first max_sort_length bytes are used when comparing BLOB values in these cases. The default value of max_sort_length value is 1024. It can be changed at server startup time. A workaround for most cases is to use a substring. For example: SELECT DISTINCT LEFT(*blob_col*,2048) FROM *tbl_name*.

- Numeric calculations are done with BIGINT or DOUBLE (both are normally 64 bits long). Which precision you get depends on the function. The general rule is that bit functions are done with BIGINT precision, IF and ELT() with BIGINT or DOUBLE precision, and the rest with DOUBLE precision. You should try to avoid using unsigned long long values if they resolve to be bigger than 63 bits (9223372036854775807) for anything other than bit fields. MySQL Server 4.0 has better BIGINT handling than 3.23.

- All string columns, except BLOB and TEXT columns, automatically have all trailing spaces removed when retrieved. For CHAR types, this is okay. The bug is that in MySQL Server, VARCHAR columns are treated the same way.

- You can have only up to 255 ENUM and SET columns in one table.

- In MIN(), MAX(), and other aggregate functions, MySQL currently compares ENUM and SET columns by their string value rather than by the string's relative position in the set.

- mysqld_safe redirects all messages from mysqld to the mysqld log. One problem with this is that if you execute mysqladmin refresh to close and reopen the log, stdout and stderr are still redirected to the old log. If you use --log extensively, you should edit mysqld_safe to log to *host_name*.err instead of *host_name*.log so that you can easily reclaim the space for the old log by deleting the old one and executing mysqladmin refresh.

- In the UPDATE statement, columns are updated from left to right. If you refer to an updated column, you get the updated value instead of the original value. For example, the following statement increments KEY by 2, not 1:

  mysql> **UPDATE** *tbl_name* **SET KEY=KEY+1,KEY=KEY+1;**

- You can refer to multiple temporary tables in the same query, but you cannot refer to any given temporary table more than once. For example, the following doesn't work:

  mysql> **SELECT * FROM temp_table, temp_table AS t2;**
  ERROR 1137: Can't reopen table: 'temp_table'

- The optimizer may handle DISTINCT differently when you are using "hidden" columns in a join than when you are not. In a join, hidden columns are counted as part of the result (even if they are not shown), whereas in normal queries, hidden columns don't participate in the DISTINCT comparison. We will probably change this in the future to never compare the hidden columns when executing DISTINCT.

  An example of this is:

  ```
  SELECT DISTINCT mp3id FROM band_downloads
         WHERE userid = 9 ORDER BY id DESC;
  ```

  and

  ```
  SELECT DISTINCT band_downloads.mp3id
         FROM band_downloads,band_mp3
         WHERE band_downloads.userid = 9
         AND band_mp3.id = band_downloads.mp3id
         ORDER BY band_downloads.id DESC;
  ```

  In the second case, you might in MySQL Server 3.23.x get two identical rows in the result set (because the values in the hidden id column may differ).

  Note that this happens only for queries where you don't have the ORDER BY columns in the result.

- Because MySQL Server allows you to work with table types that don't support transactions, and thus can't roll back data, some things behave a little differently in MySQL Server than in other SQL servers. This is just to ensure that MySQL Server never needs to do a rollback for an SQL statement. This may be a little awkward at times because column values must be checked in the application, but this will actually give you a nice speed increase because it allows MySQL Server to do some optimizations that otherwise would be very hard to do.

If you set a column to an incorrect value, MySQL Server will, instead of doing a roll-back, store the "best possible value" in the column. For information about how this occurs, see Section 1.8.6, "How MySQL Deals with Constraints."

- If you execute a PROCEDURE on a query that returns an empty set, in some cases the PROCEDURE will not transform the columns.

- Creation of a table of type MERGE doesn't check whether the underlying tables are of compatible types.

- If you use ALTER TABLE first to add a UNIQUE index to a table used in a MERGE table and then to add a normal index on the MERGE table, the key order will be different for the tables if there was an old key that was not unique in the table. This is because ALTER TABLE puts UNIQUE indexes before normal indexes to be able to detect duplicate keys as early as possible.

The following are known bugs in earlier versions of MySQL:

- In the following case you can get a core dump:
    - Delayed insert handler has pending inserts to a table.
    - LOCK TABLE with WRITE.
    - FLUSH TABLES.

- Before MySQL Server 3.23.2, an UPDATE that updated a key with a WHERE on the same key may have failed because the key was used to search for records and the same row may have been found multiple times:

```
UPDATE tbl_name SET KEY=KEY+1 WHERE KEY > 100;
```

A workaround is to use:

```
UPDATE tbl_name SET KEY=KEY+1 WHERE KEY+0 > 100;
```

This will work because MySQL Server will not use an index on expressions in the WHERE clause.

- Before MySQL Server 3.23, all numeric types were treated as fixed-point fields. That means you had to specify how many decimals a floating-point field should have. All results were returned with the correct number of decimals.

2

Installing MySQL

This chapter describes how to obtain and install MySQL:

1. **Determine whether your platform is supported.** Please note that not all supported systems are equally good for running MySQL on them. On some it is much more robust and efficient than others. See Section 2.1.1, "Operating Systems Supported by MySQL," for details.

2. **Choose which distribution to install.** Several versions of MySQL are available, and most are available in several distribution formats. You can choose from pre-packaged distributions containing binary (precompiled) programs or source code. When in doubt, use a binary distribution. We also provide public access to our current source tree for those who want to see our most recent developments and help us test new code. To determine which version and type of distribution you should use, see Section 2.1.2, "Choosing Which MySQL Distribution to Install."

3. **Download the distribution that you want to install.** For a list of sites from which you can obtain MySQL, see Section 2.1.3, "How to Get MySQL." You can verify the integrity of the distribution using the instructions in Section 2.1.4, "Verifying Package Integrity Using MD5 Checksums or GnuPG."

4. **Install the distribution.** To install MySQL from a binary distribution, use the instructions in Section 2.2, "Standard MySQL Installation Using a Binary Distribution." To install MySQL from a source distribution or from the current development source tree, use the instructions in Section 2.3, "MySQL Installation Using a Source Distribution."

   If you plan to upgrade an existing version of MySQL to a newer version rather than installing MySQL for the first time, see Section 2.5, "Upgrading/Downgrading MySQL," for information about upgrade procedures and about issues that you should consider before upgrading.

   If you encounter installation difficulties, see Section 2.6, "Operating System–Specific Notes" for information on solving problems for particular platforms.

5. **Perform any necessary post-installation setup.** After installing MySQL, read Section 2.4, "Post-Installation Setup and Testing." This section contains important information about making sure the MySQL server is working properly. It also describes

how to secure the initial MySQL user accounts, *which have no passwords* until you assign passwords. The section applies whether you install MySQL using a binary or source distribution.

6. If you want to run the MySQL benchmark scripts, Perl support for MySQL must be available. See Section 2.7, "Perl Installation Notes."

2.1 General Installation Issues

Before installing MySQL, you should do the following:

1. Determine whether or not MySQL runs on your platform.
2. Choose a distribution to install.
3. Download the distribution and verify its integrity.

This section contains the information necessary to carry out these steps. After doing so, you can use the instructions in later sections of the chapter to install the distribution that you choose.

2.1.1 Operating Systems Supported by MySQL

This section lists the operating systems on which you can expect to be able to run MySQL.

We use GNU Autoconf, so it is possible to port MySQL to all modern systems that have a C++ compiler and a working implementation of POSIX threads. (Thread support is needed for the server. To compile only the client code, the only requirement is a C++ compiler.) We use and develop the software ourselves primarily on Linux (SuSE and Red Hat), FreeBSD, and Sun Solaris (Versions 8 and 9).

MySQL has been reported to compile successfully on the following combinations of operating system and thread package. Note that for many operating systems, native thread support works only in the latest versions.

- AIX 4.x, 5.x with native threads. See Section 2.6.5.3, "IBM-AIX Notes."
- Amiga.
- BSDI 2.x with the MIT-pthreads package. See Section 2.6.4.5, "BSD/OS Version 2.x Notes."
- BSDI 3.0, 3.1 and 4.x with native threads. See Section 2.6.4.5, "BSD/OS Version 2.x Notes."
- DEC UNIX 4.x with native threads. See Section 2.6.5.5, "Alpha-DEC-Unix Notes (Tru64)."
- FreeBSD 2.x with the MIT-pthreads package. See Section 2.6.4.1, "FreeBSD Notes."
- FreeBSD 3.x and 4.x with native threads. See Section 2.6.4.1, "FreeBSD Notes."

- FreeBSD 4.x with LinuxThreads. See Section 2.6.4.1, "FreeBSD Notes."
- HP-UX 10.20 with the DCE threads or the MIT-pthreads package. See Section 2.6.5.1, "HP-UX Version 10.20 Notes."
- HP-UX 11.x with the native threads. See Section 2.6.5.2, "HP-UX Version 11.x Notes."
- Linux 2.0+ with LinuxThreads 0.7.1+ or glibc 2.0.7+. See Section 2.6.1, "Linux Notes."
- Mac OS X. See Section 2.6.2, "Mac OS X Notes."
- NetBSD 1.3/1.4 Intel and NetBSD 1.3 Alpha (requires GNU make). See Section 2.6.4.2, "NetBSD Notes."
- Novell NetWare 6.0. See Section 2.2.4, "Installing MySQL on NetWare."
- OpenBSD > 2.5 with native threads. OpenBSD < 2.5 with the MIT-pthreads package. See Section 2.6.4.3, "OpenBSD 2.5 Notes."
- OS/2 Warp 3, FixPack 29 and OS/2 Warp 4, FixPack 4. See Section 2.6.6, "OS/2 Notes."
- SCO OpenServer with a recent port of the FSU Pthreads package. See Section 2.6.5.8, "SCO Notes."
- SCO UnixWare 7.1.x. See Section 2.6.5.9, "SCO UnixWare Version 7.1.x Notes."
- SGI Irix 6.x with native threads. See Section 2.6.5.7, "SGI Irix Notes."
- Solaris 2.5 and above with native threads on SPARC and x86. See Section 2.6.3, "Solaris Notes."
- SunOS 4.x with the MIT-pthreads package. See Section 2.6.3, "Solaris Notes."
- Tru64 Unix
- Windows 9x, Me, NT, 2000, and XP. See Section 2.2.1, "Installing MySQL on Windows."

Not all platforms are equally well-suited for running MySQL. How well a certain platform is suited for a high-load mission-critical MySQL server is determined by the following factors:

- General stability of the thread library. A platform may have an excellent reputation otherwise, but MySQL will be only as stable as the thread library if that library is unstable in the code that is called by MySQL, even if everything else is perfect.
- The capability of the kernel and the thread library to take advantage of symmetric multi-processor (SMP) systems. In other words, when a process creates a thread, it should be possible for that thread to run on a different CPU than the original process.
- The capability of the kernel and the thread library to run many threads that acquire and release a mutex over a short critical region frequently without excessive context switches. If the implementation of pthread_mutex_lock() is too anxious to yield CPU time,

this will hurt MySQL tremendously. If this issue is not taken care of, adding extra CPUs will actually make MySQL slower.

- General filesystem stability and performance.
- If your tables are big, the ability of the filesystem to deal with large files at all and to deal with them efficiently.
- Our level of expertise here at MySQL AB with the platform. If we know a platform well, we enable platform-specific optimizations and fixes at compile time. We can also provide advice on configuring your system optimally for MySQL.
- The amount of testing we have done internally for similar configurations.
- The number of users that have successfully run MySQL on the platform in similar configurations. If this number is high, the chances of encountering platform-specific surprises are much smaller.

Based on the preceding criteria, the best platforms for running MySQL at this point are x86 with SuSE Linux using a 2.4 kernel, and ReiserFS (or any similar Linux distribution) and SPARC with Solaris (2.7-9). FreeBSD comes third, but we really hope it will join the top club once the thread library is improved. We also hope that at some point we will be able to include into the top category all other platforms on which MySQL currently compiles and runs okay, but not quite with the same level of stability and performance. This will require some effort on our part in cooperation with the developers of the operating system and library components that MySQL depends on. If you are interested in improving one of those components, are in a position to influence its development, and need more detailed instructions on what MySQL needs to run better, send an email message to the MySQL internals mailing list. See Section 1.7.1.1, "The MySQL Mailing Lists."

Please note that the purpose of the preceding comparison is not to say that one operating system is better or worse than another in general. We are talking only about choosing an OS for the specific purpose of running MySQL. With this in mind, the result of this comparison would be different if we considered more factors. In some cases, the reason one OS is better than the other could simply be that we have been able to put more effort into testing and optimizing for a particular platform. We are just stating our observations to help you decide which platform to use for running MySQL.

2.1.2 Choosing Which MySQL Distribution to Install

When preparing to install MySQL, you should decide which version to use. MySQL development occurs in several release series, and you can pick the one that best fits your needs. After deciding which version to install, you can choose a distribution format. Releases are available in binary or source format.

2.1.2.1 Choosing Which Version of MySQL to Install

The first decision to make is whether you want to use a production (stable) release or a development release. In the MySQL development process, multiple release series co-exist, each at a different stage of maturity:

- MySQL 5.0 is the newest development release series and is under very active development for new features. Until recently it was available only in preview form from the BitKeeper source repository. An early alpha release has now been issued to allow more widespread testing.

- MySQL 4.1 is a development release series to which major new features have been added. It is currently at beta status. Sources and binaries are available for use and testing on development systems.

- MySQL 4.0 is the current stable (production-quality) release series. New releases are issued for bugfixes. No new features are added that could diminish the code stability.

- MySQL 3.23 is the old stable (production-quality) release series. This series is retired, so new releases are issued only to fix critical bugs.

We don't believe in a complete freeze, as this also leaves out bugfixes and things that "must be done." "Somewhat frozen" means that we may add small things that "almost surely will not affect anything that's already working." Naturally, relevant bugfixes from an earlier series propagate to later series.

Normally, if you are beginning to use MySQL for the first time or trying to port it to some system for which there is no binary distribution, we recommend going with the production release series. Currently this is MySQL 4.0. All MySQL releases, even those from development series, are checked with the MySQL benchmarks and an extensive test suite before being issued.

If you are running an old system and want to upgrade, but don't want to take the chance of having a non-seamless upgrade, you should upgrade to the latest version in the same release series you are using (where only the last part of the version number is newer than yours). We have tried to fix only fatal bugs and make small, relatively safe changes to that version.

If you want to use new features not present in the production release series, you can use a version from a development series. Note that development releases are not as stable as production releases.

If you want to use the very latest sources containing all current patches and bugfixes, you can use one of our BitKeeper repositories. These are not "releases" as such, but are available as previews of the code on which future releases will be based.

The MySQL naming scheme uses release names that consist of three numbers and a suffix; for example, mysql-4.1.2-alpha. The numbers within the release name are interpreted like this:

- The first number (4) is the major version and also describes the file format. All Version 4 releases have the same file format.
- The second number (1) is the release level. Taken together, the major version and release level constitute the release series number.
- The third number (2) is the version number within the release series. This is incremented for each new release. Usually you want the latest version for the series you have chosen.

For each minor update, the last number in the version string is incremented. When there are major new features or minor incompatibilities with previous versions, the second number in the version string is incremented. When the file format changes, the first number is increased.

Release names also include a suffix to indicate the stability level of the release. Releases within a series progress through a set of suffixes to indicate how the stability level improves. The possible suffixes are:

- alpha indicates that the release contains some large section of new code that hasn't been 100% tested. Known bugs (usually there are none) should be documented in the News section of the online manual at http://dev.mysql.com/doc/mysql/en/News.html. There are also new commands and extensions in most alpha releases. Active development that may involve major code changes can occur in an alpha release, but everything will be tested before issuing a release. For this reason, there should be no known bugs in any MySQL release.
- beta means that all new code has been tested. No major new features that could cause corruption in old code are added. There should be no known bugs. A version changes from alpha to beta when there haven't been any reported fatal bugs within an alpha version for at least a month and we have no plans to add any features that could make any old command unreliable.
- gamma is a beta that has been around a while and seems to work fine. Only minor fixes are added. This is what many other companies call a release.
- If there is no suffix, it means that the version has been run for a while at many different sites with no reports of bugs other than platform-specific bugs. Only critical bugfixes are applied to the release. This is what we call a production (stable) release.

MySQL uses a naming scheme that is slightly different from most other products. In general, it's relatively safe to use any version that has been out for a couple of weeks without being replaced with a new version within the release series.

All releases of MySQL are run through our standard tests and benchmarks to ensure that they are relatively safe to use. Because the standard tests are extended over time to check for all previously found bugs, the test suite keeps getting better.

All releases have been tested at least with:

- An internal test suite

  The mysql-test directory contains an extensive set of test cases. We run these tests for virtually every server binary.

- The MySQL benchmark suite

  This suite runs a range of common queries. It is also a test to see whether the latest batch of optimizations actually made the code faster. See Section 6.1.4, "The MySQL Benchmark Suite."

- The crash-me test

  This test tries to determine what features the database supports and what its capabilities and limitations are. See Section 6.1.4, "The MySQL Benchmark Suite."

Another test is that we use the newest MySQL version in our internal production environment, on at least one machine. We have more than 100GB of data to work with.

2.1.2.2 Choosing a Distribution Format

After choosing which version of MySQL to install, you should decide whether to use a binary distribution or a source distribution. In most cases, you should probably use a binary distribution, if one exists for your platform. Binary distributions are available in native format for many platforms, such as RPM files for Linux or DMG package installers for Mac OS X. Distributions also are available as Zip archives or compressed tar files.

Reasons to choose a binary distribution include the following:

- Binary distributions generally are easier to install than source distributions.
- To satisfy different user requirements, we provide two different binary versions: one compiled with the non-transactional storage engines (a small, fast binary), and one configured with the most important extended options like transaction-safe tables. Both versions are compiled from the same source distribution. All native MySQL clients can connect to servers from either MySQL version.

  The extended MySQL binary distribution is marked with the -max suffix and is configured with the same options as mysqld-max. See Section 4.1.2, "The mysqld-max Extended MySQL Server."

  If you want to use the MySQL-Max RPM, you must first install the standard MySQL-server RPM.

Under some circumstances, you probably will be better off installing MySQL from a source distribution:

- You want to install MySQL at some explicit location. The standard binary distributions are "ready to run" at any place, but you may want to have even more flexibility to place MySQL components where you want.

- You want to configure `mysqld` with some extra features that are not included in the standard binary distributions. Here is a list of the most common extra options that you may want to use:
  - `--with-innodb` (default for MySQL 4.0 and up)
  - `-with-berkeley-db` (not available on all platforms)
  - `--with-raid`
  - `--with-libwrap`
  - `--with-named-z-libs` (this is done for some of the binaries)
  - `--with-debug[=full]`
- You want to configure `mysqld` without some features that are included in the standard binary distributions. For example, distributions normally are compiled with support for all character sets. If you want a smaller MySQL server, you can recompile it with support for only the character sets you need.
- You have a special compiler (such as `pgcc`) or want to use compiler options that are better optimized for your processor. Binary distributions are compiled with options that should work on a variety of processors from the same processor family.
- You want to use the latest sources from one of the BitKeeper repositories to have access to all current bugfixes. For example, if you have found a bug and reported it to the MySQL development team, the bugfix will be committed to the source repository and you can access it there. The bugfix will not appear in a release until a release actually is issued.
- You want to read (or modify) the C and C++ code that makes up MySQL. For this purpose, you should get a source distribution, because the source code is always the ultimate manual.
- Source distributions contain more tests and examples than binary distributions.

2.1.2.3 How and When Updates Are Released

MySQL is evolving quite rapidly here at MySQL AB and we want to share new developments with other MySQL users. We try to make a release when we have very useful features that others seem to have a need for.

We also try to help out users who request features that are easy to implement. We take note of what our licensed users want to have, and we especially take note of what our extended email-supported customers want and try to help them out.

No one has to download a new release. The News section of the online manual will tell you if the new release has something you really want. See
`http://dev.mysql.com/doc/mysql/en/News.html`.

We use the following policy when updating MySQL:

- Releases are issued within each series. For each release, the last number in the version is one more than the previous release within the same series.

- Production (stable) releases are meant to appear about 1-2 times a year. However, if small bugs are found, a release with only bugfixes will be issued.

- Working releases/bugfixes to old releases are meant to appear about every 4-8 weeks.

- Binary distributions for some platforms are made by us for major releases. Other people may make binary distributions for other systems, but probably less frequently.

- We make fixes available as soon as we have identified and corrected small or non-critical but annoying bugs. The fixes are available immediately from our public BitKeeper repositories, and will be included in the next release.

- If by any chance a fatal bug is found in a release, we will make a new release as soon as possible. (We would like other companies to do this, too!)

2.1.2.4 Release Philosophy—No Known Bugs in Releases

We put a lot of time and effort into making our releases bug-free. To our knowledge, we have not released a single MySQL version with any *known* "fatal" repeatable bugs. (A "fatal" bug is something that crashes MySQL under normal usage, produces incorrect answers for normal queries, or has a security problem.)

We have documented all open problems, bugs, and issues that are dependent on design decisions. See Section 1.8.7, "Known Errors and Design Deficiencies in MySQL."

Our aim is to fix everything that is fixable without risk of making a stable MySQL version less stable. In certain cases, this means we can fix an issue in the development versions, but not in the stable (production) version. Naturally, we document such issues so that users are aware of them.

Here is a description of how our build process works:

- We monitor bugs from our customer support list, the bugs database at http://bugs.mysql.com/, and the MySQL external mailing lists.

- All reported bugs for live versions are entered into the bugs database.

- When we fix a bug, we always try to make a test case for it and include it into our test system to ensure that the bug will never recur without being detected. (About 90% of all fixed bugs have a test case.)

- We create test cases for all new features we add to MySQL.

- Before we start to build a new MySQL release, we ensure that all reported repeatable bugs for the MySQL version (3.23.x, 4.0.x, etc) are fixed. If something is impossible to fix (due to some internal design decision in MySQL), we document this in the manual. See Section 1.8.7, "Known Errors and Design Deficiencies in MySQL."

- We do a build on all platforms for which we support binaries (15+ platforms) and run our test suite and benchmark suite on all of them.

- We will not publish a binary for a platform for which the test or benchmark suite fails. If the problem is due to a general error in the source, we fix it and do the build plus tests on all systems again from scratch.

- The build and test process takes 2-3 days. If we receive a report regarding a fatal bug during this process (for example, one that causes a core dump), we fix the problem and restart the build process.

- After publishing the binaries on `http://dev.mysql.com/`, we send out an announcement message to the `mysql` and `announce` mailing lists. See Section 1.7.1.1, "The MySQL Mailing Lists." The announcement message contains a list of all changes to the release and any known problems with the release. The Known Problems section in the release notes has been needed for only a handful of releases.

- To quickly give our users access to the latest MySQL features, we do a new MySQL release every 4-8 weeks. Source code snapshots are built daily and are available at `http://downloads.mysql.com/snapshots.php`.

- If, despite our best efforts, we get any bug reports that, after the release is done, there was something critically wrong with the build on a specific platform, we will fix it at once and build a new `'a'` release for that platform. Thanks to our large user base, problems are found quickly.

- Our track record for making good releases is quite good. In the last 150 releases, we had to do a new build for fewer than 10 releases. In three of these cases, the bug was a faulty `glibc` library on one of our build machines that took us a long time to track down.

2.1.2.5 MySQL Binaries Compiled by MySQL AB

As a service of MySQL AB, we provide a set of binary distributions of MySQL that are compiled on systems at our site or on systems where supporters of MySQL kindly have given us access to their machines.

In addition to the binaries provided in platform-specific package formats, we offer binary distributions for a number of platforms in the form of compressed tar files (`.tar.gz` files). See Section 2.2, "Standard MySQL Installation Using a Binary Distribution."

For Windows distributions, see Section 2.2.1, "Installing MySQL on Windows."

These distributions are generated using the script `Build-tools/Do-compile`, which compiles the source code and creates the binary tar.gz archive using `scripts/make_binary_distribution`.

These binaries are configured and built with the following compilers and options. This information can also be obtained by looking at the variables `COMP_ENV_INFO` and `CONFIGURE_LINE` inside the script `bin/mysqlbug` of every binary tar file distribution.

The following binaries are built on MySQL AB development systems:

- Linux 2.4.xx x86 with gcc 2.95.3:

  ```
  CFLAGS="-O2 -mcpu=pentiumpro" CXX=gcc CXXFLAGS="-O2 -mcpu=pentiumpro -felide-
  constructors" ./configure --prefix=/usr/local/mysql --with-extra-charsets=com-
  plex --enable-thread-safe-client --enable-local-infile --enable-assembler --
  disable-shared --with-client-ldflags=-all-static --with-mysqld-ldflags=-all-
  static
  ```

- Linux 2.4.xx Intel Itanium 2 with ecc (Intel C++ Itanium Compiler 7.0):

  ```
  CC=ecc CFLAGS="-O2 -tpp2 -ip -nolib_inline" CXX=ecc CXXFLAGS="-O2 -tpp2 -ip -
  nolib_inline" ./configure --prefix=/usr/local/mysql --with-extra-charsets=com-
  plex --enable-thread-safe-client --enable-local-infile
  ```

- Linux 2.4.xx Intel Itanium with ecc (Intel C++ Itanium Compiler 7.0):

  ```
  CC=ecc CFLAGS=-tpp1 CXX=ecc CXXFLAGS=-tpp1 ./configure --
  prefix=/usr/local/mysql --with-extra-charsets=complex --enable-thread-safe-
  client --enable-local-infile
  ```

- Linux 2.4.xx alpha with ccc (Compaq C V6.2-505 / Compaq C++ V6.3-006):

  ```
  CC=ccc CFLAGS="-fast -arch generic" CXX=cxx CXXFLAGS="-fast -arch generic -
  noexceptions -nortti" ./configure --prefix=/usr/local/mysql --with-extra-
  charsets=complex --enable-thread-safe-client --enable-local-infile --with-
  mysqld-ldflags=-non_shared --with-client-ldflags=-non_shared --disable-shared
  ```

- Linux 2.x.xx ppc with gcc 2.95.4:

  ```
  CC=gcc CFLAGS="-O3 -fno-omit-frame-pointer" CXX=gcc CXXFLAGS="-O3 -fno-omit-
  frame-pointer -felide-constructors -fno-exceptions -fno-rtti" ./configure --
  prefix=/usr/local/mysql --localstatedir=/usr/local/mysql/data --
  libexecdir=/usr/local/mysql/bin --with-extra-charsets=complex --enable-thread-
  safe-client --enable-local-infile --disable-shared --with-embedded-server --
  with-innodb
  ```

- Linux 2.4.xx s390 with gcc 2.95.3:

  ```
  CFLAGS="-O2" CXX=gcc CXXFLAGS="-O2 -felide-constructors" ./configure --pre-
  fix=/usr/local/mysql --with-extra-charsets=complex --enable-thread-safe-client
  --enable-local-infile --disable-shared --with-client-ldflags=-all-static --
  with-mysqld-ldflags=-all-static
  ```

- Linux 2.4.xx x86_64 (AMD64) with gcc 3.2.1:

  ```
  CXX=gcc ./configure --prefix=/usr/local/mysql --with-extra-charsets=complex --
  enable-thread-safe-client --enable-local-infile --disable-shared
  ```

- Sun Solaris 8 x86 with gcc 3.2.3:

  ```
  CC=gcc CFLAGS="-O3 -fno-omit-frame-pointer" CXX=gcc CXXFLAGS="-O3 -fno-omit-
  frame-pointer -felide-constructors -fno-exceptions -fno-rtti" ./configure
  --prefix=/usr/local/mysql --localstatedir=/usr/local/mysql/data
  --libexecdir=/usr/local/mysql/bin --with-extra-charsets=complex --enable-
  thread-safe-client --enable-local-infile --disable-shared --with-innodb
  ```

- Sun Solaris 8 SPARC with gcc 3.2:

  ```
  CC=gcc CFLAGS="-O3 -fno-omit-frame-pointer" CXX=gcc CXXFLAGS="-O3 -fno-omit-
  frame-pointer -felide-constructors -fno-exceptions -fno-rtti" ./configure
  --prefix=/usr/local/mysql --with-extra-charsets=complex --enable-thread-safe-
  client --enable-local-infile --enable-assembler --with-named-z-libs=no --with-
  named-curses-libs=-lcurses --disable-shared
  ```

- Sun Solaris 8 SPARC 64-bit with gcc 3.2:

  ```
  CC=gcc CFLAGS="-O3 -m64 -fno-omit-frame-pointer" CXX=gcc CXXFLAGS="-O3 -m64
  -fno-omit-frame-pointer -felide-constructors -fno-exceptions -fno-rtti" ./con-
  figure --prefix=/usr/local/mysql --with-extra-charsets=complex --enable-thread-
  safe-client --enable-local-infile --with-named-z-libs=no --with-named-curses-
  libs=-lcurses --disable-shared
  ```

- Sun Solaris 9 SPARC with gcc 2.95.3:

  ```
  CC=gcc CFLAGS="-O3 -fno-omit-frame-pointer" CXX=gcc CXXFLAGS="-O3 -fno-omit-
  frame-pointer -felide-constructors -fno-exceptions -fno-rtti" ./configure
  --prefix=/usr/local/mysql --with-extra-charsets=complex --enable-thread-safe-
  client --enable-local-infile --enable-assembler --with-named-curses-libs=-
  lcurses --disable-shared
  ```

- Sun Solaris 9 SPARC with cc-5.0 (Sun Forte 5.0):

  ```
  CC=cc-5.0 CXX=CC ASFLAGS="-xarch=v9" CFLAGS="-Xa -xstrconst -mt -D_FORTEC_
  -xarch=v9" CXXFLAGS="-noex -mt -D_FORTEC_ -xarch=v9" ./configure --
  prefix=/usr/local/mysql --with-extra-charsets=complex --enable-thread-safe-
  client --enable-local-infile --enable-assembler --with-named-z-libs=no
  --enable-thread-safe-client --disable-shared
  ```

- IBM AIX 4.3.2 ppc with gcc 3.2.3:

  ```
  CFLAGS="-O2 -mcpu=powerpc -Wa,-many " CXX=gcc CXXFLAGS="-O2 -mcpu=powerpc -Wa,
  -many -felide-constructors -fno-exceptions -fno-rtti" ./configure --
  prefix=/usr/local/mysql --with-extra-charsets=complex --enable-thread-safe-
  client --enable-local-infile --with-named-z-libs=no --disable-shared
  ```

- IBM AIX 4.3.3 ppc with xlC_r (IBM Visual Age C/C++ 6.0):

  ```
  CC=xlc_r CFLAGS="-ma -O2 -qstrict -qoptimize=2 -qmaxmem=8192" CXX=xlC_r
  CXXFLAGS ="-ma -O2 -qstrict -qoptimize=2 -qmaxmem=8192" ./configure
  --prefix=/usr/local/mysql --localstatedir=/usr/local/mysql/data
  ```

```
--libexecdir=/usr/local/mysql/bin --with-extra-charsets=complex --enable-
thread-safe-client --enable-local-infile --with-named-z-libs=no --disable-
shared --with-innodb
```

- IBM AIX 5.1.0 ppc with gcc 3.3:

```
CFLAGS="-O2 -mcpu=powerpc -Wa,-many" CXX=gcc CXXFLAGS="-O2 -mcpu=powerpc -Wa,
-many -felide-constructors -fno-exceptions -fno-rtti" ./configure
--prefix=/usr/local/mysql --with-extra-charsets=complex --enable-thread-safe-
client --enable-local-infile --with-named-z-libs=no --disable-shared
```

- IBM AIX 5.2.0 ppc with xlC_r (IBM Visual Age C/C++ 6.0):

```
CC=xlc_r CFLAGS="-ma -O2 -qstrict -qoptimize=2 -qmaxmem=8192" CXX=xlC_r
CXXFLAGS="-ma -O2 -qstrict -qoptimize=2 -qmaxmem=8192" ./configure
--prefix=/usr/local/mysql --localstatedir=/usr/local/mysql/data
--libexecdir=/usr/local/mysql/bin --with-extra-charsets=complex --enable-
thread-safe-client --enable-local-infile --with-named-z-libs=no --disable-
shared --with-embedded-server --with-innodb
```

- HP-UX 10.20 pa-risc1.1 with gcc 3.1:

```
CFLAGS="-DHPUX -I/opt/dce/include -O3 -fPIC" CXX=gcc CXXFLAGS="-DHPUX -
I/opt/dce /include -felide-constructors -fno-exceptions -fno-rtti -O3 -fPIC"
./configure --prefix=/usr/local/mysql --with-extra-charsets=complex --enable-
thread-safe-client --enable-local-infile --with-pthread --with-named-thread-
libs=-ldce --with-lib-ccflags=-fPIC --disable-shared
```

- HP-UX 11.00 pa-risc with aCC (HP ANSI C++ B3910B A.03.50):

```
CC=cc CXX=aCC CFLAGS=+DAportable CXXFLAGS=+DAportable ./configure
--prefix=/usr/local/mysql --localstatedir=/usr/local/mysql/data
--libexecdir=/usr/local/mysql/bin --with-extra-charsets=complex --enable-
thread-safe-client --enable-local-infile --disable-shared --with-embedded-
server --with-innodb
```

- HP-UX 11.11 pa-risc2.0 64bit with aCC (HP ANSI C++ B3910B A.03.33):

```
CC=cc CXX=aCC CFLAGS=+DD64 CXXFLAGS=+DD64 ./configure --prefix=/usr/local/mysql
--with-extra-charsets=complex --enable-thread-safe-client --enable-local-infile
--disable-shared
```

- HP-UX 11.11 pa-risc2.0 32bit with aCC (HP ANSI C++ B3910B A.03.33):

```
CC=cc CXX=aCC CFLAGS="+DAportable" CXXFLAGS="+DAportable" ./configure
--prefix=/usr/local/mysql --localstatedir=/usr/local/mysql/data --
libexecdir=/usr/local/mysql/bin --with-extra-charsets=complex --enable-thread-
safe-client --enable-local-infile --disable-shared --with-innodb
```

- HP-UX 11.22 ia64 64bit with aCC (HP aC++/ANSI C B3910B A.05.50):

```
CC=cc CXX=aCC CFLAGS="+DD64 +DSitanium2" CXXFLAGS="+DD64 +DSitanium2" ./config-
ure --prefix=/usr/local/mysql --localstatedir=/usr/local/mysql/data
```

```
--libexecdir=/usr/local/mysql/bin --with-extra-charsets=complex --enable-
thread-safe-client --enable-local-infile --disable-shared --with-embedded-
server --with-innodb
```

- Apple Mac OS X 10.2 powerpc with gcc 3.1:

```
CC=gcc CFLAGS="-O3 -fno-omit-frame-pointer" CXX=gcc CXXFLAGS="-O3 -fno-omit-
frame-pointer -felide-constructors -fno-exceptions -fno-rtti" ./configure
--prefix=/usr/local/mysql --with-extra-charsets=complex --enable-thread-safe-
client --enable-local-infile --disable-shared
```

- FreeBSD 4.7 i386 with gcc 2.95.4:

```
CFLAGS=-DHAVE_BROKEN_REALPATH ./configure --prefix=/usr/local/mysql --with-
extra-charsets=complex --enable-thread-safe-client --enable-local-infile
--enable-assembler --with-named-z-libs=not-used --disable-shared
```

- FreeBSD 4.7 i386 using LinuxThreads with gcc 2.95.4:

```
CFLAGS="-DHAVE_BROKEN_REALPATH -D__USE_UNIX98 -D_REENTRANT -D_THREAD_SAFE -
I/usr/local/include/pthread/linuxthreads" CXXFLAGS="-DHAVE_BROKEN_REALPATH -
D__USE_UNIX98 -D_REENTRANT -D_THREAD_SAFE -I/usr/local/include/pthread/linux-
threads" ./configure --prefix=/usr/local/mysql --
localstatedir=/usr/local/mysql/data --libexecdir=/usr/local/mysql/bin --enable-
thread-safe-client --enable-local-infile --enable-assembler --with-named-
thread-libs="-DHAVE_GLIBC2_STYLE_GETHOSTBYNAME_R -D_THREAD_SAFE -I
/usr/local/include/pthread/linuxthreads -L/usr/local/lib -llthread -llgcc_r"
--disable-shared --with-embedded-server --with-innodb
```

- QNX Neutrino 6.2.1 i386 with gcc 2.95.3qnx-nto 20010315:

```
CC=gcc CFLAGS="-O3 -fno-omit-frame-pointer" CXX=gcc CXXFLAGS="-O3 -fno-omit-
frame-pointer -felide-constructors -fno-exceptions -fno-rtti" ./configure
--prefix=/usr/local/mysql --with-extra-charsets=complex --enable-thread-safe-
client --enable-local-infile --disable-shared
```

The following binaries are built on third-party systems kindly provided to MySQL AB by other users. These are provided only as a courtesy; MySQL AB does not have full control over these systems, so we can provide only limited support for the binaries built on them.

- SCO Unix 3.2v5.0.6 i386 with gcc 2.95.3:

```
CFLAGS="-O3 -mpentium" LDFLAGS=-static CXX=gcc CXXFLAGS="-O3 -mpentium -felide-
constructors" ./configure --prefix=/usr/local/mysql --with-extra-charsets=com-
plex --enable-thread-safe-client --enable-local-infile --with-named-z-libs=no
--enable-thread-safe-client --disable-shared
```

- SCO OpenUnix 8.0.0 i386 with CC 3.2:

```
CC=cc CFLAGS="-O" CXX=CC ./configure --prefix=/usr/local/mysql --with-extra-
charsets=complex --enable-thread-safe-client --enable-local-infile --with-
named-z-libs=no --enable-thread-safe-client --disable-shared
```

- Compaq Tru64 OSF/1 V5.1 732 alpha with cc/cxx (Compaq C V6.3-029i / DIGITAL C++ V6.1-027):

```
CC="cc -pthread" CFLAGS="-04 -ansi_alias -ansi_args -fast -inline speed -specu-
late all" CXX="cxx -pthread" CXXFLAGS="-04 -ansi_alias -fast -inline speed
-speculate all -noexceptions -nortti" ./configure --prefix=/usr/local/mysql
--with-extra-charsets=complex --enable-thread-safe-client --enable-local-infile
--with-prefix=/usr/local/mysql --with-named-thread-libs="-lpthread -lmach -lexc
-lc" --disable-shared --with-mysqld-ldflags=-all-static
```

- SGI Irix 6.5 IP32 with gcc 3.0.1:

```
CC=gcc CFLAGS="-03 -fno-omit-frame-pointer" CXXFLAGS="-03 -fno-omit-frame-
pointer -felide-constructors -fno-exceptions -fno-rtti" ./configure
--prefix=/usr/local/mysql --with-extra-charsets=complex --enable-thread-safe-
client --enable-local-infile --disable-shared
```

- FreeBSD/sparc64 5.0 with gcc 3.2.1:

```
CFLAGS=-DHAVE_BROKEN_REALPATH ./configure --prefix=/usr/local/mysql --local-
statedir=/usr/local/mysql/data --libexecdir=/usr/local/mysql/bin --with-extra-
charsets=complex --enable-thread-safe-client --enable-local-infile --disable-
shared --with-innodb
```

The following compile options have been used for binary packages that MySQL AB provided in the past. These binaries no longer are being updated, but the compile options are listed here for reference purposes.

- Linux 2.2.xx SPARC with egcs 1.1.2:

```
CC=gcc CFLAGS="-03 -fno-omit-frame-pointer" CXX=gcc CXXFLAGS="-03 -fno-omit-
frame-pointer -felide-constructors -fno-exceptions -fno-rtti" ./configure
--prefix=/usr/local/mysql --with-extra-charsets=complex --enable-thread-safe-
client --enable-local-infile --enable-assembler --disable-shared
```

- Linux 2.2.x with x686 with gcc 2.95.2:

```
CFLAGS="-03 -mpentiumpro" CXX=gcc CXXFLAGS="-03 -mpentiumpro -felide-
constructors -fno-exceptions -fno-rtti" ./configure --prefix=/usr/local/mysql
--enable-assembler --with-mysqld-ldflags=-all-static --disable-shared --with-
extra-charsets=complex
```

- SunOS 4.1.4 2 sun4c with gcc 2.7.2.1:

```
CC=gcc CXX=gcc CXXFLAGS="-03 -felide-constructors" ./configure
--prefix=/usr/local/mysql --disable-shared --with-extra-charsets=complex
--enable-assembler
```

- SunOS 5.5.1 (and above) sun4u with egcs 1.0.3a or 2.90.27 or gcc 2.95.2 and newer:

```
CC=gcc CFLAGS="-03" CXX=gcc CXXFLAGS="-03 -felide-constructors -fno-exceptions
-fno-rtti" ./configure --prefix=/usr/local/mysql --with-low-memory --with-
extra-charsets=complex --enable-assembler
```

- SunOS 5.6 i86pc with gcc 2.8.1:

  ```
  CC=gcc CXX=gcc CXXFLAGS=-O3 ./configure --prefix=/usr/local/mysql --with-low-
  memory --with-extra-charsets=complex
  ```

- BSDI BSD/OS 3.1 i386 with gcc 2.7.2.1:

  ```
  CC=gcc CXX=gcc CXXFLAGS=-O ./configure --prefix=/usr/local/mysql --with-extra-
  charsets=complex
  ```

- BSDI BSD/OS 2.1 i386 with gcc 2.7.2:

  ```
  CC=gcc CXX=gcc CXXFLAGS=-O3 ./configure --prefix=/usr/local/mysql --with-extra-
  charsets=complex
  ```

- AIX 2 4 with gcc 2.7.2.2:

  ```
  CC=gcc CXX=gcc CXXFLAGS=-O3 ./configure --prefix=/usr/local/mysql --with-extra-
  charsets=complex
  ```

Anyone who has more optimal options for any of the preceding configurations listed can always mail them to the MySQL `internals` mailing list. See Section 1.7.1.1, "The MySQL Mailing Lists."

RPM distributions prior to MySQL 3.22 are user-contributed. Beginning with MySQL 3.22, RPM distributions are generated by MySQL AB.

If you want to compile a debug version of MySQL, you should add `--with-debug` or `--with-debug=full` to the preceding configure lines and remove any `-fomit-frame-pointer` options.

2.1.3 How to Get MySQL

Check the MySQL home page (`http://www.mysql.com/`) for information about the current version and for downloading instructions.

Our main mirror is located at `http://mirrors.sunsite.dk/mysql/`.

For a complete up-to-date list of MySQL download mirror sites, see `http://dev.mysql.com/downloads/mirrors.html`. There you will also find information about becoming a MySQL mirror site and how to report a bad or out-of-date mirror.

2.1.4 Verifying Package Integrity Using MD5 Checksums or GnuPG

After you have downloaded the MySQL package that suits your needs and before you attempt to install it, you should make sure that it is intact and has not been tampered with. MySQL AB offers three means of integrity checking:

- MD5 checksums
- Cryptographic signatures using `GnuPG`, the GNU Privacy Guard
- For RPM packages, the built-in RPM integrity verification mechanism

The following sections describe how to use these methods.

If you notice that the MD5 checksum or GPG signatures do not match, first try to download the respective package one more time, perhaps from another mirror site. If you repeatedly cannot successfully verify the integrity of the package, please notify us about such incidents, including the full package name and the download site you have been using, at webmaster@mysql.com or build@mysql.com. Do not report downloading problems using the bug-reporting system.

2.1.4.1 Verifying the MD5 Checksum

After you have downloaded a MySQL package, you should make sure that its MD5 checksum matches the one provided on the MySQL download pages. Each package has an individual checksum that you can verify with the following command, where *package_name* is the name of the package you downloaded:

```
shell> md5sum package_name
```

Example:

```
shell> md5sum mysql-standard-4.0.17-pc-linux-i686.tar.gz
60f5fe969d61c8f82e4f7f62657e1f06  mysql-standard-4.0.17-pc-linux-i686.tar.gz
```

You should verify that the resulting checksum (the string of hexadecimal digits) matches the one displayed on the download page immediately below the respective package.

Note that not all operating systems support the md5sum command. On some, it is simply called md5 and others do not ship it at all. On Linux, it is part of the GNU Text Utilities package, which is available for a wide range of platforms. You can download the source code from http://www.gnu.org/software/textutils/ as well. If you have OpenSSL installed, you can also use the command openssl md5 *package_name* instead. A DOS/Windows implementation of the md5 command is available from http://www.fourmilab.ch/md5/.

2.1.4.2 Signature Checking Using GnuPG

Another method of verifying the integrity and authenticity of a package is to use cryptographic signatures. This is more reliable than using MD5 checksums, but requires more work.

Beginning with MySQL 4.0.10 (February 2003), MySQL AB started signing downloadable packages with GnuPG (GNU Privacy Guard). GnuPG is an Open Source alternative to the very well-known Pretty Good Privacy (PGP) by Phil Zimmermann. See http://www.gnupg.org/ for more information about GnuPG and how to obtain and install it on your system. Most Linux distributions already ship with GnuPG installed by default. For more information about OpenPGP, see http://www.openpgp.org/.

To verify the signature for a specific package, you first need to obtain a copy of MySQL AB's public GPG build key. You can download the key from http://www.keyserver.net/. The key that you want to obtain is named build@mysql.com. Alternatively, you can cut and paste the key directly from the following text:

```
Key ID:
pub  1024D/5072E1F5 2003-02-03
     MySQL Package signing key (www.mysql.com) <build@mysql.com>
Fingerprint: A4A9 4068 76FC BD3C 4567  70C8 8C71 8D3B 5072 E1F5


Public Key (ASCII-armored):


-----BEGIN PGP PUBLIC KEY BLOCK-----
Version: GnuPG v1.0.6 (GNU/Linux)
Comment: For info see http://www.gnupg.org
```

```
mQGiBD4+owwRBAC14GIfUfCyEDSIePvEW3SAFUdJBtoQHH/nJKZyQT7h9bPlUWC3
RODjQReyCITRrdwyrKUGku2FmeVGwn2u2WmDMNABLnpprWPkBdCk96+OmSLN9brZ
fw2vOUgCmYv2hWOhyDHuvYlQA/BThQoADgj8AW6/OLo7V1W9/8VuHPOgQwCgvzV3
BqOxRznNCRCRxAuAuVztHRcEAJooQK1+iSiunZMYD1WufeXfshc57S/+yeJkegNW
hxwR9pRWVArNYJdDRT+rf2RUe3vpquKNQU/hnEIUHJRQqYHo8gTxvxXNQc7fJYLV
K2HtkrPbP72vwsEKMYhhrOeKCbtLGfls9krjJ6sBgACyP/Vb7hiPwxh6rDZ7ITnE
kYpXBACmWpP8NJTkamEnPCia2ZoOHODANwpUkP43I7jsDmgtobZX9qnrAXw+uNDI
QJEXM6FSbiOLLtZciNlYsafwAPEOMDKpMqAK6IyisNtPvaLd8lHObPAnWqcyefep
rvOsxxqUEMcM3o7wwgfN83POkDasDbs3pjwPhxvhz6//62zQJ7Q7TXlTUUwgUGFj
a2FnZSBzaWduaW5nIGtleSAod3d3Lm15c3FsLmNvbSkgPGJ1aWxkQG15c3FsLmNv
bT6IXQQTEQIAHQUCPj6jDAUJCWYBgAULBwoDBAMVAwIDFgIBAheAAAoJEIxxjTtQ
cuH1cY4AnilUwTXn8MatQOiG0a/bPxrvK/gCAJ4oinSNZRYTnblChwFaazt7PF3q
zIhMBBMRAgAMBQI+PqPRBYMJZgC7AAoJEE1Q4SqycpHyJOEAn1mxHijft00bKXvu
cSo/pECUmppiAJ41M9MRVj5VcdH/KN/KjRtW6tHFPYhMBBMRAgAMBQI+QoIDBYMJ
YiKJAAoJELb1zU3GuiQ/lpEAoIhpp6BozKI8p6eaabzF5MlJH58pAKCu/ROofK8J
Eg2aLos+5zEYrB/LsrkCDQQ+PqMdEAgA7+GJfxbMdY4wslPnjH9rF4N2qfWsEN/l
xaZoJYc3a6MO2WCnHl6ahT2/tBK2w1QI4YFteR47gCvtgb6O1JHffOo2HfLmRDRi
Rjd1DTCHqeyX7CHhcghj/dNR1W2Z0l5QFEcmV9U0Vhp3aFfWC4Ujfs3LU+hkAWzE
7zaD5cH9J7yv/6xuZVw411x0h4UqsTcWMuOiM1BzELqX1DY7LwoPEb/O9Rkbf4fm
Le11EzIaCa4PqARXQZc4dhSinMt6K3X4BrRsKTfozBu74F47D8I1bf5vSYHbuE5p
/1oIDznkg/p8kW+3FxuWrycciqFTcNz215yyX39LXFnlLzKUb/F5GwADBQf+Lwqq
a8CGrRfsOAJxim63CHfty5mUc5rUSnTslGYEIOCR1BeQauyPZbPDsDD9MZ1ZaSaf
anFvwFG6Llx9xkU7tzq+vKLoWkm4u5xf3vn55VjnSd1aQ9eQnUcXiL4cnBGoTbOW
I39EcyzgslzBdC++MPjcQTcA7p6JUVsP6oAB3FQWg54tuUoOEc8bsM8b3Ev42Lmu
QT5NdKHGwHsXTPtl0k1k4bQk4OajHsiy1BMahpT27jWjJlMiJc+IWJOmghkKHt92
6s/ymfdf5HkdQlcyvsz5tryVI3Fx78XeSYfQvuuwqp2H139pXGEkgOn6KdUOetdZ
Whe7OYGNPwlyjWJT1IhMBBgRAgAMBQI+PqMdBQkJZgGAAAoJEIxxjTtQcuH17p4A
n3rlQpVC9yhnW2cSAjq+kr72GX0eAJ4295kl6NxxYEuFApmr1+OuUq/SlsQ==
=YJkx
-----END PGP PUBLIC KEY BLOCK-----
```

You can import the build key into your personal public GPG keyring by using gpg --import.

For example, if you save the key in a file named `mysql_pubkey.asc`, the import command looks like this:

```
shell> gpg --import mysql_pubkey.asc
```

See the GPG documentation for more information on how to work with public keys.

After you have downloaded and imported the public build key, download your desired MySQL package and the corresponding signature, which also is available from the download page. The signature file has the same name as the distribution file with an `.asc` extension. For example:

Distribution file   `mysql-standard-4.0.17-pc-linux-i686.tar.gz`

Signature file   `mysql-standard-4.0.17-pc-linux-i686.tar.gz.asc`

Make sure that both files are stored in the same directory and then run the following command to verify the signature for the distribution file:

```
shell> gpg --verify package_name.asc
```

Example:

```
shell> gpg --verify mysql-standard-4.0.17-pc-linux-i686.tar.gz.asc
gpg: Warning: using insecure memory!
gpg: Signature made Mon 03 Feb 2003 08:50:39 PM MET
using DSA key ID 5072E1F5
gpg: Good signature from
    "MySQL Package signing key (www.mysql.com) <build@mysql.com>"
```

The `Good signature` message indicates that everything is all right. You can ignore the `insecure memory` warning.

2.1.4.3 Signature Checking Using RPM

For RPM packages, there is no separate signature. RPM packages have a built-in GPG signature and MD5 checksum. You can verify a package by running the following command:

```
shell> rpm --checksig package_name.rpm
```

Example:

```
shell> rpm --checksig MySQL-server-4.0.10-0.i386.rpm
MySQL-server-4.0.10-0.i386.rpm: md5 gpg OK
```

Note: If you are using RPM 4.1 and it complains about (GPG) NOT OK (MISSING KEYS: GPG#5072e1f5), even though you have imported the MySQL public build key into your own GPG keyring, you need to import the key into the RPM keyring first. RPM 4.1 no longer uses your personal GPG keyring (or GPG itself). Rather, it maintains its own keyring because it is a system-wide application and a user's GPG public keyring is a user-specific file. To import the MySQL public key into the RPM keyring, first obtain the key as described in the previous section. Then use `rpm --import` to import the key. For example, if you have the public key stored in a file named `mysql_pubkey.asc`, import it using this command:

```
shell> rpm --import mysql_pubkey.asc
```

2.1.5 Installation Layouts

This section describes the default layout of the directories created by installing binary or source distributions provided by MySQL AB. If you install a distribution provided by another vendor, some other layout might be used.

On Windows, the default installation directory is `C:\mysql`, which has the following subdirectories:

Directory	Contents of Directory
bin	Client programs and the `mysqld` server
data	Log files, databases
Docs	Documentation
examples	Example programs and scripts
include	Include (header) files
lib	Libraries
scripts	Utility scripts
share	Error message files

Installations created from Linux RPM distributions result in files under the following system directories:

Directory	Contents of Directory
/usr/bin	Client programs and scripts
/usr/sbin	The `mysqld` server
/var/lib/mysql	Log files, databases
/usr/share/doc/packages	Documentation
include/usr/include/mysql	Include (header) files
lib/usr/lib/mysql	Libraries
/usr/share/mysql	Error message and character set files
sql-bench/usr/share/sql-bench	Benchmarks

On Unix, a tar file binary distribution is installed by unpacking it at the installation location you choose (typically `/usr/local/mysql`) and creates the following directories in that location:

Directory	Contents of Directory
bin	Client programs and the mysqld server
data	Log files, databases
docs	Documentation, ChangeLog
include	Include (header) files
lib	Libraries
scripts	mysql_install_db
share/mysql	Error message files
sql-bench	Benchmarks

A source distribution is installed after you configure and compile it. By default, the installation step installs files under /usr/local, in the following subdirectories:

Directory	Contents of Directory
bin	Client programs and scripts
include/mysql	Include (header) files
info	Documentation in Info format
lib/mysql	Libraries
libexec	The mysqld server
share/mysql	Error message files
sql-bench	Benchmarks and crash-me test
var	Databases and log files

Within an installation directory, the layout of a source installation differs from that of a binary installation in the following ways:

- The mysqld server is installed in the libexec directory rather than in the bin directory.
- The data directory is var rather than data.
- mysql_install_db is installed in the bin directory rather than in the scripts directory.
- The header file and library directories are include/mysql and lib/mysql rather than include and lib.

You can create your own binary installation from a compiled source distribution by executing the scripts/make_binary_distribution script from the top directory of the source distribution.

2.2 Standard MySQL Installation Using a Binary Distribution

This section covers the installation of MySQL on platforms where we offer packages using the native packaging format of the respective platform. (This is also known as performing a "binary install.") However, binary distributions of MySQL are available for many other plat-forms as well. See Section 2.2.5, "Installing MySQL on Other Unix-Like Systems," for generic installation instructions for these packages that apply to all platforms.

See Section 2.1, "General Installation Issues," for more information on what other binary distributions are available and how to obtain them.

2.2.1 Installing MySQL on Windows

The installation process for MySQL on Windows has the following steps:

1. Obtain and install the distribution.

2. Set up an option file if necessary.

3. Select the server you want to use.

4. Start the server.

5. Assign passwords to the initial MySQL accounts.

MySQL for Windows is available in two distribution formats:

- The binary distribution contains a setup program that installs everything you need so that you can start the server immediately.

- The source distribution contains all the code and support files for building the executa-bles using the VC++ 6.0 compiler.

Generally speaking, you should use the binary distribution. It's simpler, and you need no additional tools to get MySQL up and running.

This section describes how to install MySQL on Windows using a binary distribution. To install using a source distribution, see Section 2.3.6, "Installing MySQL from Source on Windows."

2.2.1.1 Windows System Requirements

To run MySQL on Windows, you need the following:

- A 32-bit Windows operating system such as 9x, Me, NT, 2000, or XP. The NT family (Windows NT, 2000, and XP) permits you to run the MySQL server as a service. See Section 2.2.1.7, "Starting MySQL as a Windows Service."

- TCP/IP protocol support.

- A copy of the MySQL binary distribution for Windows, which can be downloaded from `http://dev.mysql.com/downloads/`. See Section 2.1.3, "How to Get MySQL."

  Note: If you download the distribution via FTP, we recommend the use of an adequate FTP client with a resume feature to avoid corruption of files during the download process.

- WinZip or other Windows tool that can read .zip files, to unpack the distribution file.
- Enough space on the hard drive to unpack, install, and create the databases in accordance with your requirements.
- If you plan to connect to the MySQL server via ODBC, you also need the MyODBC driver.
- If you need tables with a size larger than 4GB, install MySQL on an NTFS or newer filesystem. Don't forget to use MAX_ROWS and AVG_ROW_LENGTH when you create tables.

2.2.1.2 Installing a Windows Binary Distribution

To install MySQL on Windows using a binary distribution, follow this procedure:

1. If you are working on a Windows NT, 2000, or XP machine, make sure that you have logged in as a user with administrator privileges.

2. If you are doing an upgrade of an earlier MySQL installation, it is necessary to stop the current server. On Windows NT, 2000, or XP machines, if you are running the server as a Windows service, stop it as follows from the command prompt:

```
C:\> NET STOP MySQL
```

If you plan to use a different server after the upgrade (for example, if you want to run mysqld-max rather than mysqld), remove the existing service:

```
C:\> C:\mysql\bin\mysqld --remove
```

You can reinstall the service to use the proper server after upgrading.

If you are not running the MySQL server as a service, stop it like this:

```
C:\> C:\mysql\bin\mysqladmin -u root shutdown
```

3. Exit the WinMySQLAdmin program if it is running.

4. Unzip the distribution file to a temporary directory.

5. Run the setup.exe program to begin the installation process. If you want to install MySQL into a location other than the default directory (C:\mysql), use the Browse button to specify your preferred directory. If you do not install MySQL into the default location, you will need to specify the location whenever you start the server. The easiest way to do this is to use an option file, as described in Section 2.2.1.3, "Preparing the Windows MySQL Environment."

6. Finish the install process.

Important note: Early alpha Windows distributions for MySQL 4.1 do not contain an installer program. A 4.1 distribution is a Zip file that you just unzip in the location where you want to install MySQL. For example, to install mysql-4.1.1-alpha-win.zip as C:\mysql, unzip the distribution file on the C: drive, then rename the resulting mysql-4.1.1-alpha directory to mysql.

If you are upgrading to MySQL 4.1 from an earlier version, you will want to preserve your existing data directory that contains the grant tables in the mysql database and your own databases. Before installing 4.1, stop the server if it is running, and save your data directory to another location. Then either rename the existing C:\mysql directory or remove it. Install 4.1 as described in the preceding paragraph, and then replace its data directory with your old data directory. This will avoid the loss of your current databases. Start the new server and update the grant tables. See Section 2.5.8, "Upgrading the Grant Tables."

2.2.1.3 Preparing the Windows MySQL Environment

If you need to specify startup options when you run the server, you can indicate them on the command line or place them in an option file. For options that will be used every time the server starts, you will find it most convenient to use an option file to specify your MySQL configuration. This is true particularly under the following circumstances:

- The installation or data directory locations are different from the default locations (C:\mysql and C:\mysql\data).

- You need to tune the server settings. For example, to use the InnoDB transactional tables in MySQL 3.23, you must manually add some extra lines to the option file, as described in Section 9.4, "InnoDB Configuration." (As of MySQL 4.0, InnoDB creates its data files and log files in the data directory by default. This means you need not configure InnoDB explicitly. You may still do so if you wish, and an option file will be useful in this case, too.)

On Windows, the MySQL installer places the data directory directly under the directory where you install MySQL. If you would like to use a data directory in a different location, you should copy the entire contents of the data directory to the new location. For example, by default, the installer places MySQL in C:\mysql and the data directory in C:\mysql\data. If you want to use a data directory of E:\mydata, you must do two things:

- Move the data directory from C:\mysql\data to E:\mydata.

- Use a --datadir option to specify the new data directory location each time you start the server.

When the MySQL server starts on Windows, it looks for options in two files: the my.ini file in the Windows directory, and the C:\my.cnf file. The Windows directory typically is named something like C:\WINDOWS or C:\WinNT. You can determine its exact location from the value of the WINDIR environment variable using the following command:

```
C:\> echo %WINDIR%
```

MySQL looks for options first in the my.ini file, then in the my.cnf file. However, to avoid confusion, it's best if you use only one file. If your PC uses a boot loader where the C: drive isn't the boot drive, your only option is to use the my.ini file. Whichever option file you use, it must be a plain text file.

An option file can be created and modified with any text editor, such as the Notepad program. For example, if MySQL is installed at E:\mysql and the data directory is located at E:\mydata\data, you can create the option file and set up a [mysqld] section to specify values for the basedir and datadir parameters:

```
[mysqld]
# set basedir to your installation path
basedir=E:/mysql
# set datadir to the location of your data directory
datadir=E:/mydata/data
```

Note that Windows pathnames are specified in option files using forward slashes rather than backslashes. If you do use backslashes, you must double them.

Another way to manage an option file is to use the WinMySQLAdmin tool. You can find WinMySQLAdmin in the bin directory of your MySQL installation, as well as a help file containing instructions for using it. WinMySQLAdmin has the capability of editing your option file, but note these points:

- WinMySQLAdmin uses only the my.ini file.
- If WinMySQLAdmin finds a C:\my.cnf file, it will in fact rename it to C:\my_cnf.bak to disable it.

Now you are ready to start the server.

2.2.1.4 Selecting a Windows Server

Starting with MySQL 3.23.38, the Windows distribution includes both the normal and the MySQL-Max server binaries. Here is a list of the different MySQL servers from which you can choose:

Binary	Description
mysqld	Compiled with full debugging and automatic memory allocation checking, symbolic links, and InnoDB and BDB tables.
mysqld-opt	Optimized binary. From version 4.0 on, InnoDB is enabled. Before 4.0, this server includes no transactional table support.
mysqld-nt	Optimized binary for Windows NT, 2000, and XP with support for named pipes.
mysqld-max	Optimized binary with support for symbolic links, and InnoDB and BDB tables.
mysqld-max-nt	Like mysqld-max, but compiled with support for named pipes.

All of the preceding binaries are optimized for modern Intel processors, but should work on any Intel i386-class or higher processor.

MySQL supports TCP/IP on all Windows platforms. The mysqld-nt and mysql-max-nt servers support named pipes on NT, 2000, and XP. However, the default is to use TCP/IP regardless of the platform. (Named pipes are slower than TCP/IP in many Windows configurations.) Named pipe use is subject to these conditions:

- Starting from MySQL 3.23.50, named pipes are enabled only if you start the server with the `--enable-named-pipe` option. It is now necessary to use this option explicitly because some users have experienced problems shutting down the MySQL server when named pipes were used.

- Named pipe connections are allowed only by the `mysqld-nt` or `mysqld-max-nt` servers, and only if the server is run on a version of Windows that supports named pipes (NT, 2000, XP).

- These servers can be run on Windows 98 or Me, but only if TCP/IP is installed; named pipe connections cannot be used.

- On Windows 95, these servers cannot be used.

Note: Most of the examples in the following sections use `mysqld` as the server name. If you choose to use a different server, such as `mysqld-opt`, make the appropriate substitutions in the commands that are shown in the examples. One good reason to choose a different server is that because `mysqld` contains full debugging support, it uses more memory and runs slower than the other Windows servers.

2.2.1.5 Starting the Server for the First Time

On Windows 95, 98, or Me, MySQL clients always connect to the server using TCP/IP. (This will allow any machine on your network to connect to your MySQL server.) Because of this, you must make sure that TCP/IP support is installed on your machine before starting MySQL. You can find TCP/IP on your Windows CD-ROM.

Note that if you are using an old Windows 95 release (for example, OSR2), it's likely that you have an old Winsock package; MySQL requires Winsock 2! You can get the newest Winsock from `http://www.microsoft.com/`. Windows 98 has the new Winsock 2 library, so it is unnecessary to update the library.

On NT-based systems such as Windows NT, 2000, or XP, clients have two options. They can use TCP/IP, or they can use a named pipe if the server supports named pipe connections.

For information about which server binary to run, see Section 2.2.1.4, "Selecting a Windows Server."

This section gives a general overview of starting the MySQL server. The following sections provide more specific information for particular versions of Windows.

The examples in these sections assume that MySQL is installed under the default location of `C:\mysql`. Adjust the pathnames shown in the examples if you have MySQL installed in a different location.

Testing is best done from a command prompt in a console window (a "DOS window"). This way you can have the server display status messages in the window where they are easy to see. If something is wrong with your configuration, these messages will make it easier for you to identify and fix any problems.

To start the server, enter this command:

```
C:\> C:\mysql\bin\mysqld --console
```

For servers that include InnoDB support, you should see the following messages as the server starts:

```
InnoDB: The first specified datafile c:\ibdata\ibdata1 did not exist:
InnoDB: a new database to be created!
InnoDB: Setting file c:\ibdata\ibdata1 size to 209715200
InnoDB: Database physically writes the file full: wait...
InnoDB: Log file c:\iblogs\ib_logfile0 did not exist: new to be created
InnoDB: Setting log file c:\iblogs\ib_logfile0 size to 31457280
InnoDB: Log file c:\iblogs\ib_logfile1 did not exist: new to be created
InnoDB: Setting log file c:\iblogs\ib_logfile1 size to 31457280
InnoDB: Log file c:\iblogs\ib_logfile2 did not exist: new to be created
InnoDB: Setting log file c:\iblogs\ib_logfile2 size to 31457280
InnoDB: Doublewrite buffer not found: creating new
InnoDB: Doublewrite buffer created
InnoDB: creating foreign key constraint system tables
InnoDB: foreign key constraint system tables created
011024 10:58:25  InnoDB: Started
```

When the server finishes its startup sequence, you should see something like this, which indicates that the server is ready to service client connections:

```
mysqld: ready for connections
Version: '4.0.14-log'  socket: ''  port: 3306
```

The server will continue to write to the console any further diagnostic output it produces. You can open a new console window in which to run client programs.

If you omit the --console option, the server writes diagnostic output to the error log in the data directory (C:\mysql\data by default). The error log is the file with the .err extension.

Note: The accounts that are listed in the MySQL grant tables initially have no passwords. After starting the server, you should set up passwords for them using the instructions in Section 2.4, "Post-Installation Setup and Testing."

2.2.1.6 Starting MySQL from the Windows Command Line

The MySQL server can be started manually from the command line. This can be done on any version of Windows.

To start the `mysqld` server from the command line, you should start a console window (a "DOS window") and enter this command:

```
C:\> C:\mysql\bin\mysqld
```

On non-NT versions of Windows, this will start `mysqld` in the background. That is, after the server starts, you should see another command prompt. If you start the server this way on Windows NT, 2000, or XP, the server will run in the foreground and no command prompt will appear until the server exits. Because of this, you should open another console window to run client programs while the server is running.

You can stop the MySQL server by executing this command:

```
C:\> C:\mysql\bin\mysqladmin -u root shutdown
```

This invokes the MySQL administrative utility `mysqladmin` to connect to the server and tell it to shut down. The command connects as `root`, which is the default administrative account in the MySQL grant system. Note that users in the MySQL grant system are wholly independent from any login users under Windows.

If `mysqld` doesn't start, check the error log to see whether the server wrote any messages there to indicate the cause of the problem. The error log is located in the `C:\mysql\data` directory. It is the file with a suffix of `.err`. You can also try to start the server as `mysqld --console`; in this case, you may get some useful information on the screen that may help solve the problem.

The last option is to start `mysqld` with `--standalone --debug`. In this case, `mysqld` will write a log file `C:\mysqld.trace` that should contain the reason why `mysqld` doesn't start.

Use `mysqld --help` to display all the options that `mysqld` understands!

2.2.1.7 Starting MySQL as a Windows Service

On the NT family (Windows NT, 2000, or XP), the recommended way to run MySQL is to install it as a Windows service. Then Windows starts and stops the MySQL server automatically when Windows starts and stops. A server installed as a service can also be controlled from the command line using `NET` commands, or with the graphical `Services` utility.

The `Services` utility (the Windows `Service Control Manager`) can be found in the Windows `Control Panel` (under `Administrative Tools` on Windows 2000 or XP). It is advisable to close the `Services` utility while performing server installation or removal operations from this command line. This prevents some odd errors.

To get MySQL to work with TCP/IP on Windows NT 4, you must install service pack 3 (or newer).

Before installing MySQL as a Windows service, you should first stop the current server if it is running by using the following command:

```
C:\> C:\mysql\bin\mysqladmin -u root shutdown
```

This invokes the MySQL administrative utility `mysqladmin` to connect to the server and tell it to shut down. The command connects as `root`, which is the default administrative account in the MySQL grant system. Note that users in the MySQL grant system are wholly independent from any login users under Windows.

Now install the server as a service:

```
C:\> mysqld --install
```

If you have problems installing `mysqld` as a service using just the server name, try installing it using its full pathname:

```
C:\> C:\mysql\bin\mysqld --install
```

As of MySQL 4.0.2, you can specify a specific service name after the `--install` option. As of MySQL 4.0.3, you can in addition specify a `--defaults-file` option after the service name to indicate where the server should obtain options when it starts. The rules that determine the service name and option files the server uses are as follows:

- If you specify no service name, the server uses the default service name of `MySQL` and the server reads options from the `[mysqld]` group in the standard option files.
- If you specify a service name after the `--install` option, the server ignores the `[mysqld]` option group and instead reads options from the group that has the same name as the service. The server reads options from the standard option files.
- If you specify a `--defaults-file` option after the service name, the server ignores the standard option files and reads options only from the `[mysqld]` group of the named file.

Note: Prior to MySQL 4.0.17, a server installed as a Windows service has problems starting if its pathname or the service name contains spaces. For this reason, avoid installing MySQL in a directory such as `C:\Program Files` or using a service name containing spaces.

In the unusual case that you install the server with `--install` but no service name, the server is installed with a service name of `MySQL`.

As a more complex example, consider the following command:

```
C:\> C:\mysql\bin\mysqld --install mysql--defaults-file=C:\my-opts.cnf
```

Here, a service name is given after the `--install` option. If no `--defaults-file` option had been given, this command would have the effect of causing the server to read the `[mysql]` group from the standard option files. (This would be a bad idea, because that option group is for use by the `mysql` client program.) However, because the `--defaults-file` option is present, the server reads options only from the named file, and only from the `[mysqld]` option group.

You can also specify options as "`Start parameters`" in the Windows `Services` utility before you start the MySQL service.

Once a MySQL server is installed as a service, Windows will start the service automatically whenever Windows starts. The service also can be started immediately from the `Services` utility, or by using the command `NET START MySQL`. The `NET` command is not case sensitive.

When run as a service, `mysqld` has no access to a console window, so no messages can be seen there. If `mysqld` doesn't start, check the error log to see whether the server wrote any messages there to indicate the cause of the problem. The error log is located in the `C:\mysql\data` directory. It is the file with a suffix of `.err`.

When `mysqld` is running as a service, it can be stopped by using the `Services` utility, the command `NET STOP MySQL`, or the command `mysqladmin shutdown`. If the service is running when Windows shuts down, Windows will stop the server automatically.

From MySQL 3.23.44 on, you have the choice of installing the server as a `Manual` service if you don't wish the service to be started automatically during the boot process. To do this, use the `--install-manual` option rather than the `--install` option:

```
C:\> C:\mysql\bin\mysqld --install-manual
```

To remove a server that is installed as a service, first stop it if it is running. Then use the `--remove` option to remove it:

```
C:\> C:\mysql\bin\mysqld --remove
```

For MySQL versions older than 3.23.49, one problem with automatic MySQL service shutdown is that Windows waited only for a few seconds for the shutdown to complete, then killed the database server process if the time limit was exceeded. This had the potential to cause problems. (For example, the `InnoDB` storage engine had to perform crash recovery at the next startup.) Starting from MySQL 3.23.49, Windows waits longer for the MySQL server shutdown to complete. If you notice this still is not enough for your installation, it is safest not to run the MySQL server as a service. Instead, start it from the command-line prompt, and stop it with `mysqladmin shutdown`.

This change to tell Windows to wait longer when stopping the MySQL server works for Windows 2000 and XP. It does not work for Windows NT, where Windows waits only 20 seconds for a service to shut down, and after that kills the service process. You can increase this default by opening the Registry Editor `\winnt\system32\regedt32.exe` and editing the value of `WaitToKillServiceTimeout` at `HKEY_LOCAL_MACHINE\SYSTEM\CurrentControlSet\Control` in the Registry tree. Specify the new larger value in milliseconds. For example, the value 120000 tells Windows NT to wait up to 120 seconds.

If you don't want to start `mysqld` as a service, you can start it from the command line. For instructions, see Section 2.2.1.6, "Starting MySQL from the Windows Command Line."

2.2.1.8 Running MySQL Client Programs on Windows

You can test whether the MySQL server is working by executing any of the following commands:

```
C:\> C:\mysql\bin\mysqlshow
C:\> C:\mysql\bin\mysqlshow -u root mysql
C:\> C:\mysql\bin\mysqladmin version status proc
C:\> C:\mysql\bin\mysql test
```

If `mysqld` is slow to respond to TCP/IP connections from client programs on Windows 9x/Me, there is probably a problem with your DNS. In this case, start `mysqld` with the `--skip-name-resolve` option and use only `localhost` and IP numbers in the `Host` column of the MySQL grant tables.

You can force a MySQL client to use a named pipe connection rather than TCP/IP by specifying the `--pipe` option or by specifying . (period) as the host name. Use the `--socket` option to specify the name of the pipe. As of MySQL 4.1, you should use the `--protocol=PIPE` option.

There are two versions of the MySQL command-line tool:

Binary	Description
mysql	Compiled on native Windows, offering limited text editing capabilities.
mysqlc	Compiled with the Cygnus GNU compiler and libraries, which offers `readline` editing.

If you want to use `mysqlc`, you must have a copy of the `cygwinb19.dll` library installed somewhere that `mysqlc` can find it. Current distributions of MySQL include this library in the same directory as `mysqlc` (the `bin` directory under the base directory of your MySQL installation). If your distribution does not have the `cygwinb19.dll` library in the `bin` directory, look for it in the `lib` directory and copy it to your Windows system directory (`\Windows\system` or a similar place).

2.2.1.9 MySQL on Windows Compared to MySQL on Unix

MySQL for Windows has by now proven itself to be very stable. The Windows version of MySQL has the same features as the corresponding Unix version, with the following exceptions:

- **Windows 95 and threads**

  Windows 95 leaks about 200 bytes of main memory for each thread creation. Each connection in MySQL creates a new thread, so you shouldn't run `mysqld` for an extended time on Windows 95 if your server handles many connections! Other versions of Windows don't suffer from this bug.

- **Limited number of ports**

  Windows systems have about 4,000 ports available for client connections, and after a connection on a port closes, it takes two to four minutes before the port can be reused. In situations where clients connect to and disconnect from the server at a high rate, it is possible for all available ports to be used up before closed ports become available again. If this happens, the MySQL server will appear to have become unresponsive even though it is running. Note that ports may be used by other applications running on the machine as well, in which case the number of ports available to MySQL is lower.

- **Concurrent reads**

  MySQL depends on the `pread()` and `pwrite()` calls to be able to mix `INSERT` and `SELECT`. Currently we use mutexes to emulate `pread()`/`pwrite()`. We will, in the long run, replace the file level interface with a virtual interface so that we can use the `readfile()`/`writefile()` interface on NT, 2000, and XP to get more speed. The current implementation limits the number of open files MySQL can use to 1,024, which means that you will not be able to run as many concurrent threads on NT, 2000, and XP as on Unix.

- **Blocking read**

  MySQL uses a blocking read for each connection, which has the following implications if named pipe connections are enabled:

  - A connection will not be disconnected automatically after eight hours, as happens with the Unix version of MySQL.

  - If a connection hangs, it's impossible to break it without killing MySQL.

  - `mysqladmin kill` will not work on a sleeping connection.

  - `mysqladmin shutdown` can't abort as long as there are sleeping connections.

  We plan to fix this problem when our Windows developers have figured out a nice workaround.

- **ALTER TABLE**

  While you are executing an `ALTER TABLE` statement, the table is locked from being used by other threads. This has to do with the fact that on Windows, you can't delete a file that is in use by another thread. In the future, we may find some way to work around this problem.

- **DROP TABLE**

  `DROP TABLE` on a table that is in use by a `MERGE` table will not work on Windows because the `MERGE` handler does the table mapping hidden from the upper layer of MySQL. Because Windows doesn't allow you to drop files that are open, you first must flush all `MERGE` tables (with `FLUSH TABLES`) or drop the `MERGE` table before dropping the table. We will fix this at the same time we introduce views.

- **DATA DIRECTORY and INDEX DIRECTORY**

  The `DATA DIRECTORY` and `INDEX DIRECTORY` options for `CREATE TABLE` are ignored on Windows, because Windows doesn't support symbolic links. These options also are ignored on systems that have a non-functional `realpath()` call.

- **DROP DATABASE**

  You cannot drop a database that is in use by some thread.

- **Killing MySQL from the Task Manager**

  You cannot kill MySQL from the Task Manager or with the shutdown utility in Windows 95. You must take it down with `mysqladmin shutdown`.

- **Case-insensitive names**

  Filenames are not case sensitive on Windows, so MySQL database and table names are also not case sensitive on Windows. The only restriction is that database and table names must be specified using the same case throughout a given statement.

- **The '\' pathname separator character**

  Pathname components in Windows 95 are separated by the '\' character, which is also the escape character in MySQL. If you are using `LOAD DATA INFILE` or `SELECT ... INTO OUTFILE`, use Unix-style filenames with '/' characters:

  ```
  mysql> LOAD DATA INFILE 'C:/tmp/skr.txt' INTO TABLE skr;
  mysql> SELECT * INTO OUTFILE 'C:/tmp/skr.txt' FROM skr;
  ```

  Alternatively, you must double the '\' character:

  ```
  mysql> LOAD DATA INFILE 'C:\\tmp\\skr.txt' INTO TABLE skr;
  mysql> SELECT * INTO OUTFILE 'C:\\tmp\\skr.txt' FROM skr;
  ```

- **Problems with pipes**

  Pipes do not work reliably from the Windows command-line prompt. If the pipe includes the character ^Z / `CHAR(24)`, Windows will think it has encountered end-of-file and abort the program.

  This is mainly a problem when you try to apply a binary log as follows:

  ```
  C:\> mysqlbinlog binary-log-name | mysql --user=root
  ```

  If you have a problem applying the log and suspect that it is because of a ^Z / `CHAR(24)` character, you can use the following workaround:

  ```
  C:\> mysqlbinlog binary-log-file --result-file=/tmp/bin.sql
  C:\> mysql --user=root --execute "source /tmp/bin.sql"
  ```

  The latter command also can be used to reliably read in any SQL file that may contain binary data.

- **Can't open named pipe error**

  If you use a MySQL 3.22 server on Windows NT with the newest MySQL client programs, you will get the following error:

  ```
  error 2017: can't open named pipe to host: . pipe...
  ```

  This happens because the release version of MySQL uses named pipes on NT by default. You can avoid this error by using the `--host=localhost` option to the new

MySQL clients or by creating an option file `C:\my.cnf` that contains the following information:

```
[client]
host = localhost
```

Starting from 3.23.50, named pipes are enabled only if `mysqld-nt` or `mysqld-max-nt` is started with `--enable-named-pipe`.

- **`Access denied for user` error**

  If you attempt to run a MySQL client program to connect to a server running on the same machine, but get the error `Access denied for user: 'some-user@unknown'` to database `'mysql'`, this means that MySQL cannot resolve your hostname properly.

  To fix this, you should create a file named `\windows\hosts` containing the following information:

  ```
  127.0.0.1       localhost
  ```

Here are some open issues for anyone who might want to help us improve MySQL on Windows:

- Add some nice start and shutdown icons to the MySQL installation.
- It would be really nice to be able to kill `mysqld` from the Task Manager in Windows 95. For the moment, you must use `mysqladmin shutdown`.
- Port `readline` to Windows for use in the `mysql` command-line tool.
- GUI versions of the standard MySQL clients (`mysql`, `mysqlshow`, `mysqladmin`, and `mysqldump`) would be nice.
- It would be nice if the socket read and write functions in `net.c` were interruptible. This would make it possible to kill open threads with `mysqladmin kill` on Windows.
- Add macros to use the faster thread-safe increment/decrement methods provided by Windows.

2.2.2 Installing MySQL on Linux

The recommended way to install MySQL on Linux is by using the RPM packages. The MySQL RPMs are currently built on a SuSE Linux 7.3 system, but should work on most versions of Linux that support `rpm` and use `glibc`. To obtain RPM packages, see Section 2.1.3, "How to Get MySQL."

Note: RPM distributions of MySQL often are provided by other vendors. Be aware that they may differ in features and capabilities from those built by MySQL AB, and that the instructions in this manual do not necessarily apply to installing them. The vendor's instructions should be consulted instead.

If you have problems with an RPM file (for example, if you receive the error "`Sorry, the host 'xxxx' could not be looked up`"), see Section 2.6.1.2, "Linux Binary Distribution Notes."

In most cases, you only need to install the MySQL-server and MySQL-client packages to get a functional MySQL installation. The other packages are not required for a standard installation. If you want to run a MySQL-Max server that has additional capabilities, you should also install the MySQL-Max RPM. However, you should do so only *after* installing the MySQL-server RPM. See Section 4.1.2, "The mysqld-max Extended MySQL Server."

If you get a dependency failure when trying to install the MySQL 4.0 packages (for example, "error: removing these packages would break dependencies: libmysqlclient.so.10 is needed by ..."), you should also install the package MySQL-shared-compat, which includes both the shared libraries for backward compatibility (libmysqlclient.so.12 for MySQL 4.0 and libmysqlclient.so.10 for MySQL 3.23).

Many Linux distributions still ship with MySQL 3.23 and they usually link applications dynamically to save disk space. If these shared libraries are in a separate package (for example, MySQL-shared), it is sufficient to simply leave this package installed and just upgrade the MySQL server and client packages (which are statically linked and do not depend on the shared libraries). For distributions that include the shared libraries in the same package as the MySQL server (for example, Red Hat Linux), you could either install our 3.23 MySQL-shared RPM, or use the MySQL-shared-compat package instead.

The following RPM packages are available:

- MySQL-server-*VERSION*.i386.rpm

  The MySQL server. You will need this unless you only want to connect to a MySQL server running on another machine. Note: Server RPM files were called MySQL-*VERSION*.i386.rpm before MySQL 4.0.10. That is, they did not have -server in the name.

- MySQL-Max-*VERSION*.i386.rpm

  The MySQL-Max server. This server has additional capabilities that the one provided in the MySQL-server RPM does not. You must install the MySQL-server RPM first, because the MySQL-Max RPM depends on it.

- MySQL-client-*VERSION*.i386.rpm

  The standard MySQL client programs. You probably always want to install this package.

- MySQL-bench-*VERSION*.i386.rpm

  Tests and benchmarks. Requires Perl and the DBD::mysql module.

- MySQL-devel-*VERSION*.i386.rpm

  The libraries and include files that are needed if you want to compile other MySQL clients, such as the Perl modules.

- MySQL-shared-*VERSION*.i386.rpm

  This package contains the shared libraries (libmysqlclient.so*) that certain languages and applications need to dynamically load and use MySQL.

- `MySQL-shared-compat-VERSION.i386.rpm`

  This package includes the shared libraries for both MySQL 3.23 and MySQL 4.0.
  Install this package instead of `MySQL-shared` if you have applications installed that are
  dynamically linked against MySQL 3.23 but you want to upgrade to MySQL 4.0 without breaking the library dependencies. This package has been available since MySQL
  4.0.13.

- `MySQL-embedded-VERSION.i386.rpm`

  The embedded MySQL server library (from MySQL 4.0).

- `MySQL-VERSION.src.rpm`

  This contains the source code for all of the previous packages. It can also be used to
  rebuild the RPMs on other architectures (for example, Alpha or SPARC).

To see all files in an RPM package (for example, a `MySQL-server` RPM), run:

```
shell> rpm -qpl MySQL-server-VERSION.i386.rpm
```

To perform a standard minimal installation, run:

```
shell> rpm -i MySQL-server-VERSION.i386.rpm
shell> rpm -i MySQL-client-VERSION.i386.rpm
```

To install just the client package, run:

```
shell> rpm -i MySQL-client-VERSION.i386.rpm
```

RPM provides a feature to verify the integrity and authenticity of packages before installing
them. If you would like to learn more about this feature, see Section 2.1.4, "Verifying
Package Integrity Using MD5 Checksums or `GnuPG`."

The server RPM places data under the `/var/lib/mysql` directory. The RPM also creates a
login account for a user named `mysql` (if one does not already exist) to use for running the
MySQL server, and creates the appropriate entries in `/etc/init.d/` to start the server automatically at boot time. (This means that if you have performed a previous installation and
have made changes to its startup script, you may want to make a copy of the script so that
you don't lose it when you install a newer RPM.) See Section 2.4.3, "Starting and Stopping
MySQL Automatically," for more information on how MySQL can be started automatically
on system startup.

If you want to install the MySQL RPM on older Linux distributions that do not support
initialization scripts in `/etc/init.d` (directly or via a symlink), you should create a symbolic
link that points to the location where your initialization scripts actually are installed. For
example, if that location is `/etc/rc.d/init.d`, use these commands before installing the
RPM to create `/etc/init.d` as a symbolic link that points there:

```
shell> cd /etc
shell> ln -s rc.d/init.d .
```

However, all current major Linux distributions should already support the new directory layout that uses /etc/init.d, because it is required for LSB (Linux Standard Base) compliance.

If the RPM files that you install include MySQL-server, the mysqld server should be up and running after installation. You should now be able to start using MySQL.

If something goes wrong, you can find more information in the binary installation section. See Section 2.2.5, "Installing MySQL on Other Unix-Like Systems."

Note: The accounts that are listed in the MySQL grant tables initially have no passwords. After starting the server, you should set up passwords for them using the instructions in Section 2.4, "Post-Installation Setup and Testing."

2.2.3 Installing MySQL on Mac OS X

Beginning with MySQL 4.0.11, you can install MySQL on Mac OS X 10.2 ("Jaguar") and up using a Mac OS X binary package in PKG format instead of the binary tarball distribution. Please note that older versions of Mac OS X (for example, 10.1.x) are not supported by this package.

The package is located inside a disk image (.dmg) file that you first need to mount by double-clicking its icon in the Finder. It should then mount the image and display its contents.

To obtain MySQL, see Section 2.1.3, "How to Get MySQL."

Note: Before proceeding with the installation, be sure to shut down all running MySQL server instances by either using the MySQL Manager Application (on Mac OS X Server) or via mysqladmin shutdown on the command line.

To actually install the MySQL PKG file, double-click on the package icon. This launches the Mac OS X Package Installer, which will guide you through the installation of MySQL.

Due to a bug in the Mac OS X package installer, you may see this error message in the destination disk selection dialog:

```
You cannot install this software on this disk. (null)
```

If this error occurs, simply click the Go Back button once to return to the previous screen. Then click Continue to advance to the destination disk selection again, and you should be able to choose the destination disk correctly. We have reported this bug to Apple and it is investigating this problem.

The Mac OS X PKG of MySQL will install itself into /usr/local/mysql-*VERSION* and will also install a symbolic link, /usr/local/mysql, pointing to the new location. If a directory named /usr/local/mysql already exists, it will be renamed to /usr/local/mysql.bak first. Additionally, the installer will create the grant tables in the mysql database by executing mysql_install_db after the installation.

The installation layout is similar to that of a `tar` file binary distribution; all MySQL binaries are located in the directory `/usr/local/mysql/bin`. The MySQL socket file is created as `/tmp/mysql.sock` by default. See Section 2.1.5, "Installation Layouts."

MySQL installation requires a Mac OS X user account named `mysql`. A user account with this name should exist by default on Mac OS X 10.2 and up.

If you are running Mac OS X Server, you already have a version of MySQL installed. The versions of MySQL that ship with Mac OS X Server versions are shown in the following table:

Mac OS X Server Version	MySQL Version
10.2-10.2.2	3.23.51
10.2.3-10.2.6	3.23.53
10.3	4.0.14
10.3.2	4.0.16

This manual section covers the installation of the official MySQL Mac OS X PKG only. Make sure to read Apple's help information about installing MySQL: Run the "Help View" application, select "Mac OS X Server" help, do a search for "MySQL," and read the item entitled "Installing MySQL."

For pre-installed versions of MySQL on Mac OS X Server, note especially that you should start `mysqld` with `safe_mysqld` instead of `mysqld_safe` if MySQL is older than version 4.0.

If you previously used Marc Liyanage's MySQL packages for Mac OS X from `http://www.entropy.ch`, you can simply follow the update instructions for packages using the binary installation layout as given on his pages.

If you are upgrading from Marc's 3.23.xx versions or from the Mac OS X Server version of MySQL to the official MySQL PKG, you also need to convert the existing MySQL privilege tables to the current format, because some new security privileges have been added. See Section 2.5.8, "Upgrading the Grant Tables."

If you would like to automatically start up MySQL during system startup, you also need to install the MySQL Startup Item. Starting with MySQL 4.0.15, it is part of the Mac OS X installation disk images as a separate installation package. Simply double-click the `MySQLStartupItem.pkg` icon and follow the instructions to install it.

Note that the Startup Item need be installed only once! There is no need to install it each time you upgrade the MySQL package later.

The Startup Item will be installed into `/Library/StartupItems/MySQLCOM`. (Before MySQL 4.1.2, the location was `/Library/StartupItems/MySQL`, but that collided with the MySQL Startup Item installed by Mac OS X Server.) Startup Item installation adds a variable `MYSQLCOM=-YES-` to the system configuration file `/etc/hostconfig`. If you would like to disable the automatic startup of MySQL, simply change this variable to `MYSQLCOM=-NO-`.

On Mac OS X Server, the default MySQL installation uses the variable MYSQL in the /etc/hostconfig file. The MySQL AB Startup Item installer disables this variable by setting it to MYSQL=-NO-. This avoids boot time conflicts with the MYSQLCOM variable used by the MySQL AB Startup Item. However, it does not shut down an already running MySQL server. You should do that yourself.

After the installation, you can start up MySQL by running the following commands in a terminal window. You must have administrator privileges to perform this task.

If you have installed the Startup Item:

```
shell> sudo /Library/StartupItems/MySQL/MySQL start
(Enter your password, if necessary)
(Press Control-D or enter "exit" to exit the shell)
```

If you don't use the Startup Item, enter the following command sequence:

```
shell> cd /usr/local/mysql
shell> sudo ./bin/mysqld_safe
(Enter your password, if necessary)
(Press Control-Z)
shell> bg
(Press Control-D or enter "exit" to exit the shell)
```

You should now be able to connect to the MySQL server, for example, by running /usr/local/mysql/bin/mysql.

Note: The accounts that are listed in the MySQL grant tables initially have no passwords. After starting the server, you should set up passwords for them using the instructions in Section 2.4, "Post-Installation Setup and Testing."

You might want to add aliases to your shell's resource file to make it easier to access commonly used programs such as mysql and mysqladmin from the command line. The syntax for tcsh is:

```
alias mysql /usr/local/mysql/bin/mysql
alias mysqladmin /usr/local/mysql/bin/mysqladmin
```

For bash, use:

```
alias mysql=/usr/local/mysql/bin/mysql
alias mysqladmin=/usr/local/mysql/bin/mysqladmin
```

Even better, add /usr/local/mysql/bin to your PATH environment variable. For example, add the following line to your $HOME/.tcshrc file if your shell is tcsh:

```
setenv PATH ${PATH}:/usr/local/mysql/bin
```

If no .tcshrc file exists in your home directory, create it with a text editor.

If you are upgrading an existing installation, please note that installing a new MySQL PKG does not remove the directory of an older installation. Unfortunately, the Mac OS X Installer does not yet offer the functionality required to properly upgrade previously installed packages.

To use your existing databases with the new installation, you'll need to copy the contents of the old data directory to the new data directory. Make sure that neither the old server nor the new one is running when you do this. After you have copied over the MySQL database files from the previous installation and have successfully started the new server, you should consider removing the old installation files to save disk space. Additionally, you should also remove older versions of the Package Receipt directories located in `/Library/Receipts/mysql-VERSION.pkg`.

2.2.4 Installing MySQL on NetWare

Porting MySQL to NetWare was an effort spearheaded by Novell. Novell customers will be pleased to note that NetWare 6.5 ships with bundled MySQL binaries, complete with an automatic commercial use license for all servers running that version of NetWare.

As of version 4.0.11, the MySQL server is available for Novell NetWare in binary package form. MySQL for NetWare is compiled using a combination of `Metrowerks CodeWarrior for NetWare` and special cross-compilation versions of the GNU autotools.

The binary package for NetWare can be obtained at `http://dev.mysql.com/downloads/`. See Section 2.1.3, "How to Get MySQL."

In order to host MySQL, the NetWare server must meet these requirements:

- NetWare version 6.5, or NetWare 6.0 with Support Pack 3 installed (you can obtain this at `http://support.novell.com/filefinder/13659/index.html`).
- The system must meet Novell's minimum requirements to run the respective version of NetWare.
- MySQL data, as well as the binaries themselves, must be installed on an NSS volume; traditional volumes are not supported.

To install MySQL for NetWare, use the following procedure:

1. If you are upgrading from a prior installation, stop the MySQL server. This is done from the server console, using the following command:

   SERVER: `mysqladmin -u root shutdown`

2. Log on to the target server from a client machine with access to the location where you will install MySQL.

3. Extract the binary package Zip file onto the server. Be sure to allow the paths in the Zip file to be used. It is safe to simply extract the file to SYS:\.

If you are upgrading from a prior installation, you may need to copy the data directory (for example, SYS:MYSQL\DATA) now, as well as my.cnf, if you have customized it. You can then delete the old copy of MySQL.

4. You might want to rename the directory to something more consistent and easy to use. We recommend using SYS:MYSQL; examples in this manual use this name to refer to the installation directory in general.

5. At the server console, add a search path for the directory containing the MySQL NLMs. For example:

```
SERVER:  SEARCH ADD SYS:MYSQL\BIN
```

6. Initialize the data directory and the grant tables, if needed, by executing mysql_install_db at the server console.

7. Start the MySQL server using mysqld_safe at the server console.

8. To finish the installation, you should also add the following commands to autoexec.ncf. For example, if your MySQL installation is in SYS:MYSQL and you want MySQL to start automatically, you could add these lines:

```
#Starts the MySQL 4.0.x database server
SEARCH ADD SYS:MYSQL\BIN
MYSQLD_SAFE
```

If you are running MySQL on NetWare 6.0, we strongly suggest that you use the --skip-external-locking option on the command line:

```
#Starts the MySQL 4.0.x database server
SEARCH ADD SYS:MYSQL\BIN
MYSQLD_SAFE --skip-external-locking
```

It will also be necessary to use CHECK TABLE and REPAIR TABLE instead of myisamchk, because myisamchk makes use of external locking. External locking is known to have problems on NetWare 6.0; the problem has been eliminated in NetWare 6.5.

mysqld_safe on NetWare provides a screen presence. When you unload (shut down) the mysqld_safe NLM, the screen does not by default go away. Instead, it prompts for user input:

```
*<NLM has terminated; Press any key to close the screen>*
```

If you want NetWare to close the screen automatically instead, use the --autoclose option to mysqld_safe. For example:

```
#Starts the MySQL 4.0.x database server
SEARCH ADD SYS:MYSQL\BIN
MYSQLD_SAFE --autoclose
```

The behavior of mysqld_safe on NetWare is described further in Section 4.1.3, "The mysqld_safe Server Startup Script."

If there was an existing installation of MySQL on the server, be sure to check for existing MySQL startup commands in `autoexec.ncf`, and edit or delete them as necessary.

Note: The accounts that are listed in the MySQL grant tables initially have no passwords. After starting the server, you should set up passwords for them using the instructions in Section 2.4, "Post-Installation Setup and Testing."

2.2.5 Installing MySQL on Other Unix-Like Systems

This section covers the installation of MySQL binary distributions that are provided for various platforms in the form of compressed tar files (files with a `.tar.gz` extension). See Section 2.1.2.5, "MySQL Binaries Compiled by MySQL AB," for a detailed list.

To obtain MySQL, see Section 2.1.3, "How to Get MySQL."

MySQL tar file binary distributions have names of the form `mysql-VERSION-OS.tar.gz`, where `VERSION` is a number (for example, `4.0.17`), and `OS` indicates the type of operating system for which the distribution is intended (for example, `pc-linux-gnu-i586`).

In addition to these generic packages, we also offer binaries in platform-specific package formats for selected platforms. See Section 2.2, "Standard MySQL Installation Using a Binary Distribution," for more information on how to install these.

You need the following tools to install a MySQL `tar` file binary distribution:

- GNU `gunzip` to uncompress the distribution.
- A reasonable `tar` to unpack the distribution. GNU `tar` is known to work. Some operating systems come with a pre-installed version of `tar` that is known to have problems. For example, Mac OS X `tar` and Sun `tar` are known to have problems with long filenames. On Mac OS X, you can use the pre-installed `gnutar` program. On other systems with a deficient `tar`, you should install GNU `tar` first.

If you run into problems, *please always use `mysqlbug`* when posting questions to a MySQL mailing list. Even if the problem isn't a bug, `mysqlbug` gathers system information that will help others solve your problem. By not using `mysqlbug`, you lessen the likelihood of getting a solution to your problem. You will find `mysqlbug` in the `bin` directory after you unpack the distribution. See Section 1.7.1.3, "How to Report Bugs or Problems."

The basic commands you must execute to install and use a MySQL binary distribution are:

```
shell> groupadd mysql
shell> useradd -g mysql mysql
shell> cd /usr/local
shell> gunzip < /path/to/mysql-VERSION-OS.tar.gz | tar xvf -
shell> ln -s full-path-to-mysql-VERSION-OS mysql
shell> cd mysql
shell> scripts/mysql_install_db --user=mysql
shell> chown -R root  .
```

```
shell> chown -R mysql data
shell> chgrp -R mysql .
shell> bin/mysqld_safe --user=mysql &
```

For versions of MySQL older than 4.0, substitute `bin/safe_mysqld` for `bin/mysqld_safe` in the final command.

Note: This procedure does not set up any passwords for MySQL accounts. After following the procedure, proceed to Section 2.4, "Post-Installation Setup and Testing."

A more detailed version of the preceding description for installing a binary distribution follows:

1. Add a login user and group for `mysqld` to run as:

   ```
   shell> groupadd mysql
   shell> useradd -g mysql mysql
   ```

   These commands add the `mysql` group and the `mysql` user. The syntax for `useradd` and `groupadd` may differ slightly on different versions of Unix. They may also be called `adduser` and `addgroup`.

   You might want to call the user and group something else instead of `mysql`. If so, substitute the appropriate name in the following steps.

2. Pick the directory under which you want to unpack the distribution, and change location into it. In the following example, we unpack the distribution under `/usr/local`. (The instructions, therefore, assume that you have permission to create files and directories in `/usr/local`. If that directory is protected, you will need to perform the installation as `root`.)

   ```
   shell> cd /usr/local
   ```

3. Obtain a distribution file from one of the sites listed in Section 2.1.3, "How to Get MySQL." For a given release, binary distributions for all platforms are built from the same MySQL source distribution.

4. Unpack the distribution, which will create the installation directory. Then create a symbolic link to that directory:

   ```
   shell> gunzip < /path/to/mysql-VERSION-OS.tar.gz | tar xvf -
   shell> ln -s full-path-to-mysql-VERSION-OS mysql
   ```

   The `tar` command creates a directory named `mysql-VERSION-OS`. The `ln` command makes a symbolic link to that directory. This lets you refer more easily to the installation directory as `/usr/local/mysql`.

   With GNU `tar`, no separate invocation of `gunzip` is necessary. You can replace the first line with the following alternative command to uncompress and extract the distribution:

   ```
   shell> tar zxvf /path/to/mysql-VERSION-OS.tar.gz
   ```

5. Change location into the installation directory:

   ```
   shell> cd mysql
   ```

   You will find several files and subdirectories in the `mysql` directory. The most important for installation purposes are the `bin` and `scripts` subdirectories.

   - `bin`

   This directory contains client programs and the server. You should add the full path-name of this directory to your `PATH` environment variable so that your shell finds the MySQL programs properly. See Appendix B, "Environment Variables."

   - `scripts`

   This directory contains the `mysql_install_db` script used to initialize the `mysql` database containing the grant tables that store the server access permissions.

6. If you haven't installed MySQL before, you must create the MySQL grant tables:

   ```
   shell> scripts/mysql_install_db --user=mysql
   ```

   If you run the command as root, you should use the --user option as shown. The value of the option should be the name of the login account that you created in the first step to use for running the server. If you run the command while logged in as that user, you can omit the --user option.

   Note that for MySQL versions older than 3.22.10, `mysql_install_db` left the server running after creating the grant tables. This is no longer true; you will need to restart the server after performing the remaining steps in this procedure.

7. Change the ownership of program binaries to `root` and ownership of the data directory to the user that you will run `mysqld` as. Assuming that you are located in the installation directory (`/usr/local/mysql`), the commands look like this:

   ```
   shell> chown -R root  .
   shell> chown -R mysql data
   shell> chgrp -R mysql .
   ```

   The first command changes the owner attribute of the files to the `root` user. The second changes the owner attribute of the data directory to the `mysql` user. The third changes the group attribute to the `mysql` group.

8. If you would like MySQL to start automatically when you boot your machine, you can copy `support-files/mysql.server` to the location where your system has its startup files. More information can be found in the `support-files/mysql.server` script itself and in Section 2.4.3, "Starting and Stopping MySQL Automatically."

9. You can set up new accounts using the `bin/mysql_setpermission` script if you install the `DBI` and `DBD::mysql` Perl modules. For instructions, see Section 2.7, "Perl Installation Notes."

10. If you would like to use `mysqlaccess` and have the MySQL distribution in some non-standard place, you must change the location where `mysqlaccess` expects to find the

mysql client. Edit the `bin/mysqlaccess` script at approximately line 18. Search for a line that looks like this:

```
$MYSQL     = '/usr/local/bin/mysql';     # path to mysql executable
```

Change the path to reflect the location where `mysql` actually is stored on your system. If you do not do this, you will get a `Broken pipe` error when you run `mysqlaccess`.

After everything has been unpacked and installed, you should test your distribution.

You can start the MySQL server with the following command:

```
shell> bin/mysqld_safe --user=mysql &
```

For versions of MySQL older than 4.0, substitute `bin/safe_mysqld` for `bin/mysqld_safe` in the command.

More information about `mysqld_safe` is given in Section 4.1.3, "The `mysqld_safe` Server Startup Script."

Note: The accounts that are listed in the MySQL grant tables initially have no passwords. After starting the server, you should set up passwords for them using the instructions in Section 2.4, "Post-Installation Setup and Testing."

2.3 MySQL Installation Using a Source Distribution

Before you proceed with the source installation, check first to see whether our binary is available for your platform and whether it will work for you. We put a lot of effort into making sure that our binaries are built with the best possible options.

To obtain a source distribution for MySQL, see Section 2.1.3, "How to Get MySQL."

MySQL source distributions are provided as compressed `tar` archives and have names like `mysql-VERSION.tar.gz`, where `VERSION` is a number like `5.0.0-alpha`.

You need the following tools to build and install MySQL from source:

- GNU `gunzip` to uncompress the distribution.
- A reasonable `tar` to unpack the distribution. GNU `tar` is known to work. Some operating systems come with a pre-installed version of `tar` that is known to have problems. For example, Mac OS X `tar` and Sun `tar` are known to have problems with long filenames. On Mac OS X, you can use the pre-installed `gnutar` program. On other systems with a deficient `tar`, you should install GNU `tar` first.
- A working ANSI C++ compiler. `gcc` 2.95.2 or later, `egcs` 1.0.2 or later or `egcs` `2.91.66`, SGI C++, and SunPro C++ are some of the compilers that are known to work. `libg++` is not needed when using `gcc`. `gcc` 2.7.x has a bug that makes it impossible to compile some perfectly legal C++ files, such as `sql/sql_base.cc`. If you have only `gcc` 2.7.x, you

must upgrade your gcc to be able to compile MySQL. gcc 2.8.1 is also known to have problems on some platforms, so it should be avoided if a new compiler exists for the platform.

gcc 2.95.2 or later is recommended when compiling MySQL 3.23.x.

- A good make program. GNU make is always recommended and is sometimes required. If you have problems, we recommend trying GNU make 3.75 or newer.

If you are using a version of gcc recent enough to understand the -fno-exceptions option, it is *very important* that you use this option. Otherwise, you may compile a binary that crashes randomly. We also recommend that you use -felide-constructors and -fno-rtti along with -fno-exceptions. When in doubt, do the following:

```
CFLAGS="-O3" CXX=gcc CXXFLAGS="-O3 -felide-constructors \
       -fno-exceptions -fno-rtti" ./configure \
       --prefix=/usr/local/mysql --enable-assembler \
       --with-mysqld-ldflags=-all-static
```

On most systems, this will give you a fast and stable binary.

If you run into problems, *please always use mysqlbug* when posting questions to a MySQL mailing list. Even if the problem isn't a bug, mysqlbug gathers system information that will help others solve your problem. By not using mysqlbug, you lessen the likelihood of getting a solution to your problem. You will find mysqlbug in the scripts directory after you unpack the distribution. See Section 1.7.1.3, "How to Report Bugs or Problems."

2.3.1 Source Installation Overview

The basic commands you must execute to install a MySQL source distribution are:

```
shell> groupadd mysql
shell> useradd -g mysql mysql
shell> gunzip < mysql-VERSION.tar.gz | tar -xvf -
shell> cd mysql-VERSION
shell> ./configure --prefix=/usr/local/mysql
shell> make
shell> make install
shell> cp support-files/my-medium.cnf /etc/my.cnf
shell> cd /usr/local/mysql
shell> bin/mysql_install_db --user=mysql
shell> chown -R root  .
shell> chown -R mysql var
shell> chgrp -R mysql .
shell> bin/mysqld_safe --user=mysql &
```

For versions of MySQL older than 4.0, substitute bin/safe_mysqld for bin/mysqld_safe in the final command.

If you start from a source RPM, do the following:

```
shell> rpm --rebuild --clean MySQL-VERSION.src.rpm
```

This will make a binary RPM that you can install.

Note: This procedure does not set up any passwords for MySQL accounts. After following the procedure, proceed to Section 2.4, "Post-Installation Setup and Testing," for post-installation setup and testing.

A more detailed version of the preceding description for installing MySQL from a source distribution follows:

1. Add a login user and group for mysqld to run as:
   ```
   shell> groupadd mysql
   shell> useradd -g mysql mysql
   ```

   These commands add the mysql group and the mysql user. The syntax for useradd and groupadd may differ slightly on different versions of Unix. They may also be called adduser and addgroup.

   You might want to call the user and group something else instead of mysql. If so, substitute the appropriate name in the following steps.

2. Pick the directory under which you want to unpack the distribution, and change location into it.

3. Obtain a distribution file from one of the sites listed in Section 2.1.3, "How to Get MySQL."

4. Unpack the distribution into the current directory:
   ```
   shell> gunzip < /path/to/mysql-VERSION.tar.gz | tar xvf -
   ```

   This command creates a directory named mysql-VERSION.

   With GNU tar, no separate invocation of gunzip is necessary. You can use the following alternative command to uncompress and extract the distribution:
   ```
   shell> tar zxvf /path/to/mysql-VERSION-OS.tar.gz
   ```

5. Change location into the top-level directory of the unpacked distribution:
   ```
   shell> cd mysql-VERSION
   ```

   Note that currently you must configure and build MySQL from this top-level directory. You cannot build it in a different directory.

6. Configure the release and compile everything:
   ```
   shell> ./configure --prefix=/usr/local/mysql
   shell> make
   ```

   When you run configure, you might want to specify some options. Run ./configure --help for a list of options. Section 2.3.2, "Typical configure Options," discusses some of the more useful options.

If `configure` fails and you are going to send mail to a MySQL mailing list to ask for assistance, please include any lines from `config.log` that you think can help solve the problem. Also include the last couple of lines of output from `configure`. Post the bug report using the `mysqlbug` script. See Section 1.7.1.3, "How to Report Bugs or Problems."

If the compile fails, see Section 2.3.4, "Dealing with Problems Compiling MySQL," for help.

7. Install the distribution:

```
shell> make install
```

If you want to set up an option file, use one of those present in the `support-files` directory as a template. For example:

```
shell> cp support-files/my-medium.cnf /etc/my.cnf
```

You might need to run these commands as `root`.

If you want to configure support for `InnoDB` tables, you should edit the `/etc/my.cnf` file, remove the `#` character before the option lines that start with `innodb_...`, and modify the option values to be what you want. See Section 3.3.2, "Using Option Files," and Section 9.4, "`InnoDB` Configuration."

8. Change location into the installation directory:

```
shell> cd /usr/local/mysql
```

9. If you haven't installed MySQL before, you must create the MySQL grant tables:

```
shell> bin/mysql_install_db --user=mysql
```

If you run the command as root, you should use the --user option as shown. The value of the option should be the name of the login account that you created in the first step to use for running the server. If you run the command while logged in as that user, you can omit the --user option.

Note that for MySQL versions older than 3.22.10, `mysql_install_db` left the server running after creating the grant tables. This is no longer true; you will need to restart the server after performing the remaining steps in this procedure.

10. Change the ownership program binaries to `root` and ownership of the data directory to the user that you will run `mysqld` as. Assuming that you are located in the installation directory (`/usr/local/mysql`), the commands look like this:

```
shell> chown -R root   .
shell> chown -R mysql var
shell> chgrp -R mysql .
```

The first command changes the owner attribute of the files to the `root` user. The second changes the owner attribute of the data directory to the `mysql` user. The third changes the group attribute to the `mysql` group.

11. If you would like MySQL to start automatically when you boot your machine, you can copy `support-files/mysql.server` to the location where your system has its startup files. More information can be found in the `support-files/mysql.server` script itself and in Section 2.4.3, "Starting and Stopping MySQL Automatically."

12. You can set up new accounts using the `bin/mysql_setpermission` script if you install the `DBI` and `DBD::mysql` Perl modules. For instructions, see Section 2.7, "Perl Installation Notes."

After everything has been installed, you should initialize and test your distribution using this command:

```
shell> /usr/local/mysql/bin/mysqld_safe --user=mysql &
```

For versions of MySQL older than 4.0, substitute `safe_mysqld` for `mysqld_safe` in the command.

If that command fails immediately and prints `mysqld ended`, you can find some information in the file *host_name*.err in the data directory.

More information about `mysqld_safe` is given in Section 4.1.3, "The `mysqld_safe` Server Startup Script."

Note: The accounts that are listed in the MySQL grant tables initially have no passwords. After starting the server, you should set up passwords for them using the instructions in Section 2.4, "Post-Installation Setup and Testing."

2.3.2 Typical `configure` Options

The `configure` script gives you a great deal of control over how you configure a MySQL source distribution. Typically you do this using options on the `configure` command line. You can also affect `configure` using certain environment variables. See Appendix B, "Environment Variables." For a list of options supported by `configure`, run this command:

```
shell> ./configure --help
```

Some of the more commonly used `configure` options are described here:

- To compile just the MySQL client libraries and client programs and not the server, use the `--without-server` option:

```
shell> ./configure --without-server
```

If you don't have a C++ compiler, mysql will not compile (it is the one client program that requires C++). In this case, you can remove the code in `configure` that tests for the C++ compiler and then run `./configure` with the `--without-server` option. The compile step will still try to build mysql, but you can ignore any warnings about `mysql.cc`. (If make stops, try make `-k` to tell it to continue with the rest of the build even if errors occur.)

- If you want to build the embedded MySQL library (`libmysqld.a`) you should use the `--with-embedded-server` option.

- If you don't want your log files and database directories located under `/usr/local/var`, use a `configure` command something like one of these:

```
shell> ./configure --prefix=/usr/local/mysql
shell> ./configure --prefix=/usr/local \
         --localstatedir=/usr/local/mysql/data
```

The first command changes the installation prefix so that everything is installed under `/usr/local/mysql` rather than the default of `/usr/local`. The second command preserves the default installation prefix, but overrides the default location for database directories (normally `/usr/local/var`) and changes it to `/usr/local/mysql/data`. After you have compiled MySQL, you can change these options with option files. See Section 3.3.2, "Using Option Files."

- If you are using Unix and you want the MySQL socket located somewhere other than the default location (normally in the directory `/tmp` or `/var/run`), use a `configure` command like this:

```
shell> ./configure \
         --with-unix-socket-path=/usr/local/mysql/tmp/mysql.sock
```

The socket filename must be an absolute pathname. You can also change the location of `mysql.sock` later by using a MySQL option file. See Section A.4.5, "How to Protect or Change the MySQL Socket File `/tmp/mysql.sock`."

- If you want to compile statically linked programs (for example, to make a binary distribution, to get more speed, or to work around problems with some Red Hat Linux distributions), run `configure` like this:

```
shell> ./configure --with-client-ldflags=-all-static \
         --with-mysqld-ldflags=-all-static
```

- If you are using gcc and don't have `libg++` or `libstdc++` installed, you can tell `configure` to use gcc as your C++ compiler:

```
shell> CC=gcc CXX=gcc ./configure
```

When you use gcc as your C++ compiler, it will not attempt to link in `libg++` or `libstdc++`. This may be a good idea to do even if you have these libraries installed, because some versions of them have caused strange problems for MySQL users in the past.

The following list indicates some compilers and environment variable settings that are commonly used with each one.

- gcc 2.7.2:

```
CC=gcc CXX=gcc CXXFLAGS="-O3 -felide-constructors"
```

- egcs 1.0.3a:

```
CC=gcc CXX=gcc CXXFLAGS="-O3 -felide-constructors \
-fno-exceptions -fno-rtti"
```

- gcc 2.95.2:

```
CFLAGS="-O3 -mpentiumpro" CXX=gcc CXXFLAGS="-O3 -mpentiumpro \
-felide-constructors -fno-exceptions -fno-rtti"
```

- pgcc 2.90.29 or newer:

```
CFLAGS="-O3 -mpentiumpro -mstack-align-double" CXX=gcc \
CXXFLAGS="-O3 -mpentiumpro -mstack-align-double \
-felide-constructors -fno-exceptions -fno-rtti"
```

In most cases, you can get a reasonably optimized MySQL binary by using the options from the preceding list and adding the following options to the `configure` line:

```
--prefix=/usr/local/mysql --enable-assembler \
--with-mysqld-ldflags=-all-static
```

The full `configure` line would, in other words, be something like the following for all recent `gcc` versions:

```
CFLAGS="-O3 -mpentiumpro" CXX=gcc CXXFLAGS="-O3 -mpentiumpro \
-felide-constructors -fno-exceptions -fno-rtti" ./configure \
--prefix=/usr/local/mysql --enable-assembler \
--with-mysqld-ldflags=-all-static
```

The binaries we provide on the MySQL Web site at `http://www.mysql.com/` are all compiled with full optimization and should be perfect for most users. See Section 2.1.2.5, "MySQL Binaries Compiled by MySQL AB." There are some configuration settings you can tweak to make an even faster binary, but these are only for advanced users. See Section 6.5.3, "How Compiling and Linking Affects the Speed of MySQL."

If the build fails and produces errors about your compiler or linker not being able to create the shared library `libmysqlclient.so.#` (where '#' is a version number), you can work around this problem by giving the `--disable-shared` option to `configure`. In this case, `configure` will not build a shared `libmysqlclient.so.#` library.

- You can configure MySQL not to use DEFAULT column values for non-NULL columns (that is, columns that are not allowed to be NULL). See Section 1.8.6.2, "Constraint NOT NULL and DEFAULT Values."

```
shell> CXXFLAGS=-DDONT_USE_DEFAULT_FIELDS ./configure
```

The effect of this flag is to cause any INSERT statement to fail unless it includes explicit values for all columns that require a non-NULL value.

- By default, MySQL uses the latin1 (ISO-8859-1) character set. To change the default set, use the --with-charset option:

```
shell> ./configure --with-charset=charset
```

charset may be one of big5, cp1251, cp1257, czech, danish, dec8, dos, euc_kr, gb2312, gbk, german1, hebrew, hp8, hungarian, koi8_ru, koi8_ukr, latin1, latin2, sjis, swe7, tis620, ujis, usa7, or win1251ukr. See Section 4.7.1, "The Character Set Used for Data and Sorting."

As of MySQL 4.1.1, the default collation may also be specified. MySQL uses the latin1_swedish_ci collation. To change this, use the --with-collation option:

```
shell> ./configure --with-collation=collation
```

To change both the character set and the collation, use both the --with-charset and --with-collation options. The collation must be a legal collation for the character set. (Use the SHOW COLLATION statement to determine which collations are available for each character set.)

If you want to convert characters between the server and the client, you should take a look at the SET CHARACTER SET statement. This is discussed in the *MySQL Language Reference*.

Warning: If you change character sets after having created any tables, you will have to run myisamchk -r -q --set-character-set=*charset* on every table. Your indexes may be sorted incorrectly otherwise. (This can happen if you install MySQL, create some tables, then reconfigure MySQL to use a different character set and reinstall it.)

With the configure option --with-extra-charsets=*LIST*, you can define which additional character sets should be compiled into the server. *LIST* is either a list of character set names separated by spaces, complex to include all character sets that can't be dynamically loaded, or all to include all character sets into the binaries.

- To configure MySQL with debugging code, use the --with-debug option:

```
shell> ./configure --with-debug
```

This causes a safe memory allocator to be included that can find some errors and that provides output about what is happening.

- If your client programs are using threads, you also must compile a thread-safe version of the MySQL client library with the --enable-thread-safe-client configure option. This will create a libmysqlclient_r library with which you should link your threaded applications.

- Options that pertain to particular systems can be found in the system-specific section of this manual. See Section 2.6, "Operating System–Specific Notes."

2.3.3 Installing from the Development Source Tree

Caution: You should read this section only if you are interested in helping us test our new code. If you just want to get MySQL up and running on your system, you should use a standard release distribution (either a binary or source distribution will do).

To obtain our most recent development source tree, use these instructions:

1. Download BitKeeper from `http://www.bitmover.com/cgi-bin/download.cgi`. You will need `Bitkeeper 3.0` or newer to access our repository.

2. Follow the instructions to install it.

3. After BitKeeper has been installed, first go to the directory you want to work from, and then use one of the following commands to clone the MySQL version branch of your choice:

   To clone the old 3.23 branch, use this command:

   ```
   shell> bk clone bk://mysql.bkbits.net/mysql-3.23 mysql-3.23
   ```

   To clone the 4.0 stable (production) branch, use this command:

   ```
   shell> bk clone bk://mysql.bkbits.net/mysql-4.0 mysql-4.0
   ```

   To clone the 4.1 beta branch, use this command:

   ```
   shell> bk clone bk://mysql.bkbits.net/mysql-4.1 mysql-4.1
   ```

   To clone the 5.0 development branch, use this command:

   ```
   shell> bk clone bk://mysql.bkbits.net/mysql-5.0 mysql-5.0
   ```

   In the preceding examples, the source tree will be set up in the `mysql-3.23/`, `mysql-4.0/`, `mysql-4.1/`, or `mysql-5.0/` subdirectory of your current directory.

   If you are behind a firewall and can only initiate HTTP connections, you can also use BitKeeper via HTTP.

   If you are required to use a proxy server, set the environment variable `http_proxy` to point to your proxy:

   ```
   shell> export http_proxy="http://your.proxy.server:8080/"
   ```

   Now, simply replace the `bk://` with `http://` when doing a clone. Example:

   ```
   shell> bk clone http://mysql.bkbits.net/mysql-4.1 mysql-4.1
   ```

   The initial download of the source tree may take a while, depending on the speed of your connection. Please be patient.

4. You will need GNU `make`, `autoconf` 2.53 (or newer), `automake` 1.5, `libtool` 1.4, and `m4` to run the next set of commands. Even though many operating systems already come with their own implementation of `make`, chances are high that the compilation will fail with strange error messages. Therefore, it is highly recommended that you use GNU `make` (sometimes named `gmake`) instead.

   Fortunately, a large number of operating systems already ship with the GNU toolchain preinstalled or supply installable packages of these. In any case, they can also be downloaded from the following locations:

   - `http://www.gnu.org/software/autoconf/`
   - `http://www.gnu.org/software/automake/`

- http://www.gnu.org/software/libtool/

- http://www.gnu.org/software/m4/

- http://www.gnu.org/software/make/

If you are trying to configure MySQL 4.1 or later, you will also need GNU `bison` 1.75 or later. Older versions of `bison` may report this error:

```
sql_yacc.yy:#####: fatal error: maximum table size (32767) exceeded
```

Note: The maximum table size is not actually exceeded: the error is caused by bugs in older versions of `bison`.

Versions of MySQL before version 4.1 may also compile with other yacc implementations (for example, BSD yacc 91.7.30). For later versions, GNU `bison` is required.

The following example shows the typical commands required to configure a source tree. The first `cd` command changes location into the top-level directory of the tree; replace `mysql-4.0` with the appropriate directory name.

```
shell> cd mysql-4.0
shell> bk -r edit
shell> aclocal; autoheader; autoconf; automake
shell> (cd innobase; aclocal; autoheader; autoconf; automake)
shell> (cd bdb/dist; sh s_all)
shell> ./configure  # Add your favorite options here
make
```

The command lines that change directory into the `innobase` and `bdb/dist` directories are used to configure the `InnoDB` and Berkeley DB (`BDB`) storage engines. You can omit these command lines if you do not require `InnoDB` or `BDB` support.

If you get some strange errors during this stage, verify that you really have `libtool` installed.

A collection of our standard configuration scripts is located in the `BUILD/` subdirectory. You may find it more convenient to use the `BUILD/compile-pentium-debug` script than the preceding set of shell commands. To compile on a different architecture, modify the script by removing flags that are Pentium-specific.

5. When the build is done, run `make install`. Be careful with this on a production machine; the command may overwrite your live release installation. If you have another installation of MySQL, we recommend that you run `./configure` with different values for the `--prefix`, `--with-tcp-port`, and `--unix-socket-path` options than those used for your production server.

6. Play hard with your new installation and try to make the new features crash. Start by running `make test`.

7. If you have gotten to the `make` stage and the distribution does not compile, please report it in our bugs database at `http://bugs.mysql.com/`. If you have installed the latest versions of the required GNU tools, and they crash trying to process our configuration

files, please report that also. However, if you execute aclocal and get a command not found error or a similar problem, do not report it. Instead, make sure that all the necessary tools are installed and that your PATH variable is set correctly so that your shell can find them.

8. After the initial bk clone operation to obtain the source tree, you should run bk pull periodically to get updates.

9. You can examine the change history for the tree with all the diffs by using bk revtool. If you see some funny diffs or code that you have a question about, do not hesitate to send email to the MySQL internals mailing list. See Section 1.7.1.1, "The MySQL Mailing Lists." Also, if you think you have a better idea on how to do something, send an email message to the same address with a patch. bk diffs will produce a patch for you after you have made changes to the source. If you do not have the time to code your idea, just send a description.

10. BitKeeper has a nice help utility that you can access via bk helptool.

11. Please note that any commits (made via bk ci or bk citool) will trigger the posting of a message with the changeset to our internals mailing list, as well as the usual openlogging.org submission with just the changeset comments. Generally, you wouldn't need to use commit (since the public tree will not allow bk push), but rather use the bk diffs method described previously.

You can also browse changesets, comments, and source code online. For example, to browse this information for MySQL 4.1, go to http://mysql.bkbits.net:8080/mysql-4.1.

The manual is in a separate tree that can be cloned with:

```
shell> bk clone bk://mysql.bkbits.net/mysqldoc mysqldoc
```

There are also public BitKeeper trees for MySQL Control Center and Connector/ODBC. They can be cloned respectively as follows.

To clone MySQL Control center, use this command:

```
shell> bk clone http://mysql.bkbits.net/mysqlcc mysqlcc
```

To clone Connector/ODBC, use this command:

```
shell> bk clone http://mysql.bkbits.net/myodbc3 myodbc3
```

2.3.4 Dealing with Problems Compiling MySQL

All MySQL programs compile cleanly for us with no warnings on Solaris or Linux using gcc. On other systems, warnings may occur due to differences in system include files. See Section 2.3.5, "MIT-pthreads Notes" for warnings that may occur when using MIT-pthreads. For other problems, check the following list.

The solution to many problems involves reconfiguring. If you do need to reconfigure, take note of the following:

- If `configure` is run after it already has been run, it may use information that was gathered during its previous invocation. This information is stored in `config.cache`. When `configure` starts up, it looks for that file and reads its contents if it exists, on the assumption that the information is still correct. That assumption is invalid when you reconfigure.

- Each time you run `configure`, you must run `make` again to recompile. However, you may want to remove old object files from previous builds first because they were compiled using different configuration options.

To prevent old configuration information or object files from being used, run these commands before re-running `configure`:

```
shell> rm config.cache
shell> make clean
```

Alternatively, you can run `make distclean`.

The following list describes some of the problems when compiling MySQL that have been found to occur most often:

- If you get errors such as the ones shown here when compiling `sql_yacc.cc`, you probably have run out of memory or swap space:

```
Internal compiler error: program cc1plus got fatal signal 11
Out of virtual memory
Virtual memory exhausted
```

   The problem is that `gcc` requires a huge amount of memory to compile `sql_yacc.cc` with inline functions. Try running `configure` with the `--with-low-memory` option:

```
shell> ./configure --with-low-memory
```

   This option causes `-fno-inline` to be added to the compile line if you are using `gcc` and `-O0` if you are using something else. You should try the `--with-low-memory` option even if you have so much memory and swap space that you think you can't possibly have run out. This problem has been observed to occur even on systems with generous hardware configurations and the `--with-low-memory` option usually fixes it.

- By default, `configure` picks `c++` as the compiler name and GNU `c++` links with `-lg++`. If you are using `gcc`, that behavior can cause problems during configuration such as this:

```
configure: error: installation or configuration problem:
C++ compiler cannot create executables.
```

   You might also observe problems during compilation related to `g++`, `libg++`, or `libstdc++`.

One cause of these problems is that you may not have g++, or you may have g++ but not libg++, or libstdc++. Take a look at the config.log file. It should contain the exact reason why your C++ compiler didn't work. To work around these problems, you can use gcc as your C++ compiler. Try setting the environment variable CXX to "gcc -03". For example:

```
shell> CXX="gcc -03" ./configure
```

This works because gcc compiles C++ sources as well as g++ does, but does not link in libg++ or libstdc++ by default.

Another way to fix these problems is to install g++, libg++, and libstdc++. We would, however, like to recommend that you not use libg++ or libstdc++ with MySQL because this will only increase the binary size of mysqld without giving you any benefits. Some versions of these libraries have also caused strange problems for MySQL users in the past.

Using gcc as the C++ compiler is also required if you want to compile MySQL with RAID functionality and you are using GNU gcc version 3 and above. If you get errors like those following during the linking stage when you configure MySQL to compile with the option --with-raid, try to use gcc as your C++ compiler by defining the CXX environment variable:

```
gcc -03 -DDBUG_OFF -rdynamic -o isamchk isamchk.o sort.o  libnisam.a
../mysys/libmysys.a ../dbug/libdbug.a ../strings/libmystrings.a
 -lpthread -lz -lcrypt -lnsl -lm -lpthread
../mysys/libmysys.a(raid.o)(.text+0x79): In function
`my_raid_create':: undefined reference to `operator new(unsigned)'
../mysys/libmysys.a(raid.o)(.text+0xdd): In function
`my_raid_create':: undefined reference to `operator delete(void*)'
../mysys/libmysys.a(raid.o)(.text+0x129): In function
`my_raid_open':: undefined reference to `operator new(unsigned)'
../mysys/libmysys.a(raid.o)(.text+0x189): In function
`my_raid_open':: undefined reference to `operator delete(void*)'
../mysys/libmysys.a(raid.o)(.text+0x64b): In function
`my_raid_close':: undefined reference to `operator delete(void*)'
collect2: ld returned 1 exit status
```

- If your compile fails with errors such as any of the following, you must upgrade your version of make to GNU make:

```
making all in mit-pthreads
make: Fatal error in reader: Makefile, line 18:
Badly formed macro assignment
```

Or:

```
make: file `Makefile' line 18: Must be a separator (:
```

Or:

```
pthread.h: No such file or directory
```

Solaris and FreeBSD are known to have troublesome `make` programs.
GNU `make` Version 3.75 is known to work.

- If you want to define flags to be used by your C or C++ compilers, do so by adding the flags to the `CFLAGS` and `CXXFLAGS` environment variables. You can also specify the compiler names this way using `CC` and `CXX`. For example:

```
shell> CC=gcc
shell> CFLAGS=-O3
shell> CXX=gcc
shell> CXXFLAGS=-O3
shell> export CC CFLAGS CXX CXXFLAGS
```

See Section 2.1.2.5, "MySQL Binaries Compiled by MySQL AB," for a list of flag definitions that have been found to be useful on various systems.

- If you get an error message like this, you need to upgrade your `gcc` compiler:

```
client/libmysql.c:273: parse error before `__attribute__'
```

gcc 2.8.1 is known to work, but we recommend using gcc 2.95.2 or egcs 1.0.3a instead.

- If you get errors such as those shown here when compiling `mysqld`, `configure` didn't correctly detect the type of the last argument to `accept()`, `getsockname()`, or `getpeername()`:

```
cxx: Error: mysqld.cc, line 645: In this statement, the referenced
    type of the pointer value ''length'' is ''unsigned long'',
    which is not compatible with ''int''.
new_sock = accept(sock, (struct sockaddr *)&cAddr, &length);
```

To fix this, edit the `config.h` file (which is generated by `configure`). Look for these lines:

```
/* Define as the base type of the last arg to accept */
#define SOCKET_SIZE_TYPE XXX
```

Change *XXX* to `size_t` or `int`, depending on your operating system. (Note that you will have to do this each time you run `configure` because `configure` regenerates `config.h`.)

- The `sql_yacc.cc` file is generated from `sql_yacc.yy`. Normally the build process doesn't need to create `sql_yacc.cc`, because MySQL comes with an already generated copy. However, if you do need to re-create it, you might encounter this error:

```
"sql_yacc.yy", line xxx fatal: default action causes potential...
```

This is a sign that your version of yacc is deficient. You probably need to install `bison` (the GNU version of yacc) and use that instead.

- On Debian Linux 3.0, you need to install `gawk` instead of the default `mawk` if you want to compile MySQL 4.1 or higher with Berkeley DB support.

- If you need to debug `mysqld` or a MySQL client, run `configure` with the `--with-debug` option, then recompile and link your clients with the new client library.

- If you get a compilation error on Linux (for example, SuSE Linux 8.1 or Red Hat Linux 7.3) similar to the following one:

```
libmysql.c:1329: warning: passing arg 5 of `gethostbyname_r' from
incompatible pointer type
libmysql.c:1329: too few arguments to function `gethostbyname_r'
libmysql.c:1329: warning: assignment makes pointer from integer
without a cast
make[2]: *** [libmysql.lo] Error 1
```

By default, the configure script attempts to determine the correct number of arguments by using g++ the GNU C++ compiler. This test yields wrong results if g++ is not installed. There are two ways to work around this problem:

  - Make sure that the GNU C++ g++ is installed. On some Linux distributions, the required package is called gpp; on others, it is named gcc-c++.

  - Use gcc as your C++ compiler by setting the CXX environment variable to gcc:

    ```
    export CXX="gcc"
    ```

Please note that you need to run configure again afterward.

2.3.5 MIT-pthreads Notes

This section describes some of the issues involved in using MIT-pthreads.

On Linux, you should *not* use MIT-pthreads. Use the installed LinuxThreads implementation instead. See Section 2.6.1, "Linux Notes."

If your system does not provide native thread support, you will need to build MySQL using the MIT-pthreads package. This includes older FreeBSD systems, SunOS 4.x, Solaris 2.4 and earlier, and some others. See Section 2.1.1, "Operating Systems Supported by MySQL."

Beginning with MySQL 4.0.2, MIT-pthreads is no longer part of the source distribution. If you require this package, you need to download it separately from
http://www.mysql.com/Downloads/Contrib/pthreads-1_60_beta6-mysql.tar.gz

After downloading, extract this source archive into the top level of the MySQL source directory. It will create a new subdirectory named mit-pthreads.

- On most systems, you can force MIT-pthreads to be used by running configure with the --with-mit-threads option:

  ```
  shell> ./configure --with-mit-threads
  ```

  Building in a non-source directory is not supported when using MIT-pthreads because we want to minimize our changes to this code.

- The checks that determine whether to use MIT-pthreads occur only during the part of the configuration process that deals with the server code. If you have configured the distribution using --without-server to build only the client code, clients will not know whether MIT-pthreads is being used and will use Unix socket connections by default. Because Unix socket files do not work under MIT-pthreads on some platforms, this means you will need to use -h or --host when you run client programs.

- When MySQL is compiled using MIT-pthreads, system locking is disabled by default for performance reasons. You can tell the server to use system locking with the --external-locking option. This is needed only if you want to be able to run two MySQL servers against the same data files, which is not recommended.

- Sometimes the pthread bind() command fails to bind to a socket without any error message (at least on Solaris). The result is that all connections to the server fail. For example:

```
shell> mysqladmin version
mysqladmin: connect to server at '' failed;
error: 'Can't connect to mysql server on localhost (146)'
```

The solution to this is to kill the mysqld server and restart it. This has only happened to us when we have forced down the server and done a restart immediately.

- With MIT-pthreads, the sleep() system call isn't interruptible with SIGINT (break). This is only noticeable when you run mysqladmin --sleep. You must wait for the sleep() call to terminate before the interrupt is served and the process stops.

- When linking, you may receive warning messages like these (at least on Solaris); they can be ignored:

```
ld: warning: symbol `_iob' has differing sizes:
    (file /my/local/pthreads/lib/libpthread.a(findfp.o) value=0x4;
file /usr/lib/libc.so value=0x140);
    /my/local/pthreads/lib/libpthread.a(findfp.o) definition taken
ld: warning: symbol `__iob' has differing sizes:
    (file /my/local/pthreads/lib/libpthread.a(findfp.o) value=0x4;
file /usr/lib/libc.so value=0x140);
    /my/local/pthreads/lib/libpthread.a(findfp.o) definition taken
```

- Some other warnings also can be ignored:

```
implicit declaration of function `int strtoll(...)'
implicit declaration of function `int strtoul(...)'
```

- We haven't gotten readline to work with MIT-pthreads. (This isn't needed, but may be interesting for someone.)

2.3.6 Installing MySQL from Source on Windows

These instructions describe how to build MySQL binaries from source for versions 4.1 and above on Windows. Instructions are provided for building binaries from a standard source distribution or from the BitKeeper tree that contains the latest development source.

Note: The instructions in this document are strictly for users who want to test MySQL on Windows from the latest source distribution or from the BitKeeper tree. For production use, MySQL AB does not advise using a MySQL server built by yourself from source. Normally, it is best to use precompiled binary distributions of MySQL that are built specifically for optimal performance on Windows by MySQL AB. Instructions for installing a binary distributions are available at Section 2.2.1, "Installing MySQL on Windows."

To build MySQL on Windows from source, you need the following compiler and resources available on your Windows system:

- VC++ 6.0 compiler (updated with 4 or 5 SP and pre-processor package). The pre-processor package is necessary for the macro assembler. More details can be found at `http://msdn.microsoft.com/vstudio/downloads/updates/sp/vs6/sp5/faq.aspx`.
- Approximately 45MB disk space.
- 64MB RAM.

You'll also need a MySQL source distribution for Windows. There are two ways you can get a source distribution for MySQL version 4.1 and above:

1. Obtain a source distribution packaged by MySQL AB for the particular version of MySQL in which you are interested. Prepackaged source distributions are available for released versions of MySQL and can be obtained from `http://dev.mysql.com/downloads/`.

2. You can package a source distribution yourself from the latest BitKeeper developer source tree. If you plan to do this, you must create the package on a Unix system and then transfer it to your Windows system. (The reason for this is that some of the configuration and build steps require tools that work only on Unix.) The BitKeeper approach thus requires:

   - A system running Unix, or a Unix-like system such as Linux.
   - BitKeeper 3.0 installed on that system. You can obtain BitKeeper from `http://www.bitkeeper.com/`.

If you are using a Windows source distribution, you can go directly to Section 2.3.6.1, "Building MySQL Using VC++." To build from the BitKeeper tree, proceed to Section 2.3.6.2, "Creating a Windows Source Package from the Latest Development Source."

If you find something not working as expected, or you have suggestions about ways to improve the current build process on Windows, please send a message to the `win32` mailing list. See Section 1.7.1.1, "The MySQL Mailing Lists."

2.3.6.1 Building MySQL Using VC++

Note: VC++ workspace files for MySQL 4.1 and above are compatible with Microsoft Visual Studio 6.0 and above (7.0/.NET) editions and tested by MySQL AB staff before each release.

Follow this procedure to build MySQL:

1. Create a work directory (for example, `C:\workdir`).

2. Unpack the source distribution in the aforementioned directory using `WinZip` or other Windows tool that can read `.zip` files.

3. Start the VC++ 6.0 compiler.

4. In the `File` menu, select `Open Workspace`.

5. Open the `mysql.dsw` workspace you find in the work directory.

6. From the `Build` menu, select the `Set Active Configuration` menu.

7. Click over the screen selecting `mysqld - Win32 Debug` and click OK.

8. Press `F7` to begin the build of the debug server, libraries, and some client applications.

9. Compile the release versions that you want in the same way.

10. Debug versions of the programs and libraries are placed in the `client_debug` and `lib_debug` directories. Release versions of the programs and libraries are placed in the `client_release` and `lib_release` directories. Note that if you want to build both debug and release versions, you can select the `Build All` option from the `Build` menu.

11. Test the server. The server built using the preceding instructions will expect that the MySQL base directory and data directory are `C:\mysql` and `C:\mysql\data` by default. If you want to test your server using the source tree root directory and its data directory as the base directory and data directory, you will need to tell the server their pathnames. You can either do this on the command line with the `--basedir` and `--datadir` options, or place appropriate options in an option file (the `my.ini` file in your Windows directory or `C:\my.cnf`). If you have an existing data directory elsewhere that you want to use, you can specify its pathname instead.

12. Start your server from the `client_release` or `client_debug` directory, depending on which server you want to use. The general server startup instructions are at Section 2.2.1, "Installing MySQL on Windows." You'll need to adapt the instructions appropriately if you want to use a different base directory or data directory.

13. When the server is running in standalone fashion or as a service based on your configuration, try to connect to it from the `mysql` interactive command-line utility that exists in your `client_release` or `client_debug` directory.

When you are satisfied that the programs you have built are working correctly, stop the server. Then install MySQL as follows:

1. Create the directories where you want to install MySQL. For example, to install into `C:\mysql`, use these commands:

```
C:\> mkdir C:\mysql
C:\> mkdir C:\mysql\bin
C:\> mkdir C:\mysql\data
C:\> mkdir C:\mysql\share
C:\> mkdir C:\mysql\scripts
```

If you want to compile other clients and link them to MySQL, you should also create several additional directories:

```
C:\> mkdir C:\mysql\include
C:\> mkdir C:\mysql\lib
C:\> mkdir C:\mysql\lib\debug
C:\> mkdir C:\mysql\lib\opt
```

If you want to benchmark MySQL, create this directory:

```
C:\> mkdir C:\mysql\sql-bench
```

Benchmarking requires Perl support.

2. From the workdir directory, copy into the C:\mysql directory the following directories:

```
C:\> cd \workdir
C:\workdir> copy client_release\*.exe C:\mysql\bin
C:\workdir> copy client_debug\mysqld.exe C:\mysql\bin\mysqld-debug.exe
C:\workdir> xcopy scripts\*.* C:\mysql\scripts /E
C:\workdir> xcopy share\*.* C:\mysql\share /E
```

If you want to compile other clients and link them to MySQL, you should also copy several libraries and header files:

```
C:\workdir> copy lib_debug\mysqlclient.lib C:\mysql\lib\debug
C:\workdir> copy lib_debug\libmysql.* C:\mysql\lib\debug
C:\workdir> copy lib_debug\zlib.* C:\mysql\lib\debug
C:\workdir> copy lib_release\mysqlclient.lib C:\mysql\lib\opt
C:\workdir> copy lib_release\libmysql.* C:\mysql\lib\opt
C:\workdir> copy lib_release\zlib.* C:\mysql\lib\opt
C:\workdir> copy include\*.h C:\mysql\include
C:\workdir> copy libmysql\libmysql.def C:\mysql\include
```

If you want to benchmark MySQL, you should also do this:

```
C:\workdir> xcopy sql-bench\*.* C:\mysql\bench /E
```

Set up and start the server in the same way as for the binary Windows distribution. See Section 2.2.1, "Installing MySQL on Windows."

2.3.6.2 Creating a Windows Source Package from the Latest Development Source

To create aWindows source package from the current BitKeeper source tree, use the following instructions. Please note that this procedure must be performed on a system running a Unix or Unix-like operating system. For example, the procedure is known to work well on Linux.

1. Clone the BitKeeper source tree for MySQL (version 4.1 or above, as desired). For more information on how to clone the source tree, see the instructions at Section 2.3.3, "Installing from the Development Source Tree."

2. Configure and build the distribution so that you have a server binary to work with. One way to do this is to run the following command in the top-level directory of your source tree:

```
shell> ./BUILD/compile-pentium-max
```

3. After making sure that the build process completed successfully, run the following utility script from the top-level directory of your source tree:

```
shell> ./scripts/make_win_src_distribution
```

This script creates a Windows source package to be used on your Windows system. You can supply different options to the script based on your needs. It accepts the following options:

- --help

  Display a help message.

- --debug

  Print information about script operations, do not create package.

- --dirname

  Directory name to copy files (intermediate).

- --silent

  Do not print verbose list of files processed.

- --suffix

  Suffix name for the package.

- --tar

  Create tar.gz package instead of .zip package.

- --tmp

  Specify the temporary location.

By default, make_win_src_distribution creates a Zip-format archive with the name mysql-*VERSION*-win-src.zip, where *VERSION* represents the version of your MySQL source tree.

4. Copy or upload to your Windows machine the Windows source package that you have just created. To compile it, use the instructions in Section 2.3.6.1, "Building MySQL Using VC++."

2.3.7 Compiling MySQL Clients on Windows

In your source files, you should include `my_global.h` before `mysql.h`:

```
#include <my_global.h>
#include <mysql.h>
```

`my_global.h` includes any other files needed for Windows compatibility (such as `windows.h`) if you compile your program on Windows.

You can either link your code with the dynamic `libmysql.lib` library, which is just a wrapper to load in `libmysql.dll` on demand, or link with the static `mysqlclient.lib` library.

The MySQL client libraries are compiled as threaded libraries, so you should also compile your code to be multi-threaded.

2.4 Post-Installation Setup and Testing

After installing MySQL, there are some issues you should address. For example, on Unix, you should initialize the data directory and create the MySQL grant tables. On all platforms, an important security concern is that the initial accounts in the grant tables have no passwords. You should assign passwords to prevent unauthorized access to the MySQL server.

The following sections include post-installation procedures that are specific to Windows systems and to Unix systems. Another section, Section 2.4.4, "Starting and Troubleshooting the MySQL Server," applies to all platforms; it describes what to do if you have trouble getting the server to start. Section 2.4.5, "Securing the Initial MySQL Accounts," also applies to all platforms. You should follow its instructions to make sure that you have properly protected your MySQL accounts by assigning passwords to them.

When you are ready to create additional user accounts, you can find information on the MySQL access control system and account management in Section 4.4, "The MySQL Access Privilege System," and Section 4.5, "MySQL User Account Management."

2.4.1 Windows Post-Installation Procedures

On Windows, the data directory and the grant tables do not have to be created. MySQL Windows distributions include the grant tables already set up with a set of preinitialized accounts in the `mysql` database under the data directory. However, you should assign passwords to the accounts. The procedure for this is given in Section 2.4.5, "Securing the Initial MySQL Accounts."

Before setting up passwords, you might want to try running some client programs to make sure that you can connect to the server and that it is operating properly. Make sure the server is running (see Section 2.2.1.5, "Starting the Server for the First Time"), then issue the following commands to verify that you can retrieve information from the server. The output should be similar to what is shown here:

```
C:\> C:\mysql\bin\mysqlshow
+-----------+
| Databases |
+-----------+
| mysql     |
| test      |
+-----------+

C:\> C:\mysql\bin\mysqlshow mysql
Database: mysql
+--------------+
|    Tables    |
+--------------+
| columns_priv |
| db           |
| func         |
| host         |
| tables_priv  |
| user         |
+--------------+

C:\> C:\mysql\bin\mysql -e "SELECT Host,Db,User FROM db" mysql
+------+-------+------+
| host | db    | user |
+------+-------+------+
| %    | test% |      |
+------+-------+------+
```

If you are running a version of Windows that supports services and you want the MySQL server to run automatically when Windows starts, see Section 2.2.1.7, "Starting MySQL as a Windows Service."

2.4.2 Unix Post-Installation Procedures

After installing MySQL on Unix, you need to initialize the grant tables, start the server, and make sure that the server works okay. You may also wish to arrange for the server to be started and stopped automatically when your system starts and stops. You should also assign passwords to the accounts in the grant tables.

On Unix, the grant tables are set up by the mysql_install_db program. For some installation methods, this program is run for you automatically:

- If you install MySQL on Linux using RPM distributions, the server RPM runs mysql_install_db.
- If you install MySQL on Mac OS X using a PKG distribution, the installer runs mysql_install_db.

Otherwise, you'll need to run mysql_install_db yourself.

The following procedure describes how to initialize the grant tables (if that has not already been done) and then start the server. It also suggests some commands that you can use to test whether the server is accessible and working properly. For information about starting and stopping the server automatically, see Section 2.4.3, "Starting and Stopping MySQL Automatically."

After you complete the procedure and have the server running, you should assign passwords to the accounts created by mysql_install_db. Instructions for doing so are given in Section 2.4.5, "Securing the Initial MySQL Accounts."

In the examples shown here, the server runs under the user ID of the mysql login account. This assumes that such an account exists. Either create the account if it does not exist, or substitute the name of a different existing login account that you plan to use for running the server.

1. Change location into the top-level directory of your MySQL installation, represented here by *BASEDIR*:

```
shell> cd BASEDIR
```

BASEDIR is likely to be something like /usr/local/mysql or /usr/local. The following steps assume that you are located in this directory.

2. If necessary, run the mysql_install_db program to set up the initial MySQL grant tables containing the privileges that determine how users are allowed to connect to the server. You'll need to do this if you used a distribution type that doesn't run the program for you.

Typically, mysql_install_db needs to be run only the first time you install MySQL, so you can skip this step if you are upgrading an existing installation, However, mysql_install_db does not overwrite any existing privilege tables, so it should be safe to run in any circumstances.

To initialize the grant tables, use one of the following commands, depending on whether mysql_install_db is located in the bin or scripts directory:

```
shell> bin/mysql_install_db --user=mysql
shell> scripts/mysql_install_db --user=mysql
```

The mysql_install_db script creates the data directory, the mysql database that holds all database privileges, and the test database that you can use to test MySQL. The script also creates privilege table entries for root accounts and anonymous-user accounts. The accounts have no passwords initially. A description of their initial privileges is given in Section 2.4.5, "Securing the Initial MySQL Accounts." Briefly, these privileges allow the MySQL root user to do anything, and allow anybody to create or use databases with a name of test or starting with test_.

It is important to make sure that the database directories and files are owned by the mysql login account so that the server has read and write access to them when you run it later. To ensure this, the --user option should be used as shown if you run `mysql_install_db` as root. Otherwise, you should execute the script while logged in as `mysql`, in which case you can omit the `--user` option from the command.

`mysql_install_db` creates several tables in the `mysql` database: `user`, `db`, `host`, `tables_priv`, `columns_priv`, `func`, and possibly others depending on your version of MySQL.

If you don't want to have the `test` database, you can remove it with `mysqladmin -u root drop test` after starting the server.

If you have problems with `mysql_install_db`, see Section 2.4.2.1, "Problems Running `mysql_install_db`."

There are some alternatives to running the `mysql_install_db` script as it is provided in the MySQL distribution:

- If you want the initial privileges to be different from the standard defaults, you can modify `mysql_install_db` before you run it. However, a preferable technique is to use GRANT and REVOKE to change the privileges after the grant tables have been set up. In other words, you can run `mysql_install_db`, and then use `mysql -u root mysql` to connect to the server as the MySQL `root` user so that you can issue the GRANT and REVOKE statements.

  If you want to install MySQL on a lot of machines with the same privileges, you can put the GRANT and REVOKE statements in a file and execute the file as a script using `mysql` after running `mysql_install_db`. For example:

  ```
  shell> bin/mysql_install_db --user=mysql
  shell> bin/mysql -u root < your_script_file
  ```

  By doing this, you can avoid having to issue the statements manually on each machine.

- It is possible to re-create the grant tables completely after they have already been created. You might want to do this if you're just learning how to use GRANT and REVOKE and have made so many modifications after running `mysql_install_db` that you want to wipe out the tables and start over.

  To re-create the grant tables, remove all the `.frm`, `.MYI`, and `.MYD` files in the directory containing the `mysql` database. (This is the directory named `mysql` under the data directory, which is listed as the `datadir` value when you run `mysqld --help`.) Then run the `mysql_install_db` script again.

  Note: For MySQL versions older than 3.22.10, you should not delete the `.frm` files. If you accidentally do this, you should copy them back into the `mysql` directory from your MySQL distribution before running `mysql_install_db`.

- You can start `mysqld` manually using the `--skip-grant-tables` option and add the privilege information yourself using `mysql`:

  ```
  shell> bin/mysqld_safe --user=mysql --skip-grant-tables &
  shell> bin/mysql mysql
  ```

From `mysql`, manually execute the SQL commands contained in `mysql_install_db`. Make sure that you run `mysqladmin flush-privileges` or `mysqladmin reload` afterward to tell the server to reload the grant tables.

Note that by not using `mysql_install_db`, you not only have to populate the grant tables manually, you also have to create them first.

3. Start the MySQL server:

```
shell> bin/mysqld_safe --user=mysql &
```

For versions of MySQL older than 4.0, substitute `bin/safe_mysqld` for `bin/mysqld_safe` in this command.

It is important that the MySQL server be run using an unprivileged (non-root) login account. To ensure this, the `--user` option should be used as shown if you run `mysql_safe` as `root`. Otherwise, you should execute the script while logged in as `mysql`, in which case you can omit the `--user` option from the command.

Further instructions for running MySQL as an unprivileged user are given in Section A.3.2, "How to Run MySQL as a Normal User."

If you neglected to create the grant tables before proceeding to this step, the following message will appear in the error log file when you start the server:

```
mysqld: Can't find file: 'host.frm'
```

If you have other problems starting the server, see Section 2.4.4, "Starting and Troubleshooting the MySQL Server."

4. Use `mysqladmin` to verify that the server is running. The following commands provide simple tests to check whether the server is up and responding to connections:

```
shell> bin/mysqladmin version
shell> bin/mysqladmin variables
```

The output from `mysqladmin version` varies slightly depending on your platform and version of MySQL, but should be similar to that shown here:

```
shell> bin/mysqladmin version
mysqladmin  Ver 8.40 Distrib 4.0.18, for linux on i586
Copyright (C) 2000 MySQL AB & MySQL Finland AB & TCX DataKonsult AB
This software comes with ABSOLUTELY NO WARRANTY. This is free software,
and you are welcome to modify and redistribute it under the GPL license

Server version         4.0.18-log
Protocol version       10
Connection             Localhost via Unix socket
TCP port               3306
UNIX socket            /tmp/mysql.sock
Uptime:                16 sec
```

```
Threads: 1  Questions: 9  Slow queries: 0
Opens: 7  Flush tables: 2  Open tables: 0
Queries per second avg: 0.000
Memory in use: 132K  Max memory used: 16773K
```

To see what else you can do with `mysqladmin`, invoke it with the `--help` option.

5. Verify that you can shut down the server:

```
shell> bin/mysqladmin -u root shutdown
```

6. Verify that you can restart the server. Do this by using `mysqld_safe` or by invoking `mysqld` directly. For example:

```
shell> bin/mysqld_safe --user=mysql --log &
```

If `mysqld_safe` fails, see Section 2.4.4, "Starting and Troubleshooting the MySQL Server."

7. Run some simple tests to verify that you can retrieve information from the server. The output should be similar to what is shown here:

```
shell> bin/mysqlshow
+-----------+
| Databases |
+-----------+
| mysql     |
| test      |
+-----------+
```

```
shell> bin/mysqlshow mysql
Database: mysql
+--------------+
|    Tables    |
+--------------+
| columns_priv |
| db           |
| func         |
| host         |
| tables_priv  |
| user         |
+--------------+
```

```
shell> bin/mysql -e "SELECT Host,Db,User FROM db" mysql
+------+--------+------+
| host | db     | user |
+------+--------+------+
| %    | test   |      |
| %    | test_% |      |
+------+--------+------+
```

8. There is a benchmark suite in the `sql-bench` directory (under the MySQL installation directory) that you can use to compare how MySQL performs on different platforms. The benchmark suite is written in Perl. It uses the Perl DBI module to provide a database-independent interface to the various databases, and some other additional Perl modules are required to run the benchmark suite. You must have the following modules installed:

```
DBI
DBD::mysql
Data::Dumper
Data::ShowTable
```

These modules can be obtained from CPAN (`http://www.cpan.org/`). See Section 2.7.1, "Installing Perl on Unix."

The `sql-bench/Results` directory contains the results from many runs against different databases and platforms. To run all tests, execute these commands:

```
shell> cd sql-bench
shell> perl run-all-tests
```

If you don't have the `sql-bench` directory, you probably installed MySQL using RPM files other than the source RPM. (The source RPM includes the `sql-bench` benchmark directory.) In this case, you must first install the benchmark suite before you can use it. Beginning with MySQL 3.22, there are separate benchmark RPM files named `mysql-bench-VERSION-i386.rpm` that contain benchmark code and data.

If you have a source distribution, there are also tests in its `tests` subdirectory that you can run. For example, to run `auto_increment.tst`, execute this command from the top-level directory of your source distribution:

```
shell> mysql -vvf test < ./tests/auto_increment.tst
```

The expected result of the test can be found in the `./tests/auto_increment.res` file.

9. At this point, you should have the server running. However, none of the initial MySQL accounts have a password, so you should assign passwords using the instructions in Section 2.4.5, "Securing the Initial MySQL Accounts."

2.4.2.1 Problems Running `mysql_install_db`

The purpose of the `mysql_install_db` script is to generate new MySQL privilege tables. It will not overwrite existing MySQL privilege tables, and it will not affect any other data.

If you want to re-create your privilege tables, first stop the `mysqld` server if it's running. Then rename the `mysql` directory under the data directory to save it, and then run `mysql_install_db`. For example:

```
shell> mv mysql-data-directory/mysql mysql-data-directory/mysql-old
shell> mysql_install_db --user=mysql
```

This section lists problems you might encounter when you run `mysql_install_db`:

- **`mysql_install_db` doesn't install the grant tables**

  You may find that `mysql_install_db` fails to install the grant tables and terminates after displaying the following messages:

  ```
  Starting mysqld daemon with databases from XXXXXX
  mysqld ended
  ```

  In this case, you should examine the error log file very carefully. The log should be located in the directory *XXXXXX* named by the error message, and should indicate why `mysqld` didn't start. If you don't understand what happened, include the log when you post a bug report. See Section 1.7.1.3, "How to Report Bugs or Problems."

- **There is already a `mysqld` process running**

  This indicates that the server is already running, in which case the grant tables probably have already been created. If so, you don't have to run `mysql_install_db` at all because it need be run only once (when you install MySQL the first time).

- **Installing a second `mysqld` server doesn't work when one server is running**

  This can happen when you already have an existing MySQL installation, but want to put a new installation in a different location. For example, you might have a production installation already, but you want to create a second installation for testing purposes. Generally the problem that occurs when you try to run a second server is that it tries to use a network interface that is already in use by the first server. In this case, you will see one of the following error messages:

  ```
  Can't start server: Bind on TCP/IP port:
  Address already in use
  Can't start server: Bind on unix socket...
  ```

  For instructions on setting up multiple servers, see Section 4.9, "Running Multiple MySQL Servers on the Same Machine."

- **You don't have write access to `/tmp`**

  If you don't have write access to create temporary files or a Unix socket file in the default location (the `/tmp` directory), an error will occur when you run `mysql_install_db` or the `mysqld` server.

  You can specify different temporary directory and Unix socket file locations by executing these commands prior to starting `mysql_install_db` or `mysqld`:

  ```
  shell> TMPDIR=/some_tmp_dir/
  shell> MYSQL_UNIX_PORT=/some_tmp_dir/mysql.sock
  shell> export TMPDIR MYSQL_UNIX_PORT
  ```

  some_tmp_dir should be the full pathname to some directory for which you have write permission.

After this, you should be able to run `mysql_install_db` and start the server with these commands:

```
shell> bin/mysql_install_db --user=mysql
shell> bin/mysqld_safe --user=mysql &
```

If `mysql_install_db` is located in the `scripts` directory, modify the first command to use `scripts/mysql_install_db`.

See Section A.4.5, "How to Protect or Change the MySQL Socket File `/tmp/mysql.sock`." See also Appendix B, "Environment Variables."

2.4.3 Starting and Stopping MySQL Automatically

Generally, you start the `mysqld` server in one of these ways:

- By invoking `mysqld` directly. This works on any platform.
- By running the MySQL server as a Windows service. This can be done on versions of Windows that support services (such as NT, 2000, and XP). The service can be set to start the server automatically when Windows starts, or as a manual service that you start on request. For instructions, see Section 2.2.1.7, "Starting MySQL as a Windows Service."
- By invoking `mysqld_safe`, which tries to determine the proper options for `mysqld` and then runs it with those options. This script is used on systems based on BSD Unix. See Section 4.1.3, "The `mysqld_safe` Server Startup Script."
- By invoking `mysql.server`. This script is used primarily at system startup and shutdown on systems that use System V-style run directories, where it usually is installed under the name `mysql`. The `mysql.server` script starts the server by invoking `mysqld_safe`. See Section 4.1.4, "The `mysql.server` Server Startup Script."
- On Mac OS X, you can install a separate MySQL Startup Item package to enable the automatic startup of MySQL on system startup. The Startup Item starts the server by invoking `mysql.server`. See Section 2.2.3, "Installing MySQL on Mac OS X," for details.

The `mysql.server` and `mysqld_safe` scripts and the Mac OS X Startup Item can be used to start the server manually, or automatically at system startup time. `mysql.server` and the Startup Item also can be used to stop the server.

To start or stop the server manually using the `mysql.server` script, invoke it with `start` or `stop` arguments:

```
shell> mysql.server start
shell> mysql.server stop
```

Before `mysql.server` starts the server, it changes location to the MySQL installation directory, and then invokes `mysqld_safe`. If you want the server to run as some specific user, add an appropriate user option to the [mysqld] group of the /etc/my.cnf option file, as shown later in this section. (It is possible that you'll need to edit mysql.server if you've installed a binary distribution of MySQL in a non-standard location. Modify it to cd into the proper directory before it runs mysqld_safe. If you do this, your modified version of mysql.server may be overwritten if you upgrade MySQL in the future, so you should make a copy of your edited version that you can reinstall.)

mysql.server stop brings down the server by sending a signal to it. You can also stop the server manually by executing mysqladmin shutdown.

To start and stop MySQL automatically on your server, you need to add start and stop commands to the appropriate places in your /etc/rc* files.

If you use the Linux server RPM package (MySQL-server-VERSION.rpm), the mysql.server script will already have been installed in the /etc/init.d directory with the name mysql. You need not install it manually. See Section 2.2.2, "Installing MySQL on Linux," for more information on the Linux RPM packages.

Some vendors provide RPM packages that install a startup script under a different name such as mysqld.

If you install MySQL from a source distribution or using a binary distribution format that does not install mysql.server automatically, you can install it manually. The script can be found in the support-files directory under the MySQL installation directory or in a MySQL source tree.

To install mysql.server manually, copy it to the /etc/init.d directory with the name mysql, and then make it executable. Do this by changing location into the appropriate directory where mysql.server is located and executing these commands:

```
shell> cp mysql.server /etc/init.d/mysql
shell> chmod +x /etc/init.d/mysql
```

Older Red Hat systems use the /etc/rc.d/init.d directory rather than /etc/init.d. Adjust the preceding commands accordingly. Alternatively, first create /etc/init.d as a symbolic link that points to /etc/rc.d/init.d:

```
shell> cd /etc
shell> ln -s rc.d/init.d .
```

After installing the script, the commands needed to activate it to run at system startup depend on your operating system. On Linux, you can use chkconfig:

```
shell> chkconfig --add mysql
```

On some Linux systems, the following command also seems to be necessary to fully enable the mysql script:

```
shell> chkconfig --level 345 mysql on
```

On FreeBSD, startup scripts generally should go in /usr/local/etc/rc.d/. The rc(8) manual page states that scripts in this directory are executed only if their basename matches the *.sh shell filename pattern. Any other files or directories present within the directory are silently ignored. In other words, on FreeBSD, you should install the mysql.server script as /usr/local/etc/rc.d/mysql.server.sh to enable automatic startup.

As an alternative to the preceding setup, some operating systems also use /etc/rc.local or /etc/init.d/boot.local to start additional services on startup. To start up MySQL using this method, you could append a command like the one following to the appropriate startup file:

```
/bin/sh -c 'cd /usr/local/mysql; ./bin/mysqld_safe --user=mysql &'
```

For other systems, consult your operating system documentation to see how to install startup scripts.

You can add options for mysql.server in a global /etc/my.cnf file. A typical /etc/my.cnf file might look like this:

```
[mysqld]
datadir=/usr/local/mysql/var
socket=/var/tmp/mysql.sock
port=3306
user=mysql


[mysql.server]
basedir=/usr/local/mysql
```

The mysql.server script understands the following options: basedir, datadir, and pid-file. If specified, they *must* be placed in an option file, not on the command line. mysql.server understands only start and stop as command-line arguments.

The following table shows which option groups the server and each startup script read from option files:

Script	Option Groups
mysqld	[mysqld], [server], [mysqld-*major-version*]
mysql.server	[mysqld], [mysql.server]
mysqld_safe	[mysqld], [server], [mysqld_safe]

[mysqld-*major-version*] means that groups with names like [mysqld-4.0], [mysqld-4.1], and [mysqld-5.0] will be read by servers having versions 4.0.x, 4.1.x, 5.0.x, and so forth. This feature was added in MySQL 4.0.14. It can be used to specify options that will be read only by servers within a given release series.

For backward compatibility, mysql.server also reads the [mysql_server] group and mysqld_safe also reads the [safe_mysqld] group. However, you should update your option files to use the [mysql.server] and [mysqld_safe] groups instead when you begin using MySQL 4.0 or later.

See Section 3.3.2, "Using Option Files."

2.4.4 Starting and Troubleshooting the MySQL Server

If you have problems starting the server, here are some things you can try:

- Specify any special options needed by the storage engines you are using.
- Make sure that the server knows where to find the data directory.
- Make sure the server can use the data directory. The ownership and permissions of the data directory and its contents must be set such that the server can access and modify them.
- Check the error log to see why the server doesn't start.
- Verify that the network interfaces the server wants to use are available.

Some storage engines have options that control their behavior. You can create a my.cnf file and set startup options for the engines you plan to use. If you are going to use storage engines that support transactional tables (InnoDB, BDB), be sure that you have them configured the way you want before starting the server:

- If you are using InnoDB tables, refer to the InnoDB-specific startup options. In MySQL 3.23, you must configure InnoDB explicitly or the server will fail to start. From MySQL 4.0 on, InnoDB uses default values for its configuration options if you specify none. See Section 9.4, "InnoDB Configuration."
- If you are using BDB (Berkeley DB) tables, you should familiarize yourself with the different BDB-specific startup options. See Section 8.4.3, "BDB Startup Options."

When the mysqld server starts, it changes location to the data directory. This is where it expects to find databases and where it expects to write log files. On Unix, the server also writes the pid (process ID) file in the data directory.

The data directory location is hardwired in when the server is compiled. This is where the server looks for the data directory by default. If the data directory is located somewhere else on your system, the server will not work properly. You can find out what the default path settings are by invoking mysqld with the --verbose and --help options. (Prior to MySQL 4.1, omit the --verbose option.)

If the defaults don't match the MySQL installation layout on your system, you can override them by specifying options on the command line to mysqld or mysqld_safe. You can also list the options in an option file.

To specify the location of the data directory explicitly, use the --datadir option. However, normally you can tell mysqld the location of the base directory under which MySQL is installed and it will look for the data directory there. You can do this with the `--basedir` option.

To check the effect of specifying path options, invoke `mysqld` with those options followed by the `--verbose` and `--help` options. For example, if you change location into the directory where `mysqld` is installed, and then run the following command, it will show the effect of starting the server with a base directory of `/usr/local`:

```
shell> ./mysqld --basedir=/usr/local --verbose --help
```

You can specify other options such as `--datadir` as well, but note that `--verbose` and `--help` must be the last options. (Prior to MySQL 4.1, omit the `--verbose` option.)

Once you determine the path settings you want, start the server without `--verbose` and `--help`.

If `mysqld` is currently running, you can find out what path settings it is using by executing this command:

```
shell> mysqladmin variables
```

Or:

```
shell> mysqladmin -h host_name variables
```

host_name is the name of the MySQL server host.

If you get `Errcode 13` (which means `Permission denied`) when starting `mysqld`, this means that the access privileges of the data directory or its contents do not allow the server access. In this case, you change the permissions for the involved files and directories so that the server has the right to use them. You can also start the server as `root`, but this can raise security issues and should be avoided.

On Unix, change location into the data directory and check the ownership of the data directory and its contents to make sure the server has access. For example, if the data directory is `/usr/local/mysql/var`, use this command:

```
shell> ls -la /usr/local/mysql/var
```

If the data directory or its files or subdirectories are not owned by the account that you use for running the server, change their ownership to that account:

```
shell> chown -R mysql /usr/local/mysql/var
shell> chgrp -R mysql /usr/local/mysql/var
```

If the server fails to start up correctly, check the error log file to see if you can find out why. Log files are located in the data directory (typically `C:\mysql\data` on Windows, `/usr/local/mysql/data` for a Unix binary distribution, and `/usr/local/var` for a Unix source distribution). Look in the data directory for files with names of the form *host_name*.err and *host_name*.log, where *host_name* is the name of your server host. (Older servers on Windows use mysql.err as the error log name.) Then check the last few lines of these files. On Unix, you can use tail to display the last few lines:

```
shell> tail host_name.err
shell> tail host_name.log
```

The error log contains information that indicates why the server couldn't start. For example, you might see something like this in the log:

```
000729 14:50:10  bdb:  Recovery function for LSN 1 27595 failed
000729 14:50:10  bdb:  warning: ./test/t1.db: No such file or directory
000729 14:50:10  Can't init databases
```

This means that you didn't start mysqld with the --bdb-no-recover option and Berkeley DB found something wrong with its own log files when it tried to recover your databases. To be able to continue, you should move away the old Berkeley DB log files from the database directory to some other place, where you can later examine them. The BDB log files are named in sequence beginning with log.0000000001, where the number increases over time.

If you are running mysqld with BDB table support and mysqld dumps core at startup, this could be due to problems with the BDB recovery log. In this case, you can try starting mysqld with --bdb-no-recover. If that helps, then you should remove all BDB log files from the data directory and try starting mysqld again without the --bdb-no-recover option.

If either of the following errors occur, it means that some other program (perhaps another mysqld server) is already using the TCP/IP port or Unix socket file that mysqld is trying to use:

```
Can't start server: Bind on TCP/IP port: Address already in use
Can't start server: Bind on unix socket...
```

Use ps to determine whether you have another mysqld server running. If so, shut down the server before starting mysqld again. (If another server is running, and you really want to run multiple servers, you can find information about how to do so in Section 4.9, "Running Multiple MySQL Servers on the Same Machine.")

If no other server is running, try to execute the command telnet your-host-name tcp-ip-port-number. (The default MySQL port number is 3306.) Then press Enter a couple of times. If you don't get an error message like telnet: Unable to connect to remote host: Connection refused, some other program is using the TCP/IP port that mysqld is trying to use. You'll need to track down what program this is and disable it, or else tell mysqld to listen to a different port with the --port option. In this case, you'll also need to specify the port number for client programs when connecting to the server via TCP/IP.

Another reason the port might be inaccessible is that you have a firewall running that blocks connections to it. If so, modify the firewall settings to allow access to the port.

If the server starts but you can't connect to it, you should make sure that you have an entry in /etc/hosts that looks like this:

```
127.0.0.1       localhost
```

This problem occurs only on systems that don't have a working thread library and for which MySQL must be configured to use MIT-pthreads.

If you can't get mysqld to start, you can try to make a trace file to find the problem by using the --debug option.

2.4.5 Securing the Initial MySQL Accounts

Part of the MySQL installation process is to set up the mysql database containing the grant tables:

- Windows distributions contain preinitialized grant tables that are installed automatically.
- On Unix, the grant tables are populated by the mysql_install_db program. Some installation methods run this program for you. Others require that you execute it manually. For details, see Section 2.4.2, "Unix Post-Installation Procedures."

The grant tables define the initial MySQL user accounts and their access privileges. These accounts are set up as follows:

- Two accounts are created with a username of root. These are superuser accounts that can do anything. The initial root account passwords are empty, so anyone can connect to the MySQL server as root *without a password* and be granted all privileges.
  - On Windows, one root account is for connecting from the local host and the other allows connections from any host.
  - On Unix, both root accounts are for connections from the local host. Connections must be made from the local host by specifying a hostname of localhost for one account, or the actual hostname or IP number for the other.
- Two anonymous-user accounts are created, each with an empty username. The anonymous accounts have no passwords, so anyone can use them to connect to the MySQL server.
  - On Windows, one anonymous account is for connections from the local host. It has all privileges, just like the root accounts. The other is for connections from any host and has all privileges for the test database or other databases with names that start with test.
  - On Unix, both anonymous accounts are for connections from the local host. Connections must be made from the local host by specifying a hostname of localhost for one account, or the actual hostname or IP number for the other. These accounts have all privileges for the test database or other databases with names that start with test_.

As noted, none of the initial accounts have passwords. This means that your MySQL installation is unprotected until you do something about it:

- If you want to prevent clients from connecting as anonymous users without a password, you should either assign passwords to the anonymous accounts or else remove them.
- You should assign passwords to the MySQL root accounts.

The following instructions describe how to set up passwords for the initial MySQL accounts, first for the anonymous accounts and then for the root accounts. Replace "*newpwd*" in the examples with the actual password that you want to use. The instructions also cover how to remove the anonymous accounts, should you prefer not to allow anonymous access at all.

You might want to defer setting the passwords until later, so that you don't need to specify them while you perform additional setup or testing. However, be sure to set them before using your installation for any real production work.

To assign passwords to the anonymous accounts, you can use either SET PASSWORD or UPDATE. In both cases, be sure to encrypt the password using the PASSWORD() function.

To use SET PASSWORD on Windows, do this:

```
shell> mysql -u root
mysql> SET PASSWORD FOR ''@'localhost' = PASSWORD('newpwd');
mysql> SET PASSWORD FOR ''@'%' = PASSWORD('newpwd');
```

To use SET PASSWORD on Unix, do this:

```
shell> mysql -u root
mysql> SET PASSWORD FOR ''@'localhost' = PASSWORD('newpwd');
mysql> SET PASSWORD FOR ''@'host_name' = PASSWORD('newpwd');
```

In the second SET PASSWORD statement, replace *host_name* with the name of the server host. This is the name that is specified in the Host column of the non-localhost record for root in the user table. If you don't know what hostname this is, issue the following statement before using SET PASSWORD:

```
mysql> SELECT Host, User FROM mysql.user;
```

Look for the record that has root in the User column and something other than localhost in the Host column. Then use that Host value in the second SET PASSWORD statement.

The other way to assign passwords to the anonymous accounts is by using UPDATE to modify the user table directly. Connect to the server as root and issue an UPDATE statement that assigns a value to the Password column of the appropriate user table records. The procedure is the same for Windows and Unix. The following UPDATE statement assigns a password to both anonymous accounts at once:

```
shell> mysql -u root
mysql> UPDATE mysql.user SET Password = PASSWORD('newpwd')
    ->      WHERE User = '';
mysql> FLUSH PRIVILEGES;
```

After you update the passwords in the user table directly using UPDATE, you must tell the server to re-read the grant tables with FLUSH PRIVILEGES. Otherwise, the change will go unnoticed until you restart the server.

If you prefer to remove the anonymous accounts instead, do so as follows:

```
shell> mysql -u root
mysql> DELETE FROM mysql.user WHERE User = '';
mysql> FLUSH PRIVILEGES;
```

The DELETE statement applies both to Windows and to Unix. On Windows, if you want to remove only the anonymous account that has the same privileges as root, do this instead:

```
shell> mysql -u root
mysql> DELETE FROM mysql.user WHERE Host='localhost' AND User = '';
mysql> FLUSH PRIVILEGES;
```

This account allows anonymous access but has full privileges, so removing it improves security.

You can assign passwords to the root accounts in several ways. The following discussion demonstrates three methods:

- Use the SET PASSWORD statement
- Use the mysqladmin command-line client program
- Use the UPDATE statement

To assign passwords using SET PASSWORD, connect to the server as root and issue two SET PASSWORD statements. Be sure to encrypt the password using the PASSWORD() function.

For Windows, do this:

```
shell> mysql -u root
mysql> SET PASSWORD FOR 'root'@'localhost' = PASSWORD('newpwd');
mysql> SET PASSWORD FOR 'root'@'%' = PASSWORD('newpwd');
```

For Unix, do this:

```
shell> mysql -u root
mysql> SET PASSWORD FOR 'root'@'localhost' = PASSWORD('newpwd');
mysql> SET PASSWORD FOR 'root'@'host_name' = PASSWORD('newpwd');
```

In the second SET PASSWORD statement, replace host_name with the name of the server host. This is the same hostname that you used when you assigned the anonymous account passwords.

To assign passwords to the root accounts using mysqladmin, execute the following commands:

```
shell> mysqladmin -u root password "newpwd"
shell> mysqladmin -u root -h host_name password "newpwd"
```

These commands apply both to Windows and to Unix. In the second command, replace host_name with the name of the server host. The double quotes around the password are not always necessary, but you should use them if the password contains spaces or other characters that are special to your command interpreter.

If you are using a server from a *very* old version of MySQL, the mysqladmin commands to set the password will fail with the message parse error near 'SET password'. The solution to this problem is to upgrade the server to a newer version of MySQL.

You can also use UPDATE to modify the user table directly. The following UPDATE statement assigns a password to both root accounts at once:

```
shell> mysql -u root
mysql> UPDATE mysql.user SET Password = PASSWORD('newpwd')
    ->     WHERE User = 'root';
mysql> FLUSH PRIVILEGES;
```

The UPDATE statement applies both to Windows and to Unix.

After the passwords have been set, you must supply the appropriate password whenever you connect to the server. For example, if you want to use mysqladmin to shut down the server, you can do so using this command:

```
shell> mysqladmin -u root -p shutdown
Enter password: (enter root password here)
```

Note: If you forget your root password after setting it up, the procedure for resetting it is covered in Section A.4.1, "How to Reset the Root Password."

To set up new accounts, you can use the GRANT statement. For instructions, see Section 4.5.2, "Adding New User Accounts to MySQL."

2.5 Upgrading/Downgrading MySQL

As a general rule, we recommend that when upgrading from one release series to another, you should go to the next series rather than skipping a series. For example, if you currently are running MySQL 3.23 and wish to upgrade to a newer series, upgrade to MySQL 4.0 rather than to 4.1 or 5.0.

The following items form a checklist of things you should do whenever you perform an upgrade:

- Read the change log in the online manual for the release series to which you are upgrading to see what new features you can use. For example, before upgrading from MySQL 4.1 to 5.0, read the 5.0 news items. See `http://dev.mysql.com/doc/mysql/en/News.html`.

- Before you do an upgrade, back up your databases.

- If you are running MySQL Server on Windows, see Section 2.5.7, "Upgrading MySQL Under Windows."

- An upgrade may involve changes to the grant tables that are stored in the `mysql` database. Occasionally new columns or tables are added to support new features. To take advantage of these features, be sure that your grant tables are up to date. The upgrade procedure is described in Section 2.5.8, "Upgrading the Grant Tables."

- If you are using replication, see Section 5.6, "Upgrading a Replication Setup," for information on upgrading your replication setup.

- If you install a MySQL-Max distribution that includes a server named `mysqld-max`, then upgrade later to a non-Max version of MySQL, `mysqld_safe` will still attempt to run the old `mysqld-max` server. If you perform such an upgrade, you should manually remove the old `mysqld-max` server to ensure that `mysqld_safe` runs the new `mysqld` server.

You can always move the MySQL format files and data files between different versions on the same architecture as long as you stay within versions for the same release series of MySQL. The current production release series is 4.0. If you change the character set when running MySQL, you must run `myisamchk -r -q --set-character-set=charset` on all `MyISAM` tables. Otherwise, your indexes may not be ordered correctly, because changing the character set may also change the sort order.

If you upgrade or downgrade from one release series to another, there may be incompatibilities in table storage formats. In this case, you can use `mysqldump` to dump your tables before upgrading. After upgrading, reload the dump file using `mysql` to re-create your tables.

If you are cautious about using new versions, you can always rename your old `mysqld` before installing a newer one. For example, if you are using MySQL 4.0.18 and want to upgrade to 4.1.1, rename your current server from `mysqld` to `mysqld-4.0.18`. If your new `mysqld` then does something unexpected, you can simply shut it down and restart with your old `mysqld`.

If, after an upgrade, you experience problems with recompiled client programs, such as `Commands out of sync` or unexpected core dumps, you probably have used old header or library files when compiling your programs. In this case, you should check the date for your `mysql.h` file and `libmysqlclient.a` library to verify that they are from the new MySQL distribution. If not, recompile your programs with the new headers and libraries.

If problems occur, such as that the new `mysqld` server doesn't want to start or that you can't connect without a password, verify that you don't have some old `my.cnf` file from your previous installation. You can check this with the `--print-defaults` option (for example, `mysqld --print-defaults`). If this displays anything other than the program name, you have an active `my.cnf` file that affects server or client operation.

It is a good idea to rebuild and reinstall the Perl DBD::mysql module whenever you install a new release of MySQL. The same applies to other MySQL interfaces as well, such as the Python MySQLdb module.

2.5.1 Upgrading from Version 4.1 to 5.0

In general, you should do the following when upgrading to MySQL 5.0 from 4.1:

- Read the 5.0 news items in the online manual to see what significant new features you can use in 5.0. See http://dev.mysql.com/doc/mysql/en/News.html.
- If you are running MySQL Server on Windows, see Section 2.5.7, "Upgrading MySQL Under Windows."
- MySQL 5.0 adds support for stored procedures. This support requires the proc table in the mysql database. To create this file, you should run the mysql_fix_privilege_tables script as described in Section 2.5.8, "Upgrading the Grant Tables."
- If you are using replication, see Section 5.6, "Upgrading a Replication Setup," for information on upgrading your replication setup.

2.5.2 Upgrading from Version 4.0 to 4.1

In general, you should do the following when upgrading to MySQL 4.1 from 4.0:

- Check the items in the change lists found later in this section to see whether any of them might affect your applications.
- Read the 4.1 news items in the online manual to see what significant new features you can use in 4.1. See http://dev.mysql.com/doc/mysql/en/News.html.
- If you are running MySQL Server on Windows, see Section 2.5.7, "Upgrading MySQL Under Windows."

  Important note: Early alpha Windows distributions for MySQL 4.1 do not contain an installer program. See Section 2.2.1.2, "Installing a Windows Binary Distribution," for instructions on how to install such a distribution.

- After upgrading, update the grant tables to have the new longer Password column that is needed for secure handling of passwords. The procedure uses mysql_fix_privilege_tables and is described in Section 2.5.8, "Upgrading the Grant Tables." Implications of the password-handling change for applications are given later in this section.
- If you are using replication, see Section 5.6, "Upgrading a Replication Setup," for information on upgrading your replication setup.
- The Berkeley DB table handler is updated to DB 4.1 (from 3.2) which has a new log format. If you have to downgrade back to 4.0 you must use mysqldump to dump your BDB tables in text format and delete all log.*xxxxxxxxx* files before you start MySQL 4.0 and reload the data.

- Character set support has been improved. If you have table columns that store character data represented in a character set that the 4.1 server now supports directly, you can convert the columns to the proper character set using the instructions given later in this section.

- If you are using an old DBD-mysql module (Msql-MySQL-modules) you have to upgrade to use the newer DBD-mysql module. Anything above DBD-mysql 2.*xx* should be fine.

  If you don't upgrade, some methods (such as DBI->do()) will not notice error conditions correctly.

Several visible behaviors have changed between MySQL 4.0 and MySQL 4.1 to fix some critical bugs and make MySQL more compatible with standard SQL. These changes may affect your applications.

Some of the 4.1 behaviors can be tested in 4.0 before performing a full upgrade to 4.1. We have added to later MySQL 4.0 releases (from 4.0.12 on) a --new startup option for mysqld. See Section 4.2.1, "mysqld Command-Line Options."

This option gives you the 4.1 behavior for the most critical changes. You can also enable these behaviors for a given client connection with the SET @@new=1 command, or turn them off if they are on with SET @@new=0.

If you believe that some of the 4.1 changes will affect you, we recommend that before upgrading to 4.1, you download the latest MySQL 4.0 version and run it with the --new option by adding the following to your config file:

```
[mysqld-4.0]
new
```

That way you can test the new behaviors in 4.0 to make sure that your applications work with them. This will help you have a smooth, painless transition when you perform a full upgrade to 4.1 later. Putting the --new option in the [mysqld-4.0] option group ensures that you don't accidentally later run the 4.1 version with the --new option.

The following lists describe changes that may affect applications and that you should watch out for when upgrading to version 4.1:

Server Changes:

- All tables and string columns now have a character set. Character set information is displayed by SHOW CREATE TABLE and mysqldump. (MySQL versions 4.0.6 and above can read the new dump files; older versions cannot.) This change should not affect applications that use only one character set.

- Normally, the server runs using the latin1 character set by default. If you have been storing column data that actually is in some other character set that the 4.1 server now supports directly, you can convert the column. However, you should avoid trying to convert directly from latin1 to the "real" character set. This may result in data loss. Instead, convert the column to a binary column type, and then from the binary type to a non-binary type with the desired character set. Conversion to and from binary involves no attempt at character value conversion and preserves your data intact. For example, suppose that you have a 4.0 table with three columns that are used to store values represented in latin1, latin2, and utf8:

```
CREATE TABLE t
(
    latin1_col CHAR(50),
    latin2_col CHAR(100),
    utf8_col CHAR(150)
);
```

After upgrading to MySQL 4.1, you want to convert this table to leave latin1_col alone but change the latin2_col and utf8_col columns to have character sets of latin2 and utf8. First, back up your table, then convert the columns as follows:

```
ALTER TABLE t MODIFY latin2_col BINARY(100);
ALTER TABLE t MODIFY utf8_col BINARY(150);
ALTER TABLE t MODIFY latin2_col CHAR(100) CHARACTER SET latin2;
ALTER TABLE t MODIFY utf8_col CHAR(150) CHARACTER SET utf8;
```

The first two statements "remove" the character set information from the latin2_col and utf8_col columns. The second two statements assign the proper character sets to the two columns.

If you like, you can combine the to-binary conversions and from-binary conversions into single statements:

```
ALTER TABLE t
    MODIFY latin2_col BINARY(100),
    MODIFY utf8_col BINARY(150);
ALTER TABLE t
    MODIFY latin2_col CHAR(100) CHARACTER SET latin2,
    MODIFY utf8_col CHAR(150) CHARACTER SET utf8;
```

- The table definition format used in .frm files has changed slightly in 4.1. MySQL 4.0 versions from 4.0.11 on can read the new .frm format directly, but older versions cannot. If you need to move tables from 4.1 to a version earlier than 4.0.11, you should use mysqldump. See Section 7.8, "The mysqldump Database Backup Program."

- **Important note:** If you upgrade to MySQL 4.1.1 or higher, it is difficult to downgrade back to 4.0 or 4.1.0! That is because, for earlier versions, InnoDB is not aware of multiple tablespaces.

- If you are running multiple servers on the same Windows machine, you should use a different --shared-memory-base-name option for each server.

- The interface to aggregated UDF functions has changed a bit. You must now declare a xxx_clear() function for each aggregate function XXX().

Client Changes:

- `mysqldump` now has the `--opt` and `--quote-names` options enabled by default. You can turn them off with `--skip-opt` and `--skip-quote-names`.

SQL Changes:

- String comparison now works according to SQL standard: Instead of stripping end spaces before comparison, we now extend the shorter string with spaces. The problem with this is that now `'a' > 'a\t'`, which it wasn't before. If you have any tables where you have a `CHAR` or `VARCHAR` column in which the last character in the column may be less than `ASCII(32)`, you should use `REPAIR TABLE` or `myisamchk` to ensure that the table is correct.

- When using multiple-table `DELETE` statements, you should use the alias of the tables from which you want to delete, not the actual table name. For example, instead of this:

```
DELETE test FROM test AS t1, test2 WHERE ...
```

Do this:

```
DELETE t1 FROM test AS t1, test2 WHERE ...
```

- `TIMESTAMP` is now returned as a string in `'YYYY-MM-DD HH:MM:SS'` format. (The `--new` option can be used from 4.0.12 on to make a 4.0 server behave as 4.1 in this respect.) If you want to have the value returned as a number (as MySQL 4.0 does) you should add +0 to `TIMESTAMP` columns when you retrieve them:

```
mysql> SELECT ts_col + 0 FROM tbl_name;
```

Display widths for `TIMESTAMP` columns are no longer supported. For example, if you declare a column as `TIMESTAMP(10)`, the `(10)` is ignored.

These changes were necessary for SQL standards compliance. In a future version, a further change will be made (backward compatible with this change), allowing the timestamp length to indicate the desired number of digits for fractions of a second.

- Binary values such as `0xFFDF` now are assumed to be strings instead of numbers. This fixes some problems with character sets where it's convenient to input a string as a binary value. With this change, you should use `CAST()` if you want to compare binary values numerically as integers:

```
mysql> SELECT CAST(0xFEFF AS UNSIGNED INTEGER)
    ->         < CAST(0xFF AS UNSIGNED INTEGER);
        -> 0
```

If you don't use `CAST()`, a lexical string comparison will be done:

```
mysql> SELECT 0xFEFF < 0xFF;
        -> 1
```

Using binary items in a numeric context or comparing them using the = operator should work as before. (The --new option can be used from 4.0.13 on to make a 4.0 server behave as 4.1 in this respect.)

- For functions that produce a DATE, DATETIME, or TIME value, the result returned to the client now is fixed up to have a temporal type. For example, in MySQL 4.1, you get this result:

```
mysql> SELECT CAST('2001-1-1' AS DATETIME);
        -> '2001-01-01 00:00:00'
```

In MySQL 4.0, the result is different:

```
mysql> SELECT CAST('2001-1-1' AS DATETIME);
        -> '2001-01-01'
```

- DEFAULT values no longer can be specified for AUTO_INCREMENT columns. (In 4.0, a DEFAULT value is silently ignored; in 4.1, an error occurs.)

- LIMIT no longer accepts negative arguments. Use some large number (maximum 18446744073709551615) instead of –1.

- SERIALIZE is no longer a valid mode value for the sql_mode variable. You should use SET TRANSACTION ISOLATION LEVEL SERIALIZABLE instead. SERIALIZE is no longer valid for the --sql-mode option for mysqld, either. Use --transaction-isolation=SERIALIZABLE instead.

C API Changes:

- Some C API calls such as mysql_real_query() now return 1 on error, not -1. You may have to change some old applications if they use constructs like this:

```
if (mysql_real_query(mysql_object, query, query_length) == -1)
{
  printf("Got error");
}
```

Change the call to test for a non-zero value instead:

```
if (mysql_real_query(mysql_object, query, query_length) != 0)
{
  printf("Got error");
}
```

Password-Handling Changes:

The password hashing mechanism has changed in 4.1 to provide better security, but this may cause compatibility problems if you still have clients that use the client library from 4.0 or earlier. (It is very likely that you will have 4.0 clients in situations where clients connect from remote hosts that have not yet upgraded to 4.1.) The following list indicates some possible upgrade strategies. They represent various tradeoffs between the goal of compatibility with old clients and the goal of security.

- Only upgrade the client to use 4.1 client libraries (not the server). No behavior will change (except the return value of some API calls), but you cannot use any of the new features provided by the 4.1 client/server protocol, either. (MySQL 4.1 has an extended client/server protocol that offers such features as prepared statements and multiple result sets.)

- Upgrade to 4.1 and run the `mysql_fix_privilege_tables` script to widen the `Password` column in the `user` table so that it can hold long password hashes. But run the server with the `--old-passwords` option to provide backward compatibility that allows pre-4.1 clients to continue to connect to their short-hash accounts. Eventually, when all your clients are upgraded to 4.1, you can stop using the `--old-passwords` server option. You can also change the passwords for your MySQL accounts to use the new more secure format.

- Upgrade to 4.1 and run the `mysql_fix_privilege_tables` script to widen the `Password` column in the `user` table. If you know that all clients also have been upgraded to 4.1, don't run the server with the `--old-passwords` option. Instead, change the passwords on all existing accounts so that they have the new format. A pure-4.1 installation is the most secure.

Further background on password hashing with respect to client authentication and password-changing operations may be found in Section 4.4.9, "Password Hashing in MySQL 4.1," and Section A.2.3, "`Client does not support authentication protocol`."

2.5.3 Upgrading from Version 3.23 to 4.0

In general, you should do the following when upgrading to MySQL 4.0 from 3.23:

- Check the items in the change lists found later in this section to see whether any of them might affect your applications.

- Read the 4.0 news items in the online manual to see what significant new features you can use in 4.0. See `http://dev.mysql.com/doc/mysql/en/News.html`.

- If you are running MySQL Server on Windows, see Section 2.5.7, "Upgrading MySQL Under Windows."

- After upgrading, update the grant tables to add new privileges and features. The procedure uses the `mysql_fix_privilege_tables` script and is described in Section 2.5.8, "Upgrading the Grant Tables."

- If you are using replication, see Section 5.6, "Upgrading a Replication Setup," for information on upgrading your replication setup.

- Edit any MySQL startup scripts or option files to not use any of the deprecated options described later in this section.

- Convert your old ISAM files to MyISAM files. One way to do this is with the mysql_convert_table_format script. (This is a Perl script; it requires that DBI be installed.) To convert the tables in a given database, use this command:

```
shell> mysql_convert_table_format database db_name
```

Note that this should be used only if all tables in the given database are ISAM or MyISAM tables. To avoid converting tables of other types to MyISAM, you can explicitly list the names of your ISAM tables after the database name on the command line.

Individual tables can be changed to MyISAM by using the following ALTER TABLE statement for each table to be converted:

```
mysql> ALTER TABLE tbl_name TYPE=MyISAM;
```

If you are not sure of the table type for a given table, use this statement:

```
mysql> SHOW TABLE STATUS LIKE 'tbl_name';
```

- Ensure that you don't have any MySQL clients that use shared libraries (like the Perl DBD::mysql module). If you do, you should recompile them, because the data structures used in libmysqlclient.so have changed. The same applies to other MySQL interfaces as well, such as the Python MySQLdb module.

MySQL 4.0 will work even if you don't perform the preceding actions, but you will not be able to use the new security privileges in MySQL 4.0 and you may run into problems when upgrading later to MySQL 4.1 or newer. The ISAM file format still works in MySQL 4.0, but is deprecated and is not compiled in by default as of MySQL 4.1. MyISAM tables should be used instead.

Old clients should work with a Version 4.0 server without any problems.

Even if you perform the preceding actions, you can still downgrade to MySQL 3.23.52 or newer if you run into problems with the MySQL 4.0 series. In this case, you must use mysqldump to dump any tables that use full-text indexes and reload the dump file into the 3.23 server. This is necessary because 4.0 uses a new format for full-text indexing.

The following lists describe changes that may affect applications and that you should watch out for when upgrading to version 4.0:

Server Changes:

- MySQL 4.0 has a lot of new privileges in the mysql.user table. See Section 4.4.3, "Privileges Provided by MySQL."

To get these new privileges to work, you must update the grant tables. The procedure is described in Section 2.5.8, "Upgrading the Grant Tables." Until you do this, all accounts have the SHOW DATABASES, CREATE TEMPORARY TABLES, and LOCK TABLES privileges. SUPER and EXECUTE privileges take their value from PROCESS. REPLICATION SLAVE and REPLICATION CLIENT take their values from FILE.

If you have any scripts that create new MySQL user accounts, you may want to change them to use the new privileges. If you are not using GRANT commands in the scripts, this is a good time to change your scripts to use GRANT instead of modifying the grant tables directly.

From version 4.0.2 on, the option --safe-show-database is deprecated (and no longer does anything). See Section 4.3.3, "Startup Options for mysqld Concerning Security."

If you get Access denied errors for new users in version 4.0.2 and up, you should check whether you need some of the new grants that you didn't need before. In particular, you will need REPLICATION SLAVE (instead of FILE) for new slave servers.

- safe_mysqld has been renamed to mysqld_safe. For backward compatibility, binary distributions will for some time include safe_mysqld as a symlink to mysqld_safe.

- InnoDB support is now included by default in binary distributions. If you build MySQL from source, InnoDB is configured in by default. If you do not use InnoDB and want to save memory when running a server that has InnoDB support enabled, use the --skip-innodb server startup option. To compile MySQL without InnoDB support, run configure with the --without-innodb option.

- Values for the startup parameters myisam_max_extra_sort_file_size and myisam_max_extra_sort_file_size now are given in bytes (they were given in megabytes before 4.0.3).

- mysqld now has the option --temp-pool enabled by default because this gives better performance with some operating systems (most notably Linux).

- The mysqld startup options --skip-locking and --enable-locking were renamed to --skip-external-locking and --external-locking.

- External system locking of MyISAM/ISAM files is now turned off by default. You can turn this on with --external-locking. (However, this is never needed for most users.)

- The following startup variables and options have been renamed:

Old Name	New Name
myisam_bulk_insert_tree_size	bulk_insert_buffer_size
query_cache_startup_type	query_cache_type
record_buffer	read_buffer_size
record_rnd_buffer	read_rnd_buffer_size
sort_buffer	sort_buffer_size
warnings	log-warnings
--err-log	--log-error (for mysqld_safe)

The startup options record_buffer, sort_buffer, and warnings will still work in MySQL 4.0 but are deprecated.

SQL Changes:

- The following SQL variables have been renamed:

Old Name	New Name
SQL_BIG_TABLES	BIG_TABLES
SQL_LOW_PRIORITY_UPDATES	LOW_PRIORITY_UPDATES
SQL_MAX_JOIN_SIZE	MAX_JOIN_SIZE
SQL_QUERY_CACHE_TYPE	QUERY_CACHE_TYPE

  The old names still work in MySQL 4.0 but are deprecated.

- You have to use SET GLOBAL SQL_SLAVE_SKIP_COUNTER=*skip_count* instead of SET SQL_SLAVE_SKIP_COUNTER=*skip_count*.

- SHOW MASTER STATUS now returns an empty set if binary logging is not enabled.

- SHOW SLAVE STATUS now returns an empty set if the slave is not initialized.

- SHOW INDEX has two more columns than it had in 3.23 (Null and Index_type).

- The format of SHOW OPEN TABLES has changed.

- ORDER BY *col_name* DESC sorts NULL values last, as of MySQL 4.0.11. In 3.23 and in earlier 4.0 versions, this was not always consistent.

- CHECK, LOCALTIME, and LOCALTIMESTAMP now are reserved words.

- DOUBLE and FLOAT columns now honor the UNSIGNED flag on storage (before, UNSIGNED was ignored for these columns).

- The result of all bitwise operators (|, &, <<, >>, and ~) is now unsigned. This may cause problems if you are using them in a context where you want a signed result.

  Note: When you use subtraction between integer values where one is of type UNSIGNED, the result will be unsigned. In other words, before upgrading to MySQL 4.0, you should check your application for cases in which you are subtracting a value from an unsigned entity and want a negative answer or subtracting an unsigned value from an integer column. You can disable this behavior by using the --sql-mode= NO_UNSIGNED_SUBTRACTION option when starting mysqld. See Section 4.2.2, "The Server SQL Mode."

- You should use integers to store values in BIGINT columns (instead of using strings, as you did in MySQL 3.23). Using strings will still work, but using integers is more efficient.

- In MySQL 3.23, INSERT INTO ... SELECT always had IGNORE enabled. As of 4.0.1, MySQL will stop (and possibly roll back) by default in case of an error unless you specify IGNORE.

- You should use TRUNCATE TABLE when you want to delete all rows from a table and you don't need to obtain a count of the number of rows that were deleted. (DELETE FROM *tbl_name* returns a row count in 4.0, and TRUNCATE TABLE is faster.)

- You will get an error if you have an active transaction or LOCK TABLES statement when trying to execute TRUNCATE TABLE or DROP DATABASE.

- To use MATCH ... AGAINST (... IN BOOLEAN MODE) full-text searches with your tables, you must rebuild their indexes with REPAIR TABLE *tbl_name* USE_FRM. If you attempt a boolean full-text search without rebuilding the indexes this way, the search will return incorrect results.

- LOCATE() and INSTR() are case sensitive if one of the arguments is a binary string. Otherwise they are case insensitive.

- STRCMP() now uses the current character set when performing comparisons. This makes the default comparison behavior not case sensitive unless one or both of the operands are binary strings.

- HEX(*string*) now returns the characters in *string* converted to hexadecimal. If you want to convert a number to hexadecimal, you should ensure that you call HEX() with a numeric argument.

- RAND(*seed*) returns a different random number series in 4.0 than in 3.23; this was done to further differentiate RAND(*seed*) and RAND(*seed*+1).

- The default type returned by IFNULL(*A,B*) is now set to be the more "general" of the types of *A* and *B*. (The general-to-specific order is string, REAL, INTEGER).

C API Changes:

- The old C API functions mysql_drop_db(), mysql_create_db(), and mysql_connect() are no longer supported unless you compile MySQL with CFLAGS=-DUSE_OLD_FUNCTIONS. However, it is preferable to change client programs to use the new 4.0 API instead.

- In the MYSQL_FIELD structure, length and max_length have changed from unsigned int to unsigned long. This should not cause any problems, except that they may generate warning messages when used as arguments in the printf() class of functions.

- Multi-threaded clients should use mysql_thread_init() and mysql_thread_end().

Other Changes:

- If you want to recompile the Perl DBD::mysql module, use a recent version. Version 2.9003 is recommended. Versions older than 1.2218 should not be used because they use the deprecated mysql_drop_db() call.

2.5.4 Upgrading from Version 3.22 to 3.23

MySQL 3.22 and 3.21 clients will work without any problems with a MySQL 3.23 server.

When upgrading to MySQL 3.23 from an earlier version, note the following changes:

Table Changes:

- MySQL 3.23 supports tables of the new MyISAM type and the old ISAM type. By default, all new tables are created with type MyISAM unless you start mysqld with the --default-table-type=isam option. You don't have to convert your old ISAM tables to use them with MySQL 3.23. You can convert an ISAM table to MyISAM format with ALTER TABLE tbl_name TYPE=MyISAM or the Perl script mysql_convert_table_format.

- All tables that use the tis620 character set must be fixed with myisamchk -r or REPAIR TABLE.

- If you are using the german character sort order for ISAM tables, you must repair them with isamchk -r, because we have made some changes in the sort order.

Client Program Changes:

- The MySQL client mysql is now by default started with the --no-named-commands (-g) option. This option can be disabled with --enable-named-commands (-G). This may cause incompatibility problems in some cases—for example, in SQL scripts that use named commands without a semicolon. Long format commands still work from the first line.

- If you want your mysqldump files to be compatible between MySQL 3.22 and 3.23, you should not use the --opt or --all option to mysqldump.

SQL Changes:

- If you do a DROP DATABASE on a symbolically linked database, both the link and the original database are deleted. This didn't happen in MySQL 3.22 because configure didn't detect the availability of the readlink() system call.

- OPTIMIZE TABLE now works only for MyISAM tables. For other table types, you can use ALTER TABLE to optimize the table. During OPTIMIZE TABLE, the table is now locked to prevent it from being used by other threads.

- Date functions that work on parts of dates (such as MONTH()) will now return 0 for 0000-00-00 dates. In MySQL 3.22, these functions returned NULL.

- The default return type of IF() now depends on both arguments, not just the first one.

- AUTO_INCREMENT columns should not be used to store negative numbers. The reason for this is that negative numbers caused problems when wrapping from –1 to 0. You should not store 0 in AUTO_INCREMENT columns, either; CHECK TABLE will complain about 0 values because they may change if you dump and restore the table. AUTO_INCREMENT for MyISAM tables is now handled at a lower level and is much faster than before. In addition, for MyISAM tables, old numbers are no longer reused, even if you delete rows from the table.

- CASE, DELAYED, ELSE, END, FULLTEXT, INNER, RIGHT, THEN, and WHEN now are reserved words.

- FLOAT(p) now is a true floating-point type and not a value with a fixed number of decimals.

- When declaring columns using a DECIMAL(*length,dec*) type, the *length* argument no longer includes a place for the sign or the decimal point.

- A TIME string must now be of one of the following formats: [[[DAYS] [H]H:]MM:]SS[.fraction] or [[[[[H]H]H]H]MM]SS[.fraction].

- LIKE now compares strings using the same character comparison rules as for the = operator. If you require the old behavior, you can compile MySQL with the CXXFLAGS=-DLIKE_CMP_TOUPPER flag.

- REGEXP now is case insensitive if neither of the strings is a binary string.

- When you check or repair MyISAM (.MYI) tables, you should use the CHECK TABLE statement or the myisamchk command. For ISAM (.ISM) tables, use the isamchk command.

- Check all your calls to DATE_FORMAT() to make sure that there is a '%' before each format character. (MySQL 3.22 already allowed this syntax, but now '%' is required.)

- In MySQL 3.22, the output of SELECT DISTINCT ... was almost always sorted. In MySQL 3.23, you must use GROUP BY or ORDER BY to obtain sorted output.

- SUM() now returns NULL instead of 0 if there are no matching rows. This is required by standard SQL.

- An AND or OR with NULL values will now return NULL instead of 0. This mostly affects queries that use NOT on an AND/OR expression as NOT NULL = NULL.

- LPAD() and RPAD() now shorten the result string if it's longer than the length argument.

C API Changes:

- mysql_fetch_fields_direct() now is a function instead of a macro. It now returns a pointer to a MYSQL_FIELD instead of a MYSQL_FIELD.

- mysql_num_fields() no longer can be used on a MYSQL* object (it's now a function that takes a MYSQL_RES* value as an argument). With a MYSQL* object, you now should use mysql_field_count() instead.

2.5.5 Upgrading from Version 3.21 to 3.22

Nothing that affects compatibility has changed between versions 3.21 and 3.22. The only pitfall is that new tables that are created with DATE type columns will use the new way to store the date. You can't access these new columns from an old version of mysqld.

When upgrading to MySQL 3.23 from an earlier version, note the following changes:

- After installing MySQL Version 3.22, you should start the new server and then run the mysql_fix_privilege_tables script. This will add the new privileges that you need to use the GRANT command. If you forget this, you will get Access denied when you try to use ALTER TABLE, CREATE INDEX, or DROP INDEX. The procedure for updating the grant tables is described in Section 2.5.8, "Upgrading the Grant Tables."

- The C API interface to `mysql_real_connect()` has changed. If you have an old client program that calls this function, you must pass a 0 for the new `db` argument (or recode the client to send the `db` element for faster connections). You must also call `mysql_init()` before calling `mysql_real_connect()`. This change was done to allow the new `mysql_options()` function to save options in the `MYSQL` handler structure.

- The `mysqld` variable `key_buffer` has been renamed to `key_buffer_size`, but you can still use the old name in your startup files.

2.5.6 Upgrading from Version 3.20 to 3.21

If you are running a version older than Version 3.20.28 and want to switch to Version 3.21, you need to do the following:

You can start the `mysqld` Version 3.21 server with the `--old-protocol` option to use it with clients from a Version 3.20 distribution. In this case, the server uses the old pre-3.21 `password()` checking rather than the new method. Also, the new client function `mysql_errno()` will not return any server error, only `CR_UNKNOWN_ERROR`. The function does work for client errors.

If you are *not* using the `--old-protocol` option to `mysqld`, you will need to make the following changes:

- All client code must be recompiled. If you are using ODBC, you must get the new MyODBC 2.x driver.
- The `scripts/add_long_password` script must be run to convert the `Password` field in the `mysql.user` table to `CHAR(16)`.
- All passwords must be reassigned in the `mysql.user` table to get 62-bit rather than 31-bit passwords.
- The table format hasn't changed, so you don't have to convert any tables.

MySQL 3.20.28 and above can handle the new user table format without affecting clients. If you have a MySQL version earlier than 3.20.28, passwords will no longer work with it if you convert the user table. So to be safe, you should first upgrade to at least Version 3.20.28 and then upgrade to Version 3.21.

The new client code works with a 3.20.x `mysqld` server, so if you experience problems with 3.21.x, you can use the old 3.20.x server without having to recompile the clients again.

If you are not using the `--old-protocol` option to `mysqld`, old clients will be unable to connect and will issue the following error message:

```
ERROR: Protocol mismatch. Server Version = 10 Client Version = 9
```

The Perl DBI interface also supports the old `mysqlperl` interface. The only change you have to make if you use `mysqlperl` is to change the arguments to the `connect()` function. The new arguments are: host, database, user, and password (note that the user and password arguments have changed places).

The following changes may affect queries in old applications:

- `HAVING` must now be specified before any `ORDER BY` clause.
- The parameters to `LOCATE()` have been swapped.
- There are some new reserved words. The most notable are `DATE`, `TIME`, and `TIMESTAMP`.

2.5.7 Upgrading MySQL Under Windows

When upgrading MySQL under Windows, please follow these steps:

1. Download the latest Windows distribution of MySQL.
2. Choose a time of day with low usage, where a maintenance break is acceptable.
3. Alert the users who still are active about the maintenance break.
4. Stop the running MySQL Server (for example, with `NET STOP MySQL` or with the `Services` utility if you are running MySQL as a service, or with `mysqladmin shutdown` otherwise).
5. Exit the `WinMySQLAdmin` program if it is running.
6. Run the installation script of the Windows distribution by clicking the Install button in WinZip and following the installation steps of the script.

   Important note: Early alpha Windows distributions for MySQL 4.1 do not contain an installer program. See Section 2.2.1.2, "Installing a Windows Binary Distribution," for instructions on how to install such a distribution.
7. You may either overwrite your old MySQL installation (usually located at `C:\mysql`), or install it into a different directory, such as `C:\mysql4`. Overwriting the old installation is recommended.
8. Restart the server. For example, use `NET START MySQL` if you run MySQL as a service, or invoke `mysqld` directly otherwise.
9. Update the grant tables. The procedure is described in Section 2.5.8, "Upgrading the Grant Tables."

Possible error situations:

```
A system error has occurred.
System error 1067 has occurred.
The process terminated unexpectedly.
```

These errors mean that your option file (by default `C:\my.cnf`) contains an option that cannot be recognized by MySQL. You can verify that this is the case by trying to restart MySQL with the option file renamed to prevent the server from using it. (For example, rename `C:\my.cnf` to `C:\my_cnf.old`.) Once you have verified it, you need to identify which option is the culprit. Create a new `my.cnf` file and move parts of the old file to it (restarting the server after you move each part) until you determine which option causes server startup to fail.

2.5.8 Upgrading the Grant Tables

Some releases introduce changes to the structure of the grant tables (the tables in the `mysql` database) to add new privileges or features. To make sure that your grant tables are current when you update to a new version of MySQL, you should update your grant tables as well.

On Unix or Unix-like systems, update the grant tables by running the `mysql_fix_privilege_tables` script:

```
shell> mysql_fix_privilege_tables
```

You must run this script while the server is running. It attempts to connect to the server running on the local host as `root`. If your `root` account requires a password, indicate the password on the command line. For MySQL 4.1 and up, specify the password like this:

```
shell> mysql_fix_privilege_tables --password=root_password
```

Prior to MySQL 4.1, specify the password like this:

```
shell> mysql_fix_privilege_tables root_password
```

The `mysql_fix_privilege_tables` script performs any actions necessary to convert your grant tables to the current format. You might see some `Duplicate column name` warnings as it runs; you can ignore them.

After running the script, stop the server and restart it.

On Windows systems, there isn't an easy way to update the grant tables until MySQL 4.0.15. From version 4.0.15 on, MySQL distributions include a `mysql_fix_privilege_tables.sql` SQL script that you can run using the `mysql` client. If your MySQL installation is located at `C:\mysql`, the commands look like this:

```
C:\> C:\mysql\bin\mysql -u root -p mysql
mysql> SOURCE C:\mysql\scripts\mysql_fix_privilege_tables.sql
```

The `mysql` command will prompt you for the `root` password; enter it when prompted. If your installation is located in some other directory, adjust the pathnames appropriately.

As with the Unix procedure, you might see some `Duplicate column name` warnings as `mysql` processes the statements in the `mysql_fix_privilege_tables.sql` script; you can ignore them.

After running the script, stop the server and restart it.

2.5.9 Copying MySQL Databases to Another Machine

If you are using MySQL 3.23 or later, you can copy the `.frm`, `.MYI`, and `.MYD` files for `MyISAM` tables between different architectures that support the same floating-point format. (MySQL takes care of any byte-swapping issues.) See Section 8.1, "The `MyISAM` Storage Engine."

The MySQL ISAM data and index files (.ISD and *.ISM, respectively) are architecture dependent and in some cases operating system dependent. If you want to move your applications to another machine that has a different architecture or operating system than your current machine, you should not try to move a database by simply copying the files to the other machine. Use mysqldump instead.

By default, mysqldump will create a file containing SQL statements. You can then transfer the file to the other machine and feed it as input to the mysql client.

Try mysqldump --help to see what options are available. If you are moving the data to a newer version of MySQL, you should use mysqldump --opt to take advantage of any optimizations that result in a dump file that is smaller and can be processed faster.

The easiest (although not the fastest) way to move a database between two machines is to run the following commands on the machine on which the database is located:

```
shell> mysqladmin -h 'other hostname' create db_name
shell> mysqldump --opt db_name | mysql -h 'other hostname' db_name
```

If you want to copy a database from a remote machine over a slow network, you can use:

```
shell> mysqladmin create db_name
shell> mysqldump -h 'other hostname' --opt --compress db_name | mysql db_name
```

You can also store the result in a file, then transfer the file to the target machine and load the file into the database there. For example, you can dump a database to a file on the source machine like this:

```
shell> mysqldump --quick db_name | gzip > db_name.contents.gz
```

(The file created in this example is compressed.) Transfer the file containing the database contents to the target machine and run these commands there:

```
shell> mysqladmin create db_name
shell> gunzip < db_name.contents.gz | mysql db_name
```

You can also use mysqldump and mysqlimport to transfer the database. For big tables, this is much faster than simply using mysqldump. In the following commands, DUMPDIR represents the full pathname of the directory you use to store the output from mysqldump.

First, create the directory for the output files and dump the database:

```
shell> mkdir DUMPDIR
shell> mysqldump --tab=DUMPDIR db_name
```

Then transfer the files in the *DUMPDIR* directory to some corresponding directory on the target machine and load the files into MySQL there:

```
shell> mysqladmin create db_name         # create database
shell> cat DUMPDIR/*.sql | mysql db_name  # create tables in database
shell> mysqlimport db_name DUMPDIR/*.txt  # load data into tables
```

Also, don't forget to copy the mysql database because that is where the user, db, and host grant tables are stored. You might have to run commands as the MySQL root user on the new machine until you have the mysql database in place.

After you import the mysql database on the new machine, execute mysqladmin flush-privileges so that the server reloads the grant table information.

2.6 Operating System–Specific Notes

2.6.1 Linux Notes

This section discusses issues that have been found to occur on Linux. The first few subsections describe general operating system-related issues, problems that can occur when using binary or source distributions, and post-installation issues. The remaining subsections discuss problems that occur with Linux on specific platforms.

Note that most of these problems occur on older versions of Linux. If you are running a recent version, you likely will see none of them.

2.6.1.1 Linux Operating System Notes

MySQL needs at least Linux Version 2.0.

Warning: We have seen some strange problems with Linux 2.2.14 and MySQL on SMP systems. We also have reports from some MySQL users that they have encountered serious stability problems using MySQL with kernel 2.2.14. If you are using this kernel, you should upgrade to 2.2.19 (or newer) or to a 2.4 kernel. If you have a multiple-CPU box, then you should seriously consider using 2.4 because it will give you a significant speed boost. Your system also will be more stable.

When using LinuxThreads, you will see a minimum of three mysqld processes running. These are in fact threads. There will be one thread for the LinuxThreads manager, one thread to handle connections, and one thread to handle alarms and signals.

2.6.1.2 Linux Binary Distribution Notes

The Linux-Intel binary and RPM releases of MySQL are configured for the highest possible speed. We are always trying to use the fastest stable compiler available.

The binary release is linked with -static, which means you do not normally need to worry about which version of the system libraries you have. You need not install LinuxThreads, either. A program linked with -static is slightly larger than a dynamically linked program, but also slightly faster (3-5%). However, one problem with a statically linked program is that you can't use user-defined functions (UDFs). If you are going to write or use UDFs (this is something for C or C++ programmers only), you must compile MySQL yourself using dynamic linking.

A known issue with binary distributions is that on older Linux systems that use libc (such as Red Hat 4.x or Slackware), you will get some non-fatal problems with hostname resolution. If your system uses libc rather than glibc2, you probably will encounter some difficulties with hostname resolution and getpwnam(). This happens because glibc unfortunately depends on some external libraries to implement hostname resolution and getpwent(), even when compiled with -static. These problems manifest themselves in two ways:

- You probably will see the following error message when you run mysql_install_db:

  ```
  Sorry, the host 'xxxx' could not be looked up
  ```

  You can deal with this by executing mysql_install_db --force, which will not execute the resolveip test in mysql_install_db. The downside is that you can't use hostnames in the grant tables: Except for localhost, you must use IP numbers instead. If you are using an old version of MySQL that doesn't support --force, you must manually remove the resolveip test in mysql_install using an editor.

- You also may see the following error when you try to run mysqld with the --user option:

  ```
  getpwnam: No such file or directory
  ```

  To work around this, start mysqld by using the su command rather than by specifying the --user option. This causes the system itself to change the user ID of the mysqld process so that mysqld need not do so.

Another solution, which solves both problems, is to not use a binary distribution. Get a MySQL source distribution (in RPM or tar.gz format) and install that instead.

On some Linux 2.2 versions, you may get the error Resource temporarily unavailable when clients make a lot of new connections to a mysqld server over TCP/IP. The problem is that Linux has a delay between the time that you close a TCP/IP socket and the time that the system actually frees it. There is room for only a finite number of TCP/IP slots, so you will encounter the resource-unavailable error if clients attempt too many new TCP/IP connections during a short time. For example, you may see the error when you run the MySQL test-connect benchmark over TCP/IP.

We have inquired about this problem a few times on different Linux mailing lists but have never been able to find a suitable resolution. The only known "fix" is for the clients to use persistent connections, or, if you are running the database server and clients on the same machine, to use Unix socket file connections rather than TCP/IP connections.

2.6.1.3 Linux Source Distribution Notes

The following notes regarding glibc apply only to the situation when you build MySQL
yourself. If you are running Linux on an x86 machine, in most cases it is much better for
you to just use our binary. We link our binaries against the best patched version of glibc we
can come up with and with the best compiler options, in an attempt to make it suitable for a
high-load server. For a typical user, even for setups with a lot of concurrent connections or
tables exceeding the 2GB limit, our binary is the best choice in most cases. After reading the
following text, if you are in doubt about what to do, try our binary first to see whether it
meets your needs. If you discover that it is not good enough, then you may want to try your
own build. In that case, we would appreciate a note about it so that we can build a better
binary next time.

MySQL uses LinuxThreads on Linux. If you are using an old Linux version that doesn't
have glibc2, you must install LinuxThreads before trying to compile MySQL. You can get
LinuxThreads at http://dev.mysql.com/downloads/os-linux.html.

Note that glibc versions before and including Version 2.1.1 have a fatal bug in
pthread_mutex_timedwait() handling, which is used when you issue INSERT DELAYED statements. We recommend that you not use INSERT DELAYED before upgrading glibc.

Note that Linux kernel and the LinuxThread library can by default only have 1,024 threads.
If you plan to have more than 1,000 concurrent connections, you will need to make some
changes to LinuxThreads:

- Increase PTHREAD_THREADS_MAX in sysdeps/unix/sysv/linux/bits/local_lim.h to 4096
  and decrease STACK_SIZE in linuxthreads/internals.h to 256KB. The paths are relative
  to the root of glibc. (Note that MySQL will not be stable with around 600-1000 connections if STACK_SIZE is the default of 2MB.)

- Recompile LinuxThreads to produce a new libpthread.a library, and relink MySQL
  against it.

The page http://www.volano.com/linuxnotes.html contains additional information about
circumventing thread limits in LinuxThreads.

There is another issue that greatly hurts MySQL performance, especially on SMP systems.
The mutex implementation in LinuxThreads in glibc 2.1 is very bad for programs with
many threads that hold the mutex only for a short time. This produces a paradoxical result:
If you link MySQL against an unmodified LinuxThreads, removing processors from an
SMP actually improves MySQL performance in many cases. We have made a patch available
for glibc 2.1.3 to correct this behavior (http://www.mysql.com/Downloads/Linux/
linuxthreads-2.1-patch).

With glibc 2.2.2, MySQL 3.23.36 will use the adaptive mutex, which is much better than
even the patched one in glibc 2.1.3. Be warned, however, that under some conditions, the
current mutex code in glibc 2.2.2 overspins, which hurts MySQL performance. The likelihood that this condition will occur can be reduced by renicing the mysqld process to the

highest priority. We have also been able to correct the overspin behavior with a patch, available at `http://www.mysql.com/Downloads/Linux/linuxthreads-2.2.2.patch`. It combines the correction of overspin, maximum number of threads, and stack spacing all in one. You will need to apply it in the `linuxthreads` directory with `patch -p0 </tmp/linuxthreads-2.2.2.patch`. We hope it will be included in some form in future releases of `glibc` 2.2. In any case, if you link against `glibc` 2.2.2, you still need to correct `STACK_SIZE` and `PTHREAD_THREADS_MAX`. We hope that the defaults will be corrected to some more acceptable values for high-load MySQL setup in the future, so that the commands needed to produce your own build can be reduced to `./configure; make; make install`.

We recommend that you use these patches to build a special static version of `libpthread.a` and use it only for statically linking against MySQL. We know that the patches are safe for MySQL and significantly improve its performance, but we cannot say anything about other applications. If you link other applications that require LinuxThreads against the patched static version of the library, or build a patched shared version and install it on your system, you do so at your own risk.

If you experience any strange problems during the installation of MySQL, or with some common utilities hanging, it is very likely that they are either library or compiler related. If this is the case, using our binary will resolve them.

If you link your own MySQL client programs, you may see the following error at runtime:

```
ld.so.1: fatal: libmysqlclient.so.#:
open failed: No such file or directory
```

This problem can be avoided by one of the following methods:

- Link clients with the `-Wl,r/full/path/to/libmysqlclient.so` flag rather than with `-Lpath`).
- Copy `libmysqclient.so` to `/usr/lib`.
- Add the pathname of the directory where `libmysqlclient.so` is located to the `LD_RUN_PATH` environment variable before running your client.

If you are using the Fujitsu compiler (`fcc/FCC`), you will have some problems compiling MySQL because the Linux header files are very `gcc` oriented. The following `configure` line should work with `fcc/FCC`:

```
CC=fcc CFLAGS="-O -K fast -K lib -K omitfp -Kpreex -D_GNU_SOURCE \
    -DCONST=const -DNO_STRTOLL_PROTO" \
CXX=FCC CXXFLAGS="-O -K fast -K lib \
    -K omitfp -K preex --no_exceptions --no_rtti -D_GNU_SOURCE \
    -DCONST=const -Dalloca=__builtin_alloca -DNO_STRTOLL_PROTO \
    '-D_EXTERN_INLINE=static __inline'" \
./configure \
    --prefix=/usr/local/mysql --enable-assembler \
    --with-mysqld-ldflags=-all-static --disable-shared \
    --with-low-memory
```

2.6.1.4 Linux Post-Installation Notes

`mysql.server` can be found in the `support-files` directory under the MySQL installation directory or in a MySQL source tree. You can install it as `/etc/init.d/mysql` for automatic MySQL startup and shutdown. See Section 2.4.3, "Starting and Stopping MySQL Automatically."

If MySQL can't open enough files or connections, it may be that you haven't configured Linux to handle enough files.

In Linux 2.2 and onward, you can check the number of allocated file handles as follows:

```
shell> cat /proc/sys/fs/file-max
shell> cat /proc/sys/fs/dquot-max
shell> cat /proc/sys/fs/super-max
```

If you have more than 16MB of memory, you should add something like the following to your init scripts (for example, `/etc/init.d/boot.local` on SuSE Linux):

```
echo 65536 > /proc/sys/fs/file-max
echo 8192 > /proc/sys/fs/dquot-max
echo 1024 > /proc/sys/fs/super-max
```

You can also run the `echo` commands from the command line as `root`, but these settings will be lost the next time your computer restarts.

Alternatively, you can set these parameters on startup by using the `sysctl` tool, which is used by many Linux distributions (SuSE has added it as well, beginning with SuSE Linux 8.0). Just put the following values into a file named `/etc/sysctl.conf`:

```
# Increase some values for MySQL
fs.file-max = 65536
fs.dquot-max = 8192
fs.super-max = 1024
```

You should also add the following to `/etc/my.cnf`:

```
[mysqld_safe]
open-files-limit=8192
```

This should allow the server a limit of 8,192 for the combined number of connections and open files.

The `STACK_SIZE` constant in LinuxThreads controls the spacing of thread stacks in the address space. It needs to be large enough so that there will be plenty of room for each individual thread stack, but small enough to keep the stack of some threads from running into the global `mysqld` data. Unfortunately, as we have experimentally discovered, the Linux implementation of `mmap()` will successfully unmap an already mapped region if you ask it to map out an address already in use, zeroing out the data on the entire page instead of returning an error. So, the safety of `mysqld` or any other threaded application depends on "gentlemanly" behavior of the code that creates threads. The user must take measures to make sure that the number of running threads at any time is sufficiently low for thread stacks to stay away from the global heap. With `mysqld`, you should enforce this behavior by setting a reasonable value for the `max_connections` variable.

If you build MySQL yourself, you can patch LinuxThreads for better stack use. See Section 2.6.1.3, "Linux Source Distribution Notes." If you do not want to patch LinuxThreads, you should set `max_connections` to a value no higher than 500. It should be even less if you have a large key buffer, large heap tables, or some other things that make `mysqld` allocate a lot of memory, or if you are running a 2.2 kernel with a 2GB patch. If you are using our binary or RPM version 3.23.25 or later, you can safely set `max_connections` at 1500, assuming no large key buffer or heap tables with lots of data. The more you reduce `STACK_SIZE` in LinuxThreads the more threads you can safely create. We recommend values between 128KB and 256KB.

If you use a lot of concurrent connections, you may suffer from a "feature" in the 2.2 kernel that attempts to prevent fork bomb attacks by penalizing a process for forking or cloning a child. This causes MySQL not to scale well as you increase the number of concurrent clients. On single-CPU systems, we have seen this manifested as very slow thread creation: It may take a long time to connect to MySQL (as long as one minute), and it may take just as long to shut it down. On multiple-CPU systems, we have observed a gradual drop in query speed as the number of clients increases. In the process of trying to find a solution, we have received a kernel patch from one of our users who claimed it made a lot of difference for his site. The patch is available at `http://www.mysql.com/Downloads/Patches/linux-fork.patch`. We have now done rather extensive testing of this patch on both development and production systems. It has significantly improved MySQL performance without causing any problems and we now recommend it to our users who still run high-load servers on 2.2 kernels.

This issue has been fixed in the 2.4 kernel, so if you are not satisfied with the current performance of your system, rather than patching your 2.2 kernel, it might be easier to upgrade to 2.4. On SMP systems, upgrading also will give you a nice SMP boost in addition to fixing the fairness bug.

We have tested MySQL on the 2.4 kernel on a two-CPU machine and found MySQL scales *much* better. There was virtually no slowdown on query throughput all the way up to 1,000 clients, and the MySQL scaling factor (computed as the ratio of maximum throughput to the throughput for one client) was 180%. We have observed similar results on a four-CPU system: Virtually no slowdown as the number of clients was increased up to 1,000, and a 300% scaling factor. Based on these results, for a high-load SMP server using a 2.2 kernel, we definitely recommend upgrading to the 2.4 kernel at this point.

We have discovered that it is essential to run the `mysqld` process with the highest possible priority on the 2.4 kernel to achieve maximum performance. This can be done by adding a `renice -20 $$` command to `mysqld_safe`. In our testing on a four-CPU machine, increasing the priority resulted in a 60% throughput increase with 400 clients.

We are currently also trying to collect more information on how well MySQL performs with a 2.4 kernel on four-way and eight-way systems. If you have access such a system and have done some benchmarks, please send an email message to benchmarks@mysql.com with the results. We will review them for inclusion in the manual.

If you see a dead mysqld server process with ps, this usually means that you have found a bug in MySQL or you have a corrupted table. See Section A.4.2, "What to Do If MySQL Keeps Crashing."

To get a core dump on Linux if mysqld dies with a SIGSEGV signal, you can start mysqld with the --core-file option. Note that you also probably need to raise the core file size by adding ulimit -c 1000000 to mysqld_safe or starting mysqld_safe with --core-file-size=1000000. See Section 4.1.3, "The mysqld_safe Server Startup Script."

2.6.1.5 Linux x86 Notes

MySQL requires libc Version 5.4.12 or newer. It's known to work with libc 5.4.46. glibc Version 2.0.6 and later should also work. There have been some problems with the glibc RPMs from Red Hat, so if you have problems, check whether there are any updates. The glibc 2.0.7-19 and 2.0.7-29 RPMs are known to work.

If you are using Red Hat 8.0 or a new glibc 2.2.x library, you may see mysqld die in gethostbyaddr(). This happens because the new glibc library requires a stack size greater than 128KB for this call. To fix the problem, start mysqld with the --thread-stack=192K option. (Use -O thread_stack=192K before MySQL 4.) This stack size is now the default on MySQL 4.0.10 and above, so you should not see the problem.

If you are using gcc 3.0 and above to compile MySQL, you must install the libstdc++v3 library before compiling MySQL; if you don't do this, you will get an error about a missing __cxa_pure_virtual symbol during linking.

On some older Linux distributions, configure may produce an error like this:

```
Syntax error in sched.h. Change _P to __P in the
/usr/include/sched.h file.
See the Installation chapter in the Reference Manual.
```

Just do what the error message says. Add an extra underscore to the _P macro name that has only one underscore, then try again.

You may get some warnings when compiling. Those shown here can be ignored:

```
mysqld.cc -o objs-thread/mysqld.o
mysqld.cc: In function `void init_signals()':
mysqld.cc:315: warning: assignment of negative value `-1' to
`long unsigned int'
mysqld.cc: In function `void * signal_hand(void *)':
mysqld.cc:346: warning: assignment of negative value `-1' to
`long unsigned int'
```

If `mysqld` always dumps core when it starts, the problem may be that you have an old `/lib/libc.a`. Try renaming it, then remove `sql/mysqld` and do a new `make install` and try again. This problem has been reported on some Slackware installations.

If you get the following error when linking `mysqld`, it means that your `libg++.a` is not installed correctly:

```
/usr/lib/libc.a(putc.o): In function `_IO_putc':
putc.o(.text+0x0): multiple definition of `_IO_putc'
```

You can avoid using `libg++.a` by running `configure` like this:

```
shell> CXX=gcc ./configure
```

If `mysqld` crashes immediately and you are running Red Hat Version 5.0 with a version of `glibc` older than 2.0.7-5, you should make sure that you have installed all `glibc` patches. There is a lot of information about this in the MySQL mail archives, available online at `http://lists.mysql.com/`.

2.6.1.6 Linux SPARC Notes

In some implementations, `readdir_r()` is broken. The symptom is that the SHOW DATABASES statement always returns an empty set. This can be fixed by removing `HAVE_READDIR_R` from `config.h` after configuring and before compiling.

2.6.1.7 Linux Alpha Notes

MySQL 3.23.12 is the first MySQL version that is tested on Linux-Alpha. If you plan to use MySQL on Linux-Alpha, you should ensure that you have this version or newer.

We have tested MySQL on Alpha with our benchmarks and test suite, and it appears to work nicely.

We currently build the MySQL binary packages on SuSE Linux 7.0 for AXP, kernel 2.4.4-SMP, Compaq C compiler (V6.2-505) and Compaq C++ compiler (V6.3-006) on a Compaq DS20 machine with an Alpha EV6 processor.

You can find the preceding compilers at `http://www.support.compaq.com/alpha-tools/`. By using these compilers rather than `gcc`, we get about 9-14% better MySQL performance.

Note that until MySQL version 3.23.52 and 4.0.2, we optimized the binary for the current CPU only (by using the `-fast` compile option). This means that for older versions, you can use our Alpha binaries only if you have an Alpha EV6 processor.

For all following releases, we added the `-arch generic` flag to our compile options, which makes sure that the binary runs on all Alpha processors. We also compile statically to avoid library problems. The `configure` command looks like this:

```
CC=ccc CFLAGS="-fast -arch generic" CXX=cxx \
CXXFLAGS="-fast -arch generic -noexceptions -nortti" \
```

```
./configure --prefix=/usr/local/mysql --disable-shared \
    --with-extra-charsets=complex --enable-thread-safe-client \
    --with-mysqld-ldflags=-non_shared --with-client-ldflags=-non_shared
```

If you want to use egcs, the following configure line worked for us:

```
CFLAGS="-O3 -fomit-frame-pointer" CXX=gcc \
CXXFLAGS="-O3 -fomit-frame-pointer -felide-constructors \
    -fno-exceptions -fno-rtti" \
./configure --prefix=/usr/local/mysql --disable-shared
```

Some known problems when running MySQL on Linux-Alpha:

- Debugging threaded applications like MySQL will not work with gdb 4.18. You should use gdb 5.1 instead.
- If you try linking mysqld statically when using gcc, the resulting image will dump core at startup time. In other words, *do not* use --with-mysqld-ldflags=-all-static with gcc.

2.6.1.8 Linux PowerPC Notes

MySQL should work on MkLinux with the newest glibc package (tested with glibc 2.0.7).

2.6.1.9 Linux MIPS Notes

To get MySQL to work on Qube2 (Linux Mips), you need the newest glibc libraries. glibc-2.0.7-29C2 is known to work. You must also use the egcs C++ compiler (egcs-1.0.2-9, gcc 2.95.2 or newer).

2.6.1.10 Linux IA-64 Notes

To get MySQL to compile on Linux IA-64, we use the following configure command for building with gcc 2.96:

```
CC=gcc \
CFLAGS="-O3 -fno-omit-frame-pointer" \
CXX=gcc \
CXXFLAGS="-O3 -fno-omit-frame-pointer -felide-constructors \
    -fno-exceptions -fno-rtti" \
    ./configure --prefix=/usr/local/mysql \
    "--with-comment=Official MySQL binary" \
    --with-extra-charsets=complex
```

On IA-64, the MySQL client binaries use shared libraries. This means that if you install our binary distribution at a location other than /usr/local/mysql, you need to add the path of the directory where you have libmysqlclient.so installed either to the /etc/ld.so.conf file or to the value of your LD_LIBRARY_PATH environment variable.

See Section A.3.1, "Problems Linking to the MySQL Client Library."

2.6.2 Mac OS X Notes

On Mac OS X, `tar` cannot handle long filenames. If you need to unpack a `.tar.gz` distribution, use `gnutar` instead.

2.6.2.1 Mac OS X 10.x (Darwin)

MySQL should work without any problems on Mac OS X 10.x (Darwin).

Our binary for Mac OS X is compiled on Darwin 6.3 with the following `configure` line:

```
CC=gcc CFLAGS="-O3 -fno-omit-frame-pointer" CXX=gcc \
CXXFLAGS="-O3 -fno-omit-frame-pointer -felide-constructors \
    -fno-exceptions -fno-rtti" \
    ./configure --prefix=/usr/local/mysql \
    --with-extra-charsets=complex --enable-thread-safe-client \
    --enable-local-infile --disable-shared
```

See Section 2.2.3, "Installing MySQL on Mac OS X."

2.6.2.2 Mac OS X Server 1.2 (Rhapsody)

For current versions of Mac OS X Server, no operating system changes are necessary before compiling MySQL. Compiling for the Server platform is the same as for the client version of Mac OS X. (However, note that MySQL comes preinstalled on Mac OS X Server, so you need not build it yourself.)

For older versions (Mac OS X Server 1.2, a.k.a. Rhapsody), you must first install a pthread package before trying to configure MySQL.

See Section 2.2.3, "Installing MySQL on Mac OS X."

2.6.3 Solaris Notes

On Solaris, you may run into trouble even before you get the MySQL distribution unpacked! Solaris `tar` can't handle long filenames, so you may see an error like this when you unpack MySQL:

```
x mysql-3.22.12-beta/bench/Results/ATIS-mysql_odbc-NT_4.0-cmp-db2,
informix,ms-sql,mysql,oracle,solid,sybase, 0 bytes, 0 tape blocks
tar: directory checksum error
```

In this case, you must use GNU `tar` (`gtar`) to unpack the distribution. You can find a precompiled copy for Solaris at `http://dev.mysql.com/downloads/os-solaris.html`.

Sun native threads work only on Solaris 2.5 and higher. For Version 2.4 and earlier, MySQL automatically uses MIT-pthreads. See Section 2.3.5, "MIT-pthreads Notes."

If you get the following error from `configure`, it means that you have something wrong with your compiler installation:

```
checking for restartable system calls... configure: error can not
run test programs while cross compiling
```

In this case, you should upgrade your compiler to a newer version. You may also be able to solve this problem by inserting the following row into the `config.cache` file:

```
ac_cv_sys_restartable_syscalls=${ac_cv_sys_restartable_syscalls='no'}
```

If you are using Solaris on a SPARC, the recommended compiler is gcc 2.95.2 or 3.2. You can find this at `http://gcc.gnu.org/`. Note that egcs 1.1.1 and gcc 2.8.1 don't work reliably on SPARC!

The recommended `configure` line when using gcc 2.95.2 is:

```
CC=gcc CFLAGS="-O3" \
CXX=gcc CXXFLAGS="-O3 -felide-constructors -fno-exceptions -fno-rtti" \
./configure --prefix=/usr/local/mysql --with-low-memory \
    --enable-assembler
```

If you have an UltraSPARC system, you can get 4% better performance by adding `-mcpu=v8 -Wa,-xarch=v8plusa` to the `CFLAGS` and `CXXFLAGS` environment variables.

If you have Sun's Forte 5.0 (or newer) compiler, you can run `configure` like this:

```
CC=cc CFLAGS="-Xa -fast -native -xstrconst -mt" \
CXX=CC CXXFLAGS="-noex -mt" \
./configure --prefix=/usr/local/mysql --enable-assembler
```

To create a 64-bit binary with Sun's Forte compiler, use the following configuration options:

```
CC=cc CFLAGS="-Xa -fast -native -xstrconst -mt -xarch=v9" \
CXX=CC CXXFLAGS="-noex -mt -xarch=v9" ASFLAGS="-xarch=v9" \
./configure --prefix=/usr/local/mysql --enable-assembler
```

To create a 64-bit Solaris binary using gcc, add `-m64` to `CFLAGS` and `CXXFLAGS` and remove `--enable-assembler` from the `configure` line. This works only with MySQL 4.0 and up; MySQL 3.23 does not include the required modifications to support this.

In the MySQL benchmarks, we got a 4% speedup on an UltraSPARC when using Forte 5.0 in 32-bit mode compared to using gcc 3.2 with the `-mcpu` flag.

If you create a 64-bit `mysqld` binary, it is 4% slower than the 32-bit binary, but can handle more threads and memory.

If you get a problem with `fdatasync` or `sched_yield`, you can fix this by adding `LIBS=-lrt` to the `configure` line.

For compilers older than WorkShop 5.3, you might have to edit the configure script. Change this line:

```
#if !defined(__STDC__) || __STDC__ != 1
```

To this:

```
#if !defined(__STDC__)
```

If you turn on __STDC__ with the -Xc option, the Sun compiler can't compile with the Solaris pthread.h header file. This is a Sun bug (broken compiler or broken include file).

If mysqld issues the following error message when you run it, you have tried to compile MySQL with the Sun compiler without enabling the -mt multi-thread option:

```
libc internal error: _rmutex_unlock: rmutex not held
```

Add -mt to CFLAGS and CXXFLAGS and recompile.

If you are using the SFW version of gcc (which comes with Solaris 8), you must add /opt/sfw/lib to the environment variable LD_LIBRARY_PATH before running configure.

If you are using the gcc available from sunfreeware.com, you may have many problems. To avoid this, you should recompile gcc and GNU binutils on the machine where you will be running them.

If you get the following error when compiling MySQL with gcc, it means that your gcc is not configured for your version of Solaris:

```
shell> gcc -O3 -g -O2 -DDBUG_OFF  -o thr_alarm ...
./thr_alarm.c: In function `signal_hand':
./thr_alarm.c:556: too many arguments to function `sigwait'
```

The proper thing to do in this case is to get the newest version of gcc and compile it with your current gcc compiler. At least for Solaris 2.5, almost all binary versions of gcc have old, unusable include files that will break all programs that use threads, and possibly other programs!

Solaris doesn't provide static versions of all system libraries (libpthreads and libdl), so you can't compile MySQL with --static. If you try to do so, you will get one of the following errors:

```
ld: fatal: library -ldl: not found
undefined reference to `dlopen'
cannot find -lrt
```

If you link your own MySQL client programs, you may see the following error at runtime:

```
ld.so.1: fatal: libmysqlclient.so.#:
open failed: No such file or directory
```

This problem can be avoided by one of the following methods:

- Link clients with the -Wl,r/*full/path/to*/libmysqlclient.so flag rather than with -L*path*).
- Copy libmysqclient.so to /usr/lib.
- Add the pathname of the directory where libmysqlclient.so is located to the LD_RUN_PATH environmentvariable before running your client.

If you have problems with configure trying to link with -lz when you don't have zlib installed, you have two options:

- If you want to be able to use the compressed communication protocol, you need to get and install zlib from ftp.gnu.org.
- Run configure with the --with-named-z-libs=no option when building MySQL.

If you are using gcc and have problems with loading user-defined functions (UDFs) into MySQL, try adding -lgcc to the link line for the UDF.

If you would like MySQL to start automatically, you can copy support-files/mysql.server to /etc/init.d and create a symbolic link to it named /etc/rc3.d/S99mysql.server.

If too many processes try to connect very rapidly to mysqld, you will see this error in the MySQL log:

```
Error in accept: Protocol error
```

You might try starting the server with the --back_log=50 option as a workaround for this. (Use -O back_log=50 before MySQL 4.)

Solaris doesn't support core files for setuid() applications, so you can't get a core file from mysqld if you are using the --user option.

2.6.3.1 Solaris 2.7/2.8 Notes

Normally, you can use a Solaris 2.6 binary on Solaris 2.7 and 2.8. Most of the Solaris 2.6 issues also apply for Solaris 2.7 and 2.8.

MySQL 3.23.4 and above should be able to detect new versions of Solaris automatically and enable workarounds for the following problems.

Solaris 2.7 / 2.8 has some bugs in the include files. You may see the following error when you use gcc:

```
/usr/include/widec.h:42: warning: `getwc' redefined
/usr/include/wchar.h:326: warning: this is the location of the previous
definition
```

If this occurs, you can fix the problem by copying `/usr/include/widec.h` to `.../lib/gcc-lib/os/gcc-version/include` and changing line 41 from this:

```
#if     !defined(lint) && !defined(__lint)
```

To this:

```
#if     !defined(lint) && !defined(__lint) && !defined(getwc)
```

Alternatively, you can edit `/usr/include/widec.h` directly. Either way, after you make the fix, you should remove `config.cache` and run `configure` again.

If you get the following errors when you run `make`, it's because `configure` didn't detect the `curses.h` file (probably because of the error in `/usr/include/widec.h`):

```
In file included from mysql.cc:50:
/usr/include/term.h:1060: syntax error before `,'
/usr/include/term.h:1081: syntax error before `;'
```

The solution to this problem is to do one of the following:

- Configure with `CFLAGS=-DHAVE_CURSES_H CXXFLAGS=-DHAVE_CURSES_H ./configure`.
- Edit `/usr/include/widec.h` as indicated in the preceding discussion and re-run `configure`.
- Remove the `#define HAVE_TERM` line from the `config.h` file and run `make` again.

If your linker can't find `-lz` when linking client programs, the problem is probably that your `libz.so` file is installed in `/usr/local/lib`. You can fix this problem by one of the following methods:

- Add `/usr/local/lib` to `LD_LIBRARY_PATH`.
- Add a link to `libz.so` from `/lib`.
- If you are using Solaris 8, you can install the optional `zlib` from your Solaris 8 CD distribution.
- Run `configure` with the `--with-named-z-libs=no` option when building MySQL.

2.6.3.2 Solaris x86 Notes

On Solaris 8 on x86, `mysqld` will dump core if you remove the debug symbols using `strip`.

If you are using `gcc` or `egcs` on Solaris x86 and you experience problems with core dumps under load, you should use the following `configure` command:

```
CC=gcc CFLAGS="-O3 -fomit-frame-pointer -DHAVE_CURSES_H" \
CXX=gcc \
CXXFLAGS="-O3 -fomit-frame-pointer -felide-constructors \
    -fno-exceptions -fno-rtti -DHAVE_CURSES_H" \
./configure --prefix=/usr/local/mysql
```

This will avoid problems with the `libstdc++` library and with C++ exceptions.

If this doesn't help, you should compile a debug version and run it with a trace file or under gdb.

2.6.4 BSD Notes

This section provides information about using MySQL on variants of BSD Unix.

2.6.4.1 FreeBSD Notes

FreeBSD 4.x or newer is recommended for running MySQL, because the thread package is much more integrated. To get a secure and stable system, you should use only FreeBSD kernels that are marked -RELEASE.

The easiest (and preferred) way to install MySQL is to use the mysql-server and mysql-client ports available at http://www.freebsd.org/. Using these ports gives you the following benefits:

- A working MySQL with all optimizations enabled that are known to work on your version of FreeBSD.
- Automatic configuration and build.
- Startup scripts installed in /usr/local/etc/rc.d.
- The ability to use pkg_info -L to see which files are installed.
- The ability to use pkg_delete to remove MySQL if you no longer want it on your machine.

It is recommended you use MIT-pthreads on FreeBSD 2.x, and native threads on Versions 3 and up. It is possible to run with native threads on some late 2.2.x versions, but you may encounter problems shutting down mysqld.

Unfortunately, certain function calls on FreeBSD are not yet fully thread-safe. Most notably, this includes the gethostbyname() function, which is used by MySQL to convert hostnames into IP addresses. Under certain circumstances, the mysqld process will suddenly cause 100% CPU load and will be unresponsive. If you encounter this problem, try to start MySQL using the --skip-name-resolve option.

Alternatively, you can link MySQL on FreeBSD 4.x against the LinuxThreads library, which avoids a few of the problems that the native FreeBSD thread implementation has. For a very good comparison of LinuxThreads versus native threads, see Jeremy Zawodny's article "FreeBSD or Linux for your MySQL Server?" at http://jeremy.zawodny.com/blog/archives/000697.html.

A known problem when using LinuxThreads on FreeBSD is that the wait_timeout value is not honored (probably a signal handling problem in FreeBSD/LinuxThreads). This is supposed to be fixed in FreeBSD 5.0. The symptom is that persistent connections can hang for a very long time without getting closed down.

The MySQL build process requires GNU make (gmake) to work. If GNU make is not available, you must install it first before compiling MySQL.

The recommended way to compile and install MySQL on FreeBSD with gcc (2.95.2 and up) is:

```
CC=gcc CFLAGS="-O2 -fno-strength-reduce" \
    CXX=gcc CXXFLAGS="-O2 -fno-rtti -fno-exceptions \
    -felide-constructors -fno-strength-reduce" \
    ./configure --prefix=/usr/local/mysql --enable-assembler
gmake
gmake install
cd /usr/local/mysql
bin/mysql_install_db --user=mysql
bin/mysqld_safe &
```

If you notice that configure will use MIT-pthreads, you should read the MIT-pthreads notes. See Section 2.3.5, "MIT-pthreads Notes."

If you get an error from make install that it can't find /usr/include/pthreads, configure didn't detect that you need MIT-pthreads. To fix this problem, remove config.cache, then re-run configure with the --with-mit-threads option.

Be sure that your name resolver setup is correct. Otherwise, you may experience resolver delays or failures when connecting to mysqld. Also make sure that the localhost entry in the /etc/hosts file is correct. The file should start with a line similar to this:

```
127.0.0.1     localhost localhost.your.domain
```

FreeBSD is known to have a very low default file handle limit. See Section A.2.17, "File Not Found." Start the server by using the --open-files-limit option for mysqld_safe, or raise the limits for the mysqld user in /etc/login.conf and rebuild it with cap_mkdb /etc/login.conf. Also be sure that you set the appropriate class for this user in the password file if you are not using the default (use chpass *mysqld-user-name*). See Section 4.1.3, "The mysqld_safe Server Startup Script."

If you have a lot of memory, you should consider rebuilding the kernel to allow MySQL to use more than 512MB of RAM. Take a look at option MAXDSIZ in the LINT config file for more information.

If you get problems with the current date in MySQL, setting the TZ variable will probably help. See Appendix B, "Environment Variables."

2.6.4.2 NetBSD Notes

To compile on NetBSD, you need GNU make. Otherwise, the build process will fail when make tries to run lint on C++ files.

2.6.4.3 OpenBSD 2.5 Notes

On OpenBSD Version 2.5, you can compile MySQL with native threads with the following options:

```
CFLAGS=-pthread CXXFLAGS=-pthread ./configure --with-mit-threads=no
```

2.6.4.4 OpenBSD 2.8 Notes

Our users have reported that OpenBSD 2.8 has a threading bug that causes problems with MySQL. The OpenBSD Developers have fixed the problem, but as of January 25, 2001, it's only available in the "-current" branch. The symptoms of this threading bug are slow response, high load, high CPU usage, and crashes.

If you get an error like `Error in accept:: Bad file descriptor` or error 9 when trying to open tables or directories, the problem is probably that you have not allocated enough file descriptors for MySQL.

In this case, try starting `mysqld_safe` as `root` with the following options:

```
mysqld_safe --user=mysql --open-files-limit=2048 &
```

2.6.4.5 BSD/OS Version 2.x Notes

If you get the following error when compiling MySQL, your `ulimit` value for virtual memory is too low:

```
item_func.h: In method
`Item_func_ge::Item_func_ge(const Item_func_ge &)':
item_func.h:28: virtual memory exhausted
make[2]: *** [item_func.o] Error 1
```

Try using `ulimit -v 80000` and run make again. If this doesn't work and you are using `bash`, try switching to `csh` or `sh`; some BSDI users have reported problems with `bash` and `ulimit`.

If you are using `gcc`, you may also have to use the `--with-low-memory` flag for `configure` to be able to compile `sql_yacc.cc`.

If you get problems with the current date in MySQL, setting the `TZ` variable will probably help. See Appendix B, "Environment Variables."

2.6.4.6 BSD/OS Version 3.x Notes

Upgrade to BSD/OS Version 3.1. If that is not possible, install BSDIpatch M300-038.

Use the following command when configuring MySQL:

```
env CXX=shlicc++ CC=shlicc2 \
./configure \
    --prefix=/usr/local/mysql \
```

```
--localstatedir=/var/mysql \
--without-perl \
--with-unix-socket-path=/var/mysql/mysql.sock
```

The following is also known to work:

```
env CC=gcc CXX=gcc CXXFLAGS=-O3 \
./configure \
    --prefix=/usr/local/mysql \
    --with-unix-socket-path=/var/mysql/mysql.sock
```

You can change the directory locations if you wish, or just use the defaults by not specifying any locations.

If you have problems with performance under heavy load, try using the `--skip-thread-priority` option to `mysqld`! This will run all threads with the same priority. On BSDI Version 3.1, this gives better performance, at least until BSDI fixes its thread scheduler.

If you get the error `virtual memory exhausted` while compiling, you should try using `ulimit -v 80000` and running `make` again. If this doesn't work and you are using `bash`, try switching to `csh` or `sh`; some BSDI users have reported problems with `bash` and `ulimit`.

2.6.4.7 BSD/OS Version 4.x Notes

BSDI Version 4.x has some thread-related bugs. If you want to use MySQL on this, you should install all thread-related patches. At least M400-023 should be installed.

On some BSDI Version 4.x systems, you may get problems with shared libraries. The symptom is that you can't execute any client programs, for example, `mysqladmin`. In this case, you need to reconfigure not to use shared libraries with the `--disable-shared` option to configure.

Some customers have had problems on BSDI 4.0.1 that the `mysqld` binary after a while can't open tables. This is because some library/system-related bug causes `mysqld` to change current directory without having asked for that to happen.

The fix is to either upgrade MySQL to at least version 3.23.34 or, after running `configure`, remove the line `#define HAVE_REALPATH` from `config.h` before running `make`.

Note that this means that you can't symbolically link a database directory to another database directory or symbolic link a table to another database on BSDI. (Making a symbolic link to another disk is okay.)

2.6.5 Other Unix Notes

2.6.5.1 HP-UX Version 10.20 Notes

There are a couple of small problems when compiling MySQL on HP-UX. We recommend that you use `gcc` instead of the HP-UX native compiler, because `gcc` produces better code.

We recommend using gcc 2.95 on HP-UX. Don't use high optimization flags (such as -06) because they may not be safe on HP-UX.

The following configure line should work with gcc 2.95:

```
CFLAGS="-I/opt/dce/include -fpic" \
CXXFLAGS="-I/opt/dce/include -felide-constructors -fno-exceptions \
-fno-rtti" \
CXX=gcc \
./configure --with-pthread \
    --with-named-thread-libs='-ldce' \
    --prefix=/usr/local/mysql --disable-shared
```

The following configure line should work with gcc 3.1:

```
CFLAGS="-DHPUX -I/opt/dce/include -O3 -fPIC" CXX=gcc \
CXXFLAGS="-DHPUX -I/opt/dce/include -felide-constructors \
    -fno-exceptions -fno-rtti -O3 -fPIC" \
./configure --prefix=/usr/local/mysql \
    --with-extra-charsets=complex --enable-thread-safe-client \
    --enable-local-infile  --with-pthread \
    --with-named-thread-libs=-ldce --with-lib-ccflags=-fPIC
    --disable-shared
```

2.6.5.2 HP-UX Version 11.x Notes

For HP-UX Version 11.x, we recommend MySQL 3.23.15 or later.

Because of some critical bugs in the standard HP-UX libraries, you should install the following patches before trying to run MySQL on HP-UX 11.0:

```
PHKL_22840 Streams cumulative
PHNE_22397 ARPA cumulative
```

This will solve the problem of getting EWOULDBLOCK from recv() and EBADF from accept() in threaded applications.

If you are using gcc 2.95.1 on an unpatched HP-UX 11.x system, you will get the error:

```
In file included from /usr/include/unistd.h:11,
                 from ../include/global.h:125,
                 from mysql_priv.h:15,
                 from item.cc:19:
/usr/include/sys/unistd.h:184: declaration of C function ...
/usr/include/sys/pthread.h:440: previous declaration ...
In file included from item.h:306,
                 from mysql_priv.h:158,
                 from item.cc:19:
```

The problem is that HP-UX doesn't define `pthreads_atfork()` consistently. It has conflicting prototypes in `/usr/include/sys/unistd.h:184` and `/usr/include/sys/pthread.h:440`.

One solution is to copy `/usr/include/sys/unistd.h` into `mysql/include` and edit `unistd.h` and change it to match the definition in `pthread.h`. Look for this line:

```
extern int pthread_atfork(void (*prepare)(), void (*parent)(),
                                 void (*child)());
```

Change it to look like this:

```
extern int pthread_atfork(void (*prepare)(void), void (*parent)(void),
                                 void (*child)(void));
```

After making the change, the following `configure` line should work:

```
CFLAGS="-fomit-frame-pointer -O3 -fpic" CXX=gcc \
CXXFLAGS="-felide-constructors -fno-exceptions -fno-rtti -O3" \
./configure --prefix=/usr/local/mysql --disable-shared
```

If you are using MySQL 4.0.5 with the HP-UX compiler, you can use the following command (which has been tested with cc B.11.11.04):

```
CC=cc CXX=aCC CFLAGS=+DD64 CXXFLAGS=+DD64 ./configure \
    --with-extra-character-set=complex
```

You can ignore any errors of the following type:

```
aCC: warning 901: unknown option: `-3': use +help for online
documentation
```

If you get the following error from `configure`, verify that you don't have the path to the K&R compiler before the path to the HP-UX C and C++ compiler:

```
checking for cc option to accept ANSI C... no
configure: error: MySQL requires an ANSI C compiler (and a C++ compiler).
Try gcc. See the Installation chapter in the Reference Manual.
```

Another reason for not being able to compile is that you didn't define the +DD64 flags as just described.

Another possibility for HP-UX 11 is to use MySQL binaries for HP-UX 10.20. We have received reports from some users that these binaries work fine on HP-UX 11.00. If you encounter problems, be sure to check your HP-UX patch level.

2.6.5.3 IBM-AIX notes

Automatic detection of `xlC` is missing from Autoconf, so a number of variables need to be set before running `configure`. The following example uses the IBM compiler:

```
export CC="xlc_r -ma -O3 -qstrict -qoptimize=3 -qmaxmem=8192 "
```

```
export CXX="xlC_r -ma -O3 -qstrict -qoptimize=3 -qmaxmem=8192"
export CFLAGS="-I /usr/local/include"
export LDFLAGS="-L /usr/local/lib"
export CPPFLAGS=$CFLAGS
export CXXFLAGS=$CFLAGS


./configure --prefix=/usr/local \
                --localstatedir=/var/mysql \
                --sysconfdir=/etc/mysql \
                --sbindir='/usr/local/bin' \
                --libexecdir='/usr/local/bin' \
                --enable-thread-safe-client \
                --enable-large-files
```

The preceding options are used to compile the MySQL distribution that can be found at `http://www-frec.bull.com/`.

If you change the -O3 to -O2 in the preceding `configure` line, you must also remove the -qstrict option. This is a limitation in the IBM C compiler.

If you are using gcc or egcs to compile MySQL, you *must* use the -fno-exceptions flag, because the exception handling in gcc/egcs is not thread-safe! (This is tested with egcs 1.1.) There are also some known problems with IBM's assembler that may cause it to generate bad code when used with gcc.

We recommend the following `configure` line with egcs and gcc 2.95 on AIX:

```
CC="gcc -pipe -mcpu=power -Wa,-many" \
CXX="gcc -pipe -mcpu=power -Wa,-many" \
CXXFLAGS="-felide-constructors -fno-exceptions -fno-rtti" \
./configure --prefix=/usr/local/mysql --with-low-memory
```

The -Wa,-many option is necessary for the compile to be successful. IBM is aware of this problem but is in no hurry to fix it because of the workaround that is available. We don't know if the -fno-exceptions is required with gcc 2.95, but because MySQL doesn't use exceptions and the option generates faster code, we recommend that you should always use it with egcs / gcc.

If you get a problem with assembler code, try changing the -mcpu=xxx option to match your CPU. Typically power2, power, or powerpc may need to be used. Alternatively, you might need to use 604 or 604e. We are not positive but suspect that power would likely be safe most of the time, even on a power2 machine.

If you don't know what your CPU is, execute a uname -m command. It will produce a string that looks like 000514676700, with a format of xxyyyyyymmss where xx and ss are always 00, yyyyyy is a unique system ID and mm is the ID of the CPU Planar. A chart of these values can be found at `http://publib.boulder.ibm.com/doc_link/en_US/a_doc_lib/cmds/`

aixcmds5/uname.htm. This will give you a machine type and a machine model you can use to determine what type of CPU you have.

If you have problems with signals (MySQL dies unexpectedly under high load), you may have found an OS bug with threads and signals. In this case, you can tell MySQL not to use signals by configuring as follows:

```
CFLAGS=-DDONT_USE_THR_ALARM CXX=gcc \
CXXFLAGS="-felide-constructors -fno-exceptions -fno-rtti \
-DDONT_USE_THR_ALARM" \
./configure --prefix=/usr/local/mysql --with-debug \
    --with-low-memory
```

This doesn't affect the performance of MySQL, but has the side effect that you can't kill clients that are "sleeping" on a connection with mysqladmin kill or mysqladmin shutdown. Instead, the client will die when it issues its next command.

On some versions of AIX, linking with libbind.a makes getservbyname() dump core. This is an AIX bug and should be reported to IBM.

For AIX 4.2.1 and gcc, you have to make the following changes.

After configuring, edit config.h and include/my_config.h and change the line that says this:

```
#define HAVE_SNPRINTF 1
```

to this:

```
#undef HAVE_SNPRINTF
```

And finally, in mysqld.cc, you need to add a prototype for initgroups():

```
#ifdef _AIX41
extern "C" int initgroups(const char *,int);
#endif
```

If you need to allocate a lot of memory to the mysqld process, it's not enough to just use ulimit -d unlimited. You may also have to modify mysqld_safe to add a line something like this:

```
export LDR_CNTRL='MAXDATA=0x80000000'
```

You can find more information about using a lot of memory at http://publib16.boulder.ibm.com/pseries/en_US/aixprggd/genprogc/lrg_prg_support.htm.

2.6.5.4 SunOS 4 Notes

On SunOS 4, MIT-pthreads is needed to compile MySQL. This in turn means you will need GNU make.

Some SunOS 4 systems have problems with dynamic libraries and `libtool`. You can use the following `configure` line to avoid this problem:

```
./configure --disable-shared --with-mysqld-ldflags=-all-static
```

When compiling `readline`, you may get warnings about duplicate defines. These can be ignored.

When compiling `mysqld`, there will be some `implicit declaration of function` warnings. These can be ignored.

2.6.5.5 Alpha-DEC-Unix Notes (Tru64)

If you are using `egcs` 1.1.2 on Digital Unix, you should upgrade to `gcc` 2.95.2, because `egcs` on DEC has some serious bugs!

When compiling threaded programs under Digital Unix, the documentation recommends using the -pthread option for `cc` and `cxx` and the -lmach -lexc libraries (in addition to -lpthread). You should run `configure` something like this:

```
CC="cc -pthread" CXX="cxx -pthread -O" \
./configure --with-named-thread-libs="-lpthread -lmach -lexc -lc"
```

When compiling `mysqld`, you may see a couple of warnings like this:

```
mysqld.cc: In function void handle_connections()':
mysqld.cc:626: passing long unsigned int *' as argument 3 of
accept(int,sockadddr *, int *)'
```

You can safely ignore these warnings. They occur because `configure` can detect only errors, not warnings.

If you start the server directly from the command line, you may have problems with it dying when you log out. (When you log out, your outstanding processes receive a `SIGHUP` signal.) If so, try starting the server like this:

```
nohup mysqld [options] &
```

`nohup` causes the command following it to ignore any `SIGHUP` signal sent from the terminal. Alternatively, start the server by running `mysqld_safe`, which invokes `mysqld` using `nohup` for you. See Section 4.1.3, "The `mysqld_safe` Server Startup Script."

If you get a problem when compiling `mysys/get_opt.c`, just remove the `#define _NO_PROTO` line from the start of that file.

If you are using Compaq's CC compiler, the following `configure` line should work:

```
CC="cc -pthread"
CFLAGS="-O4 -ansi_alias -ansi_args -fast -inline speed all -arch host"
CXX="cxx -pthread"
CXXFLAGS="-O4 -ansi_alias -ansi_args -fast -inline speed all \
    -arch host -noexceptions -nortti"
```

```
export CC CFLAGS CXX CXXFLAGS
./configure \
    --prefix=/usr/local/mysql \
    --with-low-memory \
    --enable-large-files \
    --enable-shared=yes \
    --with-named-thread-libs="-lpthread -lmach -lexc -lc"
gnumake
```

If you get a problem with libtool when compiling with shared libraries as just shown, when linking mysql, you should be able to get around this by issuing these commands:

```
cd mysql
/bin/sh ../libtool --mode=link cxx -pthread  -O3 -DDBUG_OFF \
    -O4 -ansi_alias -ansi_args -fast -inline speed \
    -speculate all \ -arch host  -DUNDEF_HAVE_GETHOSTBYNAME_R \
    -o mysql  mysql.o readline.o sql_string.o completion_hash.o \
    ../readline/libreadline.a -lcurses \
    ../libmysql/.libs/libmysqlclient.so  -lm
cd ..
gnumake
gnumake install
scripts/mysql_install_db
```

2.6.5.6 Alpha-DEC-OSF/1 Notes

If you have problems compiling and have DEC CC and gcc installed, try running configure like this:

```
CC=cc CFLAGS=-O CXX=gcc CXXFLAGS=-O3 \
./configure --prefix=/usr/local/mysql
```

If you get problems with the c_asm.h file, you can create and use a 'dummy' c_asm.h file with:

```
touch include/c_asm.h
CC=gcc CFLAGS=-I./include \
CXX=gcc CXXFLAGS=-O3 \
./configure --prefix=/usr/local/mysql
```

Note that the following problems with the ld program can be fixed by downloading the latest DEC (Compaq) patch kit from: http://ftp.support.compaq.com/public/unix/.

On OSF/1 V4.0D and compiler "DEC C V5.6-071 on Digital Unix V4.0 (Rev. 878)," the compiler had some strange behavior (undefined asm symbols). /bin/ld also appears to be broken (problems with _exit undefined errors occurring while linking mysqld). On this system, we have managed to compile MySQL with the following configure line, after replacing /bin/ld with the version from OSF 4.0C:

```
CC=gcc CXX=gcc CXXFLAGS=-O3 ./configure --prefix=/usr/local/mysql
```

With the Digital compiler "C++ V6.1-029," the following should work:

```
CC=cc -pthread
CFLAGS=-O4 -ansi_alias -ansi_args -fast -inline speed \
        -speculate all -arch host
CXX=cxx -pthread
CXXFLAGS=-O4 -ansi_alias -ansi_args -fast -inline speed \
          -speculate all -arch host -noexceptions -nortti
export CC CFLAGS CXX CXXFLAGS
./configure --prefix=/usr/mysql/mysql \
            --with-mysqld-ldflags=--all-static --disable-shared \
            --with-named-thread-libs="-lmach -lexc -lc"
```

In some versions of OSF/1, the alloca() function is broken. Fix this by removing the line in config.h that defines 'HAVE_ALLOCA'.

The alloca() function also may have an incorrect prototype in /usr/include/alloca.h. The warning resulting from this can be ignored.

configure will use the following thread libraries automatically: --with-named-thread-libs="-lpthread -lmach -lexc -lc".

When using gcc, you can also try running configure like this:

```
CFLAGS=-D_PTHREAD_USE_D4 CXX=gcc CXXFLAGS=-O3 ./configure ...
```

If you have problems with signals (MySQL dies unexpectedly under high load), you may have found an OS bug with threads and signals. In this case, you can tell MySQL not to use signals by configuring with:

```
CFLAGS=-DDONT_USE_THR_ALARM \
CXXFLAGS=-DDONT_USE_THR_ALARM \
./configure ...
```

This doesn't affect the performance of MySQL, but has the side effect that you can't kill clients that are "sleeping" on a connection with mysqladmin kill or mysqladmin shutdown. Instead, the client will die when it issues its next command.

With gcc 2.95.2, you will probably run into the following compile error:

```
sql_acl.cc:1456: Internal compiler error in `scan_region',
at except.c:2566
Please submit a full bug report.
```

To fix this, you should change to the sql directory and do a cut-and-paste of the last gcc line, but change -O3 to -O0 (or add -O0 immediately after gcc if you don't have any -O option on your compile line). After this is done, you can just change back to the top-level directory and run make again.

2.6.5.7 SGI Irix Notes

If you are using Irix Version 6.5.3 or newer, `mysqld` will be able to create threads only if you run it as a user that has `CAP_SCHED_MGT` privileges (such as `root`) or give the `mysqld` server this privilege with the following shell command:

```
chcap "CAP_SCHED_MGT+epi" /opt/mysql/libexec/mysqld
```

You may have to undefine some symbols in `config.h` after running `configure` and before compiling.

In some Irix implementations, the `alloca()` function is broken. If the `mysqld` server dies on some `SELECT` statements, remove the lines from `config.h` that define `HAVE_ALLOC` and `HAVE_ALLOCA_H`. If `mysqladmin create` doesn't work, remove the line from `config.h` that defines `HAVE_READDIR_R`. You may have to remove the `HAVE_TERM_H` line as well.

SGI recommends that you install all the patches on this page as a set:

```
http://support.sgi.com/surfzone/patches/patchset/6.2_indigo.rps.html
```

At the very minimum, you should install the latest kernel rollup, the latest `rld` rollup, and the latest `libc` rollup.

You definitely need all the POSIX patches on this page, for pthreads support:

```
http://support.sgi.com/surfzone/patches/patchset/6.2_posix.rps.html
```

If you get the something like the following error when compiling `mysql.cc`:

```
"/usr/include/curses.h", line 82: error(1084):
invalid combination of type
```

Type the following in the top-level directory of your MySQL source tree:

```
extra/replace bool curses_bool < /usr/include/curses.h > include/curses.h
make
```

There have also been reports of scheduling problems. If only one thread is running, performance is slow. Avoid this by starting another client. This may lead to a two-to-tenfold increase in execution speed thereafter for the other thread. This is a poorly understood problem with Irix threads; you may have to improvise to find solutions until this can be fixed.

If you are compiling with `gcc`, you can use the following `configure` command:

```
CC=gcc CXX=gcc CXXFLAGS=-O3 \
./configure --prefix=/usr/local/mysql --enable-thread-safe-client \
    --with-named-thread-libs=-lpthread
```

On Irix 6.5.11 with native Irix C and C++ compilers ver. 7.3.1.2, the following is reported to work

```
CC=cc CXX=CC CFLAGS='-O3 -n32 -TARG:platform=IP22 -I/usr/local/include \
-L/usr/local/lib' CXXFLAGS='-O3 -n32 -TARG:platform=IP22 \
-I/usr/local/include -L/usr/local/lib' \
./configure --prefix=/usr/local/mysql --with-innodb --with-berkeley-db \
    --with-libwrap=/usr/local \
    --with-named-curses-libs=/usr/local/lib/libncurses.a
```

2.6.5.8 SCO Notes

The current port is tested only on "sco3.2v5.0.5," "sco3.2v5.0.6," and "sco3.2v5.0.7" systems. There has also been a lot of progress on a port to "sco 3.2v4.2."

For the moment, the recommended compiler on OpenServer is gcc 2.95.2. With this, you should be able to compile MySQL with just:

```
CC=gcc CXX=gcc ./configure ... (options)
```

1. For OpenServer 5.0.x, you need to use gcc-2.95.2p1 or newer from the Skunkware. Go to http://www.sco.com/skunkware/ and choose browser OpenServer packages or by FTP to ftp2.caldera.com in the pub/skunkware/osr5/devtools/gcc directory.

2. You need the port of GCC 2.5.x for this product and the Development system. They are required on this version of SCO Unix. You cannot just use the GCC Dev system.

3. You should get the FSU Pthreads package and install it first. This can be found at http://moss.csc.ncsu.edu/~mueller/ftp/pub/PART/pthreads.tar.gz. You can also get a precompiled package from http://www.mysql.com/Downloads/SCO/FSU-threads-3.5c.tar.gz.

4. FSU Pthreads can be compiled with SCO Unix 4.2 with tcpip, or using OpenServer 3.0 or Open Desktop 3.0 (OS 3.0 ODT 3.0) with the SCO Development System installed using a good port of GCC 2.5.x. For ODT or OS 3.0, you will need a good port of GCC 2.5.x. There are a lot of problems without a good port. The port for this product requires the SCO Unix Development system. Without it, you are missing the libraries and the linker that is needed.

5. To build FSU Pthreads on your system, do the following:
   1. Run ./configure in the threads/src directory and select the SCO OpenServer option. This command copies Makefile.SCO5 to Makefile.
   2. Run make.
   3. To install in the default /usr/include directory, log in as root, then cd to the thread/src directory and run make install.

6. Remember to use GNU make when making MySQL.

7. If you don't start mysqld_safe as root, you probably will get only the default 110 open files per process. mysqld will write a note about this in the log file.

8. With SCO 3.2V5.0.5, you should use FSU Pthreads version 3.5c or newer. You should also use gcc 2.95.2 or newer!

   The following `configure` command should work:

   ```
   ./configure --prefix=/usr/local/mysql --disable-shared
   ```

9. With SCO 3.2V4.2, you should use FSU Pthreads version 3.5c or newer. The following `configure` command should work:

   ```
   CFLAGS="-D_XOPEN_XPG4" CXX=gcc CXXFLAGS="-D_XOPEN_XPG4" \
   ./configure \
       --prefix=/usr/local/mysql \
       --with-named-thread-libs="-lgthreads -lsocket -lgen -lgthreads" \
       --with-named-curses-libs="-lcurses"
   ```

   You may get some problems with some include files. In this case, you can find new SCO-specific include files at http://www.mysql.com/Downloads/SCO/SCO-3.2v4.2-includes.tar.gz. You should unpack this file in the include directory of your MySQL source tree.

SCO development notes:

- MySQL should automatically detect FSU Pthreads and link mysqld with -lgthreads -lsocket -lgthreads.

- The SCO development libraries are re-entrant in FSU Pthreads. SCO claims that its library functions are re-entrant, so they must be re-entrant with FSU Pthreads. FSU Pthreads on OpenServer tries to use the SCO scheme to make re-entrant libraries.

- FSU Pthreads (at least the version at http://www.mysql.com/) comes linked with GNU malloc. If you encounter problems with memory usage, make sure that gmalloc.o is included in libgthreads.a and libgthreads.so.

- In FSU Pthreads, the following system calls are pthreads-aware: read(), write(), getmsg(), connect(), accept(), select(), and wait().

- The CSSA-2001-SCO.35.2 (the patch is listed in custom as erg711905-dscr_remap security patch (version 2.0.0)) breaks FSU threads and makes mysqld unstable. You have to remove this one if you want to run mysqld on an OpenServer 5.0.6 machine.

- SCO provides operating system patches at ftp://ftp.sco.com/pub/openserver5 for OpenServer 5.0.x.

- SCO provides security fixes and libsocket.so.2 at ftp://ftp.sco.com/pub/security/OpenServer and ftp://ftp.sco.com/pub/security/sse for OpenServer 5.0.x.

- pre-OSR506 security fixes. Also, the telnetd fix at ftp://stage.caldera.com/pub/security/openserver/ or ftp://stage.caldera.com/pub/security/openserver/CSSA-2001-SCO.10/ as both libsocket.so.2 and libresolv.so.1 with instructions for installing on pre-OSR506 systems.

   It's probably a good idea to install these patches before trying to compile/use MySQL.

2.6.5.9 SCO UnixWare Version 7.1.x Notes

On UnixWare 7.1.0, you must use a version of MySQL at least as recent as 3.22.13 to get fixes for some portability and OS problems.

We have been able to compile MySQL with the following `configure` command on UnixWare Version 7.1.x:

```
CC=cc CXX=CC ./configure --prefix=/usr/local/mysql
```

If you want to use `gcc`, you must use gcc 2.95.2 or newer.

```
CC=gcc CXX=g++ ./configure --prefix=/usr/local/mysql
```

SCO provides operating system patches at `ftp://ftp.sco.com/pub/unixware7` for UnixWare 7.1.1 and 7.1.3 and at `ftp://ftp.sco.com/pub/openunix8` for OpenUNIX 8.0.0.

SCO provides information about security fixes at `ftp://ftp.sco.com/pub/security/OpenUNIX` for OpenUNIX and at `ftp://ftp.sco.com/pub/security/UnixWare` for UnixWare.

2.6.6 OS/2 Notes

MySQL uses quite a few open files. Because of this, you should add something like the following to your `CONFIG.SYS` file:

```
SET EMXOPT=-c -n -h1024
```

If you don't do this, you will probably run into the following error:

```
File 'xxxx' not found (Errcode: 24)
```

When using MySQL with OS/2 Warp 3, FixPack 29 or above is required. With OS/2 Warp 4, FixPack 4 or above is required. This is a requirement of the Pthreads library. MySQL must be installed on a partition with a type that supports long filenames, such as HPFS, FAT32, and so on.

The `INSTALL.CMD` script must be run from OS/2's own `CMD.EXE` and may not work with replacement shells such as `40S2.EXE`.

The `scripts/mysql-install-db` script has been renamed. It is now called `install.cmd` and is a REXX script, which will set up the default MySQL security settings and create the WorkPlace Shell icons for MySQL.

Dynamic module support is compiled in but not fully tested. Dynamic modules should be compiled using the Pthreads runtime library.

```
gcc -Zdll -Zmt -Zcrtdll=pthrdrtl -I../include -I../regex -I.. \
    -o example udf_example.cc -L../lib -lmysqlclient udf_example.def
mv example.dll example.udf
```

Note: Due to limitations in OS/2, UDF module name stems must not exceed eight characters. Modules are stored in the `/mysql2/udf` directory; the `safe-mysqld.cmd` script will put this directory in the BEGINLIBPATH environment variable. When using UDF modules, specified extensions are ignored—it is assumed to be .udf. For example, in Unix, the shared module might be named example.so and you would load a function from it like this:

```
mysql> CREATE FUNCTION metaphon RETURNS STRING SONAME 'example.so';
```

In OS/2, the module would be named example.udf, but you would not specify the module extension:

```
mysql> CREATE FUNCTION metaphon RETURNS STRING SONAME 'example';
```

2.6.7 BeOS Notes

We have in the past talked with some BeOS developers who have said that MySQL is 80% ported to BeOS, but we haven't heard from them in a while.

2.7 Perl Installation Notes

Perl support for MySQL is provided by means of the DBI/DBD client interface. The interface requires Perl Version 5.6.0 or later. It *will not work* if you have an older version of Perl.

If you want to use transactions with Perl DBI, you need to have DBD::mysql version 1.2216 or newer. Version 2.9003 or newer is recommended.

If you are using the MySQL 4.1 client library, you must use DBD::mysql 2.9003 or newer.

As of MySQL 3.22.8, Perl support is no longer included with MySQL distributions. You can obtain the necessary modules from http://search.cpan.org for Unix, or by using the ActiveState ppm program on Windows. The following sections describe how to do this.

Perl support for MySQL must be installed if you want to run the MySQL benchmark scripts. See Section 6.1.4, "The MySQL Benchmark Suite."

2.7.1 Installing Perl on Unix

MySQL Perl support requires that you've installed MySQL client programming support (libraries and header files). Most installation methods install the necessary files. However, if you installed MySQL from RPM files on Linux, be sure that you've installed the developer RPM. The client programs are in the client RPM, but client programming support is in the developer RPM.

If you want to install Perl support, the files you will need can be obtained from the CPAN (Comprehensive Perl Archive Network) at http://search.cpan.org.

The easiest way to install Perl modules on Unix is to use the CPAN module. For example:

```
shell> perl -MCPAN -e shell
cpan> install DBI
cpan> install DBD::mysql
```

The DBD::mysql installation runs a number of tests. These tests require being able to connect to the local MySQL server as the anonymous user with no password. If you have removed anonymous accounts or assigned them passwords, the tests fail. You can use force install DBD::mysql to ignore the failed tests.

DBI requires the Data::Dumper module. It may already be installed; if not, you should install it before installing DBI.

It is also possible to download the module distributions in the form of compressed tar archives and build the modules manually. For example, to unpack and build a DBI distribution, use a procedure such as this:

1. Unpack the distribution into the current directory:

   ```
   shell> gunzip < DBI-VERSION.tar.gz | tar xvf -
   ```

   This command creates a directory named DBI-VERSION.

2. Change location into the top-level directory of the unpacked distribution:

   ```
   shell> cd DBI-VERSION
   ```

3. Build the distribution and compile everything:

   ```
   shell> perl Makefile.PL
   shell> make
   shell> make test
   shell> make install
   ```

The make test command is important because it verifies that the module is working. Note that when you run that command during the DBD::mysql installation to exercise the interface code, the MySQL server must be running or the test will fail.

It is a good idea to rebuild and reinstall the DBD::mysql distribution whenever you install a new release of MySQL, particularly if you notice symptoms such as that all your DBI scripts fail after you upgrade MySQL.

If you don't have access rights to install Perl modules in the system directory or if you want to install local Perl modules, the following reference may be useful: http://servers.digitaldaze.com/extensions/perl/modules.html#modules

Look under the heading "Installing New Modules that Require Locally Installed Modules."

2.7.2 Installing ActiveState Perl on Windows

On Windows, you should do the following to install the MySQL DBD module with ActiveState Perl:

- Get ActiveState Perl from http://www.activestate.com/Products/ActivePerl/ and install it.
- Open a console window (a "DOS window").

- If required, set the HTTP_proxy variable. For example, you might try:

  ```
  set HTTP_proxy=my.proxy.com:3128
  ```

- Start the PPM program:

  ```
  C:\> C:\perl\bin\ppm.pl
  ```

- If you have not already done so, install DBI:

  ```
  ppm> install DBI
  ```

- If this succeeds, run the following command:

  ```
  install \
  ftp://ftp.de.uu.net/pub/CPAN/authors/id/JWIED/DBD-mysql-1.2212.x86.ppd
  ```

This procedure should work at least with ActiveState Perl Version 5.6.

If you can't get the procedure to work, you should instead install the MyODBC driver and connect to the MySQL server through ODBC:

```
use DBI;
$dbh= DBI->connect("DBI:ODBC:$dsn",$user,$password) ||
  die "Got error $DBI::errstr when connecting to $dsn\n";
```

2.7.3 Problems Using the Perl DBI/DBD Interface

If Perl reports that it can't find the ../mysql/mysql.so module, then the problem is probably that Perl can't locate the shared library libmysqlclient.so.

You should be able to fix this by one of the following methods:

- Compile the DBD::mysql distribution with perl Makefile.PL -static -config rather than perl Makefile.PL.

- Copy libmysqlclient.so to the directory where your other shared libraries are located (probably /usr/lib or /lib).

- Modify the -L options used to compile DBD::mysql to reflect the actual location of libmysqlclient.so.

- On Linux, you can add the pathname of the directory where libmysqlclient.so is located to the /etc/ld.so.conf file.

- Add the pathname of the directory where libmysqlclient.so is located to the LD_RUN_PATH environment variable. Some systems use LD_LIBRARY_PATH instead.

Note that you may also need to modify the -L options if there are other libraries that the linker fails to find. For example, if the linker cannot find libc because it is in /lib and the link command specifies -L/usr/lib, change the -L option to -L/lib or add -L/lib to the existing link command.

If you get the following errors from DBD::mysql, you are probably using gcc (or using an old binary compiled with gcc):

```
/usr/bin/perl: can't resolve symbol '__moddi3'
/usr/bin/perl: can't resolve symbol '__divdi3'
```

Add -L/usr/lib/gcc-lib/... -lgcc to the link command when the mysql.so library gets built (check the output from make for mysql.so when you compile the Perl client). The -L option should specify the pathname of the directory where libgcc.a is located on your system.

Another cause of this problem may be that Perl and MySQL aren't both compiled with gcc. In this case, you can solve the mismatch by compiling both with gcc.

You may see the following error from DBD::mysql when you run the tests:

```
t/00base...........install_driver(mysql) failed:
Can't load '../blib/arch/auto/DBD/mysql/mysql.so' for module DBD::mysql:
../blib/arch/auto/DBD/mysql/mysql.so: undefined symbol:
uncompress at /usr/lib/perl5/5.00503/i586-linux/DynaLoader.pm line 169.
```

This means that you need to include the -lz compression library on the link line. That can be done by changing the following line in the file lib/DBD/mysql/Install.pm:

```
$sysliblist .= " -lm";
```

Change that line to:

```
$sysliblist .= " -lm -lz";
```

After this, you *must* run make realclean and then proceed with the installation from the beginning.

If you want to install DBI on SCO, you have to edit the Makefile in DBI-*xxx* and each sub-directory. Note that the following assumes gcc 2.95.2 or newer:

```
OLD:                                 NEW:
CC = cc                              CC = gcc
CCCDLFLAGS = -KPIC -W1,-Bexport      CCCDLFLAGS = -fpic
CCDLFLAGS = -w1,-Bexport             CCDLFLAGS =

LD = ld                              LD = gcc -G -fpic
LDDLFLAGS = -G -L/usr/local/lib      LDDLFLAGS = -L/usr/local/lib
LDFLAGS = -belf -L/usr/local/lib     LDFLAGS = -L/usr/local/lib

LD = ld                              LD = gcc -G -fpic
OPTIMISE = -Od                       OPTIMISE = -O1
```

```
OLD:
CCCFLAGS = -belf -dy -w0 -U M_XENIX -DPERL_SCO5 -I/usr/local/include

NEW:
CCFLAGS = -U M_XENIX -DPERL_SCO5 -I/usr/local/include
```

These changes are necessary because the Perl dynaloader will not load the DBI modules if they were compiled with icc or cc.

If you want to use the Perl module on a system that doesn't support dynamic linking (such as SCO), you can generate a static version of Perl that includes DBI and DBD::mysql. The way this works is that you generate a version of Perl with the DBI code linked in and install it on top of your current Perl. Then you use that to build a version of Perl that additionally has the DBD code linked in, and install that.

On SCO, you must have the following environment variables set:

```
LD_LIBRARY_PATH=/lib:/usr/lib:/usr/local/lib:/usr/progressive/lib
```

Or:

```
LD_LIBRARY_PATH=/usr/lib:/lib:/usr/local/lib:/usr/ccs/lib:\
    /usr/progressive/lib:/usr/skunk/lib
LIBPATH=/usr/lib:/lib:/usr/local/lib:/usr/ccs/lib:\
    /usr/progressive/lib:/usr/skunk/lib
MANPATH=scohelp:/usr/man:/usr/local1/man:/usr/local/man:\
    /usr/skunk/man:
```

First, create a Perl that includes a statically linked DBI module by running these commands in the directory where your DBI distribution is located:

```
shell> perl Makefile.PL -static -config
shell> make
shell> make install
shell> make perl
```

Then you must install the new Perl. The output of make perl will indicate the exact make command you will need to execute to perform the installation. On SCO, this is make -f Makefile.aperl inst_perl MAP_TARGET=perl.

Next, use the just-created Perl to create another Perl that also includes a statically linked DBD::mysql by running these commands in the directory where your DBD::mysql distribution is located:

```
shell> perl Makefile.PL -static -config
shell> make
shell> make install
shell> make perl
```

Finally, you should install this new Perl. Again, the output of make perl indicates the command to use.

3

Using MySQL Programs

This chapter provides a brief overview of the programs provided by MySQL AB and discusses how to specify options when you run these programs. Most programs have options that are specific to their own operation, but the syntax for specifying options is similar for all of them. Later chapters provide more detailed descriptions of individual programs, including which options they recognize.

3.1 Overview of MySQL Programs

MySQL AB provides several types of programs:

- The MYSQL server and server startup scripts:
  - `mysqld` is the MySQL server
  - `mysqld_safe`, `mysql.server`, and `mysqld_multi` are server startup scripts
  - `mysql_install_db` initializes the data directory and the initial databases

  These programs are discussed further in Chapter 4, "Database Administration."

- Client programs that access the server:
  - `mysql` is a command-line client for executing SQL statements interactively or in batch mode
  - `mysqlcc` (MySQL Control Center) is an interactive graphical tool for executing SQL statements and administration
  - `mysqladmin` is an administrative client
  - `mysqlcheck` performs table maintenance operations
  - `mysqldump` and `mysqlhotcopy` make database backups
  - `mysqlimport` imports data files
  - `mysqlshow` displays information about databases and tables

  These programs are discussed further in Chapter 7, "MySQL Client and Utility Programs."

- Utility programs that operate independently of the server:
  - `myisamchk` performs table maintenance operations
  - `myisampack` produces compressed, read-only tables
  - `mysqlbinlog` is a tool for processing binary log files
  - `perror` displays error code meanings

  `myisamchk` is discussed further in Chapter 4, "Database Administration." The other programs are discussed in Chapter 7, "MySQL Client and Utility Programs."

Most MySQL distributions include all of these programs, except for those programs that are
platform-specific. (For example, the server startup scripts are not used on Windows.) The
exception is that RPM distributions are more specialized. There is one RPM for the server,
another for the client programs, and so forth. If you appear to be missing one or more
programs, see Chapter 2, "Installing MySQL," for information on types of distributions and
what they contain. It may be that you need to install something else.

3.2 Invoking MySQL Programs

To invoke a MySQL program at the command line (that is, from your shell or command
prompt), enter the program name followed by any options or other arguments needed to
instruct the program what you want it to do. The following commands show some sample
program invocations. "`shell>`" represents the prompt for your command interpreter; it is
not part of what you type. The particular prompt you will see depends on your command
interpreter. Typical prompts are $ for sh or bash, % for csh or tcsh, and C:\> for Windows
command.com or cmd.exe.

```
shell> mysql test
shell> mysqladmin extended-status variables
shell> mysqlshow --help
shell> mysqldump --user=root personnel
```

Arguments that begin with a dash are option arguments. They typically specify the type of
connection a program should make to the server or affect its operational mode. Options
have a syntax that is described in Section 3.3, "Specifying Program Options."

Non-option arguments (arguments with no leading dash) provide additional information to
the program. For example, the `mysql` program interprets the first non-option argument as a
database name, so the command `mysql test` indicates that you want to use the `test` database.

Later sections that describe individual programs indicate which options a program understands and describe the meaning of any additional non-option arguments.

Some options are common to a number of programs. The most common of these are the
`--host`, `--user`, and `--password` options that specify connection parameters. They indicate
the host where the MySQL server is running, and the username and password of your

MySQL account. All MySQL client programs understand these options; they allow you to specify which server to connect to and the account to use on that server.

You may find it necessary to invoke MySQL programs using the pathname to the `bin` directory in which they are installed. This is likely to be the case if you get a "program not found" error whenever you attempt to run a MySQL program from any directory other than the `bin` directory. To make it more convenient to use MySQL, you can add the pathname of the `bin` directory to your `PATH` environment variable setting. Then to run a program you need only type its name, not its entire pathname.

Consult the documentation for your command interpreter for instructions on setting your `PATH`. The syntax for setting environment variables is interpreter-specific.

3.3 Specifying Program Options

You can provide options for MySQL programs in several ways:

- On the command line following the program name. This is most common for options that apply to a specific invocation of the program.
- In an option file that the program reads when it starts. This is common for options that you want the program to use each time it runs.
- In environment variables. These are useful for options that you want to apply each time the program runs, although in practice option files are used more commonly for this purpose. (Section 4.9.2, "Running Multiple Servers on Unix," discusses one situation in which environment variables can be very helpful. It describes a handy technique that uses such variables to specify the TCP/IP port number and Unix socket file for both the server and client programs.)

MySQL programs determine which options are given first by examining environment variables, then option files, and then the command line. If an option is specified multiple times, the last occurrence takes precedence. This means that environment variables have the lowest precedence and command-line options the highest.

You can take advantage of the way that MySQL programs process options by specifying the default values for a program's options in an option file. Then you need not type them each time you run the program, but can override the defaults if necessary by using command-line options.

3.3.1 Using Options on the Command Line

Program options specified on the command line follow these rules:

- Options are given after the command name.
- An option argument begins with one dash or two dashes, depending on whether it has a short name or a long name. Many options have both forms. For example, `-?` and `--help`

are the short and long forms of the option that instructs a MySQL program to display a help message.

- Option names are case sensitive. -v and -V are both legal and have different meanings. (They are the corresponding short forms of the --verbose and --version options.)

- Some options take a value following the option name. For example, -h localhost and --host=localhost indicate the MySQL server host to a client program. The option value tells the program the name of the host where the MySQL server is running.

- For a long option that takes a value, separate the option name and the value by an '=' sign. For a short option that takes a value, the option value can immediately follow the option letter, or there can be a space between. (-hlocalhost and -h localhost are equivalent.) An exception to this rule is the option for specifying your MySQL password. This option can be given in long form as --password=pass_val or as --password. In the latter case (with no password value given), the program will prompt you for the password. The password option also may be given in short form as -ppass_val or as -p. However, for the short form, if the password value is given, it must follow the option letter with *no intervening space*. The reason for this is that if a space follows the option letter, the program has no way to tell whether a following argument is supposed to be the password value or some other kind of argument. Consequently, the following two commands have two completely different meanings:

```
shell> mysql -ptest
shell> mysql -p test
```

The first command instructs mysql to use a password value of test, but specifies no default database. The second instructs mysql to prompt for the password value and to use test as the default database.

MySQL 4.0 introduced some additional flexibility in the way you specify options. These changes were made in MySQL 4.0.2. Some of them relate to the way you specify options that have "enabled" and "disabled" states, and to the use of options that might be present in one version of MySQL but not another. Those capabilities are discussed in this section. Another change pertains to the way you use options to set program variables. Section 3.3.4, "Using Options to Set Program Variables," discusses that topic further.

Some options control behavior that can be turned on or off. For example, the mysql client supports a --column-names option that determines whether or not to display a row of column names at the beginning of query results. By default, this option is enabled. However, you may want to disable it in some instances, such as when sending the output of mysql into another program that expects to see only data and not an initial header line.

To disable column names, you can specify the option using any of these forms:

```
--disable-column-names
--skip-column-names
--column-names=0
```

The `--disable` and `--skip` prefixes and the `=0` suffix all have the same effect: They turn the option off.

The "enabled" form of the option may be specified in any of these ways:

```
--column-names
--enable-column-names
--column-names=1
```

Another change to option processing introduced in MySQL 4.0 is that you can use the `--loose` prefix for command-line options. If an option is prefixed by `--loose`, the program will not exit with an error if it does not recognize the option, but instead will issue only a warning:

```
shell> mysql --loose-no-such-option
mysql: WARNING: unknown option '--no-such-option'
```

The `--loose` prefix can be useful when you run programs from multiple installations of MySQL on the same machine, at least if all the versions are as recent as 4.0.2. This prefix is particularly useful when you list options in an option file. An option that may not be recognized by all versions of a program can be given using the `--loose` prefix (or `loose` in an option file). Versions of the program that do not recognize the option will issue a warning and ignore it. This strategy requires that versions involved be 4.0.2 or later, because earlier versions know nothing of the `--loose` convention.

3.3.2 Using Option Files

MySQL programs can read startup options from option files (also sometimes called "configuration files"). Option files provide a convenient way to specify commonly used options so that they need not be entered on the command line each time you run a program. Option file capability is available from MySQL 3.22 on.

The following programs support option files: `myisamchk`, `myisampack`, `mysql`, `mysql.server`, `mysqladmin`, `mysqlbinlog`, `mysqlcc`, `mysqlcheck`, `mysqld`, `mysqld_safe`, `mysqldump`, `mysqlhotcopy`, `mysqlimport`, and `mysqlshow`.

On Windows, MySQL programs read startup options from the following files:

Filename	Purpose
`WINDIR\my.ini`	Global options
`C:\my.cnf`	Global options

`WINDIR` represents the location of your Windows directory. This is commonly `C:\Windows` or `C:\WinNT`. You can determine its exact location from the value of the `WINDIR` environment variable using the following command:

```
C:\> echo %WINDIR%
```

On Unix, MySQL programs read startup options from the following files:

Filename	Purpose
/etc/my.cnf	Global options
DATADIR/my.cnf	Server-specific options
defaults-extra-file	The file specified with --defaults-extra-file=path, if any
~/.my.cnf	User-specific options

DATADIR represents the location of the MySQL data directory. Typically this is /usr/local/mysql/data for a binary installation or /usr/local/var for a source installation. Note that this is the data directory location that was specified at configuration time, not the one specified with --datadir when mysqld starts. Use of --datadir at runtime has no effect on where the server looks for option files, because it looks for them before processing any command-line arguments.

MySQL looks for option files in the order just described and reads any that exist. If multiple option files exist, an option specified in a file read later takes precedence over the same option specified in a file read earlier.

Any long option that may be given on the command line when running a MySQL program can be given in an option file as well. To get the list of available options for a program, run it with the --help option.

The syntax for specifying options in an option file is similar to command-line syntax, except that you omit the leading two dashes. For example, --quick or --host=localhost on the command line should be specified as quick or host=localhost in an option file. To specify an option of the form --loose-opt_name in an option file, write it as loose-opt_name.

Empty lines in option files are ignored. Non-empty lines can take any of the following forms:

- #comment

  ;comment

  Comment lines start with '#' or ';'. As of MySQL 4.0.14, a '#'-comment can start in the middle of a line as well.

- [group]

  group is the name of the program or group for which you want to set options. After a group line, any opt_name or set-variable lines apply to the named group until the end of the option file or another group line is given.

- opt_name

  This is equivalent to --opt_name on the command line.

- opt_name=value

   This is equivalent to --opt_name=value on the command line. In an option file, you can have spaces around the '=' character, something that is not true on the command line. As of MySQL 4.0.16, you can quote the value with double quotes or single quotes. This is useful if the value contains a '#' comment character or whitespace.

- set-variable = var_name=value

   Set the program variable var_name to the given value. This is equivalent to --set-variable=var_name=value on the command line. Spaces are allowed around the first '=' character but not around the second. This syntax is deprecated as of MySQL 4.0. See Section 3.3.4, "Using Options to Set Program Variables," for more information on setting program variables.

Leading and trailing blanks are automatically deleted from option names and values. You may use the escape sequences '\b', '\t', '\n', '\r', '\\', and '\s' in option values to represent the backspace, tab, newline, carriage return, and space characters.

On Windows, if an option value represents a pathname, you should specify the value using '/' rather than '\' as the pathname separator. If you use '\', you must double it as '\\', because '\' is the escape character in MySQL.

If an option group name is the same as a program name, options in the group apply specifically to that program.

The [client] option group is read by all client programs (but not by mysqld). This allows you to specify options that apply to every client. For example, [client] is the perfect group to use to specify the password that you use to connect to the server. (But make sure that the option file is readable and writable only by yourself, so that other people cannot find out your password.) Be sure not to put an option in the [client] group unless it is recognized by *all* client programs that you use. Programs that do not understand the option will quit after displaying an error message if you try to run them.

As of MySQL 4.0.14, if you want to create option groups that should be read by only one specific mysqld server release series, you can do this by using groups with names of [mysqld-4.0], [mysqld-4.1], and so forth. The following group indicates that the --new option should be used only by MySQL servers with 4.0.x version numbers:

```
[mysqld-4.0]
new
```

Here is a typical global option file:

```
[client]
port=3306
socket=/tmp/mysql.sock

[mysqld]
port=3306
socket=/tmp/mysql.sock
```

```
key_buffer_size=16M
max_allowed_packet=8M

[mysqldump]
quick
```

The preceding option file uses *var_name=value* syntax for the lines that set the key_buffer_size and max_allowed_packet variables. Prior to MySQL 4.0.2, you would need to use set-variable syntax instead (described earlier in this section).

Here is a typical user option file:

```
[client]
# The following password will be sent to all standard MySQL clients
password="my_password"

[mysql]
no-auto-rehash
set-variable = connect_timeout=2

[mysqlhotcopy]
interactive-timeout
```

This option file uses set-variable syntax to set the connect_timeout variable. For MySQL 4.0.2 and up, you can also set the variable using just connect_timeout=2.

If you have a source distribution, you will find sample option files named my-*xxxx*.cnf in the support-files directory. If you have a binary distribution, look in the support-files directory under your MySQL installation directory (typically C:\mysql on Windows or /usr/local/mysql on Unix). Currently there are sample option files for small, medium, large, and very large systems. To experiment with one of these files, copy it to C:\my.cnf on Windows or to .my.cnf in your home directory on Unix.

Note: On Windows, the .cnf option file extension might not be displayed.

All MySQL programs that support option files handle the following command-line options:

- --no-defaults

  Don't read any option files.

- --print-defaults

  Print the program name and all options that it will get from option files.

- --defaults-file=*path_name*

  Use only the given option file. *path_name* is the full pathname to the file.

- --defaults-extra-file=*path_name*

  Read this option file after the global option file but before the user option file. *path_name* is the full pathname to the file.

To work properly, each of these options must immediately follow the command name on the command line, with the exception that --print-defaults may be used immediately after --defaults-file or --defaults-extra-file.

In shell scripts, you can use the my_print_defaults program to parse option files. The following example shows the output that my_print_defaults might produce when asked to show the options found in the [client] and [mysql] groups:

```
shell> my_print_defaults client mysql
--port=3306
--socket=/tmp/mysql.sock
--no-auto-rehash
```

Note for developers: Option file handling is implemented in the C client library simply by processing all matching options (that is, options in the appropriate group) before any command-line arguments. This works nicely for programs that use the last instance of an option that is specified multiple times. If you have a C or C++ program that handles multiply specified options this way but doesn't read option files, you need add only two lines to give it that capability. Check the source code of any of the standard MySQL clients to see how to do this.

Several other language interfaces to MySQL are based on the C client library, and some of them provide a way to access option file contents. These include Perl and Python. See the documentation for your preferred interface for details.

3.3.3 Using Environment Variables to Specify Options

To specify an option using an environment variable, set the variable using the syntax appropriate for your comment processor. For example, on Windows or NetWare, you can set the USER variable to specify your MySQL account name. To do so, use this syntax:

```
SET USER=your_name
```

The syntax on Unix depends on your shell. Suppose that you want to specify the TCP/IP port number using the MYSQL_TCP_PORT variable. The syntax for Bourne shell and variants (sh, bash, zsh, and so on) is:

```
MYSQL_TCP_PORT=3306
```

For csh and tcsh, use this syntax:

```
setenv MYSQL_TCP_PORT 3306
```

The commands to set environment variables can be executed at your command prompt to take effect immediately. These settings persist until you log out. To have the settings take effect each time you log in, place the appropriate command or commands in a startup file that your command interpreter reads each time it starts. Typical startup files are AUTOEXEC.BAT for Windows, .bash_profile for bash, or .tcshrc for tcsh. Consult the documentation for your command interpreter for specific details.

Appendix B, "Environment Variables," lists all environment variables that affect MySQL program operation.

3.3.4 Using Options to Set Program Variables

Many MySQL programs have internal variables that can be set at runtime. As of MySQL 4.0.2, program variables are set the same way as any other long option that takes a value. For example, mysql has a max_allowed_packet variable that controls the maximum size of its communication buffer. To set the max_allowed_packet variable for mysql to a value of 16MB, use either of the following commands:

```
shell> mysql --max_allowed_packet=16777216
shell> mysql --max_allowed_packet=16M
```

The first command specifies the value in bytes. The second specifies the value in megabytes. Variable values can have a suffix of K, M, or G (either uppercase or lowercase) to indicate units of kilobytes, megabytes, or gigabytes, respectively.

In an option file, the variable setting is given without the leading dashes:

```
[mysql]
max_allowed_packet=16777216
```

Or:

```
[mysql]
max_allowed_packet=16M
```

If you like, underscores in a variable name can be specified as dashes.

Prior to MySQL 4.0.2, program variable names are not recognized as option names. Instead, use the --set-variable option to assign a value to a variable:

```
shell> mysql --set-variable=max_allowed_packet=16777216
shell> mysql --set-variable=max_allowed_packet=16M
```

In an option file, omit the leading dashes:

```
[mysql]
set-variable = max_allowed_packet=16777216
```

Or:

```
[mysql]
set-variable = max_allowed_packet=16M
```

With --set-variable, underscores in variable names cannot be given as dashes for versions of MySQL older than 4.0.2.

The --set-variable option is still recognized in MySQL 4.0.2 and up, but is deprecated.

Some server variables can be set at runtime. For details, see Section 4.2.3.1.2, "Dynamic System Variables."

Database Administration

This chapter covers topics that deal with administering a MySQL installation, such as configuring the server, managing user accounts, and performing backups.

4.1 The MySQL Server and Server Startup Scripts

The MySQL server, `mysqld`, is the main program that does most of the work in a MySQL installation. The server is accompanied by several related scripts that perform setup operations when you install MySQL or that are helper programs to assist you in starting and stopping the server.

This section provides an overview of the server and related programs, and information about server startup scripts. Information about configuring the server itself is given in Section 4.2, "Configuring the MySQL Server."

4.1.1 Overview of the Server-Side Scripts and Utilities

All MySQL programs take many different options. However, every MySQL program provides a `--help` option that you can use to get a description of the program's options. For example, try `mysqld --help`.

You can override default options for all standard programs by specifying options on the command line or in an option file. See Section 3.3, "Specifying Program Options."

The following list briefly describes the MySQL server and server-related programs:

- `mysqld`

    The SQL daemon (that is, the MySQL server). To use client programs, this program must be running, because clients gain access to databases by connecting to the server. See Section 4.2, "Configuring the MySQL Server."

- `mysqld-max`

    A version of the server that includes additional features. See Section 4.1.2, "The `mysqld-max` Extended MySQL Server."

- `mysqld_safe`

  A server startup script. `mysqld_safe` attempts to start `mysqld-max` if it exists, and `mysqld` otherwise. See Section 4.1.3, "The `mysqld_safe` Server Startup Script."

- `mysql.server`

  A server startup script. This script is used on systems that use run directories containing scripts that start system services for particular run levels. It invokes `mysqld_safe` to start the MySQL server. See Section 4.1.4, "The `mysql.server` Server Startup Script."

- `mysqld_multi`

  A server startup script that can start or stop multiple servers installed on the system. See Section 4.1.5, "The `mysqld_multi` Program for Managing Multiple MySQL Servers."

- `mysql_install_db`

  This script creates the MySQL grant tables with default privileges. It is usually executed only once, when first installing MySQL on a system.

- `mysql_fix_privilege_tables`

  This script is used after an upgrade install operation, to update the grant tables with any changes that have been made in newer versions of MySQL.

There are several other programs that also are run on the server host:

- `myisamchk`

  A utility to describe, check, optimize, and repair `MyISAM` tables. `myisamchk` is described in Section 4.6.2, "Table Maintenance and Crash Recovery."

- `make_binary_distribution`

  This program makes a binary release of a compiled MySQL. This could be sent by FTP to `/pub/mysql/upload` on `ftp.mysql.com` for the convenience of other MySQL users.

- `mysqlbug`

  The MySQL bug reporting script. It can be used to send a bug report to the MySQL mailing list. (You can also visit `http://bugs.mysql.com/` to file a bug report online.)

4.1.2 The `mysqld-max` Extended MySQL Server

A MySQL-Max server is a version of the `mysqld` MySQL server that has been built to include additional features.

The distribution to use depends on your platform:

- For Windows, MySQL binary distributions include both the standard server (`mysqld.exe`) and the MySQL-Max server (`mysqld-max.exe`), so you need not get a special distribution. Just use a regular Windows distribution, available at `http://dev.mysql.com/downloads/mysql-4.0.html`. See Section 2.2.1, "Installing MySQL on Windows."

- For Linux, if you install MySQL using RPM distributions, use the regular `MySQL-server` RPM first to install a standard server named `mysqld`. Then use the `MySQL-Max` RPM to install a server named `mysqld-max`. The `MySQL-Max` RPM presupposes that you have already installed the regular server RPM. See Section 2.2.2, "Installing MySQL on Linux," for more information on the Linux RPM packages.

- All other MySQL-Max distributions contain a single server that is named `mysqld` but that has the additional features included.

You can find the MySQL-Max binaries on the MySQL AB Web site at `http://dev.mysql.com/downloads/mysql-max-4.0.html`.

MySQL AB builds the MySQL-Max servers by using the following `configure` options:

- `--with-server-suffix=-max`

  This option adds a `-max` suffix to the `mysqld` version string.

- `--with-innodb`

  This option enables support for the `InnoDB` storage engine. MySQL-Max servers always include `InnoDB` support, but this option actually is needed only for MySQL 3.23. From MySQL 4 on, `InnoDB` is included by default in binary distributions, so you do not need a MySQL-Max server to obtain `InnoDB` support.

- `--with-bdb`

  This option enables support for the Berkeley DB (`BDB`) storage engine.

- `CFLAGS=-DUSE_SYMDIR`

  This define enables symbolic link support for Windows.

MySQL-Max binary distributions are a convenience for those who wish to install precompiled programs. If you build MySQL using a source distribution, you can build your own Max-like server by enabling the same features at configuration time that the MySQL-Max binary distributions are built with.

MySQL-Max servers include the BerkeleyDB (`BDB`) storage engine whenever possible, but not all platforms support `BDB`. The following table shows which platforms allow MySQL-Max binaries to include `BDB`:

System	BDB Support
AIX 4.3	N
HP-UX 11.0	N
Linux-Alpha	N
Linux-IA-64	N
Linux-Intel	Y

System	BDB Support
Mac OS X	N
NetWare	N
SCO OSR5	Y
Solaris-Intel	N
Solaris-SPARC	Y
UnixWare	Y
Windows/NT	Y

To find out which storage engines your server supports, issue the following statement:

```
mysql> SHOW ENGINES;
```

Before MySQL 4.1.2, SHOW ENGINES is unavailable. Use the following statement instead and check the value of the variable for the storage engine in which you are interested:

```
mysql> SHOW VARIABLES LIKE 'have_%';
+-------------------+----------+
| Variable_name     | Value    |
+-------------------+----------+
| have_bdb          | NO       |
| have_crypt        | YES      |
| have_innodb       | YES      |
| have_isam         | NO       |
| have_raid         | NO       |
| have_symlink      | DISABLED |
| have_openssl      | NO       |
| have_query_cache  | YES      |
+-------------------+----------+
```

The values in the second column indicate the server's level of support for each feature:

Value	Meaning
YES	The feature is supported and is active.
NO	The feature is not supported.
DISABLED	The feature is supported but has been disabled.

A value of NO means that the server was compiled without support for the feature, so it cannot be activated at runtime.

A value of DISABLED occurs either because the server was started with an option that disables the feature, or because not all options required to enable it were given. In the latter case, the host_name.err error log file should contain a reason indicating why the option is disabled.

One situation in which you might see DISABLED occurs with MySQL 3.23 when the InnoDB storage engine is compiled in. In MySQL 3.23, you must supply at least the innodb_data_file_path option at runtime to set up the InnoDB tablespace. Without this option, InnoDB disables itself. See Section 9.3, "InnoDB in MySQL 3.23." You can specify configuration options for the BDB storage engine, too, but BDB will not disable itself if you do not provide them. See Section 8.4.3, "BDB Startup Options."

You might also see DISABLED for the InnoDB, BDB, or ISAM storage engines if the server was compiled to support them, but was started with the --skip-innodb, --skip-bdb, or --skip-isam options at runtime.

As of Version 3.23, all MySQL servers support MyISAM tables, because MyISAM is the default storage engine.

4.1.3 The mysqld_safe Server Startup Script

mysqld_safe is the recommended way to start a mysqld server on Unix and NetWare. mysqld_safe adds some safety features such as restarting the server when an error occurs and logging runtime information to an error log file. NetWare-specific behaviors are listed later in this section.

Note: Before MySQL 4.0, mysqld_safe is named safe_mysqld. To preserve backward compatibility, MySQL binary distributions for some time will include safe_mysqld as a symbolic link to mysqld_safe.

By default, mysqld_safe tries to start an executable named mysqld-max if it exists, or mysqld otherwise. Be aware of the implications of this behavior:

- On Linux, the MySQL-Max RPM relies on this mysqld_safe behavior. The RPM installs an executable named mysqld-max, which causes mysqld_safe to automatically use that executable from that point on.

- If you install a MySQL-Max distribution that includes a server named mysqld-max, then upgrade later to a non-Max version of MySQL, mysqld_safe will still attempt to run the old mysqld-max server. If you perform such an upgrade, you should manually remove the old mysqld-max server to ensure that mysqld_safe runs the new mysqld server.

To override the default behavior and specify explicitly which server you want to run, specify a --mysqld or --mysqld-version option to mysqld_safe.

Many of the options to mysqld_safe are the same as the options to mysqld. See Section 4.2.1, "mysqld Command-Line Options."

All options specified to mysqld_safe on the command line are passed to mysqld. If you want to use any options that are specific to mysqld_safe and that mysqld doesn't support, do not specify them on the command line. Instead, list them in the [mysqld_safe] group of an option file. See Section 3.3.2, "Using Option Files."

mysqld_safe reads all options from the [mysqld], [server], and [mysqld_safe] sections in option files. For backward compatibility, it also reads [safe_mysqld] sections, although you should rename such sections to [mysqld_safe] when you begin using MySQL 4.0 or later.

mysqld_safe supports the following options:

- --basedir=*path*

  The path to the MySQL installation directory.

- --core-file-size=*size*

  The size of the core file mysqld should be able to create. The option value is passed to ulimit -c.

- --datadir=*path*

  The path to the data directory.

- --defaults-extra-file=*path*

  The name of an option file to be read in addition to the usual option files.

- --defaults-file=*path*

  The name of an option file to be read instead of the usual option files.

- --err-log=*path*

  The old form of the --log-error option, to be used before MySQL 4.0.

- --ledir=*path*

  The path to the directory containing the mysqld program. Use this option to explicitly indicate the location of the server.

- --log-error=*path*

  Write the error log to the given file. See Section 4.8.1, "The Error Log."

- --mysqld=*prog_name*

  The name of the server program (in the ledir directory) that you want to start.

- --mysqld-version=*suffix*

  This option is similar to the --mysqld option, but you specify only the suffix for the server program name. The basename is assumed to be mysqld. For example, if you use --mysqld-version=max, mysqld_safe will start the mysqld-max program in the ledir directory. If the argument to --mysqld-version is empty, mysqld_safe uses mysqld in the ledir directory.

- --nice=*priority*

  Use the nice program to set the server's scheduling priority to the given value. This option was added in MySQL 4.0.14.

- --no-defaults

  Do not read any option files.

- `--open-files-limit=count`

  The number of files `mysqld` should be able to open. The option value is passed to `ulimit -n`. Note that you need to start `mysqld_safe` as `root` for this to work properly!

- `--pid-file=path`

  The path to the process ID file.

- `--port=port_num`

  The port number to use when listening for TCP/IP connections.

- `--socket=path`

  The Unix socket file to use for local connections.

- `--timezone=zone`

  Set the `TZ` time zone environment variable to the given option value. Consult your operating system documentation for legal time zone specification formats.

- `--user={user_name | user_id}`

  Run the `mysqld` server as the user having the name *user_name* or the numeric user ID *user_id*. ("User" in this context refers to a system login account, not a MySQL user listed in the grant tables.)

The `mysqld_safe` script is written so that it normally can start a server that was installed from either a source or a binary distribution of MySQL, even though these types of distributions typically install the server in slightly different locations. (See Section 2.1.5, "Installation Layouts.") `mysqld_safe` expects one of the following conditions to be true:

- The server and databases can be found relative to the directory from which `mysqld_safe` is invoked. For binary distributions, `mysqld_safe` looks under its working directory for `bin` and `data` directories. For source distributions, it looks for `libexec` and `var` directories. This condition should be met if you execute `mysqld_safe` from your MySQL installation directory (for example, `/usr/local/mysql` for a binary distribution).

- If the server and databases cannot be found relative to the working directory, `mysqld_safe` attempts to locate them by absolute pathnames. Typical locations are `/usr/local/libexec` and `/usr/local/var`. The actual locations are determined from the values configured into the distribution at the time it was built. They should be correct if MySQL is installed in the location specified at configuration time.

Because `mysqld_safe` will try to find the server and databases relative to its own working directory, you can install a binary distribution of MySQL anywhere, as long as you run `mysqld_safe` from the MySQL installation directory:

```
shell> cd mysql_installation_directory
shell> bin/mysqld_safe &
```

If `mysqld_safe` fails, even when invoked from the MySQL installation directory, you can specify the `--ledir` and `--datadir` options to indicate the directories in which the server and databases are located on your system.

Normally, you should not edit the `mysqld_safe` script. Instead, configure `mysqld_safe` by using command-line options or options in the `[mysqld_safe]` section of a `my.cnf` option file. In rare cases, it might be necessary to edit `mysqld_safe` to get it to start the server properly. However, if you do this, your modified version of `mysqld_safe` might be overwritten if you upgrade MySQL in the future, so you should make a copy of your edited version that you can reinstall.

On NetWare, `mysqld_safe` is a NetWare Loadable Module (NLM) that is ported from the original Unix shell script. It does the following:

1. Runs a number of system and option checks.

2. Runs a check on `MyISAM` and `ISAM` tables.

3. Provides a screen presence for the MySQL server.

4. Starts `mysqld`, monitors it, and restarts it if it terminates in error.

5. Sends error messages from `mysqld` to the *host_name*`.err` file in the data directory.

6. Sends `mysqld_safe` screen output to the *host_name*`.safe` file in the data directory.

4.1.4 The `mysql.server` Server Startup Script

MySQL distributions on Unix include a script named `mysql.server`. It can be used on systems such as Linux and Solaris that use System V-style run directories to start and stop system services. It is also used by the Mac OS X Startup Item for MySQL.

`mysql.server` can be found in the `support-files` directory under your MySQL installation directory or in a MySQL source tree.

If you use the Linux server RPM package (`MySQL-server-`*VERSION*`.rpm`), the `mysql.server` script will already have been installed in the `/etc/init.d` directory with the name `mysql`. You need not install it manually. See Section 2.2.2, "Installing MySQL on Linux," for more information on the Linux RPM packages.

Some vendors provide RPM packages that install a startup script under a different name such as `mysqld`.

If you install MySQL from a source distribution or use a binary distribution format that does not install `mysql.server` automatically, you can install it manually. Instructions are provided in Section 2.4.3, "Starting and Stopping MySQL Automatically."

`mysql.server` reads options from the `[mysql.server]` and `[mysqld]` sections of option files. For backward compatibility, it also reads `[mysql_server]` sections, although you should rename such sections to `[mysql.server]` when you begin using MySQL 4.0 or later.

4.1.5 The `mysqld_multi` Program for Managing Multiple MySQL Servers

`mysqld_multi` is meant for managing several `mysqld` processes that listen for connections on different Unix socket files and TCP/IP ports. It can start or stop servers, or report their current status.

The program searches for groups named [mysqld#] in `my.cnf` (or in the file named by the `--config-file` option). # can be any positive integer. This number is referred to in the following discussion as the option group number, or GNR. Group numbers distinguish option groups from one another and are used as arguments to `mysqld_multi` to specify which servers you want to start, stop, or obtain a status report for. Options listed in these groups are the same that you would use in the [mysqld] group used for starting `mysqld`. (See, for example, Section 2.4.3, "Starting and Stopping MySQL Automatically.") However, when using multiple servers it is necessary that each one use its own value for options such as the Unix socket file and TCP/IP port number. For more information on which options must be unique per server in a multiple-server environment, see Section 4.9, "Running Multiple MySQL Servers on the Same Machine."

To invoke `mysqld_multi`, use the following syntax:

```
shell> mysqld_multi [options] {start|stop|report} [GNR[,GNR]...]
```

start, stop, and report indicate which operation you want to perform. You can perform the designated operation on a single server or multiple servers, depending on the GNR list that follows the option name. If there is no list, `mysqld_multi` performs the operation for all servers in the option file.

Each GNR value represents an option group number or range of group numbers. The value should be the number at the end of the group name in the option file. For example, the GNR for a group named [mysqld17] is 17. To specify a range of numbers, separate the first and last numbers by a dash. The GNR value 10-13 represents groups [mysqld10] through [mysqld13]. Multiple groups or group ranges can be specified on the command line, separated by commas. There must be no whitespace characters (spaces or tabs) in the GNR list; anything after a whitespace character is ignored.

This command starts a single server using option group [mysqld17]:

```
shell> mysqld_multi start 17
```

This command stops several servers, using option groups [mysql8] and [mysqld10] through [mysqld13]:

```
shell> mysqld_multi start 8,10-13
```

For an example of how you might set up an option file, use this command:

```
shell> mysqld_multi --example
```

`mysqld_multi` supports the following options:

- `--config-file=`*`name`*

  Specify the name of an alternative option file. This affects where `mysqld_multi` looks for `[mysqld#]` option groups. Without this option, all options are read from the usual `my.cnf` file. The option does not affect where `mysqld_multi` reads its own options, which are always taken from the `[mysqld_multi]` group in the usual `my.cnf` file.

- `--example`

  Display a sample option file.

- `--help`

  Display a help message and exit.

- `--log=`*`name`*

  Specify the name of the log file. If the file exists, log output is appended to it.

- `--mysqladmin=`*`prog_name`*

  The `mysqladmin` binary to be used to stop servers.

- `--mysqld=`*`prog_name`*

  The `mysqld` binary to be used. Note that you can specify `mysqld_safe` as the value for this option also. The options are passed to `mysqld`. Just make sure that you have the directory where `mysqld` is located in your `PATH` environment variable setting or fix `mysqld_safe`.

- `--no-log`

  Print log information to `stdout` rather than to the log file. By default, output goes to the log file.

- `--password=`*`password`*

  The password of the MySQL account to use when invoking `mysqladmin`. Note that the password value is not optional for this option, unlike for other MySQL programs.

- `--tcp-ip`

  Connect to each MySQL server via the TCP/IP port instead of the Unix socket file. (If a socket file is missing, the server might still be running, but accessible only via the TCP/IP port.) By default, connections are made using the Unix socket file. This option affects `stop` and `report` operations.

- `--user=`*`user_name`*

  The username of the MySQL account to use when invoking `mysqladmin`.

- `--version`

  Display version information and exit.

Some notes about `mysqld_multi`:

- Make sure that the MySQL account used for stopping the `mysqld` servers (with the `mysqladmin` program) has the same username and password for each server. Also, make sure that the account has the `SHUTDOWN` privilege. If the servers that you want to manage have many different usernames or passwords for the administrative accounts, you might want to create an account on each server that has the same username and password. For example, you might set up a common `multi_admin` account by executing the following commands for each server:

```
shell> mysql -u root -S /tmp/mysql.sock -proot_password
mysql> GRANT SHUTDOWN ON *.*
    -> TO 'multi_admin'@'localhost' IDENTIFIED BY 'multipass';
```

See Section 4.4.2, "How the Privilege System Works." You will have to do this for each `mysqld` server. Change the connection parameters appropriately when connecting to each one. Note that the host part of the account name must allow you to connect as `multi_admin` from the host where you want to run `mysqld_multi`.

- The `--pid-file` option is very important if you are using `mysqld_safe` to start `mysqld` (for example, `--mysqld=mysqld_safe`) Every `mysqld` should have its own process ID file. The advantage of using `mysqld_safe` instead of `mysqld` is that `mysqld_safe` "guards" its `mysqld` process and will restart it if the process terminates due to a signal sent using `kill -9`, or for other reasons, such as a segmentation fault. Please note that the `mysqld_safe` script might require that you start it from a certain place. This means that you might have to change location to a certain directory before running `mysqld_multi`. If you have problems starting, please see the `mysqld_safe` script. Check especially the lines:

```
----------------------------------------------------------------
MY_PWD=`pwd`
# Check if we are starting this relative (for the binary release)
if test -d $MY_PWD/data/mysql -a -f ./share/mysql/english/errmsg.sys -a \
 -x ./bin/mysqld
----------------------------------------------------------------
```

See Section 4.1.3, "The `mysqld_safe` Server Startup Script." The test performed by these lines should be successful, or you might encounter problems.

- The Unix socket file and the TCP/IP port number must be different for every `mysqld`.

- You might want to use the `--user` option for `mysqld`, but in order to do this you need to run the `mysqld_multi` script as the Unix `root` user. Having the option in the option file doesn't matter; you will just get a warning, if you are not the superuser and the `mysqld` processes are started under your own Unix account.

- **Important**: Make sure that the data directory is fully accessible to the Unix account that the specific `mysqld` process is started as. *Do not* use the Unix root account for this, unless you *know* what you are doing.

- **Most important**: Before using mysqld_multi be sure that you understand the meanings of the options that are passed to the mysqld servers and *why* you would want to have separate mysqld processes. Beware of the dangers of using multiple mysqld servers with the same data directory. Use separate data directories, unless you *know* what you are doing. Starting multiple servers with the same data directory *will not* give you extra performance in a threaded system. See Section 4.9, "Running Multiple MySQL Servers on the Same Machine."

The following example shows how you might set up an option file for use with mysqld_multi. The first and fifth [mysqld#] group were intentionally left out from the example to illustrate that you can have "gaps" in the option file. This gives you more flexibility. The order in which the mysqld programs are started or stopped depends on the order in which they appear in the option file.

```
# This file should probably be in your home dir (~/.my.cnf)
# or /etc/my.cnf
# Version 2.1 by Jani Tolonen

[mysqld_multi]
mysqld    = /usr/local/bin/mysqld_safe
mysqladmin = /usr/local/bin/mysqladmin
user      = multi_admin
password  = multipass

[mysqld2]
socket    = /tmp/mysql.sock2
port      = 3307
pid-file  = /usr/local/mysql/var2/hostname.pid2
datadir   = /usr/local/mysql/var2
language  = /usr/local/share/mysql/english
user      = john

[mysqld3]
socket    = /tmp/mysql.sock3
port      = 3308
pid-file  = /usr/local/mysql/var3/hostname.pid3
datadir   = /usr/local/mysql/var3
language  = /usr/local/share/mysql/swedish
user      = monty

[mysqld4]
socket    = /tmp/mysql.sock4
port      = 3309
pid-file  = /usr/local/mysql/var4/hostname.pid4
datadir   = /usr/local/mysql/var4
language  = /usr/local/share/mysql/estonia
user      = tonu
```

```
[mysqld6]
socket     = /tmp/mysql.sock6
port       = 3311
pid-file   = /usr/local/mysql/var6/hostname.pid6
datadir    = /usr/local/mysql/var6
language   = /usr/local/share/mysql/japanese
user       = jani
```

See Section 3.3.2, "Using Option Files."

4.2 Configuring the MySQL Server

This section discusses MySQL server configuration topics:

- Startup options that the server supports
- How to set the server SQL mode
- Server system variables
- Server status variables

4.2.1 `mysqld` Command-Line Options

When you start the `mysqld` server, you can specify program options using any of the methods described in Section 3.3, "Specifying Program Options." The most common methods are to provide options in an option file or on the command line. However, in most cases it is desirable to make sure that the server uses the same options each time it runs. The best way to ensure this is to list them in an option file. See Section 3.3.2, "Using Option Files."

`mysqld` reads options from the `[mysqld]` and `[server]` groups. `mysqld_safe` reads options from the `[mysqld]`, `[server]`, `[mysqld_safe]`, and `[safe_mysqld]` groups. `mysql.server` reads options from the `[mysqld]` and `[mysql.server]` groups. An embedded MySQL server usually reads options from the `[server]`, `[embedded]`, and `[xxxxx_SERVER]` groups, where *xxxxx* is the name of the application into which the server is embedded.

`mysqld` accepts many command-line options. For a list, execute `mysqld --help`. Before MySQL 4.1.1, `--help` prints the full help message. As of 4.1.1, it prints a brief message; to see the full list, use `mysqld --verbose --help`.

The following list shows some of the most common server options. Additional options are described elsewhere:

- Options that affect security: See Section 4.3.3, "Startup Options for `mysqld` Concerning Security."
- SSL-related options: See Section 4.5.7.5, "SSL Command-Line Options."
- Binary log control options: See Section 4.8.4, "The Binary Log."
- Replication-related options: See Section 5.8, "Replication Startup Options."

- Options specific to particular storage engines: See Section 8.1.1, "MyISAM Startup Options," Section 8.4.3, "BDB Startup Options," and Section 9.5, "InnoDB Startup Options."

You can also set the value of a server system variable by using the variable name as an option, as described later in this section.

- `--help, -?`

   Display a short help message and exit. Before MySQL 4.1.1, `--help` displays the full help message. As of 4.1.1, it displays an abbreviated message only. Use both the `--verbose` and `--help` options to see the full message.

- `--ansi`

   Use standard SQL syntax instead of MySQL syntax. See Section 1.8.3, "Running MySQL in ANSI Mode." For more precise control over the server SQL mode, use the `--sql-mode` option instead.

- `--basedir=path, -b path`

   The path to the MySQL installation directory. All paths are usually resolved relative to this.

- `--big-tables`

   Allow large result sets by saving all temporary sets in files. This option prevents most "table full" errors, but also slows down queries for which in-memory tables would suffice. Since MySQL 3.23.2, the server is able to handle large result sets automatically by using memory for small temporary tables and switching to disk tables where necessary.

- `--bind-address=IP`

   The IP address to bind to.

- `--console`

   Write the error log messages to stderr/stdout even if `--log-error` is specified. On Windows, `mysqld` will not close the console screen if this option is used.

- `--character-sets-dir=path`

   The directory where character sets are installed. See Section 4.7.1, "The Character Set Used for Data and Sorting."

- `--chroot=path`

   Put the `mysqld` server in a closed environment during startup by using the `chroot()` system call. This is a recommended security measure as of MySQL 4.0. (MySQL 3.23 is not able to provide a `chroot()` jail that is 100% closed.) Note that use of this option somewhat limits LOAD DATA INFILE and SELECT ... INTO OUTFILE.

- `--core-file`

   Write a core file if `mysqld` dies. For some systems, you must also specify the `--core-file-size` option to `mysqld_safe`. See Section 4.1.3, "The mysqld_safe Server Startup Script." Note that on some systems, such as Solaris, you will not get a core file if you are also using the `--user` option.

- `--datadir=path, -h path`

  The path to the data directory.

- `--debug[=debug_options], -# [debug_options]`

  If MySQL is configured with `--with-debug`, you can use this option to get a trace file of what `mysqld` is doing. The `debug_options` string often is `'d:t:o,file_name'`.

- `--default-character-set=charset`

  Use `charset` as the default character set. See Section 4.7.1, "The Character Set Used for Data and Sorting."

- `--default-collation=collation`

  Use `collation` as the default collation. This option is available as of MySQL 4.1.1. See Section 4.7.1, "The Character Set Used for Data and Sorting."

- `--default-storage-engine=type`

  This option is a synonym for `--default-table-type`. It is available as of MySQL 4.1.2.

- `--default-table-type=type`

  Set the default table type for tables. See Chapter 8, "MySQL Storage Engines and Table Types."

- `--delay-key-write[= OFF | ON | ALL]`

  How the DELAYED KEYS option should be used. Delayed key writing causes key buffers not to be flushed between writes for MyISAM tables. OFF disables delayed key writes. ON enables delayed key writes for those tables that were created with the DELAYED KEYS option. ALL delays key writes for all MyISAM tables. Available as of MySQL 4.0.3. See Section 6.5.2, "Tuning Server Parameters." See Section 8.1.1, "MyISAM Startup Options."

  Note: If you set this variable to ALL, you should not use MyISAM tables from within another program (such as from another MySQL server or with `myisamchk`) when the table is in use. Doing so will lead to index corruption.

- `--delay-key-write-for-all-tables`

  Old form of `--delay-key-write=ALL` for use prior to MySQL 4.0.3. As of 4.0.3, use `--delay-key-write` instead.

- `--des-key-file=file_name`

  Read the default keys used by DES_ENCRYPT() and DES_DECRYPT() from this file.

- `--enable-named-pipe`

  Enable support for named pipes. This option applies only on Windows NT, 2000, and XP systems, and can be used only with the `mysqld-nt` and `mysqld-max-nt` servers that support named pipe connections.

- `--external-locking`

  Enable system locking. Note that if you use this option on a system on which `lockd` does not fully work (as on Linux), you will easily get `mysqld` to deadlock. This option previously was named `--enable-locking`.

Note: If you use this option to enable updates to MyISAM tables from many MySQL processes, you have to ensure that these conditions are satisfied:

- You should not use the query cache for queries that use tables that are updated by another process.
- You should not use `--delay-key-write=ALL` or `DELAY_KEY_WRITE=1` on any shared tables.

The easiest way to ensure this is to always use `--external-locking` together with `--delay-key-write=OFF --query-cache-size=0`.

(This is not done by default because in many setups it's useful to have a mixture of the above options.)

- `--exit-info[=flags]`, `-T [flags]`

This is a bit mask of different flags you can use for debugging the mysqld server. Do not use this option unless you know exactly what it does!

- `--flush`

Flush all changes to disk after each SQL statement. Normally MySQL does a write of all changes to disk only after each SQL statement and lets the operating system handle the synching to disk. See Section A.4.2, "What to Do If MySQL Keeps Crashing."

- `--init-file=file`

Read SQL statements from this file at startup. Each statement must be on a single line and should not include comments.

- `--language=lang_name`, `-L lang_name`

Client error messages in given language. `lang_name` can be given as the language name or as the full pathname to the directory where the language files are installed. See Section 4.7.2, "Setting the Error Message Language."

- `--log[=file]`, `-l [file]`

Log connections and queries to this file. See Section 4.8.2, "The General Query Log." If you don't specify a filename, MySQL will use `host_name.log` as the filename.

- `--log-bin=[file]`

The binary log file. Log all queries that change data to this file. Used for backup and replication. See Section 4.8.4, "The Binary Log." If you don't specify a filename, MySQL will use `host_name-bin` as the filename.

- `--log-bin-index[=file]`

The index file for binary log filenames. See Section 4.8.4, "The Binary Log." If you don't specify a filename, MySQL will use `host_name-bin.index` as the filename.

- `--log-error[=file]`

Log errors and startup messages to this file. See Section 4.8.1, "The Error Log." If you don't specify a filename, MySQL will use `host_name.err` as the filename.

- `--log-isam[=file]`

  Log all ISAM/MyISAM changes to this file (used only when debugging ISAM/MyISAM).

- `--log-long-format`

  Log some extra information to the log files (update log, binary update log, and slow queries log, whatever log has been activated). For example, username and timestamp are logged for queries. If you are using `--log-slow-queries` and `--log-long-format`, then queries that are not using indexes also are logged to the slow query log. Note that `--log-long-format` is deprecated as of MySQL version 4.1, when `--log-short-format` was introduced (the long log format is the default setting since version 4.1). Also note that starting with MySQL 4.1, the `--log-queries-not-using-indexes` option is available for the purpose of logging queries that do not use indexes to the slow query log.

- `--log-queries-not-using-indexes`

  If you are using this option with `--log-slow-queries`, then queries that are not using indexes also are logged to the slow query log. This option is available as of MySQL 4.1. See Section 4.8.5, "The Slow Query Log."

- `--log-short-format`

  Log less information to the log files (update log, binary update log, and slow queries log, whatever log has been activated). For example, username and timestamp are not logged for queries. This option was introduced in MySQL 4.1.

- `--log-slow-queries[=file]`

  Log all queries that have taken more than `long_query_time` seconds to execute to file. See Section 4.8.5, "The Slow Query Log." Note that the default for the amount of information logged has changed in MySQL 4.1. See the `--log-long-format` and `--log-short-format` options for details.

- `--log-update[=file]`

  Log updates to `file.#` where `#` is a unique number if not given. See Section 4.8.3, "The Update Log." The update log is deprecated and is removed in MySQL 5.0.0; you should use the binary log instead (`--log-bin`). See Section 4.8.4, "The Binary Log." Starting from version 5.0.0, using `--log-update` will just turn on the binary log instead.

- `--log-warnings, -W`

  Print out warnings such as `Aborted connection...` to the error log. Enabling this option is recommended, for example, if you use replication (you will get more information about what is happening, such as messages about network failures and reconnections). This option is enabled by default as of MySQL 4.1.2; to disable it, use `--skip-log-warnings`. See Section A.2.10, "Communication Errors and Aborted Connections."

  This option was named `--warnings` before MySQL 4.0.

- `--low-priority-updates`

  Table-modifying operations (INSERT, REPLACE, DELETE, UPDATE) will have lower priority than selects. This can also be done via {INSERT | REPLACE | DELETE | UPDATE} LOW_PRIORITY ... to lower the priority of only one query, or by SET LOW_PRIORITY_UPDATES=1 to change the priority in one thread. See Section 6.3.2, "Table Locking Issues."

- `--memlock`

  Lock the mysqld process in memory. This works on systems such as Solaris that support the mlockall() system call. This might help if you have a problem where the operating system is causing mysqld to swap on disk. Note that use of this option requires that you run the server as root, which normally is not a good idea for security reasons.

- `--myisam-recover [=option[,option...]]]`

  Set the MyISAM storage engine recovery mode. The option value is any combination of the values of DEFAULT, BACKUP, FORCE, or QUICK. If you specify multiple values, separate them by commas. You can also use a value of "" to disable this option. If this option is used, mysqld will, when it opens a MyISAM table, check whether the table is marked as crashed or wasn't closed properly. (The last option works only if you are running with --skip-external-locking.) If this is the case, mysqld will run a check on the table. If the table was corrupted, mysqld will attempt to repair it.

  The following options affect how the repair works:

Option	Description
DEFAULT	The same as not giving any option to --myisam-recover.
BACKUP	If the data file was changed during recovery, save a backup of the tbl_name.MYD file as tbl_name-datetime.BAK.
FORCE	Run recovery even if you will lose more than one row from the .MYD file.
QUICK	Don't check the rows in the table if there aren't any delete blocks.

  Before a table is automatically repaired, MySQL will add a note about this in the error log. If you want to be able to recover from most problems without user intervention, you should use the options BACKUP,FORCE. This will force a repair of a table even if some rows would be deleted, but it will keep the old data file as a backup so that you can later examine what happened.

  This option is available as of MySQL 3.23.25.

- `--new`

  From version 4.0.12, the --new option can be used to make the server behave as 4.1 in certain respects, easing a 4.0 to 4.1 upgrade:

  - TIMESTAMP is returned as a string with the format 'YYYY-MM-DD HH:MM:SS'.

  This option can be used to help you see how your applications will behave in MySQL 4.1, without actually upgrading to 4.1.

- `--pid-file=path`

  The path to the process ID file used by `mysqld_safe`.

- `--port=port_num`, `-P port_num`

  The port number to use when listening for TCP/IP connections.

- `--old-protocol`, `-o`

  Use the 3.20 protocol for compatibility with some very old clients. See Section 2.5.6, "Upgrading from Version 3.20 to 3.21."

- `--one-thread`

  Only use one thread (for debugging under Linux). This option is available only if the server is built with debugging enabled.

- `--open-files-limit=count`

  To change the number of file descriptors available to `mysqld`. If this is not set or set to 0, then `mysqld` will use this value to reserve file descriptors to use with `setrlimit()`. If this value is 0, then `mysqld` will reserve `max_connections*5` or `max_connections + table_cache*2` (whichever is larger) number of files. You should try increasing this if `mysqld` gives you the error "Too many open files."

- `--safe-mode`

  Skip some optimization stages.

- `--safe-show-database`

  With this option, the `SHOW DATABASES` statement displays only the names of those databases for which the user has some kind of privilege. As of MySQL 4.0.2, this option is deprecated and doesn't do anything (it is enabled by default), because there is now a `SHOW DATABASES` privilege that can be used to control access to database names on a per-account basis. See Section 4.4.3, "Privileges Provided by MySQL."

- `--safe-user-create`

  If this is enabled, a user can't create new users with the `GRANT` statement, if the user doesn't have the `INSERT` privilege for the `mysql.user` table or any column in the table.

- `--secure-auth`

  Disallow authentication for accounts that have old (pre-4.1) passwords. This option is available as of MySQL 4.1.1.

- `--skip-bdb`

  Disable the `BDB` storage engine. This saves memory and might speed up some operations. Do not use this option if you require `BDB` tables.

- `--skip-concurrent-insert`

  Turn off the ability to select and insert at the same time on `MyISAM` tables. (This is to be used only if you think you have found a bug in this feature.)

- `--skip-delay-key-write`

  Ignore the `DELAY_KEY_WRITE` option for all tables. As of MySQL 4.0.3, you should use `--delay-key-write=OFF` instead. See Section 6.5.2, "Tuning Server Parameters."

- `--skip-external-locking`

  Don't use system locking. To use `isamchk` or `myisamchk`, you must shut down the server. See Section 1.2.3, "MySQL Stability." In MySQL 3.23, you can use `CHECK TABLE` and `REPAIR TABLE` to check and repair `MyISAM` tables. This option previously was named `--skip-locking`.

- `--skip-grant-tables`

  This option causes the server not to use the privilege system at all. This gives everyone *full access* to all databases! (You can tell a running server to start using the grant tables again by executing a `mysqladmin flush-privileges` or `mysqladmin reload` command, or by issuing a `FLUSH PRIVILEGES` statement.)

- `--skip-host-cache`

  Do not use the internal hostname cache for faster name-to-IP resolution. Instead, query the DNS server every time a client connects. See Section 6.5.5, "How MySQL Uses DNS."

- `--skip-innodb`

  Disable the `InnoDB` storage engine. This saves memory and disk space and might speed up some operations. Do not use this option if you require `InnoDB` tables.

- `--skip-isam`

  Disable the `ISAM` storage engine. As of MySQL 4.1, `ISAM` is disabled by default, so this option applies only if the server was configured with support for `ISAM`. This option was added in MySQL 4.1.1.

- `--skip-name-resolve`

  Do not resolve hostnames when checking client connections. Use only IP numbers. If you use this option, all `Host` column values in the grant tables must be IP numbers or `localhost`. See Section 6.5.5, "How MySQL Uses DNS."

- `--skip-networking`

  Don't listen for TCP/IP connections at all. All interaction with `mysqld` must be made via named pipes (on Windows) or Unix socket files (on Unix). This option is highly recommended for systems where only local clients are allowed. See Section 6.5.5, "How MySQL Uses DNS."

- `--skip-new`

  Don't use new, possibly wrong routines.

- `--skip-symlink`

  This is the old form of `--skip-symbolic-links`, for use before MySQL 4.0.13.

- `--symbolic-links, --skip-symbolic-links`

  Enable or disable symbolic link support. This option has different effects on Windows and Unix:

  - On Windows, enabling symbolic links allows you to establish a symbolic link to a database directory by creating a `directory.sym` file that contains the path to the real directory. See Section 6.6.1.3, "Using Symbolic Links for Databases on Windows."

  - On Unix, enabling symbolic links means that you can link a `MyISAM` index file or data file to another directory with the `INDEX DIRECTORY` or `DATA DIRECTORY` options of the `CREATE TABLE` statement. If you delete or rename the table, the files that its symbolic links point to also are deleted or renamed.

  This option was added in MySQL 4.0.13.

- `--skip-safemalloc`

  If MySQL is configured with `--with-debug=full`, all MySQL programs check for memory overruns during each memory allocation and memory freeing operation. This checking is very slow, so for the server you can avoid it when you don't need it by using the `--skip-safemalloc` option.

- `--skip-show-database`

  With this option, the `SHOW DATABASES` statement is allowed only to users who have the `SHOW DATABASES` privilege, and the statement displays all database names. Without this option, `SHOW DATABASES` is allowed to all users, but displays each database name only if the user has the `SHOW DATABASES` privilege or some privilege for the database.

- `--skip-stack-trace`

  Don't write stack traces. This option is useful when you are running `mysqld` under a debugger. On some systems, you also must use this option to get a core file.

- `--skip-thread-priority`

  Disable using thread priorities for faster response time.

- `--socket=path`

  On Unix, this option specifies the Unix socket file to use for local connections. The default value is `/tmp/mysql.sock`. On Windows, the option specifies the pipe name to use for local connections that use a named pipe. The default value is `MySQL`.

- `--sql-mode=value[,value[,value...]]`

  Set the SQL mode for MySQL. See Section 4.2.2, "The Server SQL Mode." This option was added in 3.23.41.

- `--temp-pool`

  This option causes most temporary files created by the server to use a small set of names, rather than a unique name for each new file. This works around a problem in the Linux kernel dealing with creating many new files with different names. With the old behavior, Linux seems to "leak" memory, because it's being allocated to the directory entry cache rather than to the disk cache.

- `--transaction-isolation=level`

  Sets the default transaction isolation level, which can be READ-UNCOMMITTED, READ-COMMITTED, REPEATABLE-READ, or SERIALIZABLE.

- `--tmpdir=path, -t path`

  The path of the directory to use for creating temporary files. It might be useful if your default /tmp directory resides on a partition that is too small to hold temporary tables. Starting from MySQL 4.1, this option accepts several paths that are used in round-robin fashion. Paths should be separated by colon characters (':') on Unix and semi-colon characters (';') on Windows, NetWare, and OS/2. If the MySQL server is acting as a replication slave, you should not set --tmpdir to point to a directory on a memory-based filesystem or to a directory that is cleared when the server host restarts. A replication slave needs some of its temporary files to survive a machine restart so that it can replicate temporary tables or LOAD DATA INFILE operations. If files in the temporary file directory are lost when the server restarts, replication will fail.

- `--user={user_name | user_id}, -u {user_name | user_id}`

  Run the mysqld server as the user having the name *user_name* or the numeric user ID *user_id*. ("User" in this context refers to a system login account, not a MySQL user listed in the grant tables.)

  This option is *mandatory* when starting mysqld as root. The server will change its user ID during its startup sequence, causing it to run as that particular user rather than as root. See Section 4.3.1, "General Security Guidelines."

  Starting from MySQL 3.23.56 and 4.0.12: To avoid a possible security hole where a user adds a --user=root option to some my.cnf file (thus causing the server to run as root), mysqld uses only the first --user option specified and produces a warning if there are multiple --user options. Options in /etc/my.cnf and *datadir*/my.cnf are processed before command-line options, so it is recommended that you put a --user option in /etc/my.cnf and specify a value other than root. The option in /etc/my.cnf will be found before any other --user options, which ensures that the server runs as a user other than root, and that a warning results if any other --user option is found.

- `--version, -V`

  Display version information and exit.

You can assign a value to a server system variable by using an option of the form --*var_name*=*value*. For example, --key_buffer_size=32M sets the key_buffer_size variable to a value of 32MB.

Note that when setting a variable to a value, MySQL might automatically correct it to stay within a given range, or adjust the value to the closest allowable value if only certain values are allowed.

It is also possible to set variables by using --set-variable=*var_name*=*value* or -O *var_name*=*value* syntax. However, this syntax is deprecated as of MySQL 4.0.

You can find a full description for all variables in Section 4.2.3, "Server System Variables." The section on tuning server parameters includes information on how to optimize them. See Section 6.5.2, "Tuning Server Parameters."

You can change the values of most system variables for a running server with the SET statement.

If you want to restrict the maximum value to which a system variable can be set with the SET statement, you can specify this maximum by using an option of the form --maximum-var_name at server startup. For example, to prevent the value of query_cache_size from being increased to more than 32MB at runtime, use the option --maximum-query_cache_size=32M. This feature is available as of MySQL 4.0.2.

4.2.2 The Server SQL Mode

The MySQL server can operate in different SQL modes, and (as of MySQL 4.1) can apply these modes differentially for different clients. This allows applications to tailor server operation to their own requirements.

Modes define what SQL syntax MySQL should support and what kind of data validation checks it should perform. This makes it easier to use MySQL in different environments and to use MySQL together with other database servers.

You can set the default SQL mode by starting mysqld with the --sql-mode="*modes*" option. Beginning with MySQL 4.1, you can also change the mode after startup time by setting the sql_mode variable with a SET [SESSION|GLOBAL] sql_mode='*modes*' statement. Setting the GLOBAL variable affects the operation of all clients that connect from that time on. Setting the SESSION variable affects only the current client. *modes* is a list of different modes separated by comma (',') characters. You can retrieve the current mode by issuing a SELECT @@sql_mode statement. The default value is empty (no modes set).

The value also can be empty (--sql-mode="") if you want to reset it.

The following list describes the supported modes:

- ANSI_QUOTES

  Treat '"' as an identifier quote character (like the '`' quote character) and not as a string quote character. You can still use '`' to quote identifers in ANSI mode. With ANSI_QUOTES enabled, you cannot use double quotes to quote a literal string, because it will be interpreted as an identifier. (New in MySQL 4.0.0.)

- IGNORE_SPACE

  Allow spaces between a function name and the '(' character. This forces all function names to be treated as reserved words. As a result, if you want to access any database, table, or column name that is a reserved word, you must quote it. For example, because there is a USER() function, the name of the user table in the mysql database and the User column in that table become reserved, so you must quote them:

```
SELECT "User" FROM mysql."user";
```

(New in MySQL 4.0.0.)

- NO_AUTO_VALUE_ON_ZERO

  NO_AUTO_VALUE_ON_ZERO affects handling of AUTO_INCREMENT columns. Normally, you generate the next sequence number for the column by inserting either NULL or 0 into it. NO_AUTO_VALUE_ON_ZERO suppresses this behavior for 0 so that only NULL generates the next sequence number. This mode can be useful if 0 has been stored in a table's AUTO_INCREMENT column. (This is not a recommended practice, by the way.) For example, if you dump the table with mysqldump and then reload it, normally MySQL generates new sequence numbers when it encounters the 0 values, resulting in a table with different contents than the one that was dumped. Enabling NO_AUTO_VALUE_ON_ZERO before reloading the dump file solves this problem. As of MySQL 4.1.1, mysqldump automatically includes statements in the dump output to enable NO_AUTO_VALUE_ON_ZERO. (New in MySQL 4.1.1.)

- NO_DIR_IN_CREATE

  When creating a table, ignore all INDEX DIRECTORY and DATA DIRECTORY directives. This option is useful on slave replication servers. (New in MySQL 4.0.15.)

- NO_FIELD_OPTIONS

  Don't print MySQL -specific column options in the output of SHOW CREATE TABLE. This mode is used by mysqldump in portability mode. (New in MySQL 4.1.1.)

- NO_KEY_OPTIONS

  Don't print MySQL -specific index options in the output of SHOW CREATE TABLE. This mode is used by mysqldump in portability mode. (New in MySQL 4.1.1.)

- NO_TABLE_OPTIONS

  Don't print MySQL -specific table options (such as ENGINE) in the output of SHOW CRE-ATE TABLE. This mode is used by mysqldump in portability mode. (New in MySQL 4.1.1.)

- NO_UNSIGNED_SUBTRACTION

  In subtraction operations, don't mark the result as UNSIGNED if one of the operands is unsigned. Note that this makes UNSIGNED BIGINT not 100% usable in all contexts. (New in MySQL 4.0.2.)

- ONLY_FULL_GROUP_BY

  Don't allow queries that in the GROUP BY part refer to a not selected column. (New in MySQL 4.0.0.)

- PIPES_AS_CONCAT

  Treat || as a string concatenation operator (same as CONCAT()) rather than as a synonym for OR. (New in MySQL 4.0.0.)

- REAL_AS_FLOAT

  Treat REAL as a synonym for FLOAT rather than as a synonym for DOUBLE. (New in MySQL 4.0.0.)

The following special modes are provided as shorthand for combinations of mode values from the preceding list. They are available as of MySQL 4.1.1.

- ANSI

  Equivalent to REAL_AS_FLOAT, PIPES_AS_CONCAT, ANSI_QUOTES, IGNORE_SPACE, ONLY_FULL_GROUP_BY. See Section 1.8.3, "Running MySQL in ANSI Mode."

- DB2

  Equivalent to PIPES_AS_CONCAT, ANSI_QUOTES, IGNORE_SPACE, NO_KEY_OPTIONS, NO_TABLE_OPTIONS, NO_FIELD_OPTIONS.

- MAXDB

  Equivalent to PIPES_AS_CONCAT, ANSI_QUOTES, IGNORE_SPACE, NO_KEY_OPTIONS, NO_TABLE_OPTIONS, NO_FIELD_OPTIONS.

- MSSQL

  Equivalent to PIPES_AS_CONCAT, ANSI_QUOTES, IGNORE_SPACE, NO_KEY_OPTIONS, NO_TABLE_OPTIONS, NO_FIELD_OPTIONS.

- MYSQL323

  Equivalent to NO_FIELD_OPTIONS.

- MYSQL40

  Equivalent to NO_FIELD_OPTIONS.

- ORACLE

  Equivalent to PIPES_AS_CONCAT, ANSI_QUOTES, IGNORE_SPACE, NO_KEY_OPTIONS, NO_TABLE_OPTIONS, NO_FIELD_OPTIONS.

- POSTGRESQL

  Equivalent to PIPES_AS_CONCAT, ANSI_QUOTES, IGNORE_SPACE, NO_KEY_OPTIONS, NO_TABLE_OPTIONS, NO_FIELD_OPTIONS.

4.2.3 Server System Variables

The server maintains many system variables that indicate how it is configured. All of them have default values. They can be set at server startup using options on the command line or in option files. Most of them can be set at runtime using the SET statement.

Beginning with MySQL 4.0.3, the mysqld server maintains two kinds of variables. Global variables affect the overall operation of the server. Session variables affect its operation for individual client connections.

When the server starts, it initializes all global variables to their default values. These defaults can be changed by options specified in option files or on the command line. After the server starts, those global variables that are dynamic can be changed by connecting to the server and issuing a SET GLOBAL *var_name* statement. To change a global variable, you must have the SUPER privilege.

The server also maintains a set of session variables for each client that connects. The client's session variables are initialized at connect time using the current values of the corresponding global variables. For those session variables that are dynamic, the client can change them by issuing a SET SESSION *var_name* statement. Setting a session variable requires no special privilege, but a client can change only its own session variables, not those of any other client.

A change to a global variable is visible to any client that accesses that global variable. However, it affects the corresponding session variable that is initialized from the global variable only for clients that connect after the change. It does not affect the session variable for any client that is already connected (not even that of the client that issues the SET GLOBAL statement).

When setting a variable using a startup option, variable values can be given with a suffix of K, M, or G to indicate kilobytes, megabytes, or gigabytes, respectively. For example, the following command starts the server with a key buffer size of 16 megabytes:

```
mysqld --key_buffer_size=16M
```

Before MySQL 4.0, use this syntax instead:

```
mysqld --set-variable=key_buffer_size=16M
```

The lettercase of suffix letters does not matter; 16M and 16m are equivalent.

At runtime, use the SET statement to set system variables. In this context, suffix letters cannot be used, but the value can take the form of an expression:

```
mysql> SET sort_buffer_size = 10 * 1024 * 1024;
```

To specify explicitly whether to set the global or session variable, use the GLOBAL or SESSION options:

```
mysql> SET GLOBAL sort_buffer_size = 10 * 1024 * 1024;
mysql> SET SESSION sort_buffer_size = 10 * 1024 * 1024;
```

Without either option, the statement sets the session variable.

The variables that can be set at runtime are listed in Section 4.2.3.1.2, "Dynamic System Variables."

If you want to restrict the maximum value to which a system variable can be set with the SET statement, you can specify this maximum by using an option of the form --maximum-*var_name* at server startup. For example, to prevent the value of query_cache_size from being increased to more than 32MB at runtime, use the option --maximum-query_cache_size=32M. This feature is available as of MySQL 4.0.2.

You can view system variables and their values by using the SHOW VARIABLES statement. See Section 4.2.3.1, "System Variables," for more information.

```
mysql> SHOW VARIABLES;
+--------------------------------+--------------------------------+
| Variable_name                  | Value                          |
+--------------------------------+--------------------------------+
| back_log                       | 50                             |
| basedir                        | /usr/local/mysql               |
| bdb_cache_size                 | 8388572                        |
| bdb_home                       | /usr/local/mysql               |
| bdb_log_buffer_size            | 32768                          |
| bdb_logdir                     |                                |
| bdb_max_lock                   | 10000                          |
| bdb_shared_data                | OFF                            |
| bdb_tmpdir                     | /tmp/                          |
| bdb_version                    | Sleepycat Software: ...        |
| binlog_cache_size              | 32768                          |
| bulk_insert_buffer_size        | 8388608                        |
| character_set                  | latin1                         |
| character_sets                 | latin1 big5 czech euc_kr       |
| concurrent_insert              | ON                             |
| connect_timeout                | 5                              |
| convert_character_set          |                                |
| datadir                        | /usr/local/mysql/data/         |
| default_week_format            | 0                              |
| delay_key_write                | ON                             |
| delayed_insert_limit           | 100                            |
| delayed_insert_timeout         | 300                            |
| delayed_queue_size             | 1000                           |
| flush                          | OFF                            |
| flush_time                     | 0                              |
| ft_boolean_syntax              | + -><()~*:""&|                 |
| ft_max_word_len                | 84                             |
| ft_min_word_len                | 4                              |
| ft_query_expansion_limit       | 20                             |
| ft_stopword_file               | (built-in)                     |
| have_bdb                       | YES                            |
| have_innodb                    | YES                            |
| have_isam                      | YES                            |
| have_openssl                   | YES                            |
| have_query_cache               | YES                            |
| have_raid                      | NO                             |
| have_symlink                   | DISABLED                       |
| init_file                      |                                |
| innodb_additional_mem_pool_size | 1048576                       |
| innodb_buffer_pool_size        | 8388608                        |
```

```
| innodb_data_file_path            | ibdata1:10M:autoextend    |
| innodb_data_home_dir             |                           |
| innodb_fast_shutdown             | ON                        |
| innodb_file_io_threads           | 4                         |
| innodb_flush_log_at_trx_commit   | 1                         |
| innodb_flush_method              |                           |
| innodb_force_recovery            | 0                         |
| innodb_lock_wait_timeout         | 50                        |
| innodb_log_arch_dir              |                           |
| innodb_log_archive               | OFF                       |
| innodb_log_buffer_size           | 1048576                   |
| innodb_log_file_size             | 5242880                   |
| innodb_log_files_in_group        | 2                         |
| innodb_log_group_home_dir        | ./ |                      |
| innodb_mirrored_log_groups       | 1                         |
| innodb_thread_concurrency        | 8                         |
| interactive_timeout              | 28800                     |
| join_buffer_size                 | 131072                    |
| key_buffer_size                  | 16773120                  |
| key_cache_age_threshold          | 300                       |
| key_cache_block_size             | 1024                      |
| key_cache_division_limit         | 100                       |
| language                         | /usr/local/mysql/share/...|
| large_files_support              | ON                        |
| local_infile                     | ON                        |
| locked_in_memory                 | OFF                       |
| log                              | OFF                       |
| log_bin                          | OFF                       |
| log_slave_updates                | OFF                       |
| log_slow_queries                 | OFF                       |
| log_update                       | OFF                       |
| log_warnings                     | OFF                       |
| long_query_time                  | 10                        |
| low_priority_updates             | OFF                       |
| lower_case_table_names           | 0                         |
| max_allowed_packet               | 1047552                   |
| max_binlog_cache_size            | 4294967295                |
| max_binlog_size                  | 1073741824                |
| max_connect_errors               | 10                        |
| max_connections                  | 100                       |
| max_delayed_threads              | 20                        |
| max_error_count                  | 64                        |
| max_heap_table_size              | 16777216                  |
| max_join_size                    | 4294967295                |
| max_relay_log_size               | 0                         |
| max_sort_length                  | 1024                      |
| max_tmp_tables                   | 32                        |
```

```
| max_user_connections               | 0                          |
| max_write_lock_count               | 4294967295                 |
| myisam_max_extra_sort_file_size    | 268435456                  |
| myisam_max_sort_file_size          | 2147483647                 |
| myisam_recover_options             | force                      |
| myisam_repair_threads              | 1                          |
| myisam_sort_buffer_size            | 8388608                    |
| net_buffer_length                  | 16384                      |
| net_read_timeout                   | 30                         |
| net_retry_count                    | 10                         |
| net_write_timeout                  | 60                         |
| open_files_limit                   | 1024                       |
| pid_file                           | /usr/local/mysql/name.pid  |
| port                               | 3306                       |
| protocol_version                   | 10                         |
| query_cache_limit                  | 1048576                    |
| query_cache_size                   | 0                          |
| query_cache_type                   | ON                         |
| read_buffer_size                   | 131072                     |
| read_rnd_buffer_size               | 262144                     |
| rpl_recovery_rank                  | 0                          |
| server_id                          | 0                          |
| skip_external_locking              | ON                         |
| skip_networking                    | OFF                        |
| skip_show_database                 | OFF                        |
| slave_net_timeout                  | 3600                       |
| slow_launch_time                   | 2                          |
| socket                             | /tmp/mysql.sock            |
| sort_buffer_size                   | 2097116                    |
| sql_mode                           |                            |
| table_cache                        | 64                         |
| table_type                         | MYISAM                     |
| thread_cache_size                  | 3                          |
| thread_stack                       | 131072                     |
| timezone                           | EEST                       |
| tmp_table_size                     | 33554432                   |
| tmpdir                             | /tmp/:/mnt/hd2/tmp/        |
| tx_isolation                       | READ-COMMITTED             |
| version                            | 4.0.4-beta                 |
| wait_timeout                       | 28800                      |
+------------------------------------+----------------------------+
```

Most system variables are described here. Variables with no version indicated have been present since at least MySQL 3.22. InnoDB system variables are listed in Section 9.5, "InnoDB Startup Options."

Values for buffer sizes, lengths, and stack sizes are given in bytes unless otherwise specified.

Information on tuning these variables can be found in Section 6.5.2, "Tuning Server Parameters."

- `ansi_mode`

  This is `ON` if `mysqld` was started with `--ansi`. See Section 1.8.3, "Running MySQL in ANSI Mode." This variable was added in MySQL 3.23.6 and removed in 3.23.41. See the description for `--sql-mode`.

- `back_log`

  The number of outstanding connection requests MySQL can have. This comes into play when the main MySQL thread gets very many connection requests in a very short time. It then takes some time (although very little) for the main thread to check the connection and start a new thread. The `back_log` value indicates how many requests can be stacked during this short time before MySQL momentarily stops answering new requests. You need to increase this only if you expect a large number of connections in a short period of time.

  In other words, this value is the size of the listen queue for incoming TCP/IP connections. Your operating system has its own limit on the size of this queue. The manual page for the Unix `listen()` system call should have more details. Check your OS documentation for the maximum value for this variable. Attempting to set `back_log` higher than your operating system limit will be ineffective.

- `basedir`

  The MySQL installation base directory. This variable can be set with the `--basedir` option.

- `bdb_cache_size`

  The size of the buffer that is allocated for caching indexes and rows for BDB tables. If you don't use BDB tables, you should start `mysqld` with `--skip-bdb` to not waste memory for this cache. This variable was added in MySQL 3.23.14.

- `bdb_home`

  The base directory for BDB tables. This should be assigned the same value as the `datadir` variable. This variable was added in MySQL 3.23.14.

- `bdb_log_buffer_size`

  The size of the buffer that is allocated for caching indexes and rows for BDB tables. If you don't use BDB tables, you should set this to 0 or start `mysqld` with `--skip-bdb` to not waste memory for this cache. This variable was added in MySQL 3.23.31.

- `bdb_logdir`

  The directory where the BDB storage engine writes its log files. This variable can be set with the `--bdb-logdir` option. This variable was added in MySQL 3.23.14.

- `bdb_max_lock`

  The maximum number of locks you can have active on a `BDB` table (10,000 by default). You should increase this if errors such as the following occur when you perform long transactions or when `mysqld` has to examine many rows to calculate a query:

  ```
  bdb: Lock table is out of available locks
  Got error 12 from ...
  ```

  This variable was added in MySQL 3.23.29.

- `bdb_shared_data`

  This is `ON` if you are using `--bdb-shared-data`. This variable was added in MySQL 3.23.29.

- `bdb_tmpdir`

  The value of the `--bdb-tmpdir` option. This variable was added in MySQL 3.23.14.

- `bdb_version`

  The `BDB` storage engine version. This variable was added in MySQL 3.23.31.

- `binlog_cache_size`

  The size of the cache to hold the SQL statements for the binary log during a transaction. A binary log cache is allocated for each client if the server supports any transactional storage engines and, starting from MySQL 4.1.2, if the server has binary log enabled (`--log-bin` option). If you often use big, multiple-statement transactions, you can increase this to get more performance. The `Binlog_cache_use` and `Binlog_cache_disk_use` status variables can be useful for tuning the size of this variable. This variable was added in MySQL 3.23.29. See Section 4.8.4, "The Binary Log."

- `bulk_insert_buffer_size`

  MyISAM uses a special tree-like cache to make bulk inserts faster for `INSERT ... SELECT`, `INSERT ... VALUES (...), (...), ...`, and `LOAD DATA INFILE`. This variable limits the size of the cache tree in bytes per thread. Setting it to 0 disables this optimization. **Note:** This cache is used only when adding data to a non-empty table. The default value is 8MB. This variable was added in MySQL 4.0.3. This variable previously was named `myisam_bulk_insert_tree_size`.

- `character_set`

  The default character set. This variable was added in MySQL 3.23.3, then removed in MySQL 4.1.1 and replaced by the various `character_set_xxx` variables.

- `character_set_client`

  The character set for statements that arrive from the client. This variable was added in MySQL 4.1.1.

- `character_set_connection`

  The character set used for literals that do not have a character set introducer, for some functions, and for number-to-string conversion. This variable was added in MySQL 4.1.1.

- `character_set_database`

  The character set used by the default database. The server sets this variable whenever the default database changes. If there is no default database, the variable has the same value as `character_set_server`. This variable was added in MySQL 4.1.1.

- `character_set_results`

  The character set used for returning query results to the client. This variable was added in MySQL 4.1.1.

- `character_set_server`

  The server default character set. This variable was added in MySQL 4.1.1.

- `character_set_system`

  The character set used by the server for storing identifiers. The value is always `utf8`. This variable was added in MySQL 4.1.1.

- `character_sets`

  The supported character sets. This variable was added in MySQL 3.23.15.

- `collation_connection`

  The collation of the connection character set. This variable was added in MySQL 4.1.1.

- `collation_database`

  The collation used by the default database. The server sets this variable whenever the default database changes. If there is no default database, the variable has the same value as `collation_server`. This variable was added in MySQL 4.1.1.

- `collation_server`

  The server default collation. This variable was added in MySQL 4.1.1.

- `concurrent_inserts`

  If `ON` (the default), MySQL allows `INSERT` and `SELECT` statements to run concurrently for `MyISAM` tables that have no free blocks in the middle. You can turn this option off by starting `mysqld` with `--safe` or `--skip-new`. This variable was added in MySQL 3.23.7.

- `connect_timeout`

  The number of seconds the `mysqld` server waits for a connect packet before responding with `Bad handshake`.

- `datadir`

  The MySQL data directory. This variable can be set with the `--datadir` option.

- `default_week_format`

  The default mode value to use for the `WEEK()` function. This variable is available as of MySQL 4.0.14.

- `delay_key_write`

  This option applies only to MyISAM tables. It can have one of the following values to affect handling of the DELAY_KEY_WRITE table option that can be used in CREATE TABLE statements.

Option	Description
OFF	DELAYED_KEY_WRITE is ignored.
ON	MySQL honors the DELAY_KEY_WRITE option for CREATE TABLE. This is the default value.
ALL	All new opened tables are treated as if they were created with the DELAY_KEY_WRITE option enabled.

  If DELAY_KEY_WRITE is enabled, this means that the key buffer for tables with this option are not flushed on every index update, but only when a table is closed. This will speed up writes on keys a lot, but if you use this feature, you should add automatic checking of all MyISAM tables by starting the server with the --myisam-recover option (for example, --myisam-recover=BACKUP,FORCE). See Section 4.2.1, "mysqld Command-Line Options," and Section 8.1.1, "MyISAM Startup Options."

  Note that --external-locking doesn't offer any protection against index corruption for tables that use delayed key writes.

  This variable was added in MySQL 3.23.8.

- `delayed_insert_limit`

  After inserting delayed_insert_limit delayed rows, the INSERT DELAYED handler thread checks whether there are any SELECT statements pending. If so, it allows them to execute before continuing to insert delayed rows.

- `delayed_insert_timeout`

  How long an INSERT DELAYED handler thread should wait for INSERT statements before terminating.

- `delayed_queue_size`

  How many rows to queue when handling INSERT DELAYED statements. If the queue becomes full, any client that issues an INSERT DELAYED statement will wait until there is room in the queue again.

- `flush`

  This is ON if you have started mysqld with the --flush option. This variable was added in MySQL 3.22.9.

- `flush_time`

  If this is set to a non-zero value, all tables will be closed every flush_time seconds to free up resources and sync unflushed data to disk. We recommend this option only on Windows 9x or Me, or on systems with minimal resources available. This variable was added in MySQL 3.22.18.

- ft_boolean_syntax

  The list of operators supported by boolean full-text searches performed using IN BOOLEAN MODE. This variable was added in MySQL 4.0.1.

  The default variable value is '+ -><()~*:""&|'. The rules for changing the value are as follows:

  - Operator function is determined by position within the string.
  - The replacement value must be 14 characters.
  - Each character must be an ASCII non-alphanumeric character.
  - Either the first or second character must be a space.
  - No duplicates are allowed except the phrase quoting operators in positions 11 and 12. These two characters are not required to be the same, but they are the only two that may be.
  - Positions 10, 13, and 14 (which by default are set to ':', '&', and '|') are reserved for future extensions.

- ft_max_word_len

  The maximum length of the word to be included in a FULLTEXT index. This variable was added in MySQL 4.0.0.

  Note: FULLTEXT indexes must be rebuilt after changing this variable. Use REPAIR TABLE *tbl_name* QUICK.

- ft_min_word_len

  The minimum length of the word to be included in a FULLTEXT index. This variable was added in MySQL 4.0.0.

  Note: FULLTEXT indexes must be rebuilt after changing this variable. Use REPAIR TABLE *tbl_name* QUICK.

- ft_query_expansion_limit

  The number of top matches to use for full-text searches performed using WITH QUERY EXPANSION. This variable was added in MySQL 4.1.1.

- ft_stopword_file

  The file from which to read the list of stopwords for full-text searches. All the words from the file are used; comments are *not* honored. By default, a built-in list of stopwords is used (as defined in the myisam/ft_static.c file). Setting this variable to the empty string ('') disables stopword filtering. This variable was added in MySQL 4.0.10.

  Note: FULLTEXT indexes must be rebuilt after changing this variable. Use REPAIR TABLE *tbl_name* QUICK.

- group_concat_max_len

  The maximum allowed result length for the GROUP_CONCAT() function. This variable was added in MySQL 4.1.0.

- `have_bdb`

  YES if `mysqld` supports `BDB` tables. `DISABLED` if `--skip-bdb` is used. This variable was added in MySQL 3.23.30.

- `have_innodb`

  YES if `mysqld` supports `InnoDB` tables. `DISABLED` if `--skip-innodb` is used. This variable was added in MySQL 3.23.37.

- `have_isam`

  YES if `mysqld` supports `ISAM` tables. `DISABLED` if `--skip-isam` is used. This variable was added in MySQL 3.23.30.

- `have_raid`

  YES if `mysqld` supports the `RAID` option. This variable was added in MySQL 3.23.30.

- `have_openssl`

  YES if `mysqld` supports SSL (encryption) of the client/server protocol. This variable was added in MySQL 3.23.43.

- `init_connect`

  A string to be executed by the server for each client that connects. The string consists of one or more SQL statements. To specify multiple statements, separate them by semicolon characters. For example, each client begins by default with autocommit mode enabled. There is no global server variable to specify that autocommit should be disabled by default, but `init_connect` can be used to achieve the same effect:

  ```
  SET GLOBAL init_connect='SET AUTOCOMMIT=0';
  ```

  This variable can also be set on the command line or in an option file. To set the variable as just shown using an option file, include these lines:

  ```
  [mysqld]
  init_connect='SET AUTOCOMMIT=0'
  ```

  This variable was added in MySQL 4.1.2.

- `init_file`

  The name of the file specified with the `--init-file` option when you start the server. This is a file containing SQL statements that you want the server to execute when it starts. Each statement must be on a single line and should not include comments. This variable was added in MySQL 3.23.2.

- `init_slave`

  This variable is similar to `init_connect`, but is a string to be executed by a slave server each time the SQL thread starts. The format of the string is the same as for the `init_connect` variable. This variable was added in MySQL 4.1.2.

- `innodb_xxx`

  The `InnoDB` system variables are listed in Section 9.5, "`InnoDB` Startup Options."

- `interactive_timeout`

  The number of seconds the server waits for activity on an interactive connection before closing it. An interactive client is defined as a client that uses the `CLIENT_INTERACTIVE` option to `mysql_real_connect()`. See also `wait_timeout`.

- `join_buffer_size`

  The size of the buffer that is used for full joins (joins that do not use indexes). The buffer is allocated one time for each full join between two tables. Increase this value to get a faster full join when adding indexes is not possible. (Normally the best way to get fast joins is to add indexes.)

- `key_buffer_size`

  Index blocks for `MyISAM` and `ISAM` tables are buffered and are shared by all threads. `key_buffer_size` is the size of the buffer used for index blocks. The key buffer is also known as the key cache.

  Increase the value to get better index handling (for all reads and multiple writes) to as much as you can afford. Using a value that is 25% of total memory on a machine that mainly runs MySQL is quite common. However, if you make the value too large (for example, more than 50% of your total memory) your system might start to page and become extremely slow. MySQL relies on the operating system to perform filesystem caching for data reads, so you must leave some room for the filesystem cache.

  For even more speed when writing many rows at the same time, use `LOCK TABLES`.

  You can check the performance of the key buffer by issuing a `SHOW STATUS` statement and examining the `Key_read_requests`, `Key_reads`, `Key_write_requests`, and `Key_writes` status variables.

  The `Key_reads/Key_read_requests` ratio should normally be less than 0.01. The `Key_writes/Key_write_requests` ratio is usually near 1 if you are using mostly updates and deletes, but might be much smaller if you tend to do updates that affect many rows at the same time or if you are using the `DELAY_KEY_WRITE` table option.

  The fraction of the key buffer in use can be determined using `key_buffer_size` in conjunction with the `Key_blocks_used` status variable and the buffer block size. From MySQL 4.1.1 on, the buffer block size is available from the `key_cache_block_size` server variable. The fraction of the buffer in use is:

  `(Key_blocks_used * key_cache_block_size) / key_buffer_size`

  Before MySQL 4.1.1, key cache blocks are 1024 bytes, so the fraction of the key buffer in use is:

  `(Key_blocks_used * 1024) / key_buffer_size`

  See Section 6.4.6, "The `MyISAM` Key Cache."

- `key_cache_age_threshold`

  This value controls the demotion of buffers from the hot sub-chain of a key cache to the warm sub-chain. Lower values cause demotion to happen more quickly. The minimum value is 100. The default value is 300. This variable was added in MySQL 4.1.1. See Section 6.4.6, "The MyISAM Key Cache."

- `key_cache_block_size`

  The size in bytes of blocks in the key cache. The default value is 1024. This variable was added in MySQL 4.1.1. See Section 6.4.6, "The MyISAM Key Cache."

- `key_cache_division_limit`

  The division point between the hot and warm sub-chains of the key cache buffer chain. The value is the percentage of the buffer chain to use for the warm sub-chain. Allowable values range from 1 to 100. The default value is 100. This variable was added in MySQL 4.1.1. See Section 6.4.6, "The MyISAM Key Cache."

- `language`

  The language used for error messages.

- `large_file_support`

  Whether mysqld was compiled with options for large file support. This variable was added in MySQL 3.23.28.

- `local_infile`

  Whether LOCAL is supported for LOAD DATA INFILE statements. This variable was added in MySQL 4.0.3.

- `locked_in_memory`

  Whether mysqld was locked in memory with --memlock. This variable was added in MySQL 3.23.25.

- `log`

  Whether logging of all queries to the general query log is enabled. See Section 4.8.2, "The General Query Log."

- `log_bin`

  Whether the binary log is enabled. This variable was added in MySQL 3.23.14. See Section 4.8.4, "The Binary Log."

- `log_slave_updates`

  Whether updates received by a slave server from a master server should be logged to the slave's own binary log. Binary logging must be enabled on the slave for this to have any effect. This variable was added in MySQL 3.23.17. See Section 5.8, "Replication Startup Options."

- `log_slow_queries`

  Whether slow queries should be logged. "Slow" is determined by the value of the long_query_time variable. This variable was added in MySQL 4.0.2. See Section 4.8.5, "The Slow Query Log."

- `log_update`

  Whether the update log is enabled. This variable was added in MySQL 3.22.18. Note that the binary log is preferable to the update log, which is unavailable as of MySQL 5.0. See Section 4.8.3, "The Update Log."

- `long_query_time`

  If a query takes longer than this many seconds, the `Slow_queries` status variable is incremented. If you are using the `--log-slow-queries` option, the query is logged to the slow query log file. This value is measured in real time, not CPU time, so a query that is under the threshold on a lightly loaded system might be above the threshold on a heavily loaded one. See Section 4.8.5, "The Slow Query Log."

- `low_priority_updates`

  If set to 1, all `INSERT`, `UPDATE`, `DELETE`, and `LOCK TABLE WRITE` statements wait until there is no pending `SELECT` or `LOCK TABLE READ` on the affected table. This variable previously was named `sql_low_priority_updates`. It was added in MySQL 3.22.5.

- `lower_case_table_names`

  If set to 1, table names are stored in lowercase on disk and table name comparisons are not case sensitive. This variable was added in MySQL 3.23.6. If set to 2 (new in 4.0.18), table names are stored as given but compared in lowercase. From MySQL 4.0.2, this option also applies to database names. From 4.1.1, it also applies to table aliases.

  You should *not* set this variable to 0 if you are running MySQL on a system that does not have case-sensitive filenames (such as Windows or Mac OS X). New in 4.0.18: If this variable is 0 and the filesystem on which the data directory is located does not have case-sensitive filenames, MySQL automatically sets `lower_case_table_names` to 2.

- `max_allowed_packet`

  The maximum size of one packet. The message buffer is initialized to `net_buffer_length` bytes, but can grow up to `max_allowed_packet` bytes when needed. This value by default is small, to catch big (possibly wrong) packets. You must increase this value if you are using big `BLOB` columns. It should be as big as the biggest `BLOB` you want to use. The protocol limit for `max_allowed_packet` is 16MB before MySQL 4.0 and 1GB thereafter.

- `max_binlog_cache_size`

  If a multiple-statement transaction requires more than this amount of memory, you will get the error `Multi-statement transaction required more than 'max_binlog_cache_size' bytes of storage`. This variable was added in MySQL 3.23.29.

- `max_binlog_size`

  If a write to the binary log exceeds the given value, rotate the binary logs. You cannot set this variable to more than 1GB or to less than 4096 bytes. (The minimum before MYSQL 4.0.14 is 1024 bytes.) The default value is 1GB. This variable was added in MySQL 3.23.33.

Note if you are using transactions: A transaction is written in one chunk to the binary log, hence it is never split between several binary logs. Therefore, if you have big transactions, you might see binary logs bigger than `max_binlog_size`.

If `max_relay_log_size` is 0, the value of `max_binlog_size` applies to relay logs as well. `max_relay_log_size` was added in MySQL 4.0.14.

- `max_connect_errors`

If there are more than this number of interrupted connections from a host, that host is blocked from further connections. You can unblock blocked hosts with the FLUSH HOSTS statement.

- `max_connections`

The number of simultaneous client connections allowed. Increasing this value increases the number of file descriptors that `mysqld` requires. See Section 6.4.8, "How MySQL Opens and Closes Tables," for comments on file descriptor limits. Also see Section A.2.6, "Too many connections."

- `max_delayed_threads`

Don't start more than this number of threads to handle INSERT DELAYED statements. If you try to insert data into a new table after all INSERT DELAYED threads are in use, the row will be inserted as if the DELAYED attribute wasn't specified. If you set this to 0, MySQL never creates a thread to handle DELAYED rows; in effect, this disables DELAYED entirely. This variable was added in MySQL 3.23.0.

- `max_error_count`

The maximum number of error, warning, and note messages to be stored for display by SHOW ERRORS or SHOW WARNINGS. This variable was added in MySQL 4.1.0.

- `max_heap_table_size`

This variable sets the maximum size to which MEMORY (HEAP) tables are allowed to grow. The value of the variable is used to calculate MEMORY table MAX_ROWS values. Setting this variable has no effect on any existing MEMORY table, unless the table is re-created with a statement such as CREATE TABLE or TRUNCATE TABLE, or altered with ALTER TABLE. This variable was added in MySQL 3.23.0.

- `max_insert_delayed_threads`

This variable is a synonym for `max_delayed_threads`. It was added in MySQL 4.0.19.

- `max_join_size`

Don't allow SELECT statements that probably will need to examine more than `max_join_size` row combinations or are likely to do more than `max_join_size` disk seeks. By setting this value, you can catch SELECT statements where keys are not used properly and that would probably take a long time. Set it if your users tend to perform joins that lack a WHERE clause, that take a long time, or that return millions of rows.

Setting this variable to a value other than DEFAULT resets the SQL_BIG_SELECTS value to 0. If you set the SQL_BIG_SELECTS value again, the `max_join_size` variable is ignored.

If a query result already is in the query cache, no result size check is performed, because the result has already been computed and it does not burden the server to send it to the client.

This variable previously was named `sql_max_join_size`.

- `max_relay_log_size`

If a write by a replication slave to its relay log exceeds the given value, rotate the relay log. This variable enables you to put different size constraints on relay logs and binary logs. However, setting the variable to 0 makes MySQL use `max_binlog_size` for both binary logs and relay logs. You must set `max_relay_log_size` to between 4096 bytes and 1GB (inclusive), or to 0. The default value is 0. This variable was added in MySQL 4.0.14. See Section 5.3, "Replication Implementation Details."

- `max_seeks_for_key`

Limit the assumed maximum number of seeks when looking up rows based on a key. The MySQL optimizer will assume that no more than this number of key seeks will be required when searching for matching rows in a table by scanning a key, regardless of the actual cardinality of the key. By setting this to a low value (100?), you can force MySQL to prefer keys instead of table scans. This variable was added in MySQL 4.0.14.

- `max_sort_length`

The number of bytes to use when sorting BLOB or TEXT values. Only the first `max_sort_length` bytes of each value are used; the rest are ignored.

- `max_tmp_tables`

The maximum number of temporary tables a client can keep open at the same time. (This option doesn't yet do anything.)

- `max_user_connections`

The maximum number of simultaneous connections allowed to any given MySQL account. A value of 0 means "no limit." This variable was added in MySQL 3.23.34.

- `max_write_lock_count`

After this many write locks, allow some read locks to run in between. This variable was added in MySQL 3.23.7.

- `myisam_data_pointer_size`

Default pointer size in bytes to be used by CREATE TABLE for MyISAM tables when no MAX_ROWS option is specified. This variable cannot be less than 2 or larger than 8. The default value is 4. This variable was added in MySQL 4.1.2. See Section A.2.11, "The table is full."

- `myisam_max_extra_sort_file_size`

If the temporary file used for fast MyISAM index creation would be larger than using the key cache by the amount specified here, prefer the key cache method. This is mainly used to force long character keys in large tables to use the slower key cache method to create the index. This variable was added in MySQL 3.23.37. **Note:** The value is given in megabytes before 4.0.3 and in bytes thereafter.

- `myisam_max_sort_file_size`

The maximum size of the temporary file MySQL is allowed to use while re-creating a `MyISAM` index (during `REPAIR TABLE`, `ALTER TABLE`, or `LOAD DATA INFILE`). If the file size would be bigger than this value, the index will be created using the key cache instead, which is slower. This variable was added in MySQL 3.23.37. **Note:** The value is given in megabytes before 4.0.3 and in bytes thereafter.

- `myisam_recover_options`

The value of the `--myisam-recover` option. This variable was added in MySQL 3.23.36.

- `myisam_repair_threads`

If this value is greater than 1, `MyISAM` table indexes are created in parallel (each index in its own thread) during the `Repair by sorting` process. The default value is 1. **Note:** Multi-threaded repair is still *alpha* quality code. This variable was added in MySQL 4.0.13.

- `myisam_sort_buffer_size`

The buffer that is allocated when sorting `MyISAM` indexes during a `REPAIR TABLE` or when creating indexes with `CREATE INDEX` or `ALTER TABLE`. This variable was added in MySQL 3.23.16.

- `named_pipe`

On Windows, indicates whether the server supports connections over named pipes. This variable was added in MySQL 3.23.50.

- `net_buffer_length`

The communication buffer is reset to this size between queries. This should not normally be changed, but if you have very little memory, you can set it to the expected length of SQL statements sent by clients. If statements exceed this length, the buffer is automatically enlarged, up to `max_allowed_packet` bytes.

- `net_read_timeout`

The number of seconds to wait for more data from a connection before aborting the read. When the server is reading from the client, `net_read_timeout` is the timeout value controlling when to abort. When the server is writing to the client, `net_write_timeout` is the timeout value controlling when to abort. See also `slave_net_timeout`. This variable was added in MySQL 3.23.20.

- `net_retry_count`

If a read on a communication port is interrupted, retry this many times before giving up. This value should be set quite high on FreeBSD because internal interrupts are sent to all threads. This variable was added in MySQL 3.23.7.

- net_write_timeout

  The number of seconds to wait for a block to be written to a connection before aborting the write. See also net_read_timeout. This variable was added in MySQL 3.23.20.

- open_files_limit

  The number of files that the operating system allows mysqld to open. This is the real
  value allowed by the system and might be different from the value you gave mysqld as a
  startup option. The value is 0 on systems where MySQL can't change the number of
  open files. This variable was added in MySQL 3.23.20.

- pid_file

  The pathname of the process ID (PID) file. This variable can be set with the --pid-
  file option. This variable was added in MySQL 3.23.23.

- port

  The port on which the server listens for TCP/IP connections. This variable can be set
  with the --port option.

- protocol_version

  The version of the client/server protocol used by the MySQL server. This variable was
  added in MySQL 3.23.18.

- query_alloc_block_size

  The allocation size of memory blocks that are allocated for objects created during query
  parsing and execution. If you have problems with memory fragmentation, it might help
  to increase this a bit. This variable was added in MySQL 4.0.16.

- query_cache_limit

  Don't cache results that are bigger than this. The default value is 1MB. This variable
  was added in MySQL 4.0.1.

- query_cache_min_res_unit

  The minimum size for blocks allocated by the query cache. The default value is 4KB.
  Tuning information for this variable is given in Section 4.10.3, "Query Cache
  Configuration." This variable is present from MySQL 4.1.

- query_cache_size

  The amount of memory allocated for caching query results. The default value is 0,
  which disables the query cache. Note that this amount of memory will be allocated even
  if query_cache_type is set to 0. This variable was added in MySQL 4.0.1.

- query_cache_type

  Set query cache type. Setting the GLOBAL value sets the type for all clients that connect
  thereafter. Individual clients can set the SESSION value to affect their own use of the
  query cache.

Option	Description
0 or OFF	Don't cache or retrieve results. Note that this will not deallocate the query cache buffer. To do that, you should set `query_cache_size` to 0.
1 or ON	Cache all query results except for those that begin with SELECT SQL_NO_CACHE.
2 or DEMAND	Cache results only for queries that begin with SELECT SQL_CACHE.

This variable was added in MySQL 4.0.3.

- `query_cache_wlock_invalidate`

Normally, when one client acquires a WRITE lock on a MyISAM table, other clients are not blocked from issuing queries for the table if the query results are present in the query cache. Setting this variable to 1 causes acquisition of a WRITE lock for a table to invalidate any queries in the query cache that refer to the table. This forces other clients that attempt to access the table to wait while the lock is in effect. This variable was added in MySQL 4.0.19.

- `query_prealloc_size`

The size of the persistent buffer used for query parsing and execution. This buffer is not freed between queries. If you are running complex queries, a larger `query_prealloc_size` value might be helpful in improving performance, because it can reduce the need for the server to perform memory allocation during query execution operations.

This variable was added in MySQL 4.0.16.

- `range_alloc_block_size`

The size of blocks that are allocated when doing range optimization. This variable was added in MySQL 4.0.16.

- `read_buffer_size`

Each thread that does a sequential scan allocates a buffer of this size for each table it scans. If you do many sequential scans, you might want to increase this value. This variable was added in MySQL 4.0.3. Previously, it was named `record_buffer`.

- `read_only`

When the variable is set to ON for a replication slave server, it causes the slave to allow no updates except from slave threads or from users with the SUPER privilege. This can be useful to ensure that a slave server accepts no updates from clients. This variable was added in MySQL 4.0.14.

- `read_rnd_buffer_size`

When reading rows in sorted order after a sort, the rows are read through this buffer to avoid disk seeks. Setting the variable to a large value can improve ORDER BY performance by a lot. However, this is a buffer allocated for each client, so you should not set the global variable to a large value. Instead, change the session variable only from within those clients that need to run large queries. This variable was added in MySQL 4.0.3. Previously, it was named `record_rnd_buffer`.

- `safe_show_database`

  Don't show databases for which the user has no database or table privileges. This can improve security if you're concerned about people being able to see what databases other users have. See also `skip_show_database`.

  This variable was removed in MySQL 4.0.5. Instead, use the SHOW DATABASES privilege to control access by MySQL accounts to database names.

- `secure_auth`

  If the MySQL server has been started with the `--secure-auth` option, it blocks connections from all accounts that have passwords stored in the old (pre-4.1) format. In that case, the value of this variable is ON, otherwise it is OFF.

  You should enable this option if you want to prevent all usage of passwords in old format (and hence insecure communication over the network). This variable was added in MySQL 4.1.1.

  Server startup will fail with an error if this option is enabled and the privilege tables are in pre-4.1 format.

  When used as a client-side option, the client refuses to connect to a server if the server requires a password in old format for the client account.

- `server_id`

  The value of the `--server-id` option. It is used for master and slave replication servers. This variable was added in MySQL 3.23.26.

- `skip_external_locking`

  This is OFF if `mysqld` uses external locking. This variable was added in MySQL 4.0.3. Previously, it was named `skip_locking`.

- `skip_networking`

  This is ON if the server allows only local (non-TCP/IP) connections. On Unix, local connections use a Unix socket file. On Windows, local connections use a named pipe. On NetWare, only TCP/IP connections are supported, so do not set this variable to ON. This variable was added in MySQL 3.22.23.

- `skip_show_database`

  This prevents people from using the SHOW DATABASES statement if they don't have the SHOW DATABASES privilege. This can improve security if you're concerned about people being able to see what databases other users have. See also `safe_show_database`. This variable was added in MySQL 3.23.4. As of MySQL 4.0.2, its effect also depends on the SHOW DATABASES privilege: If the variable value is ON, the SHOW DATABASES statement is allowed only to users who have the SHOW DATABASES privilege, and the statement displays all database names. If the value is OFF, SHOW DATABASES is allowed to all users, but displays each database name only if the user has the SHOW DATABASES privilege or some privilege for the database.

- `slave_net_timeout`

  The number of seconds to wait for more data from a master/slave connection before aborting the read. This variable was added in MySQL 3.23.40.

- `slow_launch_time`

  If creating a thread takes longer than this many seconds, the server increments the `Slow_launch_threads` status variable. This variable was added in MySQL 3.23.15.

- `socket`

  On Unix, this is the Unix socket file used for local client connections. On Windows, this is the name of the named pipe used for local client connections.

- `sort_buffer_size`

  Each thread that needs to do a sort allocates a buffer of this size. Increase this value for faster `ORDER BY` or `GROUP BY` operations. See Section A.4.4, "Where MySQL Stores Temporary Files."

- `sql_mode`

  The current server SQL mode. This variable was added in MySQL 3.23.41. See Section 4.2.2, "The Server SQL Mode."

- `storage_engine`

  This variable is a synonym for `table_type`. It was added in MySQL 4.1.2.

- `table_cache`

  The number of open tables for all threads. Increasing this value increases the number of file descriptors that `mysqld` requires. You can check whether you need to increase the table cache by checking the `Opened_tables` status variable. See Section 4.2.4, "Server Status Variables." If the value of `Opened_tables` is large and you don't do `FLUSH TABLES` a lot (which just forces all tables to be closed and reopened), then you should increase the value of the `table_cache` variable.

  For more information about the table cache, see Section 6.4.8, "How MySQL Opens and Closes Tables."

- `table_type`

  The default table type (storage engine). To set the table type at server startup, use the `--default-table-type` option. This variable was added in MySQL 3.23.0. See Section 4.2.1, "`mysqld` Command-Line Options."

- `thread_cache_size`

  How many threads the server should cache for reuse. When a client disconnects, the client's threads are put in the cache if there aren't already `thread_cache_size` threads there. Requests for threads are satisfied by reusing threads taken from the cache if possible, and only when the cache is empty is a new thread created. This variable can be increased to improve performance if you have a lot of new connections. (Normally this doesn't give a notable performance improvement if you have a good thread implementation.) By examining the difference between the `Connections` and `Threads_created` status variables (see Section 4.2.4, "Server Status Variables," for details) you can see how efficient the thread cache is. This variable was added in MySQL 3.23.16.

- `thread_concurrency`

  On Solaris, `mysqld` calls `thr_setconcurrency()` with this value. This function allows applications to give the threads system a hint about the desired number of threads that should be run at the same time. This variable was added in MySQL 3.23.7.

- `thread_stack`

  The stack size for each thread. Many of the limits detected by the `crash-me` test are dependent on this value. The default is large enough for normal operation. See Section 6.1.4, "The MySQL Benchmark Suite."

- `timezone`

  The time zone for the server. This is set from the `TZ` environment variable when `mysqld` is started. The time zone also can be set by giving a `--timezone` argument to `mysqld_safe`. This variable was added in MySQL 3.23.15. See Section A.4.6, "Time Zone Problems."

- `tmp_table_size`

  If an in-memory temporary table exceeds this size, MySQL automatically converts it to an on-disk `MyISAM` table. Increase the value of `tmp_table_size` if you do many advanced `GROUP BY` queries and you have lots of memory.

- `tmpdir`

  The directory used for temporary files and temporary tables. Starting from MySQL 4.1, this variable can be set to a list of several paths that are used in round-robin fashion. Paths should be separated by colon characters (':') on Unix and semicolon characters (';') on Windows, NetWare, and OS/2.

  This feature can be used to spread the load between several physical disks. If the MySQL server is acting as a replication slave, you should not set `tmpdir` to point to a directory on a memory-based filesystem or to a directory that is cleared when the server host restarts. A replication slave needs some of its temporary files to survive a machine restart so that it can replicate temporary tables or `LOAD DATA INFILE` operations. If files in the temporary file directory are lost when the server restarts, replication will fail.

  This variable was added in MySQL 3.22.4.

- `transaction_alloc_block_size`

  The allocation size of memory blocks that are allocated for storing queries that are part of a transaction to be stored in the binary log when doing a commit. This variable was added in MySQL 4.0.16.

- `transaction_prealloc_size`

  The size of the persistent buffer for `transaction_alloc_blocks` that is not freed between queries. By making this big enough to fit all queries in a common transaction, you can avoid a lot of `malloc()` calls. This variable was added in MySQL 4.0.16.

- `tx_isolation`

  The default transaction isolation level. This variable was added in MySQL 4.0.3.

- `version`

  The version number for the server.

- `wait_timeout`

  The number of seconds the server waits for activity on a non-interactive connection before closing it.

  On thread startup, the session `wait_timeout` value is initialized from the global `wait_timeout` value or from the global `interactive_timeout` value, depending on the type of client (as defined by the `CLIENT_INTERACTIVE` connect option to `mysql_real_connect()`). See also `interactive_timeout`.

4.2.3.1 System Variables

Starting from MySQL 4.0.3, we provide better access to a lot of system and connection variables. Many variables can be changed dynamically while the server is running. This allows you to modify server operation without having to stop and restart it.

The `mysqld` server maintains two kinds of variables. Global variables affect the overall operation of the server. Session variables affect its operation for individual client connections.

When the server starts, it initializes all global variables to their default values. These defaults may be changed by options specified in option files or on the command line. After the server starts, those global variables that are dynamic can be changed by connecting to the server and issuing a `SET GLOBAL` *var_name* statement. To change a global variable, you must have the `SUPER` privilege.

The server also maintains a set of session variables for each client that connects. The client's session variables are initialized at connect time using the current values of the corresponding global variables. For those session variables that are dynamic, the client can change them by issuing a `SET SESSION` *var_name* statement. Setting a session variable requires no special privilege, but a client can change only its own session variables, not those of any other client.

A change to a global variable is visible to any client that accesses that global variable. However, it affects the corresponding session variable that is intialized from the global variable only for clients that connect after the change. It does not affect the session variable for any client that is already connected (not even that of the client that issues the `SET GLOBAL` statement).

Global or session variables may be set or retrieved using several syntax forms. The following examples use `sort_buffer_size` as a sample variable name.

To set the value of a GLOBAL variable, use one of the following syntaxes:

```
mysql> SET GLOBAL sort_buffer_size=value;
mysql> SET @@global.sort_buffer_size=value;
```

To set the value of a SESSION variable, use one of the following syntaxes:

```
mysql> SET SESSION sort_buffer_size=value;
mysql> SET @@session.sort_buffer_size=value;
mysql> SET sort_buffer_size=value;
```

LOCAL is a synonym for SESSION.

If you don't specify GLOBAL, SESSION, or LOCAL when setting a variable, SESSION is the default.

To retrieve the value of a GLOBAL variable, use one of the following statements:

```
mysql> SELECT @@global.sort_buffer_size;
mysql> SHOW GLOBAL VARIABLES like 'sort_buffer_size';
```

To retrieve the value of a SESSION variable, use one of the following statements:

```
mysql> SELECT @@sort_buffer_size;
mysql> SELECT @@session.sort_buffer_size;
mysql> SHOW SESSION VARIABLES like 'sort_buffer_size';
```

Here, too, LOCAL is a synonym for SESSION.

When you retrieve a variable with SELECT @@var_name (that is, you do not specify global., session., or local., MySQL returns the SESSION value if it exists and the GLOBAL value otherwise.

For SHOW VARIABLES, if you do not specify GLOBAL, SESSION, or LOCAL, MySQL returns the SESSION value.

The reason for requiring the GLOBAL keyword when setting GLOBAL-only variables but not when retrieving them is to prevent problems in the future. If we remove a SESSION variable with the same name as a SESSION variable, a client with the SUPER privilege might accidentally change the GLOBAL variable rather than just the SESSION variable for its own connection. If we add a SESSION variable with the same name as a SESSION variable, a client that intends to change the GLOBAL variable might find only its own SESSION variable changed.

4.2.3.1.1 Structured System Variables

Structured system variables are supported beginning with MySQL 4.1.1. A structured variable differs from a regular system variable in two respects:

- Its value is a structure with components that specify server parameters considered to be closely related.
- There might be several instances of a given type of structured variable. Each one has a different name and refers to a different resource maintained by the server.

Currently, MySQL supports one structured variable type. It specifies parameters that govern the operation of key caches. A key cache structured variable has these components:

- `key_buffer_size`
- `key_cache_block_size`
- `key_cache_division_limit`
- `key_cache_age_threshold`

The purpose of this section is to describe the syntax for referring to structured variables. Key cache variables are used for syntax examples, but specific details about how key caches operate are found elsewhere, in Section 6.4.6, "The MyISAM Key Cache."

To refer to a component of a structured variable instance, you can use a compound name in *instance_name.component_name* format. Examples:

```
hot_cache.key_buffer_size
hot_cache.key_cache_block_size
cold_cache.key_cache_block_size
```

For each structured system variable, an instance with the name of `default` is always predefined. If you refer to a component of a structured variable without any instance name, the `default` instance is used. Thus, `default.key_buffer_size` and `key_buffer_size` both refer to the same system variable.

The naming rules for structured variable instances and components are as follows:

- For a given type of structured variable, each instance must have a name that is unique *within* variables of that type. However, instance names need not be unique *across* structured variable types. For example, each structured variable will have an instance named `default`, so `default` is not unique across variable types.

- The names of the components of each structured variable type must be unique across all system variable names. If this were not true (that is, if two different types of structured variables could share component member names), it would not be clear which default structured variable to use for references to member names that are not qualified by an instance name.

- If a structured variable instance name is not legal as an unquoted identifier, refer to it as a quoted identifier using backticks. For example, `hot-cache` is not legal, but `` `hot-cache` `` is.

- `global`, `session`, and `local` are not legal instance names. This avoids a conflict with notation such as `@@global.var_name` for referring to non-structured system variables.

At the moment, the first two rules have no possibility of being violated because the only structured variable type is the one for key caches. These rules will assume greater significance if some other type of structured variable is created in the future.

With one exception, it is allowable to refer to structured variable components using compound names in any context where simple variable names can occur. For example, you can assign a value to a structured variable using a command-line option:

```
shell> mysqld --hot_cache.key_buffer_size=64K
```

In an option file, do this:

```
[mysqld]
hot_cache.key_buffer_size=64K
```

If you start the server with such an option, it creates a key cache named hot_cache with a size of 64KB in addition to the default key cache that has a default size of 8MB.

Suppose that you start the server as follows:

```
shell> mysqld --key_buffer_size=256K \
        --extra_cache.key_buffer_size=128K \
        --extra_cache.key_cache_block_size=2048
```

In this case, the server sets the size of the default key cache to 256KB. (You could also have written --default.key_buffer_size=256K.) In addition, the server creates a second key cache named extra_cache that has a size of 128KB, with the size of block buffers for caching table index blocks set to 2048 bytes.

The following example starts the server with three different key caches having sizes in a 3:1:1 ratio:

```
shell> mysqld --key_buffer_size=6M \
        --hot_cache.key_buffer_size=2M \
        --cold_cache.key_buffer_size=2M
```

Structured variable values may be set and retrieved at runtime as well. For example, to set a key cache named hot_cache to a size of 10MB, use either of these statements:

```
mysql> SET GLOBAL hot_cache.key_buffer_size = 10*1024*1024;
mysql> SET @@global.hot_cache.key_buffer_size = 10*1024*1024;
```

To retrieve the cache size, do this:

```
mysql> SELECT @@global.hot_cache.key_buffer_size;
```

However, the following statement does not work. The variable is not interpreted as a compound name, but as a simple string for a LIKE pattern-matching operation:

```
mysql> SHOW GLOBAL VARIABLES LIKE 'hot_cache.key_buffer_size';
```

This is the exception to being able to use structured variable names anywhere a simple variable name may occur.

4.2.3.1.2 Dynamic System Variables

Beginning with MySQL 4.0.3, many server system variables are dynamic and can be set at runtime using SET GLOBAL or SET SESSION. You can also select their values using SELECT. See Section 4.2.3.1, "System Variables."

The following table shows the full list of all dynamic system variables. The last column indicates for each variable whether GLOBAL or SESSION (or both) apply.

Variable Name	Value Type	Type
autocommit	boolean	SESSION
big_tables	boolean	SESSION
binlog_cache_size	numeric	GLOBAL
bulk_insert_buffer_size	numeric	GLOBAL | SESSION
character_set_client	string	GLOBAL | SESSION
character_set_connection	string	GLOBAL | SESSION
character_set_results	string	GLOBAL | SESSION
character_set_server	string	GLOBAL | SESSION
collation_connection	string	GLOBAL | SESSION
collation_server	string	GLOBAL | SESSION
concurrent_insert	boolean	GLOBAL
connect_timeout	numeric	GLOBAL
convert_character_set	string	GLOBAL | SESSION
default_week_format	numeric	GLOBAL | SESSION
delay_key_write	OFF | ON | ALL	GLOBAL
delayed_insert_limit	numeric	GLOBAL
delayed_insert_timeout	numeric	GLOBAL
delayed_queue_size	numeric	GLOBAL
error_count	numeric	SESSION
flush	boolean	GLOBAL
flush_time	numeric	GLOBAL
foreign_key_checks	boolean	SESSION
ft_boolean_syntax	numeric	GLOBAL
group_concat_max_len	numeric	GLOBAL | SESSION
identity	numeric	SESSION
insert_id	boolean	SESSION
interactive_timeout	numeric	GLOBAL | SESSION
join_buffer_size	numeric	GLOBAL | SESSION
key_buffer_size	numeric	GLOBAL
last_insert_id	numeric	SESSION
local_infile	boolean	GLOBAL

Variable Name	Value Type	Type
log_warnings	boolean	GLOBAL
long_query_time	numeric	GLOBAL | SESSION
low_priority_updates	boolean	GLOBAL | SESSION
max_allowed_packet	numeric	GLOBAL | SESSION
max_binlog_cache_size	numeric	GLOBAL
max_binlog_size	numeric	GLOBAL
max_connect_errors	numeric	GLOBAL
max_connections	numeric	GLOBAL
max_delayed_threads	numeric	GLOBAL
max_error_count	numeric	GLOBAL | SESSION
max_heap_table_size	numeric	GLOBAL | SESSION
max_insert_delayed_threads	numeric	GLOBAL
max_join_size	numeric	GLOBAL | SESSION
max_relay_log_size	numeric	GLOBAL
max_seeks_for_key	numeric	GLOBAL | SESSION
max_sort_length	numeric	GLOBAL | SESSION
max_tmp_tables	numeric	GLOBAL
max_user_connections	numeric	GLOBAL
max_write_lock_count	numeric	GLOBAL
myisam_max_extra_sort_file_size	numeric	GLOBAL | SESSION
myisam_max_sort_file_size	numeric	GLOBAL | SESSION
myisam_repair_threads	numeric	GLOBAL | SESSION
myisam_sort_buffer_size	numeric	GLOBAL | SESSION
net_buffer_length	numeric	GLOBAL | SESSION
net_read_timeout	numeric	GLOBAL | SESSION
net_retry_count	numeric	GLOBAL | SESSION
net_write_timeout	numeric	GLOBAL | SESSION
query_alloc_block_size	numeric	GLOBAL | SESSION
query_cache_limit	numeric	GLOBAL
query_cache_size	numeric	GLOBAL
query_cache_type	enumeration	GLOBAL | SESSION
query_cache_wlock_invalidate	boolean	GLOBAL | SESSION
query_prealloc_size	numeric	GLOBAL | SESSION
range_alloc_block_size	numeric	GLOBAL | SESSION
read_buffer_size	numeric	GLOBAL | SESSION
read_only	numeric	GLOBAL
read_rnd_buffer_size	numeric	GLOBAL | SESSION
rpl_recovery_rank	numeric	GLOBAL
safe_show_database	boolean	GLOBAL

Variable Name	Value Type	Type
server_id	numeric	GLOBAL
slave_compressed_protocol	boolean	GLOBAL
slave_net_timeout	numeric	GLOBAL
slow_launch_time	numeric	GLOBAL
sort_buffer_size	numeric	GLOBAL | SESSION
sql_auto_is_null	boolean	SESSION
sql_big_selects	boolean	SESSION
sql_big_tables	boolean	SESSION
sql_buffer_result	boolean	SESSION
sql_log_bin	boolean	SESSION
sql_log_off	boolean	SESSION
sql_log_update	boolean	SESSION
sql_low_priority_updates	boolean	GLOBAL | SESSION
sql_max_join_size	numeric	GLOBAL | SESSION
sql_quote_show_create	boolean	SESSION
sql_safe_updates	boolean	SESSION
sql_select_limit	numeric	SESSION
sql_slave_skip_counter	numeric	GLOBAL
sql_warnings	boolean	SESSION
storage_engine	enumeration	GLOBAL | SESSION
table_cache	numeric	GLOBAL
table_type	enumeration	GLOBAL | SESSION
thread_cache_size	numeric	GLOBAL
timestamp	boolean	SESSION
tmp_table_size	enumeration	GLOBAL | SESSION
transaction_alloc_block_size	numeric	GLOBAL | SESSION
transaction_prealloc_size	numeric	GLOBAL | SESSION
tx_isolation	enumeration	GLOBAL | SESSION
unique_checks	boolean	SESSION
wait_timeout	numeric	GLOBAL | SESSION
warning_count	numeric	SESSION

Variables that are marked as "string" take a string value. Variables that are marked as "numeric" take a numeric value. Variables that are marked as "boolean" can be set to 0, 1, ON or OFF. Variables that are marked as "enumeration" normally should be set to one of the available values for the variable, but can also be set to the number that corresponds to the desired enumeration value. For enumeration-valued system variables, the first enumeration value corresponds to 0. This differs from ENUM columns, for which the first enumeration value corresponds to 1.

4.2.4 Server Status Variables

The server maintains many status variables that provide information about its operations. You can view these variables and their values by using the SHOW STATUS statement:

```
mysql> SHOW STATUS;
+-------------------------+------------+
| Variable_name           | Value      |
+-------------------------+------------+
| Aborted_clients         | 0          |
| Aborted_connects        | 0          |
| Bytes_received          | 155372598  |
| Bytes_sent              | 1176560426 |
| Connections             | 30023      |
| Created_tmp_disk_tables | 0          |
| Created_tmp_files       | 60         |
| Created_tmp_tables      | 8340       |
| Delayed_errors          | 0          |
| Delayed_insert_threads  | 0          |
| Delayed_writes          | 0          |
| Flush_commands          | 1          |
| Handler_delete          | 462604     |
| Handler_read_first      | 105881     |
| Handler_read_key        | 27820558   |
| Handler_read_next       | 390681754  |
| Handler_read_prev       | 6022500    |
| Handler_read_rnd        | 30546748   |
| Handler_read_rnd_next   | 246216530  |
| Handler_update          | 16945404   |
| Handler_write           | 60356676   |
| Key_blocks_used         | 14955      |
| Key_read_requests       | 96854827   |
| Key_reads               | 162040     |
| Key_write_requests      | 7589728    |
| Key_writes              | 3813196    |
| Max_used_connections    | 0          |
| Not_flushed_delayed_rows| 0          |
| Not_flushed_key_blocks  | 0          |
| Open_files              | 2          |
| Open_streams            | 0          |
| Open_tables             | 1          |
| Opened_tables           | 44600      |
| Qcache_free_blocks      | 36         |
| Qcache_free_memory      | 138488     |
| Qcache_hits             | 79570      |
| Qcache_inserts          | 27087      |
| Qcache_lowmem_prunes    | 3114       |
| Qcache_not_cached       | 22989      |
```

```
| Qcache_queries_in_cache | 415        |
| Qcache_total_blocks     | 912        |
| Questions               | 2026873    |
| Select_full_join        | 0          |
| Select_full_range_join  | 0          |
| Select_range            | 99646      |
| Select_range_check      | 0          |
| Select_scan             | 30802      |
| Slave_open_temp_tables  | 0          |
| Slave_running           | OFF        |
| Slow_launch_threads     | 0          |
| Slow_queries            | 0          |
| Sort_merge_passes       | 30         |
| Sort_range              | 500        |
| Sort_rows               | 30296250   |
| Sort_scan               | 4650       |
| Table_locks_immediate   | 1920382    |
| Table_locks_waited      | 0          |
| Threads_cached          | 0          |
| Threads_connected       | 1          |
| Threads_created         | 30022      |
| Threads_running         | 1          |
| Uptime                  | 80380      |
+-------------------------+------------+
```

Many status variables are reset to 0 by the FLUSH STATUS statement.

The status variables have the following meanings. The Com_*xxx* statement counter variables were added beginning with MySQL 3.23.47. The Qcache_*xxx* query cache variables were added beginning with MySQL 4.0.1. Otherwise, variables with no version indicated have been present since at least MySQL 3.22.

- Aborted_clients

  The number of connections that were aborted because the client died without closing the connection properly. See Section A.2.10, "Communication Errors and Aborted Connections."

- Aborted_connects

  The number of tries to connect to the MySQL server that failed. See Section A.2.10, "Communication Errors and Aborted Connections."

- Binlog_cache_use

  The number of transactions that used the temporary binary log cache. This variable was added in MySQL 4.1.2.

- Binlog_cache_disk_use

  The number of transactions that used the temporary binary log cache but that exceeded the value of binlog_cache_size and used a temporary file to store statements from the transaction. This variable was added in MySQL 4.1.2.

- `Bytes_received`

  The number of bytes received from all clients. This variable was added in MySQL 3.23.7.

- `Bytes_sent`

  The number of bytes sent to all clients. This variable was added in MySQL 3.23.7.

- `Com_xxx`

  The number of times each *xxx* statement has been executed. There is one status variable for each type of statement. For example, `Com_delete` and `Com_insert` count `DELETE` and `INSERT` statements.

- `Connections`

  The number of connection attempts (successful or not) to the MySQL server.

- `Created_tmp_disk_tables`

  The number of temporary tables on disk created automatically by the server while executing statements. This variable was added in MySQL 3.23.24.

- `Created_tmp_files`

  How many temporary files `mysqld` has created. This variable was added in MySQL 3.23.28.

- `Created_tmp_tables`

  The number of in-memory temporary tables created automatically by the server while executing statements. If `Created_tmp_disk_tables` is big, you may want to increase the `tmp_table_size` value to cause temporary tables to be memory-based instead of disk-based.

- `Delayed_errors`

  The number of rows written with `INSERT DELAYED` for which some error occurred (probably `duplicate key`).

- `Delayed_insert_threads`

  The number of `INSERT DELAYED` handler threads in use.

- `Delayed_writes`

  The number of `INSERT DELAYED` rows written.

- `Flush_commands`

  The number of executed `FLUSH` statements.

- `Handler_commit`

  The number of internal `COMMIT` statements. This variable was added in MySQL 4.0.2.

- `Handler_delete`

  The number of times a row was deleted from a table.

- `Handler_read_first`

  The number of times the first entry was read from an index. If this is high, it suggests that the server is doing a lot of full index scans; for example, `SELECT col1 FROM foo`, assuming that `col1` is indexed.

- `Handler_read_key`

  The number of requests to read a row based on a key. If this is high, it is a good indication that your queries and tables are properly indexed.

- `Handler_read_next`

  The number of requests to read the next row in key order. This will be incremented if you are querying an index column with a range constraint or if you are doing an index scan.

- `Handler_read_prev`

  The number of requests to read the previous row in key order. This read method is mainly used to optimize `ORDER BY ... DESC`. This variable was added in MySQL 3.23.6.

- `Handler_read_rnd`

  The number of requests to read a row based on a fixed position. This will be high if you are doing a lot of queries that require sorting of the result. You probably have a lot of queries that require MySQL to scan whole tables or you have joins that don't use keys properly.

- `Handler_read_rnd_next`

  The number of requests to read the next row in the data file. This will be high if you are doing a lot of table scans. Generally this suggests that your tables are not properly indexed or that your queries are not written to take advantage of the indexes you have.

- `Handler_rollback`

  The number of internal `ROLLBACK` statements. This variable was added in MySQL 4.0.2.

- `Handler_update`

  The number of requests to update a row in a table.

- `Handler_write`

  The number of requests to insert a row in a table.

- `Key_blocks_used`

  The number of used blocks in the key cache. You can use this value to determine how much of the key cache is in use; see the discussion of `key_buffer_size` in Section 4.2.3, "Server System Variables."

- `Key_read_requests`

  The number of requests to read a key block from the cache.

- Key_reads

  The number of physical reads of a key block from disk. If Key_reads is big, then your key_buffer_size value is probably too small. The cache miss rate can be calculated as Key_reads/Key_read_requests.

- Key_write_requests

  The number of requests to write a key block to the cache.

- Key_writes

  The number of physical writes of a key block to disk.

- Max_used_connections

  The maximum number of connections that have been in use simultaneously since the server started.

- Not_flushed_delayed_rows

  The number of rows waiting to be written in INSERT DELAY queues.

- Not_flushed_key_blocks

  The number of key blocks in the key cache that have changed but haven't yet been flushed to disk.

- Open_files

  The number of files that are open.

- Open_streams

  The number of streams that are open (used mainly for logging).

- Open_tables

  The number of tables that are open.

- Opened_tables

  The number of tables that have been opened. If Opened_tables is big, your table_cache value is probably too small.

- Qcache_free_blocks

  The number of free memory blocks in query cache.

- Qcache_free_memory

  The amount of free memory for query cache.

- Qcache_hits

  The number of cache hits.

- Qcache_inserts

  The number of queries added to the cache.

- Qcache_lowmem_prunes

  The number of queries that were deleted from the cache because of low memory.

- `Qcache_not_cached`

  The number of non-cached queries (not cachable, or due to `query_cache_type`).

- `Qcache_queries_in_cache`

  The number of queries registered in the cache.

- `Qcache_total_blocks`

  The total number of blocks in the query cache.

- `Questions`

  The number of queries that have been sent to the server.

- `Rpl_status`

  The status of failsafe replication (not yet implemented).

- `Select_full_join`

  The number of joins that do not use indexes. If this value is not 0, you should carefully check the indexes of your tables. This variable was added in MySQL 3.23.25.

- `Select_full_range_join`

  The number of joins that used a range search on a reference table. This variable was added in MySQL 3.23.25.

- `Select_range`

  The number of joins that used ranges on the first table. (It's normally not critical even if this is big.) This variable was added in MySQL 3.23.25.

- `Select_range_check`

  The number of joins without keys that check for key usage after each row. (If this is not 0, you should carefully check the indexes of your tables.) This variable was added in MySQL 3.23.25.

- `Select_scan`

  The number of joins that did a full scan of the first table. This variable was added in MySQL 3.23.25.

- `Slave_open_temp_tables`

  The number of temporary tables currently open by the slave SQL thread. This variable was added in MySQL 3.23.29.

- `Slave_running`

  This is `ON` if the server is a slave that is connected to a master. This variable was added in MySQL 3.23.16.

- `Slow_launch_threads`

  The number of threads that have taken more than `slow_launch_time` seconds to create. This variable was added in MySQL 3.23.15.

- Slow_queries

  The number of queries that have taken more than long_query_time seconds. See Section 4.8.5, "The Slow Query Log."

- Sort_merge_passes

  The number of merge passes the sort algorithm has had to do. If this value is large, you should consider increasing the value of the sort_buffer_size system variable. This variable was added in MySQL 3.23.28.

- Sort_range

  The number of sorts that were done with ranges. This variable was added in MySQL 3.23.25.

- Sort_rows

  The number of sorted rows. This variable was added in MySQL 3.23.25.

- Sort_scan

  The number of sorts that were done by scanning the table. This variable was added in MySQL 3.23.25.

- Ssl_*xxx*

  Variables used for SSL connections. These variables were added in MySQL 4.0.0.

- Table_locks_immediate

  The number of times that a table lock was acquired immediately. This variable was added as of MySQL 3.23.33.

- Table_locks_waited

  The number of times that a table lock could not be acquired immediately and a wait was needed. If this is high, and you have performance problems, you should first optimize your queries, and then either split your table or tables or use replication. This variable was added as of MySQL 3.23.33.

- Threads_cached

  The number of threads in the thread cache. This variable was added in MySQL 3.23.17.

- Threads_connected

  The number of currently open connections.

- Threads_created

  The number of threads created to handle connections. If Threads_created is big, you may want to increase the thread_cache_size value. The cache hit rate can be calculated as Threads_created/Connections. This variable was added in MySQL 3.23.31.

- Threads_running

  The number of threads that are not sleeping.

- Uptime

  The number of seconds the server has been up.

4.3 General Security Issues

This section describes some general security issues to be aware of and what you can do to make your MySQL installation more secure against attack or misuse. For information specifically about the access control system that MySQL uses for setting up user accounts and checking database access, see Section 4.4, "The MySQL Access Privilege System."

4.3.1 General Security Guidelines

Anyone using MySQL on a computer connected to the Internet should read this section to avoid the most common security mistakes.

In discussing security, we emphasize the necessity of fully protecting the entire server host (not just the MySQL server) against all types of applicable attacks: eavesdropping, altering, playback, and denial of service. We do not cover all aspects of availability and fault tolerance here.

MySQL uses security based on Access Control Lists (ACLs) for all connections, queries, and other operations that users can attempt to perform. There is also some support for SSL-encrypted connections between MySQL clients and servers. Many of the concepts discussed here are not specific to MySQL at all; the same general ideas apply to almost all applications.

When running MySQL, follow these guidelines whenever possible:

- **Do not ever give anyone (except MySQL root accounts) access to the user table in the mysql database!** This is critical. **The encrypted password is the real password in MySQL.** Anyone who knows the password that is listed in the user table and has access to the host listed for the account **can easily log in as that user**.

- Learn the MySQL access privilege system. The GRANT and REVOKE statements are used for controlling access to MySQL. Do not grant any more privileges than necessary. Never grant privileges to all hosts.

  Checklist:

  - Try mysql -u root. If you are able to connect successfully to the server without being asked for a password, you have problems. Anyone can connect to your MySQL server as the MySQL root user with full privileges! Review the MySQL installation instructions, paying particular attention to the information about setting a root password. See Section 2.4.5, "Securing the Initial MySQL Accounts."

  - Use the SHOW GRANTS statement and check to see who has access to what. Then use the REVOKE statement to remove those privileges that are not necessary.

- Do not store any plain-text passwords in your database. If your computer becomes compromised, the intruder can take the full list of passwords and use them. Instead, use MD5(), SHA1(), or some other one-way hashing function.

- Do not choose passwords from dictionaries. There are special programs to break them. Even passwords like "xfish98" are very bad. Much better is "duag98" which contains the same word "fish" but typed one key to the left on a standard QWERTY keyboard. Another method is to use "Mhall" which is taken from the first characters of each word in the sentence "Mary had a little lamb." This is easy to remember and type, but difficult to guess for someone who does not know it.

- Invest in a firewall. This protects you from at least 50% of all types of exploits in any software. Put MySQL behind the firewall or in a demilitarized zone (DMZ).

  Checklist:

  - Try to scan your ports from the Internet using a tool such as nmap. MySQL uses port 3306 by default. This port should not be accessible from untrusted hosts. Another simple way to check whether or not your MySQL port is open is to try the following command from some remote machine, where *server_host* is the host on which your MySQL server runs:

    ```
    shell> telnet server_host 3306
    ```

    If you get a connection and some garbage characters, the port is open, and should be closed on your firewall or router, unless you really have a good reason to keep it open. If telnet just hangs or the connection is refused, everything is OK; the port is blocked.

- Do not trust any data entered by users of your applications. They can try to trick your code by entering special or escaped character sequences in Web forms, URLs, or whatever application you have built. Be sure that your application remains secure if a user enters something like "; DROP DATABASE mysql;". This is an extreme example, but large security leaks and data loss might occur as a result of hackers using similar techniques, if you do not prepare for them.

  A common mistake is to protect only string data values. Remember to check numeric data as well. If an application generates a query such as SELECT * FROM table WHERE ID=234 when a user enters the value 234, the user can enter the value 234 OR 1=1 to cause the application to generate the query SELECT * FROM table WHERE ID=234 OR 1=1. As a result, the server retrieves every record in the table. This exposes every record and causes excessive server load. The simplest way to protect from this type of attack is to use apostrophes around the numeric constants: SELECT * FROM table WHERE ID='234'. If the user enters extra information, it all becomes part of the string. In numeric context, MySQL automatically converts this string to a number and strips any trailing non-numeric characters from it.

  Sometimes people think that if a database contains only publicly available data, it need not be protected. This is incorrect. Even if it is allowable to display any record in the database, you should still protect against denial of service attacks (for example, those that are based on the technique in the preceding paragraph that causes the server to waste resources). Otherwise, your server becomes unresponsive to legitimate users.

Checklist:

- Try to enter '' and '"' in all your Web forms. If you get any kind of MySQL error, investigate the problem right away.

- Try to modify any dynamic URLs by adding %22 ('"'), %23 ('#'), and %27 ('') in the URL.

- Try to modify data types in dynamic URLs from numeric ones to character ones containing characters from previous examples. Your application should be safe against this and similar attacks.

- Try to enter characters, spaces, and special symbols rather than numbers in numeric fields. Your application should remove them before passing them to MySQL or else generate an error. Passing unchecked values to MySQL is very dangerous!

- Check data sizes before passing them to MySQL.

- Consider having your application connect to the database using a different username than the one you use for administrative purposes. Do not give your applications any access privileges they do not need.

- Many application programming interfaces provide a means of escaping special characters in data values. Properly used, this prevents application users from entering values that cause the application to generate statements that have a different effect than you intend:

  - MySQL C API: Use the `mysql_real_escape_string()` API call.

  - MySQL++: Use the `escape` and `quote` modifiers for query streams.

  - PHP: Use the `mysql_escape_string()` function, which is based on the function of the same name in the MySQL C API. Prior to PHP 4.0.3, use `addslashes()` instead.

  - Perl DBI: Use the `quote()` method or use placeholders.

  - Java JDBC: Use a `PreparedStatement` object and placeholders.

  Other programming interfaces might have similar capabilities.

- Do not transmit plain (unencrypted) data over the Internet. This information is accessible to everyone who has the time and ability to intercept it and use it for their own purposes. Instead, use an encrypted protocol such as SSL or SSH. MySQL supports internal SSL connections as of Version 4.0.0. SSH port-forwarding can be used to create an encrypted (and compressed) tunnel for the communication.

- Learn to use the `tcpdump` and `strings` utilities. For most cases, you can check whether MySQL data streams are unencrypted by issuing a command like the following:

```
shell> tcpdump -l -i eth0 -w - src or dst port 3306 | strings
```

(This works under Linux and should work with small modifications under other systems.) Warning: If you do not see plaintext data, this doesn't always mean that the information actually is encrypted. If you need high security, you should consult with a security expert.

4.3.2 Making MySQL Secure Against Attackers

When you connect to a MySQL server, you should use a password. The password is not transmitted in clear text over the connection. Password handling during the client connection sequence was upgraded in MySQL 4.1.1 to be very secure. If you are using an older version of MySQL, or are still using pre-4.1.1-style passwords, the encryption algorithm is less strong and with some effort a clever attacker who can sniff the traffic between the client and the server can crack the password. (See Section 4.4.9, "Password Hashing in MySQL 4.1," for a discussion of the different password handling methods.) If the connection between the client and the server goes through an untrusted network, you should use an SSH tunnel to encrypt the communication.

All other information is transferred as text that can be read by anyone who is able to watch the connection. If you are concerned about this, you can use the compressed protocol (in MySQL 3.22 and above) to make traffic much more difficult to decipher. To make the connection even more secure, you should use SSH to get an encrypted TCP/IP connection between a MySQL server and a MySQL client. You can find an Open Source SSH client at http://www.openssh.org/, and a commercial SSH client at http://www.ssh.com/.

If you are using MySQL 4.0 or newer, you can also use internal OpenSSL support. See Section 4.5.7, "Using Secure Connections."

To make a MySQL system secure, you should strongly consider the following suggestions:

- Use passwords for all MySQL users. A client program does not necessarily know the identity of the person running it. It is common for client/server applications that the user can specify any username to the client program. For example, anyone can use the mysql program to connect as any other person simply by invoking it as mysql -u other_user db_name if other_user has no password. If all users have a password, connecting using another user's account becomes much more difficult.

  To change the password for a user, use the SET PASSWORD statement. It is also possible to update the user table in the mysql database directly. For example, to change the password of all MySQL accounts that have a username of root, do this:

  ```
  shell> mysql -u root
  mysql> UPDATE mysql.user SET Password=PASSWORD('newpwd')
      -> WHERE User='root';
  mysql> FLUSH PRIVILEGES;
  ```

- Don't run the MySQL server as the Unix root user. This is very dangerous, because any user with the FILE privilege will be able to create files as root (for example, ~root/.bashrc). To prevent this, mysqld refuses to run as root unless that is specified explicitly using a --user=root option.

  mysqld can be run as an ordinary unprivileged user instead. You can also create a separate Unix account named mysql to make everything even more secure. Use the account only for administering MySQL. To start mysqld as another Unix user, add a user option that specifies the username to the [mysqld] group of the /etc/my.cnf option file or the my.cnf option file in the server's data directory. For example:

```
[mysqld]
user=mysql
```

This causes the server to start as the designated user whether you start it manually or by using mysqld_safe or mysql.server. For more details, see Section A.3.2, "How to Run MySQL as a Normal User."

Running mysql as a Unix user other than root does not mean that you need to change the root username in the user table. Usernames for MySQL accounts have nothing to do with usernames for Unix accounts.

- Don't allow the use of symlinks to tables. (This can be disabled with the --skip-symbolic-links option.) This is especially important if you run mysqld as root, because anyone that has write access to the server's data directory then could delete any file in the system! See Section 6.6.1.2, "Using Symbolic Links for Tables on Unix."

- Make sure that the only Unix user with read or write privileges in the database directories is the user that mysqld runs as.

- Don't grant the PROCESS or SUPER privilege to non-administrative users. The output of mysqladmin processlist shows the text of the currently executing queries, so any user who is allowed to execute that command might be able to see if another user issues an UPDATE user SET password=PASSWORD('not_secure') query.

    mysqld reserves an extra connection for users who have the SUPER privilege (PROCESS before MySQL 4.0.2), so that a MySQL root user can log in and check server activity even if all normal connections are in use.

    The SUPER privilege can be used to terminate client connections, change server operation by changing the value of system variables, and control replication servers.

- Don't grant the FILE privilege to non-administrative users. Any user that has this privilege can write a file anywhere in the filesystem with the privileges of the mysqld daemon! To make this a bit safer, files generated with SELECT ... INTO OUTFILE will not overwrite existing files and are writable by everyone.

    The FILE privilege may also be used to read any file that is world-readable or accessible to the Unix user that the server runs as. With this privilege, you can read any file into a database table. This could be abused, for example, by using LOAD DATA to load /etc/passwd into a table, which then can be displayed with SELECT.

- If you don't trust your DNS, you should use IP numbers rather than hostnames in the grant tables. In any case, you should be very careful about creating grant table entries using hostname values that contain wildcards!

- If you want to restrict the number of connections allowed to a single account, you can do so by setting the max_user_connections variable in mysqld. The GRANT statement also supports resource control options for limiting the extent of server use allowed to an account.

4.3.3 Startup Options for `mysqld` Concerning Security

The following `mysqld` options affect security:

- `--local-infile[={0|1}]`

  If you start the server with `--local-infile=0`, clients cannot use `LOCAL` in `LOAD DATA` statements. See Section 4.3.4, "Security Issues with `LOAD DATA LOCAL`."

- `--safe-show-database`

  With this option, the `SHOW DATABASES` statement displays the names of only those databases for which the user has some kind of privilege. As of MySQL 4.0.2, this option is deprecated and doesn't do anything (it is enabled by default), because there is now a `SHOW DATABASES` privilege that can be used to control access to database names on a per-account basis.

- `--safe-user-create`

  If this is enabled, a user cannot create new users with the `GRANT` statement unless the user has the `INSERT` privilege for the `mysql.user` table. If you want a user to have the ability to create new users with those privileges that the user has right to grant, you should grant the user the following privilege:

  ```
  mysql> GRANT INSERT(user) ON mysql.user TO 'user_name'@'host_name';
  ```

  This will ensure that the user can't change any privilege columns directly, but has to use the `GRANT` statement to give privileges to other users.

- `--secure-auth`

  Disallow authentication for accounts that have old (pre-4.1) passwords. This option is available as of MySQL 4.1.1.

- `--skip-grant-tables`

  This option causes the server not to use the privilege system at all. This gives everyone *full access* to all databases! (You can tell a running server to start using the grant tables again by executing a `mysqladmin flush-privileges` or `mysqladmin reload` command, or by issuing a `FLUSH PRIVILEGES` statement.)

- `--skip-name-resolve`

  Hostnames are not resolved. All `Host` column values in the grant tables must be IP numbers or `localhost`.

- `--skip-networking`

  Don't allow TCP/IP connections over the network. All connections to `mysqld` must be made via Unix socket files. This option is unsuitable when using a MySQL version prior to 3.23.27 with the MIT-pthreads package, because Unix socket files were not supported by MIT-pthreads at that time.

- `--skip-show-database`

  With this option, the SHOW DATABASES statement is allowed only to users who have the SHOW DATABASES privilege, and the statement displays all database names. Without this option, SHOW DATABASES is allowed to all users, but displays each database name only if the user has the SHOW DATABASES privilege or some privilege for the database.

4.3.4 Security Issues with LOAD DATA LOCAL

The LOAD DATA statement can load a file that is located on the server host, or it can load a file that is located on the client host when the LOCAL keyword is specified.

There are two potential security issues with supporting the LOCAL version of LOAD DATA statements:

- The transfer of the file from the client host to the server host is initiated by the MySQL server. In theory, a patched server could be built that would tell the client program to transfer a file of the server's choosing rather than the file named by the client in the LOAD DATA statement. Such a server could access any file on the client host to which the client user has read access.

- In a Web environment where the clients are connecting from a Web server, a user could use LOAD DATA LOCAL to read any files that the Web server process has read access to (assuming that a user could run any command against the SQL server). In this environment, the client with respect to the MySQL server actually is the Web server, not the program being run by the user connecting to the Web server.

To deal with these problems, we changed how LOAD DATA LOCAL is handled as of MySQL 3.23.49 and MySQL 4.0.2 (4.0.13 on Windows):

- By default, all MySQL clients and libraries in binary distributions are compiled with the `--enable-local-infile` option, to be compatible with MySQL 3.23.48 and before.

- If you build MySQL from source but don't use the `--enable-local-infile` option to configure, LOAD DATA LOCAL cannot be used by any client unless it is written explicitly to invoke `mysql_options(... MYSQL_OPT_LOCAL_INFILE, 0)`.

- You can disable all LOAD DATA LOCAL commands from the server side by starting `mysqld` with the `--local-infile=0` option.

- For the `mysql` command-line client, LOAD DATA LOCAL can be enabled by specifying the `--local-infile[=1]` option, or disabled with the `--local-infile=0` option. Similarly, for `mysqlimport`, the `--local` or `-L` option enables local data file loading. In any case, successful use of a local loading operation requires that the server is enabled to allow it.

- If LOAD DATA LOCAL INFILE is disabled, either in the server or the client, a client that attempts to issue such a statement receives the following error message:

  `ERROR 1148: The used command is not allowed with this MySQL version`

4.4 The MySQL Access Privilege System

MySQL has an advanced but non-standard security/privilege system. This section describes how it works.

4.4.1 What the Privilege System Does

The primary function of the MySQL privilege system is to authenticate a user connecting from a given host, and to associate that user with privileges on a database such as SELECT, INSERT, UPDATE, and DELETE.

Additional functionality includes the ability to have an anonymous user and to grant privileges for MySQL-specific functions such as LOAD DATA INFILE and administrative operations.

4.4.2 How the Privilege System Works

The MySQL privilege system ensures that all users may perform only the operations allowed to them. As a user, when you connect to a MySQL server, your identity is determined by *the host from which you connect* and *the username you specify*. The system grants privileges according to your identity and *what you want to do*.

MySQL considers both your hostname and username in identifying you because there is little reason to assume that a given username belongs to the same person everywhere on the Internet. For example, the user joe who connects from office.com need not be the same person as the user joe who connects from elsewhere.com. MySQL handles this by allowing you to distinguish users on different hosts that happen to have the same name: You can grant joe one set of privileges for connections from office.com, and a different set of privileges for connections from elsewhere.com.

MySQL access control involves two stages:

- Stage 1: The server checks whether you are even allowed to connect.
- Stage 2: Assuming that you can connect, the server checks each statement you issue to see whether you have sufficient privileges to perform it. For example, if you try to select rows from a table in a database or drop a table from the database, the server verifies that you have the SELECT privilege for the table or the DROP privilege for the database.

If your privileges are changed (either by yourself or someone else) while you are connected, those changes will not necessarily take effect immediately for the next statement you issue. See Section 4.4.7, "When Privilege Changes Take Effect," for details.

The server stores privilege information in the grant tables of the mysql database (that is, in the database named mysql). The MySQL server reads the contents of these tables into memory when it starts and re-reads them under the circumstances indicated in Section 4.4.7, "When Privilege Changes Take Effect." Access-control decisions are based on the in-memory copies of the grant tables.

Normally, you manipulate the contents of the grant tables indirectly by using the GRANT and REVOKE statements to set up accounts and control the privileges available to each one. The discussion here describes the underlying structure of the grant tables and how the server uses their contents when interacting with clients.

The server uses the user, db, and host tables in the mysql database at both stages of access control. The columns in these grant tables are shown here:

Table Name	user	db	host
SCOPE COLUMNS			
	Host	Host	Host
	User	Db	Db
	Password	User	
PRIVILEGE COLUMNS			
	Select_priv	Select_priv	Select_priv
	Insert_priv	Insert_priv	Insert_priv
	Update_priv	Update_priv	Update_priv
	Delete_priv	Delete_priv	Delete_priv
	Index_priv	Index_priv	Index_priv
	Alter_priv	Alter_priv	Alter_priv
	Create_priv	Create_priv	Create_priv
	Drop_priv	Drop_priv	Drop_priv
	Grant_priv	Grant_priv	Grant_priv
	References_priv	References_priv	References_priv
	Reload_priv		
	Shutdown_priv		
	Process_priv		
	File_priv		
	Show_db_priv		
	Super_priv		
	Create_tmp_table_priv	Create_tmp_table_priv	Create_tmp_table_priv
	Lock_tables_priv	Lock_tables_priv	Lock_tables_priv
	Execute_priv		
	Repl_slave_priv		
	Repl_client_priv		
	ssl_type		
	ssl_cipher		
	x509_issuer		

Table Name	user	db	host

PRIVILEGE COLUMNS

```
        x509_subject
        max_questions
        max_updates
        max_connections
```

During the second stage of access control (request verification), the server may, if the request involves tables, additionally consult the `tables_priv` and `columns_priv` tables that provide finer control at the table and column levels. The columns in these tables are shown here:

Table Name	tables_priv	columns_priv

SCOPE COLUMNS

```
        Host            Host
        Db              Db
        User            User
        Table_name      Table_name
                        Column_name
```

PRIVILEGE COLUMNS

```
        Table_priv      Column_priv
        Column_priv
```

OTHER COLUMNS

```
        Timestamp       Timestamp
        Grantor
```

The `Timestamp` and `Grantor` columns currently are unused and are discussed no further here.

Each grant table contains scope columns and privilege columns:

- Scope columns determine the scope of each entry (row) in the table; that is, the context in which the entry applies. For example, a `user` table entry with `Host` and `User` values of `'thomas.loc.gov'` and `'bob'` would be used for authenticating connections made to the server from the host `thomas.loc.gov` by a client that specifies a username of `bob`. Similarly, a `db` table entry with `Host`, `User`, and `Db` column values of `'thomas.loc.gov'`, `'bob'` and `'reports'` would be used when `bob` connects from the host `thomas.loc.gov` to access the `reports` database. The `tables_priv` and `columns_priv` tables contain scope columns indicating tables or table/column combinations to which each entry applies.

- Privilege columns indicate the privileges granted by a table entry; that is, what operations can be performed. The server combines the information in the various grant tables to form a complete description of a user's privileges. The rules used to do this are described in Section 4.4.6, "Access Control, Stage 2: Request Verification."

Scope columns contain strings. They are declared as shown here; the default value for each is the empty string:

Column Name	Type
Host	CHAR(60)
User	CHAR(16)
Password	CHAR(16)
Db	CHAR(64)
Table_name	CHAR(60)
Column_name	CHAR(60)

Before MySQL 3.23, the Db column is CHAR(32) in some tables and CHAR(60) in others.

For access-checking purposes, comparisons of Host values are case-insensitive. User, Password, Db, and Table_name values are case-sensitive. Column_name values are case-insensitive in MySQL 3.22.12 or later.

In the user, db, and host tables, each privilege is listed in a separate column that is declared as ENUM('N','Y') DEFAULT 'N'. In other words, each privilege can be disabled or enabled, with the default being disabled.

In the tables_priv and columns_priv tables, the privilege columns are declared as SET columns. Values in these columns can contain any combination of the privileges controlled by the table:

Table Name	Column Name	Possible Set Elements
tables_priv	Table_priv	'Select', 'Insert', 'Update', 'Delete', 'Create', 'Drop', 'Grant', 'References', 'Index', 'Alter'
tables_priv	Column_priv	'Select', 'Insert', 'Update', 'References'
columns_priv	Column_priv	'Select', 'Insert', 'Update', 'References'

Briefly, the server uses the grant tables as follows:

- The user table scope columns determine whether to reject or allow incoming connections. For allowed connections, any privileges granted in the user table indicate the user's global (superuser) privileges. These privileges apply to *all* databases on the server.
- The db table scope columns determine which users can access which databases from which hosts. The privilege columns determine which operations are allowed. A privilege granted at the database level applies to the database and to all its tables.
- The host table is used in conjunction with the db table when you want a given db table entry to apply to several hosts. For example, if you want a user to be able to use a

database from several hosts in your network, leave the Host value empty in the user's db table entry, then populate the host table with an entry for each of those hosts. This mechanism is described in more detail in Section 4.4.6, "Access Control, Stage 2: Request Verification."

Note: The host table is not affected by the GRANT and REVOKE statements. Most MySQL installations need not use this table at all.

- The tables_priv and columns_priv tables are similar to the db table, but are more fine-grained: They apply at the table and column levels rather than at the database level. A privilege granted at the table level applies to the table and to all its columns. A privilege granted at the column level applies only to a specific column.

Administrative privileges (such as RELOAD or SHUTDOWN) are specified only in the user table. This is because administrative operations are operations on the server itself and are not database-specific, so there is no reason to list these privileges in the other grant tables. In fact, to determine whether you can perform an administrative operation, the server need consult only the user table.

The FILE privilege also is specified only in the user table. It is not an administrative privilege as such, but your ability to read or write files on the server host is independent of the database you are accessing.

The mysqld server reads the contents of the grant tables into memory when it starts. You can tell it to re-read the tables by issuing a FLUSH PRIVILEGES statement or executing a mysqladmin flush-privileges or mysqladmin reload command. Changes to the grant tables take effect as indicated in Section 4.4.7, "When Privilege Changes Take Effect."

When you modify the contents of the grant tables, it is a good idea to make sure that your changes set up privileges the way you want. One way to check the privileges for a given account is to use the SHOW GRANTS statement. For example, to determine the privileges that are granted to an account with Host and User values of pc84.example.com and bob, issue this statement:

```
mysql> SHOW GRANTS FOR 'bob'@'pc84.example.com';
```

A useful diagnostic tool is the mysqlaccess script, which Yves Carlier has provided for the MySQL distribution. Invoke mysqlaccess with the --help option to find out how it works. Note that mysqlaccess checks access using only the user, db, and host tables. It does not check table or column privileges specified in the tables_priv or columns_priv tables.

For additional help in diagnosing privilege-related problems, see Section 4.4.8, "Causes of Access denied Errors." For general advice on security issues, see Section 4.3, "General Security Issues."

4.4.3 Privileges Provided by MySQL

Information about account privileges is stored in the user, db, host, tables_priv, and columns_priv tables in the mysql database. The MySQL server reads the contents of these tables into memory when it starts and re-reads them under the circumstances indicated in Section 4.4.7, "When Privilege Changes Take Effect." Access-control decisions are based on the in-memory copies of the grant tables.

The names used in this manual to refer to the privileges provided by MySQL are shown in the following table, along with the table column name associated with each privilege in the grant tables and the context in which the privilege applies. Further information about the meaning of each privilege may be found in the *MySQL Language Reference*.

Privilege	Column	Context
ALTER	Alter_priv	tables
DELETE	Delete_priv	tables
INDEX	Index_priv	tables
INSERT	Insert_priv	tables
SELECT	Select_priv	tables
UPDATE	Update_priv	tables
CREATE	Create_priv	databases, tables, or indexes
DROP	Drop_priv	databases or tables
GRANT	Grant_priv	databases or tables
REFERENCES	References_priv	databases or tables
CREATE TEMPORARY TABLES	Create_tmp_table_priv	server administration
EXECUTE	Execute_priv	server administration
FILE	File_priv	file access on server host
LOCK TABLES	Lock_tables_priv	server administration
PROCESS	Process_priv	server administration
RELOAD	Reload_priv	server administration
REPLICATION CLIENT	Repl_client_priv	server administration
REPLICATION SLAVE	Repl_slave_priv	server administration
SHOW DATABASES	Show_db_priv	server administration
SHUTDOWN	Shutdown_priv	server administration
SUPER	Super_priv	server administration

The CREATE TEMPORARY TABLES, EXECUTE, LOCK TABLES, REPLICATION CLIENT, REPLICATION SLAVE, SHOW DATABASES, and SUPER privileges were added in MySQL 4.0.2.

The EXECUTE and REFERENCES privileges currently are unused.

The SELECT, INSERT, UPDATE, and DELETE privileges allow you to perform operations on rows in existing tables in a database.

SELECT statements require the SELECT privilege only if they actually retrieve rows from a table. Some SELECT statements do not access tables and can be executed without permission for any database. For example, you can use the `mysql` client as a simple calculator to evaluate expressions that make no reference to tables:

```
mysql> SELECT 1+1;
mysql> SELECT PI()*2;
```

The CREATE and DROP privileges allow you to create new databases and tables, or to drop (remove) existing databases and tables. If you grant the DROP privilege for the `mysql` database to a user, that user can drop the database in which the MySQL access privileges are stored!

The INDEX privilege allows you to create or drop (remove) indexes. INDEX applies to existing tables. If you have the CREATE privilege for a table, you can include index definitions in the CREATE TABLE statement.

The ALTER privilege allows you to use ALTER TABLE to change the structure of or rename tables.

The GRANT privilege allows you to give to other users those privileges that you yourself possess.

The FILE privilege gives you permission to read and write files on the server host using the LOAD DATA INFILE and SELECT ... INTO OUTFILE statements. A user who has the FILE privilege can read any file on the server host that is either world-readable or readable by the MySQL server. (This implies the user can read any file in any database directory, because the server can access any of those files.) The FILE privilege also allows the user to create new files in any directory where the MySQL server has write access. Existing files cannot be overwritten.

The remaining privileges are used for administrative operations. Many of them can be performed by using the `mysqladmin` program or by issuing SQL statements. The following table shows which `mysqladmin` commands each administrative privilege allows you to execute:

Privilege	Commands Permitted to Privilege Holders
RELOAD	flush-hosts, flush-logs, flush-privileges, flush-status, flush-tables, flush-threads, refresh, reload
SHUTDOWN	shutdown
PROCESS	processlist
SUPER	kill

The `reload` command tells the server to re-read the grant tables into memory. `flush-privileges` is a synonym for `reload`. The `refresh` command closes and reopens the log files and flushes all tables. The other `flush-xxx` commands perform functions similar to `refresh`, but are more specific and may be preferable in some instances. For example, if you want to flush just the log files, `flush-logs` is a better choice than `refresh`.

The `shutdown` command shuts down the server. This command can be issued only from `mysqladmin`. There is no corresponding SQL statement.

The `processlist` command displays information about the threads executing within the server (that is, about the statements being executed by clients associated with other accounts). The `kill` command terminates server threads. You can always display or kill your own threads, but you need the `PROCESS` privilege to display threads initiated by other users and the `SUPER` privilege to kill them. Prior to MySQL 4.0.2 when `SUPER` was introduced, the `PROCESS` privilege controls the ability to both see and terminate threads for other clients.

The `CREATE TEMPORARY TABLES` privilege allows the use of the keyword `TEMPORARY` in `CREATE TABLE` statements.

The `LOCK TABLES` privilege allows the use of explicit `LOCK TABLES` statements to lock tables for which you have the `SELECT` privilege. This includes the use of write locks, which prevents anyone else from reading the locked table.

The `REPLICATION CLIENT` privilege allows the use of `SHOW MASTER STATUS` and `SHOW SLAVE STATUS`.

The `REPLICATION SLAVE` privilege should be granted to accounts that are used by slave servers when they connect to the current server as their master. Without this privilege, the slave cannot request updates that have been made to databases on the master server.

The `SHOW DATABASES` privilege allows the account to see database names by issuing the `SHOW DATABASE` statement. Accounts that do not have this privilege see only databases for which they have some privileges, and cannot use the statement at all if the server was started with the `--skip-show-database` option.

It is a good idea in general to grant privileges to only those accounts that need them, but you should exercise particular caution in granting administrative privileges:

- The `GRANT` privilege allows users to give their privileges to other users. Two users with different privileges and with the `GRANT` privilege are able to combine privileges.
- The `ALTER` privilege may be used to subvert the privilege system by renaming tables.
- The `FILE` privilege can be abused to read into a database table any files that the MySQL server can read on the server host. This includes all world-readable files and files in the server's data directory. The table can then be accessed using `SELECT` to transfer its contents to the client host.
- The `SHUTDOWN` privilege can be abused to deny service to other users entirely by terminating the server.
- The `PROCESS` privilege can be used to view the plain text of currently executing queries, including queries that set or change passwords.
- The `SUPER` privilege can be used to terminate other clients or change how the server operates.
- Privileges granted for the `mysql` database itself can be used to change passwords and other access privilege information. Passwords are stored encrypted, so a malicious user cannot simply read them to know the plain text password. However, a user with write access to the user table `Password` column can change an account's password, and then connect to the MySQL server using that account.

There are some things that you cannot do with the MySQL privilege system:

- You cannot explicitly specify that a given user should be denied access. That is, you cannot explicitly match a user and then refuse the connection.

- You cannot specify that a user has privileges to create or drop tables in a database but not to create or drop the database itself.

4.4.4 Connecting to the MySQL Server

MySQL client programs generally expect you to specify connection parameters when you want to access a MySQL server:

- The name of the host where the MySQL server is running
- Your username
- Your password

For example, the `mysql` client can be started as follows from a command-line prompt (indicated here by `shell>`):

```
shell> mysql -h host_name -u user_name -pyour_pass
```

Alternate forms of the -h, -u, and -p options are `--host=host_name`, `--user=user_name`, and `--password=your_pass`. Note that there is *no space* between -p or --password= and the password following it.

If you use a -p or --password option but do not specify the password value, the client program will prompt you to enter the password. The password is not displayed as you enter it. This is more secure than giving the password on the command line. Any user on your system may be able to see a password specified on the command line by executing a command such as `ps auxww`. See Section 4.5.6, "Keeping Your Password Secure."

MySQL client programs use default values for any connection parameter option that you do not specify:

- The default hostname is `localhost`.
- The default username is `ODBC` on Windows and your Unix login name on Unix.
- No password is supplied if -p is missing.

Thus, for a Unix user with a login name of `joe`, all of the following commands are equivalent:

```
shell> mysql -h localhost -u joe
shell> mysql -h localhost
shell> mysql -u joe
shell> mysql
```

Other MySQL clients behave similarly.

You can specify different default values to be used when you make a connection so that you need not enter them on the command line each time you invoke a client program. This can be done in a couple of ways:

- You can specify connection parameters in the [client] section of an option file. The relevant section of the file might look like this:

```
[client]
host=host_name
user=user_name
password=your_pass
```

  Option files are discussed further in Section 3.3.2, "Using Option Files."

- You can specify some connection parameters using environment variables. The host can be specified for mysql using MYSQL_HOST. The MySQL username can be specified using USER (this is for Windows and NetWare only). The password can be specified using MYSQL_PWD, although this is insecure; see Section 4.5.6, "Keeping Your Password Secure." For a list of variables, see Appendix B, "Environment Variables."

4.4.5 Access Control, Stage 1: Connection Verification

When you attempt to connect to a MySQL server, the server accepts or rejects the connection based on your identity and whether you can verify your identity by supplying the correct password. If not, the server denies access to you completely. Otherwise, the server accepts the connection, then enters Stage 2 and waits for requests.

Your identity is based on two pieces of information:

- The client host from which you connect
- Your MySQL username

Identity checking is performed using the three user table scope columns (Host, User, and Password). The server accepts the connection only if the Host and User columns in some user table record match the client hostname and username, and the client supplies the password specified in that record.

Host values in the user table may be specified as follows:

- A Host value may be a hostname or an IP number, or 'localhost' to indicate the local host.
- You can use the wildcard characters '%' and '_' in Host column values. These have the same meaning as for pattern-matching operations performed with the LIKE operator. For example, a Host value of '%' matches any hostname, whereas a value of '%.mysql.com' matches any host in the mysql.com domain.

- As of MySQL 3.23, for Host values specified as IP numbers, you can specify a netmask indicating how many address bits to use for the network number. For example:

```
mysql> GRANT ALL PRIVILEGES ON db.*
    -> TO david@'192.58.197.0/255.255.255.0';
```

This allows david to connect from any client host having an IP number client_ip for which the following condition is true:

```
client_ip & netmask = host_ip
```

That is, for the GRANT statement just shown:

```
client_ip & 255.255.255.0 = 192.58.197.0
```

IP numbers that satisfy this condition and can connect to the MySQL server are those that lie in the range from 192.58.197.0 to 192.58.197.255.

- A blank Host value in a db table record means that its privileges should be combined with those in the entry in the host table that matches the client hostname. The privileges are combined using an AND (intersection) operation, not OR (union). You can find more information about the host table in Section 4.4.6, "Access Control, Stage 2: Request Verification."

A blank Host value in the other grant tables is the same as '%'.

Because you can use IP wildcard values in the Host column (for example, '144.155.166.%' to match every host on a subnet), someone could try to exploit this capability by naming a host 144.155.166.somewhere.com. To foil such attempts, MySQL disallows matching on hostnames that start with digits and a dot. Thus, if you have a host named something like 1.2.foo.com, its name will never match the Host column of the grant tables. An IP wildcard value can match only IP numbers, not hostnames.

In the User column, wildcard characters are not allowed, but you can specify a blank value, which matches any name. If the user table entry that matches an incoming connection has a blank username, the user is considered to be an anonymous user with no name, not a user with the name that the client actually specified. This means that a blank username is used for all further access checking for the duration of the connection (that is, during Stage 2).

The Password column can be blank. This is not a wildcard and does not mean that any password matches. It means that the user must connect without specifying a password.

Non-blank Password values in the user table represent encrypted passwords. MySQL does not store passwords in plaintext form for anyone to see. Rather, the password supplied by a user who is attempting to connect is encrypted (using the PASSWORD() function). The encrypted password then is used during the connection process when checking whether the password is correct. (This is done without the encrypted password ever traveling over the connection.) From MySQL's point of view, the encrypted password is the REAL password, so you should not give anyone access to it! In particular, don't give non-administrative users read access to the tables in the mysql database!

From version 4.1 on, MySQL employs a stronger authentication method that has better password protection during the connection process than in earlier versions. It is secure even if TCP/IP packets are sniffed or the `mysql` database is captured. Password encryption is discussed further in Section 4.4.9, "Password Hashing in MySQL 4.1."

The following examples show how various combinations of `Host` and `User` values in the `user` table apply to incoming connections:

Host Value	User Value	Connections Matched by Entry
`'thomas.loc.gov'`	`'fred'`	fred, connecting from `thomas.loc.gov`
`'thomas.loc.gov'`	`''`	Any user, connecting from `thomas.loc.gov`
`'%'`	`'fred'`	fred, connecting from any host
`'%'`	`''`	Any user, connecting from any host
`'%.loc.gov'`	`'fred'`	fred, connecting from any host in the `loc.gov` domain
`'x.y.%'`	`'fred'`	fred, connecting from `x.y.net`, `x.y.com`, `x.y.edu`, and so on (this is probably not useful)
`'144.155.166.177'`	`'fred'`	fred, connecting from the host with IP address `144.155.166.177`
`'144.155.166.%'`	`'fred'`	fred, connecting from any host in the `144.155.166` class C subnet
`'144.155.166.0/255.255.255.0'`	`'fred'`	Same as previous example

It is possible for the client hostname and username of an incoming connection to match more than one entry in the `user` table. The preceding set of examples demonstrates this: Several of the entries shown match a connection from `thomas.loc.gov` by `fred`.

When multiple matches are possible, the server must determine which of them to use. It resolves this issue as follows:

- Whenever the server reads the `user` table into memory, it sorts the entries.
- When a client attempts to connect, the server looks through the entries in sorted order.
- The server uses the first entry that matches the client hostname and username.

To see how this works, suppose that the `user` table looks like this:

```
+-----------+----------+-
| Host      | User     | ...
+-----------+----------+-
| %         | root     | ...
| %         | jeffrey  | ...
| localhost | root     | ...
| localhost |          | ...
+-----------+----------+-
```

When the server reads in the table, it orders the entries with the most-specific Host values first. Literal hostnames and IP numbers are the most specific. The pattern '%' means "any host" and is least specific. Entries with the same Host value are ordered with the most-specific User values first (a blank User value means "any user" and is least specific). For the user table just shown, the result after sorting looks like this:

```
+-----------+----------+-
| Host      | User     | ...
+-----------+----------+-
| localhost | root     | ...
| localhost |          | ...
| %         | jeffrey  | ...
| %         | root     | ...
+-----------+----------+-
```

When a client attempts to connect, the server looks through the sorted entries and uses the first match found. For a connection from localhost by jeffrey, two of the entries in the table match: the one with Host and User values of 'localhost' and '', and the one with values of '%' and 'jeffrey'. The 'localhost' entry appears first in sorted order, so that is the one the server uses.

Here is another example. Suppose that the user table looks like this:

```
+----------------+----------+-
| Host           | User     | ...
+----------------+----------+-
| %              | jeffrey  | ...
| thomas.loc.gov |          | ...
+----------------+----------+-
```

The sorted table looks like this:

```
+----------------+----------+-
| Host           | User     | ...
+----------------+----------+-
| thomas.loc.gov |          | ...
| %              | jeffrey  | ...
+----------------+----------+-
```

A connection by jeffrey from thomas.loc.gov is matched by the first entry, whereas a connection by jeffrey from whitehouse.gov is matched by the second.

It is a common misconception to think that, for a given username, all entries that explicitly name that user will be used first when the server attempts to find a match for the connection. This is simply not true. The previous example illustrates this, where a connection from thomas.loc.gov by jeffrey is first matched not by the entry containing 'jeffrey' as the User column value, but by the entry with no username! As a result, jeffrey will be authenticated as an anonymous user, even though he specified a username when connecting.

If you are able to connect to the server, but your privileges are not what you expect, you probably are being authenticated as some other account. To find out what account the server used to authenticate you, use the CURRENT_USER() function. It returns a value in *user_name*@*host_name* format that indicates the User and Host values from the matching user table record. Suppose that jeffrey connects and issues the following query:

```
mysql> SELECT CURRENT_USER();
+----------------+
| CURRENT_USER() |
+----------------+
| @localhost     |
+----------------+
```

The result shown here indicates that the matching user table entry had a blank User column value. In other words, the server is treating jeffrey as an anonymous user.

The CURRENT_USER() function is available as of MySQL 4.0.6. Another thing you can do to diagnose authentication problems is to print out the user table and sort it by hand to see where the first match is being made.

4.4.6 Access Control, Stage 2: Request Verification

Once you establish a connection, the server enters Stage 2 of access control. For each request that comes in on the connection, the server determines what operation you want to perform, then checks whether you have sufficient privileges to do so. This is where the privilege columns in the grant tables come into play. These privileges can come from any of the user, db, host, tables_priv, or columns_priv tables. (You may find it helpful to refer to Section 4.4.2, "How the Privilege System Works," which lists the columns present in each of the grant tables.)

The user table grants privileges that are assigned to you on a global basis and that apply no matter what the current database is. For example, if the user table grants you the DELETE privilege, you can delete rows from any table in any database on the server host! In other words, user table privileges are superuser privileges. It is wise to grant privileges in the user table only to superusers such as database administrators. For other users, you should leave the privileges in the user table set to 'N' and grant privileges at more specific levels only. You can grant privileges for particular databases, tables, or columns.

The db and host tables grant database-specific privileges. Values in the scope columns of these tables can take the following forms:

- The wildcard characters '%' and '_' can be used in the Host and Db columns of either table. These have the same meaning as for pattern-matching operations performed with the LIKE operator. If you want to use either character literally when granting privileges, you must escape it with a backslash. For example, to include '_' character as part of a database name, specify it as '_' in the GRANT statement.

- A '%' Host value in the db table means "any host." A blank Host value in the db table means "consult the host table for further information" (a process that is described later in this section).

- A '%' or blank Host value in the host table means "any host."

- A '%' or blank Db value in either table means "any database."

- A blank User value in either table matches the anonymous user.

The server reads in and sorts the db and host tables at the same time that it reads the user table. The server sorts the db table based on the Host, Db, and User scope columns, and sorts the host table based on the Host and Db scope columns. As with the user table, sorting puts the most-specific values first and least-specific values last, and when the server looks for matching entries, it uses the first match that it finds.

The tables_priv and columns_priv tables grant table-specific and column-specific privileges. Values in the scope columns of these tables can take the following form:

- The wildcard characters '%' and '_' can be used in the Host column of either table. These have the same meaning as for pattern-matching operations performed with the LIKE operator.

- A '%' or blank Host value in either table means "any host."

- The Db, Table_name, and Column_name columns cannot contain wildcards or be blank in either table.

The server sorts the tables_priv and columns_priv tables based on the Host, Db, and User columns. This is similar to db table sorting, but simpler because only the Host column can contain wildcards.

The request verification process is described here. (If you are familiar with the access-checking source code, you will notice that the description here differs slightly from the algorithm used in the code. The description is equivalent to what the code actually does; it differs only to make the explanation simpler.)

For requests that require administrative privileges such as SHUTDOWN or RELOAD, the server checks only the user table entry because that is the only table that specifies administrative privileges. Access is granted if the entry allows the requested operation and denied otherwise. For example, if you want to execute mysqladmin shutdown but your user table entry doesn't grant the SHUTDOWN privilege to you, the server denies access without even checking the db or host tables. (They contain no Shutdown_priv column, so there is no need to do so.)

For database-related requests (INSERT, UPDATE, and so on), the server first checks the user's global (superuser) privileges by looking in the user table entry. If the entry allows the requested operation, access is granted. If the global privileges in the user table are insufficient, the server determines the user's database-specific privileges by checking the db and host tables:

1. The server looks in the db table for a match on the Host, Db, and User columns. The Host and User columns are matched to the connecting user's hostname and MySQL username. The Db column is matched to the database that the user wants to access. If there is no entry for the Host and User, access is denied.

2. If there is a matching db table entry and its Host column is not blank, that entry defines the user's database-specific privileges.

3. If the matching db table entry's Host column is blank, it signifies that the host table enumerates which hosts should be allowed access to the database. In this case, a further lookup is done in the host table to find a match on the Host and Db columns. If no host table entry matches, access is denied. If there is a match, the user's database-specific privileges are computed as the intersection (*not* the union!) of the privileges in the db and host table entries; that is, the privileges that are 'Y' in both entries. (This way you can grant general privileges in the db table entry and then selectively restrict them on a host-by-host basis using the host table entries.)

After determining the database-specific privileges granted by the db and host table entries, the server adds them to the global privileges granted by the user table. If the result allows the requested operation, access is granted. Otherwise, the server successively checks the user's table and column privileges in the tables_priv and columns_priv tables, adds those to the user's privileges, and allows or denies access based on the result.

Expressed in boolean terms, the preceding description of how a user's privileges are calculated may be summarized like this:

```
global privileges
OR (database privileges AND host privileges)
OR table privileges
OR column privileges
```

It may not be apparent why, if the global user entry privileges are initially found to be insufficient for the requested operation, the server adds those privileges to the database, table, and column privileges later. The reason is that a request might require more than one type of privilege. For example, if you execute an INSERT INTO ... SELECT statement, you need both the INSERT and the SELECT privileges. Your privileges might be such that the user table entry grants one privilege and the db table entry grants the other. In this case, you have the necessary privileges to perform the request, but the server cannot tell that from either table by itself; the privileges granted by the entries in both tables must be combined.

The host table is not affected by the GRANT or REVOKE statements, so it is unused in most MySQL installations. If you modify it directly, you can use it for some specialized purposes, such as to maintain a list of secure servers. For example, at TcX, the host table contains a list of all machines on the local network. These are granted all privileges.

You can also use the host table to indicate hosts that are *not* secure. Suppose that you have a machine public.your.domain that is located in a public area that you do not consider secure.

You can allow access to all hosts on your network except that machine by using host table entries like this:

```
+-------------------+----+-
| Host              | Db |  ...
+-------------------+----+-
| public.your.domain | % |  ... (all privileges set to 'N')
| %.your.domain      | % |  ... (all privileges set to 'Y')
+-------------------+----+-
```

Naturally, you should always test your entries in the grant tables (for example, by using SHOW GRANTS or mysqlaccess) to make sure that your access privileges are actually set up the way you think they are.

4.4.7 When Privilege Changes Take Effect

When mysqld starts, all grant table contents are read into memory and become effective for access control at that point.

When the server reloads the grant tables, privileges for existing client connections are affected as follows:

- Table and column privilege changes take effect with the client's next request.
- Database privilege changes take effect at the next USE *db_name* statement.
- Changes to global privileges and passwords take effect the next time the client connects.

If you modify the grant tables using GRANT, REVOKE, or SET PASSWORD, the server notices these changes and reloads the grant tables into memory again immediately.

If you modify the grant tables directly using statements such as INSERT, UPDATE, or DELETE, your changes have no effect on privilege checking until you either restart the server or tell it to reload the tables. To reload the grant tables manually, issue a FLUSH PRIVILEGES statement or execute a mysqladmin flush-privileges or mysqladmin reload command.

If you change the grant tables directly but forget to reload them, your changes will have *no effect* until you restart the server. This may leave you wondering why your changes don't seem to make any difference!

4.4.8 Causes of Access denied Errors

If you encounter problems when you try to connect to the MySQL server, the following items describe some courses of action you can take to correct the problem.

- Make sure that the server is running. If it is not running, you cannot connect to it. For example, if you attempt to connect to the server and see a message such as one of those following, one cause might be that the server is not running:

```
shell> mysql
ERROR 2003: Can't connect to MySQL server on 'host_name' (111)
shell> mysql
ERROR 2002: Can't connect to local MySQL server through socket
'/tmp/mysql.sock' (111)
```

It might also be that the server is running, but you are trying to connect using a TCP/IP port, named pipe, or Unix socket file different from those on which the server is listening. To correct this when you invoke a client program, specify a `--port` option to indicate the proper port, or a `--socket` option to indicate the proper named pipe or Unix socket file.

- The grant tables must be properly set up so that the server can use them for access control. For installations on Windows using a binary distribution or on Linux using a server RPM distribution, the installation process initializes the `mysql` database containing the grant tables. For other MySQL installation types, you should initialize the grant tables manually by running the `mysql_install_db` script. See Section 2.4.2, "Unix Post-Installation Procedures."

  One way to determine whether you need to initialize the grant tables is to look for a `mysql` directory under the data directory. (The data directory normally is named `data` or `var` and is located under your MySQL installation directory.) Make sure that you have a file named `user.MYD` in the `mysql` database directory. If you do not, execute the `mysql_install_db` script. After running this script and starting the server, test the initial privileges by executing this command:

  ```
  shell> mysql -u root test
  ```

  The server should let you connect without error.

- After a fresh installation, you should connect to the server and set up your users and their access permissions:

  ```
  shell> mysql -u root mysql
  ```

  The server should let you connect because the MySQL `root` user has no password initially. That is also a security risk, so setting the password for the `root` accounts is something you should do while you're setting up your other MySQL users. For instructions on setting the initial passwords, see Section 2.4.5, "Securing the Initial MySQL Accounts."

- If you have updated an existing MySQL installation to a newer version, did you run the `mysql_fix_privilege_tables` script? If not, do so. The structure of the grant tables changes occasionally when new capabilities are added, so after an upgrade you should always make sure that your tables have the current structure. For instructions, see Section 2.5.8, "Upgrading the Grant Tables."

- If a client program receives the following error message when it tries to connect, it means that the server expects passwords in a newer format than the client is capable of generating:

```
shell> mysql
Client does not support authentication protocol requested
by server; consider upgrading MySQL client
```

For information on how to deal with this, see Section 4.4.9, "Password Hashing in MySQL 4.1," and Section A.2.3, "Client does not support authentication proto-col."

- If you try to connect as root and get the following error, it means that you don't have an entry in the user table with a User column value of 'root' and that mysqld cannot resolve the hostname for your client:

```
Access denied for user: ''@'unknown' to database mysql
```

In this case, you must restart the server with the --skip-grant-tables option and edit your /etc/hosts or \windows\hosts file to add an entry for your host.

- Remember that client programs will use connection parameters specified in option files or environment variables. If a client program seems to be sending incorrect default con-nection parameters when you don't specify them on the command line, check your environment and any applicable option files. For example, if you get Access denied when you run a client without any options, make sure that you haven't specified an old password in any of your option files!

You can suppress the use of option files by a client program by invoking it with the --no-defaults option. For example:

```
shell> mysqladmin --no-defaults -u root version
```

The option files that clients use are listed in Section 3.3.2, "Using Option Files." Environment variables are listed in Appendix B, "Environment Variables."

- If you get the following error, it means that you are using an incorrect root password:

```
shell> mysqladmin -u root -pxxxx ver
Access denied for user: 'root'@'localhost' (Using password: YES)
```

If the preceding error occurs even when you haven't specified a password, it means that you have an incorrect password listed in some option file. Try the --no-defaults option as described in the previous item.

For information on changing passwords, see Section 4.5.5, "Assigning Account Passwords."

If you have lost or forgotten the root password, you can restart mysqld with --skip-grant-tables to change the password. See Section A.4.1, "How to Reset the Root Password."

- If you change a password by using SET PASSWORD, INSERT, or UPDATE, you must encrypt the password using the PASSWORD() function. If you do not use PASSWORD() for these statements, the password will not work. For example, the following statement sets a password, but fails to encrypt it, so the user will not be able to connect afterward:

```
mysql> SET PASSWORD FOR 'abe'@'host_name' = 'eagle';
```

Instead, set the password like this:

```
mysql> SET PASSWORD FOR 'abe'@'host_name' = PASSWORD('eagle');
```

The PASSWORD() function is unnecessary when you specify a password using the GRANT statement or the mysqladmin password command, both of which automatically use PASSWORD() to encrypt the password. See Section 4.5.5, "Assigning Account Passwords."

- localhost is a synonym for your local hostname, and is also the default host to which clients try to connect if you specify no host explicitly. However, connections to localhost on Unix systems do not work if you are using a MySQL version older than 3.23.27 that uses MIT-pthreads: localhost connections are made using Unix socket files, which were not supported by MIT-pthreads at that time.

  To avoid this problem on such systems, you can use a --host=127.0.0.1 option to name the server host explicitly. This will make a TCP/IP connection to the local mysqld server. You can also use TCP/IP by specifying a --host option that uses the actual hostname of the local host. In this case, the hostname must be specified in a user table entry on the server host, even though you are running the client program on the same host as the server.

- If you get an Access denied error when trying to connect to the database with mysql -u user_name, you may have a problem with the user table. Check this by executing mysql -u root mysql and issuing this SQL statement:

```
mysql> SELECT * FROM user;
```

  The result should include an entry with the Host and User columns matching your computer's hostname and your MySQL username.

- The Access denied error message will tell you who you are trying to log in as, the client host from which you are trying to connect, and whether or not you were using a password. Normally, you should have one entry in the user table that exactly matches the hostname and username that were given in the error message. For example, if you get an error message that contains Using password: NO, it means that you tried to log in without a password.

- If the following error occurs when you try to connect from a host other than the one on which the MySQL server is running, it means that there is no row in the user table with a Host value that matches the client host:

```
Host ... is not allowed to connect to this MySQL server
```

  You can fix this by setting up an account for the combination of client hostname and username that you are using when trying to connect.

If you don't know the IP number or hostname of the machine from which you are connecting, you should put an entry with '%' as the Host column value in the user table and restart mysqld with the --log option on the server machine. After trying to connect from the client machine, the information in the MySQL log will indicate how you really did connect. (Then change the '%' in the user table entry to the actual hostname that shows up in the log. Otherwise, you'll have a system that is insecure because it allows connections from any host for the given username.)

On Linux, another reason that this error might occur is that you are using a binary MySQL version that is compiled with a different version of the glibc library than the one you are using. In this case, you should either upgrade your operating system or glibc, or download a source distribution of MySQL version and compile it yourself. A source RPM is normally trivial to compile and install, so this isn't a big problem.

- If you specify a hostname when trying to connect, but get an error message where the hostname is not shown or is an IP number, it means that the MySQL server got an error when trying to resolve the IP number of the client host to a name:

```
shell> mysqladmin -u root -pxxxx -h some-hostname ver
Access denied for user: 'root'@'' (Using password: YES)
```

This indicates a DNS problem. To fix it, execute mysqladmin flush-hosts to reset the internal DNS hostname cache. See Section 6.5.5, "How MySQL Uses DNS."

Some permanent solutions are:

  - Try to find out what is wrong with your DNS server and fix it.
  - Specify IP numbers rather than hostnames in the MySQL grant tables.
  - Put an entry for the client machine name in /etc/hosts.
  - Start mysqld with the --skip-name-resolve option.
  - Start mysqld with the --skip-host-cache option.
  - On Unix, if you are running the server and the client on the same machine, connect to localhost. Unix connections to localhost use a Unix socket file rather than TCP/IP.
  - On Windows, if you are running the server and the client on the same machine and the server supports named pipe connections, connect to the hostname . (period). Connections to . use a named pipe rather than TCP/IP.

- If mysql -u root test works but mysql -h your_hostname -u root test results in Access denied (where your_hostname is the actual hostname of the local host), you may not have the correct name for your host in the user table. A common problem here is that the Host value in the user table entry specifies an unqualified hostname, but your system's name resolution routines return a fully qualified domain name (or vice versa). For example, if you have an entry with host 'tcx' in the user table, but your DNS tells MySQL that your hostname is 'tcx.subnet.se', the entry will not work. Try adding an entry to the user table that contains the IP number of your host as the Host column value. (Alternatively, you could add an entry to the user table with a Host value that contains a wildcard; for example, 'tcx.%'. However, use of hostnames ending with '%' is *insecure* and is *not* recommended!)

- If mysql -u *user_name* test works but mysql -u *user_name* *other_db_name* does not, you have not granted database access for *other_db_name* to the given user.

- If mysql -u *user_name* works when executed on the server host, but mysql -h *host_name* -u *user_name* doesn't work when executed on a remote client host, you have not enabled access to the server for the given username from the remote host.

- If you can't figure out why you get Access denied, remove from the user table all entries that have Host values containing wildcards (entries that contain '%' or '_'). A very common error is to insert a new entry with Host='%' and User='*some_user*', thinking that this will allow you to specify localhost to connect from the same machine. The reason that this doesn't work is that the default privileges include an entry with Host='localhost' and User=''. Because that entry has a Host value 'localhost' that is more specific than '%', it is used in preference to the new entry when connecting from localhost! The correct procedure is to insert a second entry with Host='localhost' and User='*some_user*', or to delete the entry with Host='localhost' and User=''. After deleting the entry, remember to issue a FLUSH PRIVILEGES statement to reload the grant tables.

- If you get the following error, you may have a problem with the db or host table:

  Access to database denied

  If the entry selected from the db table has an empty value in the Host column, make sure that there are one or more corresponding entries in the host table specifying which hosts the db table entry applies to.

- If you are able to connect to the MySQL server, but get an Access denied message whenever you issue a SELECT ... INTO OUTFILE or LOAD DATA INFILE statement, your entry in the user table doesn't have the FILE privilege enabled.

- If you change the grant tables directly (for example, by using INSERT, UPDATE, or DELETE statements) and your changes seem to be ignored, remember that you must execute a FLUSH PRIVILEGES statement or a mysqladmin flush-privileges command to cause the server to re-read the privilege tables. Otherwise, your changes have no effect until the next time the server is restarted. Remember that after you change the root password with an UPDATE command, you won't need to specify the new password until after you flush the privileges, because the server won't know you've changed the password yet!

- If your privileges seem to have changed in the middle of a session, it may be that a MySQL administrator has changed them. Reloading the grant tables affects new client connections, but it also affects existing connections as indicated in Section 4.4.7, "When Privilege Changes Take Effect."

- If you have access problems with a Perl, PHP, Python, or ODBC program, try to connect to the server with `mysql -u user_name db_name` or `mysql -u user_name -pyour_pass db_name`. If you are able to connect using the `mysql` client, the problem lies with your program, not with the access privileges. (There is no space between `-p` and the password; you can also use the `--password=your_pass` syntax to specify the password. If you use the `-p` option alone, MySQL will prompt you for the password.)

- For testing, start the `mysqld` server with the `--skip-grant-tables` option. Then you can change the MySQL grant tables and use the `mysqlaccess` script to check whether your modifications have the desired effect. When you are satisfied with your changes, execute `mysqladmin flush-privileges` to tell the `mysqld` server to start using the new grant tables. (Reloading the grant tables overrides the `--skip-grant-tables` option. This allows you to tell the server to begin using the grant tables again without stopping and restarting it.)

- If everything else fails, start the `mysqld` server with a debugging option (for example, `--debug=d,general,query`). This will print host and user information about attempted connections, as well as information about each command issued.

- If you have any other problems with the MySQL grant tables and feel you must post the problem to the mailing list, always provide a dump of the MySQL grant tables. You can dump the tables with the `mysqldump mysql` command. As always, post your problem using the `mysqlbug` script. See Section 1.7.1.3, "How to Report Bugs or Problems." In some cases, you may need to restart `mysqld` with `--skip-grant-tables` to run `mysqldump`.

4.4.9 Password Hashing in MySQL 4.1

MySQL user accounts are listed in the `user` table of the `mysql` database. Each MySQL account is assigned a password, although what is stored in the `Password` column of the `user` table is not the plaintext version of the password, but a hash value computed from it. Password hash values are computed by the `PASSWORD()` function.

MySQL uses passwords in two phases of client/server communication:

- When a client attempts to connect to the server, there is an initial authentication step in which the client must present a password that has a hash value matching the hash value stored in the `user` table for the account that the client wants to use.

- After the client connects, it can (if it has sufficient privileges) set or change the password hashes for accounts listed in the `user` table. The client can do this by using the `PASSWORD()` function to generate a password hash, or by using the `GRANT` or `SET PASSWORD` statements.

In other words, the server *uses* hash values during authentication when a client first attempts to connect. The server *generates* hash values if a connected client invokes the `PASSWORD()` function or uses a `GRANT` or `SET PASSWORD` statement to set or change a password.

The password hashing mechanism was updated in MySQL 4.1 to provide better security and to reduce the risk of passwords being intercepted. However, this new mechanism is understood only by the 4.1 server and 4.1 clients, which can result in some compatibility problems. A 4.1 client can connect to a pre-4.1 server, because the client understands both the old and new password hashing mechanisms. However, a pre-4.1 client that attempts to connect to a 4.1 server may run into difficulties. For example, a 4.0 `mysql` client that attempts to connect to a 4.1 server may fail with the following error message:

```
shell> mysql -h localhost -u root
Client does not support authentication protocol requested
by server; consider upgrading MySQL client
```

The following discussion describes the differences between the old and new password mechanisms, and what you should do if you upgrade your server to 4.1 but need to maintain backward compatibility with pre-4.1 clients. Additional information can be found in Section A.2.3, "Client does not support authentication protocol."

Note: This discussion contrasts 4.1 behavior with pre-4.1 behavior, but the 4.1 behavior described here actually begins with 4.1.1. MySQL 4.1.0 is an "odd" release because it has a slightly different mechanism than that implemented in 4.1.1 and up. Differences between 4.1.0 and more recent versions are described further in Section 4.4.9.2, "Password Hashing in MySQL 4.1.0."

Prior to MySQL 4.1, password hashes computed by the PASSWORD() function are 16 bytes long. Such hashes look like this:

```
mysql> SELECT PASSWORD('mypass');
+--------------------+
| PASSWORD('mypass') |
+--------------------+
| 6f8c114b58f2ce9e   |
+--------------------+
```

The Password column of the user table (in which these hashes are stored) also is 16 bytes long before MySQL 4.1.

As of MySQL 4.1, the PASSWORD() function has been modified to produce a longer 41-byte hash value:

```
mysql> SELECT PASSWORD('mypass');
+-------------------------------------------+
| PASSWORD('mypass')                        |
+-------------------------------------------+
| *43c8aa34cdc98eddd3de1fe9a9c2c2a9f92bb2098d75 |
+-------------------------------------------+
```

Accordingly, the Password column in the user table also must be 41 bytes long to store these values:

- If you perform a new installation of MySQL 4.1, the `Password` column will be made 41 bytes long automatically.

- If you upgrade an older installation to 4.1, you should run the `mysql_fix_privilege_tables` script to increase the length of the `Password` column from 16 to 41 bytes. (The script does not change existing password values, which remain 16 bytes long.)

A widened `Password` column can store password hashes in both the old and new formats. The format of any given password hash value can be determined two ways:

- The obvious difference is the length (16 bytes versus 41 bytes).

- A second difference is that password hashes in the new format always begin with a '`*`' character, whereas passwords in the old format never do.

The longer password hash format has better cryptographic properties, and client authentication based on long hashes is more secure than that based on the older short hashes.

The differences between short and long password hashes are relevant both for how the server uses passwords during authentication and for how it generates password hashes for connected clients that perform password-changing operations.

The way in which the server uses password hashes during authentication is affected by the width of the `Password` column:

- If the column is short, only short-hash authentication is used.

- If the column is long, it can hold either short or long hashes, and the server can use either format:

  - Pre-4.1 clients can connect, although because they know only about the old hashing mechanism, they can authenticate only for accounts that have short hashes.

  - 4.1 clients can authenticate for accounts that have short or long hashes.

For short-hash accounts, the authentication process is actually a bit more secure for 4.1 clients than for older clients. In terms of security, the gradient from least to most secure is:

- Pre-4.1 client authenticating for account with short password hash

- 4.1 client authenticating for account with short password hash

- 4.1 client authenticating for account with long password hash

The way in which the server generates password hashes for connected clients is affected by the width of the `Password` column and by the `--old-passwords` option. A 4.1 server generates long hashes only if certain conditions are met: The `Password` column must be wide enough to hold long values and the `--old-passwords` option must not be given. These conditions apply as follows:

- The `Password` column must be wide enough to hold long hashes (41 bytes). If the column has not been updated and still has the pre-4.1 width of 16 bytes, the server notices that long hashes cannot fit into it and generates only short hashes when a client performs password-changing operations using PASSWORD(), GRANT, or SET PASSWORD. This is the behavior that occurs if you have upgraded to 4.1 but have not yet run the mysql_fix_privilege_tables script to widen the Password column.

- If the Password column is wide, it can store either short or long password hashes. In this case, PASSWORD(), GRANT, and SET PASSWORD generate long hashes unless the server was started with the --old-passwords option. That option forces the server to generate short password hashes instead.

The purpose of the --old-passwords option is to allow you to maintain backward compatibility with pre-4.1 clients under circumstances where the server would otherwise generate long password hashes. The option doesn't affect authentication (4.1 clients can still use accounts that have long password hashes), but it does prevent creation of a long password hash in the user table as the result of a password-changing operation. Were that to occur, the account no longer could be used by pre-4.1 clients. Without the --old-passwords option, the following undesirable scenario is possible:

- An old client connects to an account that has a short password hash.
- The client changes its own password. Without --old-passwords, this results in the account having a long password hash.
- The next time the old client attempts to connect to the account, it cannot, because the account now has a long password hash that requires the new hashing mechanism during authentication. (Once an account has a long password hash in the user table, only 4.1 clients can authenticate for it, because pre-4.1 clients do not understand long hashes.)

This scenario illustrates that, if you must support older pre-4.1 clients, it is dangerous to run a 4.1 server without using the --old-passwords option. By running the server with --old-passwords, password-changing operations will not generate long password hashes and thus do not cause accounts to become inaccessible to older clients. (Those clients cannot inadvertently lock themselves out by changing their password and ending up with a long password hash.)

The downside of the --old-passwords option is that any passwords you create or change will use short hashes, even for 4.1 clients. Thus, you lose the additional security provided by long password hashes. If you want to create an account that has a long hash (for example, for use by 4.1 clients), you must do so while running the server without --old-passwords.

The following scenarios are possible for running a 4.1 server:

Scenario 1: Short Password column in user table:

- Only short hashes can be stored in the Password column.
- The server uses only short hashes during client authentication.

- For connected clients, password hash-generating operations involving PASSWORD(), GRANT, or SET PASSWORD use short hashes exclusively. Any change to an account's password results in that account having a short password hash.

- The --old-passwords option can be used but is superfluous because with a short Password column, the server will generate only short password hashes anyway.

Scenario 2: Long Password column; server not started with --old-passwords option:

- Short or long hashes can be stored in the Password column.
- 4.1 clients can authenticate for accounts that have short or long hashes.
- Pre-4.1 clients can authenticate only for accounts that have short hashes.
- For connected clients, password hash-generating operations involving PASSWORD(), GRANT, or SET PASSWORD use long hashes exclusively. A change to an account's password results in that account having a long password hash.

As indicated earlier, a danger in this scenario is that it is possible for accounts that have a short password hash to become inaccessible to pre-4.1 clients. A change to such an account's password made via GRANT, PASSWORD(), or SET PASSWORD results in the account being given a long password hash. From that point on, no pre-4.1 client can authenticate to that account until the client upgrades to 4.1.

To deal with this problem, you can change a password in a special way. For example, normally you use SET PASSWORD as follows to change an account password:

```
mysql> SET PASSWORD FOR 'some_user'@'some_host' = PASSWORD('mypass');
```

To change the password but create a short hash, use the OLD_PASSWORD() function instead:

```
mysql> SET PASSWORD FOR 'some_user'@'some_host' = OLD_PASSWORD('mypass');
```

OLD_PASSWORD() is useful for situations in which you explicitly want to generate a short hash.

Scenario 3: Long Password column; server started with --old-passwords option:

- Short or long hashes can be stored in the Password column.
- 4.1 clients can authenticate for accounts that have short or long hashes (but note that it is possible to create long hashes only when the server is started without --old-passwords).
- Pre-4.1 clients can authenticate only for accounts that have short hashes.
- For connected clients, password hash-generating operations involving PASSWORD(), GRANT, or SET PASSWORD use short hashes exclusively. Any change to an account's password results in that account having a short password hash.

In this scenario, you cannot create accounts that have long password hashes, because the --old-passwords option prevents generation of long hashes. Also, if you create an account with a long hash before using the --old-passwords option, changing the account's password while --old-passwords is in effect results in the account being given a short password, causing it to lose the security benefits of a longer hash.

The disadvantages for these scenarios may be summarized as follows:

In scenario 1, you cannot take advantage of longer hashes that provide more secure authentication.

In scenario 2, accounts with short hashes become inaccessible to pre-4.1 clients if you change their passwords without explicitly using OLD_PASSWORD().

In scenario 3, --old-passwords prevents accounts with short hashes from becoming inaccessible, but password-changing operations cause accounts with long hashes to revert to short hashes, and you cannot change them back to long hashes while --old-passwords is in effect.

4.4.9.1 Implications of Password Hashing Changes for Application Programs

An upgrade to MySQL 4.1 can cause a compatibility issue for applications that use PASSWORD() to generate passwords for their own purposes. Applications really should not do this, because PASSWORD() should be used only to manage passwords for MySQL accounts. But some applications use PASSWORD() for their own purposes anyway.

If you upgrade to 4.1 and run the server under conditions where it generates long password hashes, an application that uses PASSWORD() for its own passwords will break. The recommended course of action is to modify the application to use another function, such as SHA1() or MD5(), to produce hashed values. If that is not possible, you can use the OLD_PASSWORD() function, which is provided to generate short hashes in the old format. But note that OLD_PASSWORD() may one day no longer be supported.

If the server is running under circumstances where it generates short hashes, OLD_PASSWORD() is available but is equivalent to PASSWORD().

4.4.9.2 Password Hashing in MySQL 4.1.0

Password hashing in MySQL 4.1.0 differs from hashing in 4.1.1 and up. The 4.1.0 differences are:

- Password hashes are 45 bytes long rather than 41 bytes.
- The PASSWORD() function is non-repeatable. That is, with a given argument X, successive calls to PASSWORD(X) generate different results.

These differences make authentication in 4.1.0 incompatible with that of releases that follow it. If you have upgraded to MySQL 4.1.0, it is recommended that you upgrade to a newer version as soon as possible. After you do, reassign any long passwords in the user table so that they are compatible with the 41-byte format.

4.5 MySQL User Account Management

This section describes how to set up accounts for clients of your MySQL server. It discusses the following topics:

- The meaning of account names and passwords as used in MySQL and how that compares to names and passwords used by your operating system
- How to set up new accounts and remove existing accounts
- How to change passwords
- Guidelines for using passwords securely
- How to use secure connections with SSL

4.5.1 MySQL Usernames and Passwords

A MySQL account is defined in terms of a username and the client host or hosts from which the user can connect to the server. The account also has a password. There are several distinctions between the way usernames and passwords are used by MySQL and the way they are used by your operating system:

- Usernames, as used by MySQL for authentication purposes, have nothing to do with usernames (login names) as used by Windows or Unix. On Unix, most MySQL clients by default try to log in using the current Unix username as the MySQL username, but that is for convenience only. The default can be overridden easily, because client programs allow any username to be specified with a -u or --user option. Because this means that anyone can attempt to connect to the server using any username, you can't make a database secure in any way unless all MySQL accounts have passwords. Anyone who specifies a username for an account that has no password will be able to connect successfully to the server.
- MySQL usernames can be up to 16 characters long. Operating system usernames might have a different maximum length. For example, Unix usernames typically are limited to eight characters.
- MySQL passwords have nothing to do with passwords for logging in to your operating system. There is no necessary connection between the password you use to log in to a Windows or Unix machine and the password you use to access the MySQL server on that machine.
- MySQL encrypts passwords using its own algorithm. This encryption is different from that used during the Unix login process. MySQL password encryption is the same as that implemented by the PASSWORD() SQL function. Unix password encryption is the same as that implemented by the ENCRYPT() SQL function. From version 4.1 on, MySQL employs a stronger authentication method that has better password protection during the connection process than in earlier versions. It is secure even if TCP/IP

packets are sniffed or the `mysql` database is captured. (In earlier versions, even though passwords are stored in encrypted form in the `user` table, knowledge of the encrypted password value could be used to connect to the MySQL server.)

When you install MySQL, the grant tables are populated with an initial set of accounts. These accounts have names and access privileges that are described in Section 2.4.5, "Securing the Initial MySQL Accounts," which also discusses how to assign passwords to them. Thereafter, you normally set up, modify, and remove MySQL accounts using the `GRANT` and `REVOKE` statements.

When you connect to a MySQL server with a command-line client, you should specify the username and password for the account that you want to use:

```
shell> mysql --user=monty --password=guess db_name
```

If you prefer short options, the command looks like this:

```
shell> mysql -u monty -pguess db_name
```

There must be *no space* between the -p option and the following password value. See Section 4.4.4, "Connecting to the MySQL Server."

The preceding commands include the password value on the command line, which can be a security risk. See Section 4.5.6, "Keeping Your Password Secure." To avoid this, specify the `--password` or `-p` option without any following password value:

```
shell> mysql --user=monty --password db_name
shell> mysql -u monty -p db_name
```

Then the client program will print a prompt and wait for you to enter the password. (In these examples, `db_name` is *not* interpreted as a password, because it is separated from the preceding password option by a space.)

On some systems, the library call that MySQL uses to prompt for a password automatically limits the password to eight characters. That is a problem with the system library, not with MySQL. Internally, MySQL doesn't have any limit for the length of the password. To work around the problem, change your MySQL password to a value that is eight or fewer characters long, or put your password in an option file.

4.5.2 Adding New User Accounts to MySQL

You can create MySQL accounts in two ways:

- By using `GRANT` statements
- By manipulating the MySQL grant tables directly

The preferred method is to use `GRANT` statements, because they are more concise and less error-prone. `GRANT` is available as of MySQL 3.22.11; its syntax is described in the *MySQL Language Reference*.

Another option for creating accounts is to use one of several available third-party programs that offer capabilities for MySQL account administration. phpMyAdmin is one such program.

The following examples show how to use the mysql client program to set up new users. These examples assume that privileges are set up according to the defaults described in Section 2.4.5, "Securing the Initial MySQL Accounts." This means that to make changes, you must connect to the MySQL server as the MySQL root user, and the root account must have the INSERT privilege for the mysql database and the RELOAD administrative privilege.

First, use the mysql program to connect to the server as the MySQL root user:

```
shell> mysql --user=root mysql
```

If you have assigned a password to the root account, you'll also need to supply a --password or -p option for this mysql command and also for those later in this section.

After connecting to the server as root, you can add new accounts. The following statements use GRANT to set up four new accounts:

```
mysql> GRANT ALL PRIVILEGES ON *.* TO 'monty'@'localhost'
    ->     IDENTIFIED BY 'some_pass' WITH GRANT OPTION;
mysql> GRANT ALL PRIVILEGES ON *.* TO 'monty'@'%'
    ->     IDENTIFIED BY 'some_pass' WITH GRANT OPTION;
mysql> GRANT RELOAD,PROCESS ON *.* TO 'admin'@'localhost';
mysql> GRANT USAGE ON *.* TO 'dummy'@'localhost';
```

The accounts created by these GRANT statements have the following properties:

- Two of the accounts have a username of monty and a password of some_pass. Both accounts are superuser accounts with full privileges to do anything. One account ('monty'@'localhost') can be used only when connecting from the local host. The other ('monty'@'%') can be used to connect from any other host. Note that it is necessary to have both accounts for monty to be able to connect from anywhere as monty. Without the localhost account, the anonymous-user account for localhost that is created by mysql_install_db would take precedence when monty connects from the local host. As a result, monty would be treated as an anonymous user. The reason for this is that the anonymous-user account has a more specific Host column value than the 'monty'@'%' account and thus comes earlier in the user table sort order. (user table sorting is discussed in Section 4.4.5, "Access Control, Stage 1: Connection Verification.")

- One account has a username of admin and no password. This account can be used only by connecting from the local host. It is granted the RELOAD and PROCESS administrative privileges. These privileges allow the admin user to execute the mysqladmin reload, mysqladmin refresh, and mysqladmin flush-xxx commands, as well as mysqladmin processlist . No privileges are granted for accessing any databases. You could add such privileges later by issuing additional GRANT statements.

- One account has a username of dummy and no password. This account can be used only by connecting from the local host. No privileges are granted. The USAGE privilege in the GRANT statement allows you to create an account without giving it any privileges. It has the effect of setting all the global privileges to 'N'. It is assumed that you will grant specific privileges to the account later.

As an alternative to GRANT, you can create the same accounts directly by issuing INSERT statements and then telling the server to reload the grant tables:

```
shell> mysql --user=root mysql
mysql> INSERT INTO user
    ->     VALUES('localhost','monty',PASSWORD('some_pass'),
    ->     'Y','Y','Y','Y','Y','Y','Y','Y','Y','Y','Y','Y','Y','Y');
mysql> INSERT INTO user
    ->     VALUES('%','monty',PASSWORD('some_pass'),
    ->     'Y','Y','Y','Y','Y','Y','Y','Y','Y','Y','Y','Y','Y','Y');
mysql> INSERT INTO user SET Host='localhost',User='admin',
    ->     Reload_priv='Y', Process_priv='Y';
mysql> INSERT INTO user (Host,User,Password)
    ->     VALUES('localhost','dummy','');
mysql> FLUSH PRIVILEGES;
```

The reason for using FLUSH PRIVILEGES when you create accounts with INSERT is to tell the server to re-read the grant tables. Otherwise, the changes will go unnoticed until you restart the server. With GRANT, FLUSH PRIVILEGES is unnecessary.

The reason for using the PASSWORD() function with INSERT is to encrypt the password. The GRANT statement encrypts the password for you, so PASSWORD() is unnecessary.

The 'Y' values enable privileges for the accounts. Depending on your MySQL version, you may have to use a different number of 'Y' values in the first two INSERT statements. (Versions prior to 3.22.11 have fewer privilege columns, and versions from 4.0.2 on have more.) For the admin account, the more readable extended INSERT syntax using SET that is available starting with MySQL 3.22.11 is used.

In the INSERT statement for the dummy account, only the Host, User, and Password columns in the user table record are assigned values. None of the privilege columns are set explicitly, so MySQL assigns them all the default value of 'N'. This is equivalent to what GRANT USAGE does.

Note that to set up a superuser account, it is necessary only to create a user table entry with the privilege columns set to 'Y'. user table privileges are global, so no entries in any of the other grant tables are needed.

The next examples create three accounts and give them access to specific databases. Each of them has a username of custom and password of obscure.

To create the accounts with GRANT, use the following statements:

```
shell> mysql --user=root mysql
mysql> GRANT SELECT,INSERT,UPDATE,DELETE,CREATE,DROP
    ->     ON bankaccount.*
    ->     TO 'custom'@'localhost'
    ->     IDENTIFIED BY 'obscure';
mysql> GRANT SELECT,INSERT,UPDATE,DELETE,CREATE,DROP
    ->     ON expenses.*
    ->     TO 'custom'@'whitehouse.gov'
    ->     IDENTIFIED BY 'obscure';
mysql> GRANT SELECT,INSERT,UPDATE,DELETE,CREATE,DROP
    ->     ON customer.*
    ->     TO 'custom'@'server.domain'
    ->     IDENTIFIED BY 'obscure';
```

The three accounts can be used as follows:

- The first account can access the bankaccount database, but only from the local host.
- The second account can access the expenses database, but only from the host whitehouse.gov.
- The third account can access the customer database, but only from the host server.domain.

To set up the custom accounts without GRANT, use INSERT statements as follows to modify the grant tables directly:

```
shell> mysql --user=root mysql
mysql> INSERT INTO user (Host,User,Password)
    ->     VALUES('localhost','custom',PASSWORD('obscure'));
mysql> INSERT INTO user (Host,User,Password)
    ->     VALUES('whitehouse.gov','custom',PASSWORD('obscure'));
mysql> INSERT INTO user (Host,User,Password)
    ->     VALUES('server.domain','custom',PASSWORD('obscure'));
mysql> INSERT INTO db
    ->     (Host,Db,User,Select_priv,Insert_priv,
    ->     Update_priv,Delete_priv,Create_priv,Drop_priv)
    ->     VALUES('localhost','bankaccount','custom',
    ->     'Y','Y','Y','Y','Y','Y');
mysql> INSERT INTO db
    ->     (Host,Db,User,Select_priv,Insert_priv,
    ->     Update_priv,Delete_priv,Create_priv,Drop_priv)
    ->     VALUES('whitehouse.gov','expenses','custom',
    ->     'Y','Y','Y','Y','Y','Y');
mysql> INSERT INTO db
    ->     (Host,Db,User,Select_priv,Insert_priv,
    ->     Update_priv,Delete_priv,Create_priv,Drop_priv)
```

```
    ->     VALUES('server.domain','customer','custom',
    ->     'Y','Y','Y','Y','Y','Y');
mysql> FLUSH PRIVILEGES;
```

The first three INSERT statements add user table entries that allow the user custom to connect from the various hosts with the given password, but grant no global privileges (all privileges are set to the default value of 'N'). The next three INSERT statements add db table
entries that grant privileges to custom for the bankaccount, expenses, and customer databases,
but only when accessed from the proper hosts. As usual when you modify the grant tables
directly, you tell the server to reload them with FLUSH PRIVILEGES so that the privilege
changes take effect.

If you want to give a specific user access from all machines in a given domain (for example,
mydomain.com), you can issue a GRANT statement that uses the '%' wildcard character in the
host part of the account name:

```
mysql> GRANT ...
    ->     ON *.*
    ->     TO 'myname'@'%.mydomain.com'
    ->     IDENTIFIED BY 'mypass';
```

To do the same thing by modifying the grant tables directly, do this:

```
mysql> INSERT INTO user (Host,User,Password,...)
    ->     VALUES('%.mydomain.com','myname',PASSWORD('mypass'),...);
mysql> FLUSH PRIVILEGES;
```

4.5.3 Removing User Accounts from MySQL

To remove an account, use the DROP USER statement, which was added in MySQL 4.1.1. For
older versions of MySQL, use DELETE instead.

To remove a MySQL user account, you should use the following procedure, performing the
steps in the order shown:

1. Use SHOW GRANTS to determine what privileges the account has.
2. Use REVOKE to revoke the privileges displayed by SHOW GRANTS. This removes records for
   the account from all the grant tables except the user table, and revokes any global privileges listed in the user table.
3. Delete the account by using DROP USER to remove the user table record.

The DROP USER statement was added in MySQL 4.1.1. Before 4.1.1, you should first revoke
the account privileges as just described. Then delete the user table record and flush the
grant tables like this:

```
mysql> DELETE FROM mysql.user
    -> WHERE User='user_name' and Host='host_name';
mysql> FLUSH PRIVILEGES;
```

4.5.4 Limiting Account Resources

Before MySQL 4.0.2, the only available method for limiting use of MySQL server resources is to set the max_user_connections system variable to a non-zero value. But that method is strictly global. It does not allow for management of individual accounts. Also, it limits only the number of simultaneous connections made using a single account, not what a client can do once connected. Both types of control are of interest to many MySQL administrators, particularly those for Internet Service Providers.

Starting from MySQL 4.0.2, you can limit the following server resources for individual accounts:

- The number of queries that an account can issue per hour
- The number of updates that an account can issue per hour
- The number of times an account can connect to the server per hour

Any statement that a client can issue counts against the query limit. Only statements that modify databases or tables count against the update limit.

An account in this context is a single record in the user table. Each account is uniquely identified by its User and Host column values.

As a prerequisite for using this feature, the user table in the mysql database must contain the resource-related columns. Resource limits are stored in the max_questions, max_updates, and max_connections columns. If your user table doesn't have these columns, it must be upgraded; see Section 2.5.8, "Upgrading the Grant Tables."

To set resource limits with a GRANT statement, use a WITH clause that names each resource to be limited and a per-hour count indicating the limit value. For example, to create a new account that can access the customer database, but only in a limited fashion, issue this statement:

```
mysql> GRANT ALL ON customer.* TO 'francis'@'localhost'
    ->      IDENTIFIED BY 'frank'
    ->      WITH MAX_QUERIES_PER_HOUR 20
    ->           MAX_UPDATES_PER_HOUR 10
    ->           MAX_CONNECTIONS_PER_HOUR 5;
```

The limit types need not all be named in the WITH clause, but those named can be present in any order. The value for each limit should be an integer representing a count per hour. If the GRANT statement has no WITH clause, the limits are each set to the default value of zero (that is, no limit).

To set or change limits for an existing account, use a GRANT USAGE statement at the global level (ON *.*). The following statement changes the query limit for francis to 100:

```
mysql> GRANT USAGE ON *.* TO 'francis'@'localhost'
    ->      WITH MAX_QUERIES_PER_HOUR 100;
```

This statement leaves the account's existing privileges unchanged and modifies only the limit values specified.

To remove an existing limit, set its value to zero. For example, to remove the limit on how many times per hour francis can connect, use this statement:

```
mysql> GRANT USAGE ON *.* TO 'francis'@'localhost'
    ->       WITH MAX_CONNECTIONS_PER_HOUR 0;
```

Resource-use counting takes place when any account has a non-zero limit placed on its use of any of the resources.

As the server runs, it counts the number of times each account uses resources. If an account reaches its limit on number of connections within the last hour, further connections for the account are rejected until that hour is up. Similarly, if the account reaches its limit on the number of queries or updates, further queries or updates are rejected until the hour is up. In all such cases, an appropriate error message is issued.

Resource counting is done per account, not per client. For example, if your account has a query limit of 50, you cannot increase your limit to 100 by making two simultaneous client connections to the server. Queries issued on both connections are counted together.

The current resource-use counts can be reset globally for all accounts, or individually for a given count:

- To reset the current counts to zero for all accounts, issue a FLUSH USER_RESOURCES statement. The counts also can be reset by reloading the grant tables (for example, with a FLUSH PRIVILEGES statement or a mysqladmin reload command).
- The counts for an individual account can be set to zero by re-granting it any of its limits. To do this, use GRANT USAGE as described earlier and specify a limit value equal to the value that the account already has.

4.5.5 Assigning Account Passwords

Passwords may be assigned from the command line by using the mysqladmin command:

```
shell> mysqladmin -u user_name -h host_name password "newpwd"
```

The account for which this command resets the password is the one with a user table record that matches *user_name* in the User column and the client host *from which you connect* in the Host column.

Another way to assign a password to an account is to issue a SET PASSWORD statement:

```
mysql> SET PASSWORD FOR 'jeffrey'@'%' = PASSWORD('biscuit');
```

Only users such as `root` with update access to the `mysql` database can change the password for other users. If you are not connected as an anonymous user, you can change your own password by omitting the `FOR` clause:

```
mysql> SET PASSWORD = PASSWORD('biscuit');
```

You can also use a `GRANT USAGE` statement at the global level (`ON *.*`) to assign a password to an account without affecting the account's current privileges:

```
mysql> GRANT USAGE ON *.* TO 'jeffrey'@'%' IDENTIFIED BY 'biscuit';
```

Although it is generally preferable to assign passwords using one of the preceding methods, you can also do so by modifying the `user` table directly:

- To establish a password when creating a new account, provide a value for the `Password` column:

```
shell> mysql -u root mysql
mysql> INSERT INTO user (Host,User,Password)
    -> VALUES('%','jeffrey',PASSWORD('biscuit'));
mysql> FLUSH PRIVILEGES;
```

- To change the password for an existing account, use `UPDATE` to set the `Password` column value:

```
shell> mysql -u root mysql
mysql> UPDATE user SET Password = PASSWORD('bagel')
    -> WHERE Host = '%' AND User = 'francis';
mysql> FLUSH PRIVILEGES;
```

When you assign an account a password using `SET PASSWORD`, `INSERT`, or `UPDATE`, you must use the `PASSWORD()` function to encrypt it. (The only exception is that you need not use `PASSWORD()` if the password is empty.) `PASSWORD()` is necessary because the `user` table stores passwords in encrypted form, not as plaintext. If you forget that fact, you are likely to set passwords like this:

```
shell> mysql -u root mysql
mysql> INSERT INTO user (Host,User,Password)
    -> VALUES('%','jeffrey','biscuit');
mysql> FLUSH PRIVILEGES;
```

The result is that the literal value `'biscuit'` is stored as the password in the user table, not the encrypted value. When `jeffrey` attempts to connect to the server using this password, the value is encrypted and compared to the value stored in the user table. However, the stored value is the literal string `'biscuit'`, so the comparison fails and the server rejects the connection:

```
shell> mysql -u jeffrey -pbiscuit test
Access denied
```

If you set passwords using the GRANT ... IDENTIFIED BY statement or the mysqladmin password command, they both take care of encrypting the password for you. The PASSWORD() function is unnecessary.

Note: PASSWORD() encryption is different from Unix password encryption. See Section 4.5.1, "MySQL Usernames and Passwords."

4.5.6 Keeping Your Password Secure

On an administrative level, you should never grant access to the mysql.user table to any non-administrative accounts. Passwords in the user table are stored in encrypted form, but in versions of MySQL earlier than 4.1, knowing the encrypted password for an account makes it possible to connect to the server using that account.

When you run a client program to connect to the MySQL server, it is inadvisable to specify your password in a way that exposes it to discovery by other users. The methods you can use to specify your password when you run client programs are listed here, along with an assessment of the risks of each method:

- Use a -p*your_pass* or --password=*your_pass* option on the command line. For example:

  ```
  shell> mysql -u francis -pfrank db_name
  ```

  This is convenient but insecure, because your password becomes visible to system status programs such as ps that may be invoked by other users to display command lines. MySQL clients typically overwrite the command-line password argument with zeros during their initialization sequence, but there is still a brief interval during which the value is visible.

- Use a -p or --password option with no password value specified. In this case, the client program solicits the password from the terminal:

  ```
  shell> mysql -u francis -p db_name
  Enter password: ********
  ```

  The '*' characters indicate where you enter your password. The password is not displayed as you
  enter it.

  It is more secure to enter your password this way than to specify it on the command line because it is not visible to other users. However, this method of entering a password is suitable only for programs that you run interactively. If you want to invoke a client from a script that runs non-interactively, there is no opportunity to enter the password from the terminal. On some systems, you may even find that the first line of your script is read and interpreted (incorrectly) as your password!

- Store your password in an option file. For example, on Unix you can list your password in the [client] section of the .my.cnf file in your home directory:

  ```
  [client]
  password=your_pass
  ```

If you store your password in .my.cnf, the file should not be accessible to anyone but yourself. To ensure this, set the file access mode to 400 or 600. For example:

```
shell> chmod 600 .my.cnf
```

Section 3.3.2, "Using Option Files," discusses option files in more detail.

- Store your password in the MYSQL_PWD environment variable. This method of specifying your MySQL password must be considered extremely insecure and should not be used. Some versions of ps include an option to display the environment of running processes. If you set MYSQL_PWD, your password will be exposed to any other user who runs ps. Even on systems without such a version of ps, it is unwise to assume that there are no other methods by which users can examine process environments. See Appendix B, "Environment Variables."

All in all, the safest methods are to have the client program prompt for the password or to specify the password in a properly protected option file.

4.5.7 Using Secure Connections

Beginning with version 4.0.0, MySQL has support for secure (encrypted) connections between MySQL clients and the server using the Secure Sockets Layer (SSL) protocol. This section discusses how to use SSL connections. It also describes a way to set up SSH on Windows.

The standard configuration of MySQL is intended to be as fast as possible, so encrypted connections are not used by default. Doing so would make the client/server protocol much slower. Encrypting data is a CPU-intensive operation that requires the computer to do additional work and can delay other MySQL tasks. For applications that require the security provided by encrypted connections, the extra computation is warranted.

MySQL allows encryption to be enabled on a per-connection basis. You can choose a normal unencrypted connection or a secure encrypted SSL connection according to the requirements of individual applications.

4.5.7.1 Basic SSL Concepts

To understand how MySQL uses SSL, it's necessary to explain some basic SSL and X509 concepts. People who are already familiar with them can skip this part.

By default, MySQL uses unencrypted connections between the client and the server. This means that someone with access to the network could watch all your traffic and look at the data being sent or received. They could even change the data while it is in transit between client and server. To improve security a little, you can compress client/server traffic by using the --compress option when invoking client programs. However, this will not foil a determined attacker.

When you need to move information over a network in a secure fashion, an unencrypted connection is unacceptable. Encryption is the way to make any kind of data unreadable. In fact, today's practice requires many additional security elements from encryption algorithms. They should resist many kinds of known attacks such as changing the order of encrypted messages or replaying data twice.

SSL is a protocol that uses different encryption algorithms to ensure that data received over a public network can be trusted. It has mechanisms to detect any data change, loss, or replay. SSL also incorporates algorithms that provide identity verification using the X509 standard.

X509 makes it possible to identify someone on the Internet. It is most commonly used in e-commerce applications. In basic terms, there should be some company called a "Certificate Authority" (or CA) that assigns electronic certificates to anyone who needs them. Certificates rely on asymmetric encryption algorithms that have two encryption keys (a public key and a secret key). A certificate owner can show the certificate to another party as proof of identity. A certificate consists of its owner's public key. Any data encrypted with this public key can be decrypted only using the corresponding secret key, which is held by the owner of the certificate.

If you need more information about SSL, X509, or encryption, use your favorite Internet search engine to search for keywords in which you are interested.

4.5.7.2 Requirements

To use SSL connections between the MySQL server and client programs, your system must be able to support OpenSSL and your version of MySQL must be 4.0.0 or newer.

To get secure connections to work with MySQL, you must do the following:

1. Install the OpenSSL library. We have tested MySQL with OpenSSL 0.9.6. If you need OpenSSL, visit http://www.openssl.org.

2. When you configure MySQL, run the configure script with the --with-vio and --with-openssl options.

3. Make sure that you have upgraded your grant tables to include the SSL-related columns in the mysql.user table. This is necessary if your grant tables date from a version prior to MySQL 4.0.0. The upgrade procedure is described in Section 2.5.8, "Upgrading the Grant Tables."

4. To check whether a running mysqld server supports OpenSSL, examine the value of the have_openssl system variable:

```
mysql> SHOW VARIABLES LIKE 'have_openssl';
+---------------+-------+
| Variable_name | Value |
+---------------+-------+
| have_openssl  | YES   |
+---------------+-------+
```

If the value is YES, the server supports OpenSSL connections.

4.5.7.3 Setting Up SSL Certificates for MySQL

Here is an example for setting up SSL certificates for MySQL:

```
DIR=`pwd`/openssl
PRIV=$DIR/private

mkdir $DIR $PRIV $DIR/newcerts
cp /usr/share/ssl/openssl.cnf $DIR
replace ./demoCA $DIR -- $DIR/openssl.cnf

# Create necessary files: $database, $serial and $new_certs_dir
# directory (optional)

touch $DIR/index.txt
echo "01" > $DIR/serial

#
# Generation of Certificate Authority(CA)
#

openssl req -new -x509 -keyout $PRIV/cakey.pem -out $DIR/cacert.pem \
    -config $DIR/openssl.cnf

# Sample output:
# Using configuration from /home/monty/openssl/openssl.cnf
# Generating a 1024 bit RSA private key
# ................++++++
# .........++++++
# writing new private key to '/home/monty/openssl/private/cakey.pem'
# Enter PEM pass phrase:
# Verifying password - Enter PEM pass phrase:
# -----
# You are about to be asked to enter information that will be
# incorporated into your certificate request.
# What you are about to enter is what is called a Distinguished Name
# or a DN.
# There are quite a few fields but you can leave some blank
# For some fields there will be a default value,
# If you enter '.', the field will be left blank.
# -----
# Country Name (2 letter code) [AU]:FI
# State or Province Name (full name) [Some-State]:.
# Locality Name (eg, city) []:
# Organization Name (eg, company) [Internet Widgits Pty Ltd]:MySQL AB
# Organizational Unit Name (eg, section) []:
# Common Name (eg, YOUR name) []:MySQL admin
# Email Address []:
```

```
#
# Create server request and key
#
openssl req -new -keyout $DIR/server-key.pem -out \
    $DIR/server-req.pem -days 3600 -config $DIR/openssl.cnf

# Sample output:
# Using configuration from /home/monty/openssl/openssl.cnf
# Generating a 1024 bit RSA private key
# ..++++++
# .......... ++++++
# writing new private key to '/home/monty/openssl/server-key.pem'
# Enter PEM pass phrase:
# Verifying password - Enter PEM pass phrase:
# -----
# You are about to be asked to enter information that will be
# incorporated into your certificate request.
# What you are about to enter is what is called a Distinguished Name
# or a DN.
# There are quite a few fields but you can leave some blank
# For some fields there will be a default value,
# If you enter '.', the field will be left blank.
# -----
# Country Name (2 letter code) [AU]:FI
# State or Province Name (full name) [Some-State]:.
# Locality Name (eg, city) []:
# Organization Name (eg, company) [Internet Widgits Pty Ltd]:MySQL AB
# Organizational Unit Name (eg, section) []:
# Common Name (eg, YOUR name) []:MySQL server
# Email Address []:
#
# Please enter the following 'extra' attributes
# to be sent with your certificate request
# A challenge password []:
# An optional company name []:


#
# Remove the passphrase from the key (optional)
#

openssl rsa -in $DIR/server-key.pem -out $DIR/server-key.pem

#
# Sign server cert
#
```

```
openssl ca  -policy policy_anything -out $DIR/server-cert.pem \
    -config $DIR/openssl.cnf -infiles $DIR/server-req.pem


# Sample output:
# Using configuration from /home/monty/openssl/openssl.cnf
# Enter PEM pass phrase:
# Check that the request matches the signature
# Signature ok
# The Subjects Distinguished Name is as follows
# countryName             :PRINTABLE:'FI'
# organizationName        :PRINTABLE:'MySQL AB'
# commonName              :PRINTABLE:'MySQL admin'
# Certificate is to be certified until Sep 13 14:22:46 2003 GMT
# (365 days)
# Sign the certificate? [y/n]:y
#
#
# 1 out of 1 certificate requests certified, commit? [y/n]y
# Write out database with 1 new entries
# Data Base Updated


#
# Create client request and key
#
openssl req -new -keyout $DIR/client-key.pem -out \
    $DIR/client-req.pem -days 3600 -config $DIR/openssl.cnf


# Sample output:
# Using configuration from /home/monty/openssl/openssl.cnf
# Generating a 1024 bit RSA private key
# ....................................++++++
# .............................................++++++
# writing new private key to '/home/monty/openssl/client-key.pem'
# Enter PEM pass phrase:
# Verifying password - Enter PEM pass phrase:
# -----
# You are about to be asked to enter information that will be
# incorporated into your certificate request.
# What you are about to enter is what is called a Distinguished Name
# or a DN.
# There are quite a few fields but you can leave some blank
# For some fields there will be a default value,
# If you enter '.', the field will be left blank.
# -----
# Country Name (2 letter code) [AU]:FI
# State or Province Name (full name) [Some-State]:.
# Locality Name (eg, city) []:
```

```
# Organization Name (eg, company) [Internet Widgits Pty Ltd]:MySQL AB
# Organizational Unit Name (eg, section) []:
# Common Name (eg, YOUR name) []:MySQL user
# Email Address []:
#
# Please enter the following 'extra' attributes
# to be sent with your certificate request
# A challenge password []:
# An optional company name  []:

#
# Remove a passphrase from the key (optional)
#
openssl rsa -in $DIR/client-key.pem -out $DIR/client-key.pem


#
# Sign client cert
#

openssl ca  -policy policy_anything -out $DIR/client-cert.pem \
    -config $DIR/openssl.cnf -infiles $DIR/client-req.pem

# Sample output:
# Using configuration from /home/monty/openssl/openssl.cnf
# Enter PEM pass phrase:
# Check that the request matches the signature
# Signature ok
# The Subjects Distinguished Name is as follows
# countryName           :PRINTABLE:'FI'
# organizationName      :PRINTABLE:'MySQL AB'
# commonName            :PRINTABLE:'MySQL user'
# Certificate is to be certified until Sep 13 16:45:17 2003 GMT
# (365 days)
# Sign the certificate? [y/n]:y
#
#
# 1 out of 1 certificate requests certified, commit? [y/n]y
# Write out database with 1 new entries
# Data Base Updated

#
# Create a my.cnf file that you can use to test the certificates
#

cnf=""
cnf="$cnf [client]"
cnf="$cnf ssl-ca=$DIR/cacert.pem"
```

```
cnf="$cnf ssl-cert=$DIR/client-cert.pem"
cnf="$cnf ssl-key=$DIR/client-key.pem"
cnf="$cnf [mysqld]"
cnf="$cnf ssl-ca=$DIR/cacert.pem"
cnf="$cnf ssl-cert=$DIR/server-cert.pem"
cnf="$cnf ssl-key=$DIR/server-key.pem"
echo $cnf | replace " " '
' > $DIR/my.cnf
```

To test SSL connections, start the server as follows, where $DIR is the pathname to the directory where the sample my.cnf option file is located:

```
shell> mysqld --defaults-file=$DIR/my.cnf &
```

Then invoke a client program using the same option file:

```
shell> mysql --defaults-file=$DIR/my.cnf
```

If you have a MySQL source distribution, you can also test your setup by modifying the preceding my.cnf file to refer to the demonstration certificate and key files in the SSL directory of the distribution.

4.5.7.4 SSL GRANT Options

MySQL can check X509 certificate attributes in addition to the usual authentication that is based on the username and password. To specify SSL-related options for a MySQL account, use the REQUIRE clause of the GRANT statement, as described in the *MySQL Language Reference*.

4.5.7.5 SSL Command-Line Options

The following list describes options that are used for specifying the use of SSL, certificate files, and key files. These options are available beginning with MySQL 4.0. They may be given on the command line or in an option file.

- --ssl

    For the server, this option specifies that the server allows SSL connections. For a client program, it allows the client to connect to the server using SSL. This option is not sufficient in itself to cause an SSL connection to be used. You must also specify the --ssl-ca, --ssl-cert, and --ssl-key options.

    This option is more often used in its opposite form to indicate that SSL should *not* be used. To do this, specify the option as --skip-ssl or --ssl=0.

    Note that use of --ssl doesn't *require* an SSL connection. For example, if the server or client is compiled without SSL support, a normal unencrypted connection will be used.

    The secure way to ensure that an SSL connection will be used is to create an account on the server that includes a REQUIRE SSL clause in the GRANT statement. Then use this account to connect to the server, with both a server and client that have SSL support enabled.

- `--ssl-ca=file_name`

  The path to a file with a list of trusted SSL CAs.

- `--ssl-capath=directory_name`

  The path to a directory that contains trusted SSL CA certificates in pem format.

- `--ssl-cert=file_name`

  The name of the SSL certificate file to use for establishing a secure connection.

- `--ssl-cipher=cipher_list`

  A list of allowable ciphers to use for SSL encryption. `cipher_list` has the same format as the `openssl ciphers` command.

  Example: `--ssl-cipher=ALL:-AES:-EXP`

- `--ssl-key=file_name`

  The name of the SSL key file to use for establishing a secure connection.

4.5.7.6 Connecting to MySQL Remotely from Windows with SSH

Here is a note about how to connect to get a secure connection to remote MySQL server with SSH (by David Carlson `dcarlson@mplcomm.com`):

1. Install an SSH client on your Windows machine. As a user, the best non-free one I've found is from SecureCRT from `http://www.vandyke.com/`. Another option is `f-secure` from `http://www.f-secure.com/`. You can also find some free ones on Google at `http://directory.google.com/Top/Computers/Security/Products_and_Tools/Cryptography/SSH/Clients/Windows/`.

2. Start your Windows SSH client. Set `Host_Name = yourmysqlserver_URL_or_IP`. Set `userid=your_userid` to log in to your server. This `userid` value may not be the same as the username of your MySQL account.

3. Set up port forwarding. Either do a remote forward (Set `local_port: 3306`, `remote_host: yourmysqlservername_or_ip`, `remote_port: 3306`) or a local forward (Set `port: 3306, host: localhost, remote port: 3306`).

4. Save everything, otherwise you'll have to redo it the next time.

5. Log in to your server with the SSH session you just created.

6. On your Windows machine, start some ODBC application (such as Access).

7. Create a new file in Windows and link to MySQL using the ODBC driver the same way you normally do, except type in `localhost` for the MySQL host server, not `yourmysqlservername`.

You should now have an ODBC connection to MySQL, encrypted using SSH.

4.6 Disaster Prevention and Recovery

This section discusses how to make database backups and how to perform table maintenance. The syntax of the SQL statements described here is given in the *MySQL Language Reference*. Much of the information here pertains primarily to MyISAM tables. InnoDB backup procedures are given in Section 9.9, "Backing Up and Recovering an InnoDB Database."

4.6.1 Database Backups

Because MySQL tables are stored as files, it is easy to do a backup. To get a consistent backup, do a LOCK TABLES on the relevant tables, followed by FLUSH TABLES for the tables. You need only a read lock; this allows other clients to continue to query the tables while you are making a copy of the files in the database directory. The FLUSH TABLES statement is needed to ensure that the all active index pages are written to disk before you start the backup.

If you want to make an SQL-level backup of a table, you can use SELECT INTO ... OUTFILE or BACKUP TABLE. For SELECT INTO ... OUTFILE, the output file cannot already exist. For BACKUP TABLE, the same is true as of MySQL 3.23.56 and 4.0.12, because this would be a security risk.

Another way to back up a database is to use the mysqldump program or the mysqlhotcopy script. See Section 7.8, "The mysqldump Database Backup Program," and Section 7.9, "The mysqlhotcopy Database Backup Program."

1. Do a full backup of your database:

   ```
   shell> mysqldump --tab=/path/to/some/dir --opt db_name
   ```

   Or:

   ```
   shell> mysqlhotcopy db_name /path/to/some/dir
   ```

   You can also simply copy all table files (*.frm, *.MYD, and *.MYI files) as long as the server isn't updating anything. The mysqlhotcopy script uses this method. (But note that these methods will not work if your database contains InnoDB tables. InnoDB does not store table contents in database directories, and mysqlhotcopy works only for MyISAM and ISAM tables.)

2. Stop mysqld if it's running, then start it with the --log-bin[=file_name] option. See Section 4.8.4, "The Binary Log." The binary log files provide you with the information you need to replicate changes to the database that are made subsequent to the point at which you executed mysqldump.

If your MySQL server is a slave replication server, then regardless of the backup method you choose, you should also back up the master.info and relay-log.info files when you back up your slave's data. These files are always needed to resume replication after you restore the slave's data. If your slave is subject to replicating LOAD DATA INFILE commands, you should also back up any SQL_LOAD-* files that may exist in the directory specified by the --slave-load-tmpdir option. (This location defaults to the value of the tmpdir variable if not specified.) The slave needs these files to resume replication of any interrupted LOAD DATA INFILE operations.

If you have to restore MyISAM tables, try to recover them using REPAIR TABLE or myisamchk -r first. That should work in 99.9% of all cases. If myisamchk fails, try the following procedure. Note that it will work only if you have enabled binary logging by starting MySQL with the --log-bin option; see Section 4.8.4, "The Binary Log."

1. Restore the original mysqldump backup, or binary backup.

2. Execute the following command to re-run the updates in the binary logs:

```
shell> mysqlbinlog hostname-bin.[0-9]* | mysql
```

In your case, you may want to re-run only certain binary logs, from certain positions (usually you want to re-run all binary logs from the date of the restored backup, excepting possibly some incorrect queries). See Section 7.5, "The mysqlbinlog Binary Log Utility," for more information on the mysqlbinlog utility and how to use it.

If you are using the update logs instead, you can process their contents like this:

```
shell> ls -1 -t -r hostname.[0-9]* | xargs cat | mysql
```

ls is used to sort the update log filenames into the right order.

You can also do selective backups of individual files:

- To dump the table, use SELECT * INTO OUTFILE 'file_name' FROM 'tbl_name.
- To reload the table, use and restore with LOAD DATA INFILE 'file_name' REPLACE ... To avoid duplicate records, the table must have a PRIMARY KEY or a UNIQUE index. The REPLACE keyword causes old records to be replaced with new ones when a new record duplicates an old record on a unique key value.

If you have performance problems with your server while making backups, one strategy that can help is to set up replication and perform backups on the slave rather than on the master. See Section 5.1, "Introduction to Replication."

If you are using a Veritas filesystem, you can make a backup like this:

1. From a client program, execute FLUSH TABLES WITH READ LOCK.

2. From another shell, execute mount vxfs snapshot.

3. From the first client, execute UNLOCK TABLES.

4. Copy files from the snapshot.

5. Unmount the snapshot.

4.6.2 Table Maintenance and Crash Recovery

The following text discusses how to use myisamchk to check or repair MyISAM tables (tables with .MYI and .MYD files). The same concepts apply to using isamchk to check or repair ISAM tables (tables with .ISM and .ISD files). See Chapter 8, "MySQL Storage Engines and Table Types."

You can use the myisamchk utility to get information about your database tables or to check, repair, or optimize them. The following sections describe how to invoke myisamchk (including a description of its options), how to set up a table maintenance schedule, and how to use myisamchk to perform its various functions.

Even though table repair with myisamchk is quite secure, it's always a good idea to make a backup *before* doing a repair (or any maintenance operation that could make a lot of changes to a table).

myisamchk operations that affect indexes can cause FULLTEXT indexes to be rebuilt with full-text parameters that are incompatible with the values used by the MySQL server. To avoid this, read the instructions in Section 4.6.2.2, "General Options for myisamchk."

In many cases, you may find it simpler to do MyISAM table maintenance using the SQL statements that perform operations that myisamchk can do:

- To check or repair MyISAM tables, use CHECK TABLE or REPAIR TABLE.
- To optimize MyISAM tables, use OPTIMIZE TABLE.
- To analyze MyISAM tables, use ANALYZE TABLE.

These statements were introduced in different versions, but all are available from MySQL 3.23.14 on. The statements can be used directly, or by means of the mysqlcheck client program, which provides a command-line interface to them.

One advantage of these statements over myisamchk is that the server does all the work. With myisamchk, you must make sure that the server does not use the tables at the same time. Otherwise, there can be unwanted interaction betweeen myisamchk and the server.

4.6.2.1 myisamchk Invocation Syntax

Invoke myisamchk like this:

```
shell> myisamchk [options] tbl_name
```

The options specify what you want myisamchk to do. They are described in the following sections. You can also get a list of options by invoking myisamchk --help.

With no options, myisamchk simply checks your table as the default operation. To get more information or to tell myisamchk to take corrective action, specify options as described in the following discussion.

tbl_name is the database table you want to check or repair. If you run myisamchk somewhere other than in the database directory, you must specify the path to the database directory, because myisamchk has no idea where the database is located. In fact, myisamchk doesn't actually care whether the files you are working on are located in a database directory. You can copy the files that correspond to a database table into some other location and perform recovery operations on them there.

You can name several tables on the myisamchk command line if you wish. You can also specify a table by naming its index file (the file with the .MYI suffix). This allows you to specify all tables in a directory by using the pattern *.MYI. For example, if you are in a database directory, you can check all the MyISAM tables in that directory like this:

```
shell> myisamchk *.MYI
```

If you are not in the database directory, you can check all the tables there by specifying the path to the directory:

```
shell> myisamchk /path/to/database_dir/*.MYI
```

You can even check all tables in all databases by specifying a wildcard with the path to the MySQL data directory:

```
shell> myisamchk /path/to/datadir/*/*.MYI
```

The recommended way to quickly check all MyISAM and ISAM tables is:

```
shell> myisamchk --silent --fast /path/to/datadir/*/*.MYI
shell> isamchk --silent /path/to/datadir/*/*.ISM
```

If you want to check all MyISAM and ISAM tables and repair any that are corrupted, you can use the following commands:

```
shell> myisamchk --silent --force --fast --update-state \
          -O key_buffer=64M -O sort_buffer=64M \
          -O read_buffer=1M -O write_buffer=1M \
          /path/to/datadir/*/*.MYI
shell> isamchk --silent --force -O key_buffer=64M \
          -O sort_buffer=64M -O read_buffer=1M -O write_buffer=1M \
          /path/to/datadir/*/*.ISM
```

These commands assume that you have more than 64MB free. For more information about memory allocation with myisamchk, see Section 4.6.2.6, "myisamchk Memory Usage."

You must ensure that no other program is using the tables while you are running myisamchk. Otherwise, when you run myisamchk, it may display the following error message:

```
warning: clients are using or haven't closed the table properly
```

This means that you are trying to check a table that has been updated by another program (such as the mysqld server) that hasn't yet closed the file or that has died without closing the file properly.

If mysqld is running, you must force it to flush any table modifications that are still buffered in memory by using FLUSH TABLES. You should then ensure that no one is using the tables

while you are running myisamchk. The easiest way to avoid this problem is to use CHECK
TABLE instead of myisamchk to check tables.

4.6.2.2 General Options for myisamchk

The options described in this section can be used for any type of table maintenance operation performed by myisamchk. The sections following this one describe options that pertain
only to specific operations, such as table checking or repairing.

- --help, -?

  Display a help message and exit.

- --debug=*debug_options*, -# *debug_options*

  Write a debugging log. The *debug_options* string often is 'd:t:o,*file_name*'.

- --silent, -s

  Silent mode. Write output only when errors occur. You can use -s twice (-ss) to make
  myisamchk very silent.

- --verbose, -v

  Verbose mode. Print more information. This can be used with -d and -e. Use -v multiple times (-vv, -vvv) for even more output.

- --version, -V

  Display version information and exit.

- --wait, -w

  Instead of terminating with an error if the table is locked, wait until the table is
  unlocked before continuing. Note that if you are running mysqld with the --skip-
  external-locking option, the table can be locked only by another myisamchk command.

You can also set the following variables by using --*var_name*=*value* options:

Variable	Default Value
decode_bits	9
ft_max_word_len	version-dependent
ft_min_word_len	4
key_buffer_size	523264
myisam_block_size	1024
read_buffer_size	262136
sort_buffer_size	2097144
sort_key_blocks	16
write_buffer_size	262136

It is also possible to set variables by using --set-variable=*var_name*=*value* or -O
var_name=*value* syntax. However, this syntax is deprecated as of MySQL 4.0.

The possible `myisamchk` variables and their default values can be examined with `myisamchk --help`:

`sort_buffer_size` is used when the keys are repaired by sorting keys, which is the normal case when you use `--recover`.

`key_buffer_size` is used when you are checking the table with `--extend-check` or when the keys are repaired by inserting keys row by row into the table (like when doing normal inserts). Repairing through the key buffer is used in the following cases:

- You use `--safe-recover`.
- The temporary files needed to sort the keys would be more than twice as big as when creating the key file directly. This is often the case when you have large key values for CHAR, VARCHAR, or TEXT columns, because the sort operation needs to store the complete key values as it proceeds. If you have lots of temporary space and you can force `myisamchk` to repair by sorting, you can use the `--sort-recover` option.

Repairing through the key buffer takes much less disk space than using sorting, but is also much slower.

If you want a faster repair, set the `key_buffer_size` and `sort_buffer_size` variables to about 25% of your available memory. You can set both variables to large values, because only one of them is used at a time.

`myisam_block_size` is the size used for index blocks. It is available as of MySQL 4.0.0.

The `ft_min_word_len` and `ft_max_word_len` variables are available as of MySQL 4.0.0. `ft_stopword_file` is available as of MySQL 4.0.19.

`ft_min_word_len` and `ft_max_word_len` indicate the minimum and maximum word length for FULLTEXT indexes. `ft_stopword_file` names the stopword file. These need to be set under the following circumstances.

If you use `myisamchk` to perform an operation that modifies table indexes (such as repair or analyze), the FULLTEXT indexes are rebuilt using the default full-text parameter values for minimum and maximum word length and the stopword file unless you specify otherwise. This can result in queries failing.

The problem occurs because these parameters are known only by the server. They are not stored in MyISAM index files. To avoid the problem if you have modified the minimum or maximum word length or the stopword file in the server, specify the same `ft_min_word_len`, `ft_max_word_len`, and `ft_stopword_file` values to `myisamchk` that you use for `mysqld`. For example, if you have set the minimum word length to 3, you can repair a table with `myisamchk` like this:

```
shell> myisamchk --recover --ft_min_word_len=3 tbl_name.MYI
```

To ensure that `myisamchk` and the server use the same values for full-text parameters, you can place each one in both the `[mysqld]` and `[myisamchk]` sections of an option file:

```
[mysqld]
ft_min_word_len=3

[myisamchk]
ft_min_word_len=3
```

An alternative to using `myisamchk` is to use the REPAIR TABLE, ANALYZE TABLE, OPTIMIZE TABLE, or ALTER TABLE. These statements are performed by the server, which knows the proper full-text parameter values to use.

4.6.2.3 Check Options for `myisamchk`

`myisamchk` supports the following options for table checking operations:

- `--check, -c`

  Check the table for errors. This is the default operation if you specify no option that selects an operation type explicitly.

- `--check-only-changed, -C`

  Check only tables that have changed since the last check.

- `--extend-check, -e`

  Check the table very thoroughly. This is quite slow if the table has many indexes. This option should only be used in extreme cases. Normally, `myisamchk` or `myisamchk --medium-check` should be able to determine whether there are any errors in the table.

  If you are using `--extend-check` and have plenty of memory, setting the `key_buffer_size` variable to a large value will help the repair operation run faster.

- `--fast, -F`

  Check only tables that haven't been closed properly.

- `--force, -f`

  Do a repair operation automatically if `myisamchk` finds any errors in the table. The repair type is the same as that specified with the `--repair` or `-r` option.

- `--information, -i`

  Print informational statistics about the table that is checked.

- `--medium-check, -m`

  Do a check that is faster than an `--extend-check` operation. This finds only 99.99% of all errors, which should be good enough in most cases.

- `--read-only, -T`

  Don't mark the table as checked. This is useful if you use `myisamchk` to check a table that is in use by some other application that doesn't use locking, such as `mysqld` when run with the `--skip-external-locking` option.

- --update-state, -U

Store information in the .MYI file to indicate when the table was checked and whether the table crashed. This should be used to get full benefit of the --check-only-changed option, but you shouldn't use this option if the mysqld server is using the table and you are running it with the --skip-external-locking option.

4.6.2.4 Repair Options for myisamchk

myisamchk supports the following options for table repair operations:

- --backup, -B

Make a backup of the .MYD file as *file_name-time*.BAK

- --character-sets-dir=*path*

The directory where character sets are installed. See Section 4.7.1, "The Character Set Used for Data and Sorting."

- --correct-checksum

Correct the checksum information for the table.

- --data-file-length=#, -D #

Maximum length of the data file (when re-creating data file when it's "full").

- --extend-check, -e

Do a repair that tries to recover every possible row from the data file. Normally this will also find a lot of garbage rows. Don't use this option unless you are totally desperate.

- --force, -f

Overwrite old temporary files (files with names like *tbl_name*.TMD) instead of aborting.

- --keys-used=#, -k #

For myisamchk, the option value indicates which indexes to update. Each binary bit of the option value corresponds to a table index, where the first index is bit 0. For isamchk, the option value indicates that only the first # of the table indexes should be updated. In either case, an option value of 0 disables updates to all indexes, which can be used to get faster inserts. Deactivated indexes can be reactivated by using myisamchk -r or (isamchk -r).

- --no-symlinks, -l

Do not follow symbolic links. Normally myisamchk repairs the table that a symlink points to. This option doesn't exist as of MySQL 4.0, because versions from 4.0 on will not remove symlinks during repair operations.

- --parallel-recover, -p

Uses the same technique as -r and -n, but creates all the keys in parallel, using different threads. This option was added in MySQL 4.0.2. *This is alpha code. Use at your own risk!*

- `--quick, -q`

  Achieve a faster repair by not modifying the data file. You can specify this option twice to force `myisamchk` to modify the original data file in case of duplicate keys.

- `--recover, -r`

  Do a repair that can fix almost any problem except unique keys that aren't unique (which is an extremely unlikely error with `ISAM`/`MyISAM` tables). If you want to recover a table, this is the option to try first. You should try `-o` only if `myisamchk` reports that the table can't be recovered by `-r`. (In the unlikely case that `-r` fails, the data file is still intact.)

  If you have lots of memory, you should increase the value of `sort_buffer_size`.

- `--safe-recover, -o`

  Do a repair using an old recovery method that reads through all rows in order and updates all index trees based on the rows found. This is an order of magnitude slower than `-r`, but can handle a couple of very unlikely cases that `-r` cannot. This recovery method also uses much less disk space than `-r`. Normally, you should repair first with `-r`, and then with `-o` only if `-r` fails.

  If you have lots of memory, you should increase the value of `key_buffer_size`.

- `--set-character-set=name`

  Change the character set used by the table indexes.

- `--sort-recover, -n`

  Force `myisamchk` to use sorting to resolve the keys even if the temporary files should not be very big.

- `--tmpdir=path, -t path`

  Path of the directory to be used for storing temporary files. If this is not set, `myisamchk` uses the value of the `TMPDIR` environment variable. Starting from MySQL 4.1, `tmpdir` can be set to a list of directory paths that will be used successively in round-robin fashion for creating temporary files. The separator character between directory names should be colon (':') on Unix and semicolon (';') on Windows, NetWare, and OS/2.

- `--unpack, -u`

  Unpack a table that was packed with `myisampack`.

4.6.2.5 Other Options for `myisamchk`

`myisamchk` supports the following options for actions other than table checks and repairs:

- `--analyze, -a`

  Analyze the distribution of keys. This improves join performance by enabling the join optimizer to better choose the order in which to join the tables and which keys it should use. To obtain information about the distribution, use a `myisamchk` `--description --verbose tbl_name` command or the `SHOW KEYS FROM tbl_name` statement.

- `--description, -d`

  Print some descriptive information about the table.

- `--set-auto-increment[=value], -A[value]`

  Force AUTO_INCREMENT numbering for new records to start at the given value (or higher, if there are already records with AUTO_INCREMENT values this large). If value is not specified, the AUTO_INCREMENT number for new records begins with the largest value currently in the table, plus one.

- `--sort-index, -S`

  Sort the index tree blocks in high-low order. This optimizes seeks and makes table scanning by key faster.

- `--sort-records=#, -R #`

  Sort records according to a particular index. This makes your data much more localized and may speed up range-based SELECT and ORDER BY operations that use this index. (The first time you use this option to sort a table, it may be very slow.) To determine a table's index numbers, use SHOW KEYS, which displays a table's indexes in the same order that myisamchk sees them. Indexes are numbered beginning with 1.

4.6.2.6 `myisamchk` Memory Usage

Memory allocation is important when you run myisamchk. myisamchk uses no more memory than you specify with the -O options. If you are going to use myisamchk on very large tables, you should first decide how much memory you want it to use. The default is to use only about 3MB to perform repairs. By using larger values, you can get myisamchk to operate faster. For example, if you have more than 32MB RAM, you could use options such as these (in addition to any other options you might specify):

```
shell> myisamchk -O sort=16M -O key=16M -O read=1M -O write=1M ...
```

Using -O sort=16M should probably be enough for most cases.

Be aware that myisamchk uses temporary files in TMPDIR. If TMPDIR points to a memory filesystem, you may easily get out of memory errors. If this happens, set TMPDIR to point at some directory located on a filesystem with more space and run myisamchk again.

When repairing, myisamchk will also need a lot of disk space:

- Double the size of the data file (the original one and a copy). This space is not needed if you do a repair with --quick; in this case, only the index file is re-created. This space is needed on the same filesystem as the original data file! (The copy is created in the same directory as the original.)

- Space for the new index file that replaces the old one. The old index file is truncated at the start of the repair operation, so you usually ignore this space. This space is needed on the same filesystem as the original index file!

- When using --recover or --sort-recover (but not when using --safe-recover), you will need space for a sort buffer. The amount of space required is:

  (*largest_key* + *row_pointer_length*) * *number_of_rows* * 2

  You can check the length of the keys and the *row_pointer_length* with myisamchk -dv *tbl_name*. This space is allocated in the temporary directory (specified by TMPDIR or --tmpdir=*path*).

If you have a problem with disk space during repair, you can try to use --safe-recover instead of --recover.

4.6.2.7 Using myisamchk for Crash Recovery

If you run mysqld with --skip-external-locking (which is the default on some systems, such as Linux), you can't reliably use myisamchk to check a table when mysqld is using the same table. If you can be sure that no one is accessing the tables through mysqld while you run myisamchk, you only have to do mysqladmin flush-tables before you start checking the tables. If you can't guarantee this, then you must stop mysqld while you check the tables. If you run myisamchk while mysqld is updating the tables, you may get a warning that a table is corrupt even when it isn't.

If you are not using --skip-external-locking, you can use myisamchk to check tables at any time. While you do this, all clients that try to update the table will wait until myisamchk is ready before continuing.

If you use myisamchk to repair or optimize tables, you *must* always ensure that the mysqld server is not using the table (this also applies if you are using --skip-external-locking). If you don't take down mysqld, you should at least do a mysqladmin flush-tables before you run myisamchk. Your tables *may become corrupted* if the server and myisamchk access the tables simultaneously.

This section describes how to check for and deal with data corruption in MySQL databases. If your tables get corrupted frequently you should try to find the reason why. See Section A.4.2, "What to Do If MySQL Keeps Crashing."

The MyISAM table section contains reasons for why a table could be corrupted. See Section 8.1.4, "MyISAM Table Problems."

When performing crash recovery, it is important to understand that each MyISAM table *tbl_name* in a database corresponds to three files in the database directory:

File	Purpose
tbl_name.frm	Definition (format) file
tbl_name.MYD	Data file
tbl_name.MYI	Index file

Each of these three file types is subject to corruption in various ways, but problems occur most often in data files and index files.

myisamchk works by creating a copy of the .MYD data file row by row. It ends the repair stage by removing the old .MYD file and renaming the new file to the original file name. If you use --quick, myisamchk does not create a temporary .MYD file, but instead assumes that the .MYD file is correct and only generates a new index file without touching the .MYD file. This is safe, because myisamchk automatically detects whether the .MYD file is corrupt and aborts the repair if it is. You can also specify the --quick option twice to myisamchk. In this case, myisamchk does not abort on some errors (such as duplicate-key errors) but instead tries to resolve them by modifying the .MYD file. Normally the use of two --quick options is useful only if you have too little free disk space to perform a normal repair. In this case, you should at least make a backup before running myisamchk.

4.6.2.8 How to Check MyISAM Tables for Errors

To check a MyISAM table, use the following commands:

- myisamchk *tbl_name*

  This finds 99.99% of all errors. What it can't find is corruption that involves *only* the data file (which is very unusual). If you want to check a table, you should normally run myisamchk without options or with either the -s or --silent option.

- myisamchk -m *tbl_name*

  This finds 99.999% of all errors. It first checks all index entries for errors and then reads through all rows. It calculates a checksum for all keys in the rows and verifies that the checksum matches the checksum for the keys in the index tree.

- myisamchk -e *tbl_name*

  This does a complete and thorough check of all data (-e means "extended check"). It does a check-read of every key for each row to verify that they indeed point to the correct row. This may take a long time for a large table that has many indexes. Normally, myisamchk stops after the first error it finds. If you want to obtain more information, you can add the --verbose (-v) option. This causes myisamchk to keep going, up through a maximum of 20 errors.

- myisamchk -e -i *tbl_name*

  Like the previous command, but the -i option tells myisamchk to print some informational statistics, too.

In most cases, a simple myisamchk with no arguments other than the table name is sufficient to check a table.

4.6.2.9 How to Repair Tables

The discussion in this section describes how to use myisamchk on MyISAM tables (extensions .MYI and .MYD). If you are using ISAM tables (extensions .ISM and .ISD), you should use isamchk instead; the concepts are similar.

If you are using MySQL 3.23.16 and above, you can (and should) use the CHECK TABLE and REPAIR TABLE statements to check and repair MyISAM tables.

The symptoms of a corrupted table include queries that abort unexpectedly and observable errors such as these:

- *tbl_name*.frm is locked against change
- Can't find file *tbl_name*.MYI (Errcode: *###*)
- Unexpected end of file
- Record file is crashed
- Got error *###* from table handler

To get more information about the error you can run perror *###*, where *###* is the error number. The following example shows how to use perror to find the meanings for the most common error numbers that indicate a problem with a table:

```
shell> perror 126 127 132 134 135 136 141 144 145
126 = Index file is crashed / Wrong file format
127 = Record-file is crashed
132 = Old database file
134 = Record was already deleted (or record file crashed)
135 = No more room in record file
136 = No more room in index file
141 = Duplicate unique key or constraint on write or update
144 = Table is crashed and last repair failed
145 = Table was marked as crashed and should be repaired
```

Note that error 135 (no more room in record file) and error 136 (no more room in index file) are not errors that can be fixed by a simple repair. In this case, you have to use ALTER TABLE to increase the MAX_ROWS and AVG_ROW_LENGTH table option values:

```
ALTER TABLE tbl_name MAX_ROWS=xxx AVG_ROW_LENGTH=yyy;
```

If you don't know the current table option values, use SHOW CREATE TABLE *tbl_name*.

For the other errors, you must repair your tables. myisamchk can usually detect and fix most problems that occur.

The repair process involves up to four stages, described here. Before you begin, you should change location to the database directory and check the permissions of the table files. On Unix, make sure that they are readable by the user that mysqld runs as (and to you, because you need to access the files you are checking). If it turns out you need to modify files, they must also be writable by you.

The options that you can use for table maintenance with `myisamchk` and `isamchk` are described in several of the earlier subsections of Section 4.6.2, "Table Maintenance and Crash Recovery."

The following section is for the cases where the above command fails or if you want to use the extended features that `myisamchk` and `isamchk` provide.

If you are going to repair a table from the command line, you must first stop the `mysqld` server. Note that when you do `mysqladmin shutdown` on a remote server, the `mysqld` server will still be alive for a while after `mysqladmin` returns, until all queries are stopped and all keys have been flushed to disk.

Stage 1: Checking your tables

Run `myisamchk *.MYI` or `myisamchk -e *.MYI` if you have more time. Use the `-s` (silent) option to suppress unnecessary information.

If the `mysqld` server is down, you should use the `--update-state` option to tell `myisamchk` to mark the table as 'checked'.

You have to repair only those tables for which `myisamchk` announces an error. For such tables, proceed to Stage 2.

If you get weird errors when checking (such as `out of memory` errors), or if `myisamchk` crashes, go to Stage 3.

Stage 2: Easy safe repair

Note: If you want a repair operation to go much faster, you should set the values of the `sort_buffer_size` and `key_buffer_size` variables each to about 25% of your available memory when running `myisamchk` or `isamchk`.

First, try `myisamchk -r -q tbl_name` (`-r -q` means "quick recovery mode"). This will attempt to repair the index file without touching the data file. If the data file contains everything that it should and the delete links point at the correct locations within the data file, this should work, and the table is fixed. Start repairing the next table. Otherwise, use the following procedure:

1. Make a backup of the data file before continuing.
2. Use `myisamchk -r tbl_name` (`-r` means "recovery mode"). This will remove incorrect records and deleted records from the data file and reconstruct the index file.
3. If the preceding step fails, use `myisamchk --safe-recover tbl_name`. Safe recovery mode uses an old recovery method that handles a few cases that regular recovery mode doesn't (but is slower).

If you get weird errors when repairing (such as `out of memory` errors), or if `myisamchk` crashes, go to Stage 3.

Stage 3: Difficult repair

You should reach this stage only if the first 16KB block in the index file is destroyed or contains incorrect information, or if the index file is missing. In this case, it's necessary to create a new index file. Do so as follows:

1. Move the data file to some safe place.

2. Use the table description file to create new (empty) data and index files:

   ```
   shell> mysql db_name
   mysql> SET AUTOCOMMIT=1;
   mysql> TRUNCATE TABLE tbl_name;
   mysql> quit
   ```

   If your version of MySQL doesn't have TRUNCATE TABLE, use DELETE FROM tbl_name instead.

3. Copy the old data file back onto the newly created data file. (Don't just move the old file back onto the new file; you want to retain a copy in case something goes wrong.)

Go back to Stage 2. myisamchk -r -q should work now. (This shouldn't be an endless loop.)

As of MySQL 4.0.2, you can also use REPAIR TABLE tbl_name USE_FRM, which performs the whole procedure automatically.

Stage 4: Very difficult repair

You should reach this stage only if the .frm description file has also crashed. That should never happen, because the description file isn't changed after the table is created:

1. Restore the description file from a backup and go back to Stage 3. You can also restore the index file and go back to Stage 2. In the latter case, you should start with myisamchk -r.

2. If you don't have a backup but know exactly how the table was created, create a copy of the table in another database. Remove the new data file, then move the .frm description and .MYI index files from the other database to your crashed database. This gives you new description and index files, but leaves the .MYD data file alone. Go back to Stage 2 and attempt to reconstruct the index file.

4.6.2.10 Table Optimization

To coalesce fragmented records and eliminate wasted space resulting from deleting or updating records, run myisamchk in recovery mode:

```
shell> myisamchk -r tbl_name
```

You can optimize a table in the same way by using the SQL OPTIMIZE TABLE statement. OPTIMIZE TABLE does a repair of the table and a key analysis, and also sorts the index tree to give faster key lookups. There is also no possibility of unwanted interaction between a utility and the server, because the server does all the work when you use OPTIMIZE TABLE.

myisamchk also has a number of other options you can use to improve the performance of a table:

- -S, --sort-index
- -R *index_num*, --sort-records=*index_num*
- -a, --analyze

For a full description of the options, see Section 4.6.2.1, "myisamchk Invocation Syntax."

4.6.3 Setting Up a Table Maintenance Schedule

It is a good idea to perform table checks on a regular basis rather than waiting for problems to occur. One way to check and repair MyISAM tables is with the CHECK TABLE and REPAIR TABLE statements. These are available starting with MySQL 3.23.16.

Another way to check tables is to use myisamchk. For maintenance purposes, you can use myisamchk -s. The -s option (short for --silent) causes myisamchk to run in silent mode, printing messages only when errors occur.

It's also a good idea to check tables when the server starts. For example, whenever the machine has done a restart in the middle of an update, you usually need to check all the tables that could have been affected. (These are "expected crashed tables.") To check MyISAM tables automatically, start the server with the --myisam-recover option, available as of MySQL 3.23.25. If your server is too old to support this option, you could add a test to mysqld_safe that runs myisamchk to check all tables that have been modified during the last 24 hours if there is an old .pid (process ID) file left after a restart. (The .pid file is created by mysqld when it starts and removed when it terminates normally. The presence of a .pid file at system startup time indicates that mysqld terminated abnormally.)

An even better test would be to check any table whose last-modified time is more recent than that of the .pid file.

You should also check your tables regularly during normal system operation. At MySQL AB, we run a cron job to check all our important tables once a week, using a line like this in a crontab file:

```
35 0 * * 0 /path/to/myisamchk --fast --silent /path/to/datadir/*/*.MYI
```

This prints out information about crashed tables so that we can examine and repair them when needed.

Because we haven't had any unexpectedly crashed tables (tables that become corrupted for reasons other than hardware trouble) for a couple of years now (this is really true), once a week is more than enough for us.

We recommend that to start with, you execute myisamchk -s each night on all tables that have been updated during the last 24 hours, until you come to trust MySQL as much as we do.

Normally MySQL tables need little maintenance. If you are changing MyISAM tables with dynamic size rows (tables with VARCHAR, BLOB, or TEXT columns) or have tables with many deleted rows you may want to defragment/reclaim space from the tables from time to time (once a month?).

You can do this by using OPTIMIZE TABLE on the tables in question. Or, if you can stop the mysqld server for a while, change location into the data directory and use this command while the server is stopped:

```
shell> myisamchk -r -s --sort-index -O sort_buffer_size=16M */*.MYI
```

For ISAM tables, the command is similar:

```
shell> isamchk -r -s --sort-index -O sort_buffer_size=16M */*.ISM
```

4.6.4 Getting Information About a Table

To obtain a description of a table or statistics about it, use the commands shown here. We explain some of the information in more detail later:

- myisamchk -d tbl_name

  Runs myisamchk in "describe mode" to produce a description of your table. If you start the MySQL server using the --skip-external-locking option, myisamchk may report an error for a table that is updated while it runs. However, because myisamchk doesn't change the table in describe mode, there is no risk of destroying data.

- myisamchk -d -v tbl_name

  Adding -v runs myisamchk in verbose mode so that it produces more information about what it is doing.

- myisamchk -eis tbl_name

  Shows only the most important information from a table. This operation is slow because it must read the entire table.

- myisamchk -eiv tbl_name

  This is like -eis, but tells you what is being done.

Sample output for some of these commands follows. They are based on a table with these data and index file sizes:

```
-rw-rw-r--  1 monty   tcx     317235748 Jan 12 17:30 company.MYD
-rw-rw-r--  1 davida  tcx      96482304 Jan 12 18:35 company.MYM
```

Example of myisamchk -d output:

```
MyISAM file:     company.MYI
Record format:   Fixed length
Data records:    1403698  Deleted blocks:      0
Recordlength:    226
```

```
table description:
Key Start Len Index   Type
1   2     8   unique  double
2   15    10  multip. text packed stripped
3   219   8   multip. double
4   63    10  multip. text packed stripped
5   167   2   multip. unsigned short
6   177   4   multip. unsigned long
7   155   4   multip. text
8   138   4   multip. unsigned long
9   177   4   multip. unsigned long
    193   1           text
```

Example of `myisamchk -d -v` output:

```
MyISAM file:          company
Record format:        Fixed length
File-version:         1
Creation time:        1999-10-30 12:12:51
Recover time:         1999-10-31 19:13:01
Status:               checked
Data records:              1403698  Deleted blocks:          0
Datafile parts:            1403698  Deleted data:            0
Datafile pointer (bytes):        3  Keyfile pointer (bytes):       3
Max datafile length: 3791650815  Max keyfile length: 4294967294
Recordlength:              226
```

```
table description:
Key Start Len Index   Type                         Rec/key      Root Blocksize
1   2     8   unique  double                            1 15845376      1024
2   15    10  multip. text packed stripped              2 25062400      1024
3   219   8   multip. double                           73 40907776      1024
4   63    10  multip. text packed stripped              5 48097280      1024
5   167   2   multip. unsigned short                 4840 55200768      1024
6   177   4   multip. unsigned long                  1346 65145856      1024
7   155   4   multip. text                           4995 75090944      1024
8   138   4   multip. unsigned long                    87 85036032      1024
9   177   4   multip. unsigned long                   178 96481280      1024
    193   1           text
```

Example of `myisamchk -eis` output:

```
Checking MyISAM file: company
Key: 1:  Keyblocks used: 97%  Packed:   0%  Max levels: 4
Key: 2:  Keyblocks used: 98%  Packed:  50%  Max levels: 4
Key: 3:  Keyblocks used: 97%  Packed:   0%  Max levels: 4
Key: 4:  Keyblocks used: 99%  Packed:  60%  Max levels: 3
Key: 5:  Keyblocks used: 99%  Packed:   0%  Max levels: 3
```

```
Key:  6:  Keyblocks used:  99%  Packed:     0%  Max levels:  3
Key:  7:  Keyblocks used:  99%  Packed:     0%  Max levels:  3
Key:  8:  Keyblocks used:  99%  Packed:     0%  Max levels:  3
Key:  9:  Keyblocks used:  98%  Packed:     0%  Max levels:  4
Total:    Keyblocks used:  98%  Packed:    17%

Records:            1403698   M.recordlength:     226
Packed:             0%
Recordspace used:       100%  Empty space:         0%
Blocks/Record:   1.00
Record blocks:     1403698    Delete blocks:       0
Recorddata:      317235748    Deleted data:        0
Lost space:              0    Linkdata:            0

User time 1626.51, System time 232.36
Maximum resident set size 0, Integral resident set size 0
Non physical pagefaults 0, Physical pagefaults 627, Swaps 0
Blocks in 0 out 0, Messages in 0 out 0, Signals 0
Voluntary context switches 639, Involuntary context switches 28966
```

Example of myisamchk -eiv output:

```
Checking MyISAM file: company
Data records: 1403698   Deleted blocks:       0
- check file-size
- check delete-chain
block_size 1024:
index  1:
index  2:
index  3:
index  4:
index  5:
index  6:
index  7:
index  8:
index  9:
No recordlinks
- check index reference
- check data record references index: 1
Key:  1: Keyblocks used:  97%  Packed:     0%  Max levels:  4
- check data record references index: 2
Key:  2: Keyblocks used:  98%  Packed:    50%  Max levels:  4
- check data record references index: 3
Key:  3: Keyblocks used:  97%  Packed:     0%  Max levels:  4
- check data record references index: 4
Key:  4: Keyblocks used:  99%  Packed:    60%  Max levels:  3
- check data record references index: 5
```

```
Key:  5:  Keyblocks used:  99%  Packed:    0%  Max levels:  3
- check data record references index: 6
Key:  6:  Keyblocks used:  99%  Packed:    0%  Max levels:  3
- check data record references index: 7
Key:  7:  Keyblocks used:  99%  Packed:    0%  Max levels:  3
- check data record references index: 8
Key:  8:  Keyblocks used:  99%  Packed:    0%  Max levels:  3
- check data record references index: 9
Key:  9:  Keyblocks used:  98%  Packed:    0%  Max levels:  4
Total:    Keyblocks used:   9%  Packed:   17%

- check records and index references
[LOTS OF ROW NUMBERS DELETED]

Records:        1403698   M.recordlength:   226   Packed:         0%
Recordspace used:   100%  Empty space:       0%   Blocks/Record: 1.00
Record blocks:  1403698   Delete blocks:     0
Recorddata:   317235748   Deleted data:      0
Lost space:           0   Linkdata:          0

User time 1639.63, System time 251.61
Maximum resident set size 0, Integral resident set size 0
Non physical pagefaults 0, Physical pagefaults 10580, Swaps 0
Blocks in 4 out 0, Messages in 0 out 0, Signals 0
Voluntary context switches 10604, Involuntary context switches 122798
```

Explanations for the types of information myisamchk produces are given here. "Keyfile" refers to the index file. "Record" and "row" are synonymous.

- MyISAM file

  Name of the MyISAM (index) file.

- File-version

  Version of MyISAM format. Currently always 2.

- Creation time

  When the data file was created.

- Recover time

  When the index/data file was last reconstructed.

- Data records

  How many records are in the table.

- Deleted blocks

  How many deleted blocks still have reserved space. You can optimize your table to minimize this space. See Section 4.6.2.10, "Table Optimization."

- Datafile parts

  For dynamic record format, this indicates how many data blocks there are. For an optimized table without fragmented records, this is the same as Data records.

- Deleted data

  How many bytes of unreclaimed deleted data there are. You can optimize your table to minimize this space. See Section 4.6.2.10, "Table Optimization."

- Datafile pointer

  The size of the data file pointer, in bytes. It is usually 2, 3, 4, or 5 bytes. Most tables manage with 2 bytes, but this cannot be controlled from MySQL yet. For fixed tables, this is a record address. For dynamic tables, this is a byte address.

- Keyfile pointer

  The size of the index file pointer, in bytes. It is usually 1, 2, or 3 bytes. Most tables manage with 2 bytes, but this is calculated automatically by MySQL. It is always a block address.

- Max datafile length

  How long the table data file can become, in bytes.

- Max keyfile length

  How long the table index file can become, in bytes.

- Recordlength

  How much space each record takes, in bytes.

- Record format

  The format used to store table rows. The preceding examples use Fixed length. Other possible values are Compressed and Packed.

- table description

  A list of all keys in the table. For each key, myisamchk displays some low-level information:

  - Key

    This key's number.

  - Start

    Where in the record this index part starts.

  - Len

    How long this index part is. For packed numbers, this should always be the full length of the column. For strings, it may be shorter than the full length of the indexed column, because you can index a prefix of a string column.

  - Index

    Whether a key value can exist multiple times in the index. Values are unique or multip. (multiple).

- Type

  What data type this index part has. This is a MyISAM data type with the options packed, stripped, or empty.

- Root

  Address of the root index block.

- Blocksize

  The size of each index block. By default this is 1024, but the value may be changed at compile time when MySQL is built from source.

- Rec/key

  This is a statistical value used by the optimizer. It tells how many records there are per value for this key. A unique key always has a value of 1. This may be updated after a table is loaded (or greatly changed) with myisamchk -a. If this is not updated at all, a default value of 30 is given.

For the table shown in the examples, there are two table description lines for the ninth index. This indicates that it is a multiple-part index with two parts.

- Keyblocks used

  What percentage of the keyblocks are used. When a table has just been reorganized with myisamchk, as for the table in the examples, the values are very high (very near the theoretical maximum).

- Packed

  MySQL tries to pack keys with a common suffix. This can only be used for indexes on CHAR, VARCHAR, or DECIMAL columns. For long indexed strings that have similar leftmost parts, this can significantly reduce the space used. In the third example above, the fourth key is 10 characters long and a 60% reduction in space is achieved.

- Max levels

  How deep the B-tree for this key is. Large tables with long key values get high values.

- Records

  How many rows are in the table.

- M.recordlength

  The average record length. This is the exact record length for tables with fixed-length records, because all records have the same length.

- Packed

  MySQL strips spaces from the end of strings. The Packed value indicates the percentage of savings achieved by doing this.

- Recordspace used

  What percentage of the data file is used.

- Empty space

  What percentage of the data file is unused.

- Blocks/Record

  Average number of blocks per record (that is, how many links a fragmented record is composed of). This is always 1.0 for fixed-format tables. This value should stay as close to 1.0 as possible. If it gets too big, you can reorganize the table.

- Recordblocks

  How many blocks (links) are used. For fixed format, this is the same as the number of records.

- Deleteblocks

  How many blocks (links) are deleted.

- Recorddata

  How many bytes in the data file are used.

- Deleted data

  How many bytes in the data file are deleted (unused).

- Lost space

  If a record is updated to a shorter length, some space is lost. This is the sum of all such losses, in bytes.

- Linkdata

  When the dynamic table format is used, record fragments are linked with pointers (4 to 7 bytes each). Linkdata is the sum of the amount of storage used by all such pointers.

If a table has been compressed with myisampack, myisamchk -d prints additional information about each table column. See Section 7.2, "myisampack, the MySQL Compressed Read-Only Table Generator," for an example of this information and a description of what it means.

4.7 MySQL Localization and International Usage

4.7.1 The Character Set Used for Data and Sorting

By default, MySQL uses the ISO-8859-1 (Latin1) character set with sorting according to Swedish/Finnish rules. These defaults are suitable for the United States and most of western Europe.

All MySQL binary distributions are compiled with --with-extra-charsets=complex. This adds code to all standard programs that enables them to handle latin1 and all multi-byte character sets within the binary. Other character sets will be loaded from a character-set definition file when needed.

The character set determines what characters are allowed in names. It also determines how strings are sorted by the `ORDER BY` and `GROUP BY` clauses of the `SELECT` statement.

You can change the character set with the `--default-character-set` option when you start the server. The character sets available depend on the `--with-charset=`*charset* and `--with-extra-charsets=` *list-of-charsets* | `complex` | `all` | `none` options to `configure`, and the character set configuration files listed in *SHAREDIR*/charsets/Index. See Section 2.3.2, "Typical `configure` Options."

As of MySQL 4.1.1, you can also change the character set collation with the `--default-collation` option when you start the server. The collation must be a legal collation for the default character set. (Use the `SHOW COLLATION` statement to determine which collations are available for each character set.) See Section 2.3.2, "Typical `configure` Options."

If you change the character set when running MySQL, that may also change the sort order. Consequently, you must run `myisamchk -r -q --set-character-set=`*charset* on all tables, or your indexes may not be ordered correctly.

When a client connects to a MySQL server, the server indicates to the client what the server's default character set is. The client will switch to use this character set for this connection.

You should use `mysql_real_escape_string()` when escaping strings for an SQL query. `mysql_real_escape_string()` is identical to the old `mysql_escape_string()` function, except that it takes the `MYSQL` connection handle as the first parameter so that the appropriate character set can be taken into account when escaping characters.

If the client is compiled with different paths than where the server is installed and the user who configured MySQL didn't include all character sets in the MySQL binary, you must tell the client where it can find the additional character sets it will need if the server runs with a different character set than the client.

You can do this by specifying a `--character-sets-dir` option to indicate the path to the directory in which the dynamic MySQL character sets are stored. For example, you can put the following in an option file:

```
[client]
character-sets-dir=/usr/local/mysql/share/mysql/charsets
```

You can force the client to use a specific character set as follows:

```
[client]
default-character-set=charset
```

This is normally unnecessary, however.

4.7.1.1 Using the German Character Set

To get German sorting order, you should start `mysqld` with a `--default-character-set=latin1_de` option. This affects server behavior in several ways:

- When sorting and comparing strings, the following mapping is performed on the strings before doing the comparison:

```
ä  ->  ae
ö  ->  oe
ü  ->  ue
ß  ->  ss
```

- All accented characters are converted to their unaccented uppercase counterpart. All letters are converted to uppercase.

- When comparing strings with LIKE, the one-character to two-character mapping is not done. All letters are converted to uppercase. Accents are removed from all letters except Ü, ü, Ö, ö, Ä, and ä.

4.7.2 Setting the Error Message Language

By default, mysqld produces error messages in English, but they can also be displayed in any of these other languages: Czech, Danish, Dutch, Estonian, French, German, Greek, Hungarian, Italian, Japanese, Korean, Norwegian, Norwegian-ny, Polish, Portuguese, Romanian, Russian, Slovak, Spanish, or Swedish.

To start mysqld with a particular language for error messages, use the --language or -L option. The option value can be a language name or the full path to the error message file. For example:

```
shell> mysqld --language=swedish
```

Or:

```
shell> mysqld --language=/usr/local/share/swedish
```

The language name should be specified in lowercase.

The language files are located (by default) in the share/LANGUAGE directory under the MySQL base directory.

To change the error message file, you should edit the errmsg.txt file, and then execute the following command to generate the errmsg.sys file:

```
shell> comp_err errmsg.txt errmsg.sys
```

If you upgrade to a newer version of MySQL, remember to repeat your changes with the new errmsg.txt file.

4.7.3 Adding a New Character Set

This section discusses the procedure for adding another character set to MySQL. You must have a MySQL source distribution to use these instructions.

To choose the proper procedure, decide whether the character set is simple or complex:

- If the character set does not need to use special string collating routines for sorting and does not need multi-byte character support, it is simple.
- If it needs either of those features, it is complex.

For example, latin1 and danish are simple character sets, whereas big5 and czech are complex character sets.

In the following procedures, the name of your character set is represented by *MYSET*.

For a simple character set, do the following:

1. Add *MYSET* to the end of the sql/share/charsets/Index file. Assign a unique number to it.

2. Create the file sql/share/charsets/*MYSET*.conf. (You can use a copy of sql/share/charsets/latin1.conf as the basis for this file.)

   The syntax for the file is very simple:

   - Comments start with a '#' character and proceed to the end of the line.
   - Words are separated by arbitrary amounts of whitespace.
   - When defining the character set, every word must be a number in hexadecimal format.
   - The ctype array takes up the first 257 words. The to_lower[], to_upper[] and sort_order[] arrays take up 256 words each after that.

   See Section 4.7.4, "The Character Definition Arrays."

3. Add the character set name to the CHARSETS_AVAILABLE and COMPILED_CHARSETS lists in configure.in.

4. Reconfigure, recompile, and test.

For a complex character set, do the following:

1. Create the file strings/ctype-*MYSET*.c in the MySQL source distribution.

2. Add *MYSET* to the end of the sql/share/charsets/Index file. Assign a unique number to it.

3. Look at one of the existing ctype-*.c files (such as strings/ctype-big5.c) to see what needs to be defined. Note that the arrays in your file must have names like ctype_*MYSET*, to_lower_*MYSET*, and so on. These correspond to the arrays for a simple character set. See Section 4.7.4, "The Character Definition Arrays."

4. Near the top of the file, place a special comment like this:

```
/*
 * This comment is parsed by configure to create ctype.c,
 * so don't change it unless you know what you are doing.
 *
```

```
*   .configure. number_MYSET=MYNUMBER
*   .configure. strxfrm_multiply_MYSET=N
*   .configure. mbmaxlen_MYSET=N
*/
```

The `configure` program uses this comment to include the character set into the MySQL library automatically.

The `strxfrm_multiply` and `mbmaxlen` lines are explained in the following sections. You need include them only if you need the string collating functions or the multi-byte character set functions, respectively.

5. You should then create some of the following functions:

   - `my_strncoll_MYSET()`

   - `my_strcoll_MYSET()`

   - `my_strxfrm_MYSET()`

   - `my_like_range_MYSET()`

   See Section 4.7.5, "String Collating Support."

6. Add the character set name to the `CHARSETS_AVAILABLE` and `COMPILED_CHARSETS` lists in `configure.in`.

7. Reconfigure, recompile, and test.

The `sql/share/charsets/README` file includes additional instructions.

If you want to have the character set included in the MySQL distribution, mail a patch to the MySQL `internals` mailing list. See Section 1.7.1.1, "The MySQL Mailing Lists."

4.7.4 The Character Definition Arrays

`to_lower[]` and `to_upper[]` are simple arrays that hold the lowercase and uppercase characters corresponding to each member of the character set. For example:

```
to_lower['A'] should contain 'a'
to_upper['a'] should contain 'A'
```

`sort_order[]` is a map indicating how characters should be ordered for comparison and sorting purposes. Quite often (but not for all character sets) this is the same as `to_upper[]`, which means that sorting will be case-insensitive. MySQL will sort characters based on the values of `sort_order[]` elements. For more complicated sorting rules, see the discussion of string collating in Section 4.7.5, "String Collating Support."

`ctype[]` is an array of bit values, with one element for one character. (Note that `to_lower[]`, `to_upper[]`, and `sort_order[]` are indexed by character value, but `ctype[]` is indexed by character value + 1. This is an old legacy convention to be able to handle `EOF`.)

You can find the following bitmask definitions in `m_ctype.h`:

```
#define _U    01    /* Uppercase */
#define _L    02    /* Lowercase */
#define _N    04    /* Numeral (digit) */
#define _S    010   /* Spacing character */
#define _P    020   /* Punctuation */
#define _C    040   /* Control character */
#define _B    0100  /* Blank */
#define _X    0200  /* heXadecimal digit */
```

The `ctype[]` entry for each character should be the union of the applicable bitmask values that describe the character. For example, `'A'` is an uppercase character (`_U`) as well as a hexadecimal digit (`_X`), so `ctype['A'+1]` should contain the value:

```
_U + _X = 01 + 0200 = 0201
```

4.7.5 String Collating Support

If the sorting rules for your language are too complex to be handled with the simple `sort_order[]` table, you need to use the string collating functions.

Right now the best documentation for this is the character sets that are already implemented. Look at the `big5`, `czech`, `gbk`, `sjis`, and `tis160` character sets for examples.

You must specify the `strxfrm_multiply_MYSET=N` value in the special comment at the top of the file. `N` should be set to the maximum ratio the strings may grow during `my_strxfrm_MYSET` (it must be a positive integer).

4.7.6 Multi-Byte Character Support

If you want to add support for a new character set that includes multi-byte characters, you need to use the multi-byte character functions.

Right now the best documentation on this consists of the character sets that are already implemented. Look at the `euc_kr`, `gb2312`, `gbk`, `sjis`, and `ujis` character sets for examples. These are implemented in the `ctype-'charset'.c` files in the `strings` directory.

You must specify the `mbmaxlen_MYSET=N` value in the special comment at the top of the source file. `N` should be set to the size in bytes of the largest character in the set.

4.7.7 Problems with Character Sets

If you try to use a character set that is not compiled into your binary, you might run into the following problems:

- Your program has an incorrect path to where the character sets are stored. (Default `/usr/local/mysql/share/mysql/charsets`). This can be fixed by using the `--character-sets-dir` option when you run the program in question.

- The character set is a multi-byte character set that can't be loaded dynamically. In this case, you must recompile the program with support for the character set.
- The character set is a dynamic character set, but you don't have a configure file for it. In this case, you should install the configure file for the character set from a new MySQL distribution.
- If your Index file doesn't contain the name for the character set, your program will display the following error message:

```
ERROR 1105: File '/usr/local/share/mysql/charsets/?.conf'
not found (Errcode: 2)
```

In this case, you should either get a new Index file or manually add the name of any missing character sets to the current file.

For MyISAM tables, you can check the character set name and number for a table with myisam-chk -dvv tbl_name.

4.8 The MySQL Log Files

MySQL has several different log files that can help you find out what's going on inside mysqld:

Log File	Types of Information Logged to File
The error log	Logs problems encountered starting, running, or stopping mysqld.
The isam log	Logs all changes to the ISAM tables. Used only for debugging the isam code.
The query log	Logs established client connections and executed statements.
The update log	Logs statements that change data. This log is deprecated.
The binary log	Logs all statements that change data. Also used for replication.
The slow log	Logs all queries that took more than long_query_time seconds to execute or didn't use indexes.

By default, all logs are created in the mysqld data directory. You can force mysqld to close and reopen the log files (or in some cases switch to a new log) by flushing the logs. Log flushing occurs when you issue a FLUSH LOGS statement or execute mysqladmin flush-logs or mysqladmin refresh.

If you are using MySQL replication capabilities, slave replication servers maintain additional log files called relay logs. These are discussed in Chapter 5, "Replication in MySQL."

4.8.1 The Error Log

The error log file contains information indicating when mysqld was started and stopped and also any critical errors that occur while the server is running.

If `mysqld` dies unexpectedly and `mysqld_safe` needs to restart it, `mysqld_safe` will write a `restarted mysqld` message to the error log. If `mysqld` notices a table that needs to be automatically checked or repaired, it writes a message to the error log.

On some operating systems, the error log will contain a stack trace if `mysqld` dies. The trace can be used to determine where `mysqld` died.

Beginning with MySQL 4.0.10, you can specify where `mysqld` stores the error log file with the `--log-error[=file_name]` option. If no `file_name` value is given, `mysqld` uses the name `host_name.err` and writes the file in the data directory. (Prior to MySQL 4.0.10, the Windows error log name is `mysql.err`.) If you execute `FLUSH LOGS`, the error log is renamed with a suffix of `-old` and `mysqld` creates a new empty log file.

In older MySQL versions on Unix, error log handling was done by `mysqld_safe` which redirected the error file to `host_name.err`. You could change this filename by specifying a `--err-log=filename` option to `mysqld_safe`.

If you don't specify `--log-error`, or (on Windows) if you use the `--console` option, errors are written to stderr, the standard error output. Usually this is your terminal.

On Windows, error output is always written to the `.err` file if `--console` is not given.

4.8.2 The General Query Log

If you want to know what happens within `mysqld`, you should start it with the `--log[=file_name]` or `-l [file_name]` option. If no `file_name` value is given, the default name is `host_name.log` This will log all connections and statements to the log file. This log can be very useful when you suspect an error in a client and want to know exactly what the client sent to `mysqld`.

Older versions of the `mysql.server` script (from MySQL 3.23.4 to 3.23.8) pass a `--log` option to `safe_mysqld` to enable the general query log. If you need better performance when you start using MySQL in a production environment, you can remove the `--log` option from `mysql.server` or change it to `--log-bin`. See Section 4.8.4, "The Binary Log."

`mysqld` writes statements to the query log in the order that it receives them. This may be different from the order in which they are executed. This is in contrast to the update log and the binary log, which are written after the query is executed, but before any locks are released.

Server restarts and log flushing do not cause a new general query log file to be generated (although flushing closes and reopens it). On Unix, you can rename the file and create a new one by using the following commands:

```
shell> mv hostname.log hostname-old.log
shell> mysqladmin flush-logs
shell> cp hostname-old.log to-backup-directory
shell> rm hostname-old.log
```

On Windows, you cannot rename the log file while the server has it open. You must stop the server and rename the log. Then restart the server to create a new log.

4.8.3 The Update Log

Note: The update log has been deprecated and replaced by the binary log. See Section 4.8.4, "The Binary Log." The binary log can do anything the old update log could do, and more. *The update log is unavailable as of MySQL 5.0.0.*

When started with the `--log-update[=file_name]` option, `mysqld` writes a log file containing all SQL statements that update data. If no `file_name` value is given, the default name is name of the host machine. If a filename is given, but it doesn't contain a leading path, the file is written in the data directory. If `file_name` doesn't have an extension, `mysqld` creates log files with names of the form `file_name.###`, where `###` is a number that is incremented each time you start the server or flush the logs.

Note: For this naming scheme to work, you must not create your own files with the same names as those that might be used for the log file sequence.

Update logging is smart because it logs only statements that really update data. So, an UPDATE or a DELETE with a WHERE that finds no rows is not written to the log. It even skips UPDATE statements that set a column to the value it already has.

The update logging is done immediately after a query completes but before any locks are released or any commit is done. This ensures that statements are logged in execution order.

If you want to update a database from update log files, you could do the following (assuming that your update logs have names of the form `file_name.###`):

```
shell> ls -1 -t -r file_name.[0-9]* | xargs cat | mysql
```

ls is used to sort the update log filenames into the right order.

This can be useful if you have to revert to backup files after a crash and you want to redo the updates that occurred between the time of the backup and the crash.

4.8.4 The Binary Log

The binary log has replaced the old update log, which is unavailable starting from MySQL 5.0. The binary log contains all information that is available in the update log in a more efficient format and in a manner that is transactionally safe.

The binary log, like the old update log, logs only statements that really update data. So an UPDATE or a DELETE with a WHERE that finds no rows is not written to the log. It even skips UPDATE statements that set a column to the value it already has.

The binary log also contains information about how long each statement took that updated the database. It doesn't contain statements that don't modify any data. If you want to log all statements (for example, to identify a problem query) you should use the general query log. See Section 4.8.2, "The General Query Log."

The primary purpose of the binary log is to be able to update the database during a restore operation as fully as possible, because the binary log will contain all updates done after a backup was made.

The binary log is also used on master replication servers as a record of the statements to be sent to slave servers. See Chapter 5, "Replication in MySQL."

Running the server with the binary log enabled makes performance about 1% slower. However, the benefits of the binary log for restore operations and in allowing you to set up replication generally outweigh this minor performance decrement.

When started with the `--log-bin[=file_name]` option, `mysqld` writes a log file containing all SQL commands that update data. If no `file_name` value is given, the default name is the name of the host machine followed by `-bin`. If the file name is given, but it doesn't contain a path, the file is written in the data directory.

If you supply an extension in the log name (for example, `--log-bin=file_name.extension`), the extension is silently removed and ignored.

`mysqld` appends a numeric extension to the binary log name. The number is incremented each time you start the server or flush the logs. A new binary log also is created automatically when the current log's size reaches `max_binlog_size`. A binary log may become larger than `max_binlog_size` if you are using large transactions: A transaction is written to the binary log in one piece, never split between binary logs.

To be able to know which different binary log files have been used, `mysqld` also creates a binary log index file that contains the name of all used binary log files. By default this has the same name as the binary log file, with the extension `'.index'`. You can change the name of the binary log index file with the `--log-bin-index=[file_name]` option. You should not manually edit this file while `mysqld` is running; doing so would confuse `mysqld`.

You can delete all binary log files with the RESET MASTER statement, or only some of them with PURGE MASTER LOGS.

You can use the following options to `mysqld` to affect what is logged to the binary log. See also the discussion that follows this option list.

- `--binlog-do-db=db_name`

  Tells the master that it should log updates to the binary log if the current database (that is, the one selected by USE) is *db_name*. All other databases that are not explicitly mentioned are ignored. If you use this, you should ensure that you only do updates in the current database.

  An example of what does not work as you might expect: If the server is started with `binlog-do-db=sales`, and you do `USE prices; UPDATE sales.january SET amount=amount+1000;`, this statement will not be written into the binary log.

- --binlog-ignore-db=*db_name*

  Tells the master that updates where the current database (that is, the one selected by USE) is *db_name* should not be stored in the binary log. If you use this, you should ensure that you only do updates in the current database.

  An example of what does not work as you might expect: If the server is started with binlog-ignore-db=sales, and you do USE prices; UPDATE sales.january SET amount=amount+1000;, this statement will be written into the binary log.

To log or ignore multiple databases, specify the appropriate option multiple times, once for each database.

The rules for logging or ignoring updates to the binary log are evaluated in the following order:

1. Are there binlog-do-db or binlog-ignore-db rules?

   - No: Write the statement to the binary log and exit.
   - Yes: Go to the next step.

2. There are some rules (binlog-do-db or binlog-ignore-db or both). Is there a current database (has any database been selected by USE?)?

   - No: Do *not* write the statement, and exit.
   - Yes: Go to the next step.

3. There is a current database. Are there some binlog-do-db rules?

   - Yes: Does the current database match any of the binlog-do-db rules?
     - Yes: Write the statement and exit.
     - No: Do *not* write the statement, and exit.
   - No: Go to the next step.

4. There are some binlog-ignore-db rules. Does the current database match any of the binlog-ignore-db rules?

   - Yes: Do not write the statement, and exit.
   - No: Write the query and exit.

For example, a slave running with only binlog-do-db=sales will not write to the binary log any statement whose current database is different from sales (in other words, binlog-do-db can sometimes mean "ignore other databases").

If you are using replication, you should not delete old binary log files until you are sure that no slave still needs to use them. One way to do this is to do mysqladmin flush-logs once a day and then remove any logs that are more than three days old. You can remove them manually, or preferably using PURGE MASTER LOGS, which will also safely update the binary log index file for you (and which can take a date argument since MySQL 4.1).

A client with the SUPER privilege can disable binary logging of its own statements by using a SET SQL_LOG_BIN=0 statement.

You can examine the binary log file with the mysqlbinlog utility. This can be useful when you want to reprocess statements in the log. For example, you can update a MySQL server from the binary log as follows:

```
shell> mysqlbinlog log-file | mysql -h server_name
```

See Section 7.5, "The mysqlbinlog Binary Log Utility," for more information on the mysqlbinlog utility and how to use it.

If you are using transactions, you must use the MySQL binary log for backups instead of the old update log.

The binary logging is done immediately after a query completes but before any locks are released or any commit is done. This ensures that the log will be logged in the execution order.

Updates to non-transactional tables are stored in the binary log immediately after execution. For transactional tables such as BDB or InnoDB tables, all updates (UPDATE, DELETE, or INSERT) that change tables are cached until a COMMIT statement is received by the server. At that point, mysqld writes the whole transaction to the binary log before the COMMIT is executed. When the thread that handles the transaction starts, it allocates a buffer of binlog_cache_size to buffer queries. If a statement is bigger than this, the thread opens a temporary file to store the transaction. The temporary file is deleted when the thread ends.

The max_binlog_cache_size (default 4GB) can be used to restrict the total size used to cache a multiple-statement transaction. If a transaction is larger than this, it will fail and roll back.

If you are using the update log or binary log, concurrent inserts will be converted to normal inserts when using CREATE ... SELECT or INSERT ... SELECT. This is to ensure that you can re-create an exact copy of your tables by applying the log on a backup.

The binary log format is different in versions 3.23, 4.0, and 5.0.0. Those format changes were required to implement enhancements to replication. MySQL 4.1 has the same binary log format as 4.0. See Section 5.5, "Replication Compatibility Between MySQL Versions."

4.8.5 The Slow Query Log

When started with the --log-slow-queries[=file_name] option, mysqld writes a log file containing all SQL statements that took more than long_query_time seconds to execute. The time to acquire the initial table locks are not counted as execution time.

If no file_name value is given, the default is the name of the host machine with a suffix of -slow.log. If a filename is given, but doesn't contain a path, the file is written in the data directory.

A statement is logged to the slow query log after it has been executed and after all locks have been released. Log order may be different from execution order.

The slow query log can be used to find queries that take a long time to execute and are therefore candidates for optimization. However, examining a long slow query log can become a difficult task. To make this easier, you can pipe the slow query log through the `mysqldumpslow` command to get a summary of the queries that appear in the log.

If you also use the `--log-long-format` when logging slow queries, then queries that are not using indexes are logged as well. See Section 4.2.1, "`mysqld` Command-Line Options."

4.8.6 Log File Maintenance

The MySQL Server can create a number of different log files that make it easy to see what is going on. See Section 4.8, "The MySQL Log Files." However, you must clean up these files regularly to ensure that the logs don't take up too much disk space.

When using MySQL with logging enabled, you will want to back up and remove old log files from time to time and tell MySQL to start logging to new files. See Section 4.6.1, "Database Backups."

On a Linux (Red Hat) installation, you can use the `mysql-log-rotate` script for this. If you installed MySQL from an RPM distribution, the script should have been installed automatically. You should be careful with this script if you are using the binary log for replication! (You should not remove binary logs until you are certain that their contents have been processed by all slaves.)

On other systems, you must install a short script yourself that you start from `cron` to handle log files.

You can force MySQL to start using new log files by using `mysqladmin flush-logs` or by using the SQL statement FLUSH LOGS. If you are using MySQL 3.21, you must use `mysqladmin refresh`.

A log flushing operation does the following:

- If standard logging (`--log`) or slow query logging (`--log-slow-queries`) is used, closes and reopens the log file (`mysql.log` and `` `hostname`-slow.log `` as default).
- If update logging (`--log-update`) or binary logging (`--log-bin`) is used, closes the log and opens a new log file with a higher sequence number.

If you are using only an update log, you only have to rename the old log file and then flush the logs before making a backup. For example, you can do something like this:

```
shell> cd mysql-data-directory
shell> mv mysql.log mysql.old
shell> mysqladmin flush-logs
```

Then make a backup and remove `mysql.old`.

4.9 Running Multiple MySQL Servers on the Same Machine

In some cases, you might want to run multiple mysqld servers on the same machine. You might want to test a new MySQL release while leaving your existing production setup undisturbed. Or you may want to give different users access to different mysqld servers that they manage themselves. (For example, you might be an Internet Service Provider that wants to provide independent MySQL installations for different customers.)

To run multiple servers on a single machine, each server must have unique values for several operating parameters. These can be set on the command line or in option files. See Section 3.3, "Specifying Program Options."

At least the following options must be different for each server:

- --port=*port_num*

  --port controls the port number for TCP/IP connections.

- --socket=*path*

  --socket controls the Unix socket file path on Unix and the name of the named pipe on Windows. On Windows, it's necessary to specify distinct pipe names only for those servers that support named pipe connections.

- --shared-memory-base-name=*name*

  This option currently is used only on Windows. It designates the shared memory name used by a Windows server to allow clients to connect via shared memory. This option is new in MySQL 4.1.

- --pid-file=*path*

  This option is used only on Unix. It indicates the name of the file in which the server writes its process ID.

If you use the following log file options, they must be different for each server:

- --log=*path*
- --log-bin=*path*
- --log-update=*path*
- --log-error=*path*
- --log-isam=*path*
- --bdb-logdir=*path*

Log file options are described in Section 4.8.6, "Log File Maintenance."

If you want more performance, you can also specify the following options differently for each server, to spread the load between several physical disks:

- `--tmpdir=path`
- `--bdb-tmpdir=path`

Having different temporary directories is also recommended, to make it easier to determine which MySQL server created any given temporary file.

Generally, each server should also use a different data directory, which is specified using the `--datadir=path` option.

Warning: Normally you should never have two servers that update data in the same databases! This may lead to unpleasant surprises if your operating system doesn't support fault-free system locking! If (despite this warning) you run multiple servers using the same data directory and they have logging enabled, you must use the appropriate options to specify log file names that are unique to each server. Otherwise, the servers will try to log to the same files.

This warning against sharing a data directory among servers also applies in an NFS environment. Allowing multiple MySQL servers to access a common data directory over NFS is a *bad idea*!

- The primary problem is that NFS will become the speed bottleneck. It is not meant for such use.
- Another risk with NFS is that you will have to come up with a way to make sure that two or more servers do not interfere with each other. Usually NFS file locking is handled by the `lockd` daemon, but at the moment there is no platform that will perform locking 100% reliably in every situation.

Make it easy for yourself: Forget about sharing a data directory among servers over NFS. A better solution is to have one computer that contains several CPUs and use an operating system that handles threads efficiently.

If you have multiple MySQL installations in different locations, normally you can specify the base installation directory for each server with the `--basedir=path` option to cause each server to use a different data directory, log files, and PID file. (The defaults for all these values are determined relative to the base directory.) In that case, the only other options you need to specify are the `--socket` and `--port` options. For example, suppose that you install different versions of MySQL using `tar` file binary distributions. These will install in different locations, so you can start the server for each installation using the command `bin/mysqld_safe` under its corresponding base directory. `mysqld_safe` will determine the proper `--basedir` option to pass to `mysqld`, and you need specify only the `--socket` and `--port` options to `mysqld_safe`. (For versions of MySQL older than 4.0, use `safe_mysqld` rather than `mysqld_safe`.)

As discussed in the following sections, it is possible to start additional servers by setting environment variables or by specifying appropriate command-line options. However, if you need to run multiple servers on a more permanent basis, it will be more convenient to use option files to specify for each server those option values that must be unique to it.

4.9.1 Running Multiple Servers on Windows

You can run multiple servers on Windows by starting them manually from the command line, each with appropriate operating parameters. On Windows NT-based systems, you also have the option of installing several servers as Windows services and running them that way. General instructions for running MySQL servers from the command line or as services are given in Section 2.2.1, "Installing MySQL on Windows." This section describes how to make sure that you start each server with different values for those startup options that must be unique per server, such as the data directory. These options are described in Section 4.9, "Running Multiple MySQL Servers on the Same Machine."

4.9.1.1 Starting Multiple Windows Servers at the Command Line

To start multiple servers manually from the command line, you can specify the appropriate options on the command line or in an option file. It's more convenient to place the options in an option file, but it's necessary to make sure that each server gets its own set of options. To do this, create an option file for each server and tell the server the filename with a `--defaults-file` option when you run it.

Suppose that you want to run `mysqld` on port 3307 with a data directory of `C:\mydata1`, and `mysqld-max` on port 3308 with a data directory of `C:\mydata2`. (To do this, make sure that before you start the servers, each data directory exists and has its own copy of the `mysql` database that contains the grant tables.)

Then create two option files. For example, create one file named `C:\my-opts1.cnf` that looks like this:

```
[mysqld]
datadir = C:/mydata1
port = 3307
```

Create a second file named `C:\my-opts2.cnf` that looks like this:

```
[mysqld]
datadir = C:/mydata2
port = 3308
```

Then start each server with its own option file:

```
C:\> C:\mysql\bin\mysqld --defaults-file=C:\my-opts1.cnf
C:\> C:\mysql\bin\mysqld-max --defaults-file=C:\my-opts2.cnf
```

On NT, each server will start in the foreground (no new prompt appears until the server exits later); you'll need to issue those two commands in separate console windows.

To shut down the servers, you must connect to the appropriate port number:

```
C:\> C:\mysql\bin\mysqladmin --port=3307 shutdown
C:\> C:\mysql\bin\mysqladmin --port=3308 shutdown
```

Servers configured as just described will allow clients to connect over TCP/IP. If your version of Windows supports named pipes and you also want to allow named pipe connections, use the `mysqld-nt` or `mysqld-max-nt` servers and specify options that enable the named pipe and specify its name. Each server that supports named pipe connections must use a unique pipe name. For example, the `C:\my-opts1.cnf` file might be written like this:

```
[mysqld]
datadir = C:/mydata1
port = 3307
enable-named-pipe
socket = mypipe1
```

Then start the server this way:

```
C:\> C:\mysql\bin\mysqld-nt --defaults-file=C:\my-opts1.cnf
```

Modify `C:\my-opts2.cnf` similarly for use by the second server.

4.9.1.2 Starting Multiple Windows Servers as Services

On NT-based systems, a MySQL server can be run as a Windows service. The procedures for installing, controlling, and removing a single MySQL service are described in Section 2.2.1.7, "Starting MySQL as a Windows Service."

As of MySQL 4.0.2, you can install multiple servers as services. In this case, you must make sure that each server uses a different service name in addition to all the other parameters that must be unique per server.

For the following instructions, assume that you want to run the `mysqld-nt` server from two different versions of MySQL that are installed at `C:\mysql-4.0.8` and `C:\mysql-4.0.17`, respectively. (This might be the case if you're running 4.0.8 as your production server, but want to test 4.0.17 before upgrading to it.)

The following principles apply when installing a MySQL service with the `--install` or `--install-manual` option:

- If you specify no service name, the server uses the default service name of `MySQL` and the server reads options from the `[mysqld]` group in the standard option files.

- If you specify a service name after the `--install` option, the server ignores the `[mysqld]` option group and instead reads options from the group that has the same name as the service. The server reads options from the standard option files.

- If you specify a `--defaults-file` option after the service name, the server ignores the standard option files and reads options only from the `[mysqld]` group of the named file.

Note: Before MySQL 4.0.17, only a server installed using the default service name (MySQL) or one installed explicitly with a service name of mysqld will read the [mysqld] group in the standard option files. As of 4.0.17, all servers read the [mysqld] group if they read the standard option files, even if they are installed using another service name. This allows you to use the [mysqld] group for options that should be used by all MySQL services, and an option group named after each service for use by the server installed with that service name.

Based on the preceding information, you have several ways to set up multiple services. The following instructions describe some examples. Before trying any of them, be sure that you shut down and remove any existing MySQL services first.

- **Approach 1:** Specify the options for all services in one of the standard option files. To do this, use a different service name for each server. Suppose that you want to run the 4.0.8 mysqld-nt using the service name of mysqld1 and the 4.0.17 mysqld-nt using the service name mysqld2. In this case, you can use the [mysqld1] group for 4.0.8 and the [mysqld2] group for 4.0.17. For example, you can set up C:\my.cnf like this:

```
# options for mysqld1 service
[mysqld1]
basedir = C:/mysql-4.0.8
port = 3307
enable-named-pipe
socket = mypipe1

# options for mysqld2 service
[mysqld2]
basedir = C:/mysql-4.0.17
port = 3308
enable-named-pipe
socket = mypipe2
```

Install the services as follows, using the full server pathnames to ensure that Windows registers the correct executable program for each service:

```
C:\> C:\mysql-4.0.8\bin\mysqld-nt --install mysqld1
C:\> C:\mysql-4.0.17\bin\mysqld-nt --install mysqld2
```

To start the services, use the services manager, or use NET START with the appropriate service names:

```
C:\> NET START mysqld1
C:\> NET START mysqld2
```

To stop the services, use the services manager, or use NET STOP with the appropriate service names:

```
C:\> NET STOP mysqld1
C:\> NET STOP mysqld2
```

- **Approach 2:** Specify options for each server in separate files and use `--defaults-file` when you install the services to tell each server what file to use. In this case, each file should list options using a `[mysqld]` group.

With this approach, to specify options for the 4.0.8 `mysqld-nt`, create a file `C:\my-opts1.cnf` that looks like this:

```
[mysqld]
basedir = C:/mysql-4.0.8
port = 3307
enable-named-pipe
socket = mypipe1
```

For the 4.0.17 `mysqld-nt`, create a file `C:\my-opts2.cnf` that looks like this:

```
[mysqld]
basedir = C:/mysql-4.0.17
port = 3308
enable-named-pipe
socket = mypipe2
```

Install the services as follows (enter each command on a single line):

```
C:\> C:\mysql-4.0.8\bin\mysqld-nt --install mysqld1
        --defaults-file=C:\my-opts1.cnf
C:\> C:\mysql-4.0.17\bin\mysqld-nt --install mysqld2
        --defaults-file=C:\my-opts2.cnf
```

To use a `--defaults-file` option when you install a MySQL server as a service, you must precede the option with the service name.

After installing the services, start and stop them the same way as in the preceding example.

To remove multiple services, use `mysqld --remove` for each one, specifying a service name following the `--remove` option. If the service name is the default (`MySQL`), you can omit it.

4.9.2 Running Multiple Servers on Unix

The easiest way to run multiple servers on Unix is to compile them with different TCP/IP ports and Unix socket files so that each one is listening on different network interfaces. Also, by compiling in different base directories for each installation, that automatically results in different compiled-in data directory, log file, and PID file locations for each of your servers.

Assume that an existing server is configured for the default TCP/IP port number (3306) and Unix socket file (`/tmp/mysql.sock`). To configure a new server to have different operating parameters, use a `configure` command something like this:

```
shell> ./configure --with-tcp-port=port_number \
        --with-unix-socket-path=file_name \
        --prefix=/usr/local/mysql-4.0.17
```

Here, *port_number* and *file_name* must be different from the default TCP/IP port number and Unix socket file pathname, and the --prefix value should specify an installation directory different than the one under which the existing MySQL installation is located.

If you have a MySQL server listening on a given port number, you can use the following command to find out what operating parameters it is using for several important configurable variables, including the base directory and Unix socket filename:

```
shell> mysqladmin --host=host_name --port=port_number variables
```

With the information displayed by that command, you can tell what option values *not* to use when configuring an additional server.

Note that if you specify localhost as a hostname, mysqladmin will default to using a Unix socket file connection rather than TCP/IP. In MySQL 4.1, you can explicitly specify the connection protocol to use by using the --protocol={TCP | SOCKET | PIPE | MEMORY} option.

You don't have to compile a new MySQL server just to start with a different Unix socket file and TCP/IP port number. It is also possible to specify those values at runtime. One way to do so is by using command-line options:

```
shell> mysqld_safe --socket=file_name --port=port_number
```

To start a second server, provide different --socket and --port option values, and pass a --datadir=path option to mysqld_safe so that the server uses a different data directory.

Another way to achieve a similar effect is to use environment variables to set the Unix socket filename and TCP/IP port number:

```
shell> MYSQL_UNIX_PORT=/tmp/mysqld-new.sock
shell> MYSQL_TCP_PORT=3307
shell> export MYSQL_UNIX_PORT MYSQL_TCP_PORT
shell> mysql_install_db --user=mysql
shell> mysqld_safe --datadir=/path/to/datadir &
```

This is a quick way of starting a second server to use for testing. The nice thing about this method is that the environment variable settings will apply to any client programs that you invoke from the same shell. Thus, connections for those clients automatically will be directed to the second server!

Appendix B, "Environment Variables," includes a list of other environment variables you can use to affect mysqld.

For automatic server execution, your startup script that is executed at boot time should execute the following command once for each server with an appropriate option file path for each command:

```
mysqld_safe --defaults-file=path
```

Each option file should contain option values specific to a given server.

On Unix, the `mysqld_multi` script is another way to start multiple servers. See Section 4.1.5, "The `mysqld_multi` Program for Managing Multiple MySQL Servers."

4.9.3 Using Client Programs in a Multiple-Server Environment

When you want to connect with a client program to a MySQL server that is listening to different network interfaces than those compiled into your client, you can use one of the following methods:

- Start the client with `--host=host_name --port=port_number` to connect via TCP/IP to a remote server, with `--host=127.0.0.1 --port=port_number` to connect via TCP/IP to a local server, or with `--host=localhost --socket=file_name` to connect to a local server via a Unix socket file or a Windows named pipe.

- As of MySQL 4.1, start the client with `--protocol=tcp` to connect via TCP/IP, `--protocol=socket` to connect via a Unix socket file, `--protocol=pipe` to connect via a named pipe, or `--protocol=memory` to connect via shared memory. For TCP/IP connections, you may also need to specify `--host` and `--port` options. For the other types of connections, you may need to specify a `--socket` option to specify a Unix socket file or named pipe name, or a `--shared-memory-base-name` option to specify the shared memory name. Shared memory connections are supported only on Windows.

- On Unix, set the `MYSQL_UNIX_PORT` and `MYSQL_TCP_PORT` environment variables to point to the Unix socket file and TCP/IP port number before you start your clients. If you normally use a specific socket file or port number, you can place commands to set these environment variables in your `.login` file so that they apply each time you log in. See Appendix B, "Environment Variables."

- Specify the default Unix socket file and TCP/IP port number in the `[client]` group of an option file. For example, you can use `C:\my.cnf` on Windows, or the `.my.cnf` file in your home directory on Unix. See Section 3.3.2, "Using Option Files."

- In a C program, you can specify the socket file or port number arguments in the `mysql_real_connect()` call. You can also have the program read option files by calling `mysql_options()`.

- If you are using the Perl `DBD::mysql` module, you can read options from MySQL option files. For example:

```
$dsn = "DBI:mysql:test;mysql_read_default_group=client;"
     . "mysql_read_default_file=/usr/local/mysql/data/my.cnf";
$dbh = DBI->connect($dsn, $user, $password);
```

Other programming interfaces may provide similar capabilities for reading option files.

4.10 The MySQL Query Cache

From version 4.0.1 on, MySQL Server features a query cache. When in use, the query cache stores the text of a SELECT query together with the corresponding result that was sent to the client. If the identical query is received later, the server retrieves the results from the query cache rather than parsing and executing the query again.

The query cache is extremely useful in an environment where (some) tables don't change very often and you have a lot of identical queries. This is a typical situation for many Web servers that generate a lot of dynamic pages based on database content.

Note: The query cache does not return stale data. When tables are modified, any relevant entries in the query cache are flushed.

Note: The query cache does not work in an environment where you have many mysqld servers updating the same MyISAM tables.

Some performance data for the query cache follow. These results were generated by running the MySQL benchmark suite on a Linux Alpha 2 x 500MHz system with 2GB RAM and a 64MB query cache.

- If all the queries you're performing are simple (such as selecting a row from a table with one row), but still differ so that the queries cannot be cached, the overhead for having the query cache active is 13%. This could be regarded as the worst case scenario. In real life, queries tend to be much more complicated, so the overhead normally is significantly lower.

- Searches for a single row in a single-row table are 238% faster with the query cache than without it. This can be regarded as close to the minimum speedup to be expected for a query that is cached.

To disable the query cache at server startup, set the query_cache_size system variable to 0. By disabling the query cache code, there is no noticeable overhead. Query cache capabilities can be excluded from the server entirely by using the --without-query-cache option to configure when compiling MySQL.

4.10.1 How the Query Cache Operates

This section describes how the query cache works when it is operational. Section 4.10.3, "Query Cache Configuration," describes how to control whether or not it is operational.

Queries are compared before parsing, so the following two queries are regarded as different by the query cache:

```
SELECT * FROM tbl_name
Select * from tbl_name
```

Queries must be exactly the same (byte for byte) to be seen as identical. In addition, query strings that are identical may be treated as different for other reasons. Queries that use different databases, different protocol versions, or different default character sets are considered different queries and are cached separately.

If a query result is returned from query cache, the server increments the `Qcache_hits` status variable, not `Com_select`. See Section 4.10.4, "Query Cache Status and Maintenance."

If a table changes, then all cached queries that use the table become invalid and are removed from the cache. This includes queries that use `MERGE` tables that map to the changed table. A table can be changed by many types of statements, such as `INSERT`, `UPDATE`, `DELETE`, `TRUNCATE`, `ALTER TABLE`, `DROP TABLE`, or `DROP DATABASE`.

Transactional `InnoDB` tables that have been changed are invalidated when a `COMMIT` is performed.

In MySQL 4.0, the query cache is disabled within transactions (it does not return results). Beginning with MySQL 4.1.1, the query cache also works within transactions when using `InnoDB` tables (it uses the table version number to detect whether or not its contents are still current).

Before MySQL 5.0, a query that begins with a leading comment might be cached, but could not be fetched from the cache. This problem is fixed in MySQL 5.0.

The query cache works for `SELECT SQL_CALC_FOUND_ROWS ...` and `SELECT FOUND_ROWS()` type queries. `FOUND_ROWS()` returns the correct value even if the preceding query was fetched from the cache because the number of found rows is also stored in the cache.

A query cannot be cached if it contains any of the following functions:

BENCHMARK()	CONNECTION_ID()	CURDATE()
CURRENT_DATE()	CURRENT_TIME()	CURRENT_TIMESTAMP()
CURTIME()	DATABASE()	ENCRYPT() with one parameter
FOUND_ROWS()	GET_LOCK()	LAST_INSERT_ID()
LOAD_FILE()	MASTER_POS_WAIT()	NOW()
RAND()	RELEASE_LOCK()	SYSDATE()
UNIX_TIMESTAMP() with no parameters	USER()	

A query also will not be cached under these conditions:

- It contains user-defined functions (UDFs).
- It contains user variables.
- It refers to the tables in the `mysql` system database.
- It is of any of the following forms:
  ```
  SELECT ... IN SHARE MODE
  SELECT ... INTO OUTFILE ...
  SELECT ... INTO DUMPFILE ...
  ```

```
SELECT * FROM ... WHERE autoincrement_col IS NULL
```

The last form is not cached because it is used as the ODBC workaround for obtaining the last insert ID value.

- It uses TEMPORARY tables.
- It does not use any tables.
- The user has a column-level privilege for any of the involved tables.
- Before a query is fetched from the query cache, MySQL checks that the user has SELECT privilege for all the involved databases and tables. If this is not the case, the cached result is not used.

4.10.2 Query Cache SELECT Options

There are two query cache-related options that may be specified in a SELECT statement:

- SQL_CACHE

  The query result is cached if the value of the query_cache_type system variable is ON or DEMAND.

- SQL_NO_CACHE

  The query result is not cached.

Examples:

```
SELECT SQL_CACHE id, name FROM customer;
SELECT SQL_NO_CACHE id, name FROM customer;
```

4.10.3 Query Cache Configuration

The have_query_cache server system variable indicates whether the query cache is available:

```
mysql> SHOW VARIABLES LIKE 'have_query_cache';
+------------------+-------+
| Variable_name    | Value |
+------------------+-------+
| have_query_cache | YES   |
+------------------+-------+
```

Several other system variables control query cache operation. These can be set in an option file or on the command line when starting mysqld. The query cache-related system variables all have names that begin with query_cache_. They are described briefly in Section 4.2.3, "Server System Variables," with additional configuration information given here.

To set the size of the query cache, set the `query_cache_size` system variable. Setting it to 0 disables the query cache. The default cache size is 0; that is, the query cache is disabled.

If the query cache is enabled, the `query_cache_type` variable influences how it works. This variable can be set to the following values:

- A value of 0 or OFF prevents caching or retrieval of cached results.
- A value of 1 or ON allows caching except of those statements that begin with SELECT SQL_NO_CACHE.
- A value of 2 or DEMAND causes caching of only those statements that begin with SELECT SQL_CACHE.

Setting the GLOBAL value of query_cache_type determines query cache behavior for all clients that connect after the change is made. Individual clients can control cache behavior for their own connection by setting the SESSION value of query_cache_type. For example, a client can disable use of the query cache for its own queries like this:

```
mysql> SET SESSION query_cache_type = OFF;
```

To control the maximum size of individual query results that can be cached, set the `query_cache_limit` variable. The default value is 1MB.

The result of a query (the data sent to the client) is stored in the query cache during result retrieval. Therefore the data usually is not handled in one big chunk. The query cache allocates blocks for storing this data on demand, so when one block is filled, a new block is allocated. Because memory allocation operation is costly (timewise), the query cache allocates blocks with a minimum size given by the `query_cache_min_res_unit` system variable. When a query is executed, the last result block is trimmed to the actual data size so that unused memory is freed. Depending on the types of queries your server executes, you might find it helpful to tune the value of query_cache_min_res_unit:

- The default value of query_cache_min_res_unit is 4KB. This should be adequate for most cases.
- If you have a lot of queries with small results, the default block size may lead to memory fragmentation, as indicated by a large number of free blocks. Fragmentation can force the query cache to prune (delete) queries from the cache due to lack of memory. In this case, you should decrease the value of query_cache_min_res_unit. The number of free blocks and queries removed due to pruning are given by the values of the Qcache_free_blocks and Qcache_lowmem_prunes status variables.
- If most of your queries have large results (check the Qcache_total_blocks and Qcache_queries_in_cache status variables), you can increase performance by increasing query_cache_min_res_unit. However, be careful to not make it too large (see the previ-

ous item).

`query_cache_min_res_unit` is present from MySQL 4.1.

4.10.4 Query Cache Status and Maintenance

You can check whether the query cache is present in your MySQL server using the following statement:

```
mysql> SHOW VARIABLES LIKE 'have_query_cache';
+------------------+-------+
| Variable_name    | Value |
+------------------+-------+
| have_query_cache | YES   |
+------------------+-------+
```

You can defragment the query cache to better utilize its memory with the FLUSH QUERY CACHE statement. The statement does not remove any queries from the cache.

The RESET QUERY CACHE statement removes all query results from the query cache. The FLUSH TABLES statement also does this.

To monitor query cache performance, use SHOW STATUS to view the cache status variables:

```
mysql> SHOW STATUS LIKE 'Qcache%';
+-------------------------+--------+
| Variable_name           | Value  |
+-------------------------+--------+
| Qcache_free_blocks      | 36     |
| Qcache_free_memory      | 138488 |
| Qcache_hits             | 79570  |
| Qcache_inserts          | 27087  |
| Qcache_lowmem_prunes    | 3114   |
| Qcache_not_cached       | 22989  |
| Qcache_queries_in_cache | 415    |
| Qcache_total_blocks     | 912    |
+-------------------------+--------+
```

Descriptions of each of these variables are given in Section 4.2.4, "Server Status Variables." Some uses for them are described here.

The total number of SELECT queries is equal to:

```
  Com_select
+ Qcache_hits
+ queries with errors found by parser
```

The Com_select value is equal to:

```
  Qcache_inserts
+ Qcache_not_cached
+ queries with errors found during columns/rights check
```

The query cache uses variable-length blocks, so Qcache_total_blocks and Qcache_free_blocks may indicate query cache memory fragmentation. After FLUSH QUERY CACHE, only a single free block remains.

Every cached query requires a minimum of two blocks (one for the query text and one or more for the query results). Also, every table that is used by a query requires one block. However, if two or more queries use the same table, only one block needs to be allocated.

The information provided by the Qcache_lowmem_prunes status variable can help you tune the query cache size. It counts the number of queries that have been removed from the cache to free up memory for caching new queries. The query cache uses a least recently used (LRU) strategy to decide which queries to remove from the cache. Tuning information is given in Section 4.10.3, "Query Cache Configuration."

Replication in MySQL

Replication capabilities allowing the databases on one MySQL server to be duplicated on another were introduced in MySQL 3.23.15. This chapter describes the various replication features provided by MySQL. It introduces replication concepts, shows how to set up replication servers, and serves as a reference to the available replication options. It also provides a list of frequently asked questions (with answers), and troubleshooting advice for solving problems.

For a description of the syntax of replication-related SQL statements, see the *MySQL Language Reference*.

We suggest that you visit our Web site at `http://www.mysql.com` often and read updates to this chapter. Replication is constantly being improved, and we update the manual frequently with the most current information.

5.1 Introduction to Replication

MySQL 3.23.15 and up features support for one-way replication. One server acts as the master, while one or more other servers act as slaves. The master server writes updates to its binary log files, and maintains an index of the files to keep track of log rotation. These logs serve as a record of updates to be sent to slave servers. When a slave server connects to the master server, it informs the master of its last position within the logs since the last successfully propagated update. The slave catches up any updates that have occurred since then, and then blocks and waits for the master to notify it of new updates.

A slave server can also serve as a master if you want to set up chained replication servers.

Note that when you are using replication, all updates to the tables that are replicated should be performed on the master server. Otherwise, you must always be careful to avoid conflicts between updates that users make to tables on the master and updates that they make to tables on the slave.

One-way replication has benefits for robustness, speed, and system administration:

- Robustness is increased with a master/slave setup. In the event of problems with the master, you can switch to the slave as a backup.

- Better response time for clients can be achieved by splitting the load for processing client queries between the master and slave servers. SELECT queries may be sent to the slave to reduce the query processing load of the master. Statements that modify data should still be sent to the master so that the master and slave do not get out of sync. This load-balancing strategy is effective if non-updating queries dominate, but that is the normal case.

- Another benefit of using replication is that you can perform backups using a slave server without disturbing the master. The master continues to process updates while the backup is being made. See Section 4.6.1, "Database Backups."

5.2 Replication Implementation Overview

MySQL replication is based on the master server keeping track of all changes to your databases (updates, deletes, and so on) in the binary logs. Therefore, to use replication, you must enable binary logging on the master server. See Section 4.8.4, "The Binary Log."

Each slave server receives from the master the saved updates that the master has recorded in its binary log, so that the slave can execute the same updates on its copy of the data.

It is very important to realize that the binary log is simply a record starting from the fixed point in time at which you enable binary logging. Any slaves that you set up will need copies of the databases on your master as they existed at the moment you enabled binary logging on the master. If you start your slaves with databases that are not the same as what was on the master when the binary log was started, your slaves may fail.

One way to copy the master's data to the slave is to use the LOAD DATA FROM MASTER statement. Be aware that LOAD DATA FROM MASTER is available only as of MySQL 4.0.0 and currently works only if all the tables on the master are MyISAM type. Also, this statement acquires a global read lock, so no updates on the master are possible while the tables are being transferred to the slave. When we implement lock-free hot table backup (in MySQL 5.0), this global read lock will no longer be necessary.

Due to these limitations, we recommend that at this point you use LOAD DATA FROM MASTER only if the dataset on the master is relatively small, or if a prolonged read lock on the master is acceptable. While the actual speed of LOAD DATA FROM MASTER may vary from system to system, a good rule of thumb for how long it will take is 1 second per 1MB of data. That is only a rough estimate, but you should get close to it if both master and slave are equivalent to 700MHz Pentium performance and are connected through a 100MBit/s network.

After the slave has been set up with a copy of the master's data, it will simply connect to the master and wait for updates to process. If the master goes away or the slave loses connectivity with your master, it will keep trying to connect periodically until it is able to reconnect and resume listening for updates. The retry interval is controlled by the `--master-connect-retry` option. The default is 60 seconds.

Each slave keeps track of where it left off. The master server has no knowledge of how many slaves there are or which ones are up to date at any given time.

5.3 Replication Implementation Details

MySQL replication capabilities are implemented using three threads (one on the master server and two on the slave). When `START SLAVE` is issued, the slave creates an I/O thread. The I/O thread connects to the master and asks it to send the statements recorded in its binary logs. The master creates a thread to send the binary log contents to the slave. This thread can be identified as the `Binlog Dump` thread in the output of `SHOW PROCESSLIST` on the master. The slave I/O thread reads what the master `Binlog Dump` thread sends and simply copies it to some local files in the slave's data directory called relay logs. The third thread is the SQL thread, which the slave creates to read the relay logs and execute the updates they contain.

In the preceding description, there are three threads per slave. For a master that has multiple slaves, it creates one thread for each currently connected slave, and each slave has its own I/O and SQL threads.

For versions of MySQL before 4.0.2, replication involves only two threads (one on the master and one on the slave). The slave I/O and SQL threads are combined as a single thread, and no relay log files are used.

The advantage of using two slave threads is that statement reading and execution are separated into two independent tasks. The task of reading statements is not slowed down if statement execution is slow. For example, if the slave server has not been running for a while, its I/O thread can quickly fetch all the binary log contents from the master when the slave starts, even if the SQL thread lags far behind and may take hours to catch up. If the slave stops before the SQL thread has executed all the fetched statements, the I/O thread has at least fetched everything so that a safe copy of the statements is locally stored in the slave's relay logs for execution when next the slave starts. This allows the binary logs to be purged on the master, because it no longer need wait for the slave to fetch their contents.

The `SHOW PROCESSLIST` statement provides information that tells you what is happening on the master and on the slave regarding replication.

The following example illustrates how the three threads show up in `SHOW PROCESSLIST`. The output format is that used by `SHOW PROCESSLIST` as of MySQL version 4.0.15, when the content of the `State` column was changed to be more meaningful compared to earlier versions.

On the master server, the output from SHOW PROCESSLIST looks like this:

```
mysql> SHOW PROCESSLIST\G
*************************** 1. row ***************************
     Id: 2
   User: root
   Host: localhost:32931
     db: NULL
Command: Binlog Dump
   Time: 94
  State: Has sent all binlog to slave; waiting for binlog to
         be updated
   Info: NULL
```

Here, thread 2 is a replication thread for a connected slave. The information indicates that all outstanding updates have been sent to the slave and that the master is waiting for more updates to occur.

On the slave server, the output from SHOW PROCESSLIST looks like this:

```
mysql> SHOW PROCESSLIST\G
*************************** 1. row ***************************
     Id: 10
   User: system user
   Host:
     db: NULL
Command: Connect
   Time: 11
  State: Waiting for master to send event
   Info: NULL
*************************** 2. row ***************************
     Id: 11
   User: system user
   Host:
     db: NULL
Command: Connect
   Time: 11
  State: Has read all relay log; waiting for the slave I/O
         thread to update it
   Info: NULL
```

This information indicates that thread 10 is the I/O thread that is communicating with the master server, and thread 11 is the SQL thread that is processing the updates stored in the relay logs. Currently, both threads are idle, waiting for further updates.

Note that the value in the Time column can tell how late the slave is compared to the master. See Section 5.9, "Replication FAQ."

5.3.1 Replication Master Thread States

The following list shows the most common states you will see in the State column for the master's Binlog Dump thread. If you don't see any Binlog Dump threads on a master server, replication is not running. That is, no slaves currently are connected.

- Sending binlog event to slave

  Binary logs consist of events, where an event is usually an update statement plus some other information. The thread has read an event from the binary log and is sending it to the slave.

- Finished reading one binlog; switching to next binlog

  The thread has finished reading a binary log file and is opening the next one to send to the slave.

- Has sent all binlog to slave; waiting for binlog to be updated

  The thread has read all outstanding updates from the binary logs and sent them to the slave. It is idle, waiting for new events to appear in the binary log resulting from new update statements being executed on the master.

- Waiting to finalize termination

  A very brief state that occurs as the thread is stopping.

5.3.2 Replication Slave I/O Thread States

The following list shows the most common states you will see in the State column for a slave server I/O thread. Beginning with MySQL 4.1.1, this state also appears in the Slave_IO_State column displayed by the SHOW SLAVE STATUS statement. This means that you can get a good view of what is happening by using only SHOW SLAVE STATUS.

- Connecting to master

  The thread is attempting to connect to the master.

- Checking master version

  A very brief state that occurs just after the connection to the master is established.

- Registering slave on master

  A very brief state that occurs just after the connection to the master is established.

- Requesting binlog dump

  A very brief state that occurs just after the connection to the master is established. The thread sends to the master a request for the contents of its binary logs, starting from the requested binary log filename and position.

- Waiting to reconnect after a failed binlog dump request

  If the binary log dump request failed (due to disconnection), the thread goes into this state while it sleeps, then tries to reconnect periodically. The interval between retries can be specified using the --master-connect-retry option.

- Reconnecting after a failed binlog dump request

  The thread is trying to reconnect to the master.

- Waiting for master to send event

  The thread has connected to the master and is waiting for binary log events to arrive. This can last for a long time if the master is idle. If the wait lasts for slave_read_timeout seconds, a timeout will occur. At that point, the thread will consider the connection to be broken and make an attempt to reconnect.

- Queueing master event to the relay log

  The thread has read an event and is copying it to the relay log so that the SQL thread can process it.

- Waiting to reconnect after a failed master event read

  An error occurred while reading (due to disconnection). The thread is sleeping for master-connect-retry seconds before attempting to reconnect.

- Reconnecting after a failed master event read

  The thread is trying to reconnect to the master. When connection is established again, the state will become Waiting for master to send event.

- Waiting for the slave SQL thread to free enough relay log space

  You are using a non-zero relay_log_space_limit value, and the relay logs have grown so much that their combined size exceeds this value. The I/O thread is waiting until the SQL thread frees enough space by processing relay log contents so that it can delete some relay log files.

- Waiting for slave mutex on exit

  A very brief state that occurs as the thread is stopping.

5.3.3 Replication Slave SQL Thread States

The following list shows the most common states you will see in the State column for a slave server SQL thread:

- Reading event from the relay log

  The thread has read an event from the relay log so that it can process it.

- Has read all relay log; waiting for the slave I/O thread to update it

  The thread has processed all events in the relay log files and is waiting for the I/O thread to write new events to the relay log.

- Waiting for slave mutex on exit

  A very brief state that occurs as the thread is stopping.

The State column for the I/O thread may also show the text of a statement. This indicates that the thread has read an event from the relay log, extracted the statement from it, and is executing it.

5.3.4 Replication Relay and Status Files

By default, relay logs are named using filenames of the form *host_name*-relay-bin.*nnn*, where *host_name* is the name of the slave server host and *nnn* is a sequence number. Successive relay log files are created using successive sequence numbers, beginning with 001. The slave keeps track of relay logs currently in use in an index file. The default relay log index filename is *host_name*-relay-bin.index. By default, these files are created in the slave's data directory. The default filenames may be overridden with the --relay-log and --relay-log-index server options. See Section 5.8, "Replication Startup Options."

Relay logs have the same format as binary logs, so you can use mysqlbinlog to read them. A relay log is automatically deleted by the SQL thread as soon as it has executed all its events and no longer needs it). There is no explicit mechanism for deleting relay logs, because the SQL thread takes care of doing so. However, from MySQL 4.0.14, FLUSH LOGS rotates relay logs, which will influence when the SQL thread deletes them.

A new relay log is created under the following conditions:

- When the I/O thread starts for the first time after the slave server starts. (In MySQL 5.0, a new relay log is created each time the I/O thread starts, not just the first time.)
- When the logs are flushed; for example, with FLUSH LOGS or mysqladmin flush-logs. (This creates a new relay log only as of MySQL 4.0.14.)
- When the size of the current relay log file becomes too large. The meaning of "too large" is determined as follows:
  - max_relay_log_size, if max_relay_log_size > 0
  - max_binlog_size, if max_relay_log_size = 0 or MySQL is older than 4.0.14

A slave replication server creates two additional small files in the data directory. These are status files and are named master.info and relay-log.info by default. They contain information like that shown in the output of the SHOW SLAVE STATUS statement. As disk files, they survive a slave server's shutdown. The next time the slave starts up, it reads these files to determine how far it has proceeded in reading binary logs from the master and in processing its own relay logs.

The master.info file is updated by the I/O thread. Before MySQL 4.1, the correspondence between the lines in the file and the columns displayed by SHOW SLAVE STATUS is as follows:

Line	Description
1	Master_Log_File
2	Read_Master_Log_Pos
3	Master_Host
4	Master_User
5	Password (not shown by SHOW SLAVE STATUS)
6	Master_Port
7	Connect_Retry

As of MySQL 4.1, the file includes a line count and information about SSL options:

Line	Description
1	The number of lines in the file
2	Master_Log_File
3	Read_Master_Log_Pos
4	Master_Host
5	Master_User
6	Password (not shown by SHOW SLAVE STATUS)
7	Master_Port
8	Connect_Retry
9	Master_SSL_Allowed
10	Master_SSL_CA_File
11	Master_SSL_CA_Path
12	Master_SSL_Cert
13	Master_SSL_Cipher
14	Master_SSL_Key

The relay-log.info file is updated by the SQL thread. The correspondence between the lines in the file and the columns displayed by SHOW SLAVE STATUS is as follows:

Line	Description
1	Relay_Log_File
2	Relay_Log_Pos
3	Relay_Master_Log_File
4	Exec_Master_Log_Pos

When you back up your slave's data, you should back up these two small files as well, along with the relay log files. They are needed to resume replication after you restore the slave's data. If you lose the relay logs but still have the relay-log.info file, you can check it to determine how far the SQL thread has executed in the master binary logs. Then you can use CHANGE MASTER TO with the MASTER_LOG_FILE and MASTER_LOG_POS options to tell the slave to re-read the binary logs from that point. This requires that the binary logs still exist on the master server.

If your slave is subject to replicating LOAD DATA INFILE statements, you should also back up any SQL_LOAD-* files that exist in the directory that the slave uses for this purpose. The slave needs these files to resume replication of any interrupted LOAD DATA INFILE operations. The directory location is specified using the --slave-load-tmpdir option. Its default value, if not specified, is the value of the tmpdir variable.

5.4 How to Set Up Replication

Here is a quick description of how to set up complete replication of your current MySQL server. It assumes that you want to replicate all your databases and have not configured replication before. You will need to shut down your master server briefly to complete the steps outlined here.

The procedure is written in terms of setting up a single slave, but you can use it to set up multiple slaves.

While this method is the most straightforward way to set up a slave, it is not the only one. For example, if you already have a snapshot of the master's data, and the master already has its server ID set and binary logging enabled, you can set up a slave without shutting down the master or even blocking updates to it. For more details, please see Section 5.9, "Replication FAQ."

If you want to administer a MySQL replication setup, we suggest that you read this entire chapter through and try all the instructions. You should also familiarize yourself with replication startup options described in Section 5.8, "Replication Startup Options."

Note that this procedure and some of the replication SQL statements in later sections refer to the SUPER privilege. Prior to MySQL 4.0.2, use the PROCESS privilege instead.

1. Make sure that you have a recent version of MySQL installed on the master and slaves, and that these versions are compatible according to the table shown in Section 5.5, "Replication Compatibility Between MySQL Versions."

   Please do not report bugs until you have verified that the problem is present in the latest release.

2. Set up an account on the master server that the slave server can use to connect. This account must be given the REPLICATION SLAVE privilege. If the account is used only for replication (which is recommended), you don't need to grant any additional privileges.

   Suppose that your domain is mydomain.com and you want to create an account with a username of repl such that slave servers can use the account to access the master server from any host in your domain using a password of slavepass. To create the account, this use GRANT statement:

```
mysql> GRANT REPLICATION SLAVE ON *.*
    -> TO 'repl'@'%.mydomain.com' IDENTIFIED BY 'slavepass';
```

   For MySQL versions older than 4.0.2, the REPLICATION SLAVE privilege does not exist. Grant the FILE privilege instead:

```
mysql> GRANT FILE ON *.*
    -> TO 'repl'@'%.mydomain.com' IDENTIFIED BY 'slavepass';
```

If you plan to use the LOAD TABLE FROM MASTER or LOAD DATA FROM MASTER statements from the slave host, you will need to grant this account additional privileges:

- Grant the account the SUPER and RELOAD global privileges.
- Grant the SELECT privilege for all tables that you want to load. Any master tables from which the account cannot SELECT will be ignored by LOAD DATA FROM MASTER.

3. If you are using only MyISAM tables, flush all the tables and block write statements by executing a FLUSH TABLES WITH READ LOCK statement.

```
mysql> FLUSH TABLES WITH READ LOCK;
```

Leave the client running from which you issue the FLUSH TABLES statement so that the read lock remains in effect. (If you exit the client, the lock is released.) Then take a snapshot of the data on your master server.

The easiest way to create a snapshot is to use an archiving program to make a binary backup of the databases in your master's data directory. For example, use tar on Unix, or PowerArchiver, WinRAR, WinZip, or any similar software on Windows. To use tar to create an archive that includes all databases, change location into the master server's data directory, then execute this command:

```
shell> tar -cvf /tmp/mysql-snapshot.tar .
```

If you want the archive to include only a database called this_db, use this command instead:

```
shell> tar -cvf /tmp/mysql-snapshot.tar ./this_db
```

Then copy the archive file to the /tmp directory on the slave server host. On that machine, change location into the slave's data directory, and unpack the archive file using this command:

```
shell> tar -xvf /tmp/mysql-snapshot.tar
```

You may not want to replicate the mysql database if the slave server has a different set of user accounts from those that exist on the master. In this case, you should exclude it from the archive. You also need not include any log files in the archive, or the master.info or relay-log.info files.

While the read lock placed by FLUSH TABLES WITH READ LOCK is in effect, read the value of the current binary log name and offset on the master:

```
mysql > SHOW MASTER STATUS;
+---------------+----------+--------------+------------------+
| File          | Position | Binlog_Do_DB | Binlog_Ignore_DB |
+---------------+----------+--------------+------------------+
| mysql-bin.003 | 73       | test         | manual,mysql     |
+---------------+----------+--------------+------------------+
```

The `File` column shows the name of the log, while `Position` shows the offset. In this example, the binary log value is `mysql-bin.003` and the offset is 73. Record the values. You will need to use them later when you are setting up the slave. They represent the replication coordinates at which the slave should begin processing new updates from the master.

After you have taken the snapshot and recorded the log name and offset, you can re-enable write activity on the master:

```
mysql> UNLOCK TABLES;
```

If you are using `InnoDB` tables, ideally you should use the `InnoDB Hot Backup` tool. It takes a consistent snapshot without acquiring any locks on the master server, and records the log name and offset corresponding to the snapshot to be later used on the slave. `InnoDB Hot Backup` is a non-free (commercial) additional tool that is not included in the standard MySQL distribution. See the `InnoDB Hot Backup` home page at `http://www.innodb.com/manual.php` for detailed information and screenshots.

Without the `Hot Backup` tool, the quickest way to take a binary snapshot of `InnoDB` tables is to shut down the master server and copy the `InnoDB` data files, log files, and table definition files (`.frm` files). To record the current log file name and offset, you should issue the following statements before you shut down the server:

```
mysql> FLUSH TABLES WITH READ LOCK;
mysql> SHOW MASTER STATUS;
```

Then record the log name and the offset from the output of `SHOW MASTER STATUS` as was shown earlier. After recording the log name and the offset, shut down the server *without* unlocking the tables to make sure that the server goes down with the snapshot corresponding to the current log file and offset:

```
shell> mysqladmin -u root shutdown
```

An alternative that works for both `MyISAM` and `InnoDB` tables is to take an SQL dump of the master instead of a binary copy as described in the preceding discussion. For this, you can use `mysqldump --master-data` on your master and later load the SQL dump file into your slave. However, this is slower than doing a binary copy.

If the master has been previously running without `--log-bin` enabled, the log name and position values displayed by `SHOW MASTER STATUS` or `mysqldump` will be empty. In that case, the values that you will need to use later when specifying the slave's log file and position are the empty string (`' '`) and 4.

4. Make sure that the `[mysqld]` section of the `my.cnf` file on the master host includes a `log-bin` option. The section should also have a `server-id=master_id` option, where `master_id` must be a positive integer value from 1 to $2^{32} - 1$. For example:

```
[mysqld]
log-bin
server-id=1
```

If those options are not present, add them and restart the server.

5. Stop the server that is to be used as a slave server and add the following to its `my.cnf` file:

```
[mysqld]
server-id=slave_id
```

The *slave_id* value, like the *master_id* value, must be a positive integer value from 1 to $2^{32} - 1$. In addition, it is very important that the ID of the slave be different from the ID of the master. For example:

```
[mysqld]
server-id=2
```

If you are setting up multiple slaves, each one must have a unique `server-id` value that differs from that of the master and from each of the other slaves. Think of `server-id` values as something similar to IP addresses: These IDs uniquely identify each server instance in the community of replication partners.

If you don't specify a `server-id` value, it will be set to 1 if you have not defined `master-host`, otherwise it will be set to 2. Note that in the case of `server-id` omission, a master will refuse connections from all slaves, and a slave will refuse to connect to a master. Thus, omitting `server-id` is good only for backup with a binary log.

6. If you made a binary backup of the master server's data, copy it to the slave server's data directory before starting the slave. Make sure that the privileges on the files and directories are correct. The user that the server MySQL runs as must able to read and write the files, just as on the master.

If you made a backup using `mysqldump`, start the slave first (see next step).

7. Start the slave server. If it has been replicating previously, start the slave server with the `--skip-slave-start` option so that it doesn't immediately try to connect to its master. You also may want to start the slave server with the `--log-warnings` option, to get more messages about problems (for example, network or connection problems).

8. If you made a backup of the master server's data using `mysqldump`, load the dump file into the slave server:

```
shell> mysql -u root -p < dump_file.sql
```

9. Execute the following statement on the slave, replacing the option values with the actual values relevant to your system:

```
mysql> CHANGE MASTER TO
    -> MASTER_HOST='master_host_name',
    -> MASTER_USER='replication_user_name',
    -> MASTER_PASSWORD='replication_password',
    -> MASTER_LOG_FILE='recorded_log_file_name',
    -> MASTER_LOG_POS=recorded_log_position;
```

The following table shows the maximum length for the string options:

MASTER_HOST	60
MASTER_USER	16
MASTER_PASSWORD	32
MASTER_LOG_FILE	255

10. Start the slave threads:

```
mysql> START SLAVE;
```

After you have performed this procedure, the slave should connect to the master and catch up on any updates that have occurred since the snapshot was taken.

If you have forgotten to set the server-id value for the master, slaves will not be able to connect to it.

If you have forgotten to set the server-id value for the slave, you will get the following error in its error log:

```
Warning: You should set server_id to a non-0 value if master_host is set;  We force
the server id to 2, but this MySQL server will not act as a slave.
```

You will also find error messages in the slave's error log if it is not able to replicate for any other reason.

Once a slave is replicating, you will find in its data directory one file named master.info and another named relay-log.info. The slave uses these two files to keep track of how much of the master's binary log it has processed. **Do not** remove or edit these files, unless you really know what you are doing and understand the implications. Even in that case, it is preferred that you use the CHANGE MASTER TO statement.

Note: The content of master.info overrides some options specified on the command line or in my.cnf. See Section 5.8, "Replication Startup Options," for more details.

Once you have a snapshot, you can use it to set up other slaves by following the slave portion of the procedure just described. You do not need to take another snapshot of the master; you can use the same one for each slave.

5.5 Replication Compatibility Between MySQL Versions

The original binary log format was developed in MySQL 3.23. It changed in MySQL 4.0, and again in MySQL 5.0. This has consequences when you upgrade servers in a replication setup, as described in Section 5.6, "Upgrading a Replication Setup."

As far as replication is concerned, any MySQL 4.1.x version and any 4.0.x version are identical, because they all use the same binary log format. Thus, any servers from these versions are compatible, and replication between them should work seamlessly. The exceptions to this compatibility is that versions from MySQL 4.0.0 to 4.0.2 were very early development versions that should not be used anymore. (These were the alpha versions in the 4.0 release series. Compatibility for them is still documented in the manual included with their distributions.)

The following table indicates master/slave replication compatibility between different versions of MySQL.

		Master 3.23.33 and up	Master 4.0.3 and up or any 4.1.x	Master 5.0.0
Slave	3.23.33 and up	yes	no	no
Slave	4.0.3 and up	yes	yes	no
Slave	5.0.0	yes	yes	yes

As a general rule, we recommended using recent MySQL versions, because replication capabilities are continually being improved. We also recommend using the same version for both the master and the slave.

5.6 Upgrading a Replication Setup

When you upgrade servers that participate in a replication setup, the procedure for upgrading depends on the current server versions and the version to which you are upgrading.

5.6.1 Upgrading Replication to 4.0 or 4.1

This section applies to upgrading replication from MySQL 3.23 to 4.0 or 4.1. A 4.0 server should be 4.0.3 or newer, as mentioned in Section 5.5, "Replication Compatibility Between MySQL Versions."

When you upgrade a master from MySQL 3.23 to MySQL 4.0 or 4.1, you should first ensure that all the slaves of this master are already at 4.0 or 4.1. If that is not the case, you should first upgrade your slaves: Shut down each one, upgrade it, restart it, and restart replication.

The upgrade can safely be done using the following procedure, assuming that you have a 3.23 master to upgrade and the slaves are 4.0 or 4.1. Note that after the master has been upgraded, you should not restart replication using any old 3.23 binary logs, because this will unfortunately confuse the 4.0 or 4.1 slave.

1. Block all updates on the master by issuing a FLUSH TABLES WITH READ LOCK statement.
2. Wait until all the slaves have caught up with all changes from the master server. Use SHOW MASTER STATUS on the master to obtain its current binary log file and position. Then, for each slave, use those values with a SELECT MASTER_POS_WAIT() statement. The

statement will block on the slave and return when the slave has caught up. Then run STOP SLAVE on the slave.

3. Stop the master server and upgrade it to MySQL 4.0 or 4.1.

4. Restart the master server and record the name of its newly created binary log. You can obtain the name of the file by issuing a SHOW MASTER STATUS statement on the master. Then issue these statements on each slave:

```
mysql> CHANGE MASTER TO MASTER_LOG_FILE='binary_log_name',
    ->     MASTER_LOG_POS=4;
mysql> START SLAVE;
```

5.6.2 Upgrading Replication to 5.0

This section applies to upgrading replication from MySQL 3.23, 4.0, or 4.1 to 5.0.0. A 4.0 server should be 4.0.3 or newer, as mentioned in Section 5.5, "Replication Compatibility Between MySQL Versions."

First, note that MySQL 5.0.0 is an alpha release. It is intended to work better than older versions (easier upgrade, replication of some important session variables such as sql_mode). However it has not yet been extensively tested. As with any alpha release, we recommend that you not use it in critical production environments yet.

When you upgrade a master from MySQL 3.23, 4.0, or 4.1 to 5.0.0, you should first ensure that all the slaves of this master are already 5.0.0. If that's not the case, you should first upgrade your slaves. To upgrade each slave, just shut it down, upgrade it to 5.0.0, restart it, and restart replication. The 5.0.0 slave will be able to read its old relay logs that were written before the upgrade and execute the statements they contain. Relay logs created by the slave after the upgrade will be in 5.0.0 format.

After the slaves have been upgraded, shut down your master, upgrade it to 5.0.0, and restart it. The 5.0.0 master will be able to read its old binary logs that were written before the upgrade and send them to the 5.0.0 slaves. The slaves will recognize the old format and handle it properly. Binary logs created by master after the upgrade will be in 5.0.0 format. These too will be recognized by the 5.0.0 slaves.

In other words, there are no measures to take when upgrading to 5.0.0, except that slaves must be 5.0.0 before you can upgrade the master to 5.0.0. Note that downgrading from 5.0.0 to older versions does not work so automatically: You must ensure that any 5.0.0 binary logs or relay logs have been fully processed, so that you can remove them before proceeding with the downgrade.

5.7 Replication Features and Known Problems

The following list explains what is supported and what is not. Additional InnoDB-specific information about replication is given in Section 9.7.5, "InnoDB and MySQL Replication."

- Replication will be done correctly with AUTO_INCREMENT, LAST_INSERT_ID(), and TIMESTAMP values.

- The USER(), UUID(), and LOAD_FILE() functions are replicated without changes and will thus not work reliably on the slave. This is also true for CONNECTION_ID() in slave versions older than 4.1.1. The **new** PASSWORD() function in MySQL 4.1 is well replicated in masters from 4.1.1 and up; your slaves also must be 4.1.1 or above to replicate it. If you have older slaves and need to replicate PASSWORD() from your 4.1.x master, you must start your master with the --old-password option, so that it uses the old implementation of PASSWORD(). (Note that the PASSWORD() implementation in MySQL 4.1.0 differs from every other version of MySQL. It is best to avoid 4.1.0 in a replication situation.)

- The FOREIGN_KEY_CHECKS variable is replicated as of MySQL 4.0.14. The sql_mode, UNIQUE_CHECKS, and SQL_AUTO_IS_NULL variables are replicated as of 5.0.0. The SQL_SELECT_LIMIT and table_type variables are not yet replicated.

- You must use the same character set (--default-character-set) on the master and the slave. Otherwise, you may get duplicate-key errors on the slave, because a key that is regarded as unique in the master character set may not be unique in the slave character set. Character sets will be replicated in 5.0.x.

- It is possible to replicate transactional tables on the master using non-transactional tables on the slave. For example, you can replicate an InnoDB master table as a MyISAM slave table. However, if you do this, you will have problems if the slave is stopped in the middle of a BEGIN/COMMIT block, because the slave will restart at the beginning of the BEGIN block. This issue is on our TODO and will be fixed in the near future.

- Update statements that refer to user variables (that is, variables of the form @var_name) are badly replicated in 3.23 and 4.0. This is fixed in 4.1. Note that user variable names are case insensitive starting from MySQL 5.0. You should take this into account when setting up replication between 5.0 and an older version.

- The slave can connect to the master using SSL if both are 4.1.1 or newer.

- If a DATA DIRECTORY or INDEX DIRECTORY clause is used in a CREATE TABLE statement on the master server, the clause is also used on the slave. This can cause problems if no corresponding directory exists in the slave host filesystem or exists but is not accessible to the slave server. Starting from MySQL 4.0.15, there is an sql_mode option called NO_DIR_IN_CREATE. If the slave server is run with its SQL mode set to include this option, it will simply ignore the clauses before replicating the CREATE TABLE statement. The result is that the MyISAM data and index files are created in the table's database directory.

- Although we have never heard of it actually occurring, it is theoretically possible for the data on the master and slave to become different if a query is designed in such a way that the data modification is non-deterministic; that is, left to the will of the query optimizer. (That generally is not a good practice anyway, even outside of replication!) For a detailed explanation of this issue, see Section 1.8.7.3, "Open Bugs and Design Deficiencies in MySQL."

- Before MySQL 4.1.1, FLUSH, ANALYZE TABLE, OPTIMIZE TABLE, and REPAIR TABLE statements are not written to the binary log and thus are not replicated to the slaves. This is not normally a problem because these statements do not modify table data. However, it can cause difficulties under certain circumstances. If you replicate the privilege tables in the mysql database and update those tables directly without using the GRANT statement, you must issue a FLUSH PRIVILEGES statement on your slaves to put the new privileges into effect. Also if you use FLUSH TABLES when renaming a MyISAM table that is part of a MERGE table, you will have to issue FLUSH TABLES manually on the slaves. As of MySQL 4.1.1, these statements are written to the binary log (unless you specify NO_WRITE_TO_BINLOG, or its alias LOCAL). Exceptions are that FLUSH LOGS, FLUSH MASTER, FLUSH SLAVE, and FLUSH TABLES WITH READ LOCK are not logged in any case. (Any of them may cause problems if replicated to a slave.)

- MySQL only supports one master and many slaves. Later we will add a voting algorithm to automatically change master if something goes wrong with the current master. We will also introduce "agent" processes to help do load balancing by sending SELECT queries to different slaves.

- When a server shuts down and restarts, its MEMORY (HEAP) tables become empty. As of MySQL 4.0.18, the master replicates this effect as follows: The first time that the master uses each MEMORY table after startup, it notifies slaves that the table needs to be emptied by writing a DELETE FROM statement for the table to its binary log. See Section 8.3, "The MEMORY (HEAP) Storage Engine" for more details.

- Temporary tables are replicated with the exception of the case that you shut down the slave server (not just the slave threads) and you have some replicated temporary tables that are used in update statements that have not yet been executed on the slave. If you shut down the slave server, the temporary tables needed by those updates no longer are available when the slave starts again. To avoid this problem, do not shut down the slave while it has temporary tables open. Instead, use this procedure:

  1. Issue a STOP SLAVE statement.
  2. Use SHOW STATUS to check the value of the Slave_open_temp_tables variable.
  3. If the value is 0, issue a mysqladmin shutdown command to shut down the slave.
  4. If the value is not 0, restart the slave threads with START SLAVE.
  5. Repeat the procedure later to see if you have better luck next time.

  We have plans to fix this problem in the near future.

- It is safe to connect servers in a circular master/slave relationship with the `--log-slave-updates` option specified. Note, however, that many statements will not work correctly in this kind of setup unless your client code is written to take care of the potential problems that can occur from updates that occur in different sequence on different servers. This means that you can create a setup such as this:

  `A -> B -> C -> A`

  Server IDs are encoded in the binary log events, so server A will know when an event that it reads was originally created by itself and will not execute the event. Thus, there will be no infinite loop. But this circular setup will work only if you perform no conflicting updates between the tables. In other words, if you insert data in both A and C, you should never insert a row in A that may have a key that conflicts with a row inserted in C. You should also not update the same rows on two servers if the order in which the updates are applied is significant.

- If a statement on the slave produces an error, the slave SQL thread terminates, and the slave writes a message to its error log. You should then connect to the slave manually, fix the problem (for example, a non-existent table), and then run START SLAVE.

- It is safe to shut down a master server and restart it later. If a slave loses its connection to the master, the slave tries to reconnect immediately. If that fails, the slave retries periodically. (The default is to retry every 60 seconds. This may be changed with the `--master-connect-retry` option.) The slave will also be able to deal with network connectivity outages. However, the slave will notice the network outage only after receiving no data from the master for `slave_net_timeout` seconds. If your outages are short, you may want to decrease `slave_net_timeout`. See Section 4.2.3, "Server System Variables."

- Shutting down the slave (cleanly) is also safe, as it keeps track of where it left off. Unclean shutdowns might produce problems, especially if disk cache was not flushed to disk before the system went down. Your system fault tolerance will be greatly increased if you have a good uninterruptible power supply.

- Due to the non-transactional nature of MyISAM tables, it is possible to have a statement that only partially updates a table and returns an error code. This can happen, for example, on a multiple-row insert that has one row violating a key constraint, or if a long update statement is killed after updating some of the rows. If that happens on the master, the slave thread will exit and wait for the database administrator to decide what to do about it unless the error code is legitimate and the statement execution results in the same error code. If this error code validation behavior is not desirable, some or all errors can be masked out (ignored) with the `--slave-skip-errors` option. This option is available starting with MySQL 3.23.47.

- If you update transactional tables from non-transactional tables inside a BEGIN/COMMIT segment, updates to the binary log may be out of sync if some thread changes the non-transactional table before the transaction commits. This is because the transaction is written to the binary log only when it is committed.

- Before version 4.0.15, any update to a non-transactional table is written to the binary log at once when the update is made, whereas transactional updates are written on COMMIT or not written at all if you use ROLLBACK. You must take this into account when updating both transactional tables and non-transactional tables within the same transaction. (This is true not only for replication, but also if you are using binary logging for backups.) In version 4.0.15, we changed the logging behavior for transactions that mix updates to transactional and non-transactional tables, which solves the problems (order of statements is good in the binary log, and all needed statements are written to the binary log even in case of ROLLBACK). The problem that remains is when a second connection updates the non-transactional table while the first connection's transaction is not finished yet; wrong order can still occur, because the second connection's update will be written immediately after it is done.

The following table lists replication problems in MySQL 3.23 that are fixed in MySQL 4.0:

- LOAD DATA INFILE is handled properly, as long as the data file still resides on the master server at the time of update propagation.
- LOAD DATA LOCAL INFILE is no longer skipped on the slave as it was in 3.23.
- In 3.23, RAND() in updates does not replicate properly. Use RAND(*some_non_rand_expr*) if you are replicating updates with RAND(). You can, for example, use UNIX_TIMESTAMP() as the argument to RAND().

5.8 Replication Startup Options

On both the master and the slave, you must use the server-id option to establish a unique replication ID for each server. You should pick a unique positive integer in the range from 1 to $2^{32} - 1$ for each master and slave. Example: server-id=3

The options that you can use on the master server for controlling binary logging are described in Section 4.8.4, "The Binary Log."

The following table describes the options you can use on slave replication servers. You can specify them on the command line or in an option file.

Some slave server replication options are handled in a special way, in the sense that they are ignored if a master.info file exists when the slave starts and contains values for the options. The following options are handled this way:

- --master-host
- --master-user
- --master-password
- --master-port
- --master-connect-retry

As of MySQL 4.1.1, the following options also are handled specially:

- `--master-ssl`
- `--master-ssl-ca`
- `--master-ssl-capath`
- `--master-ssl-cert`
- `--master-ssl-cipher`
- `--master-ssl-key`

The `master.info` file format in 4.1.1 changed to include values corresponding to the SSL options. In addition, the 4.1.1 file format includes as its first line the number of lines in the file. If you upgrade an older server to 4.1.1, the new server upgrades the `master.info` file to the new format automatically when it starts. However, if you downgrade a 4.1.1 or newer server to a version older than 4.1.1, you should manually remove the first line before starting the older server for the first time. Note that, in this case, the downgraded server no longer can use an SSL connection to communicate with the master.

If no `master.info` file exists when the slave server starts, it uses values for those options that are specified in option files or on the command line. This will occur when you start the server as a replication slave for the very first time, or when you have run RESET SLAVE and shut down and restarted the slave server.

If the `master.info` file exists when the slave server starts, the server ignores those options. Instead, it uses the values found in the `master.info` file.

If you restart the slave server with different values of the startup options that correspond to values in the `master.info` file, the different values have no effect, because the server continues to use the `master.info` file. To use different values, you must either restart after removing the `master.info` file or (preferably) use the CHANGE MASTER TO statement to reset the values while the slave is running.

Suppose that you specify this option in your `my.cnf` file:

```
[mysqld]
master-host=some_host
```

The first time you start the server as a replication slave, it reads and uses that option from the `my.cnf` file. The server then records the value in the `master.info` file. The next time you start the server, it reads the master host value from the `master.info` file only and ignores the value in the option file. If you modify the `my.cnf` file to specify a different master host of *some_other_host*, the change still will have no effect. You should use CHANGE MASTER TO instead.

Because the server gives an existing `master.info` file precedence over the startup options just described, you might prefer not to use startup options for these values at all, and instead specify them by using the CHANGE MASTER TO statement.

This example shows a more extensive use of startup options to configure a slave server:

```
[mysqld]
server-id=2
master-host=db-master.mycompany.com
master-port=3306
master-user=pertinax
master-password=freitag
master-connect-retry=60
report-host=db-slave.mycompany.com
```

The following list describes startup options for controlling replication: Many of these options can be reset while the server is running by using the CHANGE MASTER TO statement. Others, such as the --replicate-* options, can be set only when the slave server starts. We plan to fix this.

- --log-slave-updates

  Normally, updates received from a master server by a slave are not logged to its binary log. This option tells the slave to log the updates performed by its SQL thread to the slave's own binary log. For this option to have any effect, the slave must also be started with the --log-bin option to enable binary logging. --log-slave-updates is used when you want to chain replication servers. For example, you might want a setup like this:

  ```
  A -> B -> C
  ```

  That is, A serves as the master for the slave B, and B serves as the master for the slave C. For this to work, B must be both a master and a slave. You must start both A and B with --log-bin to enable binary logging, and B with the --log-slave-updates option.

- --log-warnings

  Makes the slave print more messages about what it is doing. For example, it will warn you that it succeeded in reconnecting after a network/connection failure, and warn you about how each slave thread started.

  This option is not limited to replication use only. It produces warnings across a spectrum of server activities.

- --master-connect-retry=seconds

  The number of seconds the slave thread sleeps before retrying to connect to the master in case the master goes down or the connection is lost. The value in the master.info file takes precedence if it can be read. If not set, the default is 60.

- --master-host=host

  The hostname or IP number of the master replication server. If this option is not given, the slave thread will not be started. The value in master.info takes precedence if it can be read.

- `--master-info-file=file_name`

  The name to use for the file in which the slave records information about the master. The default name is `mysql.info` in the data directory.

- `--master-password=password`

  The password of the account that the slave thread uses for authentication when connecting to the master. The value in the `master.info` file takes precedence if it can be read. If not set, an empty password is assumed.

- `--master-port=port_number`

  The TCP/IP port the master is listening on. The value in the `master.info` file takes precedence if it can be read. If not set, the compiled-in setting is assumed. If you have not tinkered with `configure` options, this should be 3306.

- `--master-ssl`

  `--master-ssl-ca=file_name`

  `--master-ssl-capath=directory_name`

  `--master-ssl-cert=file_name`

  `--master-ssl-cipher=cipher_list`

  `--master-ssl-key=file_name`

  These options are used for setting up a secure replication connection to the master server using SSL. Their meanings are the same as the corresponding `--ssl`, `--ssl-ca`, `--ssl-capath`, `--ssl-cert`, `--ssl-cipher`, and `--ssl-key` options described in Section 4.5.8.5, "SSL Command-Line Options." The values in the `master.info` file take precedence if they can be read.

  These options are operational as of MySQL 4.1.1.

- `--master-user=username`

  The username of the account that the slave thread uses for authentication when connecting to the master. The account must have the REPLICATION SLAVE privilege. (Prior to MySQL 4.0.2, it must have the FILE privilege instead.) The value in the `master.info` file takes precedence if it can be read. If the master user is not set, user `test` is assumed.

- `--max-relay-log-size=#`

  To rotate the relay log automatically. See Section 4.2.3, "Server System Variables."

  This option is available as of MySQL 4.0.14.

- `--read-only`

  This option causes the slave to allow no updates except from slave threads or from users with the SUPER privilege. This can be useful to ensure that a slave server accepts no updates from clients.

  This option is available as of MySQL 4.0.14.

- --relay-log=*file_name*

  The name for the relay log. The default name is *host_name*-relay-bin.*nnn*, where *host_name* is the name of the slave server host and *nnn* indicates that relay logs are created in numbered sequence. You can specify the option to create hostname-independent relay log names, or if your relay logs tend to be big (and you don't want to decrease max_relay_log_size) and you need to put them in some area different from the data directory, or if you want to increase speed by balancing loads between disks.

- --relay-log-index=*file_name*

  Specifies the location and name that should be used for the relay log index file. The default name is *host_name*-relay-bin.index, where *host_name* is the name of the slave server.

- --relay-log-info-file=*file_name*

  The name to use for the file in which the slave records information about the relay logs. The default name is relay-log.info in the data directory.

- --relay-log-purge={0|1}

  Disables or enables automatic purging of relay logs as soon as they are not needed any more. The default value is 1 (enabled). This is a global variable that can be changed dynamically with SET GLOBAL relay_log_purge.

  This option is available as of MySQL 4.1.1.

- --relay-log-space-limit=#

  Places an upper limit on the total size of all relay logs on the slave (a value of 0 means "unlimited"). This is useful for a slave server host that has limited disk space. When the limit is reached, the I/O thread stops reading binary log events from the master server until the SQL thread has caught up and deleted some now unused relay logs. Note that this limit is not absolute: There are cases where the SQL thread needs more events before it can delete relay logs. In that case, the I/O thread will exceed the limit until it becomes possible for the SQL thread to delete some relay logs. Not doing so would cause a deadlock (which is what happens before MySQL 4.0.13). You should not set --relay-log-space-limit to less than twice the value of --max-relay-log-size (or --max-binlog-size if --max-relay-log-size is 0). In that case, there is a chance that the I/O thread will wait for free space because --relay-log-space-limit is exceeded, but the SQL thread will have no relay log to purge and be unable to satisfy the I/O thread. This forces the I/O thread to temporarily ignore --relay-log-space-limit.

- --replicate-do-db=*db_name*

  Tells the slave to restrict replication to statements where the default database (that is, the one selected by USE) is *db_name*. To specify more than one database, use this option multiple times, once for each database. Note that this will not replicate cross-database statements such as UPDATE *some_db*.*some_table* SET foo='bar' while having selected a different database or no database. If you need cross-database updates to work, make sure that you have MySQL 3.23.28 or later, and use --replicate-wild-do-table=*db_name*.%. Please read the notes that follow this option list.

An example of what does not work as you might expect: If the slave is started with `--replicate-do-db=sales` and you issue the following statements on the master, the UPDATE statement will not be replicated:

```
USE prices;
UPDATE sales.january SET amount=amount+1000;
```

If you need cross-database updates to work, use `--replicate-wild-do-table=db_name.%` instead.

The main reason for this "just-check-the-default-database" behavior is that it's difficult from the statement alone to know whether or not it should be replicated (for example, if you are using multiple-table DELETE or multiple-table UPDATE statements that go across multiple databases). It's also very fast to just check the default database.

- `--replicate-do-table=db_name.tbl_name`

Tells the slave thread to restrict replication to the specified table. To specify more than one table, use this option multiple times, once for each table. This will work for cross-database updates, in contrast to `--replicate-do-db`. Please read the notes that follow this option list.

- `--replicate-ignore-db=db_name`

Tells the slave to not replicate any statement where the default database (that is, the one selected by USE) is *db_name*. To specify more than one database to ignore, use this option multiple times, once for each database. You should not use this option if you are using cross-database updates and you don't want these updates to be replicated. Please read the notes that follow this option list.

An example of what does not work as you might expect: If the slave is started with `--replicate-ignore-db=sales` and you issue the following statements on the master, the UPDATE statement will be replicated:

```
USE prices;
UPDATE sales.january SET amount=amount+1000;
```

If you need cross-database updates to work, use `--replicate-wild-ignore-table=db_name.%` instead.

- `--replicate-ignore-table=db_name.tbl_name`

Tells the slave thread to not replicate any statement that updates the specified table (even if any other tables might be updated by the same statement). To specify more than one table to ignore, use this option multiple times, once for each table. This will work for cross-database updates, in contrast to `--replicate-ignore-db`. Please read the notes that follow this option list.

- `--replicate-wild-do-table=db_name.tbl_name`

Tells the slave thread to restrict replication to statements where any of the updated tables match the specified database and table name patterns. Patterns can contain the '%'

and '_' wildcard characters, which have the same meaning as for the `LIKE` pattern-matching operator. To specify more than one table, use this option multiple times, once for each table. This will work for cross-database updates. Please read the notes that follow this option list.

Example: `--replicate-wild-do-table=foo%.bar%` will replicate only updates that use a table where the database name starts with `foo` and the table name starts with `bar`.

If the table name pattern is `%`, it matches any table name and the option also applies to database-level statements (`CREATE DATABASE`, `DROP DATABASE`, and `ALTER DATABASE`). For example, if you use `--replicate-wild-do-table=foo%.%`, database-level statements are replicated if the database name matches the pattern `foo%`.

To include literal wildcard characters in the database or table name patterns, escape them with a backslash. For example, to replicate all tables of a database that is named `my_own%db`, but not replicate tables from the `my1ownAABCdb` database, you should escape the '_' and '%' characters like this: `--replicate-wild-do-table=my\_own\%db`. If you're using the option on the command line, you might need to double the backslashes or quote the option value, depending on your command interpreter. For example, with the bash shell, you would need to type `--replicate-wild-do-table=my\\_own\\%db`.

- `--replicate-wild-ignore-table=db_name.tbl_name`

Tells the slave thread to not replicate a statement where any table matches the given wildcard pattern. To specify more than one table to ignore, use this option multiple times, once for each table. This will work for cross-database updates. Please read the notes that follow this option list.

Example: `--replicate-wild-ignore-table=foo%.bar%` will not replicate updates that use a table where the database name starts with `foo` and the table name starts with `bar`.

For information about how matching works, see the description of the `--replicate-wild-ignore-table` option. The rules for including literal wildcard characters in the option value are the same as for `--replicate-wild-ignore-table` as well.

- `--replicate-rewrite-db=from_name->to_name`

Tells the slave to translate the default database (that is, the one selected by `USE`) to `to_name` if it was `from_name` on the master. Only statements involving tables are affected (not statements such as `CREATE DATABASE`, `DROP DATABASE`, and `ALTER DATABASE`), and only if `from_name` was the default database on the master. This will not work for cross-database updates. Note that the database name translation is done before `--replicate-*` rules are tested.

If you use this option on the command line and the '>' character is special to your command interpreter, quote the option value. For example:

```
shell> mysqld --replicate-rewrite-db="olddb->newdb"
```

- `--report-host=host`

  The hostname or IP number of the slave to be reported to the master during slave registration. This value will appear in the output of `SHOW SLAVE HOSTS` on the master server. Leave the value unset if you do not want the slave to register itself with the master. Note that it is not sufficient for the master to simply read the IP number of the slave from the TCP/IP socket after the slave connects. Due to NAT and other routing issues, that IP may not be valid for connecting to the slave from the master or other hosts.

  This option is available as of MySQL 4.0.0.

- `--report-port=port_number`

  The TCP/IP port for connecting to the slave, to be reported to the master during slave registration. Set it only if the slave is listening on a non-default port or if you have a special tunnel from the master or other clients to the slave. If you are not sure, leave this option unset.

  This option is available as of MySQL 4.0.0.

- `--skip-slave-start`

  Tells the slave server not to start the slave threads when the server starts. To start the threads later, use a `START SLAVE` statement.

- `--slave_compressed_protocol={0,1}`

  If this option is set to 1, use compression of the slave/client protocol if both the slave and the master support it.

- `--slave-load-tmpdir=file_name`

  The name of the directory where the slave creates temporary files. This option is by default equal to the value of the `tmpdir` system variable. When the slave SQL thread replicates a `LOAD DATA INFILE` statement, it extracts the to-be-loaded file from the relay log into temporary files, then loads these into the table. If the file loaded on the master was huge, the temporary files on the slave will be huge, too. Therefore, it might be advisable to use this option to tell the slave to put temporary files in a directory located in some filesystem that has a lot of available space. In that case, you may also use the `--relay-log` option to place the relay logs in that filesystem, because the relay logs will be huge as well. `--slave-load-tmpdir` should point to a disk-based filesystem, not a memory-based one: The slave needs the temporary files used to replicate `LOAD DATA INFILE` to survive a machine's restart. The directory also should not be one that is cleared by the operating system during the system startup process.

- `--slave-net-timeout=seconds`

  The number of seconds to wait for more data from the master before aborting the read, considering the connection broken, and trying to reconnect. The first retry occurs immediately after the timeout. The interval between retries is controlled by the `--master-connect-retry` option.

- `--slave-skip-errors= [err_code1,err_code2,... | all]`

  Normally, replication stops when an error occurs, which gives you the opportunity to resolve the inconsistency in the data manually. This option tells the slave SQL thread to continue replication when a statement returns any of the errors listed in the option value.

  Do not use this option unless you fully understand why you are getting the errors. If there are no bugs in your replication setup and client programs, and no bugs in MySQL itself, an error that stops replication should never occur. Indiscriminate use of this option will result in slaves becoming hopelessly out of sync with the master, and you will have no idea why.

  For error codes, you should use the numbers provided by the error message in your slave error log and in the output of SHOW SLAVE STATUS.

  You can (but should not) also use the very non-recommended value of all which will ignore all error messages and keep barging along regardless of what happens. Needless to say, if you use it, we make no promises regarding your data integrity. Please do not complain if your data on the slave is not anywhere close to what it is on the master in this case. You have been warned.

  Examples:

  ```
  --slave-skip-errors=1062,1053
  --slave-skip-errors=all
  ```

The `--replicate-*` rules are evaluated as follows to determine whether a statement will be executed by the slave or ignored:

1. Are there some `--replicate-do-db` or `--replicate-ignore-db` rules?
   - Yes: Test them as for `--binlog-do-db` and `--binlog-ignore-db` (see Section 4.8.4, "The Binary Log"). What is the result of the test?
     - Ignore the statement: Ignore it and exit.
     - Execute the statement: Don't execute it immediately, defer the decision, go to the next step.
   - No: Go to the next step.
2. Are there some `--replicate-*-table` rules?
   - No: Execute the query and exit.
   - Yes: Go to the next step. Only tables that are to be updated are compared to the rules (INSERT INTO sales SELECT * FROM prices: only sales will be compared to the rules). If several tables are to be updated (multiple-table statement), the first matching table (matching "do" or "ignore") wins. That is, the first table is compared to the rules. Then, if no decision could be made, the second table is compared to the rules, and so forth.

3. Are there some `--replicate-do-table` rules?
   - Yes: Does the table match any of them?
     - Yes: Execute the query and exit.
     - No: Go to the next step.
   - No: Go to the next step.

4. Are there some `--replicate-ignore-table` rules?
   - Yes: Does the table match any of them?
     - Yes: Ignore the query and exit.
     - No: Go to the next step.
   - No: Go to the next step.

5. Are there some `--replicate-wild-do-table` rules?
   - Yes: Does the table match any of them?
     - Yes: Execute the query and exit.
     - No: Go to the next step.
   - No: Go to the next step.

6. Are there some `--replicate-wild-ignore-table` rules?
   - Yes: Does the table match any of them?
     - Yes: Ignore the query and exit.
     - No: Go to the next step.
   - No: Go to the next step.

7. No `--replicate-*-table` rule was matched. Is there another table to test against these rules?
   - Yes: Loop.
   - No: We have tested all tables to be updated and could not match any rule. Are there `--replicate-do-table` or `--replicate-wild-do-table` rules?
     - Yes: Ignore the query and exit.
     - No: Execute the query and exit.

5.9 Replication FAQ

Q: How do I configure a slave if the master is already running and I do not want to stop it?

A: There are several options. If you have taken a backup of the master at some point and recorded the binary log name and offset (from the output of SHOW MASTER STATUS) corresponding to the snapshot, use the following procedure:

1. Make sure that the slave is assigned a unique server ID.

2. Execute the following statement on the slave, filling in appropriate values for each option:

```
mysql> CHANGE MASTER TO
    ->       MASTER_HOST='master_host_name',
    ->       MASTER_USER='master_user_name',
    ->       MASTER_PASSWORD='master_pass',
    ->       MASTER_LOG_FILE='recorded_log_file_name',
    ->       MASTER_LOG_POS=recorded_log_position;
```

3. Execute START SLAVE on the slave.

If you do not have a backup of the master server already, here is a quick procedure for creating one. All steps should be performed on the master host.

1. Issue this statement:

```
mysql> FLUSH TABLES WITH READ LOCK;
```

2. With the lock still in place, execute this command (or a variation of it):

```
shell> tar zcf /tmp/backup.tar.gz /var/lib/mysql
```

3. Issue this statement and make sure to record the output, which you will need later:

```
mysql> SHOW MASTER STATUS;
```

4. Release the lock:

```
mysql> UNLOCK TABLES;
```

An alternative is to make an SQL dump of the master instead of a binary copy as in the preceding procedure. To do this, you can use mysqldump --master-data on your master and later load the SQL dump into your slave. However, this is slower than making a binary copy.

No matter which of the two methods you use, afterward follow the instructions for the case when you have a snapshot and have recorded the log name and offset. You can use the same snapshot to set up several slaves. Once you have the snapshot of the master, you can wait to set up a slave as long as the binary logs of the master are left intact. The two practical limitations on the length of time you can wait are the amount of disk space available to retain binary logs on the master and the length of time it will take the slave to catch up.

You can also use LOAD DATA FROM MASTER. This is a convenient statement that transfers a snapshot to the slave and adjusts the log name and offset all at once. In the future, LOAD DATA FROM MASTER will be the recommended way to set up a slave. Be warned, however, that it works only for MyISAM tables and it may hold a read lock for a long time. It is not yet implemented as efficiently as we would like. If you have large tables, the preferred method at this time is still to make a binary snapshot on the master server after executing FLUSH TABLES WITH READ LOCK.

Q: Does the slave need to be connected to the master all the time?

A: No, it does not. The slave can go down or stay disconnected for hours or even days, then reconnect and catch up on the updates. For example, you can set up a master/slave relationship over a dial-up link where the link is up only sporadically and for short periods of time. The implication of this is that, at any given time, the slave is not guaranteed to be in sync with the master unless you take some special measures. In the future, we will have the option to block the master until at least one slave is in sync.

Q: How do I know how late a slave is compared to the master? In other words, how do I know the date of the last query replicated by the slave?

A: If the slave is 4.1.1 or newer, read the `Seconds_Behind_Master` column in `SHOW SLAVE STATUS`. For older versions, the following applies. This is possible only if `SHOW PROCESSLIST` on the slave shows that the SQL thread is running (or for MySQL 3.23, that the slave thread is running), and that the thread has executed at least one event from the master. See Section 5.3, "Replication Implementation Details."

When the slave SQL thread executes an event read from the master, it modifies its own time to the event timestamp (this is why `TIMESTAMP` is well replicated). In the `Time` column in the output of `SHOW PROCESSLIST`, the number of seconds displayed for the slave SQL thread is the number of seconds between the timestamp of the last replicated event and the real time of the slave machine. You can use this to determine the date of the last replicated event. Note that if your slave has been disconnected from the master for one hour, and then reconnects, you may immediately see `Time` values like 3600 for the slave SQL thread in `SHOW PROCESSLIST`. This would be because the slave is executing statements that are one hour old.

Q: How do I force the master to block updates until the slave catches up?

A: Use the following procedure:

1. On the master, execute these statements:

   ```
   mysql> FLUSH TABLES WITH READ LOCK;
   mysql> SHOW MASTER STATUS;
   ```

   Record the log name and the offset from the output of the `SHOW` statement. These are the replication coordinates.

2. On the slave, issue the following statement, where the arguments to the `MASTER_POS_WAIT()` function are the replication coordinate values obtained in the previous step:

   ```
   mysql> SELECT MASTER_POS_WAIT('log_name', log_offset);
   ```

   The `SELECT` statement will block until the slave reaches the specified log file and offset. At that point, the slave will be in sync with the master and the statement will return.

3. On the master, issue the following statement to allow the master to begin processing updates again:

   ```
   mysql> UNLOCK TABLES;
   ```

Q: What issues should I be aware of when setting up two-way replication?

A: MySQL replication currently does not support any locking protocol between master and slave to guarantee the atomicity of a distributed (cross-server) update. In other words, it is possible for client A to make an update to co-master 1, and in the meantime, before it propagates to co-master 2, client B could make an update to co-master 2 that will make the update of client A work differently than it did on co-master 1. Thus, when the update of client A makes it to co-master 2, it will produce tables that are different than what you have on co-master 1, even after all the updates from co-master 2 have also propagated. This means that you should not co-chain two servers in a two-way replication relationship unless you are sure that your updates can safely happen in any order, or unless you take care of mis-ordered updates somehow in the client code.

You must also realize that two-way replication actually does not improve performance very much (if at all), as far as updates are concerned. Both servers need to do the same number of updates each, as you would have one server do. The only difference is that there will be a little less lock contention, because the updates originating on another server will be serialized in one slave thread. Even this benefit might be offset by network delays.

Q: How can I use replication to improve performance of my system?

A: You should set up one server as the master and direct all writes to it. Then configure as many slaves as you have the budget and rackspace for, and distribute the reads among the master and the slaves. You can also start the slaves with the `--skip-innodb`, `--skip-bdb`, `--low-priority-updates`, and `--delay-key-write=ALL` options to get speed improvements on the slave end. In this case, the slave will use non-transactional `MyISAM` tables instead of `InnoDB` and `BDB` tables to get more speed.

Q: What should I do to prepare client code in my own applications to use performance-enhancing replication?

A: If the part of your code that is responsible for database access has been properly abstracted/modularized, converting it to run with a replicated setup should be very smooth and easy. Just change the implementation of your database access to send all writes to the master, and to send reads to either the master or a slave. If your code does not have this level of abstraction, setting up a replicated system will give you the opportunity and motivation to it clean up. You should start by creating a wrapper library or module with the following functions:

- `safe_writer_connect()`
- `safe_reader_connect()`
- `safe_reader_statement()`
- `safe_writer_statement()`

`safe_` in each function name means that the function will take care of handling all the error conditions. You can use different names for the functions. The important thing is to have a unified interface for connecting for reads, connecting for writes, doing a read, and doing a write.

You should then convert your client code to use the wrapper library. This may be a painful and scary process at first, but it will pay off in the long run. All applications that use the approach just described will be able to take advantage of a master/slave configuration, even one involving multiple slaves. The code will be a lot easier to maintain, and adding troubleshooting options will be trivial. You will just need to modify one or two functions; for example, to log how long each statement took, or which statement among your many thousands gave you an error.

If you have written a lot of code already, you may want to automate the conversion task by using the `replace` utility that comes with standard MySQL distributions, or just write your own conversion script. Ideally, your code already uses consistent programming style conventions. If not, then you are probably better off rewriting it anyway, or at least going through and manually regularizing it to use a consistent style.

Q: When and how much can MySQL replication improve the performance of my system?

A: MySQL replication is most beneficial for a system with frequent reads and infrequent writes. In theory, by using a single-master/multiple-slave setup, you can scale the system by adding more slaves until you either run out of network bandwidth, or your update load grows to the point that the master cannot handle it.

In order to determine how many slaves you can get before the added benefits begin to level out, and how much you can improve performance of your site, you need to know your query patterns, and to determine empirically by benchmarking the relationship between the throughput for reads (reads per second, or `max_reads`) and for writes (`max_writes`) on a typical master and a typical slave. The example here shows a rather simplified calculation of what you can get with replication for a hypothetical system.

Let's say that system load consists of 10% writes and 90% reads, and we have determined by benchmarking that `max_reads` is $1200 - 2 * $ `max_writes`. In other words, the system can do 1,200 reads per second with no writes, the average write is twice as slow as the average read, and the relationship is linear. Let us suppose that the master and each slave have the same capacity, and that we have one master and N slaves. Then we have for each server (master or slave):

`reads = 1200 - 2 * writes`

`reads = 9 * writes / (N + 1)` (reads are split, but writes go to all servers)

`9 * writes / (N + 1) + 2 * writes = 1200`

`writes = 1200 / (2 + 9/(N+1))`

The last equation indicates that the maximum number of writes for N slaves, given a maximum possible read rate of 1,200 per minute and a ratio of nine reads per write.

This analysis yields the following conclusions:

- If $N = 0$ (which means we have no replication), our system can handle about 1200/11 = 109 writes per second.

- If *N* = 1, we get up to 184 writes per second.
- If *N* = 8, we get up to 400 writes per second.
- If *N* = 17, we get up to 480 writes per second.
- Eventually, as *N* approaches infinity (and our budget negative infinity), we can get very close to 600 writes per second, increasing system throughput about 5.5 times. However, with only eight servers, we increased it almost four times already.

Note that these computations assume infinite network bandwidth and neglect several other factors that could turn out to be significant on your system. In many cases, you may not be able to perform a computation similar to the just shown that will accurately predict what will happen on your system if you add *N* replication slaves. However, answering the following questions should help you decide whether and how much replication will improve the performance of your system:

- What is the read/write ratio on your system?
- How much more write load can one server handle if you reduce the reads?
- For how many slaves do you have bandwidth available on your network?

Q: How can I use replication to provide redundancy/high availability?

A: With the currently available features, you would have to set up a master and a slave (or several slaves), and write a script that will monitor the master to see whether it is up. Then instruct your applications and the slaves to change master in case of failure. Some suggestions:

- To tell a slave to change its master, use the CHANGE MASTER TO statement.
- A good way to keep your applications informed as to the location of the master is by having a dynamic DNS entry for the master. With bind you can use nsupdate to dynamically update your DNS.
- You should run your slaves with the --log-bin option and without --log-slave-updates. This way the slave will be ready to become a master as soon as you issue STOP SLAVE; RESET MASTER, and CHANGE MASTER TO on the other slaves. For example, assume that you have the following setup:

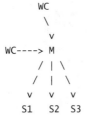

M means the master, S the slaves, WC the clients that issue database writes and reads; clients that issue only database reads are not represented, because they need not switch.

S1, S2, and S3 are slaves running with `--log-bin` and without `--log-slave-updates`. Because updates received by a slave from the master are not logged in the binary log unless `--log-slave-updates` is specified, the binary log on each slave is empty. If for some reason M becomes unavailable, you can pick one slave to become the new master. For example, if you pick S1, all WC should be redirected to S1, and S2 and S3 should replicate from S1.

Make sure that all slaves have processed any statements in their relay log. On each slave, issue `STOP SLAVE IO_THREAD`, then check the output of `SHOW PROCESSLIST` until you see `Has read all relay logs`. When this is true for all slaves, they can be reconfigured to the new setup. On the slave S1 being promoted to become the master, issue `STOP SLAVE` and `RESET MASTER`.

On the other slaves S2 and S3, use `STOP SLAVE` and `CHANGE MASTER TO MASTER_HOST='S1'` (where `'S1'` represents the real hostname of S1). To `CHANGE MASTER`, add all information about how to connect to S1 from S2 or S3 (user, password, port). In `CHANGE MASTER`, there is no need to specify the name of S1's binary log or binary log position to read from: We know it is the first binary log and position 4, which are the defaults for `CHANGE MASTER`. Finally, use `START SLAVE` on S2 and S3.

Then instruct all WC to direct their statements to S1. From that point on, all updates sent by WC to S1 are written to the binary log of S1, which will contain exactly every update statement sent to S1 since M died.

The result is this configuration:

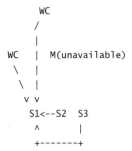

```
     WC
    /
    |
WC  | M(unavailable)
 \  |
  \ |
   v v
    S1<--S2  S3
    ^        |
    +-------+
```

When M is up again, you just have to issue on it the same `CHANGE MASTER` as the one issued on S2 and S3, so that M becomes a slave of S1 and picks all the WC writes it has missed while it was down. Now to make M a master again (because it is the most powerful machine, for example), use the preceding procedure as if S1 was unavailable and M was to be the new master. During the procedure, don't forget to run `RESET MASTER` on M before making S1, S2, and S3 slaves of M. Otherwise, they may pick up old WC writes from before the point at which M became unavailable.

We are currently working on integrating an automatic master election system into MySQL, but until it is ready, you will have to create your own monitoring tools.

5.10 Troubleshooting Replication

If you have followed the instructions, and your replication setup is not working, first check the following:

- **Check the error log for messages**. Many users have lost time by not doing this early enough.

- Is the master logging to the binary log? Check with SHOW MASTER STATUS. If it is, Position will be non-zero. If not, verify that you are running the master with the log-bin and server-id options.

- Is the slave running? Use SHOW SLAVE STATUS to check whether the Slave_IO_Running and Slave_SQL_Running values are both Yes. If not, verify the options that were used when starting the slave server.

- If the slave is running, did it establish a connection to the master? Use SHOW PROCESSLIST, find the I/O and SQL threads and check their State column to see how they display. See Section 5.3, "Replication Implementation Details." If the I/O thread state says Connecting to master, verify the privileges for the replication user on the master, master hostname, your DNS setup, whether the master is actually running, and whether it is reachable from the slave.

- If the slave was running before but now has stopped, the reason usually is that some statement that succeeded on the master failed on the slave. This should never happen if you have taken a proper snapshot of the master, and never modify the data on the slave outside of the slave thread. If it does, it is a bug or you have encountered one of the known replication limitations described in Section 5.7, "Replication Features and Known Problems." If it is a bug, see Section 5.11, "Reporting Replication Bugs," for instructions on how to report it.

- If a statement that succeeded on the master refuses to run on the slave, and it is not feasible to do a full database resynchronization (that is, to delete the slave's database and copy a new snapshot from the master), try the following:

  1. Determine whether the slave's table is different from the master's. Try to understand how this happened. Then make the slave's table identical to the master's and run START SLAVE.

  2. If the preceding step does not work or does not apply, try to understand whether it would be safe to make the update manually (if needed) and then ignore the next statement from the master.

  3. If you decide that you can skip the next statement from the master, issue the following statements:

     ```
     mysql> SET GLOBAL SQL_SLAVE_SKIP_COUNTER = n;
     mysql> START SLAVE;
     ```

     The value of *n* should be 1 if the next statement from the master does not use AUTO_INCREMENT or LAST_INSERT_ID(). Otherwise, the value should be 2. The reason for using a value of 2 for statements that use AUTO_INCREMENT or LAST_INSERT_ID() is that they take two events in the binary log of the master.

4. If you are sure that the slave started out perfectly synchronized with the master, and no one has updated the tables involved outside of slave thread, then presumably the discrepancy is the result of a bug. If you are running the most recent version, please report the problem. If you are running an older version of MySQL, try upgrading.

5.11 Reporting Replication Bugs

When you have determined that there is no user error involved, and replication still either does not work at all or is unstable, it is time to send us a bug report. We need to get as much information as possible from you to be able to track down the bug. Please do spend some time and effort preparing a good bug report.

If you have a repeatable test case that demonstrates the bug, please enter it into our bugs database at http://bugs.mysql.com/. If you have a phantom problem (one that you cannot duplicate "at will"), use the following procedure:

1. Verify that no user error is involved. For example, if you update the slave outside of the slave thread, the data will go out of sync, and you can have unique key violations on updates. In this case, the slave thread will stop and wait for you to clean up the tables manually to bring them in sync. This is not a replication problem. It is a problem of outside interference that causes replication to fail.

2. Run the slave with the --log-slave-updates and --log-bin options. They will cause the slave to log the updates that it receives from the master into its own binary logs.

3. Save all evidence before resetting the replication state. If we have no information or only sketchy information, it becomes difficult or impossible for us to track down the problem. The evidence you should collect is:

   - All binary logs from the master
   - All binary logs from the slave
   - The output of SHOW MASTER STATUS from the master at the time you have discovered the problem
   - The output of SHOW SLAVE STATUS from the master at the time you have discovered the problem
   - Error logs from the master and the slave

4. Use mysqlbinlog to examine the binary logs. The following should be helpful to find the trouble query, for example:

```
shell> mysqlbinlog -j pos_from_slave_status \
              /path/to/log_from_slave_status | head
```

Once you have collected the evidence for the phantom problem, try hard to isolate it into a separate test case first. Then enter the problem into our bugs database at http://bugs.mysql.com/ with as much information as possible.

6

MySQL Optimization

Optimization is a complex task because ultimately it requires understanding of the entire system to be optimized. Although it may be possible to perform some local optimizations with little knowledge of your system or application, the more optimal you want your system to become, the more you will have to know about it.

This chapter tries to explain and give some examples of different ways to optimize MySQL. Remember, however, that there are always additional ways to make the system even faster, although they may require increasing effort to achieve.

6.1 Optimization Overview

The most important factor in making a system fast is its basic design. You also need to know what kinds of things your system will be doing, and what your bottlenecks are.

The most common system bottlenecks are:

- Disk seeks. It takes time for the disk to find a piece of data. With modern disks, the mean time for this is usually lower than 10ms, so we can in theory do about 100 seeks a second. This time improves slowly with new disks and is very hard to optimize for a single table. The way to optimize seek time is to distribute the data onto more than one disk.

- Disk reading and writing. When the disk is at the correct position, we need to read the data. With modern disks, one disk delivers at least 10-20MB/s throughput. This is easier to optimize than seeks because you can read in parallel from multiple disks.

- CPU cycles. When we have the data in main memory (or if it was already there), we need to process it to get our result. Having small tables compared to the amount of memory is the most common limiting factor. But with small tables, speed is usually not the problem.

- Memory bandwidth. When the CPU needs more data than can fit in the CPU cache, main memory bandwidth becomes a bottleneck. This is an uncommon bottleneck for most systems, but one to be aware of.

6.1.1 MySQL Design Limitations and Tradeoffs

When using the MyISAM storage engine, MySQL uses extremely fast table locking that allows multiple readers or a single writer. The biggest problem with this storage engine occurs when you have a steady stream of mixed updates and slow selects on a single table. If this is a problem for certain tables, you can use another table type for them. See Chapter 8, "MySQL Storage Engines and Table Types."

MySQL can work with both transactional and non-transactional tables. To be able to work smoothly with non-transactional tables (which can't roll back if something goes wrong), MySQL has the following rules:

- All columns have default values.
- If you insert a "wrong" value in a column, such as a too-large numerical value into a numerical column, MySQL sets the column to the "best possible value" instead of giving an error. For numerical values, this is 0, the smallest possible value, or the largest possible value. For strings, this is either the empty string or the longest possible string that can be stored in the column.
- All calculated expressions return a value that can be used instead of signaling an error condition. For example, 1/0 returns NULL.

The implication of these rules is that you should not use MySQL to check column content. Instead, you should check values within your application before storing them in the database.

6.1.2 Designing Applications for Portability

Because all SQL servers implement different parts of standard SQL, it takes work to write portable SQL applications. It is very easy to achieve portability for very simple selects and inserts, but becomes more difficult the more capabilities you require. If you want an application that is fast with many database systems, it becomes even harder!

To make a complex application portable, you need to determine which SQL servers it must work with, then determine what features those servers support.

All database systems have some weak points. That is, they have different design compromises that lead to different behavior.

You can use the MySQL crash-me program to find functions, types, and limits that you can use with a selection of database servers. crash-me does not check for every possible feature, but it is still reasonably comprehensive, performing about 450 tests.

An example of the type of information crash-me can provide is that you shouldn't have column names longer than 18 characters if you want to be able to use Informix or DB2.

The crash-me program and the MySQL benchmarks are all very database independent. By taking a look at how they are written, you can get a feeling for what you have to do to make your own applications database independent. The programs can be found in the sql-bench directory of MySQL source distributions. They are written in Perl and use the DBI database interface. Use of DBI in itself solves part of the portability problem because it provides database-independent access methods.

For crash-me results, visit http://dev.mysql.com/tech-resources/crash-me.php. See http://dev.mysql.com/tech-resources/benchmarks/ for the results from the benchmarks.

If you strive for database independence, you need to get a good feeling for each SQL server's bottlenecks. For example, MySQL is very fast in retrieving and updating records for MyISAM tables, but will have a problem in mixing slow readers and writers on the same table. Oracle, on the other hand, has a big problem when you try to access rows that you have recently updated (until they are flushed to disk). Transactional databases in general are not very good at generating summary tables from log tables, because in this case row locking is almost useless.

To make your application *really* database independent, you need to define an easily extendable interface through which you manipulate your data. Because C++ is available on most systems, it makes sense to use a C++ class-based interface to the databases.

If you use some feature that is specific to a given database system (such as the REPLACE statement, which is specific to MySQL), you should implement the same feature for other SQL servers by coding an alternative method. Although the alternative may be slower, it will allow the other servers to perform the same tasks.

With MySQL, you can use the /*! */ syntax to add MySQL-specific keywords to a query. The code inside /**/ will be treated as a comment (and ignored) by most other SQL servers.

If high performance is more important than exactness, as in some Web applications, it is possible to create an application layer that caches all results to give you even higher performance. By letting old results "expire" after a while, you can keep the cache reasonably fresh. This provides a method to handle high load spikes, in which case you can dynamically increase the cache and set the expiration timeout higher until things get back to normal.

In this case, the table creation information should contain information of the initial size of the cache and how often the table should normally be refreshed.

An alternative to implementing an application cache is to use the MySQL query cache. By enabling the query cache, the server handles the details of determining whether a query result can be reused. This simplifies your application. See Section 4.10, "The MySQL Query Cache."

6.1.3 What We Have Used MySQL For

This section describes an early application for MySQL.

During MySQL initial development, the features of MySQL were made to fit our largest customer, which handled data warehousing for a couple of the largest retailers in Sweden.

From all stores, we got weekly summaries of all bonus card transactions, and were expected to provide useful information for the store owners to help them find how their advertising campaigns were affecting their own customers.

The volume of data was quite huge (about seven million summary transactions per month), and we had data for 4-10 years that we needed to present to the users. We got weekly requests from our customers, who wanted to get "instant" access to new reports from this data.

We solved this problem by storing all information per month in compressed "transaction" tables. We had a set of simple macros that generated summary tables grouped by different criteria (product group, customer id, store, and so on) from the tables in which the transactions were stored. The reports were Web pages that were dynamically generated by a small Perl script. This script parsed a Web page, executed the SQL statements in it, and inserted the results. We would have used PHP or mod_perl instead, but they were not available at the time.

For graphical data, we wrote a simple tool in C that could process SQL query results and produce GIF images based on those results. This tool also was dynamically executed from the Perl script that parsed the Web pages.

In most cases, a new report could be created simply by copying an existing script and modifying the SQL query in it. In some cases, we needed to add more columns to an existing summary table or generate a new one, but this also was quite simple because we kept all transaction-storage tables on disk. (This amounted to about 50GB of transaction tables and 200GB of other customer data.)

We also let our customers access the summary tables directly with ODBC so that the advanced users could experiment with the data themselves.

This system worked well and we had no problems handling the data with quite modest Sun Ultra SPARCstation hardware (2x200MHz). Eventually the system was migrated to Linux.

6.1.4 The MySQL Benchmark Suite

This section should contain a technical description of the MySQL benchmark suite (and crash-me), but that description has not yet been written. Currently, you can get a good idea of the benchmarks by looking at the code and results in the sql-bench directory in any MySQL source distribution.

This benchmark suite is meant to tell any user what operations a given SQL implementation performs well or poorly.

Note that this benchmark is single-threaded, so it measures the minimum time for the operations performed. We plan to add multi-threaded tests to the benchmark suite in the future.

To use the benchmark suite, the following requirements must be satisfied:

- The benchmark suite is provided with MySQL source distributions. You can either download a released distribution from `http://dev.mysql.com/downloads/`, or use the current development source tree (see Section 2.3.3, "Installing from the Development Source Tree").

- The benchmark scripts are written in Perl and use the Perl DBI module to access database servers, so DBI must be installed. You will also need the server-specific DBD drivers for each of the servers you want to test. For example, to test MySQL, PostgreSQL, and DB2, you must have the `DBD::mysql`, `DBD::Pg`, and `DBD::DB2` modules installed. See Section 2.7, "Perl Installation Notes."

After you obtain a MySQL source distribution, you will find the benchmark suite in its `sql-bench` directory. To run the benchmark tests, build MySQL, then change location into the `sql-bench` directory and execute the `run-all-tests` script:

```
shell> cd sql-bench
shell> perl run-all-tests --server=server_name
```

`server_name` is one of the supported servers. To get a list of all options and supported servers, invoke this command:

```
shell> perl run-all-tests --help
```

The `crash-me` script also is located in the `sql-bench` directory. `crash-me` tries to determine what features a database supports and what its capabilities and limitations are by actually running queries. For example, it determines:

- What column types are supported
- How many indexes are supported
- What functions are supported
- How big a query can be
- How big a `VARCHAR` column can be

You can find the results from `crash-me` for many different database servers at `http://dev.mysql.com/tech-resources/crash-me.php`. For more information about benchmark results, visit `http://dev.mysql.com/tech-resources/benchmarks/`.

6.1.5 Using Your Own Benchmarks

You should definitely benchmark your application and database to find out where the bottlenecks are. By fixing a bottleneck (or by replacing it with a "dummy module"), you can then easily identify the next bottleneck. Even if the overall performance for your application currently is acceptable, you should at least make a plan for each bottleneck, and decide how to solve it if someday you really need the extra performance.

For an example of portable benchmark programs, look at the MySQL benchmark suite. See Section 6.1.4, "The MySQL Benchmark Suite." You can take any program from this suite and modify it for your needs. By doing this, you can try different solutions to your problem and test which really is fastest for you.

Another free benchmark suite is the `Open Source Database Benchmark`, available at `http://osdb.sourceforge.net/`.

It is very common for a problem to occur only when the system is very heavily loaded. We have had many customers who contact us when they have a (tested) system in production and have encountered load problems. In most cases, performance problems turn out to be due to issues of basic database design (for example, table scans are *not good* at high load) or problems with the operating system or libraries. Most of the time, these problems would be a *lot* easier to fix if the systems were not already in production.

To avoid problems like this, you should put some effort into benchmarking your whole application under the worst possible load! You can use Super Smack for this. It is available at `http://jeremy.zawodny.com/mysql/super-smack/`. As the name suggests, it can bring a system to its knees if you ask it, so make sure to use it only on your development systems.

6.2 Optimizing `SELECT` Statements and Other Queries

First, one factor affects all statements: The more complex your permission setup is, the more overhead you will have.

Using simpler permissions when you issue `GRANT` statements enables MySQL to reduce permission-checking overhead when clients execute statements. For example, if you don't grant any table-level or column-level privileges, the server need not ever check the contents of the `tables_priv` and `columns_priv` tables. Similarly, if you place no resource limits on any accounts, the server does not have to perform resource counting. If you have a very high query volume, it may be worth the time to use a simplified grant structure to reduce permission-checking overhead.

If your problem is with some specific MySQL expression or function, you can use the `BENCHMARK()` function from the `mysql` client program to perform a timing test. Its syntax is `BENCHMARK(loop_count,expression)`. For example:

```
mysql> SELECT BENCHMARK(1000000,1+1);
+------------------------+
| BENCHMARK(1000000,1+1) |
+------------------------+
|                      0 |
+------------------------+
1 row in set (0.32 sec)
```

This result was obtained on a Pentium II 400MHz system. It shows that MySQL can execute 1,000,000 simple addition expressions in 0.32 seconds on that system.

All MySQL functions should be very optimized, but there may be some exceptions. BENCHMARK() is a great tool to find out if this is a problem with your query.

6.2.1 EXPLAIN Syntax (Get Information About a SELECT)

```
EXPLAIN tbl_name
```

Or:

```
EXPLAIN SELECT select_options
```

The EXPLAIN statement can be used either as a synonym for DESCRIBE or as a way to obtain information about how MySQL will execute a SELECT statement:

- The EXPLAIN tbl_name syntax is synonymous with DESCRIBE tbl_name or SHOW COLUMNS FROM tbl_name.

- When you precede a SELECT statement with the keyword EXPLAIN, MySQL explains how it would process the SELECT, providing information about how tables are joined and in which order.

This section provides information about the second use of EXPLAIN.

With the help of EXPLAIN, you can see when you must add indexes to tables to get a faster SELECT that uses indexes to find records.

You should frequently run ANALYZE TABLE to update table statistics such as cardinality of keys, which can affect the choices the optimizer makes.

You can also see whether the optimizer joins the tables in an optimal order. To force the optimizer to use a join order corresponding to the order in which the tables are named in the SELECT statement, begin the statement with SELECT STRAIGHT_JOIN rather than just SELECT.

EXPLAIN returns a row of information for each table used in the SELECT statement. The tables are listed in the output in the order that MySQL would read them while processing the query. MySQL resolves all joins using a single-sweep multi-join method. This means that MySQL reads a row from the first table, then finds a matching row in the second table, then in the third table, and so on. When all tables are processed, it outputs the selected columns and backtracks through the table list until a table is found for which there are more matching rows. The next row is read from this table and the process continues with the next table.

In MySQL version 4.1, the EXPLAIN output format was changed to work better with constructs such as UNION statements, subqueries, and derived tables. Most notable is the addition of two new columns: id and select_type. You will not see these columns when using servers older than MySQL 4.1.

Each output row from EXPLAIN provides information about one table, and each row consists of the following columns:

- id

  The SELECT identifier. This is the sequential number of the SELECT within the query.

- select_type

  The type of SELECT, which can be any of the following:

  - SIMPLE

    Simple SELECT (not using UNION or subqueries)

  - PRIMARY

    Outermost SELECT

  - UNION

    Second or later SELECT statement in a UNION

  - DEPENDENT UNION

    Second or later SELECT statement in a UNION, dependent on outer subquery

  - SUBQUERY

    First SELECT in subquery

  - DEPENDENT SUBQUERY

    First SELECT in subquery, dependent on outer subquery

  - DERIVED

    Derived table SELECT (subquery in FROM clause)

- table

  The table to which the row of output refers.

- type

  The join type. The different join types are listed here, ordered from the best type to the worst:

  - system

    The table has only one row (= system table). This is a special case of the const join type.

  - const

    The table has at most one matching row, which will be read at the start of the query. Because there is only one row, values from the column in this row can be regarded as constants by the rest of the optimizer. const tables are very fast because they are read only once!

const is used when you compare all parts of a PRIMARY KEY or UNIQUE index with constant values. In the following queries, *tbl_name* can be used as a const table:

```
SELECT * FROM tbl_name WHERE primary_key=1;

SELECT * FROM tbl_name
WHERE primary_key_part1=1 AND primary_key_part2=2;
```

- eq_ref

  One row will be read from this table for each combination of rows from the previous tables. Other than the const types, this is the best possible join type. It is used when all parts of an index are used by the join and the index is a PRIMARY KEY or UNIQUE index.

  eq_ref can be used for indexed columns that are compared using the = operator. The comparison value can be a constant or an expression that uses columns from tables that are read before this table.

  In the following examples, MySQL can use an eq_ref join to process ref_table:

  ```
  SELECT * FROM ref_table,other_table
  WHERE ref_table.key_column=other_table.column;

  SELECT * FROM ref_table,other_table
  WHERE ref_table.key_column_part1=other_table.column
  AND ref_table.key_column_part2=1;
  ```

- ref

  All rows with matching index values will be read from this table for each combination of rows from the previous tables. ref is used if the join uses only a leftmost prefix of the key or if the key is not a PRIMARY KEY or UNIQUE index (in other words, if the join cannot select a single row based on the key value). If the key that is used matches only a few rows, this is a good join type.

  ref can be used for indexed columns that are compared using the = operator.

  In the following examples, MySQL can use a ref join to process ref_table:

  ```
  SELECT * FROM ref_table WHERE key_column=expr;

  SELECT * FROM ref_table,other_table
  WHERE ref_table.key_column=other_table.column;

  SELECT * FROM ref_table,other_table
  WHERE ref_table.key_column_part1=other_table.column
  AND ref_table.key_column_part2=1;
  ```

- ref_or_null

  This join type is like ref, but with the addition that MySQL will do an extra search for rows that contain NULL values. This join type optimization is new for MySQL 4.1.1 and is mostly used when resolving subqueries.

  In the following examples, MySQL can use a ref_or_null join to process ref_table:

```
SELECT * FROM ref_table
WHERE key_column=expr OR key_column IS NULL;
```

  See Section 6.2.6, "How MySQL Optimizes IS NULL."

- index_merge

  This join type indicates that the Index Merge optimization is used. In this case, the key column contains a list of indexes used, and key_len contains a list of the longest key parts for the indexes used. For more information, see Section 6.2.5, "How MySQL Optimizes OR Clauses."

- unique_subquery

  This type replaces ref for some IN subqueries of the following form:

```
value IN (SELECT primary_key FROM single_table WHERE some_expr)
```

  unique_subquery is just an index lookup function that replaces the subquery completely for better efficiency.

- index_subquery

  This join type is similar to unique_subquery. It replaces IN subqueries, but it works for non-unique indexes in subqueries of the following form:

```
value IN (SELECT key_column FROM single_table WHERE some_expr)
```

- range

  Only rows that are in a given range will be retrieved, using an index to select the rows. The key column indicates which index is used. The key_len contains the longest key part that was used. The ref column will be NULL for this type.

  range can be used for when a key column is compared to a constant using any of the =, <>, >, >=, <, <=, IS NULL, <=>, BETWEEN, or IN operators:

```
SELECT * FROM tbl_name
WHERE key_column = 10;

SELECT * FROM tbl_name
WHERE key_column BETWEEN 10 and 20;

SELECT * FROM tbl_name
WHERE key_column IN (10,20,30);

SELECT * FROM tbl_name
WHERE key_part1= 10 AND key_part2 IN (10,20,30);
```

- index

  This join type is the same as ALL, except that only the index tree is scanned. This usually is faster than ALL, because the index file usually is smaller than the data file.

  MySQL can use this join type when the query uses only columns that are part of a single index.

- ALL

  A full table scan will be done for each combination of rows from the previous tables. This is normally not good if the table is the first table not marked const, and usually *very* bad in all other cases. Normally, you can avoid ALL by adding indexes that allow row retrieval from the table based on constant values or column values from earlier tables.

- possible_keys

  The possible_keys column indicates which indexes MySQL could use to find the rows in this table. Note that this column is totally independent of the order of the tables as displayed in the output from EXPLAIN. That means that some of the keys in possible_keys might not be usable in practice with the generated table order.

  If this column is NULL, there are no relevant indexes. In this case, you may be able to improve the performance of your query by examining the WHERE clause to see whether it refers to some column or columns that would be suitable for indexing. If so, create an appropriate index and check the query with EXPLAIN again.

  To see what indexes a table has, use SHOW INDEX FROM *tbl_name*.

- key

  The key column indicates the key (index) that MySQL actually decided to use. The key is NULL if no index was chosen. To force MySQL to use or ignore an index listed in the possible_keys column, use FORCE INDEX, USE INDEX, or IGNORE INDEX in your query.

  For MyISAM and BDB tables, running ANALYZE TABLE will help the optimizer choose better indexes. For MyISAM tables, myisamchk --analyze will do the same. See Section 4.6.2, "Table Maintenance and Crash Recovery."

- key_len

  The key_len column indicates the length of the key that MySQL decided to use. The length is NULL if the key column says NULL. Note that the value of key_len allows you to determine how many parts of a multiple-part key MySQL will actually use.

- ref

  The ref column shows which columns or constants are used with the key to select rows from the table.

- rows

  The rows column indicates the number of rows MySQL believes it must examine to execute the query.

- Extra

  This column contains additional information about how MySQL will resolve the query. Here is an explanation of the different text strings that can appear in this column:

  - Distinct

    MySQL will stop searching for more rows for the current row combination after it has found the first matching row.

  - Not exists

    MySQL was able to do a LEFT JOIN optimization on the query and will not examine more rows in this table for the previous row combination after it finds one row that matches the LEFT JOIN criteria.

    Here is an example of the type of query that can be optimized this way:

    ```
    SELECT * FROM t1 LEFT JOIN t2 ON t1.id=t2.id
    WHERE t2.id IS NULL;
    ```

    Assume that t2.id is defined as NOT NULL. In this case, MySQL will scan t1 and look up the rows in t2 using the values of t1.id. If MySQL finds a matching row in t2, it knows that t2.id can never be NULL, and will not scan through the rest of the rows in t2 that have the same id value. In other words, for each row in t1, MySQL needs to do only a single lookup in t2, regardless of how many rows actually match in t2.

  - range checked for each record (index map: #)

    MySQL found no good index to use. Instead, for each row combination in the preceding tables, it will do a check to determine which index to use (if any), and use it to retrieve the rows from the table. This is not very fast, but is faster than performing a join with no index at all.

  - Using filesort

    MySQL will need to do an extra pass to find out how to retrieve the rows in sorted order. The sort is done by going through all rows according to the join type and storing the sort key and pointer to the row for all rows that match the WHERE clause. The keys then are sorted and the rows are retrieved in sorted order.

  - Using index

    The column information is retrieved from the table using only information in the index tree without having to do an additional seek to read the actual row. This strategy can be used when the query uses only columns that are part of a single index.

  - Using temporary

    To resolve the query, MySQL will need to create a temporary table to hold the result. This typically happens if the query contains GROUP BY and ORDER BY clauses that list columns differently.

- Using where

  A WHERE clause will be used to restrict which rows to match against the next table
  or send to the client. Unless you specifically intend to fetch or examine all rows
  from the table, you may have something wrong in your query if the Extra value is
  not Using where and the table join type is ALL or index.

  If you want to make your queries as fast as possible, you should look out for Extra values of Using filesort and Using temporary.

You can get a good indication of how good a join is by taking the product of the values in
the rows column of the EXPLAIN output. This should tell you roughly how many rows
MySQL must examine to execute the query. If you restrict queries with the max_join_size
system variable, this product also is used to determine which multiple-table SELECT statements to execute. See Section 6.5.2, "Tuning Server Parameters."

The following example shows how a multiple-table join can be optimized progressively
based on the information provided by EXPLAIN.

Suppose that you have the SELECT statement shown here and you plan to examine it using
EXPLAIN:

```
EXPLAIN SELECT tt.TicketNumber, tt.TimeIn,
            tt.ProjectReference, tt.EstimatedShipDate,
            tt.ActualShipDate, tt.ClientID,
            tt.ServiceCodes, tt.RepetitiveID,
            tt.CurrentProcess, tt.CurrentDPPerson,
            tt.RecordVolume, tt.DPPrinted, et.COUNTRY,
            et_1.COUNTRY, do.CUSTNAME
      FROM tt, et, et AS et_1, do
      WHERE tt.SubmitTime IS NULL
          AND tt.ActualPC = et.EMPLOYID
          AND tt.AssignedPC = et_1.EMPLOYID
          AND tt.ClientID = do.CUSTNMBR;
```

For this example, make the following assumptions:

- The columns being compared have been declared as follows:

Table	Column	Column Type
tt	ActualPC	CHAR(10)
tt	AssignedPC	CHAR(10)
tt	ClientID	CHAR(10)
et	EMPLOYID	CHAR(15)
do	CUSTNMBR	CHAR(15)

- The tables have the following indexes:

Table	Index
tt	ActualPC
tt	AssignedPC
tt	ClientID
et	EMPLOYID (primary key)
do	CUSTNMBR (primary key)

- The tt.ActualPC values are not evenly distributed.

Initially, before any optimizations have been performed, the EXPLAIN statement produces the following information:

```
table type possible_keys key  key_len ref  rows  Extra
et    ALL  PRIMARY       NULL NULL    NULL 74
do    ALL  PRIMARY       NULL NULL    NULL 2135
et_1  ALL  PRIMARY       NULL NULL    NULL 74
tt    ALL  AssignedPC,   NULL NULL    NULL 3872
           ClientID,
           ActualPC
      range checked for each record (key map: 35)
```

Because type is ALL for each table, this output indicates that MySQL is generating a Cartesian product of all the tables; that is, every combination of rows. This will take quite a long time, because the product of the number of rows in each table must be examined. For the case at hand, this product is 74 * 2135 * 74 * 3872 = 45,268,558,720 rows. If the tables were bigger, you can only imagine how long it would take.

One problem here is that MySQL can use indexes on columns more efficiently if they are declared the same. (For ISAM tables, indexes may not be used at all unless the columns are declared the same.) In this context, VARCHAR and CHAR are the same unless they are declared as different lengths. Because tt.ActualPC is declared as CHAR(10) and et.EMPLOYID is declared as CHAR(15), there is a length mismatch.

To fix this disparity between column lengths, use ALTER TABLE to lengthen ActualPC from 10 characters to 15 characters:

```
mysql> ALTER TABLE tt MODIFY ActualPC VARCHAR(15);
```

Now tt.ActualPC and et.EMPLOYID are both VARCHAR(15). Executing the EXPLAIN statement again produces this result:

```
table type possible_keys key  key_len ref  rows  Extra
tt    ALL  AssignedPC,   NULL NULL    NULL 3872  Using
           ClientID,                            where
           ActualPC
```

```
do     ALL    PRIMARY        NULL    NULL    NULL       2135
       range checked for each record (key map: 1)
et_1   ALL    PRIMARY        NULL    NULL    NULL       74
       range checked for each record (key map: 1)
et     eq_ref PRIMARY        PRIMARY 15      tt.ActualPC 1
```

This is not perfect, but is much better: The product of the rows values is now less by a factor of 74. This version is executed in a couple of seconds.

A second alteration can be made to eliminate the column length mismatches for the tt.AssignedPC = et_1.EMPLOYID and tt.ClientID = do.CUSTNMBR comparisons:

```
mysql> ALTER TABLE tt MODIFY AssignedPC VARCHAR(15),
    ->                 MODIFY ClientID   VARCHAR(15);
```

Now EXPLAIN produces the output shown here:

table	type	possible_keys	key	key_len	ref	rows	Extra
et	ALL	PRIMARY	NULL	NULL	NULL	74	
tt	ref	AssignedPC, ClientID, ActualPC	ActualPC	15	et.EMPLOYID	52	Using where
et_1	eq_ref	PRIMARY	PRIMARY	15	tt.AssignedPC	1	
do	eq_ref	PRIMARY	PRIMARY	15	tt.ClientID	1	

This is almost as good as it can get.

The remaining problem is that, by default, MySQL assumes that values in the tt.ActualPC column are evenly distributed, and that is not the case for the tt table. Fortunately, it is easy to tell MySQL to analyze the key distribution:

```
mysql> ANALYZE TABLE tt;
```

Now the join is perfect, and EXPLAIN produces this result:

table	type	possible_keys	key	key_len	ref	rows	Extra
tt	ALL	AssignedPC ClientID, ActualPC	NULL	NULL	NULL	3872	Using where
et	eq_ref	PRIMARY	PRIMARY	15	tt.ActualPC	1	
et_1	eq_ref	PRIMARY	PRIMARY	15	tt.AssignedPC	1	
do	eq_ref	PRIMARY	PRIMARY	15	tt.ClientID	1	

Note that the rows column in the output from EXPLAIN is an educated guess from the MySQL join optimizer. You should check whether the numbers are even close to the truth. If not, you may get better performance by using STRAIGHT_JOIN in your SELECT statement and trying to list the tables in a different order in the FROM clause.

6.2.2 Estimating Query Performance

In most cases, you can estimate the performance by counting disk seeks. For small tables, you can usually find a row in one disk seek (because the index is probably cached). For bigger tables, you can estimate that, using B-tree indexes, you will need this many seeks to find a row: $\log(row\_count)$ / $\log(index\_block\_length$ / $3 * 2$ / ($index\_length$ + $data\_pointer\_length$)) + 1.

In MySQL, an index block is usually 1024 bytes and the data pointer is usually 4 bytes. For a 500,000-row table with an index length of 3 bytes (medium integer), the formula indicates $\log(500,000)/\log(1024/3*2/(3+4))$ + 1 = 4 seeks.

This index would require storage of about 500,000 * 7 * 3/2 = 5.2MB (assuming a typical index buffer fill ratio of 2/3), so you will probably have much of the index in memory and you will probably need only one or two calls to read data to find the row.

For writes, however, you will need four seek requests (as above) to find where to place the new index and normally two seeks to update the index and write the row.

Note that the preceding discussion doesn't mean that your application performance will slowly degenerate by log N! As long as everything is cached by the OS or SQL server, things will become only marginally slower as the table gets bigger. After the data gets too big to be cached, things will start to go much slower until your application is only bound by disk-seeks (which increase by log N). To avoid this, increase the key cache size as the data grows. For MyISAM tables, the key cache size is controlled by the key_buffer_size system variable. See Section 6.5.2, "Tuning Server Parameters."

6.2.3 Speed of SELECT Queries

In general, when you want to make a slow SELECT ... WHERE query faster, the first thing to check is whether you can add an index. All references between different tables should usually be done with indexes. You can use the EXPLAIN statement to determine which indexes are used for a SELECT. See Section 6.4.5, "How MySQL Uses Indexes," and Section 6.2.1, "EXPLAIN Syntax (Get Information About a SELECT)."

Some general tips for speeding up queries on MyISAM tables:

- To help MySQL optimize queries better, use ANALYZE TABLE or run myisamchk --analyze on a table after it has been loaded with data. This updates a value for each index part that indicates the average number of rows that have the same value. (For unique indexes, this is always 1.) MySQL will use this to decide which index to choose when you join two tables based on a non-constant expression. You can check the result from the table analysis by using SHOW INDEX FROM tbl_name and examining the Cardinality value. myisamchk --description --verbose shows index distribution information.

- To sort an index and data according to an index, use myisamchk --sort-index --sort-records=1 (if you want to sort on index 1). This is a good way to make queries faster if you have a unique index from which you want to read all records in order according to the index. Note that the first time you sort a large table this way, it may take a long time.

6.2.4 How MySQL Optimizes WHERE Clauses

This section discusses optimizations that can be made for processing WHERE clauses. The examples use SELECT statements, but the same optimizations apply for WHERE clauses in DELETE and UPDATE statements.

Note that work on the MySQL optimizer is ongoing, so this section is incomplete. MySQL does many optimizations, not all of which are documented here.

Some of the optimizations performed by MySQL are listed here:

- Removal of unnecessary parentheses:

```
((a AND b) AND c OR (((a AND b) AND (c AND d))))
-> (a AND b AND c) OR (a AND b AND c AND d)
```

- Constant folding:

```
(a<b AND b=c) AND a=5
-> b>5 AND b=c AND a=5
```

- Constant condition removal (needed because of constant folding):

```
(B>=5 AND B=5) OR (B=6 AND 5=5) OR (B=7 AND 5=6)
-> B=5 OR B=6
```

- Constant expressions used by indexes are evaluated only once.
- COUNT(*) on a single table without a WHERE is retrieved directly from the table information for MyISAM and HEAP tables. This is also done for any NOT NULL expression when used with only one table.
- Early detection of invalid constant expressions. MySQL quickly detects that some SELECT statements are impossible and returns no rows.
- HAVING is merged with WHERE if you don't use GROUP BY or group functions (COUNT(), MIN(), and so on).
- For each table in a join, a simpler WHERE is constructed to get a fast WHERE evaluation for the table and also to skip records as soon as possible.
- All constant tables are read first before any other tables in the query. A constant table is any of the following:
  - An empty table or a table with one row.
  - A table that is used with a WHERE clause on a PRIMARY KEY or a UNIQUE index, where all index parts are compared to constant expressions and are defined as NOT NULL.

All of the following tables are used as constant tables:

```
SELECT * FROM t WHERE primary_key=1;
SELECT * FROM t1,t2
    WHERE t1.primary_key=1 AND t2.primary_key=t1.id;
```

- The best join combination for joining the tables is found by trying all possibilities. If all columns in ORDER BY and GROUP BY clauses come from the same table, that table is preferred first when joining.

- If there is an ORDER BY clause and a different GROUP BY clause, or if the ORDER BY or GROUP BY contains columns from tables other than the first table in the join queue, a temporary table is created.

- If you use SQL_SMALL_RESULT, MySQL uses an in-memory temporary table.

- Each table index is queried, and the best index is used unless the optimizer believes that it will be more efficient to use a table scan. At one time, a scan was used based on whether the best index spanned more than 30% of the table. Now the optimizer is more complex and bases its estimate on additional factors such as table size, number of rows, and I/O block size, so a fixed percentage no longer determines the choice between using an index or a scan.

- In some cases, MySQL can read rows from the index without even consulting the data file. If all columns used from the index are numeric, only the index tree is used to resolve the query.

- Before each record is output, those that do not match the HAVING clause are skipped.

Some examples of queries that are very fast:

```
SELECT COUNT(*) FROM tbl_name;

SELECT MIN(key_part1),MAX(key_part1) FROM tbl_name;

SELECT MAX(key_part2) FROM tbl_name
    WHERE key_part1=constant;

SELECT ... FROM tbl_name
    ORDER BY key_part1,key_part2,... LIMIT 10;

SELECT ... FROM tbl_name
    ORDER BY key_part1 DESC, key_part2 DESC, ... LIMIT 10;
```

The following queries are resolved using only the index tree, assuming that the indexed columns are numeric:

```
SELECT key_part1,key_part2 FROM tbl_name WHERE key_part1=val;

SELECT COUNT(*) FROM tbl_name
    WHERE key_part1=val1 AND key_part2=val2;

SELECT key_part2 FROM tbl_name GROUP BY key_part1;
```

The following queries use indexing to retrieve the rows in sorted order without a separate
sorting pass:

```
SELECT ... FROM tbl_name
    ORDER BY key_part1,key_part2,... ;

SELECT ... FROM tbl_name
    ORDER BY key_part1 DESC, key_part2 DESC, ... ;
```

6.2.5 How MySQL Optimizes OR Clauses

The Index Merge method is used to retrieve rows with several ref, ref_or_null, or range
scans and merge the results into one. This method is employed when the table condition is a
disjunction of conditions for which ref, ref_or_null, or range could be used with different
keys.

This "join" type optimization is new in MySQL 5.0.0, and represents a significant change in
behavior with regard to indexes, because the *old* rule was that the server is only ever able to
use at most one index for each referenced table.

In EXPLAIN output, this method appears as index_merge in the type column. In this case, the
key column contains a list of indexes used, and key_len contains a list of the longest key
parts for those indexes.

Examples:

```
SELECT * FROM tbl_name WHERE key_part1 = 10 OR key_part2 = 20;

SELECT * FROM tbl_name
    WHERE (key_part1 = 10 OR key_part2 = 20) AND non_key_part=30;

SELECT * FROM t1,t2
    WHERE (t1.key1 IN (1,2) OR t1.key2 LIKE 'value%')
    AND t2.key1=t1.some_col;

SELECT * FROM t1,t2
    WHERE t1.key1=1
    AND (t2.key1=t1.some_col OR t2.key2=t1.some_col2);
```

6.2.6 How MySQL Optimizes IS NULL

MySQL can do the same optimization on col_name IS NULL that it can do with col_name =
constant_value. For example, MySQL can use indexes and ranges to search for NULL with IS
NULL.

```
SELECT * FROM tbl_name WHERE key_col IS NULL;

SELECT * FROM tbl_name WHERE key_col <=> NULL;

SELECT * FROM tbl_name
    WHERE key_col=const1 OR key_col=const2 OR key_col IS NULL;
```

If a WHERE clause includes a col_name IS NULL condition for a column that is declared as NOT NULL, that expression will be optimized away. This optimization does not occur in cases when the column might produce NULL anyway; for example, if it comes from a table on the right side of a LEFT JOIN.

MySQL 4.1.1 and up can additionally optimize the combination col_name = expr AND col_name IS NULL, a form that is common in resolved subqueries. EXPLAIN will show ref_or_null when this optimization is used.

This optimization can handle one IS NULL for any key part.

Some examples of queries that are optimized, assuming that there is an index on columns a and b or table t2:

```
SELECT * FROM t1 WHERE t1.a=expr OR t1.a IS NULL;

SELECT * FROM t1,t2 WHERE t1.a=t2.a OR t2.a IS NULL;

SELECT * FROM t1,t2
    WHERE (t1.a=t2.a OR t2.a IS NULL) AND t2.b=t1.b;

SELECT * FROM t1,t2
    WHERE t1.a=t2.a AND (t2.b=t1.b OR t2.b IS NULL);

SELECT * FROM t1,t2
    WHERE (t1.a=t2.a AND t2.a IS NULL AND ...)
    OR (t1.a=t2.a AND t2.a IS NULL AND ...);
```

ref_or_null works by first doing a read on the reference key, and then a separate search for rows with a NULL key value.

Note that the optimization can handle only one IS NULL level. In the following query, MySQL will use key lookups only on the expression (t1.a=t2.a AND t2.a IS NULL) and not be able to use the key part on b:

```
SELECT * FROM t1,t2
    WHERE (t1.a=t2.a AND t2.a IS NULL)
    OR (t1.b=t2.b AND t2.b IS NULL) ;
```

6.2.7 How MySQL Optimizes DISTINCT

DISTINCT combined with ORDER BY will need a temporary table in many cases.

Note that because DISTINCT may use GROUP BY, you should be aware of how MySQL works with columns in ORDER BY or HAVING clauses that are not part of the selected columns.

MySQL extends the use of GROUP BY so that you can use columns or calculations in the SELECT list that don't appear in the GROUP BY clause. This stands for *any possible value for this group*. You can use this to get better performance by avoiding sorting and grouping on unnecessary items. For example, you don't need to group on customer.name in the following query:

```
mysql> SELECT order.custid, customer.name, MAX(payments)
    ->         FROM order,customer
    ->         WHERE order.custid = customer.custid
    ->         GROUP BY order.custid;
```

In standard SQL, you would have to add customer.name to the GROUP BY clause. In MySQL, the name is redundant if you don't run in ANSI mode.

Do *not* use this feature if the columns you omit from the GROUP BY part are not unique in the group! You will get unpredictable results.

In some cases, you can use MIN() and MAX() to obtain a specific column value even if it isn't unique. The following gives the value of column from the row containing the smallest value in the sort column:

```
SUBSTR(MIN(CONCAT(RPAD(sort,6,' '),column)),7)
```

When combining LIMIT *row_count* with DISTINCT, MySQL stops as soon as it finds *row_count* unique rows.

If you don't use columns from all tables named in a query, MySQL stops scanning the not-used tables as soon as it finds the first match. In the following case, assuming that t1 is used before t2 (which you can check with EXPLAIN), MySQL stops reading from t2 (for any particular row in t1) when the first row in t2 is found:

```
SELECT DISTINCT t1.a FROM t1,t2 where t1.a=t2.a;
```

6.2.8 How MySQL Optimizes LEFT JOIN and RIGHT JOIN

A LEFT JOIN B *join_condition* is implemented in MySQL as follows:

- Table B is set to depend on table A and all tables on which A depends.
- Table A is set to depend on all tables (except B) that are used in the LEFT JOIN condition.
- The LEFT JOIN condition is used to decide how to retrieve rows from table B. (In other words, any condition in the WHERE clause is not used.)

- All standard join optimizations are done, with the exception that a table is always read after all tables on which it depends. If there is a circular dependence, MySQL issues an error.

- All standard WHERE optimizations are done.

- If there is a row in A that matches the WHERE clause, but there is no row in B that matches the ON condition, an extra B row is generated with all columns set to NULL.

- If you use LEFT JOIN to find rows that don't exist in some table and you have the following test: col_name IS NULL in the WHERE part, where col_name is a column that is declared as NOT NULL, MySQL stops searching for more rows (for a particular key combination) after it has found one row that matches the LEFT JOIN condition.

RIGHT JOIN is implemented analogously to LEFT JOIN, with the roles of the tables reversed.

The join optimizer calculates the order in which tables should be joined. The table read order forced by LEFT JOIN and STRAIGHT_JOIN helps the join optimizer do its work much more quickly, because there are fewer table permutations to check. Note that this means that if you do a query of the following type, MySQL will do a full scan on b because the LEFT JOIN forces it to be read before d:

```
SELECT *
    FROM a,b LEFT JOIN c ON (c.key=a.key) LEFT JOIN d ON (d.key=a.key)
    WHERE b.key=d.key;
```

The fix in this case is to rewrite the query as follows:

```
SELECT *
    FROM b,a LEFT JOIN c ON (c.key=a.key) LEFT JOIN d ON (d.key=a.key)
    WHERE b.key=d.key;
```

Starting from 4.0.14, MySQL does the following LEFT JOIN optimization: If the WHERE condition is always false for the generated NULL row, the LEFT JOIN is changed to a normal join.

For example, the WHERE clause would be false in the following query if t2.column1 would be NULL:

```
SELECT * FROM t1 LEFT JOIN t2 ON (column1) WHERE t2.column2=5;
```

Therefore, it's safe to convert the query to a normal join:

```
SELECT * FROM t1,t2 WHERE t2.column2=5 AND t1.column1=t2.column1;
```

This can be made faster because MySQL can now use table t2 before table t1 if this would result in a better query plan. To force a specific table order, use STRAIGHT_JOIN.

6.2.9 How MySQL Optimizes ORDER BY

In some cases, MySQL can use an index to satisfy an ORDER BY or GROUP BY clause without doing any extra sorting.

The index can also be used even if the ORDER BY doesn't match the index exactly, as long as all the unused index parts and all the extra ORDER BY columns are constants in the WHERE clause. The following queries will use the index to resolve the ORDER BY or GROUP BY part:

```
SELECT * FROM t1 ORDER BY key_part1,key_part2,... ;
SELECT * FROM t1 WHERE key_part1=constant ORDER BY key_part2;
SELECT * FROM t1 WHERE key_part1=constant GROUP BY key_part2;
SELECT * FROM t1 ORDER BY key_part1 DESC, key_part2 DESC;
SELECT * FROM t1
    WHERE key_part1=1 ORDER BY key_part1 DESC, key_part2 DESC;
```

In some cases, MySQL *cannot* use indexes to resolve the ORDER BY, although it still will use indexes to find the rows that match the WHERE clause. These cases include the following:

- You use ORDER BY on different keys:

  ```
  SELECT * FROM t1 ORDER BY key1, key2;
  ```

- You use ORDER BY on non-consecutive key parts:

  ```
  SELECT * FROM t1 WHERE key_part2=constant ORDER BY key_part2;
  ```

- You mix ASC and DESC:

  ```
  SELECT * FROM t1 ORDER BY key_part1 DESC, key_part2 ASC;
  ```

- The key used to fetch the rows is not the same as the one used in the ORDER BY:

  ```
  SELECT * FROM t1 WHERE key2=constant ORDER BY key1;
  ```

- You are joining many tables, and the columns in the ORDER BY are not all from the first non-constant table that is used to retrieve rows. (This is the first table in the EXPLAIN output that doesn't have a const join type.)

- You have different ORDER BY and GROUP BY expressions.

- The type of table index used doesn't store rows in order. For example, this is true for a HASH index in a HEAP table.

In those cases where MySQL must sort the result, it uses the following algorithm:

1. Read all rows according to key or by table scanning. Rows that don't match the WHERE clause are skipped.

2. Store the sort key value in a buffer. The size of the buffer is the value of the sort_buffer_size system variable.

3. When the buffer gets full, run a qsort (quicksort) on it and store the result in a temporary file. Save a pointer to the sorted block. (If all rows fit into the sort buffer, no temporary file is created.)

4. Repeat the preceding steps until all rows have been read.

5. Do a multi-merge of up to MERGEBUFF (7) regions to one block in another temporary file. Repeat until all blocks from the first file are in the second file.

6. Repeat the following until there are fewer than MERGEBUFF2 (15) blocks left.

7. On the last multi-merge, only the pointer to the row (the last part of the sort key) is written to a result file.

8. Read the rows in sorted order by using the row pointers in the result file. To optimize this, we read in a big block of row pointers, sort them, and use them to read the rows in sorted order into a row buffer. The size of the buffer is the value of the read_rnd_buffer_size system variable. The code for this step is in the sql/records.cc source file.

With EXPLAIN SELECT ... ORDER BY, you can check whether MySQL can use indexes to resolve the query. It cannot if you see Using filesort in the Extra column. See Section 6.2.1, "EXPLAIN Syntax (Get Information About a SELECT)."

If you want to increase ORDER BY speed, first see whether you can get MySQL to use indexes rather than an extra sorting phase. If this is not possible, you can try the following strategies:

- Increase the size of the sort_buffer_size variable.

- Increase the size of the read_rnd_buffer_size variable.

- Change tmpdir to point to a dedicated filesystem with lots of empty space. If you use MySQL 4.1 or later, this option accepts several paths that are used in round-robin fashion. Paths should be separated by colon characters (':') on Unix and semicolon characters (';') on Windows, NetWare, and OS/2. You can use this feature to spread the load across several directories. *Note:* The paths should be for directories in filesystems that are located on different *physical* disks, not different partitions of the same disk.

By default, MySQL sorts all GROUP BY *col1*, *col2*, ... queries as if you specified ORDER BY *col1*, *col2*, ... in the query as well. If you include an ORDER BY clause explicitly that contains the same column list, MySQL optimizes it away without any speed penalty, although the sorting still occurs. If a query includes GROUP BY but you want to avoid the overhead of sorting the result, you can suppress sorting by specifying ORDER BY NULL. For example:

```
INSERT INTO foo
SELECT a, COUNT(*) FROM bar GROUP BY a ORDER BY NULL;
```

6.2.10 How MySQL Optimizes LIMIT

In some cases, MySQL will handle a query differently when you are using LIMIT *row_count* and not using HAVING:

- If you are selecting only a few rows with LIMIT, MySQL uses indexes in some cases when normally it would prefer to do a full table scan.

- If you use LIMIT *row_count* with ORDER BY, MySQL ends the sorting as soon as it has found the first *row_count* lines rather than sorting the whole table.

- When combining LIMIT *row_count* with DISTINCT, MySQL stops as soon as it finds *row_count* unique rows.

- In some cases, a GROUP BY can be resolved by reading the key in order (or doing a sort on the key) and then calculating summaries until the key value changes. In this case, LIMIT *row_count* will not calculate any unnecessary GROUP BY values.

- As soon as MySQL has sent the required number of rows to the client, it aborts the query unless you are using SQL_CALC_FOUND_ROWS.

- LIMIT 0 always quickly returns an empty set. This is useful to check the query or to get the column types of the result columns.

- When the server uses temporary tables to resolve the query, the LIMIT *row_count* is used to calculate how much space is required.

6.2.11 How to Avoid Table Scans

The output from EXPLAIN will show ALL in the type column when MySQL uses a table scan to resolve a query. This usually happens under the following conditions:

- The table is so small that it's faster to do a table scan than a key lookup. This is a common case for tables with fewer than 10 rows and a short row length.

- There are no usable restrictions in the ON or WHERE clause for indexed columns.

- You are comparing indexed columns with constant values and MySQL has calculated (based on the index tree) that the constants cover too large a part of the table and that a table scan would be faster. See Section 6.2.4, "How MySQL Optimizes WHERE Clauses."

- You are using a key with low cardinality (many rows match the key value) through another column. In this case, MySQL assumes that by using the key it will probably do a lot of key lookups and that a table scan would be faster.

For small tables, a table scan often is appropriate. For large tables, try the following techniques to avoid having the optimizer incorrectly choose a table scan:

- Use ANALYZE TABLE *tbl_name* to update the key distributions for the scanned table.

- Use FORCE INDEX for the scanned table to tell MySQL that table scans are very expensive compared to using the given index.

  ```
  SELECT * FROM t1, t2 FORCE INDEX (index_for_column)
  WHERE t1.col_name=t2.col_name;
  ```

- Start mysqld with the --max-seeks-for-key=1000 option or use SET max_seeks_for_key=1000 to tell the optimizer to assume that no key scan will cause more than 1,000 key seeks. See Section 4.2.3, "Server System Variables."

6.2.12 Speed of INSERT Queries

The time to insert a record is determined by the following factors, where the numbers indicate approximate proportions:

- Connecting: (3)
- Sending query to server: (2)
- Parsing query: (2)
- Inserting record: (1 x size of record)
- Inserting indexes: (1 x number of indexes)
- Closing: (1)

This does not take into consideration the initial overhead to open tables, which is done once for each concurrently running query.

The size of the table slows down the insertion of indexes by log N, assuming B-tree indexes.

You can use the following methods to speed up inserts:

- If you are inserting many rows from the same client at the same time, use INSERT statements with multiple VALUES lists to insert several rows at a time. This is much faster (many times faster in some cases) than using separate single-row INSERT statements. If you are adding data to a non-empty table, you may tune the bulk_insert_buffer_size variable to make it even faster. See Section 4.2.3, "Server System Variables."

- If you are inserting a lot of rows from different clients, you can get higher speed by using the INSERT DELAYED statement.

- With MyISAM tables you can insert rows at the same time that SELECT statements are running if there are no deleted rows in the tables.

- When loading a table from a text file, use LOAD DATA INFILE. This is usually 20 times faster than using a lot of INSERT statements.

- With some extra work, it is possible to make LOAD DATA INFILE run even faster when the table has many indexes. Use the following procedure:

  1. Optionally create the table with CREATE TABLE.

  2. Execute a FLUSH TABLES statement or a mysqladmin flush-tables command.

  3. Use myisamchk --keys-used=0 -rq /path/to/db/tbl_name. This will remove all use of all indexes for the table.

  4. Insert data into the table with LOAD DATA INFILE. This will not update any indexes and will therefore be very fast.

  5. If you are going to only read the table in the future, use myisampack to make it smaller. See Section 8.1.3.3, "Compressed Table Characteristics."

  6. Re-create the indexes with myisamchk -r -q /path/to/db/tbl_name. This will create the index tree in memory before writing it to disk, which is much faster

because it avoids lots of disk seeks. The resulting index tree is also perfectly balanced.

7. Execute a FLUSH TABLES statement or a mysqladmin flush-tables command.

Note that LOAD DATA INFILE also performs the preceding optimization if you insert into an empty MyISAM table; the main difference is that you can let myisamchk allocate much more temporary memory for the index creation than you might want the server to allocate for index re-creation when it executes the LOAD DATA INFILE statement.

As of MySQL 4.0, you can also use ALTER TABLE *tbl_name* DISABLE KEYS instead of myisamchk --keys-used=0 -rq */path/to/db/tbl_name* and ALTER TABLE *tbl_name* ENABLE KEYS instead of myisamchk -r -q */path/to/db/tbl_name*. This way you can also skip the FLUSH TABLES steps.

- You can speed up INSERT operations that are done with multiple statements by locking your tables:

```
LOCK TABLES a WRITE;
INSERT INTO a VALUES (1,23),(2,34),(4,33);
INSERT INTO a VALUES (8,26),(6,29);
UNLOCK TABLES;
```

A performance benefit occurs because the index buffer is flushed to disk only once after all INSERT statements have completed. Normally there would be as many index buffer flushes as there are different INSERT statements. Explicit locking statements are not needed if you can insert all rows with a single statement.

For transactional tables, you should use BEGIN/COMMIT instead of LOCK TABLES to get a speedup.

Locking also lowers the total time of multiple-connection tests, although the maximum wait time for individual connections might go up because they wait for locks. For example:

```
Connection 1 does 1000 inserts
Connections 2, 3, and 4 do 1 insert
Connection 5 does 1000 inserts
```

If you don't use locking, connections 2, 3, and 4 will finish before 1 and 5. If you use locking, connections 2, 3, and 4 probably will not finish before 1 or 5, but the total time should be about 40% faster.

INSERT, UPDATE, and DELETE operations are very fast in MySQL, but you will obtain better overall performance by adding locks around everything that does more than about five inserts or updates in a row. If you do very many inserts in a row, you could do a LOCK TABLES followed by an UNLOCK TABLES once in a while (about each 1,000 rows) to allow other threads access to the table. This would still result in a nice performance gain.

INSERT is still much slower for loading data than LOAD DATA INFILE, even when using the strategies just outlined.

- To get some more speed for MyISAM tables, for both LOAD DATA INFILE and INSERT, enlarge the key cache by increasing the key_buffer_size system variable. See Section 6.5.2, "Tuning Server Parameters."

6.2.13 Speed of UPDATE Queries

Update queries are optimized as a SELECT query with the additional overhead of a write. The speed of the write depends on the amount of data being updated and the number of indexes that are updated. Indexes that are not changed will not be updated.

Also, another way to get fast updates is to delay updates and then do many updates in a row later. Doing many updates in a row is much quicker than doing one at a time if you lock the table.

Note that for a MyISAM table that uses dynamic record format, updating a record to a longer total length may split the record. If you do this often, it is very important to use OPTIMIZE TABLE occasionally.

6.2.14 Speed of DELETE Queries

The time to delete individual records is exactly proportional to the number of indexes. To delete records more quickly, you can increase the size of the key cache. See Section 6.5.2, "Tuning Server Parameters."

If you want to delete all rows in the table, use TRUNCATE TABLE tbl_name rather than DELETE FROM tbl_name.

6.2.15 Other Optimization Tips

This section lists a number of miscellaneous tips for improving query processing speed:

- Use persistent connections to the database to avoid connection overhead. If you can't use persistent connections and you are initiating many new connections to the database, you may want to change the value of the thread_cache_size variable. See Section 6.5.2, "Tuning Server Parameters."

- Always check whether all your queries really use the indexes you have created in the tables. In MySQL, you can do this with the EXPLAIN statement. See Section 6.2.1, "EXPLAIN Syntax (Get Information About a SELECT)."

- Try to avoid complex SELECT queries on MyISAM tables that are updated frequently, to avoid problems with table locking that occur due to contention between readers and writers.

- With MyISAM tables that have no deleted rows, you can insert rows at the end at the same time that another query is reading from the table. If this is important for you, you should consider using the table in ways that avoid deleting rows. Another possibility is to run OPTIMIZE TABLE after you have deleted a lot of rows.

- Use ALTER TABLE ... ORDER BY *expr1*, *expr2*, ... if you mostly retrieve rows in *expr1*, *expr2*, ... order. By using this option after extensive changes to the table, you may be able to get higher performance.

- In some cases, it may make sense to introduce a column that is "hashed" based on information from other columns. If this column is short and reasonably unique, it may be much faster than a big index on many columns. In MySQL, it's very easy to use this extra column:

```
SELECT * FROM tbl_name
    WHERE hash_col=MD5(CONCAT(col1,col2))
    AND col1='constant' AND col2='constant';
```

- For MyISAM tables that change a lot, you should try to avoid all variable-length columns (VARCHAR, BLOB, and TEXT). The table will use dynamic record format if it includes even a single variable-length column. See Chapter 8, "MySQL Storage Engines and Table Types."

- It's normally not useful to split a table into different tables just because the rows get "big." To access a row, the biggest performance hit is the disk seek to find the first byte of the row. After finding the data, most modern disks can read the whole row fast enough for most applications. The only cases where it really matters to split up a table is if it's a MyISAM table with dynamic record format (see above) that you can change to a fixed record size, or if you very often need to scan the table but do not need most of the columns. See Chapter 8, "MySQL Storage Engines and Table Types."

- If you very often need to calculate results such as counts based on information from a lot of rows, it's probably much better to introduce a new table and update the counter in real time. An update of the following form is very fast:

```
UPDATE tbl_name SET count_col=count_col+1 WHERE key_col=constant;
```

This is really important when you use MySQL storage engines such as MyISAM and ISAM that have only table-level locking (multiple readers / single writers). This will also give better performance with most databases, because the row locking manager in this case will have less to do.

- If you need to collect statistics from large log tables, use summary tables instead of scanning the entire log table. Maintaining the summaries should be much faster than trying to calculate statistics "live." It's much faster to regenerate new summary tables from the logs when things change (depending on business decisions) than to have to change the running application!

- If possible, you should classify reports as "live" or "statistical," where data needed for statistical reports is created only from summary tables that are generated periodically from the live data.

- Take advantage of the fact that columns have default values. Insert values explicitly only when the value to be inserted differs from the default. This reduces the parsing that MySQL needs to do and improves the insert speed.

- In some cases, it's convenient to pack and store data into a BLOB column. In this case, you must add some extra code in your application to pack and unpack information in the BLOB values, but this may save a lot of accesses at some stage. This is practical when you have data that doesn't conform to a rows-and-columns table structure.

- Normally, you should try to keep all data non-redundant (what is called "third normal form" in database theory). However, do not be afraid to duplicate information or create summary tables if necessary to gain more speed.

- Stored procedures or UDFs (user-defined functions) may be a good way to get more performance for some tasks. However, if you use a database system that does not support these capabilities, you should always have another way to perform the same tasks, even if the alternative method is slower.

- You can always gain something by caching queries or answers in your application and then performing many inserts or updates together. If your database supports table locks (like MySQL and Oracle), this should help to ensure that the index cache is only flushed once after all updates.

- Use INSERT DELAYED when you do not need to know when your data is written. This speeds things up because many records can be written with a single disk write.

- Use INSERT LOW_PRIORITY when you want to give SELECT statements higher priority than your inserts.

- Use SELECT HIGH_PRIORITY to get retrievals that jump the queue. That is, the SELECT is done even if there is another client waiting to do a write.

- Use multiple-row INSERT statements to store many rows with one SQL statement (many SQL servers support this).

- Use LOAD DATA INFILE to load large amounts of data. This is faster than using INSERT statements.

- Use AUTO_INCREMENT columns to generate unique values.

- Use OPTIMIZE TABLE once in a while to avoid fragmentation with MyISAM tables when using a dynamic table format. See Section 8.1.3, "MyISAM Table Storage Formats."

- Use HEAP tables when possible to get more speed. See Chapter 8, "MySQL Storage Engines and Table Types."

- When using a normal Web server setup, images should be stored as files. That is, store only a file reference in the database. The main reason for this is that a normal Web server is much better at caching files than database contents, so it's much easier to get a fast system if you are using files.

- Use in-memory tables for non-critical data that is accessed often, such as information about the last displayed banner for users who don't have cookies enabled in their Web browser.

- Columns with identical information in different tables should be declared to have identical data types. Before MySQL 3.23, you get slow joins otherwise.

- Try to keep column names simple. For example, in a table named `customer`, use a column name of `name` instead of `customer_name`. To make your names portable to other SQL servers, you should keep them shorter than 18 characters.

- If you need really high speed, you should take a look at the low-level interfaces for data storage that the different SQL servers support! For example, by accessing the MySQL `MyISAM` storage engine directly, you could get a speed increase of two to five times compared to using the SQL interface. To be able to do this, the data must be on the same server as the application, and usually it should only be accessed by one process (because external file locking is really slow). One could eliminate these problems by introducing low-level `MyISAM` commands in the MySQL server (this could be one easy way to get more performance if needed). By carefully designing the database interface, it should be quite easy to support this type of optimization.

- If you are using numerical data, it's faster in many cases to access information from a database (using a live connection) than to access a text file. Information in the database is likely to be stored in a more compact format than in the text file, so accessing it will involve fewer disk accesses. You will also save code in your application because you don't have to parse your text files to find line and column boundaries.

- Replication can provide a performance benefit for some operations. You can distribute client retrievals among replication servers to split up the load. To avoid slowing down the master while making backups, you can make backups using a slave server. See Chapter 5, "Replication in MySQL."

- Declaring a `MyISAM` table with the `DELAY_KEY_WRITE=1` table option makes index updates faster because they are not flushed to disk until the table is closed. The downside is that if something kills the server while such tables are open, you should ensure that they are okay by running the server with the `--myisam-recover` option, or by running `myisamchk` before restarting the server. (However, even in this case, you should not lose anything by using `DELAY_KEY_WRITE`, because the key information can always be generated from the data rows.)

6.3 Locking Issues

6.3.1 Locking Methods

Currently, MySQL supports table-level locking for `ISAM`, `MyISAM`, and `MEMORY` (`HEAP`) tables, page-level locking for `BDB` tables, and row-level locking for `InnoDB` tables.

In many cases, you can make an educated guess about which locking type is best for an application, but generally it's very hard to say that a given lock type is better than another. Everything depends on the application and different parts of an application may require different lock types.

To decide whether you want to use a storage engine with row-level locking, you will want to look at what your application does and what mix of select and update statements it uses. For example, most Web applications do lots of selects, very few deletes, updates based mainly on key values, and inserts into some specific tables. The base MySQL MyISAM setup is very well tuned for this.

Table locking in MySQL is deadlock-free for storage engines that use table-level locking. Deadlock avoidance is managed by always requesting all needed locks at once at the beginning of a query and always locking the tables in the same order.

The table-locking method MySQL uses for WRITE locks works as follows:

- If there are no locks on the table, put a write lock on it.
- Otherwise, put the lock request in the write lock queue.

The table-locking method MySQL uses for READ locks works as follows:

- If there are no write locks on the table, put a read lock on it.
- Otherwise, put the lock request in the read lock queue.

When a lock is released, the lock is made available to the threads in the write lock queue, then to the threads in the read lock queue.

This means that if you have many updates for a table, SELECT statements will wait until there are no more updates.

Starting in MySQL 3.23.33, you can analyze the table lock contention on your system by checking the Table_locks_waited and Table_locks_immediate status variables:

```
mysql> SHOW STATUS LIKE 'Table%';
+-----------------------+---------+
| Variable_name         | Value   |
+-----------------------+---------+
| Table_locks_immediate | 1151552 |
| Table_locks_waited    | 15324   |
+-----------------------+---------+
```

As of MySQL 3.23.7 (3.23.25 for Windows), you can freely mix concurrent INSERT and SELECT statements for a MyISAM table without locks if the INSERT statements are non-conflicting. That is, you can insert rows into a MyISAM table at the same time other clients are reading from it. No conflict occurs if the data file contains no free blocks in the middle, because in that case, records always are inserted at the end of the data file. (Holes can result from rows having been deleted from or updated in the middle of the table.) If there are holes, concurrent inserts are re-enabled automatically when all holes have been filled with new data.

If you want to do many INSERT and SELECT operations on a table when concurrent inserts are not possible, you can insert rows in a temporary table and update the real table with the records from the temporary table once in a while. This can be done with the following code:

```
mysql> LOCK TABLES real_table WRITE, insert_table WRITE;
mysql> INSERT INTO real_table SELECT * FROM insert_table;
mysql> TRUNCATE TABLE insert_table;
mysql> UNLOCK TABLES;
```

InnoDB uses row locks and BDB uses page locks. For the InnoDB and BDB storage engines, deadlock is possible. This is because InnoDB automatically acquires row locks and BDB acquires page locks during the processing of SQL statements, not at the start of the transaction.

Advantages of row-level locking:

- Fewer lock conflicts when accessing different rows in many threads.
- Fewer changes for rollbacks.
- Makes it possible to lock a single row a long time.

Disadvantages of row-level locking:

- Takes more memory than page-level or table-level locks.
- Is slower than page-level or table-level locks when used on a large part of the table because you must acquire many more locks.
- Is definitely much worse than other locks if you often do GROUP BY operations on a large part of the data or if you often must scan the entire table.
- With higher-level locks, you can also more easily support locks of different types to tune the application, because the lock overhead is less than for row-level locks.

Table locks are superior to page-level or row-level locks in the following cases:

- Most statements for the table are reads.
- Read and updates on strict keys, where you update or delete a row that can be fetched with a single key read:

  ```
  UPDATE tbl_name SET column=value WHERE unique_key_col=key_value;
  DELETE FROM tbl_name WHERE unique_key_col=key_value;
  ```

- SELECT combined with concurrent INSERT statements, and very few UPDATE and DELETE statements.
- Many scans or GROUP BY operations on the entire table without any writers.

Options other than row-level or page-level locking:

Versioning (such as we use in MySQL for concurrent inserts) where you can have one writer at the same time as many readers. This means that the database/table supports different views for the data depending on when you started to access it. Other names for this are time travel, copy on write, or copy on demand.

Copy on demand is in many cases much better than page-level or row-level locking. However, the worst case does use much more memory than when using normal locks.

Instead of using row-level locks, you can use application-level locks, such as GET_LOCK() and RELEASE_LOCK() in MySQL. These are advisory locks, so they work only in well-behaved applications.

6.3.2 Table Locking Issues

To achieve a very high lock speed, MySQL uses table locking (instead of page, row, or column locking) for all storage engines except InnoDB and BDB.

For InnoDB and BDB tables, MySQL only uses table locking if you explicitly lock the table with LOCK TABLES. For these table types, we recommend you to not use LOCK TABLES at all, because InnoDB uses automatic row-level locking and BDB uses page-level locking to ensure transaction isolation.

For large tables, table locking is much better than row locking for most applications, but there are some pitfalls.

Table locking enables many threads to read from a table at the same time, but if a thread wants to write to a table, it must first get exclusive access. During the update, all other threads that want to access this particular table must wait until the update is done.

Table updates normally are considered to be more important than table retrievals, so they are given higher priority. This should ensure that updates to a table are not "starved" even if there is heavy SELECT activity for the table.

Table locking causes problems in cases such as when a thread is waiting because the disk is full and free space needs to become available before the thread can proceed. In this case, all threads that want to access the problem table will also be put in a waiting state until more disk space is made available.

Table locking is also disadvantageous under the following scenario:

- A client issues a SELECT that takes a long time to run.
- Another client then issues an UPDATE on the same table. This client will wait until the SELECT is finished.
- Another client issues another SELECT statement on the same table. Because UPDATE has higher priority than SELECT, this SELECT will wait for the UPDATE to finish. It will also wait for the first SELECT to finish!

The following list describes some ways to avoid or reduce contention caused by table locking:

- Try to get the SELECT statements to run faster. You might have to create some summary tables to do this.

- Start `mysqld` with `--low-priority-updates`. This gives all statements that update (modify) a table lower priority than `SELECT` statements. In this case, the second `SELECT` statement in the preceding scenario would execute before the `INSERT` statement, and would not need to wait for the first `SELECT` to finish.

- You can specify that all updates issued in a specific connection should be done with low priority by using the `SET LOW_PRIORITY_UPDATES=1` statement.

- You can give a specific `INSERT`, `UPDATE`, or `DELETE` statement lower priority with the `LOW_PRIORITY` attribute.

- You can give a specific `SELECT` statement higher priority with the `HIGH_PRIORITY` attribute.

- Starting from MySQL 3.23.7, you can start `mysqld` with a low value for the `max_write_lock_count` system variable to force MySQL to temporarily elevate the priority of all `SELECT` statements that are waiting for a table after a specific number of inserts to the table occur. This allows `READ` locks after a certain number of `WRITE` locks.

- If you have problems with `INSERT` combined with `SELECT`, switch to using `MyISAM` tables, which support concurrent `SELECT` and `INSERT` statements.

- If you mix inserts and deletes on the same table, `INSERT DELAYED` may be of great help.

- If you have problems with mixed `SELECT` and `DELETE` statements, the `LIMIT` option to `DELETE` may help.

- Using `SQL_BUFFER_RESULT` with `SELECT` statements can help to make the duration of table locks shorter.

- You could change the locking code in `mysys/thr_lock.c` to use a single queue. In this case, write locks and read locks would have the same priority, which might help some applications.

Here are some tips about table locking in MySQL:

- Concurrent users are not a problem if you don't mix updates with selects that need to examine many rows in the same table.

- You can use `LOCK TABLES` to speed up things (many updates within a single lock is much faster than updates without locks). Splitting table contents into separate tables may also help.

- If you encounter speed problems with table locks in MySQL, you may be able to improve performance by converting some of your tables to `InnoDB` or `BDB` tables. See Chapter 9, "The `InnoDB` Storage Engine." See Section 8.4, "The `BDB` (`BerkeleyDB`) Storage Engine."

6.4 Optimizing Database Structure

6.4.1 Design Choices

MySQL keeps row data and index data in separate files. Many (almost all) other databases mix row and index data in the same table. We believe that the MySQL choice is better for a very wide range of modern systems.

Another way to store the row data is to keep the information for each column in a separate area (examples are SDBM and Focus). This will cause a performance hit for every query that accesses more than one column. Because this degenerates so quickly when more than one column is accessed, we believe that this model is not good for general-purpose databases.

The more common case is that the index and data are stored together (as in Oracle/Sybase, et al). In this case, you will find the row information at the leaf page of the index. The good thing with this layout is that it, in many cases, depending on how well the index is cached, saves a disk read. The bad things with this layout are:

- Table scanning is much slower because you have to read through the indexes to get at the data.
- You can't use only the index table to retrieve data for a query.
- You lose a lot of space, because you must duplicate indexes from the nodes (because you can't store the row in the nodes).
- Deletes will degenerate the table over time (because indexes in nodes are usually not updated on delete).
- It's harder to cache only the index data.

6.4.2 Make Your Data as Small as Possible

One of the most basic optimizations is to design your tables to take as little space on the disk as possible. This can give huge improvements because disk reads are faster, and smaller tables normally require less main memory while their contents are being actively processed during query execution. Indexing also is a lesser resource burden if done on smaller columns.

MySQL supports a lot of different table types and row formats. For each table, you can decide which storage/index method to use. Choosing the right table format for your application may give you a big performance gain. See Chapter 8, "MySQL Storage Engines and Table Types."

You can get better performance on a table and minimize storage space using the techniques listed here:

- Use the most efficient (smallest) data types possible. MySQL has many specialized types that save disk space and memory.

- Use the smaller integer types if possible to get smaller tables. For example, MEDIUMINT is often better than INT.

- Declare columns to be NOT NULL if possible. It makes everything faster and you save one bit per column. If you really need NULL in your application, you should definitely use it. Just avoid having it on all columns by default.

- For MyISAM tables, if you don't have any variable-length columns (VARCHAR, TEXT, or BLOB columns), a fixed-size record format is used. This is faster but unfortunately may waste some space. See Section 8.1.3, "MyISAM Table Storage Formats."

- The primary index of a table should be as short as possible. This makes identification of each row easy and efficient.

- Create only the indexes that you really need. Indexes are good for retrieval but bad when you need to store things fast. If you mostly access a table by searching on a combination of columns, make an index on them. The first index part should be the most used column. If you are *always* using many columns, you should use the column with more duplicates first to get better compression of the index.

- If it's very likely that a column has a unique prefix on the first number of characters, it's better to index only this prefix. MySQL supports an index on the leftmost part of a character column. Shorter indexes are faster not only because they take less disk space, but also because they will give you more hits in the index cache and thus fewer disk seeks. See Section 6.5.2, "Tuning Server Parameters."

- In some circumstances, it can be beneficial to split into two a table that is scanned very often. This is especially true if it is a dynamic format table and it is possible to use a smaller static format table that can be used to find the relevant rows when scanning the table.

6.4.3 Column Indexes

All MySQL column types can be indexed. Use of indexes on the relevant columns is the best way to improve the performance of SELECT operations.

The maximum number of indexes per table and the maximum index length is defined per storage engine. See Chapter 8, "MySQL Storage Engines and Table Types." All storage engines support at least 16 indexes per table and a total index length of at least 256 bytes. Most storage engines have higher limits.

With col_name(length) syntax in an index specification, you can create an index that uses only the first length bytes of a CHAR or VARCHAR column. Indexing only a prefix of column values like this can make the index file much smaller.

The MyISAM and (as of MySQL 4.0.14) InnoDB storage engines also support indexing on BLOB and TEXT columns. When indexing a BLOB or TEXT column, you *must* specify a prefix length for the index. For example:

```
CREATE TABLE test (blob_col BLOB, INDEX(blob_col(10)));
```

Prefixes can be up to 255 bytes long (or 1000 bytes for MyISAM and InnoDB tables as of MySQL 4.1.2). Note that prefix limits are measured in bytes, whereas the prefix length in CREATE TABLE statements is interpreted as number of characters. Take this into account when specifying a prefix length for a column that uses a multi-byte character set.

As of MySQL 3.23.23, you can also create FULLTEXT indexes. They are used for full-text searches. Only the MyISAM table type supports FULLTEXT indexes and only for CHAR, VARCHAR, and TEXT columns. Indexing always happens over the entire column and partial (prefix) indexing is not supported.

As of MySQL 4.1.0, you can create indexes on spatial column types. Currently, spatial types are supported only by the MyISAM storage engine. Spatial indexes use R-trees.

The MEMORY (HEAP) storage engine supports hash indexes. As of MySQL 4.1.0, the engine also supports B-tree indexes.

6.4.4 Multiple-Column Indexes

MySQL can create indexes on multiple columns. An index may consist of up to 15 columns. For certain column types, you can index a prefix of the column (see Section 6.4.3, "Column Indexes").

A multiple-column index can be considered a sorted array containing values that are created by concatenating the values of the indexed columns.

MySQL uses multiple-column indexes in such a way that queries are fast when you specify a known quantity for the first column of the index in a WHERE clause, even if you don't specify values for the other columns.

Suppose that a table has the following specification:

```
CREATE TABLE test (
    id INT NOT NULL,
    last_name CHAR(30) NOT NULL,
    first_name CHAR(30) NOT NULL,
    PRIMARY KEY (id),
    INDEX name (last_name,first_name));
```

The name index is an index over last_name and first_name. The index can be used for queries that specify values in a known range for last_name, or for both last_name and first_name. Therefore, the name index will be used in the following queries:

```
SELECT * FROM test WHERE last_name='Widenius';

SELECT * FROM test
    WHERE last_name='Widenius' AND first_name='Michael';
```

```
SELECT * FROM test
    WHERE last_name='Widenius'
    AND (first_name='Michael' OR first_name='Monty');

SELECT * FROM test
    WHERE last_name='Widenius'
    AND first_name >='M' AND first_name < 'N';
```

However, the name index will *not* be used in the following queries:

```
SELECT * FROM test WHERE first_name='Michael';

SELECT * FROM test
    WHERE last_name='Widenius' OR first_name='Michael';
```

The manner in which MySQL uses indexes to improve query performance is discussed further in the next section.

6.4.5 How MySQL Uses Indexes

Indexes are used to find rows with specific column values fast. Without an index, MySQL has to start with the first record and then read through the whole table to find the relevant rows. The bigger the table, the more this costs. If the table has an index for the columns in question, MySQL can quickly determine the position to seek to in the middle of the data file without having to look at all the data. If a table has 1,000 rows, this is at least 100 times faster than reading sequentially. Note that if you need to access almost all 1,000 rows, it is faster to read sequentially, because that minimizes disk seeks.

Most MySQL indexes (PRIMARY KEY, UNIQUE, INDEX, and FULLTEXT) are stored in B-trees. Exceptions are that indexes on spatial column types use R-trees, and MEMORY (HEAP) tables support hash indexes.

Strings are automatically prefix- and end-space compressed.

In general, indexes are used as described in the following discussion. Characteristics specific to hash indexes (as used in MEMORY tables) are described at the end of this section.

- To quickly find the rows that match a WHERE clause.
- To eliminate rows from consideration. If there is a choice between multiple indexes, MySQL normally uses the index that finds the smallest number of rows.
- To retrieve rows from other tables when performing joins.
- To find the MIN() or MAX() value for a specific indexed column *key_col*. This is optimized by a preprocessor that checks whether you are using WHERE *key_part_#* = *constant* on all key parts that occur before *key_col* in the index. In this case, MySQL will do a single key lookup for each MIN() or MAX() expression and replace it with a

constant. If all expressions are replaced with constants, the query will return at once. For example:

```
SELECT MIN(key_part2),MAX(key_part2)
FROM tbl_name WHERE key_part1=10;
```

- To sort or group a table if the sorting or grouping is done on a leftmost prefix of a usable key (for example, ORDER BY key_part1, key_part2). If all key parts are followed by DESC, the key is read in reverse order. See Section 6.2.9, "How MySQL Optimizes ORDER BY."

- In some cases, a query can be optimized to retrieve values without consulting the data rows. If a query uses only columns from a table that are numeric and that form a leftmost prefix for some key, the selected values may be retrieved from the index tree for greater speed:

```
SELECT key_part3 FROM tbl_name WHERE key_part1=1
```

Suppose that you issue the following SELECT statement:

```
mysql> SELECT * FROM tbl_name WHERE col1=val1 AND col2=val2;
```

If a multiple-column index exists on col1 and col2, the appropriate rows can be fetched directly. If separate single-column indexes exist on col1 and col2, the optimizer tries to find the most restrictive index by deciding which index will find fewer rows and using that index to fetch the rows.

If the table has a multiple-column index, any leftmost prefix of the index can be used by the optimizer to find rows. For example, if you have a three-column index on (col1, col2, col3), you have indexed search capabilities on (col1), (col1, col2), and (col1, col2, col3).

MySQL can't use a partial index if the columns don't form a leftmost prefix of the index. Suppose that you have the SELECT statements shown here:

```
SELECT * FROM tbl_name WHERE col1=val1;
SELECT * FROM tbl_name WHERE col2=val2;
SELECT * FROM tbl_name WHERE col2=val2 AND col3=val3;
```

If an index exists on (col1, col2, col3), only the first of the preceding queries uses the index. The second and third queries do involve indexed columns, but (col2) and (col2, col3) are not leftmost prefixes of (col1, col2, col3).

An index is used for columns that you compare with the =, >, >=, <, <=, or BETWEEN operators.

MySQL also uses indexes for LIKE comparisons if the argument to LIKE is a constant string that doesn't start with a wildcard character. For example, the following SELECT statements use indexes:

```
SELECT * FROM tbl_name WHERE key_col LIKE 'Patrick%';
SELECT * FROM tbl_name WHERE key_col LIKE 'Pat%_ck%';
```

In the first statement, only rows with `'Patrick'` <= `key_col` < `'Patricl'` are considered. In the second statement, only rows with `'Pat'` <= `key_col` < `'Pau'` are considered.

The following SELECT statements will not use indexes:

```
SELECT * FROM tbl_name WHERE key_col LIKE '%Patrick%';
SELECT * FROM tbl_name WHERE key_col LIKE other_col;
```

In the first statement, the LIKE value begins with a wildcard character. In the second statement, the LIKE value is not a constant.

MySQL 4.0 and up performs an additional LIKE optimization. If you use ... LIKE `'%string%'` and *string* is longer than three characters, MySQL will use the Turbo Boyer-Moore algorithm to initialize the pattern for the string and then use this pattern to perform the search quicker.

Searching using `col_name` IS NULL will use indexes if `col_name` is indexed.

Any index that doesn't span all AND levels in the WHERE clause is not used to optimize the query. In other words, to be able to use an index, a prefix of the index must be used in every AND group.

The following WHERE clauses use indexes:

```
... WHERE index_part1=1 AND index_part2=2 AND other_column=3
    /* index = 1 OR index = 2 */
... WHERE index=1 OR A=10 AND index=2
    /* optimized like "index_part1='hello'" */
... WHERE index_part1='hello' AND index_part3=5
    /* Can use index on index1 but not on index2 or index3 */
... WHERE index1=1 AND index2=2 OR index1=3 AND index3=3;
```

These WHERE clauses do *not* use indexes:

```
    /* index_part1 is not used */
... WHERE index_part2=1 AND index_part3=2
    /* Index is not used in both AND parts */
... WHERE index=1 OR A=10
    /* No index spans all rows  */
... WHERE index_part1=1 OR index_part2=10
```

Sometimes MySQL will not use an index, even if one is available. One way this occurs is when the optimizer estimates that using the index would require MySQL to access a large percentage of the rows in the table. (In this case, a table scan is probably much faster, because it will require many fewer seeks.) However, if such a query uses LIMIT to only retrieve part of the rows, MySQL will use an index anyway, because it can much more quickly find the few rows to return in the result.

Hash indexes have somewhat different characteristics than those just discussed:

- They are used only for = or <=> comparisons (but are *very* fast).
- The optimizer cannot use a hash index to speed up ORDER BY operations. (This type of index cannot be used to search for the next entry in order.)
- MySQL cannot determine approximately how many rows there are between two values (this is used by the range optimizer to decide which index to use). This may affect some queries if you change a MyISAM table to a hash-indexed MEMORY table.
- Only whole keys can be used to search for a row. (With a B-tree index, any prefix of the key can be used to find rows.)

6.4.6 The MyISAM Key Cache

To minimize disk I/O, the MyISAM storage engine employs a strategy that is used by many database management systems. It exploits a cache mechanism to keep the most frequently accessed table blocks in memory:

- For index blocks, a special structure called the key cache (key buffer) is maintained. The structure contains a number of block buffers where the most-used index blocks are placed.
- For data blocks, MySQL uses no special cache. Instead it relies on the native operating system filesystem cache.

This section first describes the basic operation of the MyISAM key cache. Then it discusses changes made in MySQL 4.1 that improve key cache performance and that enable you to better control cache operation:

- Access to the key cache no longer is serialized among threads. Multiple threads can access the cache concurrently.
- You can set up multiple key caches and assign table indexes to specific caches.

The key cache mechanism also is used for ISAM tables. However, the significance of this fact is on the wane. ISAM table use has been decreasing since MySQL 3.23 when MyISAM was introduced. MySQL 4.1 carries this trend further; the ISAM storage engine is disabled by default.

You can control the size of the key cache by means of the key_buffer_size system variable. If this variable is set equal to zero, no key cache is used. The key cache also is not used if the key_buffer_size value is too small to allocate the minimal number of block buffers (8).

When the key cache is not operational, index files are accessed using only the native filesystem buffering provided by the operating system. (In other words, table index blocks are accessed using the same strategy as that employed for table data blocks.)

An index block is a contiguous unit of access to the MyISAM index files. Usually the size of an index block is equal to the size of nodes of the index B-tree. (Indexes are represented on disk using a B-tree data structure. Nodes at the bottom of the tree are leaf nodes. Nodes above the leaf nodes are non-leaf nodes.)

All block buffers in a key cache structure are the same size. This size can be equal to, greater than, or less than the size of a table index block. Usually one of these two values is a multiple of the other.

When data from any table index block must be accessed, the server first checks whether it is available in some block buffer of the key cache. If it is, the server accesses data in the key cache rather than on disk. That is, it reads from the cache or writes into it rather than reading from or writing to disk. Otherwise, the server chooses a cache block buffer containing a different table index block (or blocks) and replaces the data there by a copy of required table index block. As soon as the new index block is in the cache, the index data can be accessed.

If it happens that a block selected for replacement has been modified, the block is considered "dirty." In this case, before being replaced, its contents are flushed to the table index from which it came.

Usually the server follows an LRU (Least Recently Used) strategy: When choosing a block for replacement, it selects the least recently used index block. To be able to make such a choice easy, the key cache module maintains a special queue (LRU chain) of all used blocks. When a block is accessed, it is placed at the end of the queue. When blocks need to be replaced, blocks at the beginning of the queue are the least recently used and become the first candidates for eviction.

6.4.6.1 Shared Key Cache Access

Prior to MySQL 4.1, access to the key cache is serialized: No two threads can access key cache buffers simultaneously. The server processes a request for an index block only after it has finished processing the previous request. As a result, a request for an index block not present in any key cache buffer blocks access by other threads while a buffer is being updated to contain the requested index block.

Starting from version 4.1.0, the server supports shared access to the key cache:

- A buffer that is not being updated can be accessed by multiple threads.
- A buffer that is being updated causes threads that need to use it to wait until the update is complete.
- Multiple threads can initiate requests that result in cache block replacements, as long as they do not interfere with each other (that is, as long as they need different index blocks, and thus cause different cache blocks to be replaced).

Shared access to the key cache allows the server to improve throughput significantly.

6.4.6.2 Multiple Key Caches

Shared access to the key cache improves performance but does not eliminate contention among threads entirely. They still compete for control structures that manage access to the key cache buffers. To reduce key cache access contention further, MySQL 4.1.1 offers the feature of multiple key caches. This allows you to assign different table indexes to different key caches.

When there can be multiple key caches, the server must know which cache to use when processing queries for a given MyISAM table. By default, all MyISAM table indexes are cached in the default key cache. To assign table indexes to a specific key cache, use the CACHE INDEX statement.

For example, the following statement assigns indexes from the tables t1, t2, and t3 to the key cache named hot_cache:

```
mysql> CACHE INDEX t1, t2, t3 IN hot_cache;
+---------+--------------------+----------+----------+
| Table   | Op                 | Msg_type | Msg_text |
+---------+--------------------+----------+----------+
| test.t1 | assign_to_keycache | status   | OK       |
| test.t2 | assign_to_keycache | status   | OK       |
| test.t3 | assign_to_keycache | status   | OK       |
+---------+--------------------+----------+----------+
```

Note: If the server has been built with the ISAM storage engine enabled, ISAM tables use the key cache mechanism. However, ISAM indexes use only the default key cache and cannot be reassigned to a different cache.

The key cache referred to in a CACHE INDEX statement can be created by setting its size with a SET GLOBAL parameter setting statement or by using server startup options. For example:

```
mysql> SET GLOBAL keycache1.key_buffer_size=128*1024;
```

To destroy a key cache, set its size to zero:

```
mysql> SET GLOBAL keycache1.key_buffer_size=0;
```

Key cache variables are structured system variables that have a name and components. For keycache1.key_buffer_size, keycache1 is the cache variable name and key_buffer_size is the cache component.

By default, table indexes are assigned to the main (default) key cache created at the server startup. When a key cache is destroyed, all indexes assigned to it are reassigned to the default key cache.

For a busy server, we recommend a strategy that uses three key caches:

- A hot key cache that takes up 20% of the space allocated for all key caches. This is used for tables that are heavily used for searches but that are not updated.

- A cold key cache that takes up 20% of the space allocated for all key caches. This is used for medium-sized intensively modified tables, such as temporary tables.
- A warm key cache that takes up 60% of the key cache space. This is the default key cache, to be used by default for all other tables.

One reason the use of three key caches is beneficial is that access to one key cache structure does not block access to the others. Queries that access tables assigned to one cache do not compete with queries that access tables assigned to another cache. Performance gains occur for other reasons as well:

- The hot cache is used only for retrieval queries, so its contents are never modified. Consequently, whenever an index block needs to be pulled in from disk, the contents of the cache block chosen for replacement need not be flushed first.
- For an index assigned to the hot cache, if there are no queries requiring an index scan, there is a high probability that the index blocks corresponding to non-leaf nodes of the index B-tree will remain in the cache.
- An update operation most frequently executed for temporary tables is performed much faster when the updated node already is in the cache and need not be read in from disk first. If the size of the indexes of the temporary tables are comparable with the size of cold key cache, the probability is very high that the updated node already will be in the cache.

6.4.6.3 Midpoint Insertion Strategy

By default, the key cache management system of MySQL 4.1 uses the LRU strategy for choosing key cache blocks to be evicted, but it also supports a more sophisticated method called the "midpoint insertion strategy."

When using the midpoint insertion strategy, the LRU chain is divided into two parts: a hot sub-chain and a warm sub-chain. The division point between two parts is not fixed, but the key cache management system takes care that the warm part is not "too short," always containing at least key_cache_division_limit percent of the key cache blocks. key_cache_division_limit is a component of structured key cache variables, so its value is a parameter that can be set per cache.

When an index block is read from a table into the key cache, it is placed at the end of the warm sub-chain. After a certain number of hits (accesses of the block), it is promoted to the hot sub-chain. At present, the number of hits required to promote a block (3) is the same for all index blocks. In the future, we will allow the hit count to depend on the B-tree level of the node corresponding to an index block: Fewer hits will be required for promotion of an index block if it contains a non-leaf node from the upper levels of the index B-tree than if it contains a leaf node.

A block promoted into the hot sub-chain is placed at the end of the chain. The block then circulates within this sub-chain. If the block stays at the beginning of the sub-chain for a long enough time, it is demoted to the warm chain. This time is determined by the value of the `key_cache_age_threshold` component of the key cache.

The threshold value prescribes that, for a key cache containing N blocks, the block at the beginning of the hot sub-chain not accessed within the last N*`key_cache_age_threshold`/100 hits is to be moved to the beginning of the warm sub-chain. It then becomes the first candidate for eviction, because blocks for replacement always are taken from the beginning of the warm sub-chain.

The midpoint insertion strategy allows you to keep more-valued blocks always in the cache. If you prefer to use the plain LRU strategy, leave the `key_cache_division_limit` value set to its default of 100.

The midpoint insertion strategy helps to improve performance when execution of a query that requires an index scan effectively pushes out of the cache all the index blocks corresponding to valuable high-level B-tree nodes. To avoid this, you must use a midpoint insertion strategy with the `key_cache_division_limit` set to much less than 100. Then valuable frequently hit nodes will be preserved in the hot sub-chain during an index scan operation as well.

6.4.6.4 Index Preloading

If there are enough blocks in a key cache to hold blocks of an entire index, or at least the blocks corresponding to its non-leaf nodes, then it makes sense to preload the key cache with index blocks before starting to use it. Preloading allows you to put the table index blocks into a key cache buffer in the most efficient way: by reading the index blocks from disk sequentially.

Without preloading, the blocks still will be placed into the key cache as needed by queries. Although the blocks will stay in the cache, because there are enough buffers for all of them, they will be fetched from disk in a random order, not sequentially.

To preload an index into a cache, use the LOAD INDEX INTO CACHE statement. For example, the following statement preloads nodes (index blocks) of indexes of the tables t1 and t2:

```
mysql> LOAD INDEX INTO CACHE t1, t2 IGNORE LEAVES;
+---------+--------------+----------+----------+
| Table   | Op           | Msg_type | Msg_text |
+---------+--------------+----------+----------+
| test.t1 | preload_keys | status   | OK       |
| test.t2 | preload_keys | status   | OK       |
+---------+--------------+----------+----------+
```

The IGNORE LEAVES modifier causes only blocks for the non-leaf nodes of the index to be preloaded. Thus, the statement shown preloads all index blocks from t1, but only blocks for the non-leaf nodes from t2.

If an index has been assigned to a key cache using a CACHE INDEX statement, preloading places index blocks into that cache. Otherwise, the index is loaded into the default key cache.

6.4.6.5 Key Cache Block Size

MySQL 4.1 introduces a new key_cache_block_size variable on a per-key cache basis. This variable specifies the size of the block buffers for a key cache. It is intended to allow tuning of the performance of I/O operations for index files.

The best performance for I/O operations is achieved when the size of read buffers is equal to the size of the native operating system I/O buffers. But setting the size of key nodes equal to the size of the I/O buffer does not always ensure the best overall performance. When reading the big leaf nodes, the server pulls in a lot of unnecessary data, effectively preventing reading other leaf nodes.

Currently, you cannot control the size of the index blocks in a table. This size is set by the server when the .MYI index file is created, depending on the size of the keys in the indexes present in the table definition. In most cases, it is set equal to the I/O buffer size. In the future, this will be changed and then key_cache_block_size variable will be fully employed.

6.4.6.6 Restructuring a Key Cache

A key cache can be restructured at any time by updating its parameter values. For example:

```
mysql> SET GLOBAL cold_cache.key_buffer_size=4*1024*1024;
```

If you assign to either the key_buffer_size or key_cache_block_size key cache component a value that differs from the component's current value, the server destroys the cache's old structure and creates a new one based on the new values. If the cache contains any dirty blocks, the server saves them to disk before destroying and re-creating the cache. Restructuring does not occur if you set other key cache parameters.

When restructuring a key cache, the server first flushes the contents of any dirty buffers to disk. After that, the cache contents become unavailable. However, restructuring does not block queries that need to use indexes assigned to the cache. Instead, the server directly accesses the table indexes using native filesystem caching. Filesystem caching is not as efficient as using a key cache, so although queries will execute, a slowdown can be anticipated. Once the cache has been restructured, it becomes available again for caching indexes assigned to it, and the use of filesystem caching for the indexes ceases.

6.4.7 How MySQL Counts Open Tables

When you execute a mysqladmin status command, you'll see something like this:

```
Uptime: 426 Running threads: 1 Questions: 11082
Reloads: 1 Open tables: 12
```

The Open tables value of 12 can be somewhat puzzling if you have only six tables.

MySQL is multi-threaded, so there may be many clients issuing queries for a given table simultaneously. To minimize the problem with multiple client threads having different states on the same file, the table is opened independently by each concurrent thread. This takes some memory but normally increases performance. With MyISAM tables, one extra file descriptor is required for the data file for each client that has the table open. (By contrast, the index file descriptor is shared between all threads.) The ISAM storage engine shares this behavior.

You can read more about this topic in the next section. See Section 6.4.8, "How MySQL Opens and Closes Tables."

6.4.8 How MySQL Opens and Closes Tables

The table_cache, max_connections, and max_tmp_tables system variables affect the maximum number of files the server keeps open. If you increase one or more of these values, you may run up against a limit imposed by your operating system on the per-process number of open file descriptors. Many operating systems allow you to increase the open-files limit, although the method varies widely from system to system. Consult your operating system documentation to determine whether it is possible to increase the limit and how to do so.

table_cache is related to max_connections. For example, for 200 concurrent running connections, you should have a table cache size of at least 200 * N, where N is the maximum number of tables in a join. You also need to reserve some extra file descriptors for temporary tables and files.

Make sure that your operating system can handle the number of open file descriptors implied by the table_cache setting. If table_cache is set too high, MySQL may run out of file descriptors and refuse connections, fail to perform queries, and be very unreliable. You also have to take into account that the MyISAM storage engine needs two file descriptors for each unique open table. You can increase the number of file descriptors available for MySQL with the --open-files-limit startup option to mysqld_safe. See Section A.2.17, "File Not Found."

The cache of open tables will be kept at a level of table_cache entries. The default value is 64; this can be changed with the --table_cache option to mysqld. Note that MySQL may temporarily open even more tables to be able to execute queries.

An unused table is closed and removed from the table cache under the following circumstances:

- When the cache is full and a thread tries to open a table that is not in the cache.
- When the cache contains more than table_cache entries and a thread is no longer using a table.
- When a table flushing operation occurs. This happens when someone issues a FLUSH TABLES statement or executes a mysqladmin flush-tables or mysqladmin refresh command.

When the table cache fills up, the server uses the following procedure to locate a cache entry to use:

- Tables that are not currently in use are released, in least recently used order.
- If a new table needs to be opened, but the cache is full and no tables can be released, the cache is temporarily extended as necessary.

When the cache is in a temporarily extended state and a table goes from a used to unused state, the table is closed and released from the cache.

A table is opened for each concurrent access. This means the table needs to be opened twice if two threads access the same table or if a thread accesses the table twice in the same query (for example, by joining the table to itself). Each concurrent open requires an entry in the table cache. The first open of any table takes two file descriptors: one for the data file and one for the index file. Each additional use of the table takes only one file descriptor, for the data file. The index file descriptor is shared among all threads.

If you are opening a table with the HANDLER *tbl_name* OPEN statement, a dedicated table object is allocated for the thread. This table object is not shared by other threads and is not closed until the thread calls HANDLER *tbl_name* CLOSE or the thread terminates. When this happens, the table is put back in the table cache (if the cache isn't full).

You can determine whether your table cache is too small by checking the mysqld status variable Opened_tables:

```
mysql> SHOW STATUS LIKE 'Opened_tables';
+---------------+-------+
| Variable_name | Value |
+---------------+-------+
| Opened_tables | 2741  |
+---------------+-------+
```

If the value is quite big, even when you haven't issued a lot of FLUSH TABLES statements, you should increase your table cache size. See Section 4.2.3, "Server System Variables," and Section 4.2.4, "Server Status Variables."

6.4.9 Drawbacks to Creating Many Tables in the Same Database

If you have many MyISAM or ISAM tables in a database directory, open, close, and create operations will be slow. If you execute SELECT statements on many different tables, there will be a little overhead when the table cache is full, because for every table that has to be opened, another must be closed. You can reduce this overhead by making the table cache larger.

6.5 Optimizing the MySQL Server

6.5.1 System Factors and Startup Parameter Tuning

We start with system-level factors, because some of these decisions must be made very early to achieve large performance gains. In other cases, a quick look at this section may suffice. However, it is always nice to have a sense of how much can be gained by changing things at this level.

The default operating system to use is very important! To get the best use of multiple-CPU machines, you should use Solaris (because its threads implementation works really well) or Linux (because the 2.2 kernel has really good SMP support). Note that older Linux kernels have a 2GB filesize limit by default. If you have such a kernel and a desperate need for files larger than 2GB, you should get the Large File Support (LFS) patch for the ext2 filesystem. Other filesystems such as ReiserFS and XFS do not have this 2GB limitation.

Before using MySQL in production, we advise you to test it on your intended platform.

Other tips:

- If you have enough RAM, you could remove all swap devices. Some operating systems will use a swap device in some contexts even if you have free memory.
- Use the `--skip-external-locking` MySQL option to avoid external locking. This option is on by default as of MySQL 4.0. Before that, it is on by default when compiling with MIT-pthreads, because `flock()` isn't fully supported by MIT-pthreads on all platforms. It's also on by default for Linux because Linux file locking is not yet safe.

  Note that the `--skip-external-locking` option will not affect MySQL's functionality as long as you run only one server. Just remember to take down the server (or lock and flush the relevant tables) before you run `myisamchk`. On some systems this option is mandatory, because the external locking does not work in any case.

  The only case when you can't use `--skip-external-locking` is if you run multiple MySQL *servers* (not clients) on the same data, or if you run `myisamchk` to check (not repair) a table without telling the server to flush and lock the tables first.

  You can still use LOCK TABLES/UNLOCK TABLES even if you are using `--skip-external-locking`.

6.5.2 Tuning Server Parameters

You can determine the default buffer sizes used by the `mysqld` server with this command (prior to MySQL 4.1, omit --verbose):

```
shell> mysqld --verbose --help
```

This command produces a list of all mysqld options and configurable system variables. The output includes the default variable values and looks something like this:

```
back_log                 current value: 5
bdb_cache_size           current value: 1048540
binlog_cache_size        current value: 32768
connect_timeout          current value: 5
delayed_insert_limit     current value: 100
delayed_insert_timeout   current value: 300
delayed_queue_size       current value: 1000
flush_time               current value: 0
interactive_timeout      current value: 28800
join_buffer_size         current value: 131072
key_buffer_size          current value: 1048540
long_query_time          current value: 10
lower_case_table_names   current value: 0
max_allowed_packet       current value: 1048576
max_binlog_cache_size    current value: 4294967295
max_connect_errors       current value: 10
max_connections          current value: 100
max_delayed_threads      current value: 20
max_heap_table_size      current value: 16777216
max_join_size            current value: 4294967295
max_sort_length          current value: 1024
max_tmp_tables           current value: 32
max_write_lock_count     current value: 4294967295
myisam_sort_buffer_size  current value: 8388608
net_buffer_length        current value: 16384
net_read_timeout         current value: 30
net_retry_count          current value: 10
net_write_timeout        current value: 60
read_buffer_size         current value: 131072
read_rnd_buffer_size     current value: 262144
slow_launch_time         current value: 2
sort_buffer              current value: 2097116
table_cache              current value: 64
thread_concurrency       current value: 10
thread_stack             current value: 131072
tmp_table_size           current value: 1048576
wait_timeout             current value: 28800
```

If there is a mysqld server currently running, you can see what values it actually is using for the system variables by connecting to it and issuing this statement:

```
mysql> SHOW VARIABLES;
```

You can also see some statistical and status indicators for a running server by issuing this statement:

```
mysql> SHOW STATUS;
```

System variable and status information also can be obtained using `mysqladmin`:

```
shell> mysqladmin variables
shell> mysqladmin extended-status
```

You can find a full description for all system and status variables in Section 4.2.3, "Server System Variables," and Section 4.2.4, "Server Status Variables."

MySQL uses algorithms that are very scalable, so you can usually run with very little memory. However, normally you will get better performance by giving MySQL more memory.

When tuning a MySQL server, the two most important variables to configure are `key_buffer_size` and `table_cache`. You should first feel confident that you have these set appropriately before trying to change any other variables.

The following examples indicate some typical variable values for different runtime configurations. The examples use the `mysqld_safe` script and use `--var_name=value` syntax to set the variable `var_name` to the value `value`. This syntax is available as of MySQL 4.0. For older versions of MySQL, take the following differences into account:

- Use `safe_mysqld` rather than `mysqld_safe`.
- Set variables using `--set-variable=var_name=value` or `-O var_name=value` syntax.
- For variable names that end in `_size`, you may need to specify them without `_size`. For example, the old name for `sort_buffer_size` is `sort_buffer`. The old name for `read_buffer_size` is `record_buffer`. To see which variables your version of the server recognizes, use `mysqld --help`.

If you have at least 256MB of memory and many tables and want maximum performance with a moderate number of clients, you should use something like this:

```
shell> mysqld_safe --key_buffer_size=64M --table_cache=256 \
        --sort_buffer_size=4M --read_buffer_size=1M &
```

If you have only 128MB of memory and only a few tables, but you still do a lot of sorting, you can use something like this:

```
shell> mysqld_safe --key_buffer_size=16M --sort_buffer_size=1M
```

If there are very many simultaneous connections, swapping problems may occur unless `mysqld` has been configured to use very little memory for each connection. `mysqld` performs better if you have enough memory for all connections.

With little memory and lots of connections, use something like this:

```
shell> mysqld_safe --key_buffer_size=512K --sort_buffer_size=100K \
          --read_buffer_size=100K &
```

Or even this:

```
shell> mysqld_safe --key_buffer_size=512K --sort_buffer_size=16K \
          --table_cache=32 --read_buffer_size=8K \
          --net_buffer_length=1K &
```

If you are doing GROUP BY or ORDER BY operations on tables that are much larger than your available memory, you should increase the value of read_rnd_buffer_size to speed up the reading of rows after sorting operations.

When you have installed MySQL, the support-files directory will contain some different my.cnf sample files: my-huge.cnf, my-large.cnf, my-medium.cnf, and my-small.cnf. You can use these as a basis for optimizing your system.

Note that if you specify an option on the command line for mysqld or mysqld_safe, it remains in effect only for that invocation of the server. To use the option every time the server runs, put it in an option file.

To see the effects of a parameter change, do something like this (prior to MySQL 4.1, omit --verbose):

```
shell> mysqld --key_buffer_size=32M --verbose --help
```

The variable values are listed near the end of the output. Make sure that the --verbose and --help options are last. Otherwise, the effect of any options listed after them on the command line will not be reflected in the output.

For information on tuning the InnoDB storage engine, see Section 9.12, "InnoDB Performance Tuning Tips."

6.5.3 How Compiling and Linking Affects the Speed of MySQL

Most of the following tests were performed on Linux with the MySQL benchmarks, but they should give some indication for other operating systems and workloads.

You get the fastest executables when you link with -static.

On Linux, you will get the fastest code when compiling with pgcc and -O3. You need about 200MB memory to compile sql_yacc.cc with these options, because gcc/pgcc needs a lot of memory to make all functions inline. You should also set CXX=gcc when configuring MySQL to avoid inclusion of the libstdc++ library, which is not needed. Note that with some versions of pgcc, the resulting code will run only on true Pentium processors, even if you use the compiler option indicating that you want the resulting code to work on all x586-type processors (such as AMD).

By just using a better compiler and better compiler options, you can get a 10-30% speed increase in your application. This is particularly important if you compile the MySQL server yourself.

We have tested both the Cygnus CodeFusion and Fujitsu compilers, but when we tested them, neither was sufficiently bug-free to allow MySQL to be compiled with optimizations enabled.

The standard MySQL binary distributions are compiled with support for all character sets. When you compile MySQL yourself, you should include support only for the character sets that you are going to use. This is controlled by the `--with-charset` option to `configure`.

Here is a list of some measurements that we have made:

- If you use `pgcc` and compile everything with -O6, the `mysqld` server is 1% faster than with `gcc` 2.95.2.
- If you link dynamically (without `-static`), the result is 13% slower on Linux. Note that you still can use a dynamically linked MySQL library for your client applications. It is the server that is most critical for performance.
- If you strip your `mysqld` binary with `strip mysqld`, the resulting binary can be up to 4% faster.
- For a connection from a client to a server running on the same host, if you connect using TCP/IP rather than a Unix socket file, performance is 7.5% slower. (On Unix, if you connect to the hostname `localhost`, MySQL uses a socket file by default.)
- For TCP/IP connections from a client to a server, connecting to a remote server on another host will be 8-11% slower than connecting to the local server on the same host, even for connections over 100Mb/s Ethernet.
- When running our benchmark tests using secure connections (all data encrypted with internal SSL support) performance was 55% slower than for unencrypted connections.
- If you compile with `--with-debug=full`, most queries will be 20% slower. Some queries may take substantially longer; for example, the MySQL benchmarks ran 35% slower. If you use `--with-debug` (without `=full`), the slowdown will be only 15%. For a version of `mysqld` that has been compiled with `--with-debug=full`, you can disable memory checking at runtime by starting it with the `--skip-safemalloc` option. The end result in this case should be close to that obtained when configuring with `--with-debug`.
- On a Sun UltraSPARC-IIe, a server compiled with Forte 5.0 is 4% faster than one compiled with `gcc` 3.2.
- On a Sun UltraSPARC-IIe, a server compiled with Forte 5.0 is 4% faster in 32-bit mode than in 64-bit mode.
- Compiling with `gcc` 2.95.2 for UltraSPARC with the `-mcpu=v8 -Wa,-xarch=v8plusa` options gives 4% more performance.

- On Solaris 2.5.1, MIT-pthreads is 8-12% slower than Solaris native threads on a single processor. With more load or CPUs, the difference should be larger.

- Compiling on Linux-x86 using gcc without frame pointers (`-fomit-frame-pointer` or `-fomit-frame-pointer -ffixed-ebp`) makes `mysqld` 1-4% faster.

Binary MySQL distributions for Linux that are provided by MySQL AB used to be compiled with pgcc. We had to go back to regular gcc due to a bug in pgcc that would generate code that does not run on AMD. We will continue using gcc until that bug is resolved. In the meantime, if you have a non-AMD machine, you can get a faster binary by compiling with pgcc. The standard MySQL Linux binary is linked statically to make it faster and more portable.

6.5.4 How MySQL Uses Memory

The following list indicates some of the ways that the `mysqld` server uses memory. Where applicable, the name of the system variable relevant to the memory use is given:

- The key buffer (variable `key_buffer_size`) is shared by all threads; other buffers used by the server are allocated as needed. See Section 6.5.2, "Tuning Server Parameters."

- Each connection uses some thread-specific space:
  - A stack (default 64KB, variable `thread_stack`)
  - A connection buffer (variable `net_buffer_length`)
  - A result buffer (variable `net_buffer_length`)

  The connection buffer and result buffer are dynamically enlarged up to `max_allowed_packet` when needed. While a query is running, a copy of the current query string is also allocated.

- All threads share the same base memory.

- Only compressed ISAM and MyISAM tables are memory mapped. This is because the 32-bit memory space of 4GB is not large enough for most big tables. When systems with a 64-bit address space become more common, we may add general support for memory mapping.

- Each request that performs a sequential scan of a table allocates a read buffer (variable `read_buffer_size`).

- When reading rows in "random" order (for example, after a sort), a random-read buffer may be allocated to avoid disk seeks. (variable `read_rnd_buffer_size`).

- All joins are done in one pass, and most joins can be done without even using a temporary table. Most temporary tables are memory-based (HEAP) tables. Temporary tables with a large record length (calculated as the sum of all column lengths) or that contain BLOB columns are stored on disk.

One problem before MySQL 3.23.2 is that if an internal in-memory heap table exceeds the size of `tmp_table_size`, the error `The table` `tbl_name` `is full` occurs. From 3.23.2 on, this is handled automatically by changing the in-memory heap table to a disk-based `MyISAM` table as necessary. To work around this problem for older servers, you can increase the temporary table size by setting the `tmp_table_size` option to `mysqld`, or by setting the SQL option `SQL_BIG_TABLES` in the client program.

In MySQL 3.20, the maximum size of the temporary table is `record_buffer*16`; if you are using this version, you have to increase the value of `record_buffer`. You can also start `mysqld` with the `--big-tables` option to always store temporary tables on disk. However, this will affect the speed of many complicated queries.

- Most requests that perform a sort allocate a sort buffer and zero to two temporary files depending on the result set size. See Section A.4.4, "Where MySQL Stores Temporary Files."

- Almost all parsing and calculating is done in a local memory store. No memory overhead is needed for small items, so the normal slow memory allocation and freeing is avoided. Memory is allocated only for unexpectedly large strings; this is done with `malloc()` and `free()`.

- For each `MyISAM` and `ISAM` table that is opened, the index file is opened once and the data file is opened once for each concurrently running thread. For each concurrent thread, a table structure, column structures for each column, and a buffer of size 3 `*` `N` are allocated (where `N` is the maximum row length, not counting `BLOB` columns). A `BLOB` column requires five to eight bytes plus the length of the `BLOB` data. The `MyISAM` and `ISAM` storage engines maintain one extra row buffer for internal use.

- For each table having `BLOB` columns, a buffer is enlarged dynamically to read in larger `BLOB` values. If you scan a table, a buffer as large as the largest `BLOB` value is allocated.

- Handler structures for all in-use tables are saved in a cache and managed as a FIFO. By default, the cache has 64 entries. If a table has been used by two running threads at the same time, the cache contains two entries for the table. See Section 6.4.8, "How MySQL Opens and Closes Tables."

- A `FLUSH TABLES` statement or `mysqladmin` `flush-tables` command closes all tables that are not in use and marks all in-use tables to be closed when the currently executing thread finishes. This effectively frees most in-use memory.

`ps` and other system status programs may report that `mysqld` uses a lot of memory. This may be caused by thread stacks on different memory addresses. For example, the Solaris version of `ps` counts the unused memory between stacks as used memory. You can verify this by checking available swap with `swap` `-s`. We have tested `mysqld` with several memory-leakage detectors (both commercial and open source), so there should be no memory leaks.

6.5.5 How MySQL Uses DNS

When a new client connects to mysqld, mysqld spawns a new thread to handle the request. This thread first checks whether the hostname is in the hostname cache. If not, the thread attempts to resolve the hostname:

- If the operating system supports the thread-safe gethostbyaddr_r() and gethostbyname_r() calls, the thread uses them to perform hostname resolution.
- If the operating system doesn't support the thread-safe calls, the thread locks a mutex and calls gethostbyaddr() and gethostbyname() instead. In this case, no other thread can resolve hostnames that are not in the hostname cache until the first thread unlocks the mutex.

You can disable DNS hostname lookups by starting mysqld with the --skip-name-resolve option. However, in this case, you can use only IP numbers in the MySQL grant tables.

If you have a very slow DNS and many hosts, you can get more performance by either disabling DNS lookups with --skip-name-resolve or by increasing the HOST_CACHE_SIZE define (default value: 128) and recompiling mysqld.

You can disable the hostname cache by starting the server with the --skip-host-cache option. To clear the hostname cache, issue a FLUSH HOSTS statement or execute the mysqladmin flush-hosts command.

If you want to disallow TCP/IP connections entirely, start mysqld with the --skip-networking option.

6.6 Disk Issues

- Disk seeks are a big performance bottleneck. This problem becomes more apparent when the amount of data starts to grow so large that effective caching becomes impossible. For large databases where you access data more or less randomly, you can be sure that you will need at least one disk seek to read and a couple of disk seeks to write things. To minimize this problem, use disks with low seek times.
- Increase the number of available disk spindles (and thereby reduce the seek overhead) by either symlinking files to different disks or striping the disks:
  - Using symbolic links

    This means that, for MyISAM tables, you symlink the index file and/or data file from their usual location in the data directory to another disk (that may also be striped). This makes both the seek and read times better, assuming that the disk is not used for other purposes as well. See Section 6.6.1, "Using Symbolic Links."
  - Striping

    Striping means that you have many disks and put the first block on the first disk, the second block on the second disk, and the Nth block on the (N mod *number_of_disks*) disk, and so on. This means if your normal data size is less than the stripe size (or perfectly aligned), you will get much better performance. Striping is very dependent on the operating system and the stripe size, so benchmark your application with different stripe sizes. See Section 6.1.5, "Using Your Own Benchmarks."

The speed difference for striping is *very* dependent on the parameters. Depending on how you set the striping parameters and number of disks, you may get differences measured in orders of magnitude. You have to choose to optimize for random or sequential access.

- For reliability you may want to use RAID 0+1 (striping plus mirroring), but in this case, you will need 2*N drives to hold N drives of data. This is probably the best option if you have the money for it! However, you may also have to invest in some volume-management software to handle it efficiently.

- A good option is to vary the RAID level according to how critical a type of data is. For example, store semi-important data that can be regenerated on a RAID 0 disk, but store really important data such as host information and logs on a RAID 0+1 or RAID N disk. RAID N can be a problem if you have many writes, due to the time required to update the parity bits.

- On Linux, you can get much more performance by using `hdparm` to configure your disk's interface. (Up to 100% under load is not uncommon.) The following `hdparm` options should be quite good for MySQL, and probably for many other applications:

```
hdparm -m 16 -d 1
```

Note that performance and reliability when using this command depends on your hardware, so we strongly suggest that you test your system thoroughly after using `hdparm`. Please consult the `hdparm` man page for more information. If `hdparm` is not used wisely, filesystem corruption may result, so back up everything before experimenting!

- You can also set the parameters for the filesystem that the database uses:

If you don't need to know when files were last accessed (which is not really useful on a database server), you can mount your filesystems with the `-o noatime` option. That skips updates to the last access time in inodes on the filesystem, which avoids some disk seeks.

On many operating systems, you can set a filesystem to be updated asynchronously by mounting it with the `-o async` option. If your computer is reasonably stable, this should give you more performance without sacrificing too much reliability. (This flag is on by default on Linux.)

6.6.1 Using Symbolic Links

You can move tables and databases from the database directory to other locations and replace them with symbolic links to the new locations. You might want to do this, for example, to move a database to a file system with more free space or increase the speed of your system by spreading your tables to a different disk.

The recommended way to do this is to just symlink databases to a different disk. Symlink tables only as a last resort.

6.6.1.1 Using Symbolic Links for Databases on Unix

On Unix, the way to symlink a database is to first create a directory on some disk where you have free space and then create a symlink to it from the MySQL data directory.

```
shell> mkdir /dr1/databases/test
shell> ln -s /dr1/databases/test /path/to/datadir
```

MySQL doesn't support linking one directory to multiple databases. Replacing a database directory with a symbolic link will work fine as long as you don't make a symbolic link between databases. Suppose that you have a database db1 under the MySQL data directory, and then make a symlink db2 that points to db1:

```
shell> cd /path/to/datadir
shell> ln -s db1 db2
```

Now, for any table tbl_a in db1, there also appears to be a table tbl_a in db2. If one client updates db1.tbl_a and another client updates db2.tbl_a, there will be problems.

If you really need to do this, you can change one of the source files. The file to modify depends on your version of MySQL. For MySQL 4.0 and up, look for the following statement in the mysys/my_symlink.c file:

```
if (!(MyFlags & MY_RESOLVE_LINK) ||
    (!lstat(filename,&stat_buff) && S_ISLNK(stat_buff.st_mode)))
```

Before MySQL 4.0, look for this statement in the mysys/mf_format.c file:

```
if (flag & 32 || (!lstat(to,&stat_buff) && S_ISLNK(stat_buff.st_mode)))
```

Change the statement to this:

```
if (1)
```

On Windows, you can use internal symbolic links to directories by compiling MySQL with -DUSE_SYMDIR. This allows you to put different databases on different disks. See Section 6.6.1.3, "Using Symbolic Links for Databases on Windows."

6.6.1.2 Using Symbolic Links for Tables on Unix

Before MySQL 4.0, you should not symlink tables unless you are *very* careful with them. The problem is that if you run ALTER TABLE, REPAIR TABLE, or OPTIMIZE TABLE on a symlinked table, the symlinks will be removed and replaced by the original files. This happens because these statements work by creating a temporary file in the database directory and replacing the original file with the temporary file when the statement operation is complete.

You should not symlink tables on systems that don't have a fully working realpath() call. (At least Linux and Solaris support realpath()). You can check whether your system supports symbolic links by issuing a SHOW VARIABLES LIKE 'have_symlink' statement.

In MySQL 4.0, symlinks are fully supported only for MyISAM tables. For other table types, you will probably get strange problems if you try to use symbolic links on files in the operating system with any of the preceding statements.

The handling of symbolic links for MyISAM tables in MySQL 4.0 works the following way:

- In the data directory, you will always have the table definition file, the data file, and the index file. The data file and index file can be moved elsewhere and replaced in the data directory by symlinks. The definition file cannot.

- You can symlink the data file and the index file independently to different directories.

- The symlinking can be done manually from the command line with ln -s if mysqld is not running. With SQL, you can instruct the server to perform the symlinking by using the DATA DIRECTORY and INDEX DIRECTORY options to CREATE TABLE.

- myisamchk will not replace a symlink with the data file or index file. It works directly on the file a symlink points to. Any temporary files are created in the directory where the data file or index file is located.

- When you drop a table that is using symlinks, both the symlink and the file the symlink points to are dropped. This is a good reason why you should *not* run mysqld as root or allow users to have write access to the MySQL database directories.

- If you rename a table with ALTER TABLE ... RENAME and you don't move the table to another database, the symlinks in the database directory are renamed to the new names and the data file and index file are renamed accordingly.

- If you use ALTER TABLE ... RENAME to move a table to another database, the table is moved to the other database directory. The old symlinks and the files to which they pointed are deleted. In other words, the new table will not be symlinked.

- If you are not using symlinks, you should use the --skip-symbolic-links option to mysqld to ensure that no one can use mysqld to drop or rename a file outside of the data directory.

SHOW CREATE TABLE doesn't report if a table has symbolic links prior to MySQL 4.0.15. This is also true for mysqldump, which uses SHOW CREATE TABLE to generate CREATE TABLE statements.

Table symlink operations that are not yet supported:

- ALTER TABLE ignores the DATA DIRECTORY and INDEX DIRECTORY table options.

- BACKUP TABLE and RESTORE TABLE don't respect symbolic links.

- The .frm file must *never* be a symbolic link (as indicated previously, only the data and index files can be symbolic links). Attempting to do this (for example, to make synonyms) will produce incorrect results. Suppose that you have a database db1 under the

MySQL data directory, a table `tbl1` in this database, and in the `db1` directory you make a symlink `tbl2` that points to `tbl1`:

```
shell> cd /path/to/datadir/db1
shell> ln -s tbl1.frm tbl2.frm
shell> ln -s tbl1.MYD tbl2.MYD
shell> ln -s tbl1.MYI tbl2.MYI
```

Now there will be problems if one thread reads `db1.tbl1` and another thread updates `db1.tbl2`:

- The query cache will be fooled (it will believe `tbl1` has not been updated so will return out-of-date results).
- `ALTER` statements on `tbl2` will also fail.

6.6.1.3 Using Symbolic Links for Databases on Windows

Beginning with MySQL 3.23.16, the `mysqld-max` and `mysql-max-nt` servers for Windows are compiled with the `-DUSE_SYMDIR` option. This allows you to put a database directory on a different disk by setting up a symbolic link to it. This is similar to the way that symbolic links work on Unix, although the procedure for setting up the link is different.

As of MySQL 4.0, symbolic links are enabled by default. If you don't need them, you can disable them with the `skip-symbolic-links` option:

```
[mysqld]
skip-symbolic-links
```

Before MySQL 4.0, symbolic links are disabled by default. To enable them, you should put the following entry in your `my.cnf` or `my.ini` file:

```
[mysqld]
symbolic-links
```

On Windows, you make a symbolic link to a MySQL database by creating a file in the data directory that contains the path to the destination directory. The file should be named *db_name*`.sym`, where *db_name* is the database name.

Suppose that the MySQL data directory is `C:\mysql\data` and you want to have database `foo` located at `D:\data\foo`. Set up a symlink like this:

1. Make sure that the `D:\data\foo` directory exists by creating it if necessary. If you already have a database directory named `foo` in the data directory, you should move it to `D:\data`. Otherwise, the symbolic link will be ineffective. To avoid problems, the server should not be running when you move the database directory.
2. Create a file `C:\mysql\data\foo.sym` that contains the pathname `D:\data\foo\`.

After that, all tables created in the database `foo` will be created in `D:\data\foo`. Note that the symbolic link will not be used if a directory with the database name exists in the MySQL data directory.

7

MySQL Client and Utility Programs

There are many different MySQL client programs that connect to the server to access databases or perform administrative tasks. Other utilities are available as well. These do not communicate with the server but perform MySQL-related operations.

This chapter provides a brief overview of these programs and then a more detailed description of each one. The descriptions indicate how to invoke the programs and the options they understand. See Chapter 3, "Using MySQL Programs," for general information on invoking programs and specifying program options.

7.1 Overview of the Client-Side Scripts and Utilities

The following list briefly describes the MySQL client programs and utilities:

- `myisampack`

  A utility that compresses `MyISAM` tables to produce smaller read-only tables. See Section 7.2, "`myisampack`, the MySQL Compressed Read-only Table Generator."

- `mysql`

  The command-line tool for interactively entering SQL statements or executing them from a file in batch mode. See Section 7.3, "`mysql`, the Command-Line Tool."

- `mysqlaccess`

  A script that checks the access privileges for a host, user, and database combination.

- `mysqladmin`

  A client that performs administrative operations, such as creating or dropping databases, reloading the grant tables, flushing tables to disk, and reopening log files. `mysqladmin` can also be used to retrieve version, process, and status information from the server. See Section 7.4, "`mysqladmin`, Administering a MySQL Server."

- `mysqlbinlog`

  A utility for reading statements from a binary log. The log of executed statements contained in the binary log files can be used to help recover from a crash. See Section 7.5, "The `mysqlbinlog` Binary Log Utility."

- `mysqlcc`

  A client that provides a graphical interface for interacting with the server. See Section 7.6, "`mysqlcc`, the MySQL Control Center."

- `mysqlcheck`

  A table-maintenance client that checks, repairs, analyzes, and optimizes tables. See Section 7.7, "The `mysqlcheck` Table Maintenance and Repair Program."

- `mysqldump`

  A client that dumps a MySQL database into a file as SQL statements or as tab-separated text files. Enhanced freeware originally by Igor Romanenko. See Section 7.8, "The `mysqldump` Database Backup Program."

- `mysqlhotcopy`

  A utility that quickly makes backups of `MyISAM` or `ISAM` tables while the server is running. See Section 7.9, "The `mysqlhotcopy` Database Backup Program."

- `mysqlimport`

  A client that imports text files into their respective tables using `LOAD DATA INFILE`. See Section 7.10, "The `mysqlimport` Data Import Program."

- `mysqlshow`

  A client that displays information about databases, tables, columns, and indexes. See Section 7.11, "`mysqlshow`, Showing Databases, Tables, and Columns."

- `perror`

  A utility that displays the meaning of system or MySQL error codes. See Section 7.12, "`perror`, Explaining Error Codes."

- `replace`

  A utility program that changes strings in place in files or on the standard input. See Section 7.13, "The `replace` String-Replacement Utility."

Each MySQL program takes many different options. However, every MySQL program provides a `--help` option that you can use to get a full description of the program's different options. For example, try `mysql --help`.

MySQL clients that communicate with the server using the mysqlclient library use the following environment variables:

MYSQL_UNIX_PORT	The default Unix socket file; used for connections to localhost
MYSQL_TCP_PORT	The default port number; used for TCP/IP connections
MYSQL_PWD	The default password
MYSQL_DEBUG	Debug trace options when debugging
TMPDIR	The directory where temporary tables and files are created

Use of MYSQL_PWD is insecure. See Section 4.5.6, "Keeping Your Password Secure."

You can override the default option values or values specified in environment variables for all standard programs by specifying options in an option file or on the command line. See Section 3.3, "Specifying Program Options."

7.2 myisampack, the MySQL Compressed Read-Only Table Generator

The myisampack utility compresses MyISAM tables. myisampack works by compressing each column in the table separately. Usually, myisampack packs the data file 40%-70%.

When the table is used later, the information needed to decompress columns is read into memory. This results in much better performance when accessing individual records, because you only have to uncompress exactly one record, not a much larger disk block as when using Stacker on MS-DOS.

MySQL uses mmap() when possible to perform memory mapping on compressed tables. If mmap() doesn't work, MySQL falls back to normal read/write file operations.

A similar utility, pack_isam, compresses ISAM tables. Because ISAM tables are deprecated, this section discusses only myisampack, but the general procedures for using myisampack are also true for pack_isam unless otherwise specified.

Please note the following:

- If the mysqld server was invoked with the --skip-external-locking option, it is not a good idea to invoke myisampack if the table might be updated by the server during the packing process.

- After packing a table, it becomes read-only. This is generally intended (such as when accessing packed tables on a CD). Allowing writes to a packed table is on our TODO list, but with low priority.

- myisampack can pack BLOB or TEXT columns. The older pack_isam program for ISAM tables cannot.

Invoke `myisampack` like this:

```
shell> myisampack [options] filename ...
```

Each filename should be the name of an index (.MYI) file. If you are not in the database directory, you should specify the pathname to the file. It is permissible to omit the .MYI extension.

`myisampack` supports the following options:

- `--help`, `-?`

  Display a help message and exit.

- `--backup`, `-b`

  Make a backup of the table data file using the name `tbl_name`.OLD.

- `--debug[=debug_options]`, `-# [debug_options]`

  Write a debugging log. The `debug_options` string often is 'd:t:o,`file_name`'.

- `--force`, `-f`

  Produce a packed table even if it becomes larger than the original or if the temporary file from an earlier invocation of `myisampack` exists. (`myisampack` creates a temporary file named `tbl_name`.TMD while it compresses the table. If you kill `myisampack`, the .TMD file might not be deleted.) Normally, `myisampack` exits with an error if it finds that `tbl_name`.TMD exists. With `--force`, `myisampack` packs the table anyway.

- `--join=big_tbl_name`, `-j big_tbl_name`

  Join all tables named on the command line into a single table `big_tbl_name`. All tables that are to be combined **must** have identical structure (same column names and types, same indexes, and so forth).

- `--packlength=#`, `-p #`

  Specify the record length storage size, in bytes. The value should be 1, 2, or 3. `myisampack` stores all rows with length pointers of 1, 2, or 3 bytes. In most normal cases, `myisampack` can determine the right length value before it begins packing the file, but it may notice during the packing process that it could have used a shorter length. In this case, `myisampack` will print a note that the next time you pack the same file, you could use a shorter record length.

- `--silent`, `-s`

  Silent mode. Write output only when errors occur.

- `--test`, `-t`

  Don't actually pack the table, just test packing it.

- `--tmp_dir=path`, `-T path`

  Use the named directory as the location in which to write the temporary table.

- `--verbose ,-v`

  Verbose mode. Write information about the progress of the packing operation and its result.

- `--version , -V`

  Display version information and exit.

- `--wait , -W`

  Wait and retry if the table is in use. If the `mysqld` server was invoked with the `--skip-external-locking` option, it is not a good idea to invoke `myisampack` if the table might be updated by the server during the packing process.

The following sequence of commands illustrates a typical table compression session:

```
shell> ls -l station.*
-rw-rw-r--   1 monty    my            994128 Apr 17 19:00 station.MYD
-rw-rw-r--   1 monty    my             53248 Apr 17 19:00 station.MYI
-rw-rw-r--   1 monty    my              5767 Apr 17 19:00 station.frm

shell> myisamchk -dvv station

MyISAM file:     station
Isam-version:  2
Creation time: 1996-03-13 10:08:58
Recover time:  1997-02-02  3:06:43
Data records:                1192  Deleted blocks:           0
Datafile parts:              1192  Deleted data:             0
Datafile pointer (bytes):       2  Keyfile pointer (bytes):  2
Max datafile length:     54657023  Max keyfile length:    33554431
Recordlength:                 834
Record format: Fixed length

table description:
Key Start Len Index  Type               Root  Blocksize   Rec/key
1   2     4   unique unsigned long      1024       1024         1
2   32    30  multip. text             10240       1024         1

Field Start Length Type
1     1     1
2     2     4
3     6     4
4     10    1
5     11    20
6     31    1
7     32    30
8     62    35
9     97    35
```

10	132	35
11	167	4
12	171	16
13	187	35
14	222	4
15	226	16
16	242	20
17	262	20
18	282	20
19	302	30
20	332	4
21	336	4
22	340	1
23	341	8
24	349	8
25	357	8
26	365	2
27	367	2
28	369	4
29	373	4
30	377	1
31	378	2
32	380	8
33	388	4
34	392	4
35	396	4
36	400	4
37	404	1
38	405	4
39	409	4
40	413	4
41	417	4
42	421	4
43	425	4
44	429	20
45	449	30
46	479	1
47	480	1
48	481	79
49	560	79
50	639	79
51	718	79
52	797	8
53	805	1
54	806	1
55	807	20

```
56    827   4
57    831   4
```

```
shell> myisampack station.MYI
Compressing station.MYI: (1192 records)
- Calculating statistics
```

```
normal:     20  empty-space:    16  empty-zero:     12  empty-fill: 11
pre-space:   0  end-space:      12  table-lookups:   5  zero:        7
Original trees:  57  After join: 17
- Compressing file
87.14%
Remember to run myisamchk -rq on compressed tables
```

```
shell> ls -l station.*
-rw-rw-r--   1 monty    my         127874 Apr 17 19:00 station.MYD
-rw-rw-r--   1 monty    my          55296 Apr 17 19:04 station.MYI
-rw-rw-r--   1 monty    my           5767 Apr 17 19:00 station.frm
```

```
shell> myisamchk -dvv station
```

```
MyISAM file:      station
Isam-version:  2
Creation time: 1996-03-13 10:08:58
Recover time:  1997-04-17 19:04:26
Data records:            1192  Deleted blocks:          0
Datafile parts:          1192  Deleted data:            0
Datafile pointer (bytes):   3  Keyfile pointer (bytes):    1
Max datafile length:  16777215  Max keyfile length:     131071
Recordlength:             834
Record format: Compressed
```

```
table description:
Key Start Len Index    Type            Root  Blocksize  Rec/key
1    2    4   unique   unsigned long   10240    1024        1
2   32   30   multip.  text            54272    1024        1
```

```
Field Start Length Type                        Huff tree  Bits
1     1     1      constant                         1      0
2     2     4      zerofill(1)                      2      9
3     6     4      no zeros, zerofill(1)            2      9
4    10     1                                       3      9
5    11    20      table-lookup                     4      0
6    31     1                                       3      9
7    32    30      no endspace, not_always          5      9
8    62    35      no endspace, not_always, no empty 6     9
9    97    35      no empty                         7      9
```

10	132	35	no endspace, not_always, no empty	6	9
11	167	4	zerofill(1)	2	9
12	171	16	no endspace, not_always, no empty	5	9
13	187	35	no endspace, not_always, no empty	6	9
14	222	4	zerofill(1)	2	9
15	226	16	no endspace, not_always, no empty	5	9
16	242	20	no endspace, not_always	8	9
17	262	20	no endspace, no empty	8	9
18	282	20	no endspace, no empty	5	9
19	302	30	no endspace, no empty	6	9
20	332	4	always zero	2	9
21	336	4	always zero	2	9
22	340	1		3	9
23	341	8	table-lookup	9	0
24	349	8	table-lookup	10	0
25	357	8	always zero	2	9
26	365	2		2	9
27	367	2	no zeros, zerofill(1)	2	9
28	369	4	no zeros, zerofill(1)	2	9
29	373	4	table-lookup	11	0
30	377	1		3	9
31	378	2	no zeros, zerofill(1)	2	9
32	380	8	no zeros	2	9
33	388	4	always zero	2	9
34	392	4	table-lookup	12	0
35	396	4	no zeros, zerofill(1)	13	9
36	400	4	no zeros, zerofill(1)	2	9
37	404	1		2	9
38	405	4	no zeros	2	9
39	409	4	always zero	2	9
40	413	4	no zeros	2	9
41	417	4	always zero	2	9
42	421	4	no zeros	2	9
43	425	4	always zero	2	9
44	429	20	no empty	3	9
45	449	30	no empty	3	9
46	479	1		14	4
47	480	1		14	4
48	481	79	no endspace, no empty	15	9
49	560	79	no empty	2	9
50	639	79	no empty	2	9
51	718	79	no endspace	16	9
52	797	8	no empty	2	9
53	805	1		17	1
54	806	1		3	9
55	807	20	no empty	3	9
56	827	4	no zeros, zerofill(2)	2	9
57	831	4	no zeros, zerofill(1)	2	9

myisampack displays the following kinds of information:

- normal

  The number of columns for which no extra packing is used.

- empty-space

  The number of columns containing values that are only spaces; these will occupy one bit.

- empty-zero

  The number of columns containing values that are only binary zeros; these will occupy one bit.

- empty-fill

  The number of integer columns that don't occupy the full byte range of their type; these are changed to a smaller type. For example, a BIGINT column (eight bytes) can be stored as a TINYINT column (one byte) if all its values are in the range from -128 to 127.

- pre-space

  The number of decimal columns that are stored with leading spaces. In this case, each value will contain a count for the number of leading spaces.

- end-space

  The number of columns that have a lot of trailing spaces. In this case, each value will contain a count for the number of trailing spaces.

- table-lookup

  The column had only a small number of different values, which were converted to an ENUM before Huffman compression.

- zero

  The number of columns for which all values are zero.

- Original trees

  The initial number of Huffman trees.

- After join

  The number of distinct Huffman trees left after joining trees to save some header space.

After a table has been compressed, myisamchk -dvv prints additional information about each column:

- Type

  The column type. The value may contain any of the following descriptors:

  - constant

    All rows have the same value.

- no endspace

  Don't store endspace.

- no endspace, not_always

  Don't store endspace and don't do endspace compression for all values.

- no endspace, no empty

  Don't store endspace. Don't store empty values.

- table-lookup

  The column was converted to an ENUM.

- zerofill(n)

  The most significant n bytes in the value are always 0 and are not stored.

- no zeros

  Don't store zeros.

- always zero

  Zero values are stored using one bit.

- Huff tree

  The number of the Huffman tree associated with the column.

- Bits

  The number of bits used in the Huffman tree.

After you run myisampack, you must run myisamchk to re-create any indexes. At this time, you can also sort the index blocks and create statistics needed for the MySQL optimizer to work more efficiently:

```
shell> myisamchk -rq --sort-index --analyze tbl_name.MYI
```

A similar procedure applies for ISAM tables. After using pack_isam, use isamchk to re-create the indexes:

```
shell> isamchk -rq --sort-index --analyze tbl_name.ISM
```

After you have installed the packed table into the MySQL database directory, you should execute mysqladmin flush-tables to force mysqld to start using the new table.

To unpack a packed table, use the --unpack option to myisamchk or isamchk.

7.3 mysql, the Command-Line Tool

mysql is a simple SQL shell (with GNU readline capabilities). It supports interactive and non-interactive use. When used interactively, query results are presented in an ASCII-table format. When used non-interactively (for example, as a filter), the result is presented in tab-separated format. The output format can be changed using command-line options.

If you have problems due to insufficient memory for large result sets, use the `--quick` option. This forces `mysql` to retrieve results from the server a row at a time rather than retrieving the entire result set and buffering it in memory before displaying it. This is done by using `mysql_use_result()` rather than `mysql_store_result()` to retrieve the result set.

Using `mysql` is very easy. Invoke it from the prompt of your command interpreter as follows:

```
shell> mysql db_name
```

Or:

```
shell> mysql --user=user_name --password=your_password db_name
```

Then type an SQL statement, end it with ';', \g, or \G and press Enter.

You can run a script simply like this:

```
shell> mysql db_name < script.sql > output.tab
```

`mysql` supports the following options:

- `--help`, `-?`

  Display a help message and exit.

- `--batch`, `-B`

  Print results using tab as the column separator, with each row on a new line. With this option, `mysql` doesn't use the history file.

- `--character-sets-dir=path`

  The directory where character sets are installed. See Section 4.7.1, "The Character Set Used for Data and Sorting."

- `--compress`, `-C`

  Compress all information sent between the client and the server if both support compression.

- `--database=db_name`, `-D db_name`

  The database to use. This is useful mainly in an option file.

- `--debug[=debug_options]`, `-# [debug_options]`

  Write a debugging log. The *debug_options* string often is `'d:t:o,file_name'`. The default is `'d:t:o,/tmp/mysql.trace'`.

- `--debug-info`, `-T`

  Print some debugging information when the program exits.

- `--default-character-set=charset`

  Use *charset* as the default character set. See Section 4.7.1, "The Character Set Used for Data and Sorting."

- `--execute=statement`, `-e statement`

  Execute the statement and quit. The default output format is like that produced with `--batch`.

- `--force`, `-f`

  Continue even if an SQL error occurs.

- `--host=host_name`, `-h host_name`

  Connect to the MySQL server on the given host.

- `--html`, `-H`

  Produce HTML output.

- `--ignore-space`, `-i`

  Ignore spaces after function names. The effect of this is described in the discussion for `IGNORE_SPACE` in Section 4.2.2, "The Server SQL Mode."

- `--local-infile[={0|1}]`

  Enable or disable `LOCAL` capability for `LOAD DATA INFILE`. With no value, the option enables `LOCAL`. It may be given as `--local-infile=0` or `--local-infile=1` to explicitly disable or enable `LOCAL`. Enabling `LOCAL` has no effect if the server does not also support it.

- `--named-commands`, `-G`

  Named commands are *enabled*. Long format commands are allowed as well as shortened `\*` commands. For example, `quit` and `\q` both are recognized.

- `--no-auto-rehash`, `-A`

  No automatic rehashing. This option causes `mysql` to start faster, but you must issue the `rehash` command if you want to use table and column name completion.

- `--no-beep`, `-b`

  Do not beep when errors occur.

- `--no-named-commands`, `-g`

  Named commands are disabled. Use the `\*` form only, or use named commands only at the beginning of a line ending with a semicolon (';'). As of MySQL 3.23.22, `mysql` starts with this option *enabled* by default! However, even with this option, long-format commands still work from the first line.

- `--no-pager`

  Do not use a pager for displaying query output. Output paging is discussed further in Section 7.3.1, "`mysql` Commands."

- `--no-tee`

  Do not copy output to a file. Tee files are discussed further in Section 7.3.1, "`mysql` Commands."

- `--one-database`, `-O`

  Ignore statements except those for the default database named on the command line. This is useful for skipping updates to other databases in the binary log.

- --pager[=*command*]

  Use the given command for paging query output. If the command is omitted, the default pager is the value of your PAGER environment variable. Valid pagers are less, more, cat [> filename], and so forth. This option works only on Unix. It does not work in batch mode. Output paging is discussed further in Section 7.3.1, "mysql Commands."

- --password[=*password*] , -p[*password*]

  The password to use when connecting to the server. Note that if you use the short option form (-p), you *cannot* have a space between the option and the password. If no password is given on the command line, you will be prompted for one.

- --port=*port_num* , -P *port_num*

  The TCP/IP port number to use for the connection.

- --prompt=*format_str*

  Set the prompt to the specified format. The default is mysql>. The special sequences that the prompt can contain are described in Section 7.3.1, "mysql Commands."

- --protocol={TCP | SOCKET | PIPE | MEMORY}

  The connection protocol to use. New in MySQL 4.1.

- --quick , -q

  Don't cache each query result, print each row as it is received. This may slow down the server if the output is suspended. With this option, mysql doesn't use the history file.

- --raw , -r

  Write column values without escape conversion. Often used with the --batch option.

- --reconnect

  If the connection to the server is lost, automatically try to reconnect. A single reconnect attempt is made each time the connection is lost. To suppress reconnection behavior, use --skip-reconnect. New in MySQL 4.1.0.

- --safe-updates , --i-am-a-dummy, -U

  Allow only UPDATE and DELETE statements that specify rows to affect using key values. If you have this option in an option file, you can override it by using --safe-updates on the command line. See Section 7.3.3, "mysql Tips," for more information about this option.

- --silent , -s

  Silent mode. Produce less output. This option can be given multiple times to produce less and less output.

- --skip-column-names , -N

Don't write column names in results.

- `--skip-line-numbers` , `-L`

Don't write line numbers for errors. Useful when you want to compare result files that include error messages.

- `--socket=path` , `-S path`

The socket file to use for the connection.

- `--table` , `-t`

Display output in table format. This is the default for interactive use, but can be used to produce table output in batch mode.

- `--tee=file_name`

Append a copy of output to the given file. This option does not work in batch mode. Tee files are discussed further in Section 7.3.1, "`mysql` Commands."

- `--unbuffered` , `-n`

Flush the buffer after each query.

- `--user=user_name` , `-u user_name`

The MySQL username to use when connecting to the server.

- `--verbose` , `-v`

Verbose mode. Produce more output. This option can be given multiple times to produce more and more output. (For example, `-v -v -v` produces the table output format even in batch mode.)

- `--version` , `-V`

Display version information and exit.

- `--vertical` , `-E`

Print the rows of query output vertically. Without this option, you can specify vertical output for individual statements by terminating them with `\G`.

- `--wait` , `-w`

If the connection cannot be established, wait and retry instead of aborting.

- `--xml` , `-X`

Produce XML output.

You can also set the following variables by using `--var_name=value` options:

- `connect_timeout`

The number of seconds before connection timeout. (Default value is 0.)

- `max_allowed_packet`

The maximum packet length to send to or receive from the server. (Default value is

16MB.)

- max_join_size

  The automatic limit for rows in a join when using --safe-updates. (Default value is 1,000,000.)

- net_buffer_length

  The buffer size for TCP/IP and socket communication. (Default value is 16KB.)

- select_limit

  The automatic limit for SELECT statements when using --safe-updates. (Default value is 1,000.)

It is also possible to set variables by using --set-variable=*var_name*=*value* or -O *var_name*=*value* syntax. However, this syntax is deprecated as of MySQL 4.0.

On Unix, the mysql client writes a record of executed statements to a history file. By default, the history file is named .mysql_history and is created in your home directory. To specify a different file, set the value of the MYSQL_HISTFILE environment variable.

If you do not want to maintain a history file, first remove .mysql_history if it exists, and then use either of the following techniques:

- Set the MYSQL_HISTFILE variable to /dev/null. To cause this setting to take effect each time you log in, put the setting in one of your shell's startup files.

- Create .mysql_histfile as a symbolic link to /dev/null:

  ```
  shell> ln -s /dev/null $HOME/.mysql_history
  ```

  You need do this only once.

7.3.1 mysql Commands

mysql sends SQL statements that you issue to the server to be executed. There is also a set of commands that mysql itself interprets. For a list of these commands, type help or \h at the mysql> prompt:

```
mysql> help

MySQL commands:
?          (\h)    Synonym for `help'.
clear      (\c)    Clear command.
connect    (\r)    Reconnect to the server.
                   Optional arguments are db and host.
delimiter (\d)     Set query delimiter.
edit       (\e)    Edit command with $EDITOR.
ego        (\G)    Send command to mysql server,
                   display result vertically.
exit       (\q)    Exit mysql. Same as quit.
```

```
go          (\g)    Send command to mysql server.
help        (\h)    Display this help.
nopager     (\n)    Disable pager, print to stdout.
notee       (\t)    Don't write into outfile.
pager       (\P)    Set PAGER [to_pager].
                    Print the query results via PAGER.
print       (\p)    Print current command.
prompt      (\R)    Change your mysql prompt.
quit        (\q)    Quit mysql.
rehash      (\#)    Rebuild completion hash.
source      (\.)    Execute an SQL script file.
                    Takes a file name as an argument.
status      (\s)    Get status information from the server.
system      (\!)    Execute a system shell command.
tee         (\T)    Set outfile [to_outfile].
                    Append everything into given outfile.
use         (\u)    Use another database.
                    Takes database name as argument.
```

The edit, nopager, pager, and system commands work only in Unix.

The status command provides some information about the connection and the server you are using. If you are running in --safe-updates mode, status also prints the values for the mysql variables that affect your queries.

To log queries and their output, use the tee command. All the data displayed on the screen will be appended into a given file. This can be very useful for debugging purposes also. You can enable this feature on the command line with the --tee option, or interactively with the tee command. The tee file can be disabled interactively with the notee command. Executing tee again re-enables logging. Without a parameter, the previous file will be used. Note that tee flushes query results to the file after each statement, just before mysql prints its next prompt.

Browsing or searching query results in interactive mode by using Unix programs such as less, more, or any other similar program is now possible with the --pager option. If you specify no value for the option, mysql checks the value of the PAGER environment variable and sets the pager to that. Output paging can be enabled interactively with the pager command and disabled with nopager. The command takes an optional argument; if given, the paging program is set to that. With no argument, the pager is set to the pager that was set on the command line, or stdout if no pager was specified.

Output paging works only in Unix because it uses the popen() function, which doesn't exist on Windows. For Windows, the tee option can be used instead to save query output, although this is not as convenient as pager for browsing output in some situations.

A few tips about the pager command:

- You can use it to write to a file and the results will go only to the file:

```
mysql> pager cat > /tmp/log.txt
```

You can also pass any options for the program that you want to use as your pager:

```
mysql> pager less -n -i -S
```

- In the preceding example, note the -S option. You may find it very useful for browsing wide query results. Sometimes a very wide result set is difficult to read on the screen. The -S option to less can make the result set much more readable because you can scroll it horizontally using the left-arrow and right-arrow keys. You can also use -S interactively within less to switch the horizontal-browse mode on and off. For more information, read the less manual page:

```
shell> man less
```

- You can specify very complex pager commands for handling query output:

```
mysql> pager cat | tee /dr1/tmp/res.txt \
         | tee /dr2/tmp/res2.txt | less -n -i -S
```

In this example, the command would send query results to two files in two different directories on two different filesystems mounted on /dr1 and /dr2, yet still display the results onscreen via less.

You can also combine the tee and pager functions. Have a tee file enabled and pager set to less, and you will be able to browse the results using the less program and still have every-thing appended into a file the same time. The difference between the Unix tee used with the pager command and the mysql built-in tee command is that the built-in tee works even if you don't have the Unix tee available. The built-in tee also logs everything that is printed on the screen, whereas the Unix tee used with pager doesn't log quite that much. Additionally, tee file logging can be turned on and off interactively from within mysql. This is useful when you want to log some queries to a file, but not others.

From MySQL 4.0.2 on, the default mysql> prompt can be reconfigured. The string for defining the prompt can contain the following special sequences:

Option	Description
\v	The server version
\d	The current database
\h	The server host
\p	The current TCP/IP host
\u	Your username
\U	Your full *user_name@host_name* account name
\\	A literal '\' backslash character
\n	A newline character
\t	A tab character
\	A space (a space follows the backslash)
_	A space

Option	Description
\R	The current time, in 24-hour military time (0-23)
\r	The current time, standard 12-hour time (1-12)
\m	Minutes of the current time
\y	The current year, two digits
\Y	The current year, four digits
\D	The full current date
\s	Seconds of the current time
\w	The current day of the week in three-letter format (Mon, Tue, ...)
\P	am/pm
\o	The current month in numeric format
\O	The current month in three-letter format (Jan, Feb, ...)
\c	A counter that increments for each statement you issue

'\' followed by any other letter just becomes that letter.

If you specify the prompt command with no argument, mysql resets the prompt to the default of mysql>.

You can set the prompt in several ways:

- Use an environment variable

  You can set the MYSQL_PS1 environment variable to a prompt string. For example:

  ```
  shell> export MYSQL_PS1="(\u@\h) [\d]> "
  ```

- Use an option file

  You can set the prompt option in the [mysql] group of any MySQL option file, such as /etc/my.cnf or the .my.cnf file in your home directory. For example:

  ```
  [mysql]
  prompt=(\\u@\\h) [\\d]>\\_
  ```

  In this example, note that the backslashes are doubled. If you set the prompt using the prompt option in an option file, it is advisable to double the backslashes when using the special prompt options. There is some overlap in the set of allowable prompt options and the set of special escape sequences that are recognized in option files. (These sequences are listed in Section 3.3.2, "Using Option Files.") The overlap may cause you problems if you use single backslashes. For example, \s will be interpreted as a space rather than as the current seconds value. The following example shows how to define a prompt within an option file to include the current time in HH:MM:SS> format:

  ```
  [mysql]
  prompt="\\r:\\m:\\s> "
  ```

- Use a command-line option

  You can set the --prompt option on the command line to mysql. For example:

  ```
  shell> mysql --prompt="(\u@\h) [\d]> "
  (user@host) [database]>
  ```

- Interactively

  You can change your prompt interactively by using the prompt (or \R) command. For example:

  ```
  mysql> prompt (\u@\h) [\d]>\_
  PROMPT set to '(\u@\h) [\d]>\_'
  (user@host) [database]>
  (user@host) [database]> prompt
  Returning to default PROMPT of mysql>
  mysql>
  ```

7.3.2 Executing SQL Statements from a Text File

The mysql client typically is used interactively, like this:

```
shell> mysql db_name
```

However, it's also possible to put your SQL statements in a file and then tell mysql to read its input from that file. To do so, create a text file text_file that contains the statements you wish to execute. Then invoke mysql as shown here:

```
shell> mysql db_name < text_file
```

You can also start your text file with a USE db_name statement. In this case, it is unnecessary to specify the database name on the command line:

```
shell> mysql < text_file
```

If you are already running mysql, you can execute an SQL script file using the source or \. command:

```
mysql> source filename;
mysql> \. filename
```

7.3.3 mysql Tips

This section describes some techniques that can help you use mysql more effectively.

7.3.3.1 Displaying Query Results Vertically

Some query results are much more readable when displayed vertically, instead of in the usual horizontal table format. For example, longer text values that include newlines often are much easier to read with vertical output:

```
mysql> SELECT * FROM mails WHERE LENGTH(txt) < 300 LIMIT 300,1\G
*************************** 1. row ***************************
  msg_nro: 3068
     date: 2000-03-01 23:29:50
time_zone: +0200
mail_from: Monty
    reply: monty@no.spam.com
  mail_to: "Thimble Smith" <tim@no.spam.com>
      sbj: UTF-8
      txt: >>>>> "Thimble" == Thimble Smith writes:

Thimble> Hi.  I think this is a good idea.  Is anyone familiar
Thimble> with UTF-8 or Unicode? Otherwise, I'll put this on my
Thimble> TODO list and see what happens.

Yes, please do that.

Regards,
Monty
     file: inbox-jani-1
     hash: 190402944
1 row in set (0.09 sec)
```

7.3.3.2 Using the `--safe-updates` Option

For beginners, a useful startup option is `--safe-updates` (or `--i-am-a-dummy`, which has the same effect). This option was introduced in MySQL 3.23.11. It is helpful for cases when you might have issued a DELETE FROM *tbl_name* statement but forgotten the WHERE clause. Normally, such a statement will delete all rows from the table. With `--safe-updates`, you can delete rows only by specifying the key values that identify them. This helps prevent accidents.

When you use the `--safe-updates` option, mysql issues the following statement when it connects to the MySQL server:

```
SET SQL_SAFE_UPDATES=1,SQL_SELECT_LIMIT=1000, SQL_MAX_JOIN_SIZE=1000000;
```

The SET statement has the following effects:

- You are not allowed to execute an UPDATE or DELETE statement unless you specify a key constraint in the WHERE clause or provide a LIMIT clause (or both). For example:

  ```
  UPDATE tbl_name SET not_key_column=# WHERE key_column=#;

  UPDATE tbl_name SET not_key_column=# LIMIT 1;
  ```

- All large SELECT results are automatically limited to 1,000 rows unless the statement includes a LIMIT clause.

- Multiple-table SELECT statements that will probably need to examine more than 1,000,000 row combinations are aborted.

To specify limits other than 1,000 and 1,000,000, you can override the defaults by using --select_limit and --max_join_size options:

```
shell> mysql --safe-updates --select_limit=500 --max_join_size=10000
```

7.3.3.3 Disabling mysql Auto-Reconnect

If the mysql client loses its connection to the server while sending a query, it will immediately and automatically try to reconnect once to the server and send the query again. However, even if mysql succeeds in reconnecting, your first connection has ended and all your previous session objects and settings are lost: temporary tables, the autocommit mode, and user and session variables. This behavior may be dangerous for you, as in the following example where the server was shut down and restarted without you knowing it:

```
mysql> SET @a=1;
Query OK, 0 rows affected (0.05 sec)

mysql> INSERT INTO t VALUES(@a);
ERROR 2006: MySQL server has gone away
No connection. Trying to reconnect...
Connection id:    1
Current database: test

Query OK, 1 row affected (1.30 sec)

mysql> SELECT * FROM t;
+------+
| a    |
+------+
| NULL |
+------+
1 row in set (0.05 sec)
```

The @a user variable has been lost with the connection, and after the reconnection it is undefined. If it is important to have mysql terminate with an error if the connection has been lost, you can start the mysql client with the --skip-reconnect option.

7.4 mysqladmin, Administering a MySQL Server

mysqladmin is a client for performing administrative operations. You can use it to check the server's configuration and current status, create and drop databases, and more.

Invoke `mysqladmin` like this:

```
shell> mysqladmin [options] command [command-option] command ...
```

`mysqladmin` supports the following commands:

- `create` *databasename*

  Create a new database.

- `drop` *databasename*

  Delete a database and all its tables.

- `extended-status`

  Display the server status variables and their values.

- `flush-hosts`

  Flush all information in the host cache.

- `flush-logs`

  Flush all logs.

- `flush-privileges`

  Reload the grant tables (same as `reload`).

- `flush-status`

  Clear status variables.

- `flush-tables`

  Flush all tables.

- `flush-threads`

  Flush the thread cache. (Added in MySQL 3.23.16.)

- `kill` *id,id,...*

  Kill server threads.

- `password` *new-password*

  Set a new password. This changes the password to *new-password* for the account that you use with `mysqladmin` for connecting to the server.

- `ping`

  Check whether the server is alive.

- `processlist`

  Show a list of active server threads. This is like the output of the SHOW PROCESSLIST statement. If the `--verbose` option is given, the output is like that of SHOW FULL PROCESSLIST.

- `reload`

  Reload the grant tables.

- refresh

  Flush all tables and close and open log files.

- shutdown

  Stop the server.

- start-slave

  Start replication on a slave server. (Added in MySQL 3.23.16.)

- status

  Display a short server status message.

- stop-slave

  Stop replication on a slave server. (Added in MySQL 3.23.16.)

- variables

  Display the server system variables and their values.

- version

  Display version information from the server.

All commands can be shortened to any unique prefix. For example:

```
shell> mysqladmin proc stat
+----+-------+-----------+----+-------------+------+-------+-----+
| Id | User  | Host      | db | Command     | Time | State | Info |
+----+-------+-----------+----+-------------+------+-------+-----+
| 6  | monty | localhost |    | Processlist | 0    |       |     |
+----+-------+-----------+----+-------------+------+-------+-----+
Uptime: 10077  Threads: 1  Questions: 9  Slow queries: 0
Opens: 6 Flush tables: 1  Open tables: 2
Memory in use: 1092K  Max memory used: 1116K
```

The mysqladmin status command result displays the following values:

- Uptime

  The number of seconds the MySQL server has been running.

- Threads

  The number of active threads (clients).

- Questions

  The number of questions (queries) from clients since the server was started.

- Slow queries

  The number of queries that have taken more than long_query_time seconds. See Section 4.8.5, "The Slow Query Log."

- Opens

  The number of tables the server has opened.

- Flush tables

  The number of flush ..., refresh, and reload commands the server has executed.

- Open tables

  The number of tables that currently are open.

- Memory in use

  The amount of memory allocated directly by mysqld code. This value is displayed only when MySQL has been compiled with --with-debug=full.

- Maximum memory used

  The maximum amount of memory allocated directly by mysqld code. This value is displayed only when MySQL has been compiled with --with-debug=full.

If you execute mysqladmin shutdown when connecting to a local server using a Unix socket file, mysqladmin waits until the server's process ID file has been removed, to ensure that the server has stopped properly.

mysqladmin supports the following options:

- --help , -?

  Display a help message and exit.

- --character-sets-dir=path

  The directory where character sets are installed. See Section 4.7.1, "The Character Set Used for Data and Sorting."

- --compress , -C

  Compress all information sent between the client and the server if both support compression.

- --count=# , -c #

  The number of iterations to make. This works only with --sleep (-i).

- --debug[=debug_options] , -# [debug_options]

  Write a debugging log. The debug_options string often is 'd:t:o,file_name'. The default is 'd:t:o,/tmp/mysqladmin.trace'.

- --force , -f

  Don't ask for confirmation for the drop database command. With multiple commands, continue even if an error occurs.

- --host=host_name , -h host_name

  Connect to the MySQL server on the given host.

- --password[=password] , -p[password]

  The password to use when connecting to the server. Note that if you use the short option form (-p), you *cannot* have a space between the option and the password. If no password is given on the command line, you will be prompted for one.

- `--port=port_num` , `-P port_num`

  The TCP/IP port number to use for the connection.

- `--protocol={TCP | SOCKET | PIPE | MEMORY}`

  The connection protocol to use. New in MySQL 4.1.

- `--relative` , `-r`

  Show the difference between the current and previous values when used with `-i`. Currently, this option works only with the `extended-status` command.

- `--silent` , `-s`

  Exit silently if a connection to the server cannot be established.

- `--sleep=delay` , `-i delay`

  Execute commands again and again, sleeping for *delay* seconds in between.

- `--socket=path` , `-S path`

  The socket file to use for the connection.

- `--user=user_name` , `-u user_name`

  The MySQL username to use when connecting to the server.

- `--verbose` , `-v`

  Verbose mode. Print out more information on what the program does.

- `--version` , `-V`

  Display version information and exit.

- `--vertical` , `-E`

  Print output vertically. This is similar to `--relative`, but prints output vertically.

- `--wait[=#]` , `-w[#]`

  If the connection cannot be established, wait and retry instead of aborting. If an option value is given, it indicates the number of times to retry. The default is one time.

You can also set the following variables by using `--var_name=value` options:

- `connect_timeout`

  The number of seconds before connection timeout. (Default value is 0.)

- `shutdown_timeout`

  The number of seconds to wait for shutdown. (Default value is 0.)

It is also possible to set variables by using `--set-variable=var_name=value` or `-O var_name=value` syntax. However, this syntax is deprecated as of MySQL 4.0.

7.5 The `mysqlbinlog` Binary Log Utility

The binary log files that the server generates are written in binary format. To examine these files in text format, use the `mysqlbinlog` utility. It is available as of MySQL 3.23.14.

Invoke `mysqlbinlog` like this:

```
shell> mysqlbinlog [options] log-file ...
```

For example, to display the contents of the binary log `binlog.000003`, use this command:

```
shell> mysqlbinlog binlog.0000003
```

The output includes all statements contained in `binlog.000003`, together with other information such as the time each statement took, the thread ID of the client that issued it, the timestamp when it was issued, and so forth.

Normally, you use `mysqlbinlog` to read binary log files directly and apply them to the local MySQL server. It is also possible to read binary logs from a remote server by using the `--read-from-remote-server` option. However, this is deprecated because we instead want to make it easy to apply binary logs to a local MySQL server.

When you read remote binary logs, the connection parameter options can be given to indicate how to connect to the server, but they are ignored unless you also specify the `--read-from-remote-server` option. These options are `--host`, `--password`, `--port`, `--protocol`, `--socket`, and `--user`.

You can also use `mysqlbinlog` to read relay log files written by a slave server in a replication setup. Relay logs have the same format as binary log files.

The binary log is discussed further in Section 4.8.4, "The Binary Log."

`mysqlbinlog` supports the following options:

- `--help` , `-?`

  Display a help message and exit.

- `--database=db_name` , `-d db_name`

  List entries for just this database (local log only).

- `--force-read` , `-f`

  Force reading of unknown binary log events.

- `--host=host_name` , `-h host_name`

  Get the binary log from the MySQL server on the given host.

- `--local-load=path` , `-l path`

  Prepare local temporary files for LOAD DATA INFILE in the specified directory.

- `--offset=N` , `-o N`

  Skip the first N entries.

- `--password[=password]` , `-p[password]`

  The password to use when connecting to the server. Note that if you use the short option form (-p), you *cannot* have a space between the option and the password. If no password is given on the command line, you will be prompted for one.

- `--port=port_num` , `-P port_num`

  The TCP/IP port number to use for connecting to a remote server.

- `--position=N` , `-j N`

  Start reading the binary log at position N.

- `--protocol={TCP | SOCKET | PIPE | MEMORY}`

  The connection protocol to use. New in MySQL 4.1.

- `--read-from-remote-server` , `-R`

  Read the binary log from a MySQL server. Any connection parameter options are ignored unless this option is given as well. These options are `--host`, `--password`, `--port`, `--protocol`, `--socket`, and `--user`.

- `--result-file=name` , `-r name`

  Direct output to the given file.

- `--short-form` , `-s`

  Display only the statements contained in the log, without any extra information.

- `--socket=path` , `-S path`

  The socket file to use for the connection.

- `--user=user_name` , `-u user_name`

  The MySQL username to use when connecting to a remote server.

- `--version` , `-V`

  Display version information and exit.

You can also set the following variable by using `--var_name=value` options:

- `open_files_limit`

  Specify the number of open file descriptors to reserve.

You can pipe the output of `mysqlbinlog` into a `mysql` client to execute the statements contained in the binary log. This is used to recover from a crash when you have an old backup (see Section 4.6.1, "Database Backups"):

```
shell> mysqlbinlog hostname-bin.000001 | mysql
```

Or:

```
shell> mysqlbinlog hostname-bin.[0-9]* | mysql
```

You can also redirect the output of mysqlbinlog to a text file instead, if you need to modify the statement log first (for example, to remove statements that you don't want to execute for some reason). After editing the file, execute the statements that it contains by using it as input to the mysql program.

mysqlbinlog has the --position option, which prints only those statements with an offset in the binary log greater than or equal to a given position.

If you have more than one binary log to execute on the MySQL server, the safe method is to process them all using a single connection to the server. Here is an example that demonstrates what may be *unsafe*:

```
shell> mysqlbinlog hostname-bin.000001 | mysql # DANGER!!
shell> mysqlbinlog hostname-bin.000002 | mysql # DANGER!!
```

Processing binary logs this way using different connections to the server will cause problems if the first log file contains a CREATE TEMPORARY TABLE statement and the second log contains a statement that uses the temporary table. When the first mysql process terminates, the server will drop the temporary table. When the second mysql process attempts to use the table, the server will report "unknown table."

To avoid problems like this, use a single connection to execute the contents of all binary logs that you want to process. Here is one way to do that:

```
shell> mysqlbinlog hostname-bin.000001 hostname-bin.000002 | mysql
```

Another approach is to do this:

```
shell> mysqlbinlog hostname-bin.000001 >  /tmp/statements.sql
shell> mysqlbinlog hostname-bin.000002 >> /tmp/statements.sql
shell> mysql -e "source /tmp/statements.sql"
```

In MySQL 3.23, the binary log did not contain the data to load for LOAD DATA INFILE statements. To execute such a statement from a binary log file, the original data file was needed. Starting from MySQL 4.0.14, the binary log does contain the data, so mysqlbinlog can produce output that reproduces the LOAD DATA INFILE operation without the original data file. mysqlbinlog copies the data to a temporary file and writes a LOAD DATA LOCAL INFILE statement that refers to the file. The default location of the directory where these files are written is system-specific. To specify a directory explicitly, use the --local-load option.

Because mysqlbinlog converts LOAD DATA INFILE statements to LOAD DATA LOCAL INFILE statements (that is, it adds LOCAL), both the client and the server that you use to process the statements must be configured to allow LOCAL capability.

Warning: The temporary files created for LOAD DATA LOCAL statements are *not* automatically deleted because they are needed until you actually execute those statements. You should delete the temporary files yourself after you no longer need the statement log. The files can be found in the temporary file directory and have names like *original_file_name-#-#*.

In the future, we will fix this problem by allowing `mysqlbinlog` to connect directly to a `mysqld` server. Then it will be possible to safely remove the log files automatically as soon as the `LOAD DATA INFILE` statements have been executed.

Before MySQL 4.1, `mysqlbinlog` could not prepare output suitable for `mysql` if the binary log contained intertwined statements originating from different clients that used temporary tables of the same name. This is fixed in MySQL 4.1.

7.6 `mysqlcc`, the MySQL Control Center

`mysqlcc`, the MySQL Control Center, is a platform-independent client that provides a graphical user interface (GUI) to the MySQL database server. It supports interactive use, including syntax highlighting and tab completion. It provides database and table management, and allows server administration.

`mysqlcc` is not included with MySQL distributions, but can be downloaded separately at `http://dev.mysql.com/downloads/`. Currently, `mysqlcc` runs on Windows and Linux platforms.

Invoke `mysqlcc` by double-clicking its icon in a graphical environment. From the command line, invoke it like this:

```
shell> mysqlcc [options]
```

`mysqlcc` supports the following options:

- `--help` , `-?`

  Display a help message and exit.

- `--blocking_queries` , `-b`

  Use blocking queries.

- `--compress` , `-C`

  Compress all information sent between the client and the server if both support compression.

- `--connection_name=name` , `-c name`

  This option is a synonym for `--server`.

- `--database=db_name` , `-d db_name`

  The database to use. This is useful mainly in an option file.

- `--history_size=#` , `-H #`

  The history size for the query window.

- `--host=host_name`, `-h host_name`

  Connect to the MySQL server on the given host.

- `--local-infile[={0|1}]`

  Enable or disable LOCAL capability for LOAD DATA INFILE. With no value, the option enables LOCAL. It may be given as `--local-infile=0` or `--local-infile=1` to explicitly disable or enable LOCAL. Enabling LOCAL has no effect if the server does not also support it.

- `--password[=password]` , `-p[password]`

  The password to use when connecting to the server. Note that if you use the short option form (-p), you *cannot* have a space between the option and the password. If no password is given on the command line, you will be prompted for one.

- `--plugins_path=name` , `-g name`

  The path to the directory where MySQL Control Center plugins are located.

- `--port=port_num` , `-P port_num`

  The TCP/IP port number to use for the connection.

- `--query` , `-q`

  Open a query window on startup.

- `--register` , `-r`

  Open the Register Server dialog on startup.

- `--server=name` , `-s name`

  The MySQL Control Center connection name.

- `--socket=path` , `-S path`

  The socket file to use for the connection.

- `--syntax` , `-y`

  Enable syntax highlighting and completion.

- `--syntax_file=name` , `-Y name`

  The syntax file for completion.

- `--translations_path=name` , `-T name`

  The path to the directory where MySQL Control Center translations are located.

- `--user=user_name` , `-u user_name`

  The MySQL username to use when connecting to the server.

- `--version` , `-V`

  Display version information and exit.

You can also set the following variables by using `--var_name=value` options:

- `connect_timeout`

  The number of seconds before connection timeout. (Default value is 0.)

- `max_allowed_packet`

  The maximum packet length to send to or receive from the server. (Default value is 16MB.)

- `max_join_size`

  The automatic limit for rows in a join. (Default value is 1,000,000.)

- `net_buffer_length`

  The buffer size for TCP/IP and socket communication. (Default value is 16KB.)

- `select_limit`

  The automatic limit for SELECT statements. (Default value is 1,000.)

It is also possible to set variables by using `--set-variable=var_name=value` or -0 `var_name=value` syntax. However, this syntax is deprecated as of MySQL 4.0.

7.7 The `mysqlcheck` Table Maintenance and Repair Program

The `mysqlcheck` client checks and repairs MyISAM tables. It can also optimize and analyze tables. `mysqlcheck` is available as of MySQL 3.23.38.

`mysqlcheck` is similar in function to `myisamchk`, but works differently. The main operational difference is that `mysqlcheck` must be used when the `mysqld` server is running, whereas `myisamchk` should be used when it is not. The benefit of using `mysqlcheck` is that you do not have to stop the server to check or repair your tables.

`mysqlcheck` uses the SQL statements CHECK TABLE, REPAIR TABLE, ANALYZE TABLE, and OPTIMIZE TABLE in a convenient way for the user. It determines which statements to use for the operation you want to perform, then sends the statements to the server to be executed.

There are three general ways to invoke `mysqlcheck`:

```
shell> mysqlcheck [options] db_name [tables]
shell> mysqlcheck [options] --databases DB1 [DB2 DB3...]
shell> mysqlcheck [options] --all-databases
```

If you don't name any tables or use the `--databases` or `--all-databases` option, entire databases will be checked.

`mysqlcheck` has a special feature compared to the other clients. The default behavior of checking tables (`--check`) can be changed by renaming the binary. If you want to have a tool that repairs tables by default, you should just make a copy of `mysqlcheck` named `mysqlrepair`, or make a symbolic link to `mysqlcheck` named `mysqlrepair`. If you invoke `mysqlrepair`, it will repair tables by default.

The following names can be used to change `mysqlcheck` default behavior:

`mysqlrepair`	The default option will be `--repair`
`mysqlanalyze`	The default option will be `--analyze`
`mysqloptimize`	The default option will be `--optimize`

`mysqlcheck` supports the following options:

- `--help , -?`

  Display a help message and exit.

- `--all-databases , -A`

  Check all tables in all databases. This is the same as using the `--databases` option and naming all the databases on the command line.

- `--all-in-1 , -1`

  Instead of issuing a statement for each table, execute a single statement for each database that names all the tables from that database to be processed.

- `--analyze , -a`

  Analyze the tables.

- `--auto-repair`

  If a checked table is corrupted, automatically fix it. Any necessary repairs are done after all tables have been checked.

- `--character-sets-dir=path`

  The directory where character sets are installed. See Section 4.7.1, "The Character Set Used for Data and Sorting."

- `--check , -c`

  Check the tables for errors.

- `--check-only-changed , -C`

  Check only tables that have changed since the last check or that haven't been closed properly.

- `--compress`

  Compress all information sent between the client and the server if both support compression.

- `--databases , -B`

  Process all tables in the named databases. With this option, all name arguments are regarded as database names, not as table names.

- `--debug[=debug_options] , -# [debug_options]`

  Write a debugging log. The *debug_options* string often is `'d:t:o,file_name'`.

- `--default-character-set=charset`

  Use *charset* as the default character set. See Section 4.7.1, "The Character Set Used for Data and Sorting."

- `--extended` , `-e`

  If you are using this option to check tables, it ensures that they are 100% consistent but will take a long time.

  If you are using this option to repair tables, it runs an extended repair that may not only take a long time to execute, but may produce a lot of garbage rows also!

- `--fast` , `-F`

  Check only tables that haven't been closed properly.

- `--force` , `-f`

  Continue even if an SQL error occurs.

- `--host=host_name` , `-h host_name`

  Connect to the MySQL server on the given host.

- `--medium-check` , `-m`

  Do a check that is faster than an `--extended` operation. This finds only 99.99% of all errors, which should be good enough in most cases.

- `--optimize` , `-o`

  Optimize the tables.

- `--password[=password]` , `-p[password]`

  The password to use when connecting to the server. Note that if you use the short option form (`-p`), you *cannot* have a space between the option and the password. If no password is given on the command line, you will be prompted for one.

- `--port=port_num` , `-P port_num`

  The TCP/IP port number to use for the connection.

- `--protocol={TCP | SOCKET | PIPE | MEMORY}`

  The connection protocol to use. New in MySQL 4.1.

- `--quick` , `-q`

  If you are using this option to check tables, it prevents the check from scanning the rows to check for incorrect links. This is the fastest check method.

  If you are using this option to repair tables, it tries to repair only the index tree. This is the fastest repair method.

- `--repair` , `-r`

  Do a repair that can fix almost anything except unique keys that aren't unique.

- `--silent` , `-s`

  Silent mode. Print only error messages.

- `--socket=`*path* , `-S` *path*

  The socket file to use for the connection.

- `--tables`

  Overrides the `--databases` or `-B` option. All arguments following the option are regarded as table names.

- `--user=`*user_name* , `-u` *user_name*

  The MySQL username to use when connecting to the server.

- `--verbose` , `-v`

  Verbose mode. Print information about the various stages of program operation.

- `--version` , `-V`

  Display version information and exit.

7.8 The `mysqldump` Database Backup Program

The `mysqldump` client can be used to dump a database or a collection of databases for backup or for transferring the data to another SQL server (not necessarily a MySQL server). The dump will contain SQL statements to create the table and/or populate the table.

If you are doing a backup on the server, you should consider using the `mysqlhotcopy` instead. See Section 7.9, "The `mysqlhotcopy` Database Backup Program."

There are three general ways to invoke `mysqldump`:

```
shell> mysqldump [options] db_name [tables]
shell> mysqldump [options] --databases DB1 [DB2 DB3...]
shell> mysqldump [options] --all-databases
```

If you don't name any tables or use the `--databases` or `--all-databases` option, entire databases will be dumped.

To get a list of the options your version of `mysqldump` supports, execute `mysqldump --help`.

If you run `mysqldump` without the `--quick` or `--opt` option, `mysqldump` will load the whole result set into memory before dumping the result. This will probably be a problem if you are dumping a big database. As of MySQL 4.1, `--opt` is on by default, but can be disabled with `--skip-opt`.

If you are using a recent copy of the `mysqldump` program and you are going to generate a dump that will be reloaded into a very old MySQL server, you should not use the `--opt` or `-e` options.

Out-of-range numeric values such as `-inf` and `inf`, as well as NaN (not-a-number) values are dumped by `mysqldump` as `NULL`. You can see this using the following sample table:

```
mysql> CREATE TABLE t (f DOUBLE);
mysql> INSERT INTO t VALUES(1e+111111111111111111111);
mysql> INSERT INTO t VALUES(-1e111111111111111111111);
mysql> SELECT f FROM t;
+------+
| f    |
+------+
|  inf |
| -inf |
+------+
```

For this table, `mysqldump` produces the following data output:

```
--
-- Dumping data for table `t`
--


INSERT INTO t VALUES (NULL);
INSERT INTO t VALUES (NULL);
```

The significance of this behavior is that if you dump and restore the table, the new table has contents that differ from the original contents.

`mysqldump` supports the following options:

- `--help , -?`

  Display a help message and exit.

- `--add-drop-table`

  Add a DROP TABLE statement before each CREATE TABLE statement.

- `--add-locks`

  Surround each table dump with LOCK TABLES and UNLOCK TABLES statements. This results in faster inserts when the dump file is reloaded. See Section 6.2.12, "Speed of INSERT Queries."

- `--all-databases , -A`

  Dump all tables in all databases. This is the same as using the `--databases` option and naming all the databases on the command line.

- `--allow-keywords`

  Allow creation of column names that are keywords. This works by prefixing each column name with the table name.

- `--comments[={0|1}]`

  If set to 0, suppresses additional information in the dump file such as program version, server version, and host. `--skip-comments` has the same effect as `--comments=0`. The default value is 1 to not suppress the extra information. New in MySQL 4.0.17.

- `--compatible=name`

  Produce output that is compatible with other database systems or with older MySQL servers. The value of name can be `mysql323`, `mysql40`, `postgresql`, `oracle`, `mssql`, `db2`, `sapdb`, `no_key_options`, `no_table_options`, or `no_field_options`. To use several values, separate them by commas. These values have the same meaning as the corresponding options for setting the server SQL mode. See Section 4.2.2, "The Server SQL Mode."

  This option requires a server version of 4.1.0 or higher. With older servers, it does nothing.

- `--complete-insert`, `-c`

  Use complete `INSERT` statements that include column names.

- `--compress`, `-C`

  Compress all information sent between the client and the server if both support compression.

- `--create-options`

  Include all MySQL-specific table options in the `CREATE TABLE` statements. Before MySQL 4.1.2, use `--all` instead.

- `--databases`, `-B`

  To dump several databases. Note the difference in usage. In this case, no tables are given. All name arguments on the command line are regarded as database names. A `USE` db_name statement is included in the output before each new database.

- `--debug[=debug_options]`, `-# [debug_options]`

  Write a debugging log. The debug_options string often is `'d:t:o,file_name'`.

- `--default-character-set=charset`

  Use charset as the default character set. See Section 4.7.1, "The Character Set Used for Data and Sorting." If not specified, `mysqldump` from MySQL 4.1.2 or later uses `utf8`; earlier versions use `latin1`.

- `--delayed`

  Insert rows using `INSERT DELAYED` statements.

- `--delete-master-logs`

  On a master replication server, delete the binary logs after performing the dump operation. This option automatically enables `--first-slave`. It was added in MySQL 3.23.57 (for MySQL 3.23) and MySQL 4.0.13 (for MySQL 4.0).

- `--disable-keys`, `-K`

  For each table, surround the `INSERT` statements with `/*!40000 ALTER TABLE tbl_name DISABLE KEYS */;` and `/*!40000 ALTER TABLE tbl_name ENABLE KEYS */;` statements. This makes loading the dump file into a MySQL 4.0 server faster because the indexes are created after all rows are inserted. This option is effective only for `MyISAM` tables.

- `--extended-insert` , `-e`

Use multiple-row INSERT syntax that include several VALUES lists. This results in a smaller dump file and speeds up inserts when the file is reloaded.

- `--fields-terminated-by=...`

  `--fields-enclosed-by=...`

  `--fields-optionally-enclosed-by=...`

  `--fields-escaped-by=...`

  `--lines-terminated-by=...`

These options are used with the -T option and have the same meaning as the corresponding clauses for LOAD DATA INFILE.

- `--first-slave` , `-x`

Locks all tables across all databases.

- `--flush-logs` , `-F`

Flush the MySQL server log files before starting the dump. Note that if you use this option in combination with the --all-databases (or -A) option, the logs are flushed *for each database dumped*.

- `--force` , `-f`

Continue even if an SQL error occurs during a table dump.

- `--host=`*host_name* , `-h` *host_name*

Dump data from the MySQL server on the given host. The default host is localhost.

- `--lock-tables` , `-l`

Lock all tables before starting the dump. The tables are locked with READ LOCAL to allow concurrent inserts in the case of MyISAM tables.

Please note that when dumping multiple databases, --lock-tables locks tables for each database separately. So, using this option will not guarantee that the tables in the dump file will be logically consistent between databases. Tables in different databases may be dumped in completely different states.

- `--master-data`

This option is like --first-slave, but also produces CHANGE MASTER TO statements that will make your slave server start from the correct position in the master's binary logs if you use this SQL dump of the master to set up the slave.

- `--no-create-db` , `-n`

This option suppresses the CREATE DATABASE /*!32312 IF NOT EXISTS*/ *db_name* statements that are otherwise included in the output if the --databases or --all-databases option is given.

- `--no-create-info` , `-t`

Don't write CREATE TABLE statements that re-create each dumped table.

- `--no-data , -d`

  Don't write any row information for the table. This is very useful if you just want to get a dump of the structure for a table.

- `--opt`

  This option is shorthand; it is the same as specifying `--quick --add-drop-table` `--add-locks --create-options --disable-keys --extended-insert --lock-tables`. It should give you a fast dump operation and produce a dump file that can be reloaded into a MySQL server quickly. As of MySQL 4.1, `--opt` is on by default, but can be disabled with `--skip-opt`. To disable only certain of the options enabled by `--opt`, use their `--skip` forms; for example, `--skip-add-drop-table` or `--skip-quick`.

- `--password[=password] , -p[password]`

  The password to use when connecting to the server. Note that if you use the short option form (`-p`), you *cannot* have a space between the option and the password. If no password is given on the command line, you will be prompted for one.

- `--port=port_num , -P port_num`

  The TCP/IP port number to use for the connection.

- `--protocol={TCP | SOCKET | PIPE | MEMORY}`

  The connection protocol to use. New in MySQL 4.1.

- `--quick , -q`

  This option is useful for dumping large tables. It forces `mysqldump` to retrieve rows for a table from the server a row at a time rather than retrieving the entire row set and buffering it in memory before writing it out.

- `--quote-names , -Q`

  Quote database, table, and column names within '`'` characters. If the server SQL mode includes the `ANSI_QUOTES` option, names are quoted within '"' characters. As of MySQL 4.1.1, `--quote-names` is on by default, but can be disabled with `--skip-quote-names`.

- `--result-file=file , -r file`

  Direct output to a given file. This option should be used on Windows, because it prevents newline '\n' characters from being converted to '\r\n' carriage return/newline sequences.

- `--single-transaction`

  This option issues a `BEGIN` SQL statement before dumping data from the server. It is mostly useful with `InnoDB` tables and `READ COMMITTED` transaction isolation level, because in this mode it will dump the consistent state of the database at the time when `BEGIN` was issued without blocking any applications.

  When using this option, you should keep in mind that only transactional tables will be dumped in a consistent state. For example, any `MyISAM` or `HEAP` tables dumped while using this option may still change state.

The `--single-transaction` option was added in version 4.0.2. This option is mutually exclusive with the `--lock-tables` option, because LOCK TABLES causes any pending transactions to be committed implicitly.

- `--socket=path`, `-S path`

The socket file to use when connecting to localhost (which is the default host).

- `--skip-comments`

See the description for the `--comments` option.

- `--tab=path`, `-T path`

Produces tab-separated data files. For each dumped table, mysqldump creates a `tbl_name.sql` file that contains the CREATE TABLE statement that creates the table, and a `tbl_name.txt` file that contains its data. The option value is the directory in which to write the files.

By default, the `.txt` data files are formatted using tab characters between column values and a newline at the end of each line. The format can be specified explicitly using the `--fields-xxx` and `--lines--xxx` options.

Note: This option should be used only when mysqldump is run on the same machine as the mysqld server. You must use a MySQL account that has the FILE privilege, and the server must have permission to write files in the directory you specify.

- `--tables`

Overrides the `--databases` or `-B` option. All arguments following the option are regarded as table names.

- `--user=user_name`, `-u user_name`

The MySQL username to use when connecting to the server.

- `--verbose`, `-v`

Verbose mode. Print out more information on what the program does.

- `--version`, `-V`

Display version information and exit.

- `--where='where-condition'`, `-w 'where-condition'`

Dump only records selected by the given WHERE condition. Note that quotes around the condition are mandatory if it contains spaces or characters that are special to your command interpreter.

Examples:

```
"--where=user='jimf'"
"-wuserid>1"
"-wuserid<1"
```

- `--xml`, `-X`

Write dump output as well-formed XML.

You can also set the following variables by using *--var_name=value* options:

- `max_allowed_packet`

  The maximum size of the buffer for client/server communication. The value of the variable can be up to 16MB before MySQL 4.0, and up to 1GB from MySQL 4.0 on. When creating multiple-row-insert statements (as with option `--extended-insert` or `--opt`), `mysqldump` will create rows up to `max_allowed_packet` length. If you increase this variable, you should also ensure that the `max_allowed_packet` variable in the MySQL server is at least this large.

- `net_buffer_length`

  The initial size of the buffer for client/server communication.

It is also possible to set variables by using `--set-variable=`*var_name=value* or -O *var_name=value* syntax. However, this syntax is deprecated as of MySQL 4.0.

The most common use of `mysqldump` is probably for making a backup of entire databases.

```
shell> mysqldump --opt db_name > backup-file.sql
```

You can read the dump file back into the server with:

```
shell> mysql db_name < backup-file.sql
```

Or:

```
shell> mysql -e "source /path-to-backup/backup-file.sql" db_name
```

`mysqldump` is also very useful for populating databases by copying data from one MySQL server to another:

```
shell> mysqldump --opt db_name | mysql --host=remote-host -C db_name
```

It is possible to dump several databases with one command:

```
shell> mysqldump --databases db_name1 [db_name2 ...] > my_databases.sql
```

If you want to dump all databases, use the `--all-databases` option:

```
shell> mysqldump --all-databases > all_databases.sql
```

For more information on making backups, see Section 4.6.1, "Database Backups."

7.9 The `mysqlhotcopy` Database Backup Program

`mysqlhotcopy` is a Perl script that uses LOCK TABLES, FLUSH TABLES, and cp or scp to quickly make a backup of a database. It's the fastest way to make a backup of the database or single tables, but it can be run only on the same machine where the database directories are located. `mysqlhotcopy` works only for backing up `MyISAM` and `ISAM` tables. It runs on Unix, and on NetWare as of MySQL 4.0.18.

```
shell> mysqlhotcopy db_name [/path/to/new_directory]
```

```
shell> mysqlhotcopy db_name_1 ... db_name_n /path/to/new_directory
```

```
shell> mysqlhotcopy db_name./regex/
```

`mysqlhotcopy` supports the following options:

- `--help` , `-?`

  Display a help message and exit.

- `--allowold`

  Don't abort if target already exists (rename it by adding an `_old` suffix).

- `--checkpoint=db_name.tbl_name`

  Insert checkpoint entries into the specified `db_name.tbl_name`.

- `--debug`

  Enable debug output.

- `--dryrun` , `-n`

  Report actions without doing them.

- `--flushlog`

  Flush logs after all tables are locked.

- `--keepold`

  Don't delete previous (now renamed) target when done.

- `--method=#`

  Method for copy (`cp` or `scp`).

- `--noindices`

  Don't include full index files in the backup. This makes the backup smaller and faster. The indexes can be reconstructed later with `myisamchk -rq` or `isamchk -rq`.

- `--password=password` , `-ppassword`

  The password to use when connecting to the server. Note that the password value is not optional for this option, unlike for other MySQL clients.

- `--port=port_num` , `-P port_num`

  The TCP/IP port number to use when connecting to the local server.

- `--quiet` , `-q`

  Be silent except for errors.

- `--regexp=expr`

  Copy all databases with names matching the given regular expression.

- `--socket=`*path* , `-S` *path*

  The Unix socket file to use for the connection.

- `--suffix=`*str*

  The suffix for names of copied databases.

- `--tmpdir=`*path*

  The temporary directory (instead of `/tmp`).

- `--user=`*user_name* , `-u` *user_name*

  The MySQL username to use when connecting to the server.

`mysqlhotcopy` reads the `[client]` and `[mysqlhotcopy]` option groups from option files.

To execute `mysqlhotcopy`, you must have access to the files for the tables that you are backing up, the `SELECT` privilege for those tables, and the `RELOAD` privilege (to be able to execute `FLUSH TABLES`).

Use `perldoc` for additional `mysqlhotcopy` documentation:

```
shell> perldoc mysqlhotcopy
```

7.10 The `mysqlimport` Data Import Program

The `mysqlimport` client provides a command-line interface to the `LOAD DATA INFILE` SQL statement. Most options to `mysqlimport` correspond directly to clauses of `LOAD DATA INFILE`.

Invoke `mysqlimport` like this:

```
shell> mysqlimport [options] db_name textfile1 [textfile2 ...]
```

For each text file named on the command line, `mysqlimport` strips any extension from the filename and uses the result to determine the name of the table into which to import the file's contents. For example, files named `patient.txt`, `patient.text`, and `patient` all would be imported into a table named `patient`.

`mysqlimport` supports the following options:

- `--help` , `-?`

  Display a help message and exit.

- `--columns=`*column_list* , `-c` *column_list*

  This option takes a comma-separated list of column names as its value. The order of the column names indicates how to match up data file columns with table columns.

- `--compress` , `-C`

  Compress all information sent between the client and the server if both support compression.

- `--debug[=debug_options]` , `-# [debug_options]`

  Write a debugging log. The *debug_options* string often is `'d:t:o,file_name'`.

- `--delete` , `-D`

  Empty the table before importing the text file.

- `--fields-terminated-by=...`

  `--fields-enclosed-by=...`

  `--fields-optionally-enclosed-by=...`

  `--fields-escaped-by=...`

  `--lines-terminated-by=...`

  These options have the same meaning as the corresponding clauses for LOAD DATA
  INFILE.

- `--force` , `-f`

  Ignore errors. For example, if a table for a text file doesn't exist, continue processing
  any remaining files. Without `--force`, `mysqlimport` exits if a table doesn't exist.

- `--host=host_name` , `-h host_name`

  Import data to the MySQL server on the given host. The default host is `localhost`.

- `--ignore` , `-i`

  See the description for the `--replace` option.

- `--ignore-lines=n`

  Ignore the first *n* lines of the data file.

- `--local` , `-L`

  Read input files from the client. By default, text files are assumed to be on the server if
  you connect to `localhost` (which is the default host).

- `--lock-tables` , `-l`

  Lock *all* tables for writing before processing any text files. This ensures that all tables
  are synchronized on the server.

- `--password[=password]` , `-p[password]`

  The password to use when connecting to the server. Note that if you use the short
  option form (`-p`), you *cannot* have a space between the option and the password. If no
  password is given on the command line, you will be prompted for one.

- `--port=port_num` , `-P port_num`

  The TCP/IP port number to use for the connection.

- `--protocol={TCP | SOCKET | PIPE | MEMORY}`

  The connection protocol to use. New in MySQL 4.1.

- `--replace , -r`

  The `--replace` and `--ignore` options control handling of input records that duplicate existing records on unique key values. If you specify `--replace`, new rows replace existing rows that have the same unique key value. If you specify `--ignore`, input rows that duplicate an existing row on a unique key value are skipped. If you don't specify either option, an error occurs when a duplicate key value is found, and the rest of the text file is ignored.

- `--silent , -s`

  Silent mode. Produce output only when errors occur.

- `--socket=path , -S path`

  The socket file to use when connecting to `localhost` (which is the default host).

- `--user=user_name , -u user_name`

  The MySQL username to use when connecting to the server.

- `--verbose , -v`

  Verbose mode. Print out more information what the program does.

- `--version , -V`

  Display version information and exit.

Here is a sample session that demonstrates use of `mysqlimport`:

```
shell> mysql -e 'CREATE TABLE imptest(id INT, n VARCHAR(30))' test
shell> ed
a
100     Max Sydow
101     Count Dracula
.
w imptest.txt
32
q
shell> od -c imptest.txt
0000000   1   0   0  \t   M   a   x       S   y   d   o   w  \n   1   0
0000020   1  \t   C   o   u   n   t       D   r   a   c   u   l   a  \n
0000040
shell> mysqlimport --local test imptest.txt
test.imptest: Records: 2  Deleted: 0  Skipped: 0  Warnings: 0
shell> mysql -e 'SELECT * FROM imptest' test
+------+---------------+
| id   | n             |
+------+---------------+
|  100 | Max Sydow     |
|  101 | Count Dracula |
+------+---------------+
```

7.11 mysqlshow, **Showing Databases, Tables, and Columns**

The mysqlshow client can be used to quickly look at which databases exist, their tables, and a table's columns or indexes.

mysqlshow provides a command-line interface to several SQL SHOW statements. The same information can be obtained by using those statements directly. For example, you can issue them from the mysql client program.

Invoke mysqlshow like this:

shell> **mysqlshow** [*options*] [*db_name* [*tbl_name* [*col_name*]]]

- If no database is given, all matching databases are shown.
- If no table is given, all matching tables in the database are shown.
- If no column is given, all matching columns and column types in the table are shown.

Note that in newer MySQL versions, you see only those database, tables, or columns for which you have some privileges.

If the last argument contains shell or SQL wildcard characters ('*', '?', '%', or '_'), only those names that are matched by the wildcard are shown. If a database name contains any underscores, those should be escaped with a backslash (some Unix shells will require two) in order to get a list of the proper tables or columns. '*' and '?' characters are converted into SQL '%' and '_' wildcard characters. This might cause some confusion when you try to display the columns for a table with a '_' in the name, because in this case mysqlshow shows you only the table names that match the pattern. This is easily fixed by adding an extra '%' last on the command line as a separate argument.

mysqlshow supports the following options:

- --help , -?

  Display a help message and exit.

- --character-sets-dir=*path*

  The directory where character sets are installed. See Section 4.7.1, "The Character Set Used for Data and Sorting."

- --compress , -C

  Compress all information sent between the client and the server if both support compression.

- --debug[=*debug_options*] , -# [*debug_options*]

  Write a debugging log. The *debug_options* string often is 'd:t:o,*file_name*'.

- --default-character-set=*charset*

  Use *charset* as the default character set. See Section 4.7.1, "The Character Set Used for Data and Sorting."

- --host=*host_name* , -h *host_name*

  Connect to the MySQL server on the given host.

- --keys , -k

  Show table indexes.

- --password[=*password*] , -p[*password*]

  The password to use when connecting to the server. Note that if you use the short option form (-p), you *cannot* have a space between the option and the password. If no password is given on the command line, you will be prompted for one.

- --port=*port_num* , -P *port_num*

  The TCP/IP port number to use for the connection.

- --protocol={TCP | SOCKET | PIPE | MEMORY}

  The connection protocol to use. New in MySQL 4.1.

- --socket=*path* , -S *path*

  The socket file to use when connecting to localhost (which is the default host).

- --status , -i

  Display extra information about each table.

- --user=*user_name* , -u *user_name*

  The MySQL username to use when connecting to the server.

- --verbose , -v

  Verbose mode. Print out more information what the program does. This option can be used multiple times to increase the amount of information.

- --version , -V

  Display version information and exit.

7.12 perror, Explaining Error Codes

For most system errors, MySQL displays, in addition to an internal text message, the system error code in one of the following styles:

```
message ... (errno: #)
message ... (Errcode: #)
```

You can find out what the error code means by either examining the documentation for your system or by using the perror utility.

`perror` prints a description for a system error code or for a storage engine (table handler) error code.

Invoke `perror` like this:

```
shell> perror [options] errorcode ...
```

Example:

```
shell> perror 13 64
Error code  13:  Permission denied
Error code  64:  Machine is not on the network
```

Note that the meaning of system error messages may be dependent on your operating system. A given error code may mean different things on different operating systems.

7.13 The `replace` String-Replacement Utility

The `replace` utility program changes strings in place in files or on the standard input. It uses a finite state machine to match longer strings first. It can be used to swap strings. For example, the following command swaps a and b in the given files, `file1` and `file2`:

```
shell> replace a b b a -- file1 file2 ...
```

Use the `--` option to indicate where the string-replacement list ends and the filenames begin.

Any file named on the command line is modified in place, so you may want to make a copy of the original before converting it.

If no files are named on the command line, `replace` reads the standard input and writes to the standard output. In this case, no `--` option is needed.

The `replace` program is used by `msql2mysql`.

`replace` supports the following options:

- `-?` , `-I`

    Display a help message and exit.

- `-# debug_options`

    Write a debugging log. The *debug_options* string often is `'d:t:o,file_name'`.

- `-s`

    Silent mode. Print out less information what the program does.

- `-v`

    Verbose mode. Print out more information what the program does.

- `-V`

    Display version information and exit.

8

MySQL Storage Engines and Table Types

MySQL supports several storage engines that act as handlers for different table types. MySQL storage engines include both those that handle transaction-safe tables and those that handle non-transaction-safe tables:

- The original storage engine was ISAM, which managed non-transactional tables. This engine has been replaced by MyISAM and should no longer be used. It is deprecated in MySQL 4.1, and will be removed in MySQL 5.0.

- In MySQL 3.23.0, the MyISAM and HEAP storage engines were introduced. MyISAM is an improved replacement for ISAM. The HEAP storage engine provides in-memory tables. The MERGE storage engine was added in MySQL 3.23.25. It allows a collection of identical MyISAM tables to be handled as a single table. All three of these storage engines handle non-transactional tables, and all are included in MySQL by default. Note that the HEAP storage engine now is known as the MEMORY engine.

- The InnoDB and BDB storage engines that handle transaction-safe tables were introduced in later versions of MySQL 3.23. Both are available in source distributions as of MySQL 3.23.34a. BDB is included in MySQL-Max binary distributions on those operating systems that support it. InnoDB also is included in MySQL-Max binary distributions for MySQL 3.23. Beginning with MySQL 4.0, InnoDB is included by default in all MySQL binary distributions. In source distributions, you can enable or disable either engine by configuring MySQL as you like.

This chapter describes each of the MySQL storage engines except for InnoDB, which is covered in Chapter 9, "The InnoDB Storage Engine."

When you create a new table, you can tell MySQL what type of table to create by adding an ENGINE or TYPE table option to the CREATE TABLE statement:

```
CREATE TABLE t (i INT) ENGINE = INNODB;
CREATE TABLE t (i INT) TYPE = MEMORY;
```

ENGINE is the preferred term, but cannot be used before MySQL 4.0.18. TYPE is available beginning with MySQL 3.23.0, the first version of MySQL for which multiple storage engines were available.

If you omit the ENGINE or TYPE option, the default table type is usually MyISAM. This can be changed by setting the table_type system variable.

To convert a table from one type to another, use an ALTER TABLE statement that indicates the new type:

```
ALTER TABLE t ENGINE = MYISAM;
ALTER TABLE t TYPE = BDB;
```

If you try to use a storage engine that is not compiled in or that is compiled in but deactivated, MySQL instead creates a table of type MyISAM. This behavior is convenient when you want to copy tables between MySQL servers that support different storage engines. (For example, in a replication setup, perhaps your master server supports transactional storage engines for increased safety, but the slave servers use only non-transactional storage engines for greater speed.)

This automatic substitution of the MyISAM table type when an unavailable type is specified can be confusing for new MySQL users. In MySQL 4.1 and up, a warning is generated when a table type is automatically changed.

MySQL always creates an .frm file to hold the table and column definitions. The table's index and data may be stored in one or more other files, depending on the table type. The server creates the .frm file above the storage engine level. Individual storage engines create any additional files required for the tables that they manage.

A database may contain tables of different types.

Transaction-safe tables (TSTs) have several advantages over non-transaction-safe tables (NTSTs):

- Safer. Even if MySQL crashes or you get hardware problems, you can get your data back, either by automatic recovery or from a backup plus the transaction log.
- You can combine many statements and accept them all at the same time with the COMMIT statement (if autocommit is disabled).
- You can execute ROLLBACK to ignore your changes (if autocommit is disabled).
- If an update fails, all your changes will be restored. (With non-transaction-safe tables, all changes that have taken place are permanent.)
- Transaction-safe storage engines can provide better concurrency for tables that get many updates concurrently with reads.

Note that to use the InnoDB storage engine in MySQL 3.23, you must configure at least the innodb_data_file_path startup option. In 4.0 and up, InnoDB uses default configuration values if you specify none. See Section 9.4, "InnoDB Configuration."

Non-transaction-safe tables have several advantages of their own, all of which occur because there is no transaction overhead:

- Much faster
- Lower disk space requirements
- Less memory required to perform updates

You can combine transaction-safe and non-transaction-safe tables in the same statements to get the best of both worlds. However, within a transaction with autocommit disabled, changes to non-transaction-safe tables still are committed immediately and cannot be rolled back.

8.1 The MyISAM Storage Engine

MyISAM is the default storage engine as of MySQL 3.23. It is based on the ISAM code but has many useful extensions.

Each MyISAM table is stored on disk in three files. The files have names that begin with the table name and have an extension to indicate the file type. An .frm file stores the table definition. The data file has an .MYD (MYData) extension. The index file has an .MYI (MYIndex) extension,

To specify explicitly that you want a MyISAM table, indicate that with an ENGINE or TYPE table option:

```
CREATE TABLE t (i INT) ENGINE = MYISAM;
CREATE TABLE t (i INT) TYPE = MYISAM;
```

Normally, the ENGINE or TYPE option is unnecessary; MyISAM is the default storage engine unless the default has been changed.

You can check or repair MyISAM tables with the myisamchk utility. See Section 4.6.2.7, "Using myisamchk for Crash Recovery." You can compress MyISAM tables with myisampack to take up much less space. See Section 7.2, "myisampack, the MySQL Compressed Read-Only Table Generator."

The following characteristics of the MyISAM storage engine are improvements over the older ISAM engine:

- All data values are stored with the low byte first. This makes the data machine and operating system independent. The only requirement for binary portability is that the machine uses two's-complement signed integers (as every machine for the last 20 years has) and IEEE floating-point format (also totally dominant among mainstream machines). The only area of machines that may not support binary compatibility are embedded systems, which sometimes have peculiar processors.

There is no big speed penalty for storing data low byte first; the bytes in a table row normally are unaligned and it doesn't take that much more power to read an unaligned byte in order than in reverse order. Also, the code in the server that fetches column values is not time critical compared to other code.

- Large files (up to 63-bit file length) are supported on filesystems and operating systems that support large files.

- Dynamic-sized rows are much less fragmented when mixing deletes with updates and inserts. This is done by automatically combining adjacent deleted blocks and by extending blocks if the next block is deleted.

- The maximum number of indexes per table is 64 (32 before MySQL 4.1.2). This can be changed by recompiling. The maximum number of columns per index is 16.

- The maximum key length is 1000 bytes (500 before MySQL 4.1.2). This can be changed by recompiling. For the case of a key longer than 250 bytes, a larger key block size than the default of 1024 bytes is used.

- BLOB and TEXT columns can be indexed.

- NULL values are allowed in indexed columns. This takes 0-1 bytes per key.

- All numeric key values are stored with the high byte first to allow better index compression.

- Index files are usually much smaller with MyISAM than with ISAM. This means that MyISAM normally will use less system resources than ISAM, but will need more CPU time when inserting data into a compressed index.

- When records are inserted in sorted order (as when you are using an AUTO_INCREMENT column), the index tree is split so that the high node only contains one key. This improves space utilization in the index tree.

- Internal handling of one AUTO_INCREMENT column per table. MyISAM automatically updates this column for INSERT/UPDATE. This makes AUTO_INCREMENT columns faster (at least 10%). Values at the top of the sequence are not reused after being deleted as they are with ISAM. (When an AUTO_INCREMENT column is defined as the last column of a multiple-column index, reuse of deleted values does occur.) The AUTO_INCREMENT value can be reset with ALTER TABLE or myisamchk.

- If a table doesn't have free blocks in the middle of the data file, you can INSERT new rows into it at the same time that other threads are reading from the table. (These are known as concurrent inserts.) A free block can occur as a result of deleting rows or an update of a dynamic length row with more data than its current contents. When all free blocks are used up (filled in), future inserts become concurrent again.

- You can put the data file and index file on different directories to get more speed with the DATA DIRECTORY and INDEX DIRECTORY table options to CREATE TABLE.

- As of MySQL 4.1, each character column can have a different character set.

- There is a flag in the `MyISAM` index file that indicates whether the table was closed correctly. If `mysqld` is started with the `--myisam-recover` option, `MyISAM` tables are automatically checked (and optionally repaired) when opened if the table wasn't closed properly.

- `myisamchk` marks tables as checked if you run it with the `--update-state` option. `myisamchk --fast` checks only those tables that don't have this mark.

- `myisamchk --analyze` stores statistics for key parts, not only for whole keys as in `ISAM`.

- `myisampack` can pack `BLOB` and `VARCHAR` columns; `pack_isam` cannot.

`MyISAM` also supports the following features, which MySQL will be able to use in the near future:

- Support for a true `VARCHAR` type; a `VARCHAR` column starts with a length stored in two bytes.

- Tables with `VARCHAR` may have fixed or dynamic record length.

- `VARCHAR` and `CHAR` columns may be up to 64KB.

- A hashed computed index can be used for `UNIQUE`. This will allow you to have `UNIQUE` on any combination of columns in a table. (You can't search on a `UNIQUE` computed index, however.)

8.1.1 MyISAM **Startup Options**

The following options to `mysqld` can be used to change the behavior of `MyISAM` tables:

- `--myisam-recover=mode`

  Set the mode for automatic recovery of crashed `MyISAM` tables.

- `--delay-key-write=ALL`

  Don't flush key buffers between writes for any `MyISAM` table.

  Note: If you do this, you should not use `MyISAM` tables from another program (such as from another MySQL server or with `myisamchk`) when the table is in use. Doing so will lead to index corruption.

  Using `--external-locking` will not help for tables that use `--delay-key-write`.

See Section 4.2.1, "`mysqld` Command-Line Options."

The following system variables affect the behavior of `MyISAM` tables:

- `bulk_insert_buffer_size`

  The size of the tree cache used in bulk insert optimization. **Note:** This is a limit *per thread*!

- `myisam_max_extra_sort_file_size`

  Used to help MySQL to decide when to use the slow but safe key cache index creation method. **Note:** This parameter is given in megabytes before MySQL 4.0.3, and in bytes as of 4.0.3.

- `myisam_max_sort_file_size`

  Don't use the fast sort index method to create an index if the temporary file would become larger than this. **Note:** This parameter is given in megabytes before MySQL 4.0.3, and in bytes as of 4.0.3.

- `myisam_sort_buffer_size`

  Set the size of the buffer used when recovering tables.

See Section 4.2.3, "Server System Variables."

Automatic recovery is activated if you start `mysqld` with the `--myisam-recover` option. In this case, when the server opens a `MyISAM` table, it checks whether the table is marked as crashed or whether the open count variable for the table is not 0 and you are running the server with `--skip-external-locking`. If either of these conditions is true, the following happens:

- The table is checked for errors.
- If the server finds an error, it tries to do a fast table repair (with sorting and without re-creating the data file).
- If the repair fails because of an error in the data file (for example, a duplicate-key error), the server tries again, this time re-creating the data file.
- If the repair still fails, the server tries once more with the old repair option method (write row by row without sorting). This method should be able to repair any type of error and has low disk space requirements.

If the recovery wouldn't be able to recover all rows from a previous completed statement and you didn't specify FORCE in the value of the `--myisam-recover` option, automatic repair aborts with an error message in the error log:

```
Error: Couldn't repair table: test.g00pages
```

If you specify FORCE, a warning like this is written instead:

```
Warning: Found 344 of 354 rows when repairing ./test/g00pages
```

Note that if the automatic recovery value includes BACKUP, the recovery process creates files with names of the form *tbl_name-datetime*.BAK. You should have a `cron` script that automatically moves these files from the database directories to backup media.

8.1.2 Space Needed for Keys

`MyISAM` tables use B-tree indexes. You can roughly calculate the size for the index file as `(key_length+4)/0.67`, summed over all keys. This is for the worst case when all keys are inserted in sorted order and the table doesn't have any compressed keys.

String indexes are space compressed. If the first index part is a string, it will also be prefix compressed. Space compression makes the index file smaller than the worst-case figure if the string column has a lot of trailing space or is a VARCHAR column that is not always used to the full length. Prefix compression is used on keys that start with a string. Prefix compression helps if there are many strings with an identical prefix.

In MyISAM tables, you can also prefix compress numbers by specifying PACK_KEYS=1 when you create the table. This helps when you have many integer keys that have an identical prefix when the numbers are stored high-byte first.

8.1.3 MyISAM Table Storage Formats

MyISAM supports three different storage formats. Two of them (fixed and dynamic format) are chosen automatically depending on the type of columns you are using. The third, compressed format, can be created only with the myisampack utility.

When you CREATE or ALTER a table that has no BLOB or TEXT columns, you can force the table format to FIXED or DYNAMIC with the ROW_FORMAT table option. This causes CHAR and VARCHAR columns to become CHAR for FIXED format or VARCHAR for DYNAMIC format.

In the future, you will be able to compress or decompress tables by specifying ROW_FORMAT={COMPRESSED | DEFAULT} to ALTER TABLE.

8.1.3.1 Static (Fixed-Length) Table Characteristics

Static format is the default for MyISAM tables. It is used when the table contains no variable-length columns (VARCHAR, BLOB, or TEXT). Each row is stored using a fixed number of bytes.

Of the three MyISAM storage formats, static format is the simplest and most secure (least subject to corruption). It is also the fastest of the on-disk formats. The speed comes from the easy way that rows in the data file can be found on disk: When looking up a row based on a row number in the index, multiply the row number by the row length. Also, when scanning a table, it is very easy to read a constant number of records with each disk read operation.

The security is evidenced if your computer crashes while the MySQL server is writing to a fixed-format MyISAM file. In this case, myisamchk can easily determine where each row starts and ends, so it can usually reclaim all records except the partially written one. Note that MyISAM table indexes can always be reconstructed based on the data rows.

General characteristics of static format tables:

- All CHAR, NUMERIC, and DECIMAL columns are space-padded to the column width.
- Very quick.
- Easy to cache.
- Easy to reconstruct after a crash, because records are located in fixed positions.
- Reorganization is unnecessary unless you delete a huge number of records and want to return free disk space to the operating system. To do this, use OPTIMIZE TABLE or myisamchk -r.
- Usually require more disk space than for dynamic-format tables.

8.1.3.2 Dynamic Table Characteristics

Dynamic storage format is used if a MyISAM table contains any variable-length columns (VARCHAR, BLOB, or TEXT), or if the table was created with the ROW_FORMAT=DYNAMIC option.

This format is a little more complex because each row has a header that indicates how long it is. One record can also end up at more than one location when it is made longer as a result of an update.

You can use OPTIMIZE TABLE or myisamchk to defragment a table. If you have fixed-length columns that you access or change frequently in a table that also contains some variable-length columns, it might be a good idea to move the variable-length columns to other tables just to avoid fragmentation.

General characteristics of dynamic-format tables:

- All string columns are dynamic except those with a length less than four.
- Each record is preceded by a bitmap that indicates which columns contain the empty string (for string columns) or zero (for numeric columns). Note that this does not include columns that contain NULL values. If a string column has a length of zero after trailing space removal, or a numeric column has a value of zero, it is marked in the bitmap and not saved to disk. Non-empty strings are saved as a length byte plus the string contents.
- Much less disk space usually is required than for fixed-length tables.
- Each record uses only as much space as is required. However, if a record becomes larger, it is split into as many pieces as are required, resulting in record fragmentation. For example, if you update a row with information that extends the row length, the row will be fragmented. In this case, you may have to run OPTIMIZE TABLE or myisamchk -r from time to time to get better performance. Use myisamchk -ei to obtain table statistics.
- More difficult than static-format tables to reconstruct after a crash, because a record may be fragmented into many pieces and a link (fragment) may be missing.
- The expected row length for dynamic-sized records is calculated using the following expression:

```
3
+ (number of columns + 7) / 8
+ (number of char columns)
+ (packed size of numeric columns)
+ (length of strings)
+ (number of NULL columns + 7) / 8
```

There is a penalty of 6 bytes for each link. A dynamic record is linked whenever an update causes an enlargement of the record. Each new link will be at least 20 bytes, so the next enlargement will probably go in the same link. If not, there will be another link. You may check how many links there are with myisamchk -ed. All links may be removed with myisamchk -r.

8.1.3.3 Compressed Table Characteristics

Compressed storage format is a read-only format that is generated with the myisampack tool.

All MySQL distributions as of version 3.23.19 include myisampack by default. (This version is when MySQL was placed under the GPL.) For earlier versions, myisampack was included only with licenses or support agreements, but the server still can read tables that were compressed with myisampack. Compressed tables can be uncompressed with myisamchk. (For the ISAM storage engine, compressed tables can be created with pack_isam and uncompressed with isamchk.)

Compressed tables have the following characteristics:

- Compressed tables take very little disk space. This minimizes disk usage, which is very nice when using slow disks (such as CD-ROMs).
- Each record is compressed separately, so there is very little access overhead. The header for a record is fixed (1-3 bytes) depending on the biggest record in the table. Each column is compressed differently. There is usually a different Huffman tree for each column. Some of the compression types are:
  - Suffix space compression.
  - Prefix space compression.
  - Numbers with a value of zero are stored using one bit.
  - If values in an integer column have a small range, the column is stored using the smallest possible type. For example, a BIGINT column (eight bytes) can be stored as a TINYINT column (one byte) if all its values are in the range from -128 to 127.
  - If a column has only a small set of possible values, the column type is converted to ENUM.
  - A column may use a combination of the preceding compressions.
- Can handle fixed-length or dynamic-length records.

8.1.4 MyISAM Table Problems

The file format that MySQL uses to store data has been extensively tested, but there are always circumstances that may cause database tables to become corrupted.

8.1.4.1 Corrupted MyISAM Tables

Even though the MyISAM table format is very reliable (all changes to a table made by an SQL statement are written before the statement returns), you can still get corrupted tables if some of the following things happen:

- The mysqld process is killed in the middle of a write.
- Unexpected computer shutdown occurs (for example, the computer is turned off).
- Hardware errors.

- You are using an external program (such as `myisamchk`) on a table that is being modified by the server at the same time.
- A software bug in the MySQL or `MyISAM` code.

Typical symptoms for a corrupt table are:

- You get the following error while selecting data from the table:

```
Incorrect key file for table: '...'. Try to repair it
```

- Queries don't find rows in the table or return incomplete data.

You can check whether a `MyISAM` table is okay with the CHECK TABLE statement. You can repair a corrupted `MyISAM` table with REPAIR TABLE. When `mysqld` is not running, you can also check or repair a table with the `myisamchk` command. See Section 4.6.2.1, "`myisamchk` Invocation Syntax."

If your tables become corrupted frequently, you should try to determine why this is happening. The most important thing to know is whether the table became corrupted as a result of a server crash. You can verify this easily by looking for a recent `restarted mysqld` message in the error log. If there is such a message, it is likely that that table corruption is a result of the server dying. Otherwise, corruption may have occurred during normal operation, which is a bug. You should try to create a reproducible test case that demonstrates the problem. See Section A.4.2, "What to Do If MySQL Keeps Crashing."

8.1.4.2 Problems from Tables Not Being Closed Properly

Each `MyISAM` index (`.MYI`) file has a counter in the header that can be used to check whether a table has been closed properly. If you get the following warning from CHECK TABLE or `myisamchk`, it means that this counter has gone out of sync:

```
clients are using or haven't closed the table properly
```

This warning doesn't necessarily mean that the table is corrupted, but you should at least check the table to verify that it's okay.

The counter works as follows:

- The first time a table is updated in MySQL, a counter in the header of the index files is incremented.
- The counter is not changed during further updates.
- When the last instance of a table is closed (because of a FLUSH TABLES operation or because there isn't room in the table cache), the counter is decremented if the table has been updated at any point.
- When you repair the table or check the table and it is found to be okay, the counter is reset to zero.
- To avoid problems with interaction with other processes that might check the table, the counter is not decremented on close if it was zero.

In other words, the counter can go out of sync only under these conditions:

- The MyISAM tables are copied without a preceding LOCK TABLES and FLUSH TABLES.
- MySQL has crashed between an update and the final close. (Note that the table may still be okay, because MySQL always issues writes for everything between each statement.)
- A table was modified by myisamchk --recover or myisamchk --update-state at the same time that it was in use by mysqld.
- Many mysqld servers are using the table and one server performed a REPAIR TABLE or CHECK TABLE on the table while it was in use by another server. In this setup, it is safe to use CHECK TABLE, although you might get the warning from other servers. However, REPAIR TABLE should be avoided because when one server replaces the data file with a new one, this is not signaled to the other servers.

In general, it is a bad idea to share a data directory among multiple servers. See Section 4.9, "Running Multiple MySQL Servers on the Same Machine," for additional discussion.

8.2 The MERGE Storage Engine

The MERGE storage engine was introduced in MySQL 3.23.25. It is also known as the MRG_MyISAM engine. The code is now reasonably stable.

A MERGE table is a collection of identical MyISAM tables that can be used as one. "Identical" means that all tables have identical column and index information. You can't merge tables in which the columns are packed differently, don't have exactly the same columns, or have the indexes in different order. However, any or all of the tables can be compressed with myisampack. See Section 7.2, "myisampack, the MySQL Compressed Read-Only Table Generator."

When you create a MERGE table, MySQL creates two files on disk. The files have names that begin with the table name and have an extension to indicate the file type. An .frm file stores the table definition, and an .MRG file contains the names of the tables that should be used as one. (Originally, all used tables had to be in the same database as the MERGE table itself. This restriction has been lifted as of MySQL 4.1.1.)

You can use SELECT, DELETE, UPDATE, and (as of MySQL 4.0) INSERT on the collection of tables. For the moment, you must have SELECT, UPDATE, and DELETE privileges on the tables that you map to a MERGE table.

If you DROP the MERGE table, you are dropping only the MERGE specification. The underlying tables are not affected.

When you create a MERGE table, you must specify a UNION=(list-of-tables) clause that indicates which tables you want to use as one. You can optionally specify an INSERT_METHOD option if you want inserts for the MERGE table to happen in the first or last table of the UNION list. If you don't specify any INSERT_METHOD option or specify it with a value of NO, attempts to insert records into the MERGE table result in an error.

The following example shows how to create a MERGE table:

```
mysql> CREATE TABLE t1 (
    ->     a INT NOT NULL AUTO_INCREMENT PRIMARY KEY,
    ->     message CHAR(20));
mysql> CREATE TABLE t2 (
    ->     a INT NOT NULL AUTO_INCREMENT PRIMARY KEY,
    ->     message CHAR(20));
mysql> INSERT INTO t1 (message) VALUES ('Testing'),('table'),('t1');
mysql> INSERT INTO t2 (message) VALUES ('Testing'),('table'),('t2');
mysql> CREATE TABLE total (
    ->     a INT NOT NULL AUTO_INCREMENT,
    ->     message CHAR(20), INDEX(a))
    ->     TYPE=MERGE UNION=(t1,t2) INSERT_METHOD=LAST;
```

Note that the a column is indexed in the MERGE table, but is not declared as a PRIMARY KEY as it is in the underlying MyISAM tables. This is necessary because a MERGE table cannot enforce uniqueness over the set of underlying tables.

After creating the MERGE table, you can do things like this:

```
mysql> SELECT * FROM total;
+---+---------+
| a | message |
+---+---------+
| 1 | Testing |
| 2 | table   |
| 3 | t1      |
| 1 | Testing |
| 2 | table   |
| 3 | t2      |
+---+---------+
```

Note that you can also manipulate the .MRG file directly from outside of the MySQL server:

```
shell> cd /mysql-data-directory/current-database
shell> ls -1 t1 t2 > total.MRG
shell> mysqladmin flush-tables
```

To remap a MERGE table to a different collection of MyISAM tables, you can do one of the following:

- DROP the table and re-create it.
- Use ALTER TABLE tbl_name UNION=(...) to change the list of underlying tables.
- Change the .MRG file and issue a FLUSH TABLE statement for the MERGE table and all underlying tables to force the storage engine to read the new definition file.

MERGE tables can help you solve the following problems:

- Easily manage a set of log tables. For example, you can put data from different months into separate tables, compress some of them with myisampack, and then create a MERGE table to use them as one.

- Obtain more speed. You can split a big read-only table based on some criteria, and then put individual tables on different disks. A MERGE table on this could be much faster than using the big table. (You can also use a RAID table to get the same kind of benefits.)

- Do more efficient searches. If you know exactly what you are looking for, you can search in just one of the split tables for some queries and use a MERGE table for others. You can even have many different MERGE tables that use overlapping sets of tables.

- Do more efficient repairs. It's easier to repair the individual tables that are mapped to a MERGE table than to repair a single really big table.

- Instantly map many tables as one. A MERGE table need not maintain an index of its own because it uses the indexes of the individual tables. As a result, MERGE table collections are *very* fast to create or remap. (Note that you must still specify the index definitions when you create a MERGE table, even though no indexes are created.)

- If you have a set of tables that you join as a big table on demand or batch, you should instead create a MERGE table on them on demand. This is much faster and will save a lot of disk space.

- Exceed the file size limit for the operating system. Each MyISAM table is bound by this limit, but a collection of MyISAM tables is not.

- You can create an alias or synonym for a MyISAM table by defining a MERGE table that maps to that single table. There should be no really notable performance impact of doing this (only a couple of indirect calls and memcpy() calls for each read).

The disadvantages of MERGE tables are:

- You can use only identical MyISAM tables for a MERGE table.

- MERGE tables use more file descriptors. If 10 clients are using a MERGE table that maps to 10 tables, the server uses (10*10) + 10 file descriptors. (10 data file descriptors for each of the 10 clients, and 10 index file descriptors shared among the clients.)

- Key reads are slower. When you read a key, the MERGE storage engine needs to issue a read on all underlying tables to check which one most closely matches the given key. If you then do a "read-next," the MERGE storage engine needs to search the read buffers to find the next key. Only when one key buffer is used up, the storage engine will need to read the next key block. This makes MERGE keys much slower on eq_ref searches, but not much slower on ref searches. See Section 6.2.1, "EXPLAIN Syntax (Get Information About a SELECT)," for more information about eq_ref and ref.

8.2.1 MERGE Table Problems

The following are the known problems with MERGE tables:

- If you use ALTER TABLE to change a MERGE table to another table type, the mapping to the underlying tables is lost. Instead, the rows from the underlying MyISAM tables are copied into the altered table, which then is assigned the new type.

- Before MySQL 4.1.1, all underlying tables and the MERGE table itself had to be in the same database.

- REPLACE doesn't work.

- You can't use DROP TABLE, ALTER TABLE, or DELETE FROM without a WHERE clause, REPAIR TABLE, TRUNCATE TABLE, OPTIMIZE TABLE, or ANALYZE TABLE on any of the tables that are mapped into a MERGE table that is "open." If you do this, the MERGE table may still refer to the original table and you will get unexpected results. The easiest way to work around this deficiency is to issue a FLUSH TABLES statement to ensure that no MERGE tables remain "open."

- A MERGE table cannot maintain UNIQUE constraints over the whole table. When you perform an INSERT, the data goes into the first or last MyISAM table (depending on the value of the INSERT_METHOD option). MySQL ensures that unique key values remain unique within that MyISAM table, but not across all the tables in the collection.

- Before MySQL 3.23.49, DELETE FROM merge_table used without a WHERE clause only clears the mapping for the table. That is, it incorrectly empties the .MRG file rather than deleting records from the mapped tables.

- Using RENAME TABLE on an active MERGE table may corrupt the table. This will be fixed in MySQL 4.1.x.

- When you create a MERGE table, there is no check whether the underlying tables exist and have identical structure. When the MERGE table is used, MySQL does a quick check that the record length for all mapped tables is equal, but this is not foolproof. If you create a MERGE table from dissimilar MyISAM tables, you are very likely to run into strange problems.

- Index order in the MERGE table and its underlying tables should be the same. If you use ALTER TABLE to add a UNIQUE index to a table used in a MERGE table, and then use ALTER TABLE to add a non-unique index on the MERGE table, the index order will be different for the tables if there was an old non-unique index in the underlying table. (This is because ALTER TABLE puts UNIQUE indexes before non-unique indexes to be able to detect duplicate keys as early as possible.) Consequently, queries may return unexpected results.

- DROP TABLE on a table that is in use by a MERGE table does not work on Windows because the MERGE storage engine does the table mapping hidden from the upper layer of MySQL. Because Windows doesn't allow you to delete files that are open, you first must flush all MERGE tables (with FLUSH TABLES) or drop the MERGE table before dropping the table. We will fix this at the same time we introduce views.

8.3 The MEMORY (HEAP) Storage Engine

The MEMORY storage engine creates tables with contents that are stored in memory. Before MySQL 4.1, MEMORY tables are called HEAP tables. As of 4.1, HEAP is a synonym for MEMORY, and MEMORY is the preferred term.

Each MEMORY table is associated with one disk file. The filename begins with the table name and has an extension of .frm to indicate that it stores the table definition.

To specify explicitly that you want a MEMORY table, indicate that with an ENGINE or TYPE table option:

```
CREATE TABLE t (i INT) ENGINE = MEMORY;
CREATE TABLE t (i INT) TYPE = HEAP;
```

MEMORY tables are stored in memory and use hash indexes. This makes them very fast, and very useful for creating temporary tables! However, when the server shuts down, all data stored in MEMORY tables is lost. The tables continue to exist because their definitions are stored in the .frm files on disk, but their contents will be empty when the server restarts.

Here is an example that shows how you might create, use, and remove a MEMORY table:

```
mysql> CREATE TABLE test TYPE=MEMORY
    ->     SELECT ip,SUM(downloads) AS down
    ->     FROM log_table GROUP BY ip;
mysql> SELECT COUNT(ip),AVG(down) FROM test;
mysql> DROP TABLE test;
```

MEMORY tables have the following characteristics:

- Space for MEMORY tables is allocated in small blocks. The tables use 100% dynamic hashing (on inserting). No overflow areas and no extra key space are needed. There is no extra space needed for free lists. Deleted rows are put in a linked list and are reused when you insert new data into the table. MEMORY tables also don't have problems with deletes plus inserts, which is common with hashed tables.

- MEMORY tables allow up to 32 indexes per table, 16 columns per index, and a maximum key length of 500 bytes.

- Before MySQL 4.1, the MEMORY storage engine implements only hash indexes. From MySQL 4.1 on, hash indexes are still the default, but you can specify explicitly that a MEMORY table index should be HASH or BTREE by adding a USING clause:

```
CREATE TABLE lookup
    (id INT, INDEX USING HASH (id))
    ENGINE = MEMORY;
CREATE TABLE lookup
    (id INT, INDEX USING BTREE (id))
    ENGINE = MEMORY;
```

General characteristics of B-tree and hash indexes are described in Section 6.4.5, "How MySQL Uses Indexes."

- You can have non-unique keys in a MEMORY table. (This is an uncommon feature for implementations of hash indexes.)

- If you have a hash index on a MEMORY table that has a high degree of key duplication (many index entries containing the same value), updates to the table that affect key values and all deletes will be significantly slower. The degree of slowdown is proportional to the degree of duplication (or, inversely proportional to the index cardinality). You can use a BTREE index to avoid this problem.

- MEMORY tables use a fixed record length format.

- MEMORY doesn't support BLOB or TEXT columns.

- MEMORY doesn't support AUTO_INCREMENT columns.

- Prior to MySQL 4.0.2, MEMORY doesn't support indexes on columns that can contain NULL values.

- MEMORY tables are shared between all clients (just like any other non-TEMPORARY table).

- The MEMORY table property that table contents are stored in memory is one that is shared with internal tables that the server creates on the fly while processing queries. However, internal tables also have the property that the server converts them to on-disk tables automatically if they become too large. The size limit is determined by the value of the tmp_table_size system variable.

  MEMORY tables are not converted to disk tables. To ensure that you don't accidentally do anything foolish, you can set the max_heap_table_size system variable to impose a maximum size on MEMORY tables. For individual tables, you can also specify a MAX_ROWS table option in the CREATE TABLE statement.

- The server needs enough extra memory to maintain all MEMORY tables that are in use at the same time.

- To free memory used by a MEMORY table if you no longer require its contents, you should execute DELETE or TRUNCATE TABLE, or else remove the table with DROP TABLE.

- If you want to populate a MEMORY table when the MySQL server starts, you can use the --init-file option. For example, you can put statements such as INSERT INTO ... SELECT or LOAD DATA INFILE into the file to load the table from some persistent data source. See Section 4.2.1, "mysqld Command-Line Options."

- If you are using replication, the master server's MEMORY tables become empty when it is shut down and restarted. However, a slave is not aware that these tables have become empty, so it will return out-of-date content if you select data from them. Beginning with MySQL 4.0.18, when a MEMORY table is used on the master for the first time since the master's startup, a DELETE FROM statement is written to the master's binary log automatically, thus synchronizing the slave to the master again. Note that even with this strategy, the slave still has out-of-date data in the table during the interval between the master's restart and its first use of the table. But if you use the --init-file option to populate the MEMORY table on the master at startup, it ensures that the failing time interval is zero.

- The memory needed for one row in a MEMORY table is calculated using the following expression:

```
SUM_OVER_ALL_KEYS(max_length_of_key + sizeof(char*) * 2)
+ ALIGN(length_of_row+1, sizeof(char*))
```

ALIGN() represents a round-up factor to cause the row length to be an exact multiple of the char pointer size. sizeof(char*) is 4 on 32-bit machines and 8 on 64-bit machines.

8.4 The BDB (BerkeleyDB) Storage Engine

Sleepycat Software has provided MySQL with the Berkeley DB transactional storage engine. This storage engine typically is called BDB for short. Support for the BDB storage engine is included in MySQL source distributions starting from version 3.23.34a and is activated in MySQL-Max binary distributions.

BDB tables may have a greater chance of surviving crashes and are also capable of COMMIT and ROLLBACK operations on transactions. The MySQL source distribution comes with a BDB distribution that has a couple of small patches to make it work more smoothly with MySQL. You can't use a non-patched BDB version with MySQL.

We at MySQL AB are working in close cooperation with Sleepycat to keep the quality of the MySQL/BDB interface high. (Even though Berkeley DB is in itself very tested and reliable, the MySQL interface is still considered gamma quality. We are improving and optimizing it.)

When it comes to support for any problems involving BDB tables, we are committed to helping our users locate the problem and create a reproducible test case. Any such test case will be forwarded to Sleepycat, which in turn will help us find and fix the problem. As this is a two-stage operation, any problems with BDB tables may take a little longer for us to fix than for other storage engines. However, we anticipate no significant difficulties with this procedure because the Berkeley DB code itself is used in many applications other than MySQL. See Section 1.4.1, "Support Offered by MySQL AB."

For general information about Berkeley DB, please visit the Sleepycat Web site, http://www.sleepycat.com/.

8.4.1 Operating Systems Supported by BDB

Currently, we know that the BDB storage engine works with the following operating systems:

- Linux 2.x Intel
- Sun Solaris (SPARC and x86)
- FreeBSD 4.x/5.x (x86, sparc64)

- IBM AIX 4.3.x
- SCO OpenServer
- SCO UnixWare 7.1.x

BDB does not work with the following operating systems:

- Linux 2.x Alpha
- Linux 2.x AMD64
- Linux 2.x IA-64
- Linux 2.x s390
- Mac OS X

Note: The preceding lists are not complete. We will update them as we receive more information.

If you build MySQL from source with support for BDB tables, but the following error occurs when you start mysqld, it means BDB is not supported for your architecture:

```
bdb: architecture lacks fast mutexes: applications cannot be threaded
Can't init databases
```

In this case, you must rebuild MySQL without BDB table support or start the server with the --skip-bdb option.

8.4.2 Installing BDB

If you have downloaded a binary version of MySQL that includes support for Berkeley DB, simply follow the usual binary distribution installation instructions. (MySQL-Max distributions include BDB support.)

If you build MySQL from source, you can enable BDB support by running configure with the --with-berkeley-db option in addition to any other options that you normally use. Download a distribution for MySQL 3.23.34 or newer, change location into its top-level directory, and run this command:

```
shell> ./configure --with-berkeley-db [other-options]
```

For more information, see Section 2.2.5, "Installing MySQL on Other Unix-Like Systems," Section 4.1.2, "The mysqld-max Extended MySQL Server," and Section 2.3, "MySQL Installation Using a Source Distribution."

8.4.3 BDB Startup Options

The following options to mysqld can be used to change the behavior of the BDB storage engine:

- --bdb-home=*path*

  The base directory for BDB tables. This should be the same directory you use for --datadir.

- --bdb-lock-detect=*method*

  The BDB lock detection method. The option value should be DEFAULT, OLDEST, RANDOM, or YOUNGEST.

- --bdb-logdir=*path*

  The BDB log file directory.

- --bdb-no-recover

  Don't start Berkeley DB in recover mode.

- --bdb-no-sync

  Don't synchronously flush the BDB logs.

- --bdb-shared-data

  Start Berkeley DB in multi-process mode. (Don't use DB_PRIVATE when initializing Berkeley DB.)

- --bdb-tmpdir=*path*

  The BDB temporary file directory.

- --skip-bdb

  Disable the BDB storage engine.

See Section 4.2.1, "mysqld Command-Line Options."

The following system variable affects the behavior of BDB tables:

- bdb_max_lock

  The maximum number of locks you can have active on a BDB table.

See Section 4.2.3, "Server System Variables."

If you use the --skip-bdb option, MySQL will not initialize the Berkeley DB library and this will save a lot of memory. However, if you use this option, you cannot use BDB tables. If you try to create a BDB table, MySQL will create a MyISAM table instead.

Normally, you should start mysqld without the --bdb-no-recover option if you intend to use BDB tables. However, this may give you problems when you try to start mysqld if the BDB log files are corrupted. See Section 2.4.4, "Starting and Troubleshooting the MySQL Server."

With the bdb_max_lock variable, you can specify the maximum number of locks that can be active on a BDB table. The default is 10,000. You should increase this if errors such as the following occur when you perform long transactions or when mysqld has to examine many rows to execute a query:

```
bdb: Lock table is out of available locks
Got error 12 from ...
```

You may also want to change the `binlog_cache_size` and `max_binlog_cache_size` variables if you are using large multiple-statement transactions. See Section 4.8.4, "The Binary Log."

8.4.4 Characteristics of BDB Tables

Each BDB table is stored on disk in two files. The files have names that begin with the table name and have an extension to indicate the file type. An `.frm` file stores the table definition, and a `.db` file contains the table data and indexes.

To specify explicitly that you want a BDB table, indicate that with an `ENGINE` or `TYPE` table option:

```
CREATE TABLE t (i INT) ENGINE = BDB;
CREATE TABLE t (i INT) TYPE = BDB;
```

`BerkeleyDB` is a synonym for BDB in the `ENGINE` or `TYPE` option.

The BDB storage engine provides transactional tables. The way you use these tables depends on the autocommit mode:

- If you are running with autocommit enabled (which is the default), changes to BDB tables are committed immediately and cannot be rolled back.

- If you are running with autocommit disabled, changes do not become permanent until you execute a `COMMIT` statement. Instead of committing, you can execute `ROLLBACK` to forget the changes.

  You can start a transaction with the `BEGIN WORK` statement to suspend autocommit, or with `SET AUTOCOMMIT=0` to disable autocommit explicitly.

The BDB storage engine has the following characteristics:

- BDB tables can have up to 31 indexes per table, 16 columns per index, and a maximum key size of 1024 bytes (500 bytes before MySQL 4.0).

- MySQL requires a `PRIMARY KEY` in each BDB table so that each row can be uniquely identified. If you don't create one explicitly, MySQL creates and maintains a hidden `PRIMARY KEY` for you. The hidden key has a length of five bytes and is incremented for each insert attempt.

- The `PRIMARY KEY` will be faster than any other index, because the `PRIMARY KEY` is stored together with the row data. The other indexes are stored as the key data + the `PRIMARY KEY`, so it's important to keep the `PRIMARY KEY` as short as possible to save disk space and get better speed.

  This behavior is similar to that of `InnoDB`, where shorter primary keys save space not only in the primary index but in secondary indexes as well.

- If all columns you access in a BDB table are part of the same index or part of the primary key, MySQL can execute the query without having to access the actual row. In a `MyISAM` table, this can be done only if the columns are part of the same index.

- Sequential scanning is slower than for MyISAM tables because the data in BDB tables is stored in B-trees and not in a separate data file.

- Key values are not prefix- or suffix-compressed like key values in MyISAM tables. In other words, key information takes a little more space in BDB tables compared to MyISAM tables.

- There are often holes in the BDB table to allow you to insert new rows in the middle of the index tree. This makes BDB tables somewhat larger than MyISAM tables.

- SELECT COUNT(*) FROM *tbl_name* is slow for BDB tables, because no row count is maintained in the table.

- The optimizer needs to know the approximate number of rows in the table. MySQL solves this by counting inserts and maintaining this in a separate segment in each BDB table. If you don't issue a lot of DELETE or ROLLBACK statements, this number should be accurate enough for the MySQL optimizer. However, MySQL stores the number only on close, so it may be incorrect if the server terminates unexpectedly. It should not be fatal even if this number is not 100% correct. You can update the row count by using ANALYZE TABLE or OPTIMIZE TABLE.

- Internal locking in BDB tables is done at the page level.

- LOCK TABLES works on BDB tables as with other tables. If you don't use LOCK TABLE, MySQL issues an internal multiple-write lock on the table (a lock that doesn't block other writers) to ensure that the table will be properly locked if another thread issues a table lock.

- To be able to roll back transactions, the BDB storage engine maintains log files. For maximum performance, you can use the --bdb-logdir option to place the BDB logs on a different disk than the one where your databases are located.

- MySQL performs a checkpoint each time a new BDB log file is started, and removes any BDB log files that are not needed for current transactions. You can also use FLUSH LOGS at any time to checkpoint the Berkeley DB tables.

  For disaster recovery, you should use table backups plus MySQL's binary log. See Section 4.6.1, "Database Backups."

  Warning: If you delete old log files that are still in use, BDB will not be able to do recovery at all and you may lose data if something goes wrong.

- Applications must always be prepared to handle cases where any change of a BDB table may cause an automatic rollback and any read may fail with a deadlock error.

- If you get full disk with a BDB table, you will get an error (probably error 28) and the transaction should roll back. This contrasts with MyISAM and ISAM tables, for which mysqld will wait for enough free disk before continuing.

8.4.5 Things We Need to Fix for BDB

- It's very slow to open many BDB tables at the same time. If you are going to use BDB tables, you should not have a very large table cache (for example, with a size larger than 256) and you should use the `--no-auto-rehash` option when you use the `mysql` client. We plan to partly fix this in 4.0.

- `SHOW TABLE STATUS` doesn't yet provide very much information for BDB tables.

- Optimize performance.

- Change to not use page locks at all for table scanning operations.

8.4.6 Restrictions on BDB Tables

The following list indicates restrictions that you must observe when using BDB tables:

- Each BDB table stores in the `.db` file the path to the file as it was created. This was done to be able to detect locks in a multi-user environment that supports symlinks. However, the consequence is that BDB table files cannot be moved from one database directory to another.

- When making backups of BDB tables, you must either use `mysqldump` or else make a backup that includes the files for each BDB table (the `.frm` and `.db` files) as well as the BDB log files. The BDB storage engine stores unfinished transactions in its log files and requires them to be present when `mysqld` starts. The BDB logs are the files in the data directory with names of the form `log.XXXXXXXXXX` (ten digits).

- If a column that allows NULL values has a unique index, only a single NULL value is allowed. This differs from other storage engines.

8.4.7 Errors That May Occur When Using BDB Tables

- If the following error occurs when you start `mysqld`, it means that the new BDB version doesn't support the old log file format:

```
bdb:  Ignoring log file: .../log.XXXXXXXXXX:
unsupported log version #
```

In this case, you must delete all BDB logs from your data directory (the files with names that have the format `log.XXXXXXXXXX`) and restart `mysqld`. We also recommend that you then use `mysqldump --opt` to dump your BDB tables, drop the tables, and restore them from the dump file.

- If autocommit mode is disabled and you drop a BDB table that is referenced in another transaction, you may get error messages of the following form in your MySQL error log:

```
001119 23:43:56  bdb:  Missing log fileid entry
001119 23:43:56  bdb:  txn_abort: Log undo failed for LSN:
                       1 3644744: Invalid
```

This is not fatal, but until the problem is fixed, we recommend that you not drop BDB tables except while autocommit mode is enabled. (The fix is not trivial.)

8.5 The ISAM Storage Engine

The original storage engine in MySQL was the ISAM engine. It was the only storage engine available until MySQL 3.23, when the improved MyISAM engine was introduced as the default. ISAM now is deprecated. As of MySQL 4.1, it's included in the source but not enabled in binary distributions. It will disappear in MySQL 5.0. Embedded MySQL server versions do not support ISAM tables by default.

Due to the deprecated status of ISAM, and because MyISAM is an improvement over ISAM, you are advised to convert any remaining ISAM tables to MySAM as soon as possible. To convert an ISAM table to a MyISAM table, use an ALTER TABLE statement:

```
mysql> ALTER TABLE tbl_name TYPE = MYISAM;
```

For more information about MyISAM, see Section 8.1, "The MyISAM Storage Engine."

Each ISAM table is stored on disk in three files. The files have names that begin with the table name and have an extension to indicate the file type. An .frm file stores the table definition. The data file has an .ISD extension. The index file has an .ISM extension.

ISAM uses B-tree indexes.

You can check or repair ISAM tables with the isamchk utility. See Section 4.6.2.7, "Using myisamchk for Crash Recovery."

ISAM has the following properties:

- Compressed and fixed-length keys
- Fixed and dynamic record length
- 16 indexes per table, with 16 key parts per key
- Maximum key length 256 bytes (default)
- Data values are stored in machine format; this is fast, but machine/OS dependent

Many of the properties of MyISAM tables are also true for ISAM tables. However, there are also many differences. The following list describes some of the ways that ISAM is distinct from MyISAM:

- Not binary portable across OS/platforms.
- Can't handle tables larger than 4GB.
- Only supports prefix compression on strings.
- Smaller (more restrictive) key limits.
- Dynamic tables become more fragmented.

- Doesn't support MERGE tables.
- Tables are checked and repaired with isamchk rather than with myisamchk.
- Tables are compressed with pack_isam rather than with myisampack.
- Cannot be used with the BACKUP TABLE or RESTORE TABLE backup-related statements.
- Cannot be used with the CHECK TABLE, REPAIR TABLE, OPTIMIZE TABLE, or ANALYZE TABLE table-maintenance statements.
- No support for full-text searching or spatial data types.
- No support for multiple character sets per table.
- Indexes cannot be assigned to specific key caches.

9

The InnoDB Storage Engine

9.1 InnoDB Overview

InnoDB provides MySQL with a transaction-safe (ACID compliant) storage engine with commit, rollback, and crash recovery capabilities. InnoDB does locking on the row level and also provides an Oracle-style consistent non-locking read in SELECT statements. These features increase multi-user concurrency and performance. There is no need for lock escalation in InnoDB because row-level locks in InnoDB fit in very little space. InnoDB also supports FOREIGN KEY constraints. In SQL queries you can freely mix InnoDB type tables with other table types of MySQL, even within the same query.

InnoDB has been designed for maximum performance when processing large data volumes. Its CPU efficiency is probably not matched by any other disk-based relational database engine.

Fully integrated with MySQL Server, the InnoDB storage engine maintains its own buffer pool for caching data and indexes in main memory. InnoDB stores its tables and indexes in a tablespace, which may consist of several files (or raw disk partitions). This is different from, for example, MyISAM tables where each table is stored using separate files. InnoDB tables can be of any size even on operating systems where file size is limited to 2GB.

InnoDB is included in binary distributions by default as of MySQL 4.0. For information about InnoDB support in MySQL 3.23, see Section 9.3, "InnoDB in MySQL 3.23."

InnoDB is used in production at numerous large database sites requiring high performance. The famous Internet news site Slashdot.org runs on InnoDB. Mytrix, Inc. stores over 1TB of data in InnoDB, and another site handles an average load of 800 inserts/updates per second in InnoDB.

InnoDB is published under the same GNU GPL License Version 2 (of June 1991) as MySQL. If you distribute MySQL/InnoDB, and your application does not satisfy the provisions of the GPL license, you must purchase a commercial **MySQL Pro** license from https://order.mysql.com/?sub=pg&pg_no=1.

9.2 InnoDB **Contact Information**

Contact information for Innobase Oy, producer of the InnoDB engine:

```
Web site: http://www.innodb.com/
Email: sales@innodb.com
Phone: +358-9-6969 3250 (office)
       +358-40-5617367 (mobile)


Innobase Oy Inc.
World Trade Center Helsinki
Aleksanterinkatu 17
P.O.Box 800
00101 Helsinki
Finland
```

9.3 InnoDB **in MySQL 3.23**

Beginning with MySQL 4.0, InnoDB is enabled by default, so the following information applies only to MySQL 3.23.

InnoDB tables are included in the MySQL source distribution starting from 3.23.34a and are activated in the MySQL-Max binaries of the 3.23 series. For Windows, the MySQL-Max binaries are included in the standard distribution.

If you have downloaded a binary version of MySQL that includes support for InnoDB, simply follow the instructions of the MySQL manual for installing a binary version of MySQL. If you already have MySQL 3.23 installed, the simplest way to install MySQL-Max is to replace the executable mysqld server with the corresponding executable from the MySQL-Max distribution. MySQL and MySQL-Max differ only in the server executable. See Section 2.2.5, "Installing MySQL on Other Unix-Like Systems," and Section 4.1.2, "The mysqld-max Extended MySQL Server."

To compile the MySQL source code with InnoDB support, download MySQL 3.23.34a or newer from http://www.mysql.com/ and configure MySQL with the --with-innodb option. See Section 2.3, "MySQL Installation Using a Source Distribution."

To use InnoDB tables with MySQL 3.23, you must specify configuration parameters in the [mysqld] section of the my.cnf option file. On Windows, you can use my.ini instead. If you do not configure InnoDB in the option file, InnoDB will not start. (From MySQL 4.0 on, InnoDB uses default parameters if you do not specify any. However, to get best performance, it is still recommended that you use parameters appropriate for your system, as discussed in Section 9.4, "InnoDB Configuration.")

In MySQL 3.23, you must specify at the minimum an `innodb_data_file_path` value to configure the `InnoDB` data files. For example, to configure `InnoDB` to use a single 10MB auto-extending data file, place the following setting in the `[mysqld]` section of your option file:

```
[mysqld]
innodb_data_file_path=ibdata1:10M:autoextend
```

`InnoDB` will create the `ibdata1` file in the MySQL data directory by default. To specify the location explicitly, specify an `innodb_data_home_dir` setting. See Section 9.4, "InnoDB Configuration."

9.4 InnoDB **Configuration**

To enable `InnoDB` tables in MySQL 3.23, see Section 9.3, "InnoDB in MySQL 3.23."

From MySQL 4.0 on, the `InnoDB` storage engine is enabled by default. If you don't want to use `InnoDB` tables, you can add the `skip-innodb` option to your MySQL option file.

Two important disk-based resources managed by the `InnoDB` storage engine are its tablespace data files and its log files.

If you specify no `InnoDB` configuration options, MySQL 4.0 and above creates an auto-extending 10MB data file named `ibdata1` and two 5MB log files named `ib_logfile0` and `ib_logfile1` in the MySQL data directory. (In MySQL 4.0.0 and 4.0.1, the data file is 64MB and not auto-extending.) In MySQL 3.23, `InnoDB` will not start if you provide no configuration options.

Note: To get good performance, you should explicitly provide `InnoDB` parameters as discussed in the following examples. Naturally, you should edit the settings to suit your hardware and requirements.

To set up the `InnoDB` tablespace files, use the `innodb_data_file_path` option in the `[mysqld]` section of the `my.cnf` option file. On Windows, you can use `my.ini` instead. The value of `innodb_data_file_path` should be a list of one or more data file specifications. If you name more than one data file, separate them by semicolon (';') characters:

```
innodb_data_file_path=datafile_spec1[;datafile_spec2]...
```

For example, a setting that explicitly creates a tablespace having the same characteristics as the MySQL 4.0 default is as follows:

```
[mysqld]
innodb_data_file_path=ibdata1:10M:autoextend
```

This setting configures a single 10MB data file named `ibdata1` that is auto-extending. No location for the file is given, so the default is the MySQL data directory.

Sizes are specified using `M` or `G` suffix letters to indicate units of MB or GB.

A tablespace containing a fixed-size 50MB data file named ibdata1 and a 50MB auto-extending file named ibdata2 in the data directory can be configured like this:

```
[mysqld]
innodb_data_file_path=ibdata1:50M;ibdata2:50M:autoextend
```

The full syntax for a data file specification includes the filename, its size, and several optional attributes:

```
file_name:file_size[:autoextend[:max:max_file_size]]
```

The autoextend attribute and those following can be used only for the last data file in the innodb_data_file_path line. autoextend is available starting from MySQL 3.23.50 and 4.0.2.

If you specify the autoextend option for the last data file, InnoDB extends the data file if it runs out of free space in the tablespace. The increment is 8MB at a time.

If the disk becomes full, you might want to add another data file on another disk. Instructions for reconfiguring an existing tablespace are given in Section 9.8, "Adding and Removing InnoDB Data and Log Files."

InnoDB is not aware of the maximum file size, so be cautious on filesystems where the maximum file size is 2GB. To specify a maximum size for an auto-extending data file, use the max attribute. The following configuration allows ibdata1 to grow up to a limit of 500MB:

```
[mysqld]
innodb_data_file_path=ibdata1:10M:autoextend:max:500M
```

InnoDB creates tablespace files in the MySQL data directory by default. To specify a location explicitly, use the innodb_data_home_dir option. For example, to use two files named ibdata1 and ibdata2 but create them in the /ibdata directory, configure InnoDB like this:

```
[mysqld]
innodb_data_home_dir = /ibdata
innodb_data_file_path=ibdata1:50M;ibdata2:50M:autoextend
```

Note: InnoDB does not create directories, so make sure that the /ibdata directory exists before you start the server. This is also true of any log file directories that you configure. Use the Unix or DOS mkdir command to create any necessary directories.

InnoDB forms the directory path for each data file by textually concatenating the value of innodb_data_home_dir to the data file name, adding a slash or backslash between if needed. If the innodb_data_home_dir option is not mentioned in my.cnf at all, the default value is the "dot" directory ./, which means the MySQL data directory.

If you specify innodb_data_home_dir as an empty string, you can specify absolute paths for the data files listed in the innodb_data_file_path value. The following example is equivalent to the preceding one:

```
[mysqld]
innodb_data_home_dir =
innodb_data_file_path=/ibdata/ibdata1:50M;/ibdata/ibdata2:50M:autoextend
```

A simple `my.cnf` example. Suppose that you have a computer with 128MB RAM and one hard disk. The following example shows possible configuration parameters in `my.cnf` or `my.ini` for InnoDB. The example assumes the use of MySQL-Max 3.23.50 or later or MySQL 4.0.2 or later because it makes use of the `autoextend` attribute.

This example suits most users, both on Unix and Windows, who do not want to distribute `InnoDB` data files and log files on several disks. It creates an auto-extending data file `ibdata1` and two `InnoDB` log files `ib_logfile0` and `ib_logfile1` in the MySQL data directory. Also, the small archived `InnoDB` log file `ib_arch_log_0000000000` that `InnoDB` creates automatically ends up in the data directory.

```
[mysqld]
# You can write your other MySQL server options here
# ...
# Data files must be able to hold your data and indexes.
# Make sure that you have enough free disk space.
innodb_data_file_path = ibdata1:10M:autoextend
#
# Set buffer pool size to 50-80% of your computer's memory
set-variable = innodb_buffer_pool_size=70M
set-variable = innodb_additional_mem_pool_size=10M
#
# Set the log file size to about 25% of the buffer pool size
set-variable = innodb_log_file_size=20M
set-variable = innodb_log_buffer_size=8M
#
innodb_flush_log_at_trx_commit=1
```

Make sure that the MySQL server has the proper access rights to create files in the data directory. More generally, the server must have access rights in any directory where it needs to create data files or log files.

Note that data files must be less than 2GB in some filesystems. The combined size of the log files must be less than 4GB. The combined size of data files must be at least 10MB.

When you create an `InnoDB` tablespace for the first time, it is best that you start the MySQL server from the command prompt. `InnoDB` will then print the information about the database creation to the screen, so you can see what is happening. For example, on Windows, if `mysqld-max` is located in `C:\mysql\bin`, you can start it like this:

`C:\> C:\mysql\bin\mysqld-max --console`

If you do not send server output to the screen, check the server's error log to see what `InnoDB` prints during the startup process.

See Section 9.6, "Creating the `InnoDB` Tablespace," for an example of what the information displayed by `InnoDB` should look like.

Where to specify options on Windows? The rules for option files on Windows are as follows:

- Only one of my.cnf or my.ini should be created.

- The my.cnf file should be placed in the root directory of the C: drive.

- The my.ini file should be placed in the WINDIR directory; for example, C:\WINDOWS or C:\WINNT. You can use the SET command at the command prompt in a console window to print the value of WINDIR:

```
C:\> SET WINDIR
windir=C:\WINNT
```

- If your PC uses a boot loader where the C: drive is not the boot drive, your only option is to use the my.ini file.

Where to specify options on Unix? On Unix, mysqld reads options from the following files, if they exist, in the following order:

- /etc/my.cnf

  Global options.

- *DATADIR*/my.cnf

  Server-specific options.

- defaults-extra-file

  The file specified with the --defaults-extra-file option.

- ~/.my.cnf

  User-specific options.

DATADIR represents the MySQL data directory that was specified as a configure option when mysqld was compiled (typically /usr/local/mysql/data for a binary installation or /usr/local/var for a source installation).

If you want to make sure that mysqld reads options only from a specific file, you can use the --defaults-option as the first option on the command line when starting the server:

```
mysqld --defaults-file=your_path_to_my_cnf
```

An advanced my.cnf example. Suppose that you have a Linux computer with 2GB RAM and three 60GB hard disks (at directory paths /, /dr2 and /dr3). The following example shows possible configuration parameters in my.cnf for InnoDB.

```
[mysqld]
# You can write your other MySQL server options here
# ...
innodb_data_home_dir =
#
```

```
# Data files must be able to hold your data and indexes
# Enter the entire innodb_data_file_path value on a single line
innodb_data_file_path = /ibdata/ibdata1:2000M;
/dr2/ibdata/ibdata2:2000M:autoextend
#
# Set buffer pool size to 50-80% of your computer's memory,
# but make sure on Linux x86 total memory usage is < 2GB
set-variable = innodb_buffer_pool_size=1G
set-variable = innodb_additional_mem_pool_size=20M
innodb_log_group_home_dir = /dr3/iblogs
#
# innodb_log_arch_dir must be the same as innodb_log_group_home_dir
# (starting from 4.0.6, you can omit it)
innodb_log_arch_dir = /dr3/iblogs
set-variable = innodb_log_files_in_group=2
#
# Set the log file size to about 25% of the buffer pool size
set-variable = innodb_log_file_size=250M
set-variable = innodb_log_buffer_size=8M
#
innodb_flush_log_at_trx_commit=1
set-variable = innodb_lock_wait_timeout=50
#
# Uncomment the next lines if you want to use them
#innodb_flush_method=fdatasync
#set-variable = innodb_thread_concurrency=5
```

Note that the example places the two data files on different disks. InnoDB will fill the tablespace beginning with the first data file. In some cases, it will improve the performance of the database if all data is not placed on the same physical disk. Putting log files on a different disk from data is very often beneficial for performance. You can also use raw disk partitions (raw devices) as InnoDB data files, which may speed up I/O. See Section 9.15.2, "Using Raw Devices for the Tablespace."

Warning: On GNU/Linux x86, you must be careful not to set memory usage too high. glibc will allow the process heap to grow over thread stacks, which will crash your server. It is a risk if the value of the following expression is close to or exceeds 2GB:

```
innodb_buffer_pool_size
+ key_buffer_size
+ max_connections*(sort_buffer_size+read_buffer_size+binlog_cache_size)
+ max_connections*2MB
```

Each thread will use a stack (often 2MB, but only 256KB in MySQL AB binaries) and in the worst case also uses sort_buffer_size + read_buffer_size additional memory.

Starting from MySQL 4.1, you can use up to 64GB of physical memory in 32-bit Windows. See the description for innodb_buffer_pool_awe_mem_mb in Section 9.5, "InnoDB Startup Options."

How to tune other `mysqld` server parameters? The following values are typical and suit most users:

```
[mysqld]
skip-external-locking
set-variable = max_connections=200
set-variable = read_buffer_size=1M
set-variable = sort_buffer_size=1M
#
# Set key_buffer to 5 - 50% of your RAM depending on how much
# you use MyISAM tables, but keep key_buffer_size + InnoDB
# buffer pool size < 80% of your RAM
set-variable = key_buffer_size=...
```

9.5 InnoDB **Startup Options**

This section describes the `InnoDB`-related server options. In MySQL 4.0 and up, all of them can be specified in `--opt_name=value` form on the command line or in option files. Before MySQL 4.0, numeric options should be specified using `--set-variable=opt_name=value` or `-O opt_name=value` syntax.

- `innodb_additional_mem_pool_size`

  The size of a memory pool `InnoDB` uses to store data dictionary information and other internal data structures. The more tables you have in your application, the more memory you will need to allocate here. If `InnoDB` runs out of memory in this pool, it will start to allocate memory from the operating system and write warning messages to the MySQL error log. The default value is 1MB.

- `innodb_buffer_pool_awe_mem_mb`

  The size of the buffer pool (in MB), if it is placed in the AWE memory of 32-bit Windows. Available from MySQL 4.1.0 and relevant only in 32-bit Windows. If your 32-bit Windows operating system supports more than 4GB memory, so-called "Address Windowing Extensions," you can allocate the `InnoDB` buffer pool into the AWE physical memory using this parameter. The maximum possible value for this is 64000. If this parameter is specified, `innodb_buffer_pool_size` is the window in the 32-bit address space of `mysqld` where `InnoDB` maps that AWE memory. A good value for `innodb_buffer_pool_size` is 500MB.

- `innodb_buffer_pool_size`

  The size of the memory buffer `InnoDB` uses to cache data and indexes of its tables. The larger you set this value, the less disk I/O is needed to access data in tables. On a dedicated database server, you may set this to up to 80% of the machine's physical memory size. However, do not set it too large because competition for the physical memory might cause paging in the operating system.

- `innodb_data_file_path`

  The paths to individual data files and their sizes. The full directory path to each data file is acquired by concatenating `innodb_data_home_dir` to each path specified here. The file sizes are specified in megabytes or gigabytes (1024MB) by appending M or G to the size value. The sum of the sizes of the files must be at least 10MB. On some operating systems, files must be less than 2GB. If you do not specify `innodb_data_file_path`, the default behavior starting from 4.0 is to create a single 10MB auto-extending data file named `ibdata1`. Starting from 3.23.44, you can set the file size bigger than 4GB on those operating systems that support big files. You can also use raw disk partitions as data files. See Section 9.15.2, "Using Raw Devices for the Tablespace."

- `innodb_data_home_dir`

  The common part of the directory path for all `InnoDB` data files. If you do not set this value, the default is the MySQL data directory. You can specify this also as an empty string, in which case you can use absolute file paths in `innodb_data_file_path`.

- `innodb_fast_shutdown`

  By default, `InnoDB` does a full purge and an insert buffer merge before a shutdown. These operations can take minutes, or even hours in extreme cases. If you set this parameter to 1, `InnoDB` skips these operations at shutdown. This option is available starting from MySQL 3.23.44 and 4.0.1. Its default value is 1 starting from 3.23.50.

- `innodb_file_io_threads`

  The number of file I/O threads in `InnoDB`. Normally this should be left at the default value of 4, but disk I/O on Windows may benefit from a larger number. On Unix, increasing the number has no effect; `InnoDB` always uses the default value. This option is available as of MySQL 3.23.37.

- `innodb_file_per_table`

  This option causes `InnoDB` to create each new table using its own `.ibd` file for storing data and indexes, rather than in the shared tablespace. See Section 9.7.6, "Using Per-Table Tablespaces." This option is available as of MySQL 4.1.1.

- `innodb_flush_log_at_trx_commit`

  Normally you set this to 1, meaning that at a transaction commit, the log is flushed to disk, and the modifications made by the transaction become permanent and survive a database crash. If you are willing to compromise this safety, and you are running small transactions, you may set this to 0 or 2 to reduce disk I/O to the logs. A value of 0 means that the log is only written to the log file and the log file flushed to disk approximately once per second. A value of 2 means the log is written to the log file at each commit, but the log file is only flushed to disk approximately once per second. The default value is 1 (prior to MySQL 4.0.13, the default is 0).

- `innodb_flush_method`

  This option is relevant only on Unix systems. If set to `fdatasync`, `InnoDB` uses `fsync()` to flush both the data and log files. If set to `O_DSYNC`, `InnoDB` uses `O_SYNC` to open and flush the log files, but uses `fsync()` to flush the data files. If `O_DIRECT` is specified (available on some GNU/Linux versions starting from MySQL 4.0.14), InnoDB uses `O_DIRECT` to open the data files, and uses `fsync()` to flush both the data and log files. Note that InnoDB does not use `fdatasync` or `O_DSYNC` by default because there have been problems with them on many Unix flavors. This option is available as of MySQL 3.23.40.

- `innodb_force_recovery`

Warning: This option should be defined only in an emergency situation when you want to dump your tables from a corrupt database! Possible values are from 1 to 6. The meanings of these values are described in Section 9.9.1, "Forcing Recovery." As a safety measure, InnoDB prevents a user from modifying data when this option is greater than 0. This option is available starting from MySQL 3.23.44.

- `innodb_lock_wait_timeout`

The timeout in seconds an InnoDB transaction may wait for a lock before being rolled back. InnoDB automatically detects transaction deadlocks in its own lock table and rolls back the transaction. If you use the `LOCK TABLES` statement, or other transaction-safe storage engines than InnoDB in the same transaction, a deadlock may arise that InnoDB cannot notice. In cases like this, the timeout is useful to resolve the situation. The default is 50 seconds.

- `innodb_log_arch_dir`

The directory where fully written log files would be archived if we used log archiving. The value of this parameter should currently be set the same as `innodb_log_group_home_dir`. Starting from MySQL 4.0.6, you may omit this option.

- `innodb_log_archive`

This value should currently be set to 0. Because recovery from a backup is done by MySQL using its own log files, there is currently no need to archive InnoDB log files. The default for this option is 0.

- `innodb_log_buffer_size`

The size of the buffer that InnoDB uses to write to the log files on disk. Sensible values range from 1MB to 8MB. The default is 1MB. A large log buffer allows large transactions to run without a need to write the log to disk before the transactions commit. Thus, if you have big transactions, making the log buffer larger will save disk I/O.

- `innodb_log_file_size`

The size of each log file in a log group. The combined size of log files must be less than 4GB on 32-bit computers. The default is 5MB. Sensible values range from 1MB to $1/N$-th of the size of the buffer pool, below, where N is the number of log files in the group. The larger the value, the less checkpoint flush activity is needed in the buffer pool, saving disk I/O. But larger log files also mean that recovery will be slower in case of a crash.

- `innodb_log_files_in_group`

  The number of log files in the log group. `InnoDB` writes to the files in a circular fashion. The default is 2 (recommended).

- `innodb_log_group_home_dir`

  The directory path to the `InnoDB` log files. It must have the same value as `innodb_log_arch_dir`. If you do not specify any `InnoDB` log parameters, the default is to create two 5MB files named `ib_logfile0` and `ib_logfile1` in the MySQL data directory.

- `innodb_max_dirty_pages_pct`

  This is an integer in the range from 0 to 100. The default is 90. The main thread in `InnoDB` tries to flush pages from the buffer pool so that at most this many percent of pages may not yet have been flushed at any particular time. Available starting from 4.0.13 and 4.1.1. If you have the `SUPER` privilege, this percentage can be changed while the server is running:

  ```
  SET GLOBAL innodb_max_dirty_pages_pct = value;
  ```

- `innodb_mirrored_log_groups`

  The number of identical copies of log groups we keep for the database. Currently this should be set to 1.

- `innodb_open_files`

  This option is relevant only if you use multiple tablespaces in `InnoDB`. It specifies the maximum number of `.ibd` files that `InnoDB` can keep open at one time. The minimum value is 10. The default is 300. This option is available as of MySQL 4.1.1.

  The file descriptors used for `.ibd` files are for `InnoDB` only. They are independent of those specified by the `--open-files-limit` server option, and do not affect the operation of the table cache.

- `innodb_thread_concurrency`

  `InnoDB` tries to keep the number of operating system threads concurrently inside `InnoDB` less than or equal to the limit given by this parameter. The default value is 8. If you have low performance and `SHOW INNODB STATUS` reveals many threads waiting for semaphores, you may have thread thrashing and should try setting this parameter lower or higher. If you have a computer with many processors and disks, you can try setting the value higher to better utilize the resources of your computer. A recommended value is the sum of the number of processors and disks your system has. A value of 500 or greater disables the concurrency checking. This option is available starting from MySQL 3.23.44 and 4.0.1.

9.6 Creating the `InnoDB` Tablespace

Suppose that you have installed MySQL and have edited your option file so that it contains the necessary `InnoDB` configuration parameters. Before starting MySQL, you should verify that the directories you have specified for `InnoDB` data files and log files exist and that the MySQL server has access rights to those directories. `InnoDB` cannot create directories, only files. Check also that you have enough disk space for the data and log files.

It is best to run the MySQL server `mysqld` from the command prompt when you create an `InnoDB` database, not from the `mysqld_safe` wrapper or as a Windows service. When you run from a command prompt you see what `mysqld` prints and what is happening. On Unix, just invoke `mysqld`. On Windows, use the `--console` option.

When you start the MySQL server after initially configuring `InnoDB` in your option file, `InnoDB` creates your data files and log files. `InnoDB` will print something like the following:

```
InnoDB: The first specified datafile /home/heikki/data/ibdata1
did not exist:
InnoDB: a new database to be created!
InnoDB: Setting file /home/heikki/data/ibdata1 size to 134217728
InnoDB: Database physically writes the file full: wait...
InnoDB: datafile /home/heikki/data/ibdata2 did not exist:
new to be created
InnoDB: Setting file /home/heikki/data/ibdata2 size to 262144000
InnoDB: Database physically writes the file full: wait...
InnoDB: Log file /home/heikki/data/logs/ib_logfile0 did not exist:
new to be created
InnoDB: Setting log file /home/heikki/data/logs/ib_logfile0 size
to 5242880
InnoDB: Log file /home/heikki/data/logs/ib_logfile1 did not exist:
new to be created
InnoDB: Setting log file /home/heikki/data/logs/ib_logfile1 size
to 5242880
InnoDB: Doublewrite buffer not found: creating new
InnoDB: Doublewrite buffer created
InnoDB: Creating foreign key constraint system tables
InnoDB: Foreign key constraint system tables created
InnoDB: Started
mysqld: ready for connections
```

A new `InnoDB` database has now been created. You can connect to the MySQL server with the usual MySQL client programs like `mysql`. When you shut down the MySQL server with `mysqladmin shutdown`, the output will be like the following:

```
010321 18:33:34  mysqld: Normal shutdown
010321 18:33:34  mysqld: Shutdown Complete
InnoDB: Starting shutdown...
InnoDB: Shutdown completed
```

You can now look at the data file and log directories and you will see the files created. The log directory will also contain a small file named `ib_arch_log_0000000000`. That file resulted from the database creation, after which `InnoDB` switched off log archiving. When MySQL is started again, the data files and log files will already have been created, so the output will be much briefer:

```
InnoDB: Started
mysqld: ready for connections
```

9.6.1 Dealing with `InnoDB` Initialization Problems

If `InnoDB` prints an operating system error in a file operation, usually the problem is one of the following:

- You did not create the `InnoDB` data file or log directories.
- `mysqld` does not have access rights to create files in those directories.
- `mysqld` does not read the proper `my.cnf` or `my.ini` option file, and consequently does not see the options you specified.
- The disk is full or a disk quota is exceeded.
- You have created a subdirectory whose name is equal to a data file you specified.
- There is a syntax error in `innodb_data_home_dir` or `innodb_data_file_path`.

If something goes wrong when `InnoDB` attempts to initialize its tablespace or its log files, you should delete all files created by `InnoDB`. This means all data files, all log files, and the small archived log file. In case you already created some `InnoDB` tables, delete the corresponding `.frm` files for these tables (and any `.ibd` files if you are using multiple tablespaces) from the MySQL database directories as well. Then you can try the `InnoDB` database creation again. It is best to start the MySQL server from a command prompt so that you see what is happening.

9.7 Creating `InnoDB` Tables

Suppose that you have started the MySQL client with the command `mysql test`. To create an `InnoDB` table, you must specify an `ENGINE = InnoDB` or `TYPE = InnoDB` option in the table creation SQL statement:

```
CREATE TABLE customers (a INT, b CHAR (20), INDEX (a)) ENGINE=InnoDB;
CREATE TABLE customers (a INT, b CHAR (20), INDEX (a)) TYPE=InnoDB;
```

The SQL statement creates a table and an index on column a in the `InnoDB` tablespace that consists of the data files you specified in `my.cnf`. In addition, MySQL creates a file `customers.frm` in the `test` directory under the MySQL database directory. Internally, `InnoDB` adds to its own data dictionary an entry for table `'test/customers'`. This means you can create a table of the same name `customers` in some other database, and the table names will not collide inside `InnoDB`.

You can query the amount of free space in the InnoDB tablespace by issuing a SHOW TABLE STATUS statement for any InnoDB table. The amount of free space in the tablespace appears in the Comment section in the output of SHOW TABLE STATUS. An example:

```
SHOW TABLE STATUS FROM test LIKE 'customers'
```

Note that the statistics SHOW gives about InnoDB tables are only approximate. They are used in SQL optimization. Table and index reserved sizes in bytes are accurate, though.

9.7.1 How to Use Transactions in InnoDB with Different APIs

By default, each client that connects to the MySQL server begins with autocommit mode enabled, which automatically commits every SQL statement you run. To use multiple-statement transactions, you can switch autocommit off with the SQL statement SET AUTO-COMMIT = 0 and use COMMIT and ROLLBACK to commit or roll back your transaction. If you want to leave autocommit on, you can enclose your transactions between START TRANSACTION and COMMIT or ROLLBACK. Before MySQL 4.0.11, you have to use the keyword BEGIN instead of START TRANSACTION. The following example shows two transactions. The first is committed and the second is rolled back.

```
shell> mysql test
Welcome to the MySQL monitor.  Commands end with ; or \g.
Your MySQL connection id is 5 to server version: 3.23.50-log
Type 'help;' or '\h' for help. Type '\c' to clear the buffer.
mysql> CREATE TABLE CUSTOMER (A INT, B CHAR (20), INDEX (A))
    -> TYPE=InnoDB;
Query OK, 0 rows affected (0.00 sec)
mysql> BEGIN;
Query OK, 0 rows affected (0.00 sec)
mysql> INSERT INTO CUSTOMER VALUES (10, 'Heikki');
Query OK, 1 row affected (0.00 sec)
mysql> COMMIT;
Query OK, 0 rows affected (0.00 sec)
mysql> SET AUTOCOMMIT=0;
Query OK, 0 rows affected (0.00 sec)
mysql> INSERT INTO CUSTOMER VALUES (15, 'John');
Query OK, 1 row affected (0.00 sec)
mysql> ROLLBACK;
Query OK, 0 rows affected (0.00 sec)
mysql> SELECT * FROM CUSTOMER;
+------+--------+
| A    | B      |
+------+--------+
|   10 | Heikki |
+------+--------+
1 row in set (0.00 sec)
mysql>
```

In APIs like PHP, Perl DBI/DBD, JDBC, ODBC, or the standard C call interface of MySQL, you can send transaction control statements such as COMMIT to the MySQL server as strings just like any other SQL statements such as SELECT or INSERT. Some APIs also offer separate special transaction commit and rollback functions or methods.

9.7.2 Converting MyISAM Tables to InnoDB

Important: You should not convert MySQL system tables in the mysql database (such as user or host) to the InnoDB type. The system tables must always be of the MyISAM type.

If you want all your (non-system) tables to be created as InnoDB tables, you can, starting from the MySQL 3.23.43, add the line default-table-type=innodb to the [mysqld] section of your my.cnf or my.ini file.

InnoDB does not have a special optimization for separate index creation the way the MyISAM storage engine does. Therefore, it does not pay to export and import the table and create indexes afterward. The fastest way to alter a table to InnoDB is to do the inserts directly to an InnoDB table. That is, use ALTER TABLE ... TYPE=INNODB, or create an empty InnoDB table with identical definitions and insert the rows with INSERT INTO ... SELECT * FROM ....

If you have UNIQUE constraints on secondary keys, starting from MySQL 3.23.52, you can speed up a table import by turning off the uniqueness checks temporarily during the import session: SET UNIQUE_CHECKS=0; For big tables, this saves a lot of disk I/O because InnoDB can then use its insert buffer to write secondary index records in a batch.

To get better control over the insertion process, it might be good to insert big tables in pieces:

```
INSERT INTO newtable SELECT * FROM oldtable
   WHERE yourkey > something AND yourkey <= somethingelse;
```

After all records have been inserted, you can rename the tables.

During the conversion of big tables, you should increase the size of the InnoDB buffer pool to reduce disk I/O. Do not use more than 80% of the physical memory, though. You can also increase the sizes of the InnoDB log files.

Make sure that you do not fill up the tablespace: InnoDB tables require a lot more disk space than MyISAM tables. If an ALTER TABLE runs out of space, it will start a rollback, and that can take hours if it is disk-bound. For inserts, InnoDB uses the insert buffer to merge secondary index records to indexes in batches. That saves a lot of disk I/O. In rollback, no such mechanism is used, and the rollback can take 30 times longer than the insertion.

In the case of a runaway rollback, if you do not have valuable data in your database, it may be advisable to kill the database process rather than wait for millions of disk I/O operations to complete. For the complete procedure, see Section 9.9.1, "Forcing Recovery."

9.7.3 How an AUTO_INCREMENT Column Works in InnoDB

If you specify an AUTO_INCREMENT column for a table, the InnoDB table handle in the data dictionary will contain a special counter called the auto-increment counter that is used in assigning new values for the column. The auto-increment counter is stored only in main memory, not on disk.

InnoDB uses the following algorithm to initialize the auto-increment counter for a table T that contains an AUTO_INCREMENT column named ai_col: After a server startup, when a user first does an insert to a table T, InnoDB executes the equivalent of this statement:

```
SELECT MAX(ai_col) FROM T FOR UPDATE;
```

The value retrieved by the statement is incremented by one and assigned to the column and the auto-increment counter of the table. If the table is empty, the value 1 is assigned. If the auto-increment counter is not initialized and the user invokes a SHOW TABLE STATUS statement that displays output for the table T, the counter is initialized (but not incremented) and stored for use by later inserts. Note that in this initialization we do a normal exclusive-locking read on the table and the lock lasts to the end of the transaction.

InnoDB follows the same procedure for initializing the auto-increment counter for a freshly created table.

Note that if the user specifies NULL or 0 for the AUTO_INCREMENT column in an INSERT, InnoDB treats the row as if the value had not been specified and generates a new value for it.

After the auto-increment counter has been initialized, if a user inserts a row that explicitly specifies the column value, and the value is bigger than the current counter value, the counter is set to the specified column value. If the user does not explicitly specify a value, InnoDB increments the counter by one and assigns the new value to the column.

When accessing the auto-increment counter, InnoDB uses a special table level AUTO-INC lock that it keeps to the end of the current SQL statement, not to the end of the transaction. The special lock release strategy was introduced to improve concurrency for inserts into a table containing an AUTO_INCREMENT column. Two transactions cannot have the AUTO-INC lock on the same table simultaneously.

Note that you may see gaps in the sequence of values assigned to the AUTO_INCREMENT column if you roll back transactions that have gotten numbers from the counter.

The behavior of the auto-increment mechanism is not defined if a user assigns a negative value to the column or if the value becomes bigger than the maximum integer that can be stored in the specified integer type.

9.7.4 FOREIGN KEY Constraints

Starting from MySQL 3.23.44b, InnoDB features foreign key constraints.

The syntax of a foreign key constraint definition in InnoDB looks like this:

```
[CONSTRAINT symbol] FOREIGN KEY [id] (index_col_name, ...)
    REFERENCES tbl_name (index_col_name, ...)
    [ON DELETE {CASCADE | SET NULL | NO ACTION | RESTRICT | SET DEFAULT}]
    [ON UPDATE {CASCADE | SET NULL | NO ACTION | RESTRICT | SET DEFAULT}]
```

Both tables must be InnoDB type. In the referencing table, there must be an index where the foreign key columns are listed as the *first* columns in the same order. In the referenced table, there must be an index where the referenced columns are listed as the *first* columns in the same order. Index-prefixed columns on foreign keys are not supported.

InnoDB does not automatically create indexes on foreign keys or referenced keys: You must create them explicitly. The indexes are needed so that foreign key checks can be fast and not require a table scan.

Corresponding columns in the foreign key and the referenced key must have similar internal data types inside InnoDB so that they can be compared without a type conversion. The **size and the signedness of integer types has to be the same**. The length of string types need not be the same. If you specify a SET NULL action, make sure you have **not declared the columns in the child table** as NOT NULL.

If MySQL reports an error number 1005 from a CREATE TABLE statement, and the error message string refers to errno 150, this means that the table creation failed because a foreign key constraint was not correctly formed. Similarly, if an ALTER TABLE fails and it refers to errno 150, that means a foreign key definition would be incorrectly formed for the altered table. Starting from MySQL 4.0.13, you can use SHOW INNODB STATUS to display a detailed explanation of the latest InnoDB foreign key error in the server.

Starting from MySQL 3.23.50, InnoDB does not check foreign key constraints on those foreign key or referenced key values that contain a NULL column.

A deviation from SQL standards: If in the parent table there are several rows that have the same referenced key value, then InnoDB acts in foreign key checks as if the other parent rows with the same key value do not exist. For example, if you have defined a RESTRICT type constraint, and there is a child row with several parent rows, InnoDB does not allow the deletion of any of those parent rows.

Starting from MySQL 3.23.50, you can also associate the ON DELETE CASCADE or ON DELETE SET NULL clause with the foreign key constraint. Corresponding ON UPDATE options are available starting from 4.0.8. If ON DELETE CASCADE is specified, and a row in the parent table is deleted, InnoDB automatically deletes also all those rows in the child table whose foreign key values are equal to the referenced key value in the parent row. If ON DELETE SET NULL is specified, the child rows are automatically updated so that the columns in the foreign key are set to the SQL NULL value. SET DEFAULT is parsed but ignored.

InnoDB performs cascading operations through a depth-first algorithm, based on records in the indexes corresponding to the foreign key constraints.

A deviation from SQL standards: If ON UPDATE CASCADE or ON UPDATE SET NULL recurses to update the *same table* it has already updated during the cascade, it acts like RESTRICT. This means that you cannot use self-referential ON UPDATE CASCADE or ON UPDATE SET NULL operations. This is to prevent infinite loops resulting from cascaded updates. A self-referential ON DELETE SET NULL, on the other hand, is possible from 4.0.13. A self-referential ON DELETE CASCADE has been possible since ON DELETE was implemented.

A simple example that relates parent and child tables through a single-column foreign key:

```
CREATE TABLE parent(id INT NOT NULL,
                    PRIMARY KEY (id)
) TYPE=INNODB;
CREATE TABLE child(id INT, parent_id INT,
                    INDEX par_ind (parent_id),
                    FOREIGN KEY (parent_id) REFERENCES parent(id)
                        ON DELETE CASCADE
) TYPE=INNODB;
```

A more complex example in which a product_order table has foreign keys for two other tables. One foreign key references a two-column index in the product table. The other references a single-column index in the customer table:

```
CREATE TABLE product (category INT NOT NULL, id INT NOT NULL,
                    price DECIMAL,
                    PRIMARY KEY(category, id)) TYPE=INNODB;
CREATE TABLE customer (id INT NOT NULL,
                    PRIMARY KEY (id)) TYPE=INNODB;
CREATE TABLE product_order (no INT NOT NULL AUTO_INCREMENT,
                    product_category INT NOT NULL,
                    product_id INT NOT NULL,
                    customer_id INT NOT NULL,
                    PRIMARY KEY(no),
                    INDEX (product_category, product_id),
                    FOREIGN KEY (product_category, product_id)
                      REFERENCES product(category, id)
                      ON UPDATE CASCADE ON DELETE RESTRICT,
                    INDEX (customer_id),
                    FOREIGN KEY (customer_id)
                      REFERENCES customer(id)) TYPE=INNODB;
```

Starting from MySQL 3.23.50, InnoDB allows you to add a new foreign key constraint to a table by using ALTER TABLE:

```
ALTER TABLE yourtablename
    ADD [CONSTRAINT symbol] FOREIGN KEY [id] (index_col_name, ...)
    REFERENCES tbl_name (index_col_name, ...)
    [ON DELETE {CASCADE | SET NULL | NO ACTION | RESTRICT | SET DEFAULT}]
    [ON UPDATE {CASCADE | SET NULL | NO ACTION | RESTRICT | SET DEFAULT}]
```

Remember to create the required indexes first. You can also add a self-referential foreign key constraint to a table using ALTER TABLE.

Starting from MySQL 4.0.13, InnoDB supports the use of ALTER TABLE to drop foreign keys:

```
ALTER TABLE yourtablename DROP FOREIGN KEY fk_symbol;
```

If the FOREIGN KEY clause included a CONSTRAINT name when you created the foreign key, you can refer to that name to drop the foreign key. (A constraint name can be given as of MySQL 4.0.18.) Otherwise, the fk_symbol value is internally generated by InnoDB when the foreign key is created. To find out the symbol when you want to drop a foreign key, use the SHOW CREATE TABLE statement. An example:

```
mysql> SHOW CREATE TABLE ibtest11c\G
*************************** 1. row ***************************
       Table: ibtest11c
Create Table: CREATE TABLE `ibtest11c` (
  `A` int(11) NOT NULL auto_increment,
  `D` int(11) NOT NULL default '0',
  `B` varchar(200) NOT NULL default '',
  `C` varchar(175) default NULL,
  PRIMARY KEY  (`A`,`D`,`B`),
  KEY `B` (`B`,`C`),
  KEY `C` (`C`),
  CONSTRAINT `0_38775` FOREIGN KEY (`A`, `D`)
REFERENCES `ibtest11a` (`A`, `D`)
ON DELETE CASCADE ON UPDATE CASCADE,
  CONSTRAINT `0_38776` FOREIGN KEY (`B`, `C`)
REFERENCES `ibtest11a` (`B`, `C`)
ON DELETE CASCADE ON UPDATE CASCADE
) TYPE=InnoDB CHARSET=latin1
1 row in set (0.01 sec)

mysql> ALTER TABLE ibtest11c DROP FOREIGN KEY 0_38775;
```

Starting from MySQL 3.23.50, the InnoDB parser allows you to use backticks around table and column names in a FOREIGN KEY ... REFERENCES ... clause. Starting from MySQL 4.0.5, the InnoDB parser also takes into account the lower_case_table_names system variable setting.

Before MySQL 3.23.50, ALTER TABLE or CREATE INDEX should not be used in connection with tables that have foreign key constraints or that are referenced in foreign key constraints: Any ALTER TABLE removes all foreign key constraints defined for the table. You should not use ALTER TABLE with the referenced table, either. Instead, use DROP TABLE and CREATE TABLE to modify the schema. When MySQL does an ALTER TABLE it may internally use RENAME TABLE, and that will confuse the foreign key constraints that refer to the table. In MySQL, a CREATE INDEX statement is processed as an ALTER TABLE, so the same considerations apply.

Starting from MySQL 3.23.50, InnoDB returns the foreign key definitions of a table as part of the output of the SHOW CREATE TABLE statement:

```
SHOW CREATE TABLE tbl_name;
```

From this version, mysqldump also produces correct definitions of tables to the dump file, and does not forget about the foreign keys.

You can display the foreign key constraints for a table like this:

```
SHOW TABLE STATUS FROM db_name LIKE 'tbl_name'
```

The foreign key constraints are listed in the Comment column of the output.

When performing foreign key checks, InnoDB sets shared row level locks on child or parent records it has to look at. InnoDB checks foreign key constraints immediately; the check is not deferred to transaction commit.

To make it easier to reload dump files for tables that have foreign key relationships, mysqldump automatically includes a statement in the dump output to set FOREIGN_KEY_CHECKS to 0 as of MySQL 4.1.1. This avoids problems with tables having to be reloaded in a particular order when the dump is reloaded. For earlier versions, you can disable the variable manually within mysql when loading the dump file like this:

```
mysql> SET FOREIGN_KEY_CHECKS = 0;
mysql> SOURCE dump_file_name;
mysql> SET FOREIGN_KEY_CHECKS = 1;
```

This allows you to import the tables in any order if the dump file contains tables that are not correctly ordered for foreign keys. It also speeds up the import operation. FOREIGN_KEY_CHECKS is available starting from MySQL 3.23.52 and 4.0.3.

Setting FOREIGN_KEY_CHECKS to 0 also can be useful for ignoring foreign key constraints during LOAD DATA operations.

InnoDB allows you to drop any table, even though that would break the foreign key constraints that reference the table. When you drop a table, the constraints that were defined in its create statement are also dropped.

If you re-create a table that was dropped, it must have a definition that conforms to the foreign key constraints referencing it. It must have the right column names and types, and it must have indexes on the referenced keys, as stated earlier. If these are not satisfied, MySQL returns error number 1005 and refers to errno 150 in the error message string.

9.7.5 InnoDB and MySQL Replication

MySQL replication works for InnoDB tables as it does for MyISAM tables. It is also possible to use replication in a way where the table type on the slave is not the same as the original table type on the master. For example, you can replicate modifications to an InnoDB table on the master to a MyISAM table on the slave.

To set up a new slave for a master, you have to make a copy of the InnoDB tablespace and the log files, as well as the .frm files of the InnoDB tables, and move the copies to the slave. For the proper procedure to do this, see Section 9.10, "Moving an InnoDB Database to Another Machine."

If you can shut down the master or an existing slave, you can take a cold backup of the InnoDB tablespace and log files and use that to set up a slave. To make a new slave without taking down any server you can also use the non-free (commercial) InnoDB Hot Backup tool (order.html).

There are minor limitations in InnoDB replication:

- LOAD TABLE FROM MASTER does not work for InnoDB type tables. There are workarounds: 1) dump the table on the master and import the dump file into the slave, or 2) use ALTER TABLE *tbl_name* TYPE=MyISAM on the master before setting up replication with LOAD TABLE *tbl_name* FROM MASTER, and then use ALTER TABLE to alter the master table back to the InnoDB type afterward.

- Before MySQL 4.0.6, SLAVE STOP did not respect the boundary of a multiple-statement transaction. An incomplete transaction would be rolled back, and the next SLAVE START would only execute the remaining part of the half transaction. That would cause replication to fail.

- Before MySQL 4.0.6, a slave crash in the middle of a multiple-statement transaction would cause the same problem as SLAVE STOP.

- Before MySQL 4.0.11, replication of the SET FOREIGN_KEY_CHECKS=0 statement does not work properly.

Most of these limitations can be eliminated by using more recent server versions for which the limitations do not apply.

Transactions that fail on the master do not affect replication at all. MySQL replication is based on the binary log where MySQL writes SQL statements that modify data. A slave reads the binary log of the master and executes the same SQL statements. However, statements that occur within a transaction are not written to the binary log until the transaction commits, at which point all statements in the transaction are written at once. If a statement fails, for example, because of a foreign key violation, or if a transaction is rolled back, no SQL statements are written to the binary log, and the transaction is not executed on the slave at all.

9.7.6 Using Per-Table Tablespaces

Starting from MySQL 4.1.1, you can store each InnoDB table and its indexes into its own file. This feature is called "multiple tablespaces" because in effect each table has its own tablespace.

Important note: If you upgrade to MySQL 4.1.1 or higher, it is difficult to downgrade back to 4.0 or 4.1.0! That is because, for earlier versions, InnoDB is not aware of multiple tablespaces.

If you need to downgrade to 4.0, you have to take table dumps and re-create the whole InnoDB tablespace. If you have not created new InnoDB tables under MySQL 4.1.1 or above, and need to downgrade quickly, you can also do a direct downgrade to MySQL 4.0.18 or later in the 4.0 series. Before doing the direct downgrade to 4.0.x, you have to end all client connections to the mysqld server that is to be downgraded, and let it run the purge and insert buffer merge operations to completion, so that SHOW INNODB STATUS shows the main thread in the state waiting for server activity. Then you can shut down mysqld and start 4.0.18 or later in the 4.0 series. A direct downgrade is not recommended, however, because it has not been extensively tested.

You can enable multiple tablespaces by adding a line to the [mysqld] section of my.cnf:

```
[mysqld]
innodb_file_per_table
```

After restarting the server, InnoDB will store each newly created table into its own file tbl_name.ibd in the database directory where the table belongs. This is similar to what the MyISAM storage engine does, but MyISAM divides the table into a data file tbl_name.MYD and the index file tbl_name.MYI. For InnoDB, the data and the indexes are stored together in the .ibd file. The tbl_name.frm file is still created as usual.

If you remove the innodb_file_per_table line from my.cnf and restart the server, InnoDB creates tables inside the shared tablespace files again.

innodb_file_per_table affects only table creation. If you start the server with this option, new tables are created using .idb files, but you can still access tables that exist in the shared tablespace. If you remove the option, new tables are created in the shared tablespace, but you can still access any tables that were created using multiple tablespaces.

InnoDB always needs the shared tablespace. The .ibd files are not sufficient for InnoDB to operate. The shared tablespace consists of the familiar ibdata files where InnoDB puts its internal data dictionary and undo logs.

You cannot freely move .ibd files around between database directories the way you can with MyISAM table files. This is because the table definition is stored in the InnoDB shared tablespace, and also because InnoDB must preserve the consistency of transaction IDs and log sequence numbers.

Within a given MySQL installation, you can move an .ibd file and the associated table from one database to another with the familiar RENAME TABLE statement:

```
RENAME TABLE old_db_name.tbl_name TO new_db_name.tbl_name;
```

If you have a "clean" backup of an .ibd file, you can restore it to the MySQL installation from which it originated as follows:

1. Issue this ALTER TABLE statement:

   ```
   ALTER TABLE tbl_name DISCARD TABLESPACE;
   ```

   Caution: This deletes the current .ibd file.

2. Put the backup .ibd file back in the proper database directory.

3. Issue this ALTER TABLE statement:

   ```
   ALTER TABLE tbl_name IMPORT TABLESPACE;
   ```

In this context, a "clean" .ibd file backup means:

- There are no uncommitted modifications by transactions in the .ibd file.
- There are no unmerged insert buffer entries in the .ibd file.
- Purge has removed all delete-marked index records from the .ibd file.
- mysqld has flushed all modified pages of the .ibd file from the buffer pool to the file.

You can make such a clean backup .ibd file with the following method:

1. Stop all activity from the mysqld server and commit all transactions.

2. Wait until SHOW INNODB STATUS shows that there are no active transactions in the database, and the main thread status of InnoDB is Waiting for server activity. Then you can make a copy of the .ibd file.

Another method for making a clean copy of an .ibd file is to use the commercial InnoDB Hot Backup tool:

1. Use InnoDB Hot Backup to back up the InnoDB installation.

2. Start a second mysqld server on the backup and let it clean up the .ibd files in the backup.

It is in the TODO to also allow moving clean .ibd files to another MySQL installation. This requires resetting of transaction IDs and log sequence numbers in the .ibd file.

9.8 Adding and Removing InnoDB Data and Log Files

This section describes what you can do when your InnoDB tablespace runs out of room or when you want to change the size of the log files.

From MySQL 3.23.50 and 4.0.2, the easiest way to increase the size of the InnoDB tablespace is to configure it from the beginning to be auto-extending. Specify the autoextend attribute for the last data file in the tablespace definition. Then InnoDB will increase the size of that file automatically in 8MB increments when it runs out of space.

Alternatively, you can increase the size of your tablespace by adding another data file. To do this, you have to shut down the MySQL server, edit the my.cnf file to add a new data file to the end of innodb_data_file_path, and start the server again.

If your last data file already was defined with the keyword autoextend, the procedure to edit my.cnf must take into account the size to which the last data file has grown. You have to look at the size of the data file, round the size downward to the closest multiple of 1024 * 1024 bytes (= 1MB), and specify the rounded size explicitly in innodb_data_file_path. Then you can add another data file. Remember that only the last data file in the innodb_data_file_path can be specified as auto-extending.

As an example, assume that the tablespace has just one auto-extending data file ibdata1:

```
innodb_data_home_dir =
innodb_data_file_path = /ibdata/ibdata1:10M:autoextend
```

Suppose that this data file, over time, has grown to 988MB. Below is the configuration line after adding another auto-extending data file.

```
innodb_data_home_dir =
innodb_data_file_path = /ibdata/ibdata1:988M;/disk2/ibdata2:50M:autoextend
```

When you add a new file to the tablespace, make sure that it does not exist. InnoDB will create and initialize it when you restart the server,

Currently, you cannot remove a data file from the tablespace. To decrease the size of your tablespace, use this procedure:

1. Use mysqldump to dump all your InnoDB tables.
2. Stop the server.
3. Remove all the existing tablespace files.
4. Configure a new tablespace.
5. Restart the server.
6. Import the dump files.

If you want to change the number or the size of your InnoDB log files, you have to stop the MySQL server and make sure that it shuts down without errors. Then copy the old log files into a safe place just in case something went wrong in the shutdown and you will need them to recover the tablespace. Delete the old log files from the log file directory, edit my.cnf to change the log file configuration, and start the MySQL server again. mysqld will see that no log files exist at startup and tell you that it is creating new ones.

9.9 Backing Up and Recovering an `InnoDB` Database

The key to safe database management is taking regular backups.

`InnoDB Hot Backup` is an online backup tool you can use to backup your `InnoDB` database while it is running. `InnoDB Hot Backup` does not require you to shut down your database and it does not set any locks or disturb your normal database processing. `InnoDB Hot Backup` is a non-free (commercial) additional tool whose annual license fee is 390 euros per computer where the MySQL server is run. See the `InnoDB Hot Backup` home page (`http://www.innodb.com/order.html`) for detailed information and screenshots.

If you are able to shut down your MySQL server, you can make a "binary" backup that consists of all files used by `InnoDB` to manage its tables. Use the following procedure:

1. Shut down your MySQL server and make sure that it shuts down without errors.
2. Copy all your data files into a safe place.
3. Copy all your `InnoDB` log files to a safe place.
4. Copy your `my.cnf` configuration file or files to a safe place.
5. Copy all the `.frm` files for your `InnoDB` tables to a safe place.

Replication works with `InnoDB` type tables, so you can use MySQL replication capabilities to keep a copy of your database at database sites requiring high availability.

In addition to taking binary backups as just described, you should also regularly take dumps of your tables with `mysqldump`. The reason for this is that a binary file might be corrupted without you noticing it. Dumped tables are stored into text files that are human-readable, so spotting table corruption becomes easier. Also, since the format is simpler, the chance for serious data corruption is smaller. `mysqldump` also has a `--single-transaction` option that you can use to take a consistent snapshot without locking out other clients.

To be able to recover your `InnoDB` database to the present from the binary backup described above, you have to run your MySQL server with binary logging turned on. Then you can apply the binary log to the backup database to achieve point-in-time recovery:

```
mysqlbinlog yourhostname-bin.123 | mysql
```

To recover from a crash of your MySQL server process, the only thing you have to do is to restart it. `InnoDB` will automatically check the logs and perform a roll-forward of the database to the present. `InnoDB` will automatically roll back uncommitted transactions that were present at the time of the crash. During recovery, `mysqld` will display output something like this:

```
InnoDB: Database was not shut down normally.
InnoDB: Starting recovery from log files...
InnoDB: Starting log scan based on checkpoint at
```

```
InnoDB: log sequence number 0 13674004
InnoDB: Doing recovery: scanned up to log sequence number 0 13739520
InnoDB: Doing recovery: scanned up to log sequence number 0 13805056
InnoDB: Doing recovery: scanned up to log sequence number 0 13870592
InnoDB: Doing recovery: scanned up to log sequence number 0 13936128
...
InnoDB: Doing recovery: scanned up to log sequence number 0 20555264
InnoDB: Doing recovery: scanned up to log sequence number 0 20620800
InnoDB: Doing recovery: scanned up to log sequence number 0 20664692
InnoDB: 1 uncommitted transaction(s) which must be rolled back
InnoDB: Starting rollback of uncommitted transactions
InnoDB: Rolling back trx no 16745
InnoDB: Rolling back of trx no 16745 completed
InnoDB: Rollback of uncommitted transactions completed
InnoDB: Starting an apply batch of log records to the database...
InnoDB: Apply batch completed
InnoDB: Started
mysqld: ready for connections
```

If your database gets corrupted or your disk fails, you have to do the recovery from a backup. In the case of corruption, you should first find a backup that is not corrupted. After restoring the base backup, do the recovery from the binary log files.

In some cases of database corruption it is enough just to dump, drop, and re-create one or a few corrupt tables. You can use the CHECK TABLE SQL statement to check whether a table is corrupt, though CHECK TABLE naturally cannot detect every possible kind of corruption. You can use innodb_tablespace_monitor to check the integrity of the file space management inside the tablespace files.

In some cases, apparent database page corruption is actually due to the operating system corrupting its own file cache, and the data on disk may be okay. It is best first to try restarting your computer. It may eliminate errors that appeared to be database page corruption.

9.9.1 Forcing Recovery

If there is database page corruption, you may want to dump your tables from the database with SELECT INTO OUTFILE, and usually most of the data will be intact and correct. But the corruption may cause SELECT * FROM *tbl_name* or InnoDB background operations to crash or assert, or even the InnoDB roll-forward recovery to crash. Starting from MySQL 3.23.44, there is an InnoDB variable that you can use to force the InnoDB storage engine to start up, and you can also prevent background operations from running, so that you will be able to dump your tables. For example, you can add the following line to the [mysqld] section of your option file before restarting the server:

```
[mysqld]
innodb_force_recovery = 4
```

Before MySQL 4.0, use this syntax instead:

```
[mysqld]
set-variable = innodb_force_recovery=4
```

The allowable non-zero values for `innodb_force_recovery` follow. A larger number includes all precautions of lower numbers. If you are able to dump your tables with an option value of at most 4, then you are relatively safe that only some data on corrupt individual pages is lost. A value of 6 is more dramatic because database pages are left in an obsolete state, which in turn may introduce more corruption into B-trees and other database structures.

- 1 (SRV_FORCE_IGNORE_CORRUPT)

  Let the server run even if it detects a corrupt page; try to make SELECT * FROM *tbl_name* jump over corrupt index records and pages, which helps in dumping tables.

- 2 (SRV_FORCE_NO_BACKGROUND)

  Prevent the main thread from running. If a crash would occur in the purge operation, this prevents it.

- 3 (SRV_FORCE_NO_TRX_UNDO)

  Do not run transaction rollbacks after recovery.

- 4 (SRV_FORCE_NO_IBUF_MERGE)

  Prevent also insert buffer merge operations. If they would cause a crash, better not do them; do not calculate table statistics.

- 5 (SRV_FORCE_NO_UNDO_LOG_SCAN)

  Do not look at undo logs when starting the database: InnoDB will treat even incomplete transactions as committed.

- 6 (SRV_FORCE_NO_LOG_REDO)

  Do not do the log roll-forward in connection with recovery.

The database must not otherwise be used with any of these options enabled! As a safety measure, InnoDB prevents users from doing INSERT, UPDATE, or DELETE when `innodb_force_recovery` is set to a value greater than 0.

Starting from MySQL 3.23.53 and 4.0.4, you are allowed to DROP or CREATE a table even if forced recovery is used. If you know that a certain table is causing a crash in rollback, you can drop it. You can use this also to stop a runaway rollback caused by a failing mass import or ALTER TABLE. You can kill the `mysqld` process and set `innodb_force_recovery` to 3 to bring your database up without the rollback. Then DROP the table that is causing the runaway rollback.

9.9.2 Checkpoints

InnoDB implements a checkpoint mechanism called a "fuzzy checkpoint." InnoDB will flush modified database pages from the buffer pool in small batches. There is no need to flush the buffer pool in one single batch, which would in practice stop processing of user SQL statements for a while.

In crash recovery, InnoDB looks for a checkpoint label written to the log files. It knows that all modifications to the database before the label are already present in the disk image of the database. Then InnoDB scans the log files forward from the place of the checkpoint, applying the logged modifications to the database.

InnoDB writes to the log files in a circular fashion. All committed modifications that make the database pages in the buffer pool different from the images on disk must be available in the log files in case InnoDB has to do a recovery. This means that when InnoDB starts to reuse a log file in the circular fashion, it has to make sure that the database page images on disk already contain the modifications logged in the log file InnoDB is going to reuse. In other words, InnoDB has to make a checkpoint and often this involves flushing of modified database pages to disk.

The preceding description explains why making your log files very big may save disk I/O in checkpointing. It can make sense to set the total size of the log files as big as the buffer pool or even bigger. The drawback of big log files is that crash recovery can take longer because there will be more logged information to apply to the database.

9.10 Moving an InnoDB Database to Another Machine

On Windows, InnoDB internally always stores database and table names in lowercase. To move databases in a binary format from Unix to Windows or from Windows to Unix, you should have all table and database names in lowercase. A convenient way to accomplish this on Unix is to add the following line to the [mysqld] section of your my.cnf before you start creating your databases and tables:

```
[mysqld]
set-variable = lower_case_table_names=1
```

On Windows, lower_case_table_names is set to 1 by default.

Like MyISAM data files, InnoDB data and log files are binary-compatible on all platforms if the floating-point number format on the machines is the same. You can move an InnoDB database simply by copying all the relevant files, which were listed in Section 9.9, "Backing Up and Recovering an InnoDB Database." If the floating-point formats on the machines are different but you have not used FLOAT or DOUBLE data types in your tables, then the procedure is the same: Just copy the relevant files. If the formats are different and your tables contain floating-point data, you have to use mysqldump to dump your tables on one machine and then import the dump files on the other machine.

A performance tip is to switch off autocommit mode when you import data into your database, assuming that your tablespace has enough space for the big rollback segment the big import transaction will generate. Do the commit only after importing a whole table or a segment of a table.

9.11 InnoDB **Transaction Model and Locking**

In the InnoDB transaction model, the goal has been to combine the best properties of a multi-versioning database with traditional two-phase locking. InnoDB does locking on the row level and runs queries as non-locking consistent reads by default, in the style of Oracle. The lock table in InnoDB is stored so space-efficiently that lock escalation is not needed: Typically several users are allowed to lock every row in the database, or any random subset of the rows, without InnoDB running out of memory.

9.11.1 InnoDB **and** AUTOCOMMIT

In InnoDB, all user activity occurs inside a transaction. If the autocommit mode is enabled, each SQL statement forms a single transaction on its own. MySQL always starts a new connection with autocommit enabled.

If the autocommit mode is switched off with SET AUTOCOMMIT = 0, then we can consider that a user always has a transaction open. An SQL COMMIT or ROLLBACK statement ends the current transaction and a new one starts. Both statements will release all InnoDB locks that were set during the current transaction. A COMMIT means that the changes made in the current transaction are made permanent and become visible to other users. A ROLLBACK statement, on the other hand, cancels all modifications made by the current transaction.

If the connection has autocommit enabled, the user can still perform a multiple-statement transaction by starting it with an explicit START TRANSACTION or BEGIN statement and ending it with COMMIT or ROLLBACK.

9.11.2 InnoDB **and** TRANSACTION ISOLATION LEVEL

In terms of the SQL:1992 transaction isolation levels, the InnoDB default is REPEATABLE READ. Starting from MySQL 4.0.5, InnoDB offers all four different transaction isolation levels described by the SQL standard. You can set the default isolation level for all connections by using the --transaction-isolation option on the command line or in option files. For example, you can set the option in the [mysqld] section of my.cnf like this:

```
[mysqld]
transaction-isolation = {READ-UNCOMMITTED | READ-COMMITTED
                  | REPEATABLE-READ | SERIALIZABLE}
```

A user can change the isolation level of a single session or all new incoming connections with the SET TRANSACTION statement. Its syntax is as follows:

```
SET [SESSION | GLOBAL] TRANSACTION ISOLATION LEVEL
               {READ UNCOMMITTED | READ COMMITTED
                | REPEATABLE READ | SERIALIZABLE}
```

Note that there are hyphens in the level names for the `--transaction-isolation` option, but not for the `SET TRANSACTION` statement.

The default behavior is to set the isolation level for the next (not started) transaction. If you use the `GLOBAL` keyword, the statement sets the default transaction level globally for all new connections created from that point on (but not existing connections). You need the `SUPER` privilege to do this. Using the `SESSION` keyword sets the default transaction level for all future transactions performed on the current connection.

Any client is free to change the session isolation level (even in the middle of a transaction), or the isolation level for the next transaction.

Before MySQL 3.23.50, `SET TRANSACTION` had no effect on `InnoDB` tables. Before 4.0.5, only `REPEATABLE READ` and `SERIALIZABLE` were available.

You can query the global and session transaction isolation levels with these statements:

```
SELECT @@global.tx_isolation;
SELECT @@tx_isolation;
```

In row-level locking, `InnoDB` uses so-called "next-key locking." That means that besides index records, `InnoDB` can also lock the "gap" before an index record to block insertions by other users immediately before the index record. A next-key lock refers to a lock that locks an index record and the gap before it. A gap lock refers to a lock that only locks a gap before some index record.

A detailed description of each isolation level in `InnoDB`:

- `READ UNCOMMITTED`

  `SELECT` statements are performed in a non-locking fashion, but a possible earlier version of a record might be used. Thus, using this isolation level, such reads are not "consistent." This is also called "dirty read." Other than that, this isolation level works like `READ COMMITTED`.

- `READ COMMITTED`

  A somewhat Oracle-like isolation level. All `SELECT ... FOR UPDATE` and `SELECT ... LOCK IN SHARE MODE` statements lock only the index records, not the gaps before them, and thus allow free inserting of new records next to locked records. `UPDATE` and `DELETE` statements that use a unique index with a unique search condition lock only the index record found, not the gap before it. In range-type `UPDATE` and `DELETE` statements, `InnoDB` must set next-key or gap locks and block insertions by other users to the gaps covered by the range. This is necessary because "phantom rows" must be blocked for MySQL replication and recovery to work.

  Consistent reads behave as in Oracle: Each consistent read, even within the same transaction, sets and reads its own fresh snapshot. See Section 9.11.3, "Consistent Non-Locking Read."

- REPEATABLE READ

  This is the default isolation level of InnoDB. SELECT ... FOR UPDATE, SELECT ... LOCK IN SHARE MODE, UPDATE, and DELETE statements that use a unique index with a unique search condition lock only the index record found, not the gap before it. With other search conditions, these operations employ next-key locking, locking the index range scanned with next-key or gap locks, and block new insertions by other users.

  In consistent reads, there is an important difference from the previous isolation level: In this level, all consistent reads within the same transaction read the same snapshot established by the first read. This convention means that if you issue several plain SELECT statements within the same transaction, these SELECT statements are consistent also with respect to each other. See Section 9.11.3, "Consistent Non-Locking Read."

- SERIALIZABLE

  This level is like REPEATABLE READ, but all plain SELECT statements are implicitly converted to SELECT ... LOCK IN SHARE MODE.

9.11.3 Consistent Non-Locking Read

A consistent read means that InnoDB uses its multi-versioning to present to a query a snapshot of the database at a point in time. The query will see the changes made by exactly those transactions that committed before that point of time, and no changes made by later or uncommitted transactions. The exception to this rule is that the query will see the changes made by the transaction itself that issues the query.

If you are running with the default REPEATABLE READ isolation level, then all consistent reads within the same transaction read the snapshot established by the first such read in that transaction. You can get a fresher snapshot for your queries by committing the current transaction and after that issuing new queries.

Consistent read is the default mode in which InnoDB processes SELECT statements in READ COMMITTED and REPEATABLE READ isolation levels. A consistent read does not set any locks on the tables it accesses, and therefore other users are free to modify those tables at the same time a consistent read is being performed on the table.

9.11.4 Locking Reads SELECT ... FOR UPDATE and SELECT ... LOCK IN SHARE MODE

In some circumstances, a consistent read is not convenient. For example, you might want to add a new row into your table child, and make sure that the child already has a parent in table parent. The following example shows how to implement referential integrity in your application code.

Suppose that you use a consistent read to read the table parent and indeed see the parent of the child in the table. Can you now safely add the child row to table child? No, because it may happen that meanwhile some other user deletes the parent row from the table parent, without you being aware of it.

The solution is to perform SELECT in a locking mode using LOCK IN SHARE MODE:

```
SELECT * FROM parent WHERE NAME = 'Jones' LOCK IN SHARE MODE;
```

Performing a read in share mode means that we read the latest available data, and set a shared mode lock on the rows we read. A shared mode lock prevents others from updating or deleting the row we have read. Also, if the latest data belongs to a yet uncommitted transaction of another client connection, we will wait until that transaction commits. After we see that the preceding query returns the parent 'Jones', we can safely add the child record to the child table and commit our transaction.

Let us look at another example: We have an integer counter field in a table child_codes that we use to assign a unique identifier to each child added to table child. Obviously, using a consistent read or a shared mode read to read the present value of the counter is not a good idea, since two users of the database may then see the same value for the counter, and a duplicate-key error will occur if two users attempt to add children with the same identifier to the table.

Here, LOCK IN SHARE MODE is not a good solution because if two users read the counter at the same time, at least one of them will end up in deadlock when attempting to update the counter.

In this case, there are two good ways to implement the reading and incrementing of the counter: (1) update the counter first by incrementing it by 1 and only after that read it, or (2) read the counter first with a lock mode FOR UPDATE, and increment after that. The latter approach can be implemented as follows:

```
SELECT counter_field FROM child_codes FOR UPDATE;
UPDATE child_codes SET counter_field = counter_field + 1;
```

A SELECT ... FOR UPDATE reads the latest available data, setting exclusive locks on each row it reads. Thus it sets the same locks a searched SQL UPDATE would set on the rows.

Please note that the above is merely an example of how SELECT ... FOR UPDATE works. In MySQL, the specific task of generating a unique identifier actually can be accomplished using only a single access to the table:

```
UPDATE child_codes SET counter_field = LAST_INSERT_ID(counter_field + 1);
SELECT LAST_INSERT_ID();
```

The SELECT statement merely retrieves the identifier information (specific to the current connection). It does not access any table.

9.11.5 Next-Key Locking: Avoiding the Phantom Problem

In row-level locking, InnoDB uses an algorithm called "next-key locking." InnoDB does the row-level locking in such a way that when it searches or scans an index of a table, it sets shared or exclusive locks on the index records it encounters. Thus the row-level locks are actually index record locks.

The locks InnoDB sets on index records also affect the "gap" before that index record. If a user has a shared or exclusive lock on record R in an index, another user cannot insert a new index record immediately before R in the index order. This locking of gaps is done to prevent the so-called "phantom problem." Suppose that you want to read and lock all children from the child table with an identifier value larger than 100, with the intent of updating some column in the selected rows later:

```
SELECT * FROM child WHERE id > 100 FOR UPDATE;
```

Suppose that there is an index on the id column. The query will scan that index starting from the first record where id is bigger than 100. Now, if the locks set on the index records would not lock out inserts made in the gaps, a new row might meanwhile be inserted to the table. If you now execute the same SELECT within the same transaction, you would see a new row in the result set returned by the query. This is contrary to the isolation principle of transactions: A transaction should be able to run so that the data it has read does not change during the transaction. If we regard a set of rows as a data item, the new "phantom" child would violate this isolation principle.

When InnoDB scans an index, it can also lock the gap after the last record in the index. Just that happens in the previous example: The locks set by InnoDB prevent any insert to the table where id would be bigger than 100.

You can use next-key locking to implement a uniqueness check in your application: If you read your data in share mode and do not see a duplicate for a row you are going to insert, then you can safely insert your row and know that the next-key lock set on the successor of your row during the read will prevent anyone meanwhile inserting a duplicate for your row. Thus the next-key locking allows you to "lock" the non-existence of something in your table.

9.11.6 An Example of How the Consistent Read Works in InnoDB

Suppose that you are running in the default REPEATABLE READ isolation level. When you issue a consistent read, that is, an ordinary SELECT statement, InnoDB will give your transaction a timepoint according to which your query sees the database. If another transaction deletes a row and commits after your timepoint was assigned, you will not see the row as having been deleted. Inserts and updates are treated similarly.

You can advance your timepoint by committing your transaction and then doing another SELECT.

This is called "multi-versioned concurrency control."

```
              User A                    User B

         SET AUTOCOMMIT=0;     SET AUTOCOMMIT=0;
time
 |       SELECT * FROM t;
 |       empty set
 |                             INSERT INTO t VALUES (1, 2);
 |
 v       SELECT * FROM t;
         empty set
                               COMMIT;

         SELECT * FROM t;
         empty set

         COMMIT;

         SELECT * FROM t;
         --------------------
         |   1   |   2   |
         --------------------
         1 row in set
```

In this example, user A sees the row inserted by B only when B has committed the insert and A has committed as well, so that the timepoint is advanced past the commit of B.

If you want to see the "freshest" state of the database, you should use either the READ COMMITTED isolation level or a locking read:

```
SELECT * FROM t LOCK IN SHARE MODE;
```

9.11.7 Locks Set by Different SQL Statements in InnoDB

A locking read, an UPDATE, or a DELETE generally set record locks on every index record that is scanned in the processing of the SQL query. It does not matter if there are WHERE conditions in the query that would exclude the row from the result set of the query. InnoDB does not remember the exact WHERE condition, but only knows which index ranges were scanned. The record locks are normally next-key locks that also block inserts to the "gap" immediately before the record.

If the locks to be set are exclusive, then InnoDB always retrieves also the clustered index record and sets a lock on it.

If you do not have indexes suitable for your query and MySQL has to scan the whole table to process the query, every row of the table will become locked, which in turn blocks all inserts by other users to the table. It is important to create good indexes so that your queries do not unnecessarily need to scan many rows.

- SELECT ... FROM is a consistent read, reading a snapshot of the database and setting no locks unless the transaction isolation level is set to SERIALIZABLE. For SERIALIZABLE level, this sets shared next-key locks on the index records it encounters.

- SELECT ... FROM ... LOCK IN SHARE MODE sets shared next-key locks on all index records the read encounters.

- SELECT ... FROM ... FOR UPDATE sets exclusive next-key locks on all index records the read encounters.

- INSERT INTO ... VALUES (...) sets an exclusive lock on the inserted row. Note that this lock is not a next-key lock and does not prevent other users from inserting to the gap before the inserted row. If a duplicate-key error occurs, a shared lock on the duplicate index record is set.

- While initializing a previously specified AUTO_INCREMENT column on a table, InnoDB sets an exclusive lock on the end of the index associated with the AUTO_INCREMENT column. In accessing the auto-increment counter, InnoDB uses a specific table lock mode AUTO-INC where the lock lasts only to the end of the current SQL statement, instead of to the end of the whole transaction. See Section 9.11.1, "InnoDB and AUTOCOMMIT."

  Before MySQL 3.23.50, SHOW TABLE STATUS applied to a table with an AUTO_INCREMENT column sets an exclusive row-level lock to the high end of the AUTO_INCREMENT index. This means also that SHOW TABLE STATUS could cause a deadlock of transactions, something that may surprise users. Starting from MySQL 3.23.50, InnoDB fetches the value of a previously initialized AUTO_INCREMENT column without setting any locks.

- INSERT INTO T SELECT ... FROM S WHERE ... sets an exclusive (non-next-key) lock on each row inserted into T. It does the search on S as a consistent read, but sets shared next-key locks on S if MySQL binary logging is turned on. InnoDB has to set locks in the latter case: In roll-forward recovery from a backup, every SQL statement has to be executed in exactly the same way it was done originally.

- CREATE TABLE ... SELECT ... performs the SELECT as a consistent read or with shared locks, as in the previous item.

- REPLACE is done like an insert if there is no collision on a unique key. Otherwise, an exclusive next-key lock is placed on the row that has to be updated.

- UPDATE ... WHERE ... sets an exclusive next-key lock on every record the search encounters.

- DELETE FROM ... WHERE ... sets an exclusive next-key lock on every record the search encounters.

- If a FOREIGN KEY constraint is defined on a table, any insert, update, or delete that requires checking of the constraint condition sets shared record-level locks on the records it looks at to check the constraint. InnoDB also sets these locks in the case where the constraint fails.

- LOCK TABLES sets table locks, but it is the higher MySQL layer above the InnoDB layer that sets these locks. The automatic deadlock detection of InnoDB cannot detect deadlocks where such table locks are involved. See Section 9.11.9, "Deadlock Detection and Rollback."

  Also, since the higher MySQL layer does not know about row-level locks, it is possible to get a table lock on a table where another user currently has row-level locks. But that does not put transaction integrity in danger. See Section 9.17, "Restrictions on InnoDB Tables."

9.11.8 When Does MySQL Implicitly Commit or Roll Back a Transaction?

MySQL begins each client connection with autocommit mode enabled by default. When autocommit is enabled, MySQL does a commit after each SQL statement if that statement did not return an error.

If you have the autocommit mode off and close a connection without performing an explicit commit of your transaction, then MySQL will roll back your transaction.

If an error is returned by an SQL statement, the commit/rollback behavior depends on the error. See Section 9.16, "Error Handling."

The following SQL statements cause an implicit commit of the current transaction in MySQL:

- ALTER TABLE, BEGIN, CREATE INDEX, DROP DATABASE, DROP INDEX, DROP TABLE, LOAD MASTER DATA, LOCK TABLES, RENAME TABLE, SET AUTOCOMMIT=1, START TRANSACTION, TRUNCATE, UNLOCK TABLES.
- CREATE TABLE (this commits only if before MySQL 4.0.13 and MySQL binary logging is used).
- The CREATE TABLE statement in InnoDB is processed as a single transaction. This means that a ROLLBACK from the user does not undo CREATE TABLE statements the user made during that transaction.

9.11.9 Deadlock Detection and Rollback

InnoDB automatically detects a deadlock of transactions and rolls back a transaction or transactions to prevent the deadlock. Starting from MySQL 4.0.5, InnoDB tries to pick small transactions to roll back. The size of a transaction is determined by the number of rows it has inserted, updated, or deleted. Prior to 4.0.5, InnoDB always rolled back the transaction whose lock request was the last one to build a deadlock, that is, a cycle in the "waits-for" graph of transactions.

InnoDB cannot detect deadlocks where a table lock set by a MySQL LOCK TABLES statement is involved, or if a lock set by another storage engine than InnoDB is involved. You have to resolve these situations by setting the value of the innodb_lock_wait_timeout system variable.

When InnoDB performs a complete rollback of a transaction, all the locks of the transaction are released. However, if just a single SQL statement is rolled back as a result of an error, some of the locks set by the SQL statement may be preserved. This is because InnoDB stores row locks in a format such that it cannot know afterward which lock was set by which SQL statement.

9.11.10 How to Cope with Deadlocks

Deadlocks are a classic problem in transactional databases, but they are not dangerous unless they are so frequent that you cannot run certain transactions at all. Normally, you must write your applications so that they are always prepared to re-issue a transaction if it gets rolled back because of a deadlock.

InnoDB uses automatic row-level locking. You can get deadlocks even in the case of transactions that just insert or delete a single row. That is because these operations are not really "atomic"; they automatically set locks on the (possibly several) index records of the row inserted or deleted.

You can cope with deadlocks and reduce the likelihood of their occurrence with the following techniques:

- Use SHOW INNODB STATUS to determine the cause of the latest deadlock. That can help you to tune your application to avoid deadlocks. This strategy can be used as of MySQL 3.23.52 and 4.0.3, depending on your MySQL series.

- Always be prepared to re-issue a transaction if it fails due to deadlock. Deadlocks are not dangerous. Just try again.

- Commit your transactions often. Small transactions are less prone to collide.

- If you are using locking reads (SELECT ... FOR UPDATE or ... LOCK IN SHARE MODE), try using a lower isolation level such as READ COMMITTED.

- Access your tables and rows in a fixed order. Then transactions form nice queues and do not deadlock.

- Add well-chosen indexes to your tables. Then your queries need to scan fewer index records and consequently set fewer locks. Use EXPLAIN SELECT to determine which indexes the MySQL server regards as the most appropriate for your queries.

- Use less locking. If you can afford to allow a SELECT to return data from an old snapshot, do not add the clause FOR UPDATE or LOCK IN SHARE MODE to it. Using READ COMMITTED isolation level is good here, because each consistent read within the same transaction reads from its own fresh snapshot.

- If nothing helps, serialize your transactions with table-level locks. For example, if you need to write table t1 and read table t2, you can do this:

```
LOCK TABLES t1 WRITE, t2 READ, ...;
[do something with tables t1 and t2 here];
UNLOCK TABLES;
```

  Table-level locks make your transactions queue nicely, and deadlocks are avoided. Note that LOCK TABLES implicitly starts a transaction, just like the statement BEGIN, and UNLOCK TABLES implicitly ends the transaction in a COMMIT.

- Another way to serialize transactions is to create an auxiliary "semaphore" table that contains just a single row. Have each transaction update that row before accessing other tables. In that way, all transactions happen in a serial fashion. Note that the InnoDB instant deadlock detection algorithm also works in this case, because the serializing lock is a row-level lock. With MySQL table-level locks, the timeout method must be used to resolve deadlocks.

9.12 InnoDB **Performance Tuning Tips**

- If the Unix top tool or the Windows Task Manager shows that the CPU usage percentage with your workload is less than 70%, your workload is probably disk-bound. Maybe you are making too many transaction commits, or the buffer pool is too small. Making the buffer pool bigger can help, but do not set it bigger than 80% of physical memory.

- Wrap several modifications into one transaction. InnoDB must flush the log to disk at each transaction commit if that transaction made modifications to the database. Since the rotation speed of a disk is typically at most 167 revolutions/second, that constrains the number of commits to the same 167/second if the disk does not fool the operating system.

- If you can afford the loss of some of the latest committed transactions, you can set the my.cnf parameter innodb_flush_log_at_trx_commit to 0. InnoDB tries to flush the log once per second anyway, although the flush is not guaranteed.

- Make your log files big, even as big as the buffer pool. When InnoDB has written the log files full, it has to write the modified contents of the buffer pool to disk in a checkpoint. Small log files will cause many unnecessary disk writes. The drawback of big log files is that recovery time will be longer.

- Make the log buffer quite big as well (say, 8MB).

- Use the VARCHAR column type instead of CHAR if you are storing variable-length strings or if the column may contain many NULL values. A CHAR(N) column always takes N bytes to store data, even if the string is shorter or its value is NULL. Smaller tables fit better in the buffer pool and reduce disk I/O.

- (Relevant from 3.23.39 up.) In some versions of GNU/Linux and Unix, flushing files to disk with the Unix fsync() and other similar methods is surprisingly slow. The default method InnoDB uses is the fsync() function. If you are not satisfied with the database write performance, you might try setting innodb_flush_method in my.cnf to O_DSYNC, though O_DSYNC seems to be slower on most systems.

- When importing data into InnoDB, make sure that MySQL does not have autocommit mode enabled because that would require a log flush to disk for every insert. To disable autocommit during your import operation, surround it with SET AUTOCOMMIT and COMMIT statements:

```
SET AUTOCOMMIT=0;
/* SQL import statements ... */
COMMIT;
```

  If you use the mysqldump option --opt, you will get dump files that are fast to import into an InnoDB table, even without wrapping them with the SET AUTOCOMMIT and COMMIT statements.

- Beware of big rollbacks of mass inserts: InnoDB uses the insert buffer to save disk I/O in inserts, but no such mechanism is used in a corresponding rollback. A disk-bound rollback can take 30 times the time of the corresponding insert. Killing the database process will not help because the rollback will start again at the server startup. The only way to get rid of a runaway rollback is to increase the buffer pool so that the rollback becomes CPU-bound and runs fast, or to use a special procedure. See Section 9.9.1, "Forcing Recovery."

- Beware also of other big disk-bound operations. Use DROP TABLE or TRUNCATE TABLE (from MySQL 4.0 up) to empty a table, not DELETE FROM tbl_name.

- Use the multiple-row INSERT syntax to reduce communication overhead between the client and the server if you need to insert many rows:

```
INSERT INTO yourtable VALUES (1,2), (5,5), ...;
```

  This tip is valid for inserts into any table type, not just InnoDB.

- If you have UNIQUE constraints on secondary keys, starting from MySQL 3.23.52 and 4.0.3, you can speed up table imports by temporarily turning off the uniqueness checks during the import session:

```
SET UNIQUE_CHECKS=0;
```

  For big tables, this saves a lot of disk I/O because InnoDB can use its insert buffer to write secondary index records in a batch.

- If you have FOREIGN KEY constraints in your tables, starting from MySQL 3.23.52 and 4.0.3, you can speed up table imports by turning the foreign key checks off for a while in the import session:

```
SET FOREIGN_KEY_CHECKS=0;
```

For big tables, this can save a lot of disk I/O.

- If you often have recurring queries to tables that are not updated frequently, use the query cache available as of MySQL 4.0:

```
[mysqld]
query_cache_type = ON
query_cache_size = 10M
```

In MySQL 4.0, the query cache works only with autocommit enabled. This restriction is removed in MySQL 4.1.1 and up.

9.12.1 SHOW INNODB STATUS and the InnoDB Monitors

Starting from MySQL 3.23.42, InnoDB includes InnoDB Monitors that print information about the InnoDB internal state. Starting from MySQL 3.23.52 and 4.0.3, you can use the SQL statement SHOW INNODB STATUS to fetch the output of the standard InnoDB Monitor to your SQL client. The information is useful in performance tuning. If you are using the mysql interactive SQL client, the output is more readable if you replace the usual semicolon statement terminator by \G:

```
mysql> SHOW INNODB STATUS\G
```

Another way to use InnoDB Monitors is to let them continuously write data to the standard output of the server mysqld. In this case, no output is sent to clients. When switched on, InnoDB Monitors print data about every 15 seconds. Server output usually is directed to the .err log in the MySQL data directory. This data is useful in performance tuning. On Windows, you must start the server from a command prompt in a console window with the --console option if you want to direct the output to the window rather than to the error log.

Monitor output includes information of the following types:

- Table and record locks held by each active transaction
- Lock waits of transactions
- Semaphore waits of threads
- Pending file I/O requests
- Buffer pool statistics
- Purge and insert buffer merge activity of the main InnoDB thread

To cause the standard InnoDB Monitor to write to the standard output of mysqld, use the following SQL statement:

```
CREATE TABLE innodb_monitor(a INT) TYPE=InnoDB;
```

The monitor can be stopped by issuing the following statement:

```
DROP TABLE innodb_monitor;
```

The CREATE TABLE syntax is just a way to pass a command to the InnoDB engine through the MySQL SQL parser: The only things that matter are the table name innodb_monitor and that it be an InnoDB table. The structure of the table is not relevant at all for the InnoDB Monitor. If you shut down the server when the monitor is running, and you want to start the monitor again, you have to drop the table before you can issue a new CREATE TABLE statement to start the monitor. This syntax may change in a future release.

In a similar way, you can start innodb_lock_monitor, which is otherwise the same as innodb_monitor but also prints a lot of lock information. A separate innodb_tablespace_monitor prints a list of created file segments existing in the tablespace and also validates the tablespace allocation data structures. Starting from 3.23.44, there is innodb_table_monitor with which you can print the contents of the InnoDB internal data dictionary.

A sample of InnoDB Monitor output:

```
mysql> SHOW INNODB STATUS\G
*************************** 1. row ***************************
Status:
=====================================
030709 13:00:59 INNODB MONITOR OUTPUT
=====================================
Per second averages calculated from the last 18 seconds
----------
SEMAPHORES
----------
OS WAIT ARRAY INFO: reservation count 413452, signal count 378357
--Thread 32782 has waited at btr0sea.c line 1477 for 0.00 seconds the
semaphore:
X-lock on RW-latch at 41a28668 created in file btr0sea.c line 135
a writer (thread id 32782) has reserved it in mode wait exclusive
number of readers 1, waiters flag 1
Last time read locked in file btr0sea.c line 731
Last time write locked in file btr0sea.c line 1347
Mutex spin waits 0, rounds 0, OS waits 0
RW-shared spins 108462, OS waits 37964; RW-excl spins 681824, OS waits 375485
------------------------
LATEST FOREIGN KEY ERROR
------------------------
030709 13:00:59 Transaction:
TRANSACTION 0 290328284, ACTIVE 0 sec, process no 3195, OS thread id 34831 inser
ting
15 lock struct(s), heap size 2496, undo log entries 9
MySQL thread id 25, query id 4668733 localhost heikki update
insert into ibtest11a (D, B, C) values (5, 'khDk' ,'khDk')
Foreign key constraint fails for table test/ibtest11a:
,
  CONSTRAINT `0_219242` FOREIGN KEY (`A`, `D`) REFERENCES `ibtest11b` (`A`, `D`)
ON DELETE CASCADE ON UPDATE CASCADE
```

Trying to add in child table, in index PRIMARY tuple:
 0: len 4; hex 80000101; asc ....;; 1: len 4; hex 80000005; asc ....;; 2: len 4;
 hex 6b68446b; asc khDk;; 3: len 6; hex 0000114e0edc; asc ...N..;; 4: len 7; hex
 00000000c3e0a7; asc ....;; 5: len 4; hex 6b68446b; asc khDk;;
But in parent table test/ibtest11b, in index PRIMARY,
the closest match we can find is record:
RECORD: info bits 0 0: len 4; hex 8000015b; asc ...[;; 1: len 4; hex 80000005; a
sc ....;; 2: len 3; hex 6b6864; asc khd;; 3: len 6; hex 0000111ef3eb; asc ......
;; 4: len 7; hex 800001001e0084; asc ....;; 5: len 3; hex 6b6864; asc khd;;

LATEST DETECTED DEADLOCK

030709 12:59:58
*** (1) TRANSACTION:
TRANSACTION 0 290252780, ACTIVE 1 sec, process no 3185, OS thread id 30733 inser
ting
LOCK WAIT 3 lock struct(s), heap size 320, undo log entries 146
MySQL thread id 21, query id 4553379 localhost heikki update
INSERT INTO alex1 VALUES(86, 86, 794,'aA35818','bb','c79166','d4766t','e187358f'
,'g84586','h794',date_format('2001-04-03 12:54:22','%Y-%m-%d %H:%i'),7
*** (1) WAITING FOR THIS LOCK TO BE GRANTED:
RECORD LOCKS space id 0 page no 48310 n bits 568 table test/alex1 index symbole
trx id 0 290252780 lock mode S waiting
Record lock, heap no 324 RECORD: info bits 0 0: len 7; hex 61613335383138; asc a
a35818;; 1:
*** (2) TRANSACTION:
TRANSACTION 0 290251546, ACTIVE 2 sec, process no 3190, OS thread id 32782 inser
ting
130 lock struct(s), heap size 11584, undo log entries 437
MySQL thread id 23, query id 4554396 localhost heikki update
REPLACE INTO alex1 VALUES(NULL, 32, NULL,'aa3572','','c3572','d6012t','', NULL,'
h396', NULL, NULL, 7.31,7.31,7.31,200)
*** (2) HOLDS THE LOCK(S):
RECORD LOCKS space id 0 page no 48310 n bits 568 table test/alex1 index symbole
trx id 0 290251546 lock_mode X locks rec but not gap
Record lock, heap no 324 RECORD: info bits 0 0: len 7; hex 61613335383138; asc a
a35818;; 1:
*** (2) WAITING FOR THIS LOCK TO BE GRANTED:
RECORD LOCKS space id 0 page no 48310 n bits 568 table test/alex1 index symbole
trx id 0 290251546 lock_mode X locks gap before rec insert intention waiting
Record lock, heap no 82 RECORD: info bits 0 0: len 7; hex 61613335373230; asc aa
35720;; 1:
*** WE ROLL BACK TRANSACTION (1)

TRANSACTIONS

```
Trx id counter 0 290328385
Purge done for trx's n:o < 0 290315608 undo n:o < 0 17
Total number of lock structs in row lock hash table 70
LIST OF TRANSACTIONS FOR EACH SESSION:
---TRANSACTION 0 0, not started, process no 3491, OS thread id 42002
MySQL thread id 32, query id 4668737 localhost heikki
show innodb status
---TRANSACTION 0 290328384, ACTIVE 0 sec, process no 3205, OS thread id 38929 in
serting
1 lock struct(s), heap size 320
MySQL thread id 29, query id 4668736 localhost heikki update
insert into speedc values (1519229,1, 'hgjhjgghgggjgjgjgjgjgggjgjgjgjgjgggjgjgjlhh
gghggggghhjhghgggggghjhghghghghghghhhhghghghjhhjghjghjghjkghjghjghjghjfhjfh
---TRANSACTION 0 290328383, ACTIVE 0 sec, process no 3180, OS thread id 28684 co
mmitting
1 lock struct(s), heap size 320, undo log entries 1
MySQL thread id 19, query id 4668734 localhost heikki update
insert into speedcm values (1603393,1, 'hgjhjgghggjgjgjgjgjgggjgjgjgjgjgggjgjgjlh
hgghggggghhjhghgggggghjhghghghghghghhhhghghghjhhjghjghjkghjghjghjghjfhjf
---TRANSACTION 0 290328327, ACTIVE 0 sec, process no 3200, OS thread id 36880 st
arting index read
LOCK WAIT 2 lock struct(s), heap size 320
MySQL thread id 27, query id 4668644 localhost heikki Searching rows for update
update ibtest11a set B = 'kHdkkkk' where A = 89572
------- TRX HAS BEEN WAITING 0 SEC FOR THIS LOCK TO BE GRANTED:
RECORD LOCKS space id 0 page no 65556 n bits 232 table test/ibtest11a index PRIM
ARY trx id 0 290328327 lock_mode X waiting
Record lock, heap no 1 RECORD: info bits 0 0: len 9; hex 73757072656d756d00; asc
 supremum.;;
------------------
---TRANSACTION 0 290328284, ACTIVE 0 sec, process no 3195, OS thread id 34831 ro
llback of SQL statement
ROLLING BACK 14 lock struct(s), heap size 2496, undo log entries 9
MySQL thread id 25, query id 4668733 localhost heikki update
insert into ibtest11a (D, B, C) values (5, 'khDk' ,'khDk')
---TRANSACTION 0 290327208, ACTIVE 1 sec, process no 3190, OS thread id 32782
58 lock struct(s), heap size 5504, undo log entries 159
MySQL thread id 23, query id 4668732 localhost heikki update
REPLACE INTO alex1 VALUES(86, 46, 538,'aa95666','bb','c95666','d9486t','e200498f
','g86814','h538',date_format('2001-04-03 12:54:22','%Y-%m-%d %H:%i'),
---TRANSACTION 0 290323325, ACTIVE 3 sec, process no 3185, OS thread id 30733 in
serting
4 lock struct(s), heap size 1024, undo log entries 165
MySQL thread id 21, query id 4668735 localhost heikki update
INSERT INTO alex1 VALUES(NULL, 49, NULL,'aa42837','','c56319','d1719t','', NULL,
'h321', NULL, NULL, 7.31,7.31,7.31,200)
```

```
--------
FILE I/O
--------
I/O thread 0 state: waiting for i/o request (insert buffer thread)
I/O thread 1 state: waiting for i/o request (log thread)
I/O thread 2 state: waiting for i/o request (read thread)
I/O thread 3 state: waiting for i/o request (write thread)
Pending normal aio reads: 0, aio writes: 0,
 ibuf aio reads: 0, log i/o's: 0, sync i/o's: 0
Pending flushes (fsync) log: 0; buffer pool: 0
151671 OS file reads, 94747 OS file writes, 8750 OS fsyncs
25.44 reads/s, 18494 avg bytes/read, 17.55 writes/s, 2.33 fsyncs/s
-------------------------------------
INSERT BUFFER AND ADAPTIVE HASH INDEX
-------------------------------------
Ibuf for space 0: size 1, free list len 19, seg size 21,
85004 inserts, 85004 merged recs, 26669 merges
Hash table size 207619, used cells 14461, node heap has 16 buffer(s)
1877.67 hash searches/s, 5121.10 non-hash searches/s
---
LOG
---
Log sequence number 18 1212842764
Log flushed up to   18 1212665295
Last checkpoint at  18 1135877290
0 pending log writes, 0 pending chkp writes
4341 log i/o's done, 1.22 log i/o's/second
---------------------
BUFFER POOL AND MEMORY
---------------------
Total memory allocated 84966343; in additional pool allocated 1402624
Buffer pool size   3200
Free buffers       110
Database pages     3074
Modified db pages  2674
Pending reads 0
Pending writes: LRU 0, flush list 0, single page 0
Pages read 171380, created 51968, written 194688
28.72 reads/s, 20.72 creates/s, 47.55 writes/s
Buffer pool hit rate 999 / 1000
--------------
ROW OPERATIONS
--------------
0 queries inside InnoDB, 0 queries in queue
Main thread process no. 3004, id 7176, state: purging
Number of rows inserted 3738558, updated 127415, deleted 33707, read 755779
```

```
1586.13 inserts/s, 50.89 updates/s, 28.44 deletes/s, 107.88 reads/s
----------------------------
END OF INNODB MONITOR OUTPUT
============================
1 row in set (0.05 sec)
```

Some notes on the output:

- If the TRANSACTIONS section reports lock waits, your application may have lock contention. The output can also help to trace the reasons for transaction deadlocks.

- The SEMAPHORES section reports threads waiting for a semaphore and statistics on how many times threads have needed a spin or a wait on a mutex or an rw-lock semaphore. A large number of threads waiting for semaphores may be a result of disk I/O, or contention problems inside InnoDB. Contention can be due to heavy parallelism of queries, or problems in operating system thread scheduling. Setting innodb_thread_concurrency smaller than the default value of 8 can help in such situations.

- The BUFFER POOL AND MEMORY section gives you statistics on pages read and written. You can calculate from these numbers how many data file I/O operations your queries currently are doing.

- The ROW OPERATIONS section shows what the main thread is doing.

9.13 Implementation of Multi-Versioning

Because InnoDB is a multi-versioned database, it must keep information about old versions of rows in the tablespace. This information is stored in a data structure called a rollback segment after an analogous data structure in Oracle.

Internally, InnoDB adds two fields to each row stored in the database. A 6-byte field indicates the transaction identifier for the last transaction that inserted or updated the row. Also, a deletion is treated internally as an update where a special bit in the row is set to mark it as deleted. Each row also contains a 7-byte field called the roll pointer. The roll pointer points to an undo log record written to the rollback segment. If the row was updated, the undo log record contains the information necessary to rebuild the content of the row before it was updated.

InnoDB uses the information in the rollback segment to perform the undo operations needed in a transaction rollback. It also uses the information to build earlier versions of a row for a consistent read.

Undo logs in the rollback segment are divided into insert and update undo logs. Insert undo logs are needed only in transaction rollback and can be discarded as soon as the transaction commits. Update undo logs are used also in consistent reads, and they can be discarded only after there is no transaction present for which InnoDB has assigned a snapshot that in a consistent read could need the information in the update undo log to build an earlier version of a database row.

You must remember to commit your transactions regularly, including those transactions that only issue consistent reads. Otherwise, InnoDB cannot discard data from the update undo logs, and the rollback segment may grow too big, filling up your tablespace.

The physical size of an undo log record in the rollback segment is typically smaller than the corresponding inserted or updated row. You can use this information to calculate the space need for your rollback segment.

In the InnoDB multi-versioning scheme, a row is not physically removed from the database immediately when you delete it with an SQL statement. Only when InnoDB can discard the update undo log record written for the deletion can it also physically remove the corresponding row and its index records from the database. This removal operation is called a purge, and it is quite fast, usually taking the same order of time as the SQL statement that did the deletion.

9.14 Table and Index Structures

MySQL stores its data dictionary information for tables in .frm files in database directories. This is true for all MySQL storage engines. But every InnoDB table also has its own entry in InnoDB internal data dictionaries inside the tablespace. When MySQL drops a table or a database, it has to delete both an .frm file or files, and the corresponding entries inside the InnoDB data dictionary. This is the reason why you cannot move InnoDB tables between databases simply by moving the .frm files. It is also the reason why DROP DATABASE did not work for InnoDB type tables before MySQL 3.23.44.

Every InnoDB table has a special index called the clustered index where the data of the rows is stored. If you define a PRIMARY KEY on your table, the index of the primary key will be the clustered index.

If you do not define a PRIMARY KEY for your table, MySQL picks the first UNIQUE index that has only NOT NULL columns as the primary key and InnoDB uses it as the clustered index. If there is no such index in the table, InnoDB internally generates a clustered index where the rows are ordered by the row ID that InnoDB assigns to the rows in such a table. The row ID is a 6-byte field that increases monotonically as new rows are inserted. Thus the rows ordered by the row ID will be physically in the insertion order.

Accessing a row through the clustered index is fast because the row data will be on the same page where the index search leads. If a table is large, the clustered index architecture often saves a disk I/O when compared to the traditional solution. (In many databases, the data is traditionally stored on a different page from the index record.)

In InnoDB, the records in non-clustered indexes (also called secondary indexes) contain the primary key value for the row. InnoDB uses this primary key value to search for the row from the clustered index. Note that if the primary key is long, the secondary indexes use more space.

InnoDB compares CHAR and VARCHAR strings of different lengths such that the remaining length in the shorter string is treated as if padded with spaces.

9.14.1 Physical Structure of an Index

All indexes in InnoDB are B-trees where the index records are stored in the leaf pages of the tree. The default size of an index page is 16KB. When new records are inserted, InnoDB tries to leave 1/16 of the page free for future insertions and updates of the index records.

If index records are inserted in a sequential order (ascending or descending), the resulting index pages will be about 15/16 full. If records are inserted in a random order, the pages will be from 1/2 to 15/16 full. If the fillfactor of an index page drops below 1/2, InnoDB tries to contract the index tree to free the page.

9.14.2 Insert Buffering

It is a common situation in a database application that the primary key is a unique identifier and new rows are inserted in the ascending order of the primary key. Thus the insertions to the clustered index do not require random reads from a disk.

On the other hand, secondary indexes are usually non-unique, and insertions into secondary indexes happen in a relatively random order. This would cause a lot of random disk I/O operations without a special mechanism used in InnoDB.

If an index record should be inserted to a non-unique secondary index, InnoDB checks whether the secondary index page is already in the buffer pool. If that is the case, InnoDB does the insertion directly to the index page. If the index page is not found in the buffer pool, InnoDB inserts the record to a special insert buffer structure. The insert buffer is kept so small that it fits entirely in the buffer pool, and insertions can be done very fast.

Periodically, the insert buffer is merged into the secondary index trees in the database. Often it is possible to merge several insertions to the same page of the index tree, saving disk I/O operations. It has been measured that the insert buffer can speed up insertions into a table up to 15 times.

9.14.3 Adaptive Hash Indexes

If a table fits almost entirely in main memory, the fastest way to perform queries on it is to use hash indexes. InnoDB has an automatic mechanism that monitors index searches made to the indexes defined for a table. If InnoDB notices that queries could benefit from building a hash index, it does so automatically.

Note that the hash index is always built based on an existing B-tree index on the table. InnoDB can build a hash index on a prefix of any length of the key defined for the B-tree, depending on the pattern of searches that InnoDB observes for the B-tree index. A hash index can be partial: It is not required that the whole B-tree index is cached in the buffer pool. InnoDB will build hash indexes on demand for those pages of the index that are often accessed.

In a sense, InnoDB tailors itself through the adaptive hash index mechanism to ample main memory, coming closer to the architecture of main memory databases.

9.14.4 Physical Record Structure

Records in InnoDB tables have the following characteristics:

- Each index record in InnoDB contains a header of six bytes. The header is used to link consecutive records together, and also in row-level locking.
- Records in the clustered index contain fields for all user-defined columns. In addition, there is a six-byte field for the transaction ID and a seven-byte field for the roll pointer.
- If no primary key was defined for a table, each clustered index record also contains a six-byte row ID field.
- Each secondary index record contains also all the fields defined for the clustered index key.
- A record contains also a pointer to each field of the record. If the total length of the fields in a record is less than 128 bytes, the pointer is one byte; otherwise, two bytes.
- Internally, InnoDB stores fixed-length character columns such as CHAR(10) in a fixed-length format. InnoDB truncates trailing spaces from VARCHAR columns. Note that MySQL may internally convert CHAR columns to VARCHAR.
- An SQL NULL value reserves zero bytes if stored in a variable-length column. In a fixed-length column, it reserves the fixed length of the column. The motivation behind reserving the fixed space for NULL values is that then an update of the column from NULL to a non-NULL value can be done in place and does not cause fragmentation of the index page.

9.15 File Space Management and Disk I/O

9.15.1 Disk I/O

InnoDB uses simulated asynchronous disk I/O: InnoDB creates a number of threads to take care of I/O operations, such as read-ahead.

There are two read-ahead heuristics in InnoDB:

- In sequential read-ahead, if InnoDB notices that the access pattern to a segment in the tablespace is sequential, it posts in advance a batch of reads of database pages to the I/O system.
- In random read-ahead, if InnoDB notices that some area in a tablespace seems to be in the process of being fully read into the buffer pool, it posts the remaining reads to the I/O system.

Starting from MySQL 3.23.40b, InnoDB uses a novel file flush technique called doublewrite. It adds safety to crash recovery after an operating system crash or a power outage, and improves performance on most Unix flavors by reducing the need for fsync() operations.

Doublewrite means that before writing pages to a data file, InnoDB first writes them to a contiguous tablespace area called the doublewrite buffer. Only after the write and the flush to the doublewrite buffer has completed does InnoDB write the pages to their proper positions in the data file. If the operating system crashes in the middle of a page write, InnoDB later will find a good copy of the page from the doublewrite buffer during recovery.

9.15.2 Using Raw Devices for the Tablespace

Starting from MySQL 3.23.41, you can use raw disk partitions as tablespace data files. By using a raw disk, you can perform non-buffered I/O on Windows and on some Unix systems without filesystem overhead, which might improve performance.

When you create a new data file, you must put the keyword newraw immediately after the data file size in innodb_data_file_path. The partition must be at least as large as the size that you specify. Note that 1MB in InnoDB is 1024 * 1024 bytes, whereas 1MB usually means 1,000,000 bytes in disk specifications.

```
[mysqld]
innodb_data_home_dir=
innodb_data_file_path=/dev/hdd1:3Gnewraw;/dev/hdd2:2Gnewraw
```

The next time you start the server, InnoDB notices the newraw keyword and initializes the new partition. However, do not create or change any InnoDB tables yet. Otherwise, when you next restart the server, InnoDB will reinitialize the partition and your changes will be lost. (Starting from 3.23.44, as a safety measure InnoDB prevents users from modifying data when any partition with newraw is specified.)

After InnoDB has initialized the new partition, stop the server, change newraw in the data file specification to raw:

```
[mysqld]
innodb_data_home_dir=
innodb_data_file_path=/dev/hdd1:5Graw;/dev/hdd2:2Graw
```

Then restart the server and InnoDB will allow changes to be made.

On Windows, starting from 4.1.1, you can allocate a disk partition as a data file like this:

```
[mysqld]
innodb_data_home_dir=
innodb_data_file_path=//./D::10Gnewraw
```

The //./ corresponds to the Windows syntax of \\.\ for accessing physical drives.

When you use raw disk partitions, be sure that they have permissions that allow read and write access by the account used for running the MySQL server.

9.15.3 File Space Management

The data files you define in the configuration file form the tablespace of InnoDB. The files are simply concatenated to form the tablespace. There is no striping in use. Currently you cannot define where in the tablespace your tables will be allocated. However, in a newly created tablespace, InnoDB allocates space starting from the first data file.

The tablespace consists of database pages with a default size of 16KB. The pages are grouped into extents of 64 consecutive pages. The "files" inside a tablespace are called "segments" in InnoDB. The name of the "rollback segment" is somewhat confusing because it actually contains many segments in the tablespace.

Two segments are allocated for each index in InnoDB. One is for non-leaf nodes of the B-tree, the other is for the leaf nodes. The idea here is to achieve better sequentiality for the leaf nodes, which contain the data.

When a segment grows inside the tablespace, InnoDB allocates the first 32 pages to it individually. After that InnoDB starts to allocate whole extents to the segment. InnoDB can add to a large segment up to four extents at a time to ensure good sequentiality of data.

Some pages in the tablespace contain bitmaps of other pages, and therefore a few extents in an InnoDB tablespace cannot be allocated to segments as a whole, but only as individual pages.

When you ask for available free space in the tablespace by issuing a SHOW TABLE STATUS, InnoDB reports the extents that are definitely free in the tablespace. InnoDB always reserves some extents for cleanup and other internal purposes; these reserved extents are not included in the free space.

When you delete data from a table, InnoDB will contract the corresponding B-tree indexes. It depends on the pattern of deletes whether that frees individual pages or extents to the tablespace, so that the freed space becomes available for other users. Dropping a table or deleting all rows from it is guaranteed to release the space to other users, but remember that deleted rows will be physically removed only in an (automatic) purge operation after they are no longer needed in transaction rollback or consistent read.

9.15.4 Defragmenting a Table

If there are random insertions into or deletions from the indexes of a table, the indexes may become fragmented. Fragmentation means that the physical ordering of the index pages on the disk is not close to the index ordering of the records on the pages, or that there are many unused pages in the 64-page blocks that were allocated to the index.

It can speed up index scans if you periodically perform a "null" ALTER TABLE operation:

```
ALTER TABLE tbl_name TYPE=InnoDB
```

That causes MySQL to rebuild the table. Another way to perform a defragmentation operation is to use `mysqldump` to dump the table to a text file, drop the table, and reload it from the dump file.

If the insertions to an index are always ascending and records are deleted only from the end, the `InnoDB` file space management algorithm guarantees that fragmentation in the index will not occur.

9.16 Error Handling

Error handling in `InnoDB` is not always the same as specified in the SQL standard. According to the standard, any error during an SQL statement should cause the rollback of that statement. `InnoDB` sometimes rolls back only part of the statement, or the whole transaction. The following items describe how `InnoDB` performs error handling:

- If you run out of file space in the tablespace, you will get the MySQL `Table is full` error and `InnoDB` rolls back the SQL statement.

- A transaction deadlock or a timeout in a lock wait causes `InnoDB` to roll back the whole transaction.

- A duplicate-key error rolls back only the insert of that particular row, even in a statement like `INSERT INTO ... SELECT`. This will probably change so that the SQL statement will be rolled back if you have not specified the `IGNORE` option in your statement.

- A "row too long" error rolls back the SQL statement.

- Other errors are mostly detected by the MySQL layer of code (above the `InnoDB` storage engine level), and they roll back the corresponding SQL statement.

9.16.1 InnoDB **Error Codes**

The following is a non-exhaustive list of common `InnoDB`-specific errors that you may encounter, with information about why they occur and how to resolve the problem.

- 1005 (ER_CANT_CREATE_TABLE)

  Cannot create table. If the error message string refers to `errno` 150, table creation failed because a foreign key constraint was not correctly formed.

- 1016 (ER_CANT_OPEN_FILE)

  Cannot find the `InnoDB` table from the `InnoDB` data files though the `.frm` file for the table exists. See Section 9.18.1, "Troubleshooting `InnoDB` Data Dictionary Operations."

- 1114 (ER_RECORD_FILE_FULL)

  `InnoDB` has run out of free space in the tablespace. You should reconfigure the tablespace to add a new data file.

- 1205 (ER_LOCK_WAIT_TIMEOUT)

  Lock wait timeout expired. Transaction was rolled back.

- 1213 (ER_LOCK_DEADLOCK)

  Transaction deadlock. You should rerun the transaction.

- 1216 (ER_NO_REFERENCED_ROW)

  You are trying to add a row but there is no parent row, and a foreign key constraint fails. You should add the parent row first.

- 1217 (ER_ROW_IS_REFERENCED)

  You are trying to delete a parent row that has children, and a foreign key constraint fails. You should delete the children first.

9.16.2 Operating System Error Codes

To print the meaning of an operating system error number, use the perror program that comes with the MySQL distribution.

The following table provides a list of some common Linux system error codes. For a more complete list, see Linux source code (http://www.iglu.org.il/lxr/source/include/asm-i386/errno.h).

- 1 (EPERM)

  Operation not permitted

- 2 (ENOENT)

  No such file or directory

- 3 (ESRCH)

  No such process

- 4 (EINTR)

  Interrupted system call

- 5 (EIO)

  I/O error

- 6 (ENXIO)

  No such device or address

- 7 (E2BIG)

  Arg list too long

- 8 (ENOEXEC)

  Exec format error

- 9 (EBADF)

  Bad file number

- 10 (ECHILD)

  No child processes

- 11 (EAGAIN)

  Try again

- 12 (ENOMEM)

  Out of memory

- 13 (EACCES)

  Permission denied

- 14 (EFAULT)

  Bad address

- 15 (ENOTBLK)

  Block device required

- 16 (EBUSY)

  Device or resource busy

- 17 (EEXIST)

  File exists

- 18 (EXDEV)

  Cross-device link

- 19 (ENODEV)

  No such device

- 20 (ENOTDIR)

  Not a directory

- 21 (EISDIR)

  Is a directory

- 22 (EINVAL)

  Invalid argument

- 23 (ENFILE)

  File table overflow

- 24 (EMFILE)

  Too many open files

- 25 (ENOTTY)

  Inappropriate ioctl for device

- 26 (ETXTBSY)

  Text file busy

- 27 (EFBIG)

  File too large

- 28 (ENOSPC)

  No space left on device

- 29 (ESPIPE)

  Illegal seek

- 30 (EROFS)

  Read-only filesystem

- 31 (EMLINK)

  Too many links

The following table provides a list of some common Windows system error codes. For a complete list see the Microsoft Web site (http://msdn.microsoft.com/library/default.asp?url=/library/en-us/debug/base/system_error_codes.asp).

- 1 (ERROR_INVALID_FUNCTION)

  Incorrect function.

- 2 (ERROR_FILE_NOT_FOUND)

  The system cannot find the file specified.

- 3 (ERROR_PATH_NOT_FOUND)

  The system cannot find the path specified.

- 4 (ERROR_TOO_MANY_OPEN_FILES)

  The system cannot open the file.

- 5 (ERROR_ACCESS_DENIED)

  Access is denied.

- 6 (ERROR_INVALID_HANDLE)

  The handle is invalid.

- 7 (ERROR_ARENA_TRASHED)

  The storage control blocks were destroyed.

- 8 (ERROR_NOT_ENOUGH_MEMORY)

  Not enough storage is available to process this command.

- 9 (ERROR_INVALID_BLOCK)

  The storage control block address is invalid.

- 10 (ERROR_BAD_ENVIRONMENT)

  The environment is incorrect.

- 11 (ERROR_BAD_FORMAT)

  An attempt was made to load a program with an incorrect format.

- 12 (ERROR_INVALID_ACCESS)

  The access code is invalid.

- 13 (ERROR_INVALID_DATA)

  The data is invalid.

- 14 (ERROR_OUTOFMEMORY)

  Not enough storage is available to complete this operation.

- 15 (ERROR_INVALID_DRIVE)

  The system cannot find the drive specified.

- 16 (ERROR_CURRENT_DIRECTORY)

  The directory cannot be removed.

- 17 (ERROR_NOT_SAME_DEVICE)

  The system cannot move the file to a different disk drive.

- 18 (ERROR_NO_MORE_FILES)

  There are no more files.

- 19 (ERROR_WRITE_PROTECT)

  The media is write protected.

- 20 (ERROR_BAD_UNIT)

  The system cannot find the device specified.

- 21 (ERROR_NOT_READY)

  The device is not ready.

- 22 (ERROR_BAD_COMMAND)

  The device does not recognize the command.

- 23 (ERROR_CRC)

  Data error (cyclic redundancy check).

- 24 (ERROR_BAD_LENGTH)

  The program issued a command but the command length is incorrect.

- 25 (ERROR_SEEK)

  The drive cannot locate a specific area or track on the disk.

- 26 (ERROR_NOT_DOS_DISK)

  The specified disk or diskette cannot be accessed.

- 27 (ERROR_SECTOR_NOT_FOUND)

  The drive cannot find the sector requested.

- 28 (ERROR_OUT_OF_PAPER)

  The printer is out of paper.

- 29 (ERROR_WRITE_FAULT)

  The system cannot write to the specified device.

- 30 (ERROR_READ_FAULT)

  The system cannot read from the specified device.

- 31 (ERROR_GEN_FAILURE)

  A device attached to the system is not functioning.

- 32 (ERROR_SHARING_VIOLATION)

  The process cannot access the file because it is being used by another process.

- 33 (ERROR_LOCK_VIOLATION)

  The process cannot access the file because another process has locked a portion of the file.

- 34 (ERROR_WRONG_DISK)

  The wrong diskette is in the drive. Insert %2 (Volume Serial Number: %3) into drive %1.

- 36 (ERROR_SHARING_BUFFER_EXCEEDED)

  Too many files opened for sharing.

- 38 (ERROR_HANDLE_EOF)

  Reached the end of the file.

- 39 (ERROR_HANDLE_DISK_FULL)

  The disk is full.

- 112 (ERROR_DISK_FULL)

  The disk is full.

- 123 (ERROR_INVALID_NAME)

  The filename, directory name, or volume label syntax is incorrect.

- 1450 (ERROR_NO_SYSTEM_RESOURCES)

  Insufficient system resources exist to complete the requested service.

9.17 Restrictions on InnoDB Tables

- A table cannot contain more than 1000 columns.
- The maximum key length is 1024 bytes.
- The maximum row length, except for BLOB and TEXT columns, is slightly less than half of a database page; that is, the maximum row length is about 8000 bytes. LONGBLOB and LONGTEXT columns must be less than 4GB, and the total row length, including also BLOB and TEXT columns, must be less than 4GB. InnoDB stores the first 512 bytes of a BLOB or TEXT column in the row, and the rest into separate pages.

- On some operating systems, data files must be less than 2GB.

- The combined size of the InnoDB log files must be less than 4GB.

- The minimum tablespace size is 10MB. The maximum tablespace size is four billion database pages (64TB). This is also the maximum size for a table.

- InnoDB tables do not support FULLTEXT indexes.

- On Windows, InnoDB always stores database and table names internally in lowercase. To move databases in binary format from Unix to Windows or from Windows to Unix, you should have all database and table names in lowercase.

- **Warning:** Do *not* convert MySQL system tables in the mysql database from MyISAM to InnoDB tables! This is an unsupported operation. If you do this, MySQL will not restart until you restore the old system tables from a backup or regenerate them with the mysql_install_db script.

- InnoDB does not keep an internal count of rows in a table. (This would actually be somewhat complicated because of multi-versioning.) To process a SELECT COUNT(*) FROM T statement, InnoDB must scan an index of the table, which will take some time if the table is not entirely in the buffer pool. To get a fast count, you have to use a counter table you create yourself and let your application update it according to the inserts and deletes it does. If your table does not change often, using the MySQL query cache is a good solution. SHOW TABLE STATUS also can be used if an approximate row count is sufficient. See Section 9.12, "InnoDB Performance Tuning Tips."

- For an AUTO_INCREMENT column, you must always define an index for the table, and that index must contain just the AUTO_INCREMENT column. In MyISAM tables, the AUTO_INCREMENT column may be part of a multi-column index.

- InnoDB does not support the AUTO_INCREMENT table option for setting the initial sequence value in a CREATE TABLE or ALTER TABLE statement. To set the value with InnoDB, insert a dummy row with a value one less and delete that dummy row, or insert the first row with an explicit value specified.

- When you restart the MySQL server, InnoDB may reuse an old value for an AUTO_INCREMENT column (that is, a value that was assigned to an old transaction that was rolled back).

- When an AUTO_INCREMENT column runs out of values, InnoDB wraps a BIGINT to -9223372036854775808 and BIGINT UNSIGNED to 1. However, BIGINT values have 64 bits, so do note that if you were to insert one million rows per second, it would still take about a million years before BIGINT reached its upper bound. With all other integer type columns, a duplicate-key error will result. This is similar to how MyISAM works, as it is mostly general MySQL behavior and not about any storage engine in particular.

- DELETE FROM *tbl_name* does not regenerate the table but instead deletes all rows, one by one.

- TRUNCATE *tbl_name* is mapped to DELETE FROM *tbl_name* for InnoDB and doesn't reset the AUTO_INCREMENT counter.

- SHOW TABLE STATUS does not give accurate statistics on InnoDB tables, except for the physical size reserved by the table. The row count is only a rough estimate used in SQL optimization.

- If you try to create a unique index on a prefix of a column you will get an error:
  CREATE TABLE T (A CHAR(20), B INT, UNIQUE (A(5))) TYPE = InnoDB;

  If you create a non-unique index on a prefix of a column, InnoDB will create an index over the whole column.

  These restrictions are removed starting from MySQL 4.0.14 and 4.1.1.

- INSERT DELAYED is not supported for InnoDB tables.

- The MySQL LOCK TABLES operation does not know about InnoDB row-level locks set by already completed SQL statements. This means that you can get a table lock on a table even if there still exist transactions by other users that have row-level locks on the same table. Thus your operations on the table may have to wait if they collide with these locks of other users. Also a deadlock is possible. However, this does not endanger trans- action integrity, because the row-level locks set by InnoDB will always take care of the integrity. Also, a table lock prevents other transactions from acquiring more row-level locks (in a conflicting lock mode) on the table.

- Before MySQL 3.23.52, replication always ran with autocommit enabled. Therefore consistent reads in the slave would also see partially processed transactions, and thus the read would not be really consistent in the slave. This restriction was removed in MySQL 3.23.52.

- The LOAD TABLE FROM MASTER statement for setting up replication slave servers does not yet work for InnoDB tables. A workaround is to alter the table to MyISAM on the master, do then the load, and after that alter the master table back to InnoDB.

- The default database page size in InnoDB is 16KB. By recompiling the code, you can set it to values ranging from 8KB to 64KB. You have to update the values of UNIV_PAGE_SIZE and UNIV_PAGE_SIZE_SHIFT in the univ.i source file.

9.18 InnoDB **Troubleshooting**

- A general rule is that when an operation fails or you suspect a bug, you should look at the MySQL server error log, which typically has a name something like *host_name*.err, or mysql.err on Windows.

- When doing troubleshooting, it is usually best to run the MySQL server from the com- mand prompt, not through the mysqld_safe wrapper or as a Windows service. You will then see what mysqld prints to the command prompt window, and you have a better grasp of what is going on. On Windows, you must start the server with the --console option to direct the output to the console window.

- Use the InnoDB Monitors to obtain information about a problem. If the problem is performance-related, or your server appears to be hung, you should use innodb_monitor to print information about the internal state of InnoDB. If the problem is with locks, use innodb_lock_monitor. If the problem is in creation of tables or other data dictionary operations, use innodb_table_monitor to print the contents of the InnoDB internal data dictionary.

- If you suspect a table is corrupt, run CHECK TABLE on that table.

9.18.1 Troubleshooting InnoDB Data Dictionary Operations

A specific issue with tables is that the MySQL server keeps data dictionary information in .frm files it stores in the database directories, while InnoDB also stores the information into its own data dictionary inside the tablespace files. If you move .frm files around, or use DROP DATABASE in MySQL versions before 3.23.44, or the server crashes in the middle of a data dictionary operation, the .frm files may end up out of sync with the InnoDB internal data dictionary.

A symptom of an out-of-sync data dictionary is that a CREATE TABLE statement fails. If this occurs, you should look in the server's error log. If the log says that the table already exists inside the InnoDB internal data dictionary, you have an orphaned table inside the InnoDB tablespace files that has no corresponding .frm file. The error message looks like this:

```
InnoDB: Error: table test/parent already exists in InnoDB internal
InnoDB: data dictionary. Have you deleted the .frm file
InnoDB: and not used DROP TABLE? Have you used DROP DATABASE
InnoDB: for InnoDB tables in MySQL version <= 3.23.43?
InnoDB: See the Restrictions section of the InnoDB manual.
InnoDB: You can drop the orphaned table inside InnoDB by
InnoDB: creating an InnoDB table with the same name in another
InnoDB: database and moving the .frm file to the current database.
InnoDB: Then MySQL thinks the table exists, and DROP TABLE will
InnoDB: succeed.
```

You can drop the orphaned table by following the instructions given in the error message.

Another symptom of an out-of-sync data dictionary is that MySQL prints an error that it cannot open an .InnoDB file:

```
ERROR 1016: Can't open file: 'child2.InnoDB'. (errno: 1)
```

In the error log you will find a message like this:

```
InnoDB: Cannot find table test/child2 from the internal data dictionary
InnoDB: of InnoDB though the .frm file for the table exists. Maybe you
InnoDB: have deleted and recreated InnoDB data files but have forgotten
InnoDB: to delete the corresponding .frm files of InnoDB tables?
```

This means that there is an orphaned `.frm` file without a corresponding table inside `InnoDB`. You can drop the orphaned `.frm` file by deleting it manually.

If MySQL crashes in the middle of an `ALTER TABLE` operation, you may end up with an orphaned temporary table inside the `InnoDB` tablespace. With `innodb_table_monitor` you see a table whose name is `#sql...`, but since MySQL does not allow accessing any table with such a name, you cannot dump or drop it. The solution is to use a special mechanism available starting from MySQL 3.23.48.

When you have an orphaned table `#sql_id` inside the tablespace, you can cause `InnoDB` to rename it to `rsql_id_recover_innodb_tmp_table` with the following statement:

```
CREATE TABLE `rsql_id_recover_innodb_tmp_table`(...) TYPE=InnoDB;
```

The backticks around the table name are needed because a temporary table name contains the character '-'.

The table definition must be similar to that of the temporary table. If you do not know the definition of the temporary table, you can use an arbitrary definition in the preceding `CREATE TABLE` statement, and after that replace the file `rsql_id.frm` by the file `#sql_id.frm` of the temporary table. Note that to copy or rename a file in the shell, you need to put the filename in double quotes if the filename contains '#'. Then you can dump and drop the renamed table.

Introduction to MaxDB

MaxDB is an enterprise-level database. MaxDB is the new name of a database management system formerly called SAP DB.

10.1 History of MaxDB

The history of SAP DB goes back to the early 1980s when it was developed as a commercial product (Adabas). The database has changed names several times since then. When SAP AG, a company based in Walldorf, Germany, took over the development of that database system, it was called SAP DB.

SAP developed that database system to serve as a storage system for all heavy-duty SAP applications, namely R/3. SAP DB was meant to provide an alternative to third-party database systems such as Oracle, Microsoft SQL Server, and DB2 by IBM. In October 2000, SAP AG released SAP DB under the GNU GPL license, thus making it open source software. In October 2003, more than 2,000 customers of SAP AG were using SAP DB as their main database system, and more than another 2,000 customers were using it as a separate database system besides their main database, as part of the APO/LiveCache solution.

In May 2003, a technology partnership was formed between MySQL AB and SAP AG. That partnership entitles MySQL AB to further develop SAP DB, rename it, and sell commercial licenses of the renamed SAP DB to customers who do not want to be bound to the restrictions imposed on them when using that database system under the GNU GPL. In August 2003, SAP DB was renamed MaxDB by MySQL AB.

10.2 Licensing and Support

MaxDB can be used under the same licenses available for the other products distributed by MySQL AB. Thus, MaxDB will be available under the GNU General Public License and a commercial license. For more information about licensing and support options, see Section 1.4, "MySQL Support and Licensing."

MySQL will offer MaxDB support to non-SAP customers.

The first rebranded version was MaxDB 7.5.00, which was released in November 2003.

10.3 MaxDB-Related Links

The main page for information about MaxDB is `http://www.mysql.com/products/maxdb`. Information formerly available at `http://www.sapdb.org` has been moved there.

10.4 Basic Concepts of MaxDB

MaxDB operates as a client/server product. It was developed to meet the demands of installations processing a high volume of online transactions. Both online backup and expansion of the database are supported. Microsoft Clustered Server is supported directly for multiple server implementations; other failover solutions must be scripted manually. Database management tools are provided in both Windows and browser-based implementations.

10.5 Feature Differences Between MaxDB and MySQL

The following list provides a short summary of the main differences between MaxDB and MySQL; it is not complete.

- MaxDB runs as a client/server system. MySQL can run as a client/server system or as an embedded system.

- MaxDB might not run on all platforms supported by MySQL. For example, MaxDB does not run on IBM's OS/2.

- MaxDB uses a proprietary network protocol for client/server communication. MySQL uses either TCP/IP (with or without SSL encryption), sockets (under Unix-like systems), or named pipes (under Windows NT-family systems).

- MaxDB supports stored procedures. For MySQL, stored procedures are implemented in version 5.0. MaxDB also supports programming of triggers through an SQL extension, which is scheduled for MySQL 5.1. MaxDB contains a debugger for stored procedure languages, can cascade nested triggers, and supports multiple triggers per action and row.

- MaxDB is distributed with user interfaces that are text-based, graphical, or Web-based. MySQL is distributed with text-based user interfaces only; graphical user interfaces (MySQL Control Center, MySQL Administrator) are shipped separately from the main distributions. Web-based user interfaces for MySQL are offered by third parties.

- MaxDB supports a number of programming interfaces that also are supported by MySQL. However, MaxDB does not support RDO, ADO, or .NET, all of which are supported by MySQL. MaxDB supports embedded SQL only with C/C++.
- MaxDB includes administrative features that MySQL does not have: job scheduling by time, event, and alert, and sending messages to a database administrator on alert thresholds.

10.6 Interoperability Features Between MaxDB and MySQL

The following features will be included in MaxDB versions to be released shortly after the first 7.5.00 version. These features will allow interoperation between MaxDB and MySQL.

- There will be a MySQL proxy enabling connections to MaxDB using the MySQL protocol. This makes it possible to use MySQL client programs for MaxDB, such as the `mysql` command-line user interface, the `mysqldump` dump utility, or the `mysqlimport` import program. Using `mysqldump`, you can easily dump data from one database system and export (or even pipe) those data to the other database system.
- Replication between MySQL and MaxDB will be supported in both directions. That is, either MySQL or MaxDB can be used as the master replication server. The long-range plan is to converge and extend the replication syntax so that both database systems understand the same syntax. See Section 5.1, "Introduction to Replication."

10.7 Reserved Words in MaxDB

Like MySQL, MaxDB has a number of reserved words that have special meanings. Normally, they cannot be used as names of identifiers, such as database or table names. The following table lists reserved words in MaxDB, indicates the context in which those words are used, and indicates whether or not they have counterparts in MySQL. If such a counterpart exists, the meaning in MySQL might be identical or differing in some aspects. The main purpose is to list in which respects MaxDB differs from MySQL; therefore, this list is not complete.

For the list of reserved words in MySQL, see the *MySQL Language Reference*.

Reserved in MaxDB	Context of Usage in MaxDB	MySQL Counterpart
@	Can prefix identifier, like "@table"	Not allowed
ADDDATE()	SQL function	ADDDATE();new in MySQL 4.1.1
ADDTIME()	SQL function	ADDTIME(); new in MySQL 4.1.1

Reserved in MaxDB	Context of Usage in MaxDB	MySQL Counterpart
ALPHA	SQL function	Nothing comparable
ARRAY	Data type	Not implemented
ASCII()	SQL function	ASCII(), but implemented with a different meaning
AUTOCOMMIT	Transactions; ON by default	Transactions; OFF by default
BOOLEAN	Column types; BOOLEAN accepts as values only TRUE, FALSE, and NULL	BOOLEAN was added in MySQL 4.1.0; it is a synonym for BOOL which is mapped to TINYINT(1). It accepts integer values in the same range as TINYINT as well as NULL. TRUE and FALSE can be used as aliases for 1 and 0.
CHECK	CHECK TABLE	CHECK TABLE; similar, but not identical usage
COLUMN	Column types	COLUMN; noise word
CHAR()	SQL function	CHAR(); identical syntax; similar, not identical usage
COMMIT	Implicit commits of transactions happen when data definition statements are issued	Implicit commits of transactions happen when data definition statements are issued, and also with a number of other statements
COSH()	SQL function	Nothing comparable
COT()	SQL function	COT();identical syntax and implementation
CREATE	SQL, data definition language	CREATE
DATABASE	SQL function	DATABASE(); DATABASE is used in a different context; for example, CREATE DATABASE
DATE()	SQL function	CURRENT_DATE

Reserved in MaxDB	Context of Usage in MaxDB	MySQL Counterpart
DATEDIFF()	SQL function	DATEDIFF(); new in MySQL 4.1.1
DAY()	SQL function	Nothing comparable
DAYOFWEEK()	SQL function	DAYOFWEEK(); by default, 1 represents Monday in MaxDB and Sunday in MySQL
DISTINCT	SQL functions AVG, MAX, MIN, SUM	DISTINCT; but used in a different context: SELECT DISTINCT
DROP	DROP INDEX, for example	DROP INDEX; similar, but not identical usage
EBCDIC()	SQL function	Nothing comparable
EXPAND()	SQL function	Nothing comparable
EXPLAIN	Optimization	EXPLAIN; similar, but not identical usage
FIXED()	SQL function	Nothing comparable
FLOAT()	SQL function	Nothing comparable
HEX()	SQL function	HEX(); similar, but not identical usage
INDEX()	SQL function	INSTR() or LOCATE(); similar, but not identical syntaxes and meanings
INDEX	USE INDEX, IGNORE INDEX and similar hints are used right after SELECT; for example, in SELECT ... USE INDEX	USE INDEX, IGNORE INDEX and similar hints are used in the FROM clause of a SELECT query; for example, in SELECT ... FROM ... USE INDEX
INITCAP()	SQL function	Nothing comparable
LENGTH()	SQL function	LENGTH(); identical syntax, but slightly different implementation
LFILL()	SQL function	Nothing comparable
LIKE	Comparisons	LIKE; but the extended LIKE MaxDB provides rather resembles the MySQL REGEX

Reserved in MaxDB	Context of Usage in MaxDB	MySQL Counterpart
LIKE wildcards	MaxDB supports "%", "_", "Control-underline", "Control-up arrow", "*", and "?" as wildcards in LIKE comparisons	MySQL supports "%", and "_" as wildcards in LIKE comparisons
LPAD()	SQL function	LPAD(); slightly different implementation
LTRIM()	SQL function	LTRIM(); slightly different implementation
MAKEDATE()	SQL function	MAKEDATE(); new in MySQL 4.1.1
MAKETIME()	SQL function	MAKETIME(); new in MySQL 4.1.1
MAPCHAR()	SQL function	Nothing comparable
MICROSECOND()	SQL function	MICROSECOND(); new in MySQL 4.1.1
NOROUND()	SQL function	Nothing comparable
NULL	Column types; comparisons	NULL; MaxDB supports special NULL values that are returned by arithmetic operations that lead to an overflow or a division by zero; MySQL does not support such special values
PI	SQL function	PI(); identical syntax and implementation, but parentheses are mandatory in MySQL
REF	Data type	Nothing comparable
RFILL()	SQL function	Nothing comparable
ROWNO	Predicate in WHERE clause	Similar to LIMIT clause
RPAD()	SQL function	RPAD(); slightly different implementation
RTRIM()	SQL function	RTRIM(); slightly different implementation
SEQUENCE	CREATE SEQUENCE, DROP SEQUENCE	AUTO_INCREMENT; similar concept, but different implementation
SINH()	SQL function	Nothing comparable

Reserved in MaxDB	Context of Usage in MaxDB	MySQL Counterpart
SOUNDS()	SQL function	SOUNDEX(); slightly different syntax
STATISTICS	UPDATE STATISTICS	ANALYZE TABLE; similar concept, but different implementation
SUBSTR()	SQL function	SUBSTRING(); slightly different implementation
SUBTIME()	SQL function	SUBTIME(); new in MySQL 4.1.1
SYNONYM	Data definition language: CREATE [PUBLIC] SYNONYM, RENAME SYNONYM, DROP SYNONYM	Nothing comparable
TANH()	SQL function	Nothing comparable
TIME()	SQL function	CURRENT_TIME
TIMEDIFF()	SQL function	TIMEDIFF(); new in MySQL 4.1.1
TIMESTAMP()	SQL function	TIMESTAMP(); new in MySQL 4.1.1
TIMESTAMP() as argument to DAYOFMONTH() and DAYOFYEAR()	SQL function	Nothing comparable
TIMEZONE()	SQL function	Nothing comparable
TRANSACTION()	Returns the ID of the current transaction	Nothing comparable
TRANSLATE()	SQL function	REPLACE(); identical syntax and implementation
TRIM()	SQL function	TRIM(); slightly different implementation
TRUNC()	SQL function	TRUNCATE(); slightly different syntax and implementation
USE	Termmates connection to current database; switches to new database	Switches to new database
USER	SQL function	USER(); identical syntax, but slightly different implementation, and parentheses are mandatory in MySQL

Reserved in MaxDB	Context of Usage in MaxDB	MySQL Counterpart
UTC_DIFF()	SQL function	UTC_DATE(); provides a means to calculate the same result as UTC_DIFF()
VALUE()	SQL function, alias for COALESCE()	COALESCE(); identical syntax and implementation
VARIANCE()	SQL function	VARIANCE();new in MySQL 4.1.0
WEEKOFYEAR()	SQL function	WEEKOFYEAR(); new in MySQL 4.1.1

A

Troubleshooting Problems with MySQL Programs

This appendix lists some common problems and error messages that you may encounter when running MySQL programs. It describes how to determine the causes of the problems and what to do to solve them.

A.1 How to Determine What Is Causing a Problem

When you run into a problem, the first thing you should do is to find out which program or piece of equipment is causing it:

- If you have one of the following symptoms, then it is probably a hardware problem (such as memory, motherboard, CPU, or hard disk) or kernel problem:

  - The keyboard doesn't work. This can normally be checked by pressing the Caps Lock key. If the Caps Lock light doesn't change, you have to replace your keyboard. (Before doing this, you should try to restart your computer and check all cables to the keyboard.)

  - The mouse pointer doesn't move.

  - The machine doesn't answer to a remote machine's pings.

  - Other programs that are not related to MySQL don't behave correctly.

  - Your system restarted unexpectedly. (A faulty user-level program should never be able to take down your system.)

  In this case, you should start by checking all your cables and run some diagnostic tool to check your hardware! You should also check whether there are any patches, updates, or service packs for your operating system that could likely solve your problem. Check also that all your libraries (such as glibc) are up to date.

  It's always good to use a machine with ECC memory to discover memory problems early.

- If your keyboard is locked up, you may be able to recover by logging in to your machine from another machine and executing `kbd_mode -a`.

- Please examine your system log file (`/var/log/messages` or similar) for reasons for your problem. If you think the problem is in MySQL, you should also examine MySQL's log files. See Section 4.8, "The MySQL Log Files."

- If you don't think you have hardware problems, you should try to find out which program is causing problems. Try using `top`, `ps`, Task Manager, or some similar program, to check which program is taking all CPU or is locking the machine.

- Use `top`, `df`, or a similar program to check whether you are out of memory, disk space, file descriptors, or some other critical resource.

- If the problem is some runaway process, you can always try to kill it. If it doesn't want to die, there is probably a bug in the operating system.

If after you have examined all other possibilities and you have concluded that the MySQL server or a MySQL client is causing the problem, it's time to create a bug report for our mailing list or our support team. In the bug report, try to give a very detailed description of how the system is behaving and what you think is happening. You should also state why you think that MySQL is causing the problem. Take into consideration all the situations in this chapter. State any problems exactly how they appear when you examine your system. Use the "copy and paste" method for any output and error messages from programs and log files.

Try to describe in detail which program is not working and all symptoms you see. We have in the past received many bug reports that state only "the system doesn't work." This doesn't provide us with any information about what could be the problem.

If a program fails, it's always useful to know the following information:

- Has the program in question made a segmentation fault (did it dump core)?

- Is the program taking up all available CPU time? Check with `top`. Let the program run for a while, it may simply be evaluating something computationally intensive.

- If the `mysqld` server is causing problems, can you get any response from it with `mysqladmin -u root ping` or `mysqladmin -u root processlist`?

- What does a client program say when you try to connect to the MySQL server? (Try with `mysql`, for example.) Does the client jam? Do you get any output from the program?

When sending a bug report, you should follow the outline described in Section 1.7.1.2, "Asking Questions or Reporting Bugs."

A.2 Common Errors When Using MySQL Programs

This section lists some errors that users frequently encounter when running MySQL programs. Although the problems show up when you try to run client programs, the solutions to many of the problems involves changing the configuration of the MySQL server.

A.2.1 Access denied

An Access denied error can have many causes. Often the problem is related to the MySQL accounts that the server allows client programs to use when connecting. See Section 4.4.8, "Causes of Access denied Errors." See Section 4.4.2, "How the Privilege System Works."

A.2.2 Can't connect to [local] MySQL server

A MySQL client on Unix can connect to the mysqld server in two different ways: By using a Unix socket file to connect through a file in the filesystem (default /tmp/mysql.sock), or by using TCP/IP, which connects through a port number. A Unix socket file connection is faster than TCP/IP, but can be used only when connecting to a server on the same computer. A Unix socket file is used if you don't specify a hostname or if you specify the special hostname localhost.

If the MySQL server is running on Windows 9x or Me, you can connect only via TCP/IP. If the server is running on Windows NT, 2000, or XP and is started with the --enable-named-pipe option, you can also connect with named pipes if you run the client on the host where the server is running. The name of the named pipe is MySQL by default. If you don't give a hostname when connecting to mysqld, a MySQL client first will try to connect to the named pipe. If that doesn't work, it will connect to the TCP/IP port. You can force the use of named pipes on Windows by using . as the hostname.

The error (2002) Can't connect to ... normally means that there is no MySQL server running on the system or that you are using an incorrect Unix socket filename or TCP/IP port number when trying to connect to the server.

Start by checking whether there is a process named mysqld running on your server host. (Use ps on Unix or the Task Manager on Windows.) If there is no such process, you should start the server. See Section 2.4.4, "Starting and Troubleshooting the MySQL Server."

If a mysqld process is running, you can check it by trying the following commands. The port number or Unix socket filename might be different in your setup. host_ip represents the IP number of the machine where the server is running.

```
shell> mysqladmin version
shell> mysqladmin variables
shell> mysqladmin -h `hostname` version variables
shell> mysqladmin -h `hostname` --port=3306 version
shell> mysqladmin -h host_ip version
shell> mysqladmin --protocol=socket --socket=/tmp/mysql.sock version
```

Note the use of backticks rather than forward quotes with the hostname command; these cause the output of hostname (that is, the current hostname) to be substituted into the mysqladmin command. If you have no hostname command or are running on Windows, you can manually type the hostname of your machine (without backticks) following the -h option. You can also try -h 127.0.0.1 to connect with TCP/IP to the local host.

Here are some reasons the `Can't connect to local MySQL server` error might occur:

- `mysqld` is not running.
- You are running on a system that uses MIT-pthreads. If you are running on a system that doesn't have native threads, `mysqld` uses the MIT-pthreads package. See Section 2.1.1, "Operating Systems Supported by MySQL." However, not all MIT-pthreads versions support Unix socket files. On a system without socket file support, you must always specify the hostname explicitly when connecting to the server. Try using this command to check the connection to the server:

```
shell> mysqladmin -h `hostname` version
```

- Someone has removed the Unix socket file that `mysqld` uses (`/tmp/mysql.sock` by default). For example, you might have a `cron` job that removes old files from the `/tmp` directory. You can always run `mysqladmin version` to check whether the Unix socket file that `mysqladmin` is trying to use really exists. The fix in this case is to change the `cron` job to not remove `mysql.sock` or to place the socket file somewhere else. See Section A.4.5, "How to Protect or Change the MySQL Socket File `/tmp/mysql.sock`."
- You have started the `mysqld` server with the `--socket=/path/to/socket` option, but forgotten to tell client programs the new name of the socket file. If you change the socket pathname for the server, you must also notify the MySQL clients. You can do this by providing the same `--socket` option when you run client programs. See Section A.4.5, "How to Protect or Change the MySQL Socket File `/tmp/mysql.sock`."
- You are using Linux and one server thread has died (dumped core). In this case, you must kill the other `mysqld` threads (for example, with `kill` or with the `mysql_zap` script) before you can restart the MySQL server. See Section A.4.2, "What to Do If MySQL Keeps Crashing."
- The server or client program might not have the proper access privileges for the directory that holds the Unix socket file or the socket file itself. In this case, you must either change the access privileges for the directory or socket file so that the server and clients can access them, or restart `mysqld` with a `--socket` option that specifies a socket filename in a directory where the server can create it and where client programs can access it.

If you get the error message `Can't connect to MySQL server on` *some_host*, you can try the following things to find out what the problem is:

- Check whether the server is running on that host by executing `telnet` *some_host* `3306` and pressing the Enter key a couple of times. (3306 is the default MySQL port number. Change the value if your server is listening to a different port.) If there is a MySQL server running and listening to the port, you should get a response that includes the server's version number. If you get an error such as `telnet: Unable to connect to remote host: Connection refused`, then there is no server running on the given port.

- If the server is running on the local host, try using `mysqladmin -h localhost variables` to connect using the Unix socket file. Verify the TCP/IP port number that the server is configured to listen to (it is the value of the `port` variable.)

- Make sure that your `mysqld` server was not started with the `--skip-networking` option. If it was, you will not be able to connect to it using TCP/IP.

A.2.3 `Client does not support authentication protocol`

MySQL 4.1 and up uses an authentication protocol based on a password hashing algorithm that is incompatible with that used by older clients. If you upgrade the server to 4.1, attempts to connect to it with an older client may fail with the following message:

```
shell> mysql
Client does not support authentication protocol requested
by server; consider upgrading MySQL client
```

To solve this problem, you should use one of the following approaches:

- Upgrade all client programs to use a 4.1.1 or newer client library.

- When connecting to the server with a pre-4.1 client program, use an account that still has a pre-4.1-style password.

- Reset the password to pre-4.1 style for each user that needs to use a pre-4.1 client program. This can be done using the SET PASSWORD statement and the OLD_PASSWORD() function:

```
mysql> SET PASSWORD FOR
    -> 'some_user'@'some_host' = OLD_PASSWORD('newpwd');
```

Alternatively, use UPDATE and FLUSH PRIVILEGES:

```
mysql> UPDATE mysql.user SET Password = OLD_PASSWORD('newpwd')
    -> WHERE Host = 'some_host' AND User = 'some_user';
mysql> FLUSH PRIVILEGES;
```

Substitute the password you want to use for "*newpwd*" in the preceding examples. MySQL cannot tell you what the original password was, so you'll need to pick a new one.

- Tell the server to use the older password hashing algorithm:

    1. Start `mysqld` with the `--old-passwords` option.

    2. Assign an old-format password to each account that has had its password updated to the longer 4.1 format. You can identify these accounts with the following query:

```
mysql> SELECT Host, User, Password FROM mysql.user
    -> WHERE LENGTH(Password) > 16;
```

For each account record displayed by the query, use the Host and User values and assign a password using the OLD_PASSWORD() function and either SET PASSWORD or UPDATE, as described earlier.

For additional background on password hashing and authentication, see Section 4.4.9, "Password Hashing in MySQL 4.1."

A.2.4 Password Fails When Entered Interactively

MySQL client programs prompt for a password when invoked with a --password or -p option that has no following password value:

```
shell> mysql -u user_name -p
Enter password:
```

On some systems, you may find that your password works when specified in an option file or on the command line, but not when you enter it interactively at the Enter password: prompt. This occurs when the library provided by the system to read passwords limits password values to a small number of characters (typically eight). That is a problem with the system library, not with MySQL. To work around it, change your MySQL password to a value that is eight or fewer characters long, or put your password in an option file.

A.2.5 Host 'host_name' is blocked

If you get the following error, it means that mysqld has received many connect requests from the host 'host_name' that have been interrupted in the middle:

```
Host 'host_name' is blocked because of many connection errors.
Unblock with 'mysqladmin flush-hosts'
```

The number of interrupted connect requests allowed is determined by the value of the max_connect_errors system variable. After max_connect_errors failed requests, mysqld assumes that something is wrong (for example, that someone is trying to break in), and blocks the host from further connections until you execute a mysqladmin flush-hosts command or issue a FLUSH HOSTS statement. See Section 4.2.3, "Server System Variables."

By default, mysqld blocks a host after 10 connection errors. You can adjust the value by starting the server like this:

```
shell> mysqld_safe --max_connect_errors=10000 &
```

If you get this error message for a given host, you should first verify that there isn't anything wrong with TCP/IP connections from that host. If you are having network problems, it will do you no good to increase the value of the max_connect_errors variable.

A.2.6 Too many connections

If you get a Too many connections error when you try to connect to the mysqld server, this means that all available connections already are used by other clients.

The number of connections allowed is controlled by the max_connections system variable. Its default value is 100. If you need to support more connections, you should restart mysqld with a larger value for this variable.

mysqld actually allows max_connections+1 clients to connect. The extra connection is reserved for use by accounts that have the SUPER privilege. By granting the SUPER privilege to administrators and not to normal users (who should not need it), an administrator can connect to the server and use SHOW PROCESSLIST to diagnose problems even if the maximum number of unprivileged clients already are connected.

The maximum number of connections MySQL can support depends on the quality of the thread library on a given platform. Linux or Solaris should be able to support 500-1000 simultaneous connections, depending on how much RAM you have and what your clients are doing.

A.2.7 Out of memory

If you issue a query using the mysql client program and receive an error like the following one, it means that mysql does not have enough memory to store the entire query result:

```
mysql: Out of memory at line 42, 'malloc.c'
mysql: needed 8136 byte (8k), memory in use: 12481367 bytes (12189k)
ERROR 2008: MySQL client ran out of memory
```

To remedy the problem, first check whether your query is correct. Is it reasonable that it should return so many rows? If not, correct the query and try again. Otherwise, you can invoke mysql with the --quick option. This causes it to use the mysql_use_result() C API function to retrieve the result set, which places less of a load on the client (but more on the server).

A.2.8 MySQL server has gone away

This section also covers the related Lost connection to server during query error.

The most common reason for the MySQL server has gone away error is that the server timed out and closed the connection. In this case, you normally get one of the following error codes (which one you get is operating system-dependent):

Error Code	Description
CR_SERVER_GONE_ERROR	The client couldn't send a question to the server.
CR_SERVER_LOST	The client didn't get an error when writing to the server, but it didn't get a full answer (or any answer) to the question.

By default, the server closes the connection after eight hours if nothing has happened. You can change the time limit by setting the `wait_timeout` variable when you start `mysqld`. See Section 4.2.3, "Server System Variables."

If you have a script, you just have to issue the query again for the client to do an automatic reconnection.

You will also get an error if someone has killed the running thread with a `KILL` statement or a `mysqladmin kill` command.

Another common reason the `MySQL server has gone away` error occurs within an application program is that you tried to run a query after closing the connection to the server. This indicates a logic error in the application that should be corrected.

You can check whether the MySQL server died and restarted by executing `mysqladmin version` and examining the server's uptime. If the client connection was broken because `mysqld` crashed and restarted, you should concentrate on finding the reason for the crash. Start by checking whether issuing the query again kills the server again. See Section A.4.2, "What to Do If MySQL Keeps Crashing."

You can also get these errors if you send a query to the server that is incorrect or too large. If `mysqld` receives a packet that is too large or out of order, it assumes that something has gone wrong with the client and closes the connection. If you need big queries (for example, if you are working with big `BLOB` columns), you can increase the query limit by setting the server's `max_allowed_packet` variable, which has a default value of 1MB. You may also need to increase the maximum packet size on the client end. More information on setting the packet size is given in Section A.2.9, "Packet too large."

You will also get a lost connection if you are sending a packet 16MB or larger if your client is older than 4.0.8 and your server is 4.0.8 and above, or the other way around.

If you want to create a bug report regarding this problem, be sure that you include the following information:

- Indicate whether or not the MySQL server died. You can find information about this in the server error log. See Section A.4.2, "What to Do If MySQL Keeps Crashing."
- If a specific query kills `mysqld` and the tables involved were checked with `CHECK TABLE` before you ran the query, can you provide a reproducible test case?
- What is the value of the `wait_timeout` system variable in the MySQL server? (`mysqladmin variables` gives you the value of this variable.)
- Have you tried to run `mysqld` with the `--log` option to determine whether the problem query appears in the log?

See Section 1.7.1.2, "Asking Questions or Reporting Bugs."

A.2.9 `Packet too large`

A communication packet is a single SQL statement sent to the MySQL server or a single row that is sent to the client.

In MySQL 3.23, the largest possible packet is 16MB, due to limits in the client/server protocol. In MySQL 4.0.1 and up, the limit is 1GB.

When a MySQL client or the `mysqld` server receives a packet bigger than `max_allowed_packet` bytes, it issues a `Packet too large` error and closes the connection. With some clients, you may also get a `Lost connection to MySQL server during query` error if the communication packet is too large.

Both the client and the server have their own `max_allowed_packet` variable, so if you want to handle big packets, you must increase this variable both in the client and in the server.

If you are using the `mysql` client program, its default `max_allowed_packet` variable is 16MB. That is also the maximum value before MySQL 4.0. To set a larger value from 4.0 on, start `mysql` like this:

```
mysql> mysql --max_allowed_packet=32M
```

That sets the packet size to 32MB.

The server's default `max_allowed_packet` value is 1MB. You can increase this if the server needs to handle big queries (for example, if you are working with big `BLOB` columns). For example, to set the variable to 16MB, start the server like this:

```
mysql> mysqld --max_allowed_packet=16M
```

Before MySQL 4.0, use this syntax instead:

```
mysql> mysqld --set-variable=max_allowed_packet=16M
```

You can also use an option file to set `max_allowed_packet`. For example, to set the size for the server to 16MB, add the following lines in an option file:

```
[mysqld]
max_allowed_packet=16M
```

Before MySQL 4.0, use this syntax instead:

```
[mysqld]
set-variable = max_allowed_packet=16M
```

It's safe to increase the value of this variable because the extra memory is allocated only when needed. For example, `mysqld` allocates more memory only when you issue a long query or when `mysqld` must return a large result row. The small default value of the variable is a precaution to catch incorrect packets between the client and server and also to ensure that you don't run out of memory by using large packets accidentally.

You can also get strange problems with large packets if you are using large BLOB values but have not given mysqld access to enough memory to handle the query. If you suspect this is the case, try adding ulimit -d 256000 to the beginning of the mysqld_safe script and restarting mysqld.

A.2.10 Communication Errors and Aborted Connections

The server error log can be a useful source of information about connection problems. See Section 4.8.1, "The Error Log." Starting with MySQL 3.23.40, if you start the server with the --warnings option (or --log-warnings from MySQL 4.0.3 on), you might find messages like this in your error log:

```
010301 14:38:23  Aborted connection 854 to db: 'users' user: 'josh'
```

If Aborted connections messages appear in the error log, the cause can be any of the following:

- The client program did not call mysql_close() before exiting.
- The client had been sleeping more than wait_timeout or interactive_timeout seconds without issuing any requests to the server. See Section 4.2.3, "Server System Variables."
- The client program ended abruptly in the middle of a data transfer.

When any of these things happen, the server increments the Aborted_clients status variable.

The server increments the Aborted_connects status variable when the following things happen:

- A client doesn't have privileges to connect to a database.
- A client uses an incorrect password.
- A connection packet doesn't contain the right information.
- It takes more than connect_timeout seconds to get a connect packet. See Section 4.2.3, "Server System Variables."

If these kinds of things happen, it might indicate that someone is trying to break into your server!

Other reasons for problems with aborted clients or aborted connections:

- Use of Ethernet protocol with Linux, both half and full duplex. Many Linux Ethernet drivers have this bug. You should test for this bug by transferring a huge file via FTP between the client and server machines. If a transfer goes in burst-pause-burst-pause mode, you are experiencing a Linux duplex syndrome. The only solution is switching the duplex mode for both your network card and hub/switch to either full duplex or to half duplex and testing the results to determine the best setting.
- Some problem with the thread library that causes interrupts on reads.

- Badly configured TCP/IP.

- Faulty Ethernets, hubs, switches, cables, and so forth. This can be diagnosed properly only by replacing hardware.

- The `max_allowed_packet` variable value is too small or queries require more memory than you have allocated for `mysqld`. See Section A.2.9, "`Packet too large`."

A.2.11 The `table is full`

There are several ways a full-table error can occur:

- You are using a MySQL server older than 3.23 and an in-memory temporary table becomes larger than `tmp_table_size` bytes. To avoid this problem, you can use the `-O tmp_table_size=#` option to make `mysqld` increase the temporary table size or use the SQL option `SQL_BIG_TABLES` before you issue the problematic query.

  You can also start `mysqld` with the `--big-tables` option. This is exactly the same as using `SQL_BIG_TABLES` for all queries.

  As of MySQL 3.23, this problem should not occur. If an in-memory temporary table becomes larger than `tmp_table_size`, the server automatically converts it to a disk-based `MyISAM` table.

- You are using `InnoDB` tables and run out of room in the `InnoDB` tablespace. In this case, the solution is to extend the `InnoDB` tablespace. See Section 9.8, "Adding and Removing `InnoDB` Data and Log Files."

- You are using `ISAM` or `MyISAM` tables on an operating system that supports files only up to 2GB in size and you have hit this limit for the data file or index file.

- You are using a `MyISAM` table and the space required for the table exceeds what is allowed by the internal pointer size. (If you don't specify the `MAX_ROWS` table option when you create a table, MySQL uses the `myisam_data_pointer_size` system variable. Its default value of 4 bytes is enough to allow only 4GB of data.) See Section 4.2.3, "Server System Variables."

  You can check the maximum data/index sizes by using this statement:

  `SHOW TABLE STATUS FROM database LIKE 'tbl_name';`

  You also can use `myisamchk -dv /path/to/table-index-file`.

  If the pointer size is too small, you can fix the problem by using `ALTER TABLE`:

  `ALTER TABLE tbl_name MAX_ROWS=1000000000 AVG_ROW_LENGTH=nnn;`

  You have to specify `AVG_ROW_LENGTH` only for tables with `BLOB` or `TEXT` columns; in this case, MySQL can't optimize the space required based only on the number of rows.

A.2.12 Can't create/write to file

If you get an error of the following type for some queries, it means that MySQL cannot create a temporary file for the result set in the temporary directory:

```
Can't create/write to file '\\sqla3fe_0.ism'.
```

The preceding error is a typical message for Windows; the Unix message is similar. The fix is to start mysqld with the --tmpdir option or to add the option to the [mysqld] section of your option file. For example, to specify a directory of C:\temp, use these lines:

```
[mysqld]
tmpdir=C:/temp
```

The C:\temp directory must already exist. See Section 3.3.2, "Using Option Files."

Check also the error code that you get with perror. One reason the server cannot write to a table is that the filesystem is full:

```
shell> perror 28
Error code  28:  No space left on device
```

A.2.13 Commands out of sync

If you get Commands out of sync; you can't run this command now in your client code, you are calling client functions in the wrong order.

This can happen, for example, if you are using mysql_use_result() and try to execute a new query before you have called mysql_free_result(). It can also happen if you try to execute two queries that return data without calling mysql_use_result() or mysql_store_result() in between.

A.2.14 Ignoring user

If you get the following error, it means that when mysqld was started or when it reloaded the grant tables, it found an account in the user table that had an invalid password.

```
Found wrong password for user: 'some_user'@'some_host'; ignoring user
```

As a result, the account is simply ignored by the permission system.

The following list indicates possible causes of and fixes for this problem:

- You may be running a new version of mysqld with an old user table. You can check this by executing mysqlshow mysql user to see whether the Password column is shorter than 16 characters. If so, you can correct this condition by running the scripts/add_long_password script.

- The account has an old password (eight characters long) and you didn't start mysqld with the --old-protocol option. Update the account in the user table to have a new password or restart mysqld with the --old-protocol option.

- You have specified a password in the user table without using the PASSWORD() function. Use mysql to update the account in the user table with a new password, making sure to use the PASSWORD() function:

```
mysql> UPDATE user SET Password=PASSWORD('newpwd')
    -> WHERE User='some_user' AND Host='some_host';
```

A.2.15 Table 'tbl_name' doesn't exist

If you get either of the following errors, it usually means that no table exists in the current database with the given name:

```
Table 'tbl_name' doesn't exist
Can't find file: 'tbl_name' (errno: 2)
```

In some cases, it may be that the table does exist but that you are referring to it incorrectly:

- Because MySQL uses directories and files to store databases and tables, database and table names are case sensitive if they are located on a filesystem that has case-sensitive filenames.
- Even for filesystems that are not case sensitive, such as on Windows, all references to a given table within a query must use the same lettercase.

You can check which tables are in the current database with SHOW TABLES.

A.2.16 Can't initialize character set

You might see an error like this if you have character set problems:

```
MySQL Connection Failed: Can't initialize character set charset_name
```

This error can have any of the following causes:

- The character set is a multi-byte character set and you have no support for the character set in the client. In this case, you need to recompile the client by running configure with the --with-charset=charset_name or --with-extra-charsets=charset_name option. See Section 2.3.2, "Typical configure Options."

  All standard MySQL binaries are compiled with --with-extra-character-sets=complex, which enables support for all multi-byte character sets. See Section 4.7.1, "The Character Set Used for Data and Sorting."
- The character set is a simple character set that is not compiled into mysqld, and the character set definition files are not in the place where the client expects to find them.

  In this case, you need to use one of the following methods to solve the problem:

  - Recompile the client with support for the character set. See Section 2.3.2, "Typical configure Options."

- Specify to the client the directory where the character set definition files are located. For many clients, you can do this with the `--character-sets-dir` option.
- Copy the character definition files to the path where the client expects them to be.

A.2.17 File Not Found

If you get ERROR '...' not found (errno: 23), Can't open file: ... (errno: 24), or any other error with errno 23 or errno 24 from MySQL, it means that you haven't allocated enough file descriptors for the MySQL server. You can use the `perror` utility to get a description of what the error number means:

```
shell> perror 23
File table overflow
shell> perror 24
Too many open files
shell> perror 11
Resource temporarily unavailable
```

The problem here is that `mysqld` is trying to keep open too many files simultaneously. You can either tell `mysqld` not to open so many files at once or increase the number of file descriptors available to `mysqld`.

To tell `mysqld` to keep open fewer files at a time, you can make the table cache smaller by reducing the value of the `table_cache` system variable (the default value is 64). Reducing the value of `max_connections` also will reduce the number of open files (the default value is 100).

To change the number of file descriptors available to `mysqld`, you can use the `--open-files-limit` option to `mysqld_safe` or (as of MySQL 3.23.30) set the `open_files_limit` system variable. See Section 4.2.3, "Server System Variables." The easiest way to set these values is to add an option to your option file. See Section 3.3.2, "Using Option Files." If you have an old version of `mysqld` that doesn't support setting the open files limit, you can edit the `mysqld_safe` script. There is a commented-out line `ulimit -n 256` in the script. You can remove the '#' character to uncomment this line, and change the number 256 to set the number of file descriptors to be made available to `mysqld`.

`--open-files-limit` and `ulimit` can increase the number of file descriptors, but only up to the limit imposed by the operating system. There is also a "hard" limit that can be overridden only if you start `mysqld_safe` or `mysqld` as `root` (just remember that you also need to start the server with the `--user` option in this case so that it does not continue to run as `root` after it starts up). If you need to increase the operating system limit on the number of file descriptors available to each process, consult the documentation for your system.

Note: If you run the `tcsh` shell, `ulimit` will not work! `tcsh` will also report incorrect values when you ask for the current limits. In this case, you should start `mysqld_safe` using `sh`.

A.3 Installation-Related Issues

A.3.1 Problems Linking to the MySQL Client Library

When you are linking an application program to use the MySQL client library, you might get undefined reference errors for symbols that start with mysql_, such as those shown here:

```
/tmp/ccFKsdPa.o: In function `main':
/tmp/ccFKsdPa.o(.text+0xb): undefined reference to `mysql_init'
/tmp/ccFKsdPa.o(.text+0x31): undefined reference to `mysql_real_connect'
/tmp/ccFKsdPa.o(.text+0x57): undefined reference to `mysql_real_connect'
/tmp/ccFKsdPa.o(.text+0x69): undefined reference to `mysql_error'
/tmp/ccFKsdPa.o(.text+0x9a): undefined reference to `mysql_close'
```

You should be able to solve this problem by adding -L*dir_path* -lmysqlclient at the end of your link command, where *dir_path* represents the pathname of the directory where the client library is located. To determine the correct directory, try this command:

```
shell> mysql_config --libs
```

The output from mysql_config might indicate other libraries that should be specified on the link command as well.

If you get undefined reference errors for the uncompress or compress function, add -lz to the end of your link command and try again.

If you get undefined reference errors for a function that should exist on your system, such as connect, check the manual page for the function in question to determine which libraries you should add to the link command.

You might get undefined reference errors such as the following for functions that don't exist on your system:

```
mf_format.o(.text+0x201): undefined reference to `__lxstat'
```

This usually means that your MySQL client library was compiled on a system that is not 100% compatible with yours. In this case, you should download the latest MySQL source distribution and compile MySQL yourself. See Section 2.3, "MySQL Installation Using a Source Distribution."

You might get undefined reference errors at runtime when you try to execute a MySQL program. If these errors specify symbols that start with mysql_ or indicate that the mysqlclient library can't be found, it means that your system can't find the shared libmysqlclient.so library. The fix for this is to tell your system to search for shared libraries where the library is located. Use whichever of the following methods is appropriate for your system:

- Add the path to the directory where libmysqlclient.so is located to the LD_LIBRARY_PATH environment variable.

- Add the path to the directory where libmysqlclient.so is located to the LD_LIBRARY environment variable.

- Copy libmysqlclient.so to some directory that is searched by your system, such as /lib, and update the shared library information by executing ldconfig.

Another way to solve this problem is by linking your program statically with the -static option, or by removing the dynamic MySQL libraries before linking your code. Before trying the second method, you should be sure that no other programs are using the dynamic libraries.

A.3.2 How to Run MySQL as a Normal User

On Windows, you can run the server as a Windows service using normal user accounts beginning with MySQL 4.0.17 and 4.1.2. (Older MySQL versions required you to have administrator rights. This was a bug introduced in MySQL 3.23.54.)

On Unix, the MySQL server mysqld can be started and run by any user. However, you should avoid running the server as the Unix root user for security reasons. In order to change mysqld to run as a normal unprivileged Unix user user_name, you must do the following:

1. Stop the server if it's running (use mysqladmin shutdown).

2. Change the database directories and files so that user_name has privileges to read and write files in them (you might need to do this as the Unix root user):

   shell> **chown -R** user_name /path/to/mysql/datadir

   If you do not do this, the server will not be able to access databases or tables when it runs as user_name.

   If directories or files within the MySQL data directory are symbolic links, you'll also need to follow those links and change the directories and files they point to. chown -R might not follow symbolic links for you.

3. Start the server as user user_name. If you are using MySQL 3.22 or later, another alternative is to start mysqld as the Unix root user and use the --user=user_name option. mysqld will start up, then switch to run as the Unix user user_name before accepting any connections.

4. To start the server as the given user automatically at system startup time, specify the username by adding a user option to the [mysqld] group of the /etc/my.cnf option file or the my.cnf option file in the server's data directory. For example:

   [mysqld]
   user=user_name

If your Unix machine itself isn't secured, you should assign passwords to the MySQL root accounts in the grant tables. Otherwise, any user with a login account on that machine can run the `mysql` `client` with a `--user=root` option and perform any operation. (It is a good idea to assign passwords to MySQL accounts in any case, but especially so when other login accounts exist on the server host.) See Section 2.4, "Post-Installation Setup and Testing."

A.3.3 Problems with File Permissions

If you have problems with file permissions, the `UMASK` environment variable might be set incorrectly when `mysqld` starts. For example, MySQL might issue the following error message when you create a table:

```
ERROR: Can't find file: 'path/with/filename.frm' (Errcode: 13)
```

The default `UMASK` value is `0660`. You can change this behavior by starting `mysqld_safe` as follows:

```
shell> UMASK=384  # = 600 in octal
shell> export UMASK
shell> mysqld_safe &
```

By default, MySQL creates database and `RAID` directories with an access permission value of `0700`. You can modify this behavior by setting the `UMASK_DIR` variable. If you set its value, new directories are created with the combined `UMASK` and `UMASK_DIR` values. For example, if you want to give group access to all new directories, you can do this:

```
shell> UMASK_DIR=504  # = 770 in octal
shell> export UMASK_DIR
shell> mysqld_safe &
```

In MySQL 3.23.25 and above, MySQL assumes that the value for `UMASK` and `UMASK_DIR` is in octal if it starts with a zero.

See Appendix B, "Environment Variables."

A.4 Administration-Related Issues

A.4.1 How to Reset the Root Password

If you have never set a `root` password for MySQL, the server will not require a password at all for connecting as `root`. However, it is recommended to set a password for each account. See Section 4.3.1, "General Security Guidelines."

If you set a `root` password previously, but have forgotten what it was, you can set a new password. The following procedure is for Windows systems. The procedure for Unix systems is given later in this section.

The procedure under Windows:

1. Log on to your system as Administrator.
2. Stop the MySQL server if it is running. For a server that is running as a Windows service, go to the Services manager:

   ```
   Start Menu -> Control Panel -> Administrative Tools -> Services
   ```

   Then find the MySQL service in the list, and stop it.

   If your server is not running as a service, you may need to use the Task Manager to force it to stop.
3. Open a console window to get to the DOS command prompt:

   ```
   Start Menu -> Run -> cmd
   ```

4. We are assuming that you installed MySQL to C:\mysql. If you installed MySQL to another location, adjust the following commands accordingly.

   At the DOS command prompt, execute this command:

   ```
   C:\> C:\mysql\bin\mysqld-nt --skip-grant-tables
   ```

   This starts the server in a special mode that does not check the grant tables to control access.
5. Keeping the first console window open, open a second console window and execute the following commands (type each on a single line):

   ```
   C:\> C:\mysql\bin\mysqladmin -u root
           flush-privileges password "newpwd"
   C:\> C:\mysql\bin\mysqladmin -u root -p shutdown
   ```

   Replace "newpwd" with the actual root password that you want to use. The second command will prompt you to enter the new password for access. Enter the password that you assigned in the first command.
6. Stop the MySQL server, then restart it in normal mode again. If you run the server as a service, start it from the Windows Services window. If you start the server manually, use whatever command you normally use.
7. You should now be able to connect using the new password.

In a Unix environment, the procedure for resetting the root password is as follows:

1. Log on to your system as either the Unix root user or as the same user that the mysqld server runs as.
2. Locate the .pid file that contains the server's process ID. The exact location and name of this file depend on your distribution, hostname, and configuration. Common locations are /var/lib/mysql/, /var/run/mysqld/, and /usr/local/mysql/data/. Generally, the filename has the extension of .pid and begins with either mysqld or your system's hostname.

Now you can stop the MySQL server by sending a normal `kill` (not `kill -9`) to the `mysqld` process, using the pathname of the `.pid` file in the following command:

```
shell> kill `cat /mysql-data-directory/host_name.pid`
```

Note the use of backticks rather than forward quotes with the `cat` command; these cause the output of `cat` to be substituted into the `kill` command.

3. Restart the MySQL server with the special `--skip-grant-tables` option:

```
shell> mysqld_safe --skip-grant-tables &
```

4. Set a new password for the `root@localhost` MySQL account:

```
shell> mysqladmin -u root flush-privileges password "newpwd"
```

Replace "*newpwd*" with the actual `root` password that you want to use.

5. Stop the MySQL server, then restart it in normal mode again.

6. You should now be able to connect using the new password.

Alternatively, on any platform, you can set the new password using the `mysql` client:

1. Stop `mysqld` and restart it with the `--skip-grant-tables` option as described earlier.

2. Connect to the `mysqld` server with this command:

```
shell> mysql -u root
```

3. Issue the following statements in the `mysql` client:

```
mysql> UPDATE mysql.user SET Password=PASSWORD('newpwd')
    ->                   WHERE User='root';
mysql> FLUSH PRIVILEGES;
```

Replace "*newpwd*" with the actual `root` password that you want to use.

4. Stop the MySQL server, then restart it in normal mode again.

5. You should now be able to connect using the new password.

A.4.2 What to Do If MySQL Keeps Crashing

Each MySQL version is tested on many platforms before it is released. This doesn't mean that there are no bugs in MySQL, but if there are bugs, they should be very few and can be hard to find. If you have a problem, it will always help if you try to find out exactly what crashes your system, because you will have a much better chance of getting the problem fixed quickly.

First, you should try to find out whether the problem is that the `mysqld` server dies or whether your problem has to do with your client. You can check how long your `mysqld` server has been up by executing `mysqladmin version`. If `mysqld` has died and restarted, you may find the reason by looking in the server's error log. See Section 4.8.1, "The Error Log."

On some systems, you can find in the error log a stack trace of where mysqld died that you can resolve with the resolve_stack_dump program. Note that the variable values written in the error log may not always be 100% correct.

Many server crashes are caused by corrupted data files or index files. MySQL will update the files on disk with the write() system call after every SQL statement and before the client is notified about the result. (This is not true if you are running with --delay-key-write, in which case data files are written but not index files.) This means that data file contents are safe even if mysqld crashes, because the operating system will ensure that the unflushed data is written to disk. You can force MySQL to flush everything to disk after every SQL statement by starting mysqld with the --flush option.

The preceding means that normally you should not get corrupted tables unless one of the following happens:

- The MySQL server or the server host was killed in the middle of an update.
- You have found a bug in mysqld that caused it to die in the middle of an update.
- Some external program is manipulating data files or index files at the same time as mysqld without locking the table properly.
- You are running many mysqld servers using the same data directory on a system that doesn't support good filesystem locks (normally handled by the lockd lock manager), or you are running multiple servers with the --skip-external-locking option.
- You have a crashed data file or index file that contains very corrupt data that confused mysqld.
- You have found a bug in the data storage code. This isn't likely, but it's at least possible. In this case, you can try to change the table type to another storage engine by using ALTER TABLE on a repaired copy of the table.

Because it is very difficult to know why something is crashing, first try to check whether things that work for others crash for you. Please try the following things:

- Stop the mysqld server with mysqladmin shutdown, run myisamchk --silent --force */*.MYI from the data directory to check all MyISAM tables, and restart mysqld. This will ensure that you are running from a clean state. See Chapter 4, "Database Administration."
- Start mysqld with the --log option and try to determine from the information written to the log whether some specific query kills the server. About 95% of all bugs are related to a particular query. Normally, this will be one of the last queries in the log file just before the server restarts. See Section 4.8.2, "The General Query Log." If you can repeatedly kill MySQL with a specific query, even when you have checked all tables just before issuing it, then you have been able to locate the bug and should submit a bug report for it. See Section 1.7.1.3, "How to Report Bugs or Problems."
- Try to make a test case that we can use to repeat the problem.

- Try running the tests in the `mysql-test` directory and the MySQL benchmarks. They should test MySQL rather well. You can also add code to the benchmarks that simulates your application. The benchmarks can be found in the `sql-bench` directory in a source distribution or, for a binary distribution, in the `sql-bench` directory under your MySQL installation directory.

- Try the `fork_big.pl` script. (It is located in the `tests` directory of source distributions.)

- If you configure MySQL for debugging, it will be much easier to gather information about possible errors if something goes wrong. Configuring MySQL for debugging causes a safe memory allocator to be included that can find some errors. It also provides a lot of output about what is happening. Reconfigure MySQL with the `--with-debug` or `--with-debug=full` option to `configure` and then recompile.

- Make sure that you have applied the latest patches for your operating system.

- Use the `--skip-external-locking` option to `mysqld`. On some systems, the `lockd` lock manager does not work properly; the `--skip-external-locking` option tells `mysqld` not to use external locking. (This means that you cannot run two `mysqld` servers on the same data directory and that you must be careful if you use `myisamchk`. Nevertheless, it may be instructive to try the option as a test.)

- Have you tried `mysqladmin -u root processlist` when `mysqld` appears to be running but not responding? Sometimes `mysqld` is not comatose even though you might think so. The problem may be that all connections are in use, or there may be some internal lock problem. `mysqladmin -u root processlist` usually will be able to make a connection even in these cases, and can provide useful information about the current number of connections and their status.

- Run the command `mysqladmin -i 5 status` or `mysqladmin -i 5 -r status` in a separate window to produce statistics while you run your other queries.

- Try the following:

  1. Start `mysqld` from `gdb` (or another debugger).

  2. Run your test scripts.

  3. Print the backtrace and the local variables at the three lowest levels. In `gdb`, you can do this with the following commands when `mysqld` has crashed inside `gdb`:

     ```
     backtrace
     info local
     up
     info local
     up
     info local
     ```

     With `gdb`, you can also examine which threads exist with `info threads` and switch to a specific thread with `thread #`, where # is the thread ID.

- Try to simulate your application with a Perl script to force MySQL to crash or misbehave.

- Send a normal bug report. See Section 1.7.1.3, "How to Report Bugs or Problems." Be even more detailed than usual. Because MySQL works for many people, it may be that the crash results from something that exists only on your computer (for example, an error that is related to your particular system libraries).

- If you have a problem with tables containing dynamic-length rows and you are using only VARCHAR columns (not BLOB or TEXT columns), you can try to change all VARCHAR to CHAR with ALTER TABLE. This will force MySQL to use fixed-size rows. Fixed-size rows take a little extra space, but are much more tolerant to corruption.

  The current dynamic row code has been in use at MySQL AB for several years with very few problems, but dynamic-length rows are by nature more prone to errors, so it may be a good idea to try this strategy to see whether it helps.

A.4.3 How MySQL Handles a Full Disk

When a disk-full condition occurs, MySQL does the following:

- It checks once every minute to see whether there is enough space to write the current row. If there is enough space, it continues as if nothing had happened.

- Every six minutes it writes an entry to the log file, warning about the disk-full condition.

To alleviate the problem, you can take the following actions:

- To continue, you only have to free enough disk space to insert all records.

- To abort the thread, you must use mysqladmin kill. The thread will be aborted the next time it checks the disk (in one minute).

- Other threads might be waiting for the table that caused the disk-full condition. If you have several "locked" threads, killing the one thread that is waiting on the disk-full condition will allow the other threads to continue.

Exceptions to the preceding behavior are when you use REPAIR TABLE or OPTIMIZE TABLE or when the indexes are created in a batch after LOAD DATA INFILE or after an ALTER TABLE statement. All of these statements may create large temporary files that, if left to themselves, would cause big problems for the rest of the system. If the disk becomes full while MySQL is doing any of these operations, it will remove the big temporary files and mark the table as crashed. The exception is that for ALTER TABLE, the old table will be left unchanged.

A.4.4 Where MySQL Stores Temporary Files

MySQL uses the value of the TMPDIR environment variable as the pathname of the directory in which to store temporary files. If you don't have TMPDIR set, MySQL uses the system default, which is normally `/tmp`, `/var/tmp`, or `/usr/tmp`. If the filesystem containing your temporary file directory is too small, you can use the `--tmpdir` option to `mysqld` to specify a directory in a filesystem where you have enough space.

Starting from MySQL 4.1, the `--tmpdir` option can be set to a list of several paths that are used in round-robin fashion. Paths should be separated by colon characters (':') on Unix and semicolon characters (';') on Windows, NetWare, and OS/2. **Note:** To spread the load effectively, these paths should be located on different *physical* disks, not different partitions of the same disk.

If the MySQL server is acting as a replication slave, you should not set `--tmpdir` to point to a directory on a memory-based filesystem or to a directory that is cleared when the server host restarts. A replication slave needs some of its temporary files to survive a machine restart so that it can replicate temporary tables or `LOAD DATA INFILE` operations. If files in the temporary file directory are lost when the server restarts, replication will fail.

MySQL creates all temporary files as hidden files. This ensures that the temporary files will be removed if `mysqld` is terminated. The disadvantage of using hidden files is that you will not see a big temporary file that fills up the filesystem in which the temporary file directory is located.

When sorting (`ORDER BY` or `GROUP BY`), MySQL normally uses one or two temporary files. The maximum disk space required is determined by the following expression:

```
(length of what is sorted + sizeof(row pointer))
* number of matched rows
* 2
```

The row pointer size is usually four bytes, but may grow in the future for really big tables.

For some `SELECT` queries, MySQL also creates temporary SQL tables. These are not hidden and have names of the form `SQL_*`.

`ALTER TABLE` creates a temporary table in the same directory as the original table.

A.4.5 How to Protect or Change the MySQL Socket File `/tmp/mysql.sock`

The default location for the Unix socket file that the server uses for communication with local clients is `/tmp/mysql.sock`. This might cause problems, because on some versions of Unix, anyone can delete files in the `/tmp` directory.

On most versions of Unix, you can protect your `/tmp` directory so that files can be deleted only by their owners or the superuser (`root`). To do this, set the `sticky` bit on the `/tmp` directory by logging in as `root` and using the following command:

```
shell> chmod +t /tmp
```

You can check whether the `sticky` bit is set by executing `ls -ld /tmp`. If the last permission character is `t`, the bit is set.

Another approach is to change the place where the server creates the Unix socket file. If you do this, you should also let client programs know the new location of the file. You can specify the file location in several ways:

- Specify the path in a global or local option file. For example, put the following lines in `/etc/my.cnf`:

  ```
  [mysqld]
  socket=/path/to/socket
  ```

  ```
  [client]
  socket=/path/to/socket
  ```

  See Section 3.3.2, "Using Option Files."

- Specify a `--socket` option on the command line to `mysqld_safe` and when you run client programs.

- Set the `MYSQL_UNIX_PORT` environment variable to the path of the Unix socket file.

- Recompile MySQL from source to use a different default Unix socket file location. Define the path to the file with the `--with-unix-socket-path` option when you run `configure`. See Section 2.3.2, "Typical `configure` Options."

You can test whether the new socket location works by attempting to connect to the server with this command:

```
shell> mysqladmin --socket=/path/to/socket version
```

A.4.6 Time Zone Problems

If you have a problem with `SELECT NOW()` returning values in GMT and not your local time, you have to tell the server your current time zone. The same applies if `UNIX_TIMESTAMP()` returns the wrong value. This should be done for the environment in which the server runs; for example, in `mysqld_safe` or `mysql.server`. See Appendix B, "Environment Variables."

You can set the time zone for the server with the `--timezone=timezone_name` option to `mysqld_safe`. You can also set it by setting the `TZ` environment variable before you start `mysqld`.

The allowable values for `--timezone` or `TZ` are system-dependent. Consult your operating system documentation to see what values are acceptable.

B

Environment Variables

This appendix lists all the environment variables that are used directly or indirectly by MySQL. Most of these can also be found in other places in this manual.

Note that any options on the command line take precedence over values specified in option files and environment variables, and values in option files take precedence over values in environment variables.

In many cases, it's preferable to use an option file instead of environment variables to modify the behavior of MySQL. See Section 3.3.2, "Using Option Files."

Variable	Description
CXX	The name of your C++ compiler (for running `configure`).
CC	The name of your C compiler (for running `configure`).
CFLAGS	Flags for your C compiler (for running `configure`).
CXXFLAGS	Flags for your C++ compiler (for running `configure`).
DBI_USER	The default username for Perl DBI.
DBI_TRACE	Trace options for Perl DBI.
HOME	The default path for the `mysql` history file is `$HOME/.mysql_history`.
LD_RUN_PATH	Used to specify where your `libmysqlclient.so` is located.
MYSQL_DEBUG	Debug trace options when debugging.
MYSQL_HISTFILE	The path to the `mysql` history file. If this variable is set, its value overrides the default of `$HOME/.mysql_history`.
MYSQL_HOST	The default hostname used by the `mysql` command-line client.
MYSQL_PS1	The command prompt to use in the `mysql` command-line client.
MYSQL_PWD	The default password when connecting to `mysqld`. Note that use of this is insecure! See Section 4.5.6, "Keeping Your Password Secure."
MYSQL_TCP_PORT	The default TCP/IP port number.
MYSQL_UNIX_PORT	The default Unix socket filename; used for connections to `localhost`.
PATH	Used by the shell to find MySQL programs.
TMPDIR	The directory where temporary files are created.

Variable	Description
TZ	This should be set to your local time zone. See Section A.4.6, "Time Zone Problems."
UMASK_DIR	The user-directory creation mask when creating directories. Note that this is ANDed with UMASK!
UMASK	The user-file creation mask when creating files.
USER	The default username on Windows and NetWare to use when connecting to mysqld.

Index

Symbols

{} (braces), 3
... (ellipsis), 3
[ ] (square brackets), 3
| (vertical bar), 3

Numbers

3.23 troubleshooting, 387
4.0 upgrades, replication setups, 382-383
5.0 upgrades, replication setups, 383
1005 error, 555
2002 error (Can't connect to local MySQL server), 609-611

A

Aborted clients error, 616-617
Aborted connections error, 616-617
access
    servers, client programs, 197
    shared, MyISAM key cache, 447
    write, tmp files, 134
Access Control Lists. *See* ACLs
Access denied errors, 290-296, 609
access privilege system
    Access denied errors, 290-296
    accounts, 141

administrative privileges, 281
    changes, implementing, 290
    connecting, 274-278, 282-287
    functions, 274
    grant tables, 274-282
    password hashing, 296-301
    requests, verification, 287-290
accounts
    access privileges, 141
    anonymous, 141
    creating, 303-307
    deleting, 307
    managing, 302-303
    passwords, 142-144
        assigning, 309-311
        securing, 311-312
    resources, limiting, 308-309
    security, 141-144
    SSL (Secure Sockets Layer)
        command-line options, 318-319
        encryption, 312
        GRANT statement options, 318
        requirements, 313
        setting, 314-318
    SSH (Secure Shell), 319
    X509 certificates, 313

ACID (atomicity, consistency, isolation, and durability)

compliance, 48

InnoDB storage engine

backup/recovery, 563-566

configuring, 541-546

contact information, 540

creating, 551-559

data files, adding/removing, 561-562

defragmenting tables, 588

doublewrite, 587

dumping, 563

error handling, 589-594

fields, 583

file space management, 588

I/O (input/output), 586-588

indexes, 584-586

locking, 567-576

log files, adding/removing, 561-562

moving, 566-567

multi-versioning, 583-584

overview, 539

per-table tablespaces, 559-561

performance tuning, 576-583

read-aheads, 586

restrictions, 594-596

startup parameters, 546-549

sizing, 562

tablespaces, 550-551, 588

troubleshooting, 596-598

undo logs, 583

version 3.23, 540-541

ACLs (Access Control Lists), access privilege system, 267

Access denied errors, 290-296

administrative privileges, 281

changes, implementing, 290

connecting, 274-278, 282-287

functions, 274

grant tables, 274-282

password hashing, 296-301

requests, verification, 287-290

ActiveState Perl, 192-193

administration

access privilege system

Access denied errors, 290-296

administrative privileges, 281

changes, implementing, 290

connecting, 274-278, 282-287

functions, 274

grant tables, 274-282

password hashing, 296-301

requests, verification, 287-290

MySQL server configuration

mysqld command-line options, 219-229

server system variables, dynamic, 257-259

server system variables, global, 231-232, 253-254

server system variables, options, 236-253

server system variables, session, 231, 253-254

server system variables, SHOW VARIABLES statement, 233-235

server system variables, status, 260-266

server system variables, structured, 254-256

SQL modes, 229-231

server

mysqladmin program, 487-491

mysqld-max, 208-211

startup scripts, 207-208

  mysql.server, 214

  mysqld_multi, 215-219

  mysqld_safe, 211-214

user account management

  creating accounts, 303-307

  deleting accounts, 307

  limiting resources, 308-309

  passwords, 302-303, 309-312

  SSL (Secure Sockets Layer), 312-319

  usernames, 302-303

administrative privileges, granting, 281

Alpha Linux, notes, 169-170

Alpha-DEC-OSF/1 notes, 185-186

Alpha-DEC-Unix (Tru64) notes, 184-185

anonymous users, 141, 284, 287

ANSI modes, 44

ANSI/ISO SQL compatibility, 42-43

ANSI modes, 44

constraints, 54-56

differences

  atomic operations, 48-51

  comments, 53-54

  foreign keys, 51-52

  SELECT INTO TABLE extension, 48

  stored procedures, 51

  subqueries, 47

  transactions, 48-51

  triggers, 51

  views, 52-53

extensions, 44-47

known errors, 56-61

SQL modes, 43

application-level locking, 438

applications. *See* **programs**

arguments, option, 198

arrays, definition, 346-347

atomic operations, 48-51

attacks, avoiding, 270-271

authentication, Client does not support authentication protocol error, 611-612

AUTO-INCREMENT column, InnoDB storage engine, 554

auto-increment counter, 554

auto-reconnect option (mysql program), 487

autocommit mode

BDB (BerkeleyDB) storage engine, 534

InnoDB storage engine, locking, 567

automatic recovery, MyISAM storage engine, 520

automatic startup, 100

B

backups

databases, 320-321, 506-508

files, 321

InnoDB storage engine, 563-566

batch option (mysql program), 477

BDB (BerkeleyDB) storage engine

autocommit mode, 534

errors, 536-537

features, 534-535

files, 534

installing, 532

limitations, 536

mysqld-max server, 209-210

operating systems, 531-532

startup parameters, 532-534

tables, 48

troubleshooting, 536

BENCHMARK function, queries, 411

benchmarks, 406-408

downloading, 409

Open Source Database Benchmark, 410

performance, 409-410

scripts, 409

testing, 409

BeOS notes, 191

BerkeleyDB (BDB) storage engine

autocommit mode, 534

errors, 536-537

features, 534-535

files, 534

installing, 532

limitations, 536

mysqld-max server, 209-210

operating systems, 531-532

startup parameters, 532-534

troubleshooting, 536

binary distributions, 72-78

choosing, 67-70

Linux, 162-163

MySQL installation, 83

Linux, 96-99

Mac OS X, 99-102

Novell NetWare, 102-104

tar files, 104-107

Windows, 84-96

binary installation, Windows, 83

preparations, 86-87

servers, 87-93

system requirements, 84-85

versus Unix, 93-96

binary log files, 350, 353, 370-371, 494-495

mysqld options, 351

mysqlbinlog program, options, 492-493

rules, 352

temporary files, deleting, 494

BitKeeper repositories, 67

BitKeeper tree, MySQL installation, 114-117

BLOB columns, indexing, 441

block size, key cache, 451

blocking indexes, 447

blocking_queries option (mysqlcc program), 495

bottlenecks, troubleshooting, 405

braces ({}), 3

BSD Unix, notes

FreeBSD, 176-177

NetBSD, 177

OpenBSD 2.5, 178

OpenBSD 2.8, 178

version 2.x, 178

version 3.x, 178

version 4.x, 179

buffer pools, flushing, 565

buffer sizes, mysqld server, 454-457

bug reports

creating, 608, 614

reports, criteria, 38-41

bugs

known

design issues, 56-61

version 3.23, 56

version 4.0, 56

reporting, 17, 37-42, 404

version releases, 71-72

bugs database, 37-42

bugs.mysql.com Web site, 37

C

C API

  3.23 upgrade changes, 157

  4.0 upgrade changes, 150, 155

C++ compiler, 112, 118

cache

  hostnames, 461

  key, MyISAM storage engine, 446

    block size, 451

    index preloading, 450-451

    midpoint insertion strategy, 449-450

    multiple, 448-449

    restructuring, 451

    shared access, 447

  optimization, 407

  query

    configuring, 365-366

    implementing, 363-365

    maintaining, 367-368

    SELECT statement options, 365

    status, 367-368

  tables, 452-453

Can't connect to local MySQL server (2002) error, 609-611

Can't create/write to file error, 618

Can't find file error, 623

Can't initialize character set error, 619-620

case sensitivity

  access privilege system, 277

  database names, 45

  table names, 45

CC environment variable, 631

cc1plus, troubleshooting, 118

certificates, X509 (Secure Sockets Layer), 313

certification, MySQL AB, 14

CFLAGS environment variable, 631

character sets, 113-114, 342

  adding, 344-346

  Can't initialize character set error, 619-620

  definition arrays, 346-347

  German, 343-344

  limitations, 347-348

  multi-byte, 347

  replicating, 384

character-sets-dir option (mysql program), 477

characters, wildcard, 511

check options, myisamchk utility, 326-327

checking tables, mysqlcheck program, 497-500

checkpoints, InnoDB storage engine, 565-566

clauses

  DISTINCT, optimizing, 425

  IS NULL

    indexes, 445

    optimizing, 423-424

  LEFT JOIN, optimizing, 425-426

  LIMIT, optimizing, 428-429

  OR, optimizing, 423

  ORDER BY, optimizing, 426-428

  RIGHT JOIN, optimizing, 426

  WHERE, optimizing, 421-423

clean .idb files, 561

Client does not support authentication protocol error, 611-612

client libraries, linking, 621-622

client programs, 8

    4.0 upgrading changes, 149

    Aborted clients error, 616-617

    compiling, Windows, 127

    multiple servers, running, 362

    server access, 197

    startup parameters, 203

    version 3.23 upgrade changes, 156

clustered indexes, InnoDB storage engine, 584

code, source code, 540

collating strings, 347

columns

    AUTO-INCREMENT, InnoDB storage engine, 554

    BLOB, indexing, 441

    compressed tables, 475-476

    displaying, mysqlshow program, 511-512

    EXPLAIN statement, 412-417

    grant tables, 276-282

    indexes, database optimization, 441-443

    TEXT, indexing, 441

    types, 6

columns_priv table, wildcards, 288

command line

    invoking programs, 198-199

    multiple servers, running (Windows), 357-358

    mysqld options, 219-229

    options, SSL (Secure Sockets Layer), 318-319

    program options, 199-201

    startup parameters, 204

    Windows startup, 89-90

command-line history, .mysql_history file, 481

command-line options

    mysql program, 477-480

    mysqladmin program, 490-491

    mysqlcc program, 495-496

command-line tools

    mysql, 476

        auto-reconnect option, 487

        commands, 481-485

        executing statements, 485

        options, 477-480

        query results, displaying vertically, 485-486

        safe-updates option, 486-487

        SQL scripts, running, 477

        variables, setting, 480-481

Commands out of sync error, 618

comments, starting, 53-54

commercial licenses, 19

    contact information, 16

    MySQL AB, 15

    Web sites, 20

commercial support, types, 17

committing transactions, InnoDB storage engine, 574

compatibility

    ANSI/ISO SQL, 42

        ANSI modes, 44

        constraints, 54-56

        differences, 47-54

        extensions, 44-47

        known errors, 56-61

        SQL modes, 43

    Oracle, 45

    PostgreSQL, 47

    protocols, 158

replication, versions, 381-382

upgrading, versions, 145-146

    3.21, 158-159

    3.22, 157

    3.23, 156-157

    4.0, 147-155

compile options, binary distributions, 77-78

compilers

    C++, 112, 118

    troubleshooting, 118

compiling

    clients, Windows, 127

    optimizing, 454

    source code, 540

    speed, 457-459

    static, 112

compliance, Y2K (Year 2000), 11-12

compress option (mysql program), 477

compress option (mysqlcc program), 495

compressed file formats, MyISAM storage engine, 523

compressing tables, myisampack program, 469-470

    columns, 475-476

    examples, 471-476

concurrency, multi-versioned concurrency control, 571-572

Conditional Use logos, 21

config.cache file, 117-121

configuration options, MySQL installation, 111-114

configuration

    InnoDB storage engine

        my.cnf files, 543-545

        mysqld server parameters, 546

    tablespace files, setting up, 541-542

    Unix option files, 544

    Windows option files, 544

    master/slave setup, 396-397

    MySQL server

        mysqld command-line options, 219-229

        server system variables, dynamic, 257-259

        server system variables, global, 231-232, 253-254

        server system variables, options, 236-253

        server system variables, session, 231, 253-254

        server system variables, SHOW VARIABLES statement, 233-235

        server system variables, status, 260-266

        server system variables, structured, 254-256

        SQL modes, 229-231

    query cache, 365-366

configure options, MySQL installation, 111-114

connect_timeout variable, 480

connections

    Aborted connections error, 616-617

    access privilege system, 274-278, 282-287

    Lost connection to server during query error, 613-614

    master/slave setup, 398

    resources, limiting (user accounts), 309

    Too many connections error, 613

connection_name option (mysqlcc program), 495

connectivity, 7

connect_timeout variable, 491, 496

consistent reads

    InnoDB storage engine, 569-572

    non-locking, InnoDB storage engine, 569

const tables, 412

constraints

    default values, 55

    ENUM, 56

    FOREIGN KEY, 554-558

    NOT NULL, 55

    PRIMARY KEY, 54

    SET, 56

    UNIQUE, 54

consulting MySQL AB, 14

contact information, MySQL AB, 16-17

conventions, typographical, 2-4

converting table types, 516

copy on demand, 438

copyrights, 18

corrupted MyISAM tables, troubleshooting, 523-524

corrupted tables, troubleshooting, 626

costs, support, 17

counters, auto-increment, 554

crash recovery

    error checking, 331

    maintenance scheduling, 335-336

    myisamchk utility, 321, 331

        invocation syntax, 322-324

        memory usage, 329-330

        options, 324-329

        variables, 324-325

tables

    optimizing, 334

    repairing, 331-334

    retrieving information, 336-342

crash-me program, 406-409

crashes, troubleshooting, 625-628

cryptographic signatures, verifying download integrity, 79-81

customer support

    mailing address, 41

    MySQL AB, 14

customer uses, 407-408

CXX environment variable, 631

CXXFLAGS environment variable, 631

D

data

    character sets, 342-344

    importing, mysqlimport program, 508-510

data dictionary operations, troubleshooting (InnoDB storage engine), 597-598

data directory

    creating, 127

    server startup, troubleshooting, 138-139

data files, adding/removing (InnoDB storage engine), 561-562

database option (mysql program), 477

database option (mysqlcc program), 495

databases

    backing up, 320-321, 506-508

    bugs, 37-42

    copying, 160-162

    defined, 4

displaying, mysqlshow program, 511-512

dumping, mysqldump program, 500-506

maintenance, myisamchk utility, 321

    check options, 326-327

    crash recovery, 330-331

    error checking, 331

    invocation syntax, 322-324

    memory usage, 329-330

    options, 324-329

    repair options, 327-328

    retrieving information, 336-342

    scheduling, 335-336

    table optimization, 334

    table repair, 331-334

    variables, 324-325

MaxDB

    concepts, 600

    features, 600-601

    history, 599

    interoperability, 601

    licensing, 599

    reserved words, 601-606

    resource links, 600

    versus MySQL, 600-601

name case-sensitivity, 45

optimizing

    design, 440

    indexes, 441-446

    MyISAM key cache, 446-451

    reducing size, 440-441

    tables, 451-453

relational, defined, 4

replicating

    binary logs, 370-371

    implementing, 370-374

    master/slave setup, 396-398

    overview, 369-370

    performance improvements, 399-401

    redundancy/high availability, 401-402

    relay logs, 375-376

    setup, 377-383

    startup options, 387-396

    status files, 375-376

    support, 384-387

    troubleshooting, 384-387

    two-way replication, 399

    version compatibility, 381-382

restoring, 321

Unix, symbolic links, 463

Windows, symbolic links, 465

date functions, Y2K compliance, 11-12

db table

    sorting, 288

    wildcards, 287

.db files, 534

DBI_TRACE environment variable, 631

DBI_USER environment variable, 631

deadlocked transactions, InnoDB storage engine, 574-576

debug option (mysql program), 477

debug-info option (mysql program), 477

default installation directories, 82-83

default values, 406

default-character-set option (mysql program), 477

definition arrays, character sets, 346-347

defragmenting tables, 336, 588

DELETE queries, optimizing, 432

design

    benefits/limitations, 406

    database optimization, 440

    portability, 406-407

development source tree, MySQL installation, 114-117

directories

    data, creating, 127

    installation structures, 82-83

disk image files, 99

disk seeks, 420

disks

    data, splitting, 465

    full, troubleshooting, 628

    optimizing

        filesystem parameters, 462

        hdparm command, 462

        RAID, 462

        spindles, 461

        striping, 461

        symbolic links, 461-465

displaying database information, mysqlshow program, 511-512

DISTINCT clause, optimizing, 425

distributions

    binary, 72-78

        Linux, 162-163

        MySQL installation, 83

    commands, 108-109

    formats, choosing, 69-70

    MySQL installation

        Linux, 96-99

        Mac OS X, 99-102

        Novell NetWare, 102-104

        tar files, 104-107

        Windows, 84-96

source

    Linux, 164-165

    MySQL installation, 107-111

testing, MySQL installation

    configure options, 111-114

    development source tree, 114-117

    MIT-pthreads, 121-122

    requirements, 107-108

    troubleshooting, 117-121

    Windows, 122-127

.dmg files, 99

DNS, optimizing, 461

dolphin logo, 21

doublewrite, InnoDB storage engine, 587

downgrades, 144-146, 560

downloading

    benchmarks, 409

    versions, 78

Dual Licensing, 15

dumping InnoDB tables, 563

dumping databases, mysqldump program, 500-506

dynamic file format, MyISAM storage engine, 522

dynamic system variables, 257-259

E

ellipsis (...), 3

embedded server, version 4.0, 25

encryption, SSL (Secure Sockets Layer), 312

ENUM constraint, 56

environment variables

    list of, 631-632

    PATH, 199

    programs, 199, 205-206, 469

UMASK, 623

UMASK_DIR, 623

Errcode, 512-513

errno, 512-513

error handling, InnoDB storage engine, 589-594

error log file, 348-349

error messages

displaying, perror program, 512-513

languages, 344

errors, 608

1005 error, 555

2002 error, 609-611

Aborted clients, 616-617

Aborted connections, 616-617

Access denied, 290-296, 609

BDB (BerkeleyDB) storage engine, 536-537

Can't connect to local MySQL server (2002), 609-611

Can't create/write to file, 618

Can't find file, 623

Can't initialize character set, 619-620

checking, myisamchk utility, 331

Client does not support authentication protocol, 611-612

Commands out of sync, 618

File Not Found, 620

Host 'host name' is blocked, 612

Ignoring user, 618-619

known, 56-61

Lost connection to server during query, 613-614

MySQL server has gone away, 613-614

Out of memory, 613

Packet too large, 615-616

Password Fails When Entered Interactively, 612

reporting, mailing lists, 33-35

answering questions, 42

archive location, 36-37

bugs database, 37-42

IRC (Internet Relay Chat), 42

subscribing/unsubscribing, 33

Table 'tbl_name' doesn't exist, 619

The table is full, 617

Too many connections, 613

undefined reference, 621

execute option (mysql program), 478

EXPLAIN statement, 411-419

extensions

ANSI, modes, 44

GROUP BY, 425

MySQL differences

atomic operations, 48-51

SELECT INTO TABLE extension, 48

subqueries, 47

transactions, 48-51

SQL, 42-43

standard SQL, 44-47

F

fatal signal 11, 118

features

clients, 8

columns, 6

commands, 7

connectivity, 7

functions, 7

internals, 6

localization, 8

mid-term future, 32-33

near future, 29-32

portability, 6

scalability, 7

security, 7

tools, 8

versions, 22-27

fields, InnoDB storage engine, 583

file formats

master.info, 388

MyISAM storage engine, 521-523

File Not Found error, 620

file permissions, troubleshooting, 623

file space management, InnoDB storage engine, 588

files

backing up, 321

BDB (BerkeleyDB) storage engine, 534

config.cache, 117-121

data, adding/removing, InnoDB storage engine, 561-562

error messages, 344

.db, 534

.dmg, 99

.frm, 517, 525, 534, 537

.idb, 560-561

index, MyISAM storage engine, 520

ISAM storage engine, 537

.ISD, 537

log

adding/removing, InnoDB storage engine, 561-562

binary, 350-353

binary, mysqld options, 351

binary, rules, 352

error, 348-349

maintaining, 354

names, 320

query, 349-350

slow, 353-354

update, 350

MERGE storage engine, 525

.MRG, 525

my.cnf, 380, 543-545

.MYD, 517

.MYI, 517

.mysql_history, 481

mysql.sock, modifying/protecting, 629-630

option, program options, 199-201

clients, 203

command line, 204

non-empty lines, 202-203

shell scripts, 205

syntax, 202-204

Unix, 202

Windows, 201

size limits, 9-10

status, 375-376

tablespace, setting up, 541-542

tar

binary distributions, 72

MySQL installation, 104-107

Solaris installation, troubleshooting, 171-174

temporary

deleting, 494

storing, 628-629

text

importing, mysqlimport program, 508-510

statements, executing, 485

tmp, write access, 134

Unix options, InnoDB storage engine, 544

Windows options, InnoDB storage engine, 544

filesystem parameters, disk optimization, 462

fixed file formats, MyISAM storage engine, 521

floating-point formats, 566

FLOSS (Free/Libre and Open Source Software), 18

flush tables value (status command), 490

flushing
buffer pools, 565
log files, 354

for update mode, consistent reads (InnoDB storage engine), 570

force option (mysql program), 478

forcing recovery, InnoDB storage engine, 564-565

FOREIGN KEY constraints, InnoDB storage engine, 554
indexes, 557-558
SQL standards, 555-556

foreign keys, 51-52

formats, floating-point, 566

Free/Libre and Open Source Software (FLOSS), 18

FreeBSD
notes, 176-177
troubleshooting, 120

.frm files, 517, 525, 534, 537

full disks, troubleshooting, 628

functions, 7
BENCHMARK, queries, 411
PASSWORD, 284, 619
troubleshooting, 411

future
mid-term future features, 32-33
near future features, 29-32

version 4.1, 27
version 5.0, 28-29
version 5.1, 29

fuzzy checkpoints, InnoDB storage engine, 565-566

G

gcc compiler, 112

General Public License (GPL), 4, 15, 18-21

global system variables, 231-232, 253-254

GNR (group number), 215

GnuPG (GNU Privacy Guard), verifying download integrity, 79-81

GPG build key, importing, 81

GPL (General Public License), 4, 15, 18-21

GRANT statement, 303-307, 318

grant tables
access privilege system, 274-282
columns, 276-278
creating, 127-128
re-creating, 130
sorting, 286-288
upgrades, 160

graphical tools, mysqlcc program, 495-497

GROUP BY extensions, 425

group number (GNR), 215

GUI (graphical user interface) tools, mysqlcc program, 495-497

H

hardware, determining problems, 607-608

hash indexes, 446, 529, 585

hashing passwords, access privilege system, 296-301

hdparm command, 462

HEAP tables (MEMORY storage engine). 529-531

help option (mysql program), 477

help option (mysqlcc program), 495

high availability, replication, 401-402

history, 5

history_size option (mysqlcc program), 495

HOME environment variable, 631

Host 'host_name' is blocked error, 612

host option (mysql program), 478

host option (mysqlcc program), 495

host table, 287-289

hostname caching, 461

HP-UX version 10.20 notes, 179-180

HP-UX version 11.x notes, 180-181

html option (mysql program), 478

I

I/O (input/output)
  InnoDB storage engine, 586-588
  slave threads, 373-374
  threads, 371

IA-64 Linux, notes, 170

IBM-AIX Unix notes, 181-183

.idb files, 560-561

ignore-space option (mysql program), 478

Ignoring user error, 618-619

importing
  data, mysqlimport program, 508-510
  GPG build key, 81

index blocks, 447

index files, MyISAM storage engine, 520

indexes
  BLOB columns, 441
  block sizes, 242
  columns, database optimization, 441-443
  creating, FOREIGN KEY constraints, 557-558
  hash, 446, 529
  InnoDB storage engine, 584-586
  IS NULL clause, 445
  leftmost prefix, 444
  LIKE values, 444
  preloading, 450-451
  sorting, 420
  storing, 443
  string, 520
  TEXT columns, 441
  uses of, database optimization, 443-446

initialization, troubleshooting (InnoDB storage engine), 551

InnoDB Hot Backup tool, 563

InnoDB Monitors, 578-583

InnoDB storage engine
  ACID compliance, 48
  backup/recovery, 563-566
  configuring
    my.cnf files, 543-545
    mysqld server parameters, 546
    tablespace files, 541-542
    Unix option files, 544
    Windows option files, 544
  contact information, 540

creating, 551
    AUTO_INCREMENT column,
    554
    converted MyISAM tables, 553
    FOREIGN KEY constraints,
    554-558
    per-table tablespaces, 559-561
    replication, 558-559
    transactions, 552-553
data files, adding/removing, 561-562
defragmenting tables, 588
doublewrite, 587
dumping, 563
error handling, 589-594
fields, 583
file space management, 588
I/O (input/output), 586-588
indexes
    clustered, 584
    hash, 585
    insert buffering, 585
    non-clustered, 584
    record structure, 585-586
locking
    autocommit mode, 567
    consistent non-locking reads, 569
    consistent reads, 569-572
    next-key locking, 571
    setup, 572-574
    transaction isolation levels,
    567-569
    transactions, 574-576
log files, adding/removing, 561-562
maximum size, 10
moving, 566-567
multi-versioning, 583-584
overview, 539
performance tuning, 576-583

read-aheads, 586
restrictions, 594-596
startup parameters, 546-549
tablespaces
    creating, 550-551
    segments, 588
    sizing, 562
    troubleshooting initialization, 551
troubleshooting, 596-598
undo logs, 583
version 3.23, 540-541
input/output. *See* **I/O**
**insert buffering, InnoDB storage
engine, 585**
**INSERT queries, optimizing,
430-432**
**INSERT statement, grant privileges,
305-307**
installation
BDB (BerkeleyDB) storage engine,
532
binary distributions, 83
    Linux, 96-99
    Mac OS X, 99-102
    Novell NetWare, 102-104
    tar files, 104-107
    Windows, 84-96
file permissions, troubleshooting, 623
MySQL-Max, 540
overview, 63-64
Perl
    troubleshooting, 193-195
    Unix, 191-192
    Windows, 192-193
post
    Linux, 166-168
    setup/testing, account security,
    141-144

setup/testing, startup problems, 138-141

setup/testing, startup/shutdown, 135-138

setup/testing, Unix procedures, 128-135

setup/testing, Windows procedures, 127-128

preparation

layouts, 82-83

supported operating systems, 64-66

versions, binary distributions, 72-78

versions, bug-free releases, 71-72

versions, choosing, 66-69

versions, distribution formats, 69-70

versions, downloads, 78

versions, updates, 70-71

versions, verifying download integrity, 78-81

source distributions, 110

commands, 108-109

configure options, 111-114

development source tree, 114-117

MIT-pthreads, 121-122

requirements, 107-108

testing, 111

troubleshooting, 117-121

Windows, 122-127

troubleshooting

client library links, 621-622

startup, 622-623

internal compilers, troubleshooting, 118

internal locking, 435-438

Internet Relay Chat (IRC), 42

Internet service provider (ISP), 20

interoperability, MaxDB, 601

invoking programs, command line, 198-199

IRC (Internet Relay Chat), 42

IS NULL clause

indexes, 445

optimizing, 423-424

ISAM storage engine, 537-538

isamchk utility, 537

.ISD files, 537

isolation levels, transaction (InnoDB storage engine), 567-569

ISP (Internet service provider), 20

J-K

joins

multiple tables, 417-419

OR clauses, 423

single-sweep multi-join method, 411

key cache, MyISAM storage engine, 446

block size, 451

index preloading, 450-451

midpoint insertion strategy, 449-450

multiple, 448-449

restructuring, 451

shared access, 447

key cache structured variable, 255

keys, foreign, 51-52

keywords, adding, 407

killing running threads, 614

L

languages, error messages, 344

Large File Support (LFS), 10

layouts, installation, 82-83

LD_RUN_PATH environment variable, 631

Least Recently Used (LRU), midpoint insertion strategy, 449-450

LEFT JOIN clause, optimizing, 425-426

leftmost prefix, indexes, 444

levels, locking, 435-439

LFS (Large File Support), 10

libraries, client, 621-622

licenses
  commercial, 15, 19-20
  Dual Licensing, 15
  free, 20-21
  GPL (General Public License), 4, 15, 18-21
  logos, 21-22
  Open Source, 18
  trademarks, 21-22

licensing
  contact information, 16-17
  MaxDB databases, 599
  MySQL, 1
  support costs, 17

LIKE values, indexes, 444

LIMIT clause, optimizing, 428-429

links
  client libraries, troubleshooting, 621-622
  resource, MaxDB databases, 600
  speed, 457-459

symbolic, 461-462
  Unix databases, 463
  Unix tables, 463-465
  Windows databases, 465

symbolic links, tables, 271

Linux
  compiling, 457
  error codes, InnoDB storage engine, 590-592
  MySQL installation, 96-99
  mysqld-max server, 209
  notes
    Alpha, 169-170
    binary distributions, 162-163
    IA-64, 170
    MIPS, 170
    post-installation, 166-168
    PowerPC, 170
    source distributions, 164-165
    SPARC, 169
    version 2.0, 162
    x86, 168-169

LinuxThreads, mutex implementation, 164

LOAD DATA LOCAL statement, 273

LOAD DATA statement, 273

local-infile option (mysql program), 478

local-infile option (mysqlcc program), 496

localization, 8

lock in share mode, consistent reads (InnoDB storage engine), 569-570

locking, 454

  InnoDB storage engine

    autocommit mode, 567

    consistent non-locking reads, 569

    consistent reads, 569-572

    next-key locking, 571

    setup, 572-574

    transaction isolation levels, 567-569

    transactions, 574-576

  methods, 435-438

  row-level, 51

  table-level, 437-439

log files

  adding/removing, InnoDB storage engine, 561-562

  binary, 350-353, 370-371, 495

    mysqlbinlog program, options, 492-493

    temporary files, deleting, 494

  error, 348-349

  flushing, 354

  maintaining, 354

  names, 320

  query, 349-350

  relay, 375-376

  slow, 353-354

  update, 350

Log, undo (InnoDB storage engine), 583

logos, 21-22

Lost connection to server during query error, 613-614

LRU (Least Recently Used), mid-point insertion strategy, 449-450

M

Mac OS X

  MySQL installation, 99-102

  notes, 171

mailing lists, 34-35

  answering questions, 42

  archive location, 36-37

  bugs database, 37-42

  IRC (Internet Relay Chat), 42

  postings, 104

  subscribing/unsubscribing, 33

maintaining databases, myisamchk utility, 321

  crash recovery, 330-331

  error checking, 331

  invocation syntax, 322-324

  memory usage, 329-330

  options, 324-325, 329

    check, 326-327

    repair, 327-328

  retrieving information, 336-342

  scheduling, 335-336

  tables

    optimizing, 334

    repairing, 331-334

  variables, 324-325

maintaining log files, 354

maintaining query cache, 367-368

make_binary_distribution script, 208

mapping MERGE tables, 526

master thread, 373

master.info file format, 388

master/slave setup, 369

  binary logs, 370-371

  blocking updates, 398

  configuration, 396-397

connections, 398

query dates, 398

MaxDB database system

concepts, 600

features, 600-601

history, 599

interoperability, 601

licensing, 599

reserved words, 601-606

resource links, 600

versus MySQL, 600-601

maximum memory used value (status command), 490

max_allowed_packet variable, 480, 497

max_join_size variable, 481, 497

MD5 checksum, verifying download integrity, 79

memory

determining problems, 608

myisamchk utility, 329-330

optimizing, 459-460

Out of memory error, 613

virtual, compiling problems, 118

memory in use value (status command), 490

MEMORY storage engine, 529-531

MERGE storage engine

files, 525

limitations, 527

problem solving features, 527

remapping, 526

troubleshooting, 528

midpoint insertion strategy, MyISAM key cache, 449-450

MIPS, Linux, notes, 170

mirror sites, 78

MIT-pthreads, MySQL installation, 121-122

modes

ANSI, 44

autocommit

BDB (BerkeleyDB) storage engine, 534

InnoDB storage engine, locking, 567

for update mode, consistent reads (InnoDB storage engine), 570

lock in share, consistent reads (InnoDB storage engine), 569-570

SQL, 43

setting, 229-231

special, 231

supported, 229-231

modules, 9, 214

monitors, InnoDB, 578-583

moving InnoDB tables, 566-567

.MRG files, 525

MRG_MyISAM engine. *See* **MERGE storage engine**

multi-byte characters, 347, 619-620

multi-versioned concurrency control, 571-572

multi-versioning, InnoDB storage engine, 583-584

multiple columns, indexes, 442-443

multiple MyISAM key cache, 448-449

multiple servers

managing, mysqld_multi script, 215-219

running, 355-356

client programs, 362

Unix, 360-362

Windows, 357-360

multiple tablespaces, InnoDB storage engine, 559-561

multiple-table joins, 417-419

mutex, implementing, 164

my.cnf files, 380, 543-545

.MYD file, 517

.MYI file, 517

MyISAM storage engine, 469-470

automatic recovery, 520

columns, 475-476

converting tables to InnoDB, 553

examples, 471-476

features, 519

file formats, 521-523

files, 517

improvements, 517-519

index files, 520

key cache, 446

   block size, 451

   index preloading, 450-451

   midpoint insertion strategy, 449-450

   multiple, 448-449

   restructuring, 451

   shared access, 447

maximum size, 10

queries, speed, 420

startup options, 519-520

symbolic links, 464

troubleshooting, 523-525

myisamchk utility, 114, 208, 467

database maintenance, 321

   crash recovery, 330-331

   error checking, 331

   invocation syntax, 322-324

   memory usage, 329-330

   options, 324-326, 328-329

   retrieving information, 336-342

   scheduling, 335-336

   table optimization, 334

   table repair, 331-334

   variables, 324-325

options, 470-471

tables, compressing, 469-470

   columns, 475-476

   examples, 471-476

MySQL 3.23, InnoDB storage engine, 540-541

MySQL 4.0, features, 23-25

MySQL 4.1 features, 25-27

MySQL 5.0, 27-29

MySQL 5.1, future, 29

MySQL AB

business model, 13

   certification, 14

   commercial licenses, 15

   consulting, 14

   contact information, 16-17

   customer support, 14

   partnerships, 15

   training, 14

core values, 13

overview, 12-13

MySQL Certification Program Web site, 14

MySQL Control Center. *See* **mysqlcc program**

MySQL Database Software, 1

***MySQL Language Reference*, 1**

mysql program, 467, 476

auto-reconnect option, 487

command-line options, 477-480

commands, 481-485

executing statements, 485

query results, displaying vertically, 485-486

safe-updates option, 486-487

SQL scripts, running, 477

variables, setting, 480-481

MySQL server has gone away error, 613-614

MySQL version 3.20, upgrading, 158-159

MySQL version 3.21, upgrading, 157

MySQL version 3.22, upgrading, 155-157

MySQL version 3.23

InnoDB storage engine, 540-541

known errors, 56

upgrading, 151-155

MySQL version 4.0

known errors, 56

upgrading, 146-151

MySQL version 5.0, upgrading, 146

MySQL Web site, 1, 369

MySQL-Max, installing, 540

MYSQL_PS1 environment variable, 631

mysql_install_db script, troubleshooting, 133-135

mysql.server script, 208, 214

mysql.sock file, 112, 629-630

mysqlaccess program, 467

mysqladmin program, 468, 487

command-line options, 490-491

commands, 488-489

status command, 489-490

variables, 491

mysqlbinlog program, 468, 495

options, 492-493

temporary files, deleting, 494

mysqlbug script, 37, 104, 208

mysqlcc program, 468, 495-497

mysqlcheck program, 468, 497-500

mysqld servers

buffer sizes, 454-457

command-line options, 219-229

options, 351, 455-457

parameters, InnoDB storage engine, 546

process, checking, 609

script, 207

startup options, security, 272-273

mysqld-max server 207, 211

BDB storage engine, 209-210

creating, 209

Unix, 209

Windows, 208

mysqldump program, 161, 468, 500-506

mysqld_multi script, 208, 215-219

mysqld_safe script, 208, 211-214

mysqlhotcopy program, 468, 506-508

mysqlimport program, 161, 468, 508-510

mysqlshow program, 468, 511-512

MYSQL_DEBUG environment variable, 631

mysql_fix_privilege_tables script, 208, 291

.mysql_history file, 481, 631

MYSQL_HOST environment variable, 631

mysql_install_db script, 208

MYSQL_PWD environment variable, 631

MYSQL_TCP_PORT environment variable, 631

MYSQL_UNIX_PORT environment variable, 631

N

named pipes, 87, 93

named-commands option (mysql program), 478

naming schemes, MySQL versions, 67-68

native thread support, 64-66

NetBSD notes, 177

netmask notation, user table, 284

NetWare (Novell), MySQL installation, 102-104

NetWare Loadable Module (NLM), 214

net_buffer_length variable, 481, 497

next-key locking, InnoDB storage engine, 571

NLM (NetWare Loadable Module), 214

no-auto-rehash option (mysql program), 478

no-beep option (mysql program), 478

no-named-commands option (mysql program), 478

no-pager option (mysql program), 478

no-tee option (mysql program), 478

non-clustered indexes, InnoDB storage engine, 584

non-locking consistent reads, InnoDB storage engine, 569

non-transaction-safe tables (NTSTs), 516-517

non-transactional tables
  default values, 406
  versus transactional tables, 48-50

NOT NULL constraint, 55

Novell NetWare, MySQL installation, 102-104

NTSTs (non-transaction-safe tables), 516-517

O

one-database option (mysql program), 478

Open Source
  defined, 4
  license, 18

Open Source Database Benchmark, 410

open tables
  counting, 451
  value (status command), 490

OpenBSD 2.5 notes, 178

OpenBSD 2.8 notes, 178

OpenPGP Web site, 79

opens value (status command), 489

open_files_limit variable, 493

operating system support, 64-66

operating systems
  BDB (BerkeleyDB) storage engine, 531-532
  BeOS notes, 191
  BSD Unix notes
    BSD/OS 2.x, 178
    BSD/OS 3.x, 178
    BSD/OS 4.x, 179
    FreeBSD, 176-177
    NetBSD, 177
    OpenBSD 2.5, 178
    OpenBSD 2.8, 178
  error codes, InnoDB storage engine, 590-594
  file-size limits, 9-10
  Linux notes
    Alpha, 169-170
    binary distributions, 162-163
    IA-64, 170
    MIPS, 170

post-installation procedures,
166-168
PowerPC, 170
source distributions, 164-165
SPARC, 169
version 2.0, 162
x86, 168-169
Mac OS X notes, 171
OS/2 notes, 190-191
Solaris notes, 171-175
supported, 64-66
Unix notes
Alpha-DEC-OSF/1, 185-186
Alpha-DEC-Unix (Tru64),
184-185
HP-UX version 10.20, 179-180
HP-UX version 11.x, 180-181
IBM-AIX, 181-183
SCO, 188-189
SCO UnixWare version 7.1.x, 190
SGI Irix, 187-188
SunOS 4, 183
operations, atomic, 48-51
optimization
bottlenecks, 405
compiling, 457-459
databases
design, 440
indexes, 441-446
MyISAM key cache, 446-451
reducing size, 440-441
tables, 451-453
disks
filesystem parameters, 462
hdparm command, 462
RAID, 462

spindles, 461
striping, 461
symbolic links, 461-465
DNS, 461
linking, 457-459
locking, 454
methods, 435-438
table-level, limitations, 438-439
memory, 459-460
overview, 405
benchmarks, 408-410
design benefits/limitations, 406
design portability, 406-407
queries, 410
DELETE, 432
DISTINCT clause, 425
estimating performance, 420
EXPLAIN, 411-419
INSERT, 430-432
IS NULL clause, 423-424
LEFT JOIN clause, 425-426
LIMIT clause, 428-429
OR clause, 423
ORDER BY clause, 426-428
RIGHT JOIN clause, 426
SELECT statement speed, 420
table scans, avoiding, 429
tips, 432-435
UPDATE, 432
WHERE clause, 421-423
server parameters, tuning, 454-457
system, 454
tables, myisamchk utility, 334
option arguments, 198
**option files, program options,
199-201**
clients, 203
command line, 204

non-empty lines, 202-203

shell scripts, 205

syntax, 202-204

Unix, 202

Windows, 201

OR clause, optimizing, 423

OR Index Merge optimization, 423

Oracle, compatibility, 45

ORDER BY clause, optimizing, 426-428

OS/2 notes, 190-191

Out of memory error, 613

P

Packet too large error, 615-616

pack_isam program, 469

page-level locking, 435-438

pager option (mysql program), 479

parameters. *See* **startup parameters**

partitions, raw disk (InnoDB storage engine I/O), 587-588

partnerships

logos, 22

MySQL AB, 15

Password Fails When Entered Interactively error, 612

password hashing, access privilege system, 296-301

password option (mysql program), 479

password option (mysqlcc program), 496

PASSWORD function, 284, 619

passwords, 270

4.0 upgrading changes, 150-151

accounts, 142-144

assigning, user accounts, 309-311

resetting, 623-625

root, 144

securing, user accounts, 311-312

troubleshooting, 623-625

user accounts, 302-303

patches, LFS (Large File Support), 10

PATH environment variable, 199, 631

pathnames, Windows, 87

paths, temporary file directory, 629

per-table tablespaces, InnoDB storage engine, 559-561

performance

benchmarks, 409-410

disks

filesystem parameters, 462

hdparm command, 462

RAID, 462

spindles, 461

striping, 461

symbolic links, 461-465

improving, replication, 399-401

queries, estimating, 420

tuning, InnoDB storage engine, 576-583

Perl

benchmark scripts, 409

installing

troubleshooting, 193-195

Unix, 191-192

Windows, 192-193

scripts, mysqlhotcopy program, 506-508

permissions

files, troubleshooting, 623

logos, 21-22

perror program, 468, 512-513

plugins_path option (mysqlcc program), 496

port option (mysql program), 479

port option (mysqlcc program), 496

portability, 6, 406-407

ports, server startup, 140

post-installation procedures

  Linux, 166-168

  setup/testing

    account security, 141-144

    startup, troubleshooting, 138-141

    startup/shutdown, 135-138

    Unix procedures, 128-135

    Windows procedures, 127-128

PostgreSQL, compatibility, 47

posting mailing lists, 104

PowerPC, Linux, notes, 170

preloading indexes, 450-451

PRIMARY KEY constraint, 54

privileges

  access system, 274

    accounts, 141

    Access denied errors, 290-296

    administrative privileges, 281

    connecting, 274-278, 282-287

    functions, 274

    grant tables, 274-282

    password hashing, 296-301

  adding, 303-307

  columns, grant tables, 276-278

  deleting, 307

  requests, verification, 287-290

  tables, creating, 133

processes, mysqld, 609

program variables, setting, 206

programs

  client

    multiple server environment, 362

    server access, 197

  crash-me, 406-409

  determining problems, 608

environment variables, 469

invoking, command line, 198-199

list of, 467-469

myisampack, 467

  options, 470-471

  tables, compressing, 469-476

mysql, 467, 476

  auto-reconnect option, 487

  command-line options, 477-480

  commands, 481-485

  executing statements, 485

  query results, displaying vertically, 485-486

  safe-updates option, 486-487

  SQL scripts, running, 477

  variables, setting, 480-481

mysqlaccess, 467

mysqladmin, 468, 487

  command-line options, 490-491

  commands, 488-489

  status command, 489-490

  variables, 491

mysqlbinlog, 468, 492-495

  options, 492-493

  temporary files, deleting, 494

mysqlcc, 468, 495-497

mysqlcheck, 468, 497-500

mysqldump, 468, 500-506

mysqlhotcopy, 468, 506-508

mysqlimport, 468, 508-510

mysqlshow, 468, 511-512

options

  command line, 199-201

  environment variables, 199, 205-206

  option files, 199-205

  program variables, setting, 206

pack_isam, 469
perror, 468, 512-513
replace, 468, 513
server startup scripts, 197
utility, 198
prompt command, 484-485
prompt option (mysql program), 479
protocol option (mysql program), 479
protocols
compatibility, 158
TCP/IP (Transmission Control
Protocol/Internet Protocol),
Windows servers, 88-96

Q

queries
InnoDB storage engine, hash indexes,
585
keywords, adding, 407
master/slave setup, 398
optimizing, 410
DELETE, 432
DISTINCT clause, 425
estimating performance, 420
EXPLAIN, 411-419
INSERT, 430-432
IS NULL clause, 423-424
LEFT JOIN clause, 425-426
LIMIT clause, 428-429
OR clause, 423
ORDER BY clause, 426-428
RIGHT JOIN clause, 426
SELECT statement speed, 420
table scans, avoiding, 429
tips, 432-435
UPDATE, 432
WHERE clause, 421-423

query cache
configuring, 365-366
implementing, 363-365
log file, 349-350
maintaining, 367-368
SELECT statement options, 365
status, 367-368
resources, limiting (user accounts),
308
results, displaying vertically, 485-486
subqueries, 47
troubleshooting, BENCHMARK
function, 411
query option (mysqlcc program), 496
**questions value (status command),
489**
quick option (mysql program), 479

R

**RAID (redundant array of independ-
ent disks), 119, 462**
**random read-aheads, InnoDB storage
engine, 586**
**raw disk partitions, InnoDB storage
engine I/O, 587-588**
raw option (mysql program), 479
**read-aheads, InnoDB storage engine,
586**
**records, InnoDB storage engine
indexes, 585-586**
recovery
automatic, MyISAM storage engine,
520
InnoDB storage engine, 563
forcing, 564-565
fuzzy checkpoints, 565-566
recovery mode, storage engines, 224
redundancy, replication, 401-402

ref_or_null, 423-424

register option (mysqlcc program), 496

relational databases, defined, 4

relay log files, 375-376

releases. *See* versions

remote connections, SSH (Secure Shell), 319

repair options, myisamchk utility, 327-328

repairing tables

  myisamchk utility, 331-334

  mysqlcheck program, 497-500

replace program, 468, 513

replication

  benefits, 370

  binary logs, 370-371

  implementing, threads, 370-374

  InnoDB storage engine, 558-559

  limitations, 370-371

  master/slave setup

    blocking updates, 398

    configurations, 396-397

    connections, 398

    query dates, 398

  overview, 369-370

  performance, improving, 399-401

  redundancy/high availability, 401-402

  relay logs, 375-376

  setup, 377

    my.cnf files, 380

    troubleshooting, 381

    upgrading, 382-383

  speed, increasing, 370

  startup options, 387-394

    master.info file format, 388

    statement execution, 395-396

    status files, 375-376

    support, 384-387

    troubleshooting, 384-387, 403-404

    two-way, 399

    version compatibility, 381-382

reporting errors, mailing lists, 34-35

  answering questions, 42

  archive location, 36-37

  bugs database, 37-42

  IRC (Internet Relay Chat), 42

  subscribing/unsubscribing, 33

reports, bug reports, 608, 614

repositories, BitKeeper, 67

requests, access privilege system verification, 287-290

reserved words, MaxDB, 601-602, 604-606

resource links, MaxDB, 600

resources, limiting (user accounts), 308-309

restoring

  databases, 321

  .idb files, 561

RIGHT JOIN clause, optimizing, 426

roll pointers, InnoDB storage engine, 583

rolling back transactions, InnoDB storage engine, 574

root password, 144

root user, resetting passwords, 623-625

row-level locking, 51, 435-438

RPM Package Manager, MySQL installation, 96-99

  files, MySQL installation, 96-99

  verifying version integrity, 81

running

ANSI mode, 44

servers, multiple, 355-356

   client programs, 362

   Unix, 360-362

   Windows, 357-360

SQL scripts, 477

threads, killing, 614

Web servers, 20

S

safe_mysqld startup script. *See* mysqld_safe script

safe-updates option (mysql program), 479, 486-487

Sakila, 5

SAP DB. *See* **MaxDB database system**

scalability, 7

scans, table, 429

scheduling table maintenance, 335-336

SCO notes, 188-190

scope columns, grant tables, 276-278

scripts

benchmarks, 409

mysqlbug, 37

mysql_fix_privilege_tables, 291

mysql_install_db, troubleshooting, 133-135

Perl, mysqlhotcopy program, 506-508

server startup, 197

SQL, running, 477

startup, 207-208

   mysql.server, 214

   mysqld_multi, 215-219

   mysqld_safe, 211-214

secondary indexes, InnoDB storage engine, 584

Secure Shell (SSH), user accounts, 319

Secure Sockets Layer (SSL)

command-line options, 318-319

encryption, 312

GRANT statement, options, 318

requirements, 313

setting, 314-318

SSH (Secure Shell), 319

X509 certificates, 313

security, 7

access privilege system

   Access denied errors, 290-296

   administrative privileges, 281

   changes, implementing, 290

   connecting, 274-278, 282-287

   functions, 274

   grant tables, 274-282

   password hashing, 296-301

   requests, verification, 287-290

accounts, 141-144

attacks, avoiding, 270-271

guidelines, 267-269

LOAD DATA LOCAL statement, 273

LOAD DATA statement, 273

mysqld startup options, 272-273

passwords, 270

seeks, disk, 420

segments, tablespace, 588

SELECT statement

optimizing, EXPLAIN statement, 410-411

   columns, 412-413, 415-417

   multiple-table joins, 417-419

options, 365

speed, 420

select_limit variable, 481, 497

sequential read-aheads, InnoDB storage engine, 586

server option (mysqlcc program), 496

server parameters, tuning, 454-457

server startup scripts, 197

server system variables

dynamic, 257-259

global, 231-232, 253-254

options, 236-253

session, 253-254

SHOW VARIABLES statement, 233-235

status, 260-266

structured, 254-256

server

4.0 upgrade changes, 147-148, 152-153

accessing, client programs, 197

administration, mysqladmin program, 487

command-line options, 490-491

commands, 488-489

status command, 489-490

variables, 491

embedded, version 4.0, 25

master/slave setup, 369

binary logs, 370-371

blocking updates, 398

configuration, 396-397

connections, 398

multiple

managing, mysqld_multi script, 215-219

running, 355-362

mysqld

buffer sizes, 454-457

options, 455-457

mysqld-max, 211

BDB storage engine, 209-210

creating, 209

Unix, 209

Windows, 208

shutdown, 135-138

startup, 135-141

Unix, 129, 132

Windows, 87

starting, 88-93

versus Unix, 93-96

services, running multiple servers (Windows), 358-360

session system variables, 231, 253-254

SET constraints, 56

SET PASSWORD statement, 309-311

setup, post-installation

account security, 141-144

startup, troubleshooting, 138-141

startup/shutdown, 135-138

Unix procedures, 128-135

Windows procedures, 127-128

SGI Irix notes, 187-188

shared access, MyISAM key cache, 447

shell command, 2

shell scripts, startup parameters, 205

shell syntax, 3

SHOW INNODB STATUS statement, 578-583

SHOW STATUS statement, 260-261

SHOW VARIABLES statement, 233-235

showing database information, mysql-show program, 511-512

shutdown

servers, 135-138

Unix servers, 132

shutdown_timeout variable, 491

signatures, cryptographic, 79-81

silent option (mysql program), 479

single-sweep multi-join method, 411

sites. *See* **Web sites**

skip-column-names option (mysql program), 479

skip-line-numbers option (mysql program), 480

slave thread, 371-374

slow log file, 353-354

slow queries value (status command), 489

SMP (symmetric multi-processor), 65

snapshot, master server, 378-379

socket

files, modifying/protecting, 629-630

locations, changing, 112, 137

option (mysqlcc program), 496

socket option (mysql program), 480

Solaris

notes, 171-175

troubleshooting, 120

sorting

character sets, 342-344

grant tables, 286-288

indexes, 420

source code, compiling, 540

source distributions

choosing, 67-70

Linux, 164-165

MySQL installation, 107, 110

commands, 108-109

configure options, 111-114

development source tree, 114-117

MIT-pthreads, 121-122

testing, 111

troubleshooting, 117-121

Windows, 122-127

MySQL installation, requirements, 107-108

source packages, MySQL installation (Windows), 125-126

SPARC Linux, notes, 169

speed

compiling, 457-459

increasing via replication, 370

linking, 457-459

queries, 410

DELETE, 432

DISTINCT clause, 425

estimating performance, 420

EXPLAIN, 411-419

INSERT, 430-432

IS NULL clause, 423-424

LEFT JOIN clause, 425-426

LIMIT clause, 428-429

optimization tips, 432-435

OR clause, 423

ORDER BY clause, 426-428

RIGHT JOIN clause, 426

SELECT statement, 420

table scans, avoiding, 429

UPDATE, 432

WHERE clause, 421-423

spindles, disks, 461

SQL (Structured Query Language)

4.0 upgrade changes, 149-150, 154-155

defined, 4

modes, 43

  setting, 229-231

  special, 231

  supported, 229-231

scripts, running, 477

slave thread, 374

standards, FOREIGN KEY constraints (InnoDB storage engine), 555-556

version 3.23 upgrade changes, 156-157

SQL-92, extensions, 42

sql_yacc.cc, troubleshooting, 118

square brackets ([ ]), 3

SSH (Secure Shell), user account, 319

SSL (Secure Sockets Layer)

command-line options, 318-319

encryption, 312

GRANT statement, options, 318

requirements, 313

setting, 314-318

SSH (Secure Shell), 319

X509 certificates, 313

stability, 8-9

standards compliance, 42

ANSI modes, 44

constraints, 54-56

foreign keys, 51-52

known errors, 56-61

MySQL differences, 47-51

SELECT INTO TABLE extension, 48

SQL extensions, 44-47

SQL modes, 43

stored procedures, 51

subqueries, 47

transactions, 48-51

triggers, 51

views, 52-53

startup

automatic, 100

replication options, 387-394

  master.info file format, 388

  statement execution, 395-396

running, normal user account, 622-623

servers, 135-141

Unix servers, 129

Windows servers, 88-96

startup parameters, 454-457

BDB (BerkeleyDB) storage engine, 532-534

InnoDB storage engine, 546-549

MyISAM storage engine, 519-520

mysql program, 477-480

mysqladmin program, 490-491

mysqlcc program, 495-496

mysqld, security, 272-273

programs

  clients, 203

  command line, 204

  shell scripts, 205

  syntax, 202-204

  Unix, 202

  Windows, 201

tuning, 454

startup scripts, 207-208

mysql.server, 214

mysqld_multi, 215-219

mysqld_safe, 211-214

servers, 197

statements
EXPLAIN, 411-419
GRANT, 303-307, 318
INSERT, 305-307
LOAD DATA, 273
LOAD DATA LOCAL, 273
SELECT
  optimizing, 410-419
  options, 365
  speed, 420
SET PASSWORD, 309-311
SHOW INNODB STATUS, 578-583
static compilation, 112
static file format, MyISAM storage engine, 521
status
command, 482, 489-490
files, 375-376
query cache, 367-368
system variables, 260-266
storage engines
BDB (BerkeleyDB)
  autocommit mode, 534
  errors, 536-537
  features, 534-535
  files, 534
  installing, 532
  limitations, 536
  operating systems, 531-532
  startup parameters, 532-534
  troubleshooting, 536
choosing, 515-517
InnoDB
  backup/recovery, 563-566
  configuring, 541-546
  contact information, 540
  creating, 551-561

data files, adding/removing, 561-562
defragmenting tables, 588
doublewrite, 587
dumping, 563
error handling, 589-594
fields, 583
file space management, 588
I/O (input/output), 586-588
indexes, 584-586
locking, 567-576
log files, adding/removing, 561-562
moving, 566-567
multi-versioning, 583-584
overview, 539
performance tuning, 576-583
read-aheads, 586
restrictions, 594-596
startup parameters, 546-549
tablespaces, creating, 550-551, 562, 588
troubleshooting, 596-598
undo logs, 583
version 3.23, 540-541
ISAM, 537-538
MEMORY, features, 529-531
MERGE, 525-528
MyISAM
  automatic recovery, 520
  converting tables to InnoDB storage engine, 553
  features, 519
  file formats, 521-523
  files, 517
  improvements, 517-519
  index files, 520
  key cache, 446-451

query speed, 420

startup options, 519-520

symbolic links, 464

troubleshooting, corruption, 523-525

recovery mode, 224

server startup, troubleshooting, 138

storage. *See also* **databases**

indexes, 443

temporary files, 628-629

stored procedures, 51

strings

collating, 347

indexes, 520

replacing, replace program, 513

striping, 461

Structured Query Language. *See* **SQL**

structured system variables, 254-256

subqueries, 47

SunOS 4 notes, 183

Super Smack, 410

support, mailing address, 41

symbolic links, 461-465

symbolic links, tables, 271

symmetric multi-processor (SMP), 65

synchronization, data dictionary (InnoDB storage engine), 597

syntax

global variables, 254

myisamchk utility, 322-324

session variables, 254

shell, 3

startup parameters, 202-204

syntax option (mysqlcc program), 496

syntax_file option (mysqlcc program), 496

T

Table 'tbl_name' doesn't exist error, 619

table option (mysql program), 480

table scans, avoiding, 429

table-level locking, 435-436

benefits, 437

limitations, 438-439

tables_priv table, wildcards, 288

tables. *See also* **databases**

backing up, mysqlhotcopy program, 506-508

BDB (BerkeleyDB), 48

autocommit mode, 534

errors, 536-537

features, 534-535

files, 534

installing, 532

limitations, 536

operating systems, 531-532

startup parameters, 532-534

troubleshooting, 536

checking/repairing, mysqlcheck program, 497-500

columns_priv table, wildcards, 288

compressing, myisampack program, 469-470

columns, 475-476

examples, 471-476

const, 412

corrupted, troubleshooting, 626

db table, wildcards, 287

defragmenting, 336, 588

displaying, mysqlshow program, 511-512

dumping, mysqldump program, 500-506

How can we make this index more useful? Email us at indexes@samspublishing.com

grant
    columns, 276-278
    creating, 127-128
    re-creating, 130
    sorting, 286-288
    upgrading, 160
host, 289
host table, wildcards, 287
InnoDB
    ACID compliance, 48
    backup/recovery, 563-566
    configuring, 541-546
    contact information, 540
    creating, 551-559
    data files, adding/removing, 561-562
    doublewrite, 587
    dumping, 563
    error handling, 589-594
    fields, 583
    file space management, 588
    I/O (input/output), 586-588
    indexes, 584-586
    locking, 567-576
    log files, adding/removing, 561-562
    moving, 566-567
    multi-versioning, 583-584
    overview, 539
    per-table tablespaces, 559-561
    performance tuning, 576-583
    read-aheads, 586
    restrictions, 594-596
    startup parameters, 546-549
    table defragmenting, 588
    tablespaces, 550-551, 562, 588
    troubleshooting, 596-598

    undo logs, 583
    version 3.23, 540-541
ISAM, 537-538
maximum size, 9-10
MEMORY, features, 529-531
MERGE, 525-528
MyISAM
    automatic recovery, 520
    converting tables to InnoDB storage engine, 553
    features, 519
    file formats, 521-523
    files, 517
    improvements, 517-519
    index files, 520
    key cache, 446-451
    query speed, 420
    startup options, 519-520
    symbolic links, 464
    troubleshooting, 523-525
name case sensitivity, 45
non-transactional tables
    default values, 406
    versus transactional tables, 48-50
NTSTs (non-transaction-safe tables), 516-517
open, counting, 451
opening/closing, 452-453
optimizing, myisamchk utility, 334
privilege, creating, 133
reducing number of, 453
repairing, myisamchk utility, 331-334
symbolic links, 271
system, 412
tables_priv table, wildcards, 288
temporary, replicating, 385
The table is full error, 617

TSTs (transaction-safe tables),
516-517

types, 515-517

Unix, symbolic links, 463-465

user table, 283-284

version 3.23 upgrade changes, 156

tablespace files, setting up, 541-542

tablespaces

creating, 550-551

initialization, troubleshooting, 551

InnoDB storage engine, per-table
tablespaces, 559-561

segments, 588

sizing, 562

table_cache option, 452-453

tar files

binary distributions, 72

MySQL installation, 104-107

Solaris installation, troubleshooting,
171-174

**TCP/IP (Transmission Control
Protocol/Internet Protocol)**

Windows servers

starting, 88-93

versus Unix, 93-96

Windows support, 87

technical support

mailing address, 41

types, 17

tee option (mysql program), 480

temporary file directory, 629

temporary files

deleting, 494

storing, 628-629

write access, 134

temporary tables, replicating, 385

testing

benchmarks, 409

connections, access privilege system,
283-287

post-installation

account security, 141-144

startup problems, 138-141

startup/shutdown, 135-138

Unix procedures, 128-135

Windows procedures, 127-128

requests, access privilege system,
287-290

source distribution installation, 111

versions, 69

TEXT columns, indexing, 441

text files

importing, mysqlimport program,
508-510

statements, executing, 485

The table is full error, 617

threads

LinuxThreads, 164

master, 373

running, killing, 614

slave, 371-374

support, non-native, 121-122

threads value (status command), 489

time zone, setting, 630

timeout

connect_timeout variable, 480, 491,
496

shutdown_timeout variable, 491

tmp files, write access, 134

TMPDIR environment variable, 631

ToDo list

mid-term future features, 32-33

near future features, 29-32

version 4.1, 27

version 5.0, 28-29

version 5.1, 29

Too many connections error, 613

tools, 8. *See also* **command-line tools**

GUI (graphical user interface), mysqlcc program, 495-497

InnoDB Hot Backup, 563

WinMySQLAdmin, 87

trademarks, 21-22

transaction isolation levels, InnoDB storage engine, 567-569

transaction-safe tables (TSTs), 516-517

transactional tables versus non-transactional tables, 48-50

transactions, 48-51

rolling/rolling back (InnoDB storage engine), 574

deadlock (InnoDB storage engine), 575-576

deadlock/rollback (InnoDB storage engine), 574

InnoDB storage engine, 552-553

translations_path option (mysqlcc program), 496

Transmission Control Protocol/Internet Protocol (TCP/IP)

Windows servers

starting, 88-93

versus Unix, 93-96

Windows support, 87

triggers, 51

troubleshooting

BDB (BerkeleyDB) storage engine, 536

bottlenecks, 405

corrupted tables, 626

crashes, 625-628

determining problems, 607-608

errors, 608

Aborted clients, 616-617

Aborted connections, 616-617

Access denied, 609

Can't connect to local MySQL server (2002), 609-611

Can't create/write to file, 618

Can't initialize character set, 619-620

Client does not support authentication protocol, 611-612

Commands out of sync error, 618

File Not Found, 620

Host 'host_name' is blocked, 612

Ignoring user, 618-619

Lost connection to server during query, 613-614

MySQL server has gone away, 613-614

Out of memory, 613

Packet too large, 615-616

Password Fails When Entered Interactively, 612

Table 'tbl_name' doesn't exist, 619

The table is full error, 617

Too many connections, 613

FreeBSD, 120

full disks, 628

InnoDB storage engine, 596

data dictionary operations, 597-598

initialization, 551

installation, 621-623

MERGE tables, 528

MyISAM storage engine, 523-525

MySQL installation, 117-121

mysql.sock file, 629-630

mysql_install_db script, 133-135

passwords, 623-625

Perl installation, 193-195

programs, missing, 198

queries, BENCHMARK function, 411

replication, 381, 384-387, 403-404

servers, startup, 138-141

Solaris, 120, 171-175

temporary file storage, 628-629

time zones, 630

transactions, deadlock, 574-576

upgrading, 145

version 3.23, 387

Windows upgrades, 159

TSTs (transaction-safe tables), 516-517

tuning parameters, 454-457

two-way replication, 399

typographical conventions, 2-4

TZ environment variable, 632

U

UMASK environment variable, 623, 632

UMASK_DIR environment variable, 623, 632

unbuffered option (mysql program), 480

undefined reference errors, 621

undo log, InnoDB storage engine, 583

UNIQUE constraint, 54

Unix

BSD notes

BSD/OS 2.x, 178

BSD/OS 3.x, 178

BSD/OS 4.x, 179

FreeBSD, 176-177

NetBSD, 177

OpenBSD 2.5, 178

OpenBSD 2.8, 178

databases, symbolic links, 463

grant tables, upgrading, 160

InnoDB tables, moving, 566-567

multiple servers, running, 360-362

notes

Alpha-DEC-OSF/1, 185-186

Alpha-DEC-Unix (Tru64), 184-185

HP-UX version 10.20, 179-180

HP-UX version 11.x, 180-181

IBM-AIX, 181-183

SCO, 188-190

SGI Irix, 187-188

SunOS 4, 183

option files, InnoDB storage engine, 544

Perl installation, 191-192

post-installation procedures, setup/testing, 128-135

root passwords, setting, 624-625

servers, 129, 132

startup parameters, 202

tables, symbolic links, 463-465

troubleshooting, Can't connect to local MySQL server (2002) error, 609-611

versus Windows, 93-96

update log files, 350

UPDATE queries, optimizing, 432

updates

blocking, master/slave setup, 398

resources, limiting (user accounts), 308

versions, 70-71

views, 53

upgrades. *See also* **downgrades**
  compatibility, 145
  databases, copying, 160-162
  grant tables, 160
  preparation, 144-145
  replication setup, 382-383
  troubleshooting, 145
  version 3.20 to 3.21, 158-159
  version 3.21 to 3.22, 157
  version 3.22 to 3.23, 155-157
  version 3.23 to 4.0, 151-155
  version 4.0 to 4.1, 146-151
  version 5.0, 146
  version compatibility, 146
    3.21, 158-159
    3.22, 157
    3.23 changes, 156-157
    4.0 changes, 147-155
  Windows, 159
uptime value (status command), 489
user account management
  creating accounts, 303-307
  deleting accounts, 307
  limiting resources, 308-309
  passwords, 302-303
    assigning, 309-311
    securing, 311-312
  SSL (Secure Sockets Layer)
    command-line options, 318-319
    encryption, 312
    GRANT statement options, 318
    requirements, 313
    setting, 314-318
    SSH (Secure Shell), 319
    X509 certificates, 313
  usernames, 302-303
USER environment variable, 632

user option (mysql program), 480
user option (mysqlcc program), 496
user table, 283-286
usernames, 302-303
utilities. *See* **programs**

V

variables. *See also* **environment variables**
  assigning, values, 228
  myisamchk utility, 324-325
  mysqladmin program, 491
  mysqld server, 455-457
  program, setting, 206
  server system
    dynamic, 257-259
    global, 231-232, 253-254
    options, 236-253
    session, 231, 253-254
    SHOW VARIABLES statement, 233-235
    status, 260-266
    structured, 254-256
  setting, mysql program, 480-481
VC++, MySQL installation (Windows), 123-125
verbose option (mysql program), 480
verification, download integrity, 78
  GnuPG (GNU Privacy Guard), 79-81
  MD5 checksum, 79
  RPM, 81
verifying
  connections, access privilege system, 283-287
  requests, access privilege system, 287-290
Veritas filesystem, 321

version option (mysql program), 480

version option (mysqlcc program), 496

versioning, 437

versions, MySQL, 66

    4.1, future, 27

    5.0, future, 28-29

    5.1, future, 29

    binary distributions, 72-78

    bug-free releases, 71-72

    choosing, 67-69

    distribution formats, 69-70

    downloading, verifying integrity, 78

        GnuPG (GNU Privacy Guard), 79-81

        MD5 checksum, 79

        RPM, 81

    features, 22-23

        4.0, 23-25

        4.1, 25-27

        5.0, 27,

    Linux 2.0, troubleshooting, 162

    multi-versioning, InnoDB storage engine, 583-584

    naming schemes, 67-68

    replication compatibility, 381-382

    testing, 69

    updates, 70-71

    upgrade compatibility, 146

        3.21, 158-159

        3.22, 157

        3.23 changes, 156-157

        4.0 changes, 147-155

vertical bar (|), 3

vertical option (mysql program), 480

views, 52-53

virtual memory, problems during compiling, 118

W

wait option (mysql program), 480

Web sites

    bugs.mysql.com, 37

    commercial licenses, 20

    InnoDB Hot Backup, 563

    MySQL 1, 369

    MySQL Certification Program, 14

    MySQL downloads, 78

    OpenPGP, 79

    Reference Manual, 1

    Super Smack, 410

    Winsock, 88

WHERE clause, optimizing, 421-423

wildcards

    characters, 511

    columns_priv table, 288

    db table, 287

    host table, 287

    LIKE values, 444

    tables_priv table, 288

    user table, 283

Windows

    databases, symbolic links, 465

    error codes, InnoDB storage engine, 592-594

    grant tables, upgrading, 160

    InnoDB storage engine, moving, 566-567

    multiple servers, running

        command line, 357-358

        services, 358-360

    MySQL installation, 122

        clients, compiling, 127

        preparation, 86-87

        servers, 87-88

        servers, starting, 88-93

source packages, 125-126

system requirements, 84-85

VC++, 123-125

versus Unix, 93-96

mysqld-max servers, 208

open issues, 96

option files, InnoDB storage engine,
544

pathnames, 87

Perl installation, 192-193

post-installation procedures,
setup/testing, 127-128

root passwords, setting, 624

startup parameters, 201

TCP/IP (Transmission Control
Protocol/Internet Protocol) support, 87

upgrades, 159

**Windows service, running MySQL as,
90-92**

WinMySQLAdmin tool, 87

Winsock Web site, 88

write access, tmp files, 134

writing logos, permissions, 21-22

X-Z

**X509 certificates, SSL (Secure
Sockets Layer), 313**

x86 Linux, notes, 168-169

xml option (mysql program), 480

Y2K (Year 2000) compliance, 11-12

Your Guide to Computer Technology

www.informit.com